Corporate Social Responsibility

Corporate Social Responsibility

FOURTH EDITION

Michael Blowfield

Alan Murray

OXFORD
UNIVERSITY PRESS

Great Clarendon Street, Oxford, OX2 6DP,
United Kingdom

Oxford University Press is a department of the University of Oxford. It furthers the University's objective of excellence in research, scholarship, and education by publishing worldwide. Oxford is a registered trade mark of Oxford University Press in the UK and in certain other countries

First edition 2008
Second edition 2011
Third edition 2014

Impression: 2

Published in the United States of America by Oxford University Press
198 Madison Avenue, New York, NY 10016, United States of America

British Library Cataloguing in Publication Data
Data available

Library of Congress Control Number: 2018966911

ISBN 978-0-19-879775-3

Printed and bound by CPI Group (UK) Ltd, Croydon, CR0 4YY

Preface

This is the fourth edition of a book that first saw the light of day in 2008. The original aim was to provide a strong introduction to the theory and practice of corporate social responsibility at a time when what had initially been a movement was becoming a common aspect of business management. Over a decade later, that aim has not changed, but it has been fascinating to watch the field twist and turn.

If anyone doubts the power of CSR in the corporate psyche, they only need to look at the Responsibility or Sustainability sections of company websites and reports. In the first edition, there was a lively debate about where CSR sat in the management curriculum: whether it should be taught separately or integrated into other courses from accounting to strategy. That discussion continues to this day, but what is undeniable is that issues to do with the responsibilities of business to the societies they operate within, and how those responsibilities are managed, are recurring elements of management. The business world is now in an era where few managers will not have been taught about and had to practise CSR. Practices that in 2008 were considered radical and outside of the mainstream, such as working conditions in supply chains and the special issues affecting female workers in poor countries, are now widely accepted as legitimate even if they are not tackled perfectly.

In part, the continuing importance of CSR is due to recurrent corporate missteps, crimes, and misdemeanours. In the third edition, we highlighted corporate taxation, financial misselling, and austerity as areas where companies were at fault. Scandals to do with these issues continue to grab the headlines, and the fines reach ever new heights. But the importance of CSR is also to do with the changing nature of business. Concepts such as the gig economy and firms such as Deliveroo or Uber did not exist when the first edition was published. Academics wrote about the rights of workers in factories, and few envisaged the growth of part-time work and the new kinds of contract between company and a very different kind of workforce. At the same time, global tensions have shifted and perhaps escalated, be this in the area of terrorism, protectionism, or climate change. The meaning of what companies are responsible for has changed profoundly and CSR is an important lens through which these shifts can be observed.

This book is intended for students and tutors of CSR at both undergraduate and graduate levels, but we are proud that it has also been taken up by other disciplines concerned about the role of business in modern society. The text provides a strong framework for studying CSR, which links a wealth of theoretical analysis with more practitioner-oriented materials. Its fourteen chapters are divided into three broad themes: the origins and meaning of CSR; how it is being managed and implemented; and its impact to date and its likely future directions. Under these themes, we examine such topics as the social and historical context of CSR and its business case; key areas of management practice including stakeholder engagement, partnership, ethical supply chains, social auditing, and corporate governance; and the role of responsible investment, as well as that of government and civil society.

We provide an international dimension in that the theories and examples are drawn from around the world. We provide a critical perspective in that we do not advocate any particular ideas about CSR, preferring instead to compare and contrast a host of differing perspectives. Our aim above all is to assist in building an understanding of the potential and limitations of the private sector in areas of extra-financial performance.

Michael Blowfield
Alan Murray

Acknowledgements

MEB

This book reflects our experiences as academics, practitioners, and consultants working in the field of corporate social responsibility for companies, civil societies, and government organizations. I am grateful to the many friends and colleagues who have knowingly, or unknowingly, contributed to that experience. It would be unfair to single out anyone in particular, but this in no way diminishes my accumulated gratitude over the years, and I trust that those involved will understand why the only people mentioned by name are John MacLean, Catherine, Ieuan, Lucy, and Terry.

AM

I would like to acknowledge the work of the Centre for Social and Environmental Accounting Research at the University of St Andrews—particularly the efforts of Rob and Sue Gray, and all the researchers who have attended the annual summer schools over the past decade or so, whose scholarship and rigour has helped to develop and inform my views and opinions. I would also like to acknowledge the love of Kathryn, Rosie, Ellie, and Florence in supporting me in this endeavour.

We are grateful to the anonymous reviewers whose comments have added immensely to the text, and to Cary Krosinsky, William Frederick, the Center for Corporate Citizenship at Boston College, CANOPUS, and the Ethical Trading Initiative, each of which has granted us permission to use some of their materials.

Contents

List of Figures

List of Tables

List of Boxes

List of Snapshots

List of Case Studies

List of Abbreviations

ACCA	Association of Chartered Certified Accountants
ASriA.	Association of Sustainable and Responsible Investment in Asia
BATNEEC	Best Available Technology Not Entailing Excessive Cost
BAU	business-as-usual
BCCI	Bank of Credit and Commerce International
BEE	Black Economic Empowerment
BITC	Business in the Community
BOP	bottom of the pyramid
BSE	bovine spongiform encephalopathy
BSR	Business for Social Responsibility
CATNIP	Currently Available Technology Not Involving Prosecution
CC	Center for Corporate Citizenship
CCAB	Consultative Committee of Accountancy Bodies
CDO	collateralized debt obligation
CEFIC	European Chemical Industry Council
CEO	chief executive officer
CERES	Coalition for Environmentally Responsible Economies
CFA	chartered financial analyst
CFO	chief finance officer
CIC	community-investment company
COO	chief operating officer
CPI	University of Cambridge Programme for Industry
CR	corporate responsibility
CSEAR	Centre for Social and Environmental Accounting Research
CSO	civil society organization
CSP	corporate social performance
CSR	corporate social responsibility
CTF	conservation trust funds
DFID	Department for International Development
DJSI	Dow Jones Sustainability Index
DSI	Domini 400 Social Index
EAI	Enhanced Analytics Initiative
EBITDA	earnings before interest, taxes, depreciation, and amortization
EIL	Environmental Impairment Liability Centre for Competence

EIRIS	Ethical Investment Research Service
EITI	Extractive Industries Transparency Initiative
EIU	Economist Intelligence Unit
EMAS	Eco-Management and Audit System
EPA	Environmental Protection Agency
EPZ	export processing zone
ESG	environmental, social, and governance
ETF	exchange traded fund
ETI	Ethical Trading Initiative
ETS	EU Emissions Trading Scheme
EU	European Union
EurepGAP	European Retailers Group Guidelines on Good Agricultural Practice
Eurosif	European Sustainable and Responsible Investment Forum
EVPA	European Venture Philanthropy Association
FASB	Financial Accounting Standards Board
FDI	foreign direct investment
FEE	Fédération des Experts Compatibles Européens
FLA	Fair Labor Association
FRC	Financial Reporting Council
FSC	Forest Stewardship Council
FWF	Fair Wear Foundation
GAAP	generally accepted accounting principles
GEMI	Global Environmental Management Initiative
GeSI	Global e-Sustainability Initiative
GHG	greenhouse gas
GRI	Global Reporting Initiative
IBLF	International Business Leaders' Forum
ICAEW	Institute of Chartered Accountants in England and Wales
ICCA	International Council of Chemical Associations
ICGN	International Corporate Governance Network
ICMM	International Council on Mining and Metals
ICT	information and communications technology
IFA	International Federation of Accountants
IFRS	International Financial Reporting Standard
IIRC	International Integrated Reporting Committee
ILO	International Labour Organization
IMF	infant milk formula
IPCC	United Nations Intergovernmental Panel on Climate Change
ISC	Institutional Shareholders' Committee

ISO	International Organization for Standardization
LEAF	Linking Environment and Farming
LGBT	lesbian, gay, bisexual, and transgender
LSE	London Stock Exchange
MDGs	Millennium Development Goals
MFA	Multi-Fibre Agreement
MIC	methyl isocyanate
MIMCO	Mattel Independent Monitoring Council for Global Manufacturing Principles
MNC	multinational company
MSC	Marine Stewardship Council
NGO	non-government organization
NPV	net present value
OECD	Organisation for Economic Co-operation and Development
OFR	Operating and Financial Review
ONS	Office for National Statistics
OPEC	Organization of Petroleum Exporting Countries
PETA	People for the Ethical Treatment of Animals
P&L	profit and loss
PPP	public–private sector partnership
PRI	United Nations Principles for Responsible Investing
RAN	Rainforest Action Network
ROI	return on investment
RSPA	Roundtable on Sustainable Palm Oil
SAI	Social Accountability International
SASIX	South African Social Investment Exchange
SCP	sustainable consumption and production
SDG	Sustainable Development Goals
SEAT	Socio-Economic Assessment Toolbox
SIF	Social Investment Forum
SIV	structured investment vehicle
SME	small and medium-sized enterprise
SRI	socially responsible investing/investment
SROI	social return on investment
SSE	social stock exchange
TfL	Transport for London
toe	tonnes of oil equivalent
UN	United Nations
UNCED	United Nations Conference on Environment and Development

UNCTAD	United Nations Conference on Trade and Development
UNDP	United Nations Development Programme
UNEP	United Nations Environment Programme
UNEP-FI	United Nations Global Compact and United Nations Environment Programme's finance initiative
UNICEF	United Nations Children's Fund
UNIDO	United Nations Industrial Development Organization
UNFCC	United Nations Framework Convention on Climate Change
UNGC	United Nations Global Compact
UNRISD	United Nations Research Institute for Social Development
VBLI	Vietnam Business Links Initiative
WBCSD	World Business Council for Sustainable Development
WCED	World Commission on Economic Development
WEF	World Economic Forum
WMO	World Meteorological Organization
WRAP	Worldwide Responsible Apparel Production
WRI	World Resources Institute
WTO	World Trade Organization
WWF	World Wildlife Fund

How to Use this Book

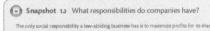

Chapter overview

In this chapter, we introduce the idea of corporate social responsibility (CSR): its concerns, its meanings, and why it is a significant part of the business agenda. In particular, we will:

- set out the context within which contemporary CSR has flourished;
- examine the different perspectives on and definitions of CSR;
- discuss the values that companies are being asked to uphold;
- look at the main issues with which contemporary CSR is wrestling.

Chapter overview and main topics

These chapter-opening features provide a route map through the material, and summarize the goals and main topics of each chapter.

Limitations of CSR frameworks

Key terms

Business and society	Legal responsibility
Business ethics and values	Economic responsibility
Corporate philanthropy	Sustainability

Key terms

Navigate the terminology of CSR with an overview of the key terms at the start of each chapter, later defined in the end-of-book glossary.

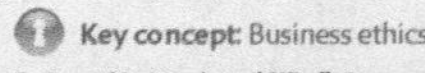

Key concept: Business ethics

Business ethics is a subset of CSR offering a crucial analytical tool for understanding, concept and legitimizing whether the actions and behaviour of companies are *morally* right or wrong. comprises two broad areas: (a) normative business ethics with its roots in theoretical philosop focus on understanding what is moral or immoral in a particular situation; and (b) descriptive ethics rooted in a wider range of disciplines (e.g. psychology, organizational behaviour, anthr and a focus on ethical decisions, how they are made, and what influences the process and ou (Visser et al., 2007).

One could argue that business ethics underpins the entire field of CSR theory and practic while it is important (and is supported by a vast number of publications), it is not the only le through which CSR is being viewed. The influential idea of a 'business case' for CSR (see Ch

Key concepts

These boxes highlight and discuss seminal concepts at the relevant places in each chapter to help you understand the main ideas covered.

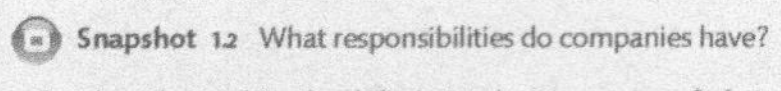

Snapshot 1.2 What responsibilities do companies have?

The only social responsibility a law-abiding business has is to maximize profits for its share

This, in short, is economist Milton Friedman's theory of free market CSR. It is a controversial v among CSR theorists because it appears to say that what's good for investors is good for ever That is a difficult position to defend because profit maximization can drive companies to ben break the law to the point of self-destruction (e.g. Enron, Lehman Brothers, Carillion). But Frie isn't saying that everything is justified by the share price: he believes that government sets the the game, and companies have to operate within them. An important question, therefore, is governments do a good job at regulating business behaviour, and the answer to that might b different in today's globalized economy than it was when many companies primarily operat

Snapshots

Snapshots present concise, topical examples that place the content of the chapter into a practical context that is relevant to businesses today. Each Snapshot is followed by quick questions to check your understanding and link the snapshot back to the theory of the chapter.

and inequality are intertwined; on the other, it must promote capitalism as
key social and environmental issues of the age.

Discussion points

Surveys of executives and the public repeatedly show that business is distrusted as a me

- Why do you think there is a high degree of distrust?
- Is CSR a good way to restore business's reputation?
- How would you factor distrust into a company's business plan?

Discussion points

Alternative viewpoints and insightful questions invite you to reflect on and challenge various aspects of CSR, developing your critical thinking and argument skills.

Case study 1 Too big to jail? Guilt and innocence in the aero
industry

Aerospace is an industry, much like defence, in which there is a constant drum-beat of allega
bribery, corruption, and other scandals. It is not surprising: aircraft are big-budget items man
by large companies requiring huge amounts of investment and specialist skills. Aerospace co
do not pop up overnight. They are also large employers, and are closely associated with natio
prestige. Boeing, the largest company in the industry, is typically portrayed as a standard-bea
prestige, while Airbus, its main competitor, carries the flag for European engineering, particul
Germany, France, and the UK.

In 2014 alone, Boeing was accused by competitor Elon Musk of using corrupt practices to
rocket project, and a procurement officer, Deon Anderson, was jailed for twenty months fo

Case Studies

Each chapter closes with a longer, integrative case study, which provides the opportunity to apply what you have learnt in a practical context. Accompanying extended questions promote deeper thinking and reasoning.

How to Use the Online Resources

Visit **www.oup.com/uk/blowfield-murray4e/** to access supporting content including web exercises, sources of further information, and a 'Journal Club' for students; and all the figures and tables from the text for registered lecturers.

Part 1

The meaning and origins of corporate social responsibility

Introducing corporate social responsibility

Chapter overview

In this chapter, we introduce the idea of corporate social responsibility (CSR): its concerns, its meanings, and why it is a significant part of the business agenda. In particular, we will:

- set out the context within which contemporary CSR has flourished;
- examine the different perspectives on and definitions of CSR;
- discuss the values that companies are being asked to uphold;
- look at the main issues with which contemporary CSR is wrestling.

Main topics

Key terms

Business and society
Business ethics and values
Corporate philanthropy
Legal responsibility
Economic responsibility
Sustainability

Why CSR?

In 2005, *The Economist* published a series of articles castigating CSR and the folly of managers who thought it would benefit their companies. Corporate-responsibility-conscious managers were accused of taking their eye off shareholder interests. Accusations were made that CSR and bad governance went hand in hand. In an accompanying survey, the Economist Intelligence Unit found that only 35% of managers felt CSR was a priority.

Fast forward to 2008, and *The Economist* again runs a feature on CSR. But this time the tone is different. Now it says that 96% of managers believe that CSR offers value for money, and 56% of managers surveyed by the Economist Intelligence Unit say that it is a high priority. Three years after dismissing it, *The Economist* was now professing that few big companies could ignore CSR. Ten years after *The Economist* embraced CSR, and despite speculation that interest in it would wane during economic recessions, the field is still thriving. Much of what was once considered CSR is now categorized as corporate sustainability, as the overview reports produced by Accenture with the UN Global Compact (the *CEO Study on Sustainability*, 2013) and the Business for Social Responsibility's annual *Sustainable Business Survey* make apparent. But whatever the title, these reports show continuing executive interest in the impact of business on society as a management issue.

We live in a world in which the richest 20% of people possess 86% of gross national product, in which one country accounts for 23% of worldwide energy consumption, and in which the USA and Europe account for 65% of annual wealth creation. It is a highly unequal world in which over a billion people live on under $1.25 a day, and a woman is one hundred times more likely to die during pregnancy in Africa than she is in Scandinavia. Yet it is a world in which emerging economies such as China and India are outperforming developed ones in many respects, and in which so-called advanced economies often rely on poorer countries to buy their vast debts.

In this world, prosperity is nearly always measured in terms of economic growth, made possible by greater productivity and cost reduction. The drive for growth increases the demand for natural resources, cheap labour, and new markets. Often these three trends come together in what was once called the Third World, but which is now divided between emerging, developing, and least-developed nations. One can celebrate this growth because it creates new jobs, stimulates local economies, and raises living standards. One can also criticize it because it has been linked to human rights abuses, environmental disasters, and poverty.

Moreover, the concept of growth itself has become problematic. The latest report by the International Panel on Climate Change concludes that there is 95% certainty among scientists worldwide that climate change caused by humans is a real phenomenon. That is a high degree of certainty, exceeding, for instance, the certainty about the benefits of many approved drugs and far more sure than the economic predictions that rule government policy-making. To prevent uncertain, perhaps catastrophic, climate change, energy use in society will have to change by altering the energy mix and/or reducing energy consumption. Yet, historically, economic growth and rising energy consumption have always gone hand in hand, begging the questions: How can society decouple economic growth from increased climate change? Is it possible to maintain growth without jeopardizing the Earth's sustainability?

Business sits in the midst of these complex and vital questions. There are many examples over several decades of business leaders pushing for greater globalization and the interconnected free-flowing world we now inhabit. But even if that were not the case, it is impossible for companies, large or small, to ignore the changing nature of the world they inhabit and the roles they play within it. The fish restaurant on the high street is affected by overfishing and sustainable fisheries—both CSR issues. The fresh fruit importer is affected by campaigns for healthier food and fair treatment of labourers. The small manufacturer is concerned about how its multinational competitor avoids taxes. The multinational company, be it in mining, retail, fast-moving consumer goods, or whatever industry, knows that issues such as water scarcity, responsible investment, carbon emissions, and child labour are not just potential PR problems; they are central to company performance.

The private sector creates wealth, generates employment, utilizes natural resources, and attracts investment at unprecedented levels. Consumption plays a pivotal role in our social lives and our personal identities. Brands have a significance that is not dissimilar to that of religion and ideology in previous eras. The vloggers who have risen to prominence since the last edition of this book show just how much brands matter to individuals. Companies play important roles in public policy, not least in countries where the standard of governance is low, or in situations in which international governance mechanisms are inadequate.

In today's world it is impossible to imagine the absence of the private sector. Despite the financial collapse starting in 2007, alternatives to a free market economy are scarce and have garnered little popular support. In contrast with the 1920s or 1960s, for instance, protest movements in the wake of the financial crisis have focused on reforming—not replacing—private-sector capitalism. Governments around the world have stepped in to save business—from investment banking to manufacturing—from its own failings. In the UK, the government has consistently put the blame for the nation's debt at the feet of politicians, despite the fact that corporate and financial industry debt is 300% of GDP compared with government debt of about 100%.[1] Despite the ethical, financial, and management failings of companies from Lehman Brothers to A4e, J.P. Morgan and HSBC to G4S and Juventus FC, the private sector is still widely admired as the exemplar of efficiency and prosperity. Goldman Sachs' Lloyd Blankfein might be overstating the case when he says he is 'doing God's work', but many believe the statement by Whole Foods' John Mackey that 'Great companies have great purposes.' Allowing widespread business failure is unthinkable, because we seem unable to imagine an alternative to the free market economy.

People in business are often vexed that the contribution of private enterprise to society is not better understood. Yet in 2017, Merrill Lynch, part of Bank of America Group, was fined £34.5 million for failing to report exchange traded derivative transactions.[2] This is by no means the largest fine in corporate history, but it came on the back of a $415 million settlement to settle allegations about misuse of customer money. What's more, in 2014, when the previous edition of this book was put together, Bank of America paid the biggest penalty in US corporate history, $16.65 billion for its packaging of mortgage-backed securities. Some days, it feels like you cannot go anywhere without seeing examples of corporate wrong-doing.

Not surprisingly, therefore, for all the private sector's importance to the global economy, company behaviour is often a cause for concern. Firms are being subjected to new levels of transparency, whether in terms of the demands that the largest stock markets make for greater disclosure and changes to corporate governance, or in terms of public outcry on issues as diverse as environmental pollution, consumer rights, child labour, corruption, and support for military regimes. Adverse disclosure threatens shareholder confidence, brand reputation, production stability, employee trust, and other corporate assets, both tangible and intangible.

What is more, the conditions that leave companies open to charges of irresponsibility, when looked at differently, can become business opportunities. Public opinion is becoming less tolerant of corporate excess and malfeasance, but there are also increasing expectations that business will come up with solutions to some of the twenty-first century's main social and environmental challenges, such as water accessibility, global warming, and affordable health care. New types of business are starting to appear that claim to have a specific social purpose. These are the twin hemispheres that CSR is charged to embrace: on the one hand, it must deal with what Baker called 'capitalism's Achilles heel',[3] within which capital, poverty, and inequality are intertwined; on the other, it must promote capitalism as a solution to the key social and environmental issues of the age.

Discussion points

Surveys of executives and the public repeatedly show that business is distrusted as a member of society.

- Why do you think there is a high degree of distrust?
- Is CSR a good way to restore business's reputation?
- How would you factor distrust into a company's business plan?

Definitions of CSR

The above is the context within which CSR has come to the fore—but what does the term itself actually mean? There never has been a straightforward answer to this, and growing interest in the field—whether from companies, governments, the general public, academics, or civil society organizations—has only served to extend the array of definitions.

Long before there was a name for CSR, there were ideas about what it meant for business to make a positive contribution to the rest of society. Owen, Rowntree, and Lever were among the many individuals who utilized company assets to improve the conditions of nineteenth-century workers. Throughout the twentieth century, companies such as Norsk Hydro would take responsibility for social conditions in their often isolated company towns; many logging, mining, plantation, and oil operations throughout the world set up housing, schools, clinics, and other social amenities. Just as importantly, many more were criticized for failing to take on such responsibilities.[4]

The positive and negative impacts that business had on society generated public, political, and academic debate. While it was quite clear that business sought a profit from providing goods and services in response to society's demands, it was much less obvious what constraints should be put on its activities and who should impose them. Was all profit legitimate? Was all profit legitimate provided that the company stayed within the law? What was a fair distribution of the wealth business created between shareholders, employees, and wider society? Should companies give part of their wealth back to the communities within which they operated? Could markets be relied upon to set a fair price, whether for labour, products, or natural resources? Could governments reliably decide what was in the public interest?

Questions such as these gave rise to different notions of CSR. The field began with a focus on the role of business leaders, particularly on how they managed their companies with a view to society and how they gave back to their local communities. In the 1950s, the focus of CSR shifted to the behaviour of companies rather than that of individuals. This generated a fair degree of academic debate about what companies should be responsible for; it also spawned the concepts of 'corporate social responsiveness' and then 'corporate social performance' which, in the 1980s, put less stress on the philosophical meaning of responsibility and more on the act of being responsible (Rayman-Bacchus, 2017).

Other terms were introduced. 'Corporate sustainability', for example, was used in the 1990s to emphasize how environmental concerns were increasingly an area in which companies were expected to exhibit responsibility. For a while, 'corporate citizenship' (originally used to refer to the types of corporate philanthropy common in the USA) was used as a development of CSR that emphasized the role of business as a citizen in global society and its function in delivering the citizenship rights of individuals.[5] Now, terms such as social entrepreneurship, green enterprise, and benefit corporation have gained popularity, particularly in relation to new types of business. Furthermore, whether it be the USA, Europe, or Indonesia, the precise meanings of these terms can vary from country to country (Patrisia, 2016).

Changes in the focus of CSR inevitably affect the way it is defined. For Davis (1973), CSR begins where the law ends. In other words, it is about what companies do to make a positive contribution to society above and beyond that which constitutes their legal obligations. This simple parameter gets to the heart of much of the debate about CSR in recent years, i.e. the desirability and effectiveness of market-based solutions to social and environmental challenges, and, in particular, their voluntary and self-regulatory nature.

The different definitions of CSR shown in Box 1.1 share in common the belief that companies have a responsibility for the public good—but they emphasize different elements of this. The definitions used by the *Financial Times* and Chiquita, for example, highlight that responsibility is gauged by how companies listen and respond to stakeholders' concerns. PricewaterhouseCoopers' definition sets out the kinds of stakeholder groups to whom companies are responsible. It also stresses that responsibility involves balancing profit maximization and stakeholders' needs. The Confederation of British Industry's definition sheds light on what some of the responsibilities to stakeholders are, while that of the European Commission stresses that actions under the CSR umbrella are voluntary in nature. Finally, the ISO 26000 standard, which provides guidance to companies, sets out seven areas business should be responsible for (see Box 1.1), reiterates the importance of stakeholder involvement and accountability, and adds that responsibility should be integrated into organizational practices.

Box 1.1 Definitions of CSR

Corporations have a responsibility to those groups and individuals that they can affect, i.e. its stakeholders, and to society at large. Stakeholders are usually defined as customers, suppliers, employees, communities, and shareholders or other financiers.

Financial Times Lexicon, http://lexicon.ft.com

CSR commits us to operate in a socially responsible way everywhere we do business, fairly balancing the needs and concerns of our various stakeholders—all those who impact, are impacted by, or have a legitimate interest in the Company's actions and performance.

Chiquita, http://www.chiquita.com

CSR [is] the proposition that companies are responsible not only for maximising profits, but also for recognising the needs of such stakeholders as employees, customers, demographic groups and even the regions they serve.

PricewaterhouseCoopers, http://www.pwc.com

(continued . . .)

The seven core subjects of CSR are organizational governance, community involvement/development, labour practices, consumer issues, fair operating practices, human rights, and the environment.

ISO 26000, http://www.iso.org/files/live/sites/isoorg/files/archive/pdf/en/sr_7_core_subjects.pdf

[CSR is] a concept whereby companies integrate social and environmental concerns in their business operations and in their interactions with their stakeholders on a voluntary basis.

European Commission, Directorate General for Employment and Social Affairs

These broad definitions reflect claims about the values that companies wish to uphold, such as honesty, fairness, and integrity, and these may be set out in standards or codes of practice (see Box 1.2). The values can be quite diverse, and Paine et al. (2005) have tried to categorize them, differentiating, for example, between management's responsibility to investors (fiduciary responsibilities), respecting human rights (dignity principle), and a duty to honour commitments (reliability principle).

Box 1.2 Published standards of CSR

The following is a selection of standards, guidelines, and declarations that set out some of the rights that companies are being asked to uphold.

Beijing Declaration

An international declaration on the rights of women.

http://www.un.org/womenwatch/daw/beijing/platform/declar.htm

CERES Principles

Model corporate code of environmental conduct.

https://www.gdrc.org/sustbiz/ceres-principles.html

Global Reporting Initiative

A framework for reporting on social, environmental, and economic performance.

http://www.globalreporting.org

Marine Stewardship Council

Standards for sustainable fishing and seafood traceability.

http://www.msc.org

Organisation for Economic Co-operation and Development (OECD) guidelines for multinational enterprises

Government recommendations on responsible business conduct.

http://www.oecd.org

Principles for Responsible Investment

Principles on environmental, social, and corporate governance issues pertaining to investors.

http://www.unpri.org

(continued . . .)

Social Accountability 8000

Workplace standard against which to assure worker rights and welfare.

http://www.sa-intl.org

Wolfsberg Anti-Money Laundering Principles

Principles for private banks to counter money laundering.

http://www.wolfsberg-principles.com

There are also companies and individuals that define CSR in terms of its commercial benefits, emphasizing the instrumental value (the business case) that acts of responsibility can bring. Windsor says that the degree and types of responsibility that individual companies have are a factor of the wealth and power of the company, so that a multinational corporation will have different responsibilities to those of a small or medium-sized enterprise.[6] Equally, separate industries have distinctive social and environmental impacts, so that, for example, good performance in cosmetics will look quite different from that in transportation. Indeed, according to Chandler (2016), there are so many variables that it is impossible to prescribe what mix of responsibilities any company faces; companies should not look for universal definitions, but should instead build their strategies around the perspectives of their stakeholders (even though that term is itself subject to multiple interpretations—see Chapter 9).

Corporate governance

In the US tradition of CSR which shaped much of the thinking in the field until fairly recently, corporate governance was not given much consideration. However, as CSR theory has stopped being the preserve of academe, other thinkers—notably those in socially responsible investing (see Chapter 10)—have argued that it needs to be part of CSR's scope. Hence, the Certified Financial Analyst Institute's material refers to CSR as ESG—environmental, social, and governance—as do fund managers such as Jupiter Asset Management.

A valid criticism of CSR practice is that companies have not taken the governance dimension seriously enough, and that it played no discernible part in identifying or addressing the various crises of governance affecting Western markets in the early and late 2000s (see Chapter 13). We explore the evolution of corporate governance and how it relates to CSR more widely in Chapter 7, and tend to agree that governance is an important (if underdeveloped) aspect of the business-society relationship. In so far as governance is the primary responsibility of boards, and the board's role is to 'create tomorrow's company out of today's',[7] CSR would seem to offer useful frameworks for board-level governance. However, CSR is also part of the reconstruction of governance: something that is connected to globalization (see Chapter 5) and social accounting (see Chapter 8), and is evident, for instance, in phenomena such as civil governance, when companies are affected as much by the beliefs and actions of groups such as online protest communities as they are by the interests of the investors that conventional governance is intended to protect (Chapter 9).

A framework for understanding CSR

Snapshot 1.1 demonstrates the wide variety of CSR activities currently being practised by companies. Furthermore, observers such as academics have a multitude of perspectives on the meaning of CSR (see Chapter 2). Given this array, it is not surprising that no single definition adequately captures the range of issues, policies, processes, and initiatives covered in this book. As we will explore in the coming chapters, the notion of stakeholders, the way issues become recognized, and the role of values are all important elements of CSR today. Likewise, the tensions that arise because of competing interests, priorities, and goals affect what CSR means in practise.

Snapshot 1.1 Types of CSR

How many kinds of CSR are there? An early study found nearly 150, but some people are happy to say that CSR is 'just this' or 'just that'. Table 1.1 highlights seven main areas of CSR activity.

Table 1.1 Seven areas of CSR activity

Type of CSR	What it includes	Examples
Leadership, vision, and values	(a) Defining and setting the corporate purpose, values, and vision (b) Translating this into policies and procedures (c) Putting it into practice, including empowering and embedding (d) Ethical leadership and championing	Common Objective Interface
Marketplace activities	(a) Responsible customer relations, including marketing and advertising (b) Product responsibility (c) Using CSR product labelling (d) Ethical competition (e) Making markets work for all	Fairtrade Roundtable for Sustainable Palm Oil
Workforce activities	(a) Employee communication and representation (b) Ensuring employability and skills development (c) Diversity and equality (d) Responsible/fair remuneration (e) Work-life balance (f) Health, safety, and well-being (g) Responsible restructuring	Innocent Lincoln Electric
Supply chain activities	(a) Being a fair customer (b) Driving social and environmental standards through the supply chain (c) Promoting social and economic inclusion via the supply chain	Ethical Trading Initiative Fair Labor Association

(continued...)

Type of CSR	What it includes	Examples
Stakeholder engagement	(a) Mapping key stakeholders and their main concerns (b) Stakeholder consultation (c) Responding to and managing stakeholders (d) Transparent reporting and communication	Extractive Industries Transparency Initiative International Council on Mining and Metals
Community activities	(a) Financial donations (b) Volunteering employee time (c) Giving gifts in kind (d) Being a good neighbour	IKEA Newman's Own
Environmental activities	(a) Resource and energy use (b) Pollution and waste management (c) Environmental product responsibility (d) Transport planning	Philips Siemens

(*Sources:* Ashridge Centre for Business and Society, 2005; Moon, 2014; Jamali, Karam, and Blowfield, 2015)

Quick questions

Different companies adopt different CSR focuses, and ones that are good in one area are not necessarily good in another.

1 Which of the seven types of CSR above do you think are most important for companies you know?

2 Why do you think the companies listed as examples in Table 1.1 have been chosen?

3 Are there aspects of CSR that are not covered in the table?

However, rather than try to adopt and defend a particular definition, in this book we use CSR as an umbrella term that captures the variety of ways in which business's relationship with society is being defined, managed, and acted upon. Therefore, for us, CSR comprises: (a) the responsibilities of business in the context of wider society; (b) how those responsibilities are defined and negotiated; and (c) how they are managed and organized. The chapters of this book emphasize one or other of these dimensions, highlighting where the various observers and practitioners share common ground, and where they disagree.

Key concept: Corporate social responsibility (CSR)

Corporate social responsibility is an umbrella term that captures the variety of ways in which business's relationship with society is being defined, managed, and acted upon. It comprises:

- the responsibilities of business in the context of wider society;
- how those responsibilities are defined and negotiated; and
- how they are managed and organized.

Readers will see soon enough that we do not pretend that there is a unifying vision of CSR. However, there are two broad motivations for companies to treat CSR as a management issue: (a) because companies, like people, have values that guide their interactions with other society members (values motivation); and (b) because to succeed companies need to manage their relationship with wider society (materiality motivation) (see Figure 1.1). We tackle these ways of thinking in the following sections.

Discussion points

Historically, many companies interpret CSR as 'giving back to their communities' through philanthropy and community affairs, yet in the following sections we show that today other types of responsibility are considered more important.

- Why do you think that 'giving back' is increasingly less acceptable as a definition of CSR?
- When some executives say that their companies do not give back to communities because they have 'already given', what do they mean?
- Why do you think there is a stronger tradition of corporate philanthropy in the USA than in Europe?

Values motivation

When executives talk about CSR, many stress the importance of their companies' values. In 1972, then Danone chief executive officer (CEO), Antoine Riboud, made one of the earliest statements on 'modern' CSR:

> CSR does not end at the factory gate or the office door. The jobs a business creates are central to the lives of employees, and the energy and raw materials we consume change the shape of our planet. Public opinion is there to remind us of our responsibilities in the industrial world of today. It is clear that growth should no longer be an end in itself, but rather a tool used to serve quality of life without ever being detrimental to it.
>
> (Danone, undated)

He called this the 'dual purpose' company, but it took a back seat in the late 1990s and early 2000s when publicly listed firms had a strong growth and stock price orientation. However, the dual purpose came to the fore again after the 2007–2008 financial crisis, when Danone returned to the vision set out by Riboud, and the commitments of companies such as Danone, IBM, and Nestlé reflect what Waddock (2001) identified as being the core value of what she calls 'corporate citizenship':

1. a company's adoption of policies, procedures, and processes that are based on integrity (i.e. honesty to oneself and to others), and which allow it to build values-based practices;
2. a company's capacity to perceive and evaluate the long-term consequences of its behaviour, and its willingness to make short-term sacrifices to realize long-term gains.

Others flesh out what those policies, procedures, and processes might embrace (e.g. transparency, empowering stakeholders, managing a triple bottom line of economic, social, and

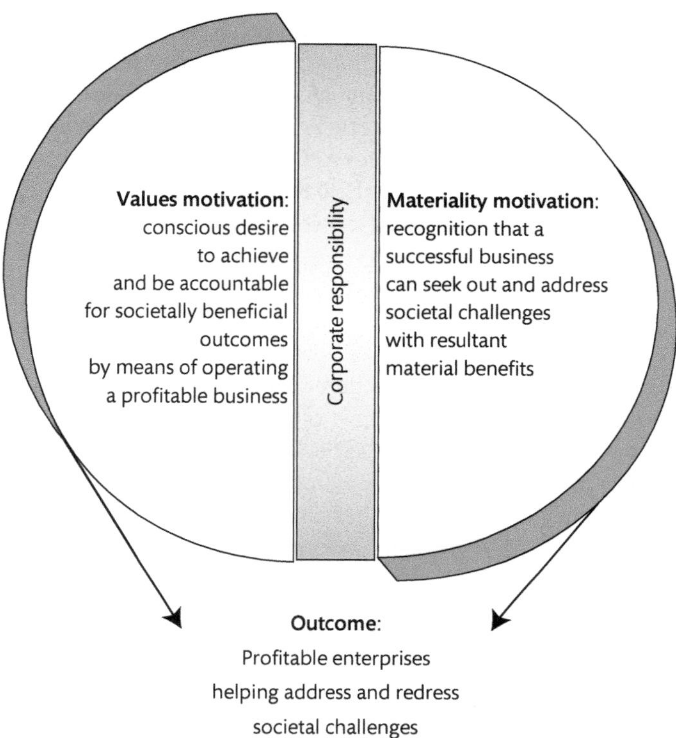

Figure 1.1 Relationship between CSR motivations and outcomes

environmental value added, etc.), offering different political and philosophical frameworks for understanding what ethical constructs should be included (e.g. human liberty, social justice, communitarianism, a duty of care).[8] Although some critics of CSR might view it as being a kind of anti-capitalism intrusion into business, it is notable that CSR can reflect the views of libertarians such as the heads of Whole Foods and Koch Industries (Mackey and Sisodia, 2013; Koch, 2015), as well as the more famous left-leaning figures of Anita Roddick, Jerry Greenfield, or Ben Cohen.

There is debate about who decides the values to which business should adhere: companies themselves or the societies within which they operate. For those who see CSR as a choice that business makes, companies face three competing cases that will ultimately determine their CSR strategy: the moral case (obligations that the company has to society); the rational case (taking proactive steps that will minimize the restrictions society imposes on business); and the economic case (adding financial value to the company by preserving its legitimacy with its stakeholders).[9] For others, however, companies do not choose to practise CSR; rather, it is an integral part of the free enterprise system, and the issues and problems at the heart of CSR are:

> a natural consequence of the industrialized quest for profits [and] represent the raw edge of business values rubbing against the social values of human communities and the ecosystems that sustain those communities.
>
> (Frederick, 2006, p 59)

Underlying these different vantage points is a common acceptance that a legal construct such as a corporation can have values, and that notions of ethics, justice, responsibility, and obligation rooted in human experience can be meaningfully adapted to guide corporate behaviour. As we discuss in Chapter 2, these are debatable assumptions, and an important question is whether CSR practice today makes companies sufficiently accountable for adhering to society's values in the same way that people are held to account, or whether it, de facto, allows companies to pick and choose those things for which they want to be responsible in a way that would seem preposterous if the choices were to be made by individuals.

Business ethics

Not surprisingly, this pushes us in the direction of the field called 'business ethics', which refers to ethical systems applied in the context of profit-oriented organizations. Some will argue that business ethics should be treated as the overarching framework within which CSR theories and practices are devised and implemented. For example, under a theory of environmental ethics, humanity may have a duty of care to the planet, and hence CSR practices should be guided by that duty. If we were concerned only with views on what ideologies should inform corporate behaviour, we might treat CSR and business ethics as synonymous. However, our interest is something broader which embraces theory, management practice, and the societal context within which business exists. Just as neither politics nor religion can be entirely explained by reference to theoretical principles, neither can CSR.

There are many fascinating introductions to business ethics, and we are not going to attempt to duplicate them here. Some of these are concerned with the behaviour of individuals as members of the company and wider society, but others concentrate on business as an institution and how a company integrates values, such as honesty, trust, integrity, respect, and fairness, into its policies, practices, and decision-making. This can involve ensuring that employees abide by the law and are not left in a position in which, in order to achieve one set of targets (e.g. earnings), they are necessarily encouraged to bend or break the law. It can also involve going beyond legal requirements and adhering to company, industry, or professional codes of conduct, such as those that have long been adopted in the medical, military, and legal professions.

It might be argued that, before business management can be considered a mature profession, it too needs to develop comprehensive and relevant codes of ethics. Khurana (2007) claims that business schools were originally intended to educate managers in how to lead socially responsible institutions, but that these 'higher aims' were sacrificed to a focus on profit maximization so that managers today are simply the hired hands of investors. Certainly, there is now a resurgence of interest in business ethics, both in companies and in business schools, as a result of the corporate corruption scandals of the late 1990s and 2000s. The changing nature of business also presents new ethical challenges in order to resolve issues arising from operating globally and within multiple cultural norms, from new industries such as biohacking and information technology, and from increasing public scrutiny of business behaviour. Some companies and industries have invested in internal mechanisms to manage the ethical dimensions of their operations, such as the medical company Baxter International's overarching set of bioethics principles, and defence and aircraft manufacturer Raytheon's appointment of a corporate director for ethics compliance and ethics officers in its major business segments.

Key concept: Business ethics

Business ethics is a subset of CSR offering a crucial analytical tool for understanding, conceptualizing, and legitimizing whether the actions and behaviour of companies are *morally* right or wrong. The field comprises two broad areas: (a) normative business ethics with its roots in theoretical philosophy, and a focus on understanding what is moral or immoral in a particular situation; and (b) descriptive business ethics rooted in a wider range of disciplines (e.g. psychology, organizational behaviour, anthropology), and a focus on ethical decisions, how they are made, and what influences the process and outcomes (Visser et al., 2007).

One could argue that business ethics underpins the entire field of CSR theory and practice, but while it is important (and is supported by a vast number of publications), it is not the only lens through which CSR is being viewed. The influential idea of a 'business case' for CSR (see Chapter 6) largely relies on societal consensus to set out a moral case which is then addressed by harnessing the capacities of business. Or, if one takes the example of stakeholder theory (see Chapter 9), while it can be used to help understand what is moral or not for business, ethics is not an intrinsic element of it, and it can be (and often is) used just to analyse corporate self-interest. Therefore, even if almost every action involving human beings has an ethical dimension at some level, it can be too regressive and unhelpful to resort to first principles in each discussion of CSR.

There are, however, two readily identifiable difficulties with how companies currently implement business ethics. First, there are many examples of even companies with strong ethical policies and processes being found in breach of the law. This was the case with Boeing, which, despite its extensive ethical guidelines on procurement, corruption, and marketing, used confidential materials stolen from rival Lockheed Martin to win nearly $2 billion worth of defence procurement contracts with the US government in 1998, an action that later led the company to be suspended from bidding for defence contracts.[10]

The second difficulty is that company codes and guidelines mostly take the form of usable algorithms that are intended to guide managers through ethically contentious situations, rather than help them to develop a coherent ethical theory that will inform overall business practice.[11] Consequently, ethics is often described as something that is necessary to achieve business imperatives such as profitability, growth, and shareholder value, rather than as something that is at the heart of business behaviour and a prime determinant of what that behaviour should be, especially if there is conflict between instrumental and moral imperatives.

This may seem odd given that much of business ethics seeks to apply ethical theory to the business context. Thus, we find a variety of texts seeking to adapt the ideas of Aristotle, Kant, Mill, Locke, Heidegger, and others to the needs of business.[12] Scherer and Palazzo (2007) argue that companies should not expect to act in accordance with a specific ethical theory but rather, in line with Habermas's view of contemporary ethics, they should adopt the values that emerge from an informed and inclusive negotiation with different sections of society. In what has been characterized as part of a distinct European as opposed to American school of business ethics, companies are seen as uniquely placed organizations in relation to issues with distinct ethical dimensions. For example, Crane and Matten (2015) focus on three core themes that influence the ethical dimension to business behaviour—globalization, sustainability, and citizenship—and, in doing so, refer as much to sociology, political economy, and international relations as they do to philosophy. They highlight, for example, how the Rhenish model of capitalism, found in Italy, Germany, Spain, France, and elsewhere, creates different expectations and challenges to those of the Anglo-Saxon model that is typical of the UK and USA. They also describe how factors such as age, gender, national identity and culture, level of education, personal integrity, and moral imagination all affect individuals' ethical decisions. And they make clear that the concerns of business ethics are affected by the role, capacity, and responsibilities of government and other social institutions.

The online resources contain a more detailed overview of business ethics in relation to CSR, including examples of current ethical controversies affecting companies such as Uber and Facebook. But what the new European school of business ethics highlights is that ethics itself is a social construct—not an absolute value that business should adopt or be judged against, but something that companies as institutions or collectives of individuals both shape and are shaped by. It is insufficient to apply values to business. Rather, values should be seen as an element of what business needs to be cognisant of in building its societal relationships.

Materiality motivation—managing business and society

Central to this European school of business ethics is the idea that the relationship between business and society is subject to continual renegotiation. This counters a criticism of some other forms of business ethics which encourage the idea that responsibility is an end state, or a goal to be strived for, rather than a way of thinking about the role of business in wider society. According to Jonkers, it is confusing to managers to portray responsibility as something that can be accomplished, rather:

> [CSR] is a 'sensitising concept': a term that draws attention to a complex range of issues and elements that are all related to the position and function of the business enterprise in contemporary society.
>
> (Jonkers, 2005, p 20)

There is a strong belief that CSR means something different in the USA than in most of Europe because of the different social contracts that business is a part of in these regions. Equally, various authors discuss the fundamental difference in CSR between developed and developing economies.[13] Concepts such as sensitizing help discussions of CSR steer clear of national relativism, but we should be aware that in countries such as the USA and the UK, where the welfare state is relatively weak by Western standards, the responsibilities of corporations will be different than in Germany or Denmark, where government provides greater workplace protection and social security. However, we should also steer clear of convenient stereotypes, and recognize, for example, that the USA has stronger legal protections in areas such as disability rights and consumer protection than in most of the world.

There is a long tradition of business and society as an area of academic study and public policy, but its primary concern has been how to regulate and motivate business so as to contribute more to the public good. Thus, for example, governments have passed legislation on issues ranging from working hours to sexual harassment, maternity leave, and equal pay so as to enhance workers' well-being. Business and government are depicted as having separate concerns: the former, to do with creating wealth; the latter, to do with social cohesion and security, which has often required intervening in the world of business through both regulation and redistribution.

Since the 1950s, it has become clear that this idea of separate sectors with discrete responsibilities is confusing and, moreover, that different societies around the world have very specific, and often complex, expectations of the role that business should play, which go well beyond paying taxes and abiding by the law. These became apparent in the flurry of literature in the 1960s and 1970s, which provided the theoretical context for contemporary CSR (see Chapter 2). In 1979, Carroll offered what is perhaps the most widely cited framework for understanding the different aspects of social responsibility that had emerged (see Figure 1.2). He identified four types of responsibility under which the various actions taken to manage business's relationship with society should fall, and we examine these individually now.

Economic responsibility

Economic responsibility refers to the fundamental responsibility of business to produce goods and services that society wants, and which it sells at a profit. Many eminent theorists and business leaders would argue that this is the limit of a company's responsibilities, and to attempt any more is at best folly, and at worst a misuse of owners' capital (see Snapshot 1.2). They argue that under the free enterprise system, creating jobs, shareholder value, and goods and services—and doing this in a law-abiding manner—are all inherent ways in which business contributes to society. Managers as agents of the company's owners do not need to worry about the different outcomes because ultimately the company's value will reflect its utility. Indeed, as soon as managers do anything more than focus on profit they risk creating an enterprise with multiple objective functions that ends up having no clear accountability or definition of good performance.[14]

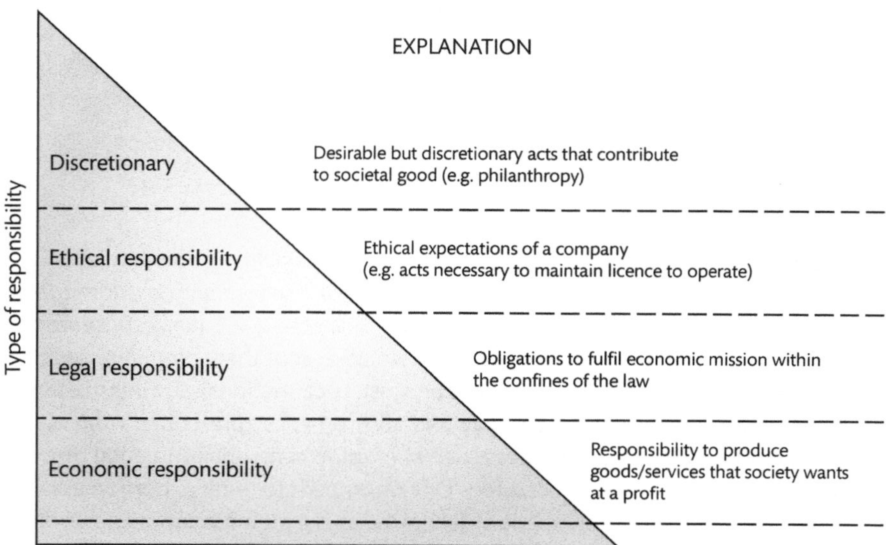

Figure 1.2 Carroll's typology of corporate responsibilities

(*Source:* Adapted from Carroll (1979))

Table 1.2 How the value of CSR depends on your viewpoint

If your starting point is this...	Then the value of CSR to you is likely to be this...
Capitalism is fundamentally wrong	CSR has little if anything to offer you, although it might help you to criticize capitalism
Free markets are self-regulating and successful companies inherently contribute to the social good	CSR has nothing to offer you, and may appear a threat to your beliefs
Some forms of capitalism are worse than others	CSR theory offers some insight: see, for instance, Reich, 2007 and Vogel, 2005
Free market capitalism is essentially good but needs controlling or moderating	CSR theory has a lot to offer in areas from strategy to social accounting
There are business models within the capitalist framework that offer particular social and environmental benefits	Certain aspects under CSR help you understand and manage these models, such as fair trade, social enterprise, and socially responsible investment
Responsible behaviour is a driver for business success	CSR can provide a framework for identifying behaviour that will deliver value to the financial bottom line
Companies can choose to behave more or less ethically	Business ethics as a subset of CSR can help you to understand and manage ethical behaviour
Individuals within companies can be unethical	Individual ethics in the workplace is a subset of CSR

As we shall see in other chapters of this book, there are various counter-arguments to this view. But the idea that companies have a purpose other than simply to make money—that, at the very least, they should consider not only profitability, but also the way in which profits are made—is central to understanding CSR in terms of business's relationship to society. Indeed, where you stand on this argument can significantly influence what you see as the value of CSR (see Table 1.2).

Legal responsibility

Legal responsibility refers to the obligation of business to fulfil its economic mission within the confines of the law. Most people who believe CSR is synonymous with economic responsibility would add the caveat that companies must abide by the law. Equally, those who think that CSR is much more than profit maximization would accept that companies need to be lawful, at least in so far as the laws are legitimate and just. Local, national, and international law sets out the rules by which corporations play, and, over time, has prescribed what companies can and cannot do with regard to areas such as employment, environmental protection, corruption, human rights, and product safety. One only needs to think of pornography, arms sales, and narcotics to realize how the law defines what is legitimate business activity; one need only consider corporate law to appreciate how it spells out the purpose of the company.

Public outrage about the financial crisis since 2007 and the fact that heads of financial institutions have not been put on trial highlights that in many areas of corporate life the law may not be fit for purpose. On top of this, there is growing public and political consternation that it is legal—indeed, by some definitions responsible—to avoid paying corporation taxes in countries where a company does business. But even without these examples, there are good reasons for saying that CSR is concerned with more than legal compliance. Forceful arguments have been made that CSR refers to the actions companies take without legal compulsion. In other words, CSR as a field is about voluntary, not mandatory actions.

The distinction between voluntary and compulsory behaviour may be useful for demarcating a particular subset of CSR theory and practice. Legislation is not comprehensive, and is often the final resort to address a major issue when neither societal norms nor other means of resolution prove adequate. This means that the law by itself will never define everything that society expects companies to take responsibility for. Moreover, companies can have significant influence on what is passed as law, and spend large sums of money persuading law-makers about how to apply their powers. For example, the Trump Administration has been accused of putting individuals and policies in place at the Environmental Protection Agency that favour chemical, oil, and gas companies.[15] In 2013, GSK saw at least thirty staff arrested in a scandal about bribing doctors to prescribe its drugs. Indeed, company wealth can be used to influence the meaning of acceptable or unacceptable influence, while some companies, as part of their CSR strategies, have said that they will simply not engage in political debate.

The use of company wealth to influence politicians has been linked to wider debates about the diminishing power of government. Globalization, including the increased international flows of capital, goods, and services (see Chapter 2) has in some respects increased the scope of corporate influence. Headlines along the lines of '*Tesco: Richer than Peru*',[16] raise fears about unfettered corporate power and the lack of regulation, especially once one looks beyond national borders. Such information should be treated with caution. For example, to say that a company is richer than a country is a bit like saying a short person standing up is taller than a fat person lying down: it is not an accurate, or even useful, comparison.

Despite arguments that if governments are too harsh on companies, business will invest elsewhere, by some measures governments have become stricter on business. For instance, the European Union's Pollution Prevention and Control Directive has raised the bar on controlling industrial pollution, the EU fined Microsoft €899 million because of anti-competitive practices, and in 2017 HSBC had to pay over HK$400 million in fines for its role in selling Lehman Brothers-linked financial products.[17] Nonetheless, fears that business wields too much power are widespread and not totally without foundation. For example, in 2006 the British government refused to enforce anti-corruption laws against BAE, the defence company, following what were later described as 'blatant threats',[18] and Total successfully prevented a case about human rights abuse in Burma from going to court in Belgium.

But, even if it is true that governments find it harder to regulate business than in the past, it is a mistake to ignore the very real power that legislation has. For example, the Alien Torts Claims Act 1789, despite being a US law, has been used to make companies legally accountable for their behaviour overseas, and laws modelled on the US Foreign Corrupt Practices Act 1977 are starting to find their way onto statute books in other countries. There is also a complex body of international law on issues such as labour rights, slavery, economic rights, and the environment, which, despite being incomplete, unwieldy, and poorly enforced, nonetheless offers the basis for regulating business in the coming years.

However, legal requirements that vary greatly from country to country present (depending on one's perspective) a problem or an opportunity for business. For example, the work week in China is 44 hours, in France it is 35, and in South Korea it is over 50. Will companies choose to invest where the legal work week is longest? Is it immoral for investors to refuse to let a company relocate to a country where environmental management costs are low due to weak environmental laws? If it is legal in Indonesia to use lead paint, why should a retailer there insist that its suppliers use more expensive non-toxic paints? Time and again in the contemporary world corporations are finding themselves held to account not for abiding by the laws in a particular country of operation, but for upholding the non-legislated norms and values of globally dispersed groups and individuals.

Similar developments are taking place in the corporate governance field. For example, both Harvard University's Kennedy School and the environmental non-government organization (NGO) CERES have, in different ways, put governance to the fore of their work on CSR. Companies such as Walt Disney, IBM, and Intel include corporate governance as part of their CSR reports, while pressure groups such as the Interfaith Center on CSR see aspects of governance, such as executive compensation, the independence and inclusivity of boards of directors, and transparency and accountability to shareholders and other stakeholders as important parts of the CSR agenda. Transparency and disclosure are recurring themes in debates about good governance and CSR more broadly.

Another area where the legal requirements of one region are being spread into other countries is corruption. Business has long been criticized from different parts of the ideological spectrum for using bribery and corruption to influence policy, win contracts, and otherwise distort both the functioning of free markets and the political process. Transparency International, an international NGO that lobbies against corrupt practices, defines corruption as the abuse of entrusted power for private gain. Although often portrayed as a victimless crime, corruption has been associated with low wages, unsafe counterfeit products, and hazardous living and working conditions. It is also blamed for undermining democracy and sound governance, stifling private-sector growth, and encouraging inefficient business management (because winning contracts comes down to influence rather than competency).

Industries such as mining, construction, and defence have been especially criticized for paying commissions to win business, not least in countries with limited transparency and accountability. Although in advanced democracies industries from banking to pharmaceuticals to football have all been implicated in corruption scandals, nonetheless the traditional targets have been at the forefront of CSR initiatives in this area, including the Extractive Industries Transparency Initiative, which enables the public to compare company payments with declared government revenues from oil, gas, and mining. Combating corruption has also been added to the principles of the United Nations Global Compact, but, despite these developments, some still downplay its importance, either because it is held to be culturally acceptable in some parts of the world, or because of fears that, by getting too strict with certain governments, companies will lose business to less scrupulous competitors.

Ethical responsibility

Ethical responsibility refers to the responsibilities of companies that go beyond legal compliance, and which are not determined by economic calculations. For some people, this is the most interesting part of CSR because it is asking what companies can do beyond what is demanded by regulation and economic rationality. Sometimes, companies preempt tougher legislation (e.g. the chemical industry's Responsible Care standard) believing that voluntary agreements will be easier to manage, and perhaps less stringent. But ethical responsibility is not always so pragmatically motivated. In the 1980s, The Body Shop gave a significant boost to campaigners who, since the publication of Harrison's *Animal machines* in 1964, had wanted the testing of cosmetics on animals outlawed. Today, campaign groups such as People for the Ethical Treatment of Animals (PETA) are successful in getting companies such as McDonald's to improve animal welfare.

The environment is one area where in the past companies relied on government to say what was permissible, but in the face of global challenges from climate change to water availability to deforestation they are, at least to some degree, willing to go beyond legal compliance. IKEA, for instance, is committed to '100% renewable energy' by 2020, producing as much renewable energy as it consumes using renewable sources, such as the wind and sun.[19] This is part of a trend commencing in the 1980s when the effectiveness of command-and-control regulatory solutions started to be questioned, and both companies and regulators began to accept that preventing pollution could be a more effective way forward than simply punishing it after the event. Environmental issues found their way into marketing strategies, and industries focusing on environmental technologies and services emerged. In the 1990s, environmental management standards such as BS 7750, the EU Eco-Management and Audit System (EMAS), and the ISO 14000 series provided new ways for companies to understand and manage their environmental impacts. Companies began to realize that, in certain situations, improved environmental performance could have a positive impact on the financial bottom line. In what came to be called the 'greening revolution', the business–environment relationship became, for some companies, less a costly problem than a strategic opportunity.[20]

The greening revolution was accompanied by a shift in government attitude, notably in Europe, where the legal responsibility of producers for their products began to cover more of the product life cycle, so that factors such as disposal and recycling had to be considered in product design, manufacturing, and marketing. 'Cradle-to-grave' thinking has become part of design philosophy in industries ranging from electrical goods to footwear to automotives. Major chemical companies have invested heavily in developing more environmentally beneficial substitutes for harmful materials. At the same time, new industries, such as biotechnology, have presented new environmental challenges (e.g. the perceived environmental consequences of genetically modified organisms) and established industries, such as energy, have generated new debates by investing in renewable energy at the same time as they remain dependent on environmentally damaging carbon-based fuels.

With its emphasis on financial and environmental benefits, the greening revolution marked a significant step forward in CSR and one that most CSR theorists failed to predict. The term 'eco-efficiency' has become widely used, highlighting that there need not be a trade-off between business and environmental performance. As McDonough and Braungart

(2002) point out, however, there is a significant difference between being eco-efficient and eco-effective: it is the distinction between being *less bad* and consciously striving to do *more good*. If the greening revolution helped companies to think about making their products less harmful, eco-effectiveness (what has been called 'beyond greening') requires companies to rethink their technologies, their products, and their whole vision of the contribution that business makes to society.

The importance of beyond greening has grown as sustainability has become a major public concern. Sustainability—the ability to sustain a high quality of life for current and future generations—requires companies to rethink what they produce and how they do so. It also involves society rethinking what it wants from commercial enterprise—a question that is capturing widespread attention, as the potentially catastrophic consequences of global climate change become more widely believed.

Although 'sustainability' is still used in some CSR literature to refer to an eco-efficiency agenda, in its fullest sense it refers to something that cannot be captured only by reference to an environmental or a business rationale.[21] The triple bottom line was developed to address this by encouraging companies to think in terms of adding economic, social, and environmental value.[22] This provides the framework for some companies' sustainability reports, but merging these three dimensions of value in a way that shows the company's relationship to sustainable development has proved difficult and there is a marked tendency to treat each topic in isolation.

The distinction between doing less harm compared with doing more good is also evident among entrepreneurs whose motivation for going into business is measured by their social or environmental success. In the 1950s, faith-based and other organizations began responding to their members' concerns about unequal distribution of the wealth created by trade by establishing alternative trade organizations. Oxfam Trading, Traidcraft, and others invested in building the capacity of producers in poor countries, and sold their handicrafts and other products in Western markets. Later, beginning in the Netherlands, fairtrade labelling organizations were formed, guaranteeing to the consumer that certified producers and traders, in commodities such as coffee, tea, and cocoa, met specified fairtrade standards which include a minimum price to growers that exceeds the cost of production and payment of a social development premium. For several years now, companies such as Starbucks, Virgin Atlantic, and J Sainsbury have offered fairtrade-certified products, and a new generation of social enterprises has tried to take the social impact of business a step further by offering goods and services with a defined social or environmental purpose.

The same principle of harnessing the power of the markets for the benefit of the poor is found in initiatives popularized under the headings 'bottom of the pyramid' and 'corporate social opportunity'.[23] A well-known example of this is the microfinance model, originally developed in Bangladesh, but now found throughout the world. Microfinance provides poor people with financial capital without the need for collateral, helping them to avoid high usury charges and providing them with a safe place to keep their money. Initially, it was promoted by NGOs and aid organizations, but then major banks such as Citigroup and Deutsche Bank have started to offer microfinance services. A variety of models have evolved, such as the pioneering Grameen Bank, BRI in Indonesia with 30 million savers, and ProCredit with banks throughout Eastern Europe (see Chapter 10). BRAC Bank, for example, which grew out of a NGO's social development work, is now the fastest-growing bank in Bangladesh, with over

350 branches. Investment in microfinance is also made possible by organizations such as Kiva, an internet platform that links small-scale investors with individual entrepreneurs in the Global South.

Discretionary responsibilities

Discretionary responsibilities are ones, such as philanthropy, which a company can assume even if there are no clear-cut societal expectations. As noted, for some, CSR is what lies beyond the law, and an important area of discretionary responsibility has been the idea of 'giving back' to society through philanthropic donations. Business leaders such as Carnegie, Rowntree, and Ford gave back large amounts of their individual wealth to establish foundations or to invest in favoured projects. Companies such as Hitachi, ExxonMobil, and Tata, often encouraged by tax regimes, gave as much as 5% of their pre-tax income to the arts, community development, education, and other valued causes. Even though it no longer defines CSR, philanthropy remains important, as the multi-billion-dollar endowments by Bill Gates and Warren Buffet show. In the USA, where 2,600 companies have charitable foundations, corporate giving by firms of all sizes was estimated to be $18.5 billion in 2012.[24] In the UK, corporate donations are reckoned to be less than £800 million and, unlike the USA, are in decline.[25]

In the 1990s, companies increasingly began to take a more strategic view of philanthropy, seeking out causes that were aligned with their business goals. For example, AT&T's foundation used its funding of education projects to win the ear of government policy advisers and this gave it an inside track in subsequent policy-making about the information superhighway. This has led some companies to adopt cause-related or affinity marketing, under which companies invest in social causes that complement their brands. But companies are wary of criticism that anything they do to give back is perceived as a public relations exercise and have sought to emphasize the win-win nature of investing in communities, while also taking a more critical view of staff volunteering and product gifting. Company-backed initiatives, such as the Partnership for Quality Medical Product Donation and Lloyds Banking Group, have helped focus attention on what constitutes good practice and the impact that philanthropy can have.

Discussion points

We have set out two ways of thinking about CSR: company values and materiality.

- Which of these do you find most useful as a way of starting to think about the meaning of 'CSR'?
- Which of these do you think would resonate most with business managers?
- Do you think the type and size of a company and its industry affect how it approaches CSR?

Limitations of CSR frameworks

There are now more sophisticated frameworks for comprehending CSR than that of Carroll (1979), as we explore in Chapter 6, and some of these put much greater emphasis on the process of managing the relationship with wider society. Interestingly, although

Carroll denied that his was a hierarchical framework under which some types of responsibility were more important than others, many of these subsequent theories have perpetuated and expanded on the idea that there are qualitatively different tiers of responsibility. This, in turn, has encouraged the idea that companies undergo different evolutionary stages within which their responsibilities and the nature of their relationship with other elements of society discernibly change. Prominent areas of CSR activity today include:

- business ethics
- human rights (including gender and sexuality)
- legal compliance
- worker rights and welfare
- philanthropy and community investment
- market relations
- environmental management
- corruption
- sustainability
- corporate governance
- animal rights.

Demonstrating that these transitions are beneficial either to business or society is an important part of the debate about CSR, as we discuss in Chapters 6 and 13. Transitions comprise new issues that business is having to address (e.g. climate change and shifts to a low-carbon economy), and also new concepts (e.g. responsibility to stakeholders). But when thinking about such changes, one should be as alert to the responsibilities that are seldom mentioned as one is to the those highlighted in CSR reports or at conferences. Moreover, one should be prepared to ask why issue A has been included whereas issue B has not. For example, companies such as Unilever, IBM, and Barclays celebrate their commitment to CSR, but do not include the closing of their company pension schemes or its consequences for workers as a responsibility issue. Likewise, accounting firms such as KPMG and PWC provide CSR consulting services, but are not especially vociferous on corporate taxation as a dimension of CSR.

Issues such as tax and pensions draw attention to the importance of long-term corporate performance. In considering how companies negotiate their responsibilities to society, an important test is whether they use their power and resources for the long-term benefit of society, even if there are short-term costs to the company. In an early *Citizenship report* (GE, 2005), multinational conglomerate GE stressed that good citizenship has a more positive and enduring purpose than tackling the ills of the moment: it is about delivering high performance with high integrity over a sustained period of time, so as to create benefits for the long-term health of society and the enterprise. Commentators on business and society have pointed to a number of situations in which private enterprise is most at odds with society's interests, such as when monopolies replace competitive markets, or when companies become so powerful that they unduly influence public policy. These threats exist today, but to these has been added a situation in which the short-term interests of investors prevent companies from taking a long-term view of the well-being of either the enterprise or society.

It is interesting to note that economist Milton Friedman, who made probably the most forceful statement that companies are responsible only to shareholders (see Snapshot 1.2), introduced his theory of CSR at a time when investors were more inclined to hold shares for the longer term. Nowadays, notably in the Anglo-Saxon model that has become the norm against which other business systems are examined, many of Friedman's unspoken assumptions about what underpins the business–society relationship no longer hold, because investors look for higher and speedier returns, employees are more mobile, and senior managers are rewarded for pushing up the price of shares and increasing productivity, regardless of the human cost. Furthermore, increasingly these investors are less interested in publicly traded firms. The number of publicly listed companies and the number of initial public offerings in the UK have fallen by half in the 2000s (Franks and Mayer, 2017), while a growing number of firms are owned by private equity funds.

It is these types of change that some feel CSR should redress, either by putting limits on what is acceptable behaviour in the short run, or by encouraging companies to pay more attention to long-term performance. As one group of managers within the World Business Council for Sustainable Development (WBCSD) has concluded, CSR (specifically sustainability) becomes a logical element of profit maximization as soon as one insists that shareholder value equates with *long-term* shareholder value.[26] The reality for many companies, however, is that they have to straddle the demands of both the short and the long term. In the words of an oil industry CEO who had to contend with pressure from both the financial markets and civil society:

> On the one hand, you've got Wall Street squeezing you harder and harder for shorter and shorter term performance. On the other hand, you have a broader constituent base that wants more than financial results . . . Most CEOs will tell you, 'This is damn hard work'.
>
> (Blowfield and Googins, 2007, p 22)

Snapshot 1.2 What responsibilities do companies have?

The only social responsibility a law-abiding business has is to maximize profits for its shareholders.

This, in short, is economist Milton Friedman's theory of free market CSR. It is a controversial viewpoint among CSR theorists because it appears to say that what's good for investors is good for everyone. That is a difficult position to defend because profit maximization can drive companies to bend or break the law to the point of self-destruction (e.g. Enron, Lehman Brothers, Carillion). But Friedman isn't saying that everything is justified by the share price: he believes that government sets the rules of the game, and companies have to operate within them. An important question, therefore, is whether governments do a good job at regulating business behaviour, and the answer to that might be very different in today's globalized economy than it was when many companies primarily operated within national boundaries.

Another important question is, 'What do we mean by shareholder?' In the 1960s, it was common for individuals and institutions to hold shares for many years, and people's wealth was closely related to the long-term well-being of the firm. That has changed with the emergence of day-traders, the high turnover in shares even among institutional investors, the emphasis put on publicly traded companies' quarterly earnings, and the way success is defined by private equity firms. The shareholder is not the long-term owner that he or she once was.

(continued . . .)

Even among libertarian entrepreneurs, who would typically favour markets over governments as arbiters of the social good, Friedman's view of the firm has been criticized as outdated. For example, John Mackey, CEO of US retailer Whole Foods and a self-proclaimed libertarian, has said: 'The enlightened corporation should try to create value for all of its constituencies.' In a dialogue with Friedman, he argued that shareholders are one group with an interest in the company and that they want the firm to maximize profits. According to Mackey, it is too narrow to say that shareholder interests are paramount: the entrepreneur defines the company's purpose, and if he says from the outset that part of that purpose is, for example, to give a stated percentage of net profits to philanthropy, then subsequent investors have no right to dispute that—they know what they are buying into.

(*Sources:* Friedman, 1962; *Wall Street Journal*, 2005; Mackey and Sisodia, 2013; Rogers, 2018)

Quick questions

CSR is often depicted as a 'left-wing' intervention to disrupt market capitalism, yet people on 'the right' also disagree about its value and importance.

1 What changes have taken place in society since the 1960s that might make Friedman's notion of CSR outdated?

2 How convincing is Mackey's argument that profits are not the purpose, but a means to realizing social and environmental ends?

3 Do you think the example of Carillion in 2018 supports Mackey's argument or Friedman's?

Case study 1 Too big to jail? Guilt and innocence in the aerospace industry

Aerospace is an industry, much like defence, in which there is a constant drum-beat of allegations about bribery, corruption, and other scandals. It is not surprising: aircraft are big-budget items manufactured by large companies requiring huge amounts of investment and specialist skills. Aerospace companies do not pop up overnight. They are also large employers, and are closely associated with national prestige. Boeing, the largest company in the industry, is typically portrayed as a standard-bearer of US prestige, while Airbus, its main competitor, carries the flag for European engineering, particularly for Germany, France, and the UK.

In 2014 alone, Boeing was accused by competitor Elon Musk of using corrupt practices to win a rocket project, and a procurement officer, Deon Anderson, was jailed for twenty months for providing confidential information to help a supplier win bids. But some would say Anderson was unlucky. Despite the number of allegations made about the industry, not many people are indicted.

In 2017, Tom Enders, CEO of Airbus, agreed to step down in part because he was investigated in Austria over fighter-jet sales. His chief operating officer (COO), Fabrice Brégier, has officially stood down but numerous media articles claim the departure of the CEO's bitter rival was a condition for Enders's own exit. In both cases, the departure of Airbus's number 1 and 2 executives has been strongly linked to a series of corruption allegations in Britain and France that have dogged the company.

Airbus is not alone. In 2017, a smaller competitor, Bombardier, had to be saved after Boeing accused it of illegal subsidies which led to its C-Series jet being hit by 300% tariffs in the USA. This case illustrates the political nature of the industry, with various governments accused of helping Bombardier, Boeing accused of pressuring the US government into agreeing the tariffs, and US–British relations being damaged because of the possible loss of jobs in Northern Ireland.

(*continued . . .*)

The political nature of the industry was also highlighted by the case of Rolls-Royce, which reached a \$1.8 million settlement with the Indian government in 2014 to end a bribery investigation, and in 2016 paid multi-million pound settlements in Britain, Brazil, and the USA. And the industry is not just on the paying end of corrupt practices. In 2017, Boeing's 787 aircraft came under scrutiny from safety bodies worried about components in its wings. The components were made by Kobe Steel, which announced that for several years it had been falsifying quality checks on thousands of metal products, including parts for the 787.

Whether it be Boeing, Kobe Steel, Rolls-Royce, or Airbus, what is noticeable is that the executives involved have walked away without fines or jail terms. Shareholders have taken a hit in terms of dividends or share prices (Rolls-Royce made a loss of £4.03 billion in 2016, and its share price fell 4%) and jobs are at risk (4,000 people work at the Bombardier plant near Belfast), but when Rolls-Royce announced 2,600 job cuts in 2014, its chief finance officer (CFO) left the company with a £900,000 pay-off. After the bailing out of financial institutions around the world after the 2007 financial crisis led to accusations that some businesses had become 'too big to fail', now according to financial reporter, Jesse Eisinger, some executives have become 'too big to jail'.

(*Sources:* Economist 2017; Eisinger, 2017; Frangos, 2017; Monaghan 2017; Sage 2017)

Questions

1 Industries such as oil and gas, aerospace, and arms and defence involve large companies with highly skilled staff, operating around the world. Because they are so large, they have huge influence and importance, and close relationships with national governments.

   a Why are these industries so often caught up in bribery and corruption scandals?

   b Do you think that the prestige of these industries means they should be treated as a special case by national governments?

   c What are the main CSR issues that the aerospace industry needs to address?

2 Eisinger says that it has become difficult for executives in large corporations to be brought to account for their actions, even when they seem unethical or against the law.

   a Is being forced to step down a sufficient sanction for someone such as Tom Enders?

   b Deon Anderson was jailed; Hiroya Kawasaki, CEO of Kobe Steel, was not. Is this fair?

   c What other industries do you think have executives who are too big for jail?

Summary

CSR is the newest 'old' thing in business management. What we mean by 'CSR' is constantly changing as society itself evolves, affecting our expectations of business and the way in which its relationship with society is handled. The discussion about what CSR means can be entered into from several doors. We can think of the company as an entity with its own values, or at least as a vessel that has to accommodate the competing values and moral principles of different people. We can also think of it as a member of society that has to uphold certain duties and obligations in order to be a good citizen.

Each doorway has its advantages and disadvantages from an analytical standpoint, but it would be a mistake to conclude that CSR is diminished because there is no universal definition or overarching theory. Instead, what these different perspectives reveal are a multitude of ways in which business impacts upon, and is affected by, the rest of society and hence a multiplicity of reasons why companies might want to manage that relationship. They will do this differently, depending on such variables as the type of company, the moment in history, the nature of the industry, and the geopolitical context. Similar variables will also determine the benefits of addressing the relationship. But the constant and central concern of CSR is how the relationship between business and wider society is defined and acted upon, whether by business as a whole, through collective action, or by single corporate actors.

Further reading

Barrett, R. 1998, *Liberating the corporate soul: building a visionary organization*, Butterworth-Heinemann, Boston, MA.

An interesting approach to blending and aligning personal and organizational values.

Chandler, D. 2016, *Strategic corporate social responsibility: sustainable value creation*, 4th edn, Harvard University Press, Cambridge, MA.

Concise overview of the main drivers and hurdles affecting CSR today.

Crane, A. and Matten, D. 2015, *Business ethics: managing corporate citizenship and sustainability in the age of globalization*, Oxford University Press, Oxford.

Comprehensive introduction to business ethics, with an interesting focus on the company as a member of society.

Davis, I. 2005, 'Ian Davis on business and society', *The Economist*, 26 May, online at http://piglossary.pbwors.com/f/davis+-+The+Biggest+Contract.pdf.

Provocative take on the need to rethink the role of business, from the head of McKinsey's management consultancy.

Frederick, W.C. 2006, *Corporation be good!: the story of corporate social responsibility*, Dog Ear Publishing, Indianapolis, IN.

Several decades of CSR thinking collected together by an American academic.

Krawcheck, S., 2017, *Own it: the power of women at work*, Crown Business, New York.

American entrepreneur on the importance of feminism in management.

http://www.oup.com/uk/blowfield_murray4e

Visit the online resources that accompany this book to enrich your understanding of this chapter. Among the resources available are web links, exercises, and additional case studies.

Endnotes

1. http://www.economicshelp.org/blog/4060/economics/total-uk-debt, accessed 5 April 2018.
2. http://www.fca.org.uk/news/press-releases/fca-fines-merrill-lynch-failing-report-transactions, accessed 5 September 2018.

3. Baker, 2005.
4. May et al., 2007.
5. For overviews of CSR, see Carroll, 1999; Birch, 2001; Basu and Palazzo, 2005. For a discussion of corporate social responsiveness and performance, see Wartick and Cochran, 1985. Bennett et al., 1999, contains essays on the progress of corporate sustainability. Wood and Logsdon, 2001, 2002; Moon et al., 2005; Matten and Moon, 2008 provide different viewpoints on corporate citizenship.
6. Windsor, 2001.
7. Harvey-Jones, 1988.
8. See e.g. Birch, 2001; Dion, 2001; Wood and Logsdon, 2001.
9. Werther and Chandler, 2011.
10. Anderson, 2003, 2005.
11. Davies, 1997.
12. See e.g. Chryssides and Kaler, 1993; Sorell and Hendry, 1994; Donaldson and Dunfee, 1999; Ladkin, 2006.
13. Jamali and Mirshak, 2007; Visser and Tolhurst, 2010.
14. Jensen and Meckling, 1976; for a fuller discussion, see Chapter 8.
15. http://www.theguardian.com/us-news/2017/dec/12/big-oil-lobby-get-what-it-wants-epa-trump-pruitt, accessed 5 April 2018.
16. http://www.guardian.co.uk/business/2007/apr/15/supermarkets.uknews, accessed 5 April 2018.
17. https://www.telegraph.co.uk/business/2017/11/21/hsbc-slapped-record-hong-kong-fine-sale-products-linked-lehman, accessed 25 April 2018.
18. Gibb and Webster, 2008.
19. http://www.ikea.com/gb/en/this-is-ikea/people-planet/energy-resources/climate-energy, accessed 5 September 2018.
20. Freeman et al., 2000; Schaltegger et al., 2003.
21. Renn, 1995, cited by Schaltegger et al., 2003.
22. Elkington, 1998.
23. Grayson and Hodges, 2004; Prahalad, 2005.
24. https://philanthropy.com/article/Big-Businesses-Expect-Modest/140341, accessed 5 April 2018.
25. http://www.thirdsector.co.uk/Fundraising/article/1187212/corporate-donations-fell-almost-third-past-two-years, accessed 5 April 2018.
26. WBCSD, 2006.

The origins of corporate social responsibility

Chapter overview

In this chapter, we set out the theoretical and historical origins of modern-day CSR. In particular, we will:

- plot the evolution of the modern corporation and its relevance for the business–society relationship;
- explore how CSR has evolved from the Industrial Revolution to the current era of globalization;
- trace the development of theories of CSR.

Main topics

Key terms

Capitalism
Corporate philanthropy
Industrial Revolution
Welfare state
Globalization
Licence to operate
Limited liability
New Deal
Social contract

Introduction

In 1909, George Cadbury found himself in court because the company bearing his name had been buying cocoa produced by slaves in Africa.[1] In 2000, the company found itself accused once more of the same offence. These incidents demonstrate that issues such as slavery do not go away. More to the point, when corporate behaviour clashes with people's sense of justice and permissibility, companies are held responsible even if there is no legal liability and despite the absence or presence of shareholder interest.

The issues that matter, why they come to the fore, and what a company does to address them vary according to the company, the industry, the location, and the time. Cadbury's response in 1909 was very different to what it was in 2000 (see Case study 2), even if slavery was always more likely to be more of an issue for the chocolate manufacturer than for its Birmingham neighbour, the car-maker Rover, which in 2000, faced with bankruptcy and allegations of pension fund fraud, had its own CSR headaches to deal with.

CSR is constant, yet variable and dynamic. In this chapter, we examine how society has consistently held expectations of business that go beyond the narrow sphere of wealth creation. We begin by exploring the relationship that business has had with society during different historical periods and in different countries. Then we examine how various theories of CSR have emerged to help understand and manage that relationship.

What the following sections reveal is that private enterprise has always been the subject of public scrutiny. What we mean by 'CSR' today has been influenced enormously by our economic systems, the evolution of the modern corporation, and the emergence of theories of CSR itself. This chapter is a discussion of that heritage.

The Cadbury case is a useful starting point for putting CSR in context. The issues in 1909 were, in many ways, the same as those today. First, companies were then, and are now, felt by many to have a duty to uphold certain human rights, even when there is no legal liability. Second, companies that purchase commodities or manufactured goods are held to have influence over, and responsibility for, the behaviour of their producers. These principles were apparent in the 1909 court case and are central to areas of modern CSR, such as ethical trade.

Echoes of the Cadbury experience can be heard throughout this chapter as we explore the origins of CSR. The company's experiences are not unique; stick a pin anywhere in the timeline of corporate evolution and the issues of what a company should be responsible for, who decides, and where accountability lies are recurring themes. Responses can vary, as do the levels of trust in corporations (see Figure 2.1), but what this chapter shows

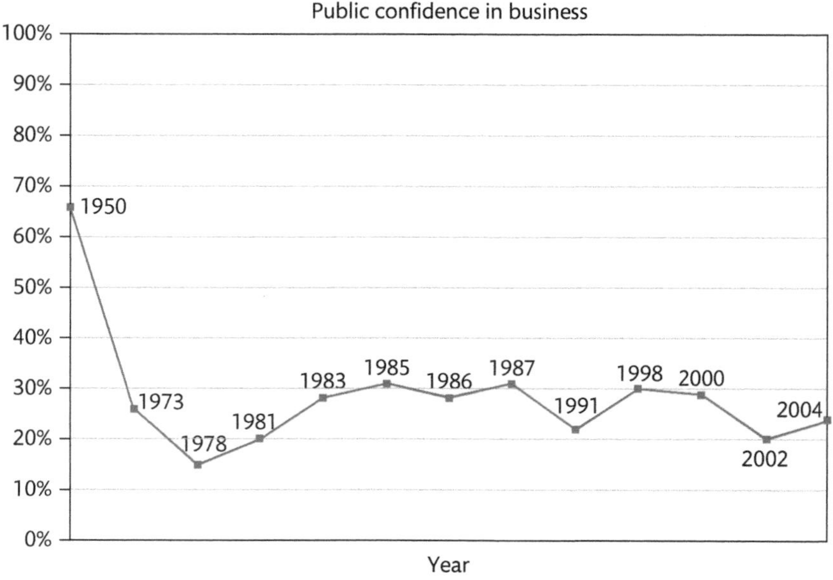

Figure 2.1 Levels of public confidence in business over the years

(*Source:* Based on data from Frederick, 2006)

is that the issues of CSR and the role of commercial endeavour in society are constants throughout human history.

Three eras of responsibility

The Cadbury experience straddles three historical periods, during which the nature of business's relationship with society has changed significantly:

1 the Industrial Revolution;
2 the mid-twentieth-century welfare state;
3 the Globalization era.

Each period has raised new issues about what business should be responsible for, but, as we shall see, many of the issues remain relevant from one era to the next.

The Industrial Revolution

Throughout much of Europe, the biggest change in human demographics and human working life came with the Industrial Revolution, as the poor from the countryside headed towards the cities in search of work. In the UK, the first industrial power, the proportion of the population engaged in manufacturing increased from one-fifth to nearly two-thirds between 1801 and 1871.[2]

But this massive increase in urban living brought with it problems of overcrowding and disease. Children were employed in sweeping chimneys, domestic service, and manufacturing, as depicted in the popular novels of Dickens and Kingsley. Factories and mines were responsible for a large number of injuries and fatalities. Slave labour on the African and American continents produced many of the raw materials that industrialization required. In some industries, women became important components of the workforce, not out of choice, but due to poverty.

Industrialization provoked civil unrest. From the late 1770s, there were numerous popular, and frequently violent, protests aimed at resisting industrialization or improving the lives of those affected by it. Information about human exploitation spurred various reform movements, such as Wilberforce's anti-slavery society, while the UK's first Factory Acts were passed in 1819 and laws to control conditions in mines were passed in 1842.

In addition to government intervention, it was around this time that writers such as Carlyle and Arnold began to suggest how heads of industry might behave, marking the start of the era of Victorian philanthropy. Robert Owen had already set up his mills at New Lanark and was an instigator of the early Factory Acts. He strove to establish a new model of industrial development in Scotland and the USA, based on the belief that a man's character was formed by his surroundings and the conditions under which he worked and lived. This vision was developed later in the century by the likes of Cadbury and Rowntree, who established villages at Bournville and New Earswick, respectively, within which their workers could live in supportive communities with open spaces, shops, and schools in easy reach.

Carnegie—who famously said that the wealthy should consider their wealth to be trust funds that they should use for the good of the community—pursued a different form of benevolence, using his fortune from steel to embark on a philanthropic quest that saw him donate some $350 million to charitable and other philanthropic causes, including the building of libraries, the establishment of educational trusts, and contributions towards creating such iconic buildings as the Carnegie Hall in New York and the Peace Palace in The Hague.

Each industrial economy has its own history of industrialization, and we only have to look at the different timelines of the abolition of slavery in the UK, the USA, and Belgium, for example, to see that change happened at different speeds and in different ways. And some countries' toleration of slavery overseas when it had been outlawed at home is but one example of how standards of business behaviour were affected by location. Similar aspects of industrialization have arisen again today with the emergence of new industrial powers. For example, in countries such as China, the massive influx of rural people into urban areas is one trend that has redefined notions of CSR, as have aspects of economic growth and overseas investment that appear to be at the expense of human and environmental well-being (see Chapter 5).

The evolution and rise of the modern corporation

In the mind's eye, the first Industrial Revolution in Europe and the USA conjures up images of technological innovation: steam engines, mills, belching factory chimneys, and the like. But this was as much an institutional as an industrial revolution. Work life changed, governed by clocks and machines rather than by seasons. Also the idea of business itself changed as well. As important as technology was institutional innovation, not least the emergence of the 'limited liability company' and changes in the meaning of 'incorporation'. These legal constructs were to have a profound effect on the business-society relationship, not only on where liability fell, but what the rights and responsibilities of the company were. Today, the meaning of 'business' is either taken for granted, or the subject of typically polarized arguments over whether it is a good or a bad thing. But in capitalism's early days, the advantages and disadvantages of different types of company were widely debated. Limited liability—the construct by which shareholders in a company are not liable for its debts beyond the nominal value of their shares—was a major factor that allowed the modern corporation to emerge. The economist Adam Smith disliked this idea and favoured partnerships over corporations, because he felt that separating the owner from direct control of the company opens the way for professional managers to pursue their own self-interest.[3] But, despite the fact that the limited liability company is only one of several forms of commercial enterprise, it has nonetheless come to dominate the modern business world.

Limited liability encourages entrepreneurship, but has also been singled out as the root cause of problems in the business-society relationship. It has made possible the emergence of multinational corporations, the power of which Korten (1995) views as a threat to society and Henderson (2004) sees as an asset. It also creates the tension between shareholders and corporate officials that is central to arguments about where a company's responsibilities lie. For some, such as Friedman (1962) and Novak (1982), the primacy given to shareholder interests is the genius of capitalism; for others, such as Mitchell (2001) and Ellsworth (2002), it is the reason why managers focus on short-term results and therefore restricts their freedom to serve the interests of others in society. Thus, limited liability is central to the roles that companies play in creating jobs, paying taxes, and generating wealth, but also to aspects of corporate behaviour such as downsizing, bankruptcy, and who has claim to the company's assets. We discuss these issues in other chapters, not least in the context of the socially responsible investment movement which seeks to change the investor-company relationship (see Chapter 10).

The twentieth century–a more mature capitalism

From corporate to government responsibility

By the early twentieth century, changes in the legal definition of the firm led to a huge increase in the number of mergers, and corporations came to be seen by some as huge impersonal monoliths that were beginning to exert political pressure as never before, leading to public calls for greater regulation and supervision (see Snapshot 2.1). Private enterprise had flourished in the late nineteenth century until the period prior to World War I. Yes, it could be highly exploitative of people and nature. Yes, it was often the bedfellow of imperialism and militarism. Yes, it frequently relied on monopoly and oligopoly to the point where John D. Rockefeller, who famously stated that 'competition is a sin', owned wealth equivalent to nearly 2% of US GDP (Bill Gates is worth 0.65%).[4] Capitalism took various forms and had many facets, making it difficult to generalize. But for all its weaknesses and failings, capitalist free enterprise, and with it global free trade, flourished before World War I, corporate power grew, and private self-interest was promoted as serving the public good. This triumphalism faded after the war; momentum increased for greater equality and a rethinking of the social order following the leadership failures that had left 8 million dead on battlefields around the world, and the image of the capitalist as war profiteer depicted in Shaw's play *Major Barbara* was commonplace. The International Labour Organization (ILO), founded in 1919 as part of the League of Nations, brought together government, business, and trade unions, and explicitly recognized the dangers of an unjust political or economic order. Business leaders were forced to consider the impact that their activities were having on wider society, and some engaged in movements such as 'New Capitalism',[5] promoting the idea that business should voluntarily take steps to portray itself and its activities as beneficial to society at large.

But such ideas gained limited traction, partly because of the greater struggle between managers and organized labour that was a feature of the post-war period, and also because economic growth (particularly increases in share value in some countries) encouraged a belief that markets could be the ultimate guarantors of the public good. This came to a head with the Great Depression, when corporate greed was blamed as one of the possible causes of the 1929 Wall Street Crash that left millions destitute in the USA, with ramifications throughout the world's economy. It was time to rein in corporate and shareholder excess, and where possible government stepped in to rescue the economy. In Germany, the National Socialist Party struck alliances with big business to align private enterprise with the national good. In the USA, President Franklin D. Roosevelt initiated the 'New Deal', a series of measures that were, in part, designed to limit the power of corporations. If the 1920s view of corporate managers is encapsulated in the phrase of General Motors' President, Alfred Sloan, 'The business of business is business', Roosevelt's view can be seen in the quote, 'We consider too much the good luck of the early bird, and not enough the bad luck of the early worm.' Despite the very different fortunes of countries such as Germany, the USA, and Japan, the idea of social welfare as a safety net for when capitalism wobbled or fell remained a platform of the social order for the rest of the twentieth century, at least in wealthier nations. In countries from Argentina to Indonesia governments have continued to step in to tackle market failure, and the interventions by major economic powers around the world to save the finance industry in 2008 show that in the world of *realpolitik*, free markets are not trusted to serve the public good.

Snapshot 2.1 Is big business desirable, inevitable, or irredeemable?

Ever since the nineteenth century the size of companies has grown and grown. When people think about CSR, they often think about the giant multinational companies and conglomerates that dominate industries from information and communication technologies to retail to pharmaceuticals. Most private-sector workers may work for small firms, but it is large business that attracts attention. Unilever, Tata, BHP Billiton, and Samsung are a handful of the many multinational companies that put CSR on the front pages of their websites. But are these companies too big to be responsible members of society?

Thomas Quinn called such companies *'monster business'*. The monster business was the inevitable end result of business evolution where companies evolved from small enterprising firms to large ones, then into giant corporations, and finally into monsters. Monster companies not only stifle competition—something that has led to antitrust laws around the world—but also affect social and political institutions, and even pose a menace to the democratic way of life.

Although Quinn was writing during the 1930s Depression, his views find echoes in CSR discussions today. For example, he pointed to big-banker trustees who control voting at the dominant corporations, representing what he called *'the highest degree of concentrated economic power in our history'*. Reflecting recent criticisms about board responsibility, he claimed that directors were responsible for setting *'wholly arbitrary, self-serving judgments, compensation and recognition awards'*. He also blamed corporate officials for paying themselves excessive salaries, bonuses, pensions, and stock options, and went on to explain why monster business was inherently antisocial.

Quinn was no radical outsider—certainly not the 1930s equivalent of Naomi Klein or Joel Bakan. He was a star executive at that quintessential 'monster business' General Electric—the man who established that company's refrigerator division. In the economic and social upheaval of his time, his views were part of the cauldron of public debate. Now, when executives are typically portrayed as conservatives, his cry to limit the size of business is in marked contrast to right-wing thinkers such as Rand and Hayek, who treated a company's growth within the free market as the best way to increase shareholder value, lower prices, and serve the general good.

Quinn's views are more aligned with the political left, but even here things are not clear-cut. Canadian economist J.K. Galbraith did not necessarily favour big business, but saw its growth as inevitable as perfect competition disappeared beneath its shadow. He agreed with Quinn that, by itself, this would have undesirable outcomes across society. However, we should not worry about this because the interests of capital and management, he argued, would be counterbalanced by trade unions and other organized groups. It was what he called this *'countervailing power'* that would keep monster business honest and continuing to serve the public good.

(*Sources:* Galbraith, 1952; Quinn, 1962; Rand, 1966)

Quick questions

1. Does the fact that parts of what Quinn observed still resonate today suggest that 'the problem' of big business is nothing new and is something that society adequately controls through conventional political processes?
2. Do you agree with Galbraith that the power of 'business' can be controlled by 'countervailing powers'?
3. Is Rand right to argue that controls on the size of business such as antitrust laws stifle innovation, success, and economic rewards?

Post-World War II

Business emerged from World War II with a mixed reputation. Companies such as Mitsubishi and Mercedes had been part of their nations' war machines, while firms from IBM to Coca-Cola were to spend years cleansing themselves of associations with fascism. But business had played a key part in winning the war, whether it be through unprecedented levels of production or fast-track innovation. Where the war had hit hardest, there was exhaustion and an appetite for change. In the UK, the post-war Labour government put in place a system of welfare safety nets. It also acted on its belief in state-owned industry by nationalizing major industries such as coal, railways, steel, gas distribution, and power generation. The idea that business best served the public good if it was state-controlled took hold in much of Western Europe and, of course, in the Eastern Bloc of Communist countries, in which private enterprise was outlawed. It also characterized the role of business in newly independent countries such as Indonesia and India, which saw the nationalization of industry as essential to the long-held dream of independence.

In West Germany and Italy, new models of governance were put in place to ensure that workers, as well as shareholders, had a say in how companies were run. In the USA, a seemingly spontaneous interplay between business and society emerged, similar to what chaos theory would later term 'complex adaptive systems', but which at the time was seen as a debate over how much of its power business would cede to wider society.[6]

These different approaches to managing the role of business in society all marked a significant change in thinking from that of the days when it was assumed that business best benefited others by being left largely to its own devices. The welfare state was primarily concerned with a more equitable distribution of the benefits of economic prosperity. Distribution was the responsibility of government and the primary role of business was to create jobs, obey the law, and pay taxes. However, the concerns of the welfare state, such as health care, living wages, and education, influence what we think of as 'CSR' today. Equally, the renewed interest in human rights shown by national governments in the aftermath of the war gave rise to such agreements as the United Nations Universal Declaration of Human Rights, which is now referenced in important CSR initiatives.

It is easy to idealize the post-World War II contract between business and government. In the former colonies, new governments lacked the expertise or wealth to deliver the comprehensive safety nets enjoyed in wealthier countries. Companies such as Zambia Consolidated Copper Mines found themselves directly involved in community development. Equally, prosperity brought with it new social concerns. In the early 1950s, smog claimed the lives of many citizens in both the UK and USA, with serious instances in London, New York, and Los Angeles. Pollution became a political issue, resulting in the passing of the US Air Pollution Control Act in 1955 and the UK Clean Air Act in 1956. A year later, Scripps Oceanographic Institute scientists were surprised to discover rising carbon dioxide levels in the world's oceans.

In 1962, Carson's *Silent spring* was published, detailing the effect of man-made pesticides, and throughout the decade scientific discovery of the effects of leaded petroleum, water pollution, and chemical seepage served to make increasing numbers of people aware of the connection between environmental degradation and corporate activity. In the following decades, regular instances of corporate malfeasance, such as the Love Canal, Bhopal, Chernobyl, and the *Exxon Valdez*, served to reinforce this connection.

Non-government environmental groups, such as Greenpeace (founded in 1971), began advocating for change outside the mainstream political process. In terms of organization and strategy, they set the agenda for a much broader range of rights-focused activists, such as those protecting the interests of workers, indigenous people, animals, children, bonded labour, etc.—the advocacy groups that play an important role in contemporary CSR today.

The women's rights movement also became more visible in the 1970s and, among other things, raised issues of equality in the workplace. One aspect of this was equal treatment in terms of remuneration and working conditions, and another was equality of opportunity. The movement worldwide has had an enormous impact in a relatively short space of time, most notably in the area of legislation (e.g. maternity rights, equal pay). In terms of CSR, the women's rights movement established the basic principle that companies shall not discriminate against women. Similar principles have been applied in relation to age, ethnicity, race, disability, and sexual orientation, and, in the USA especially, racial discrimination has been a significant part of the CSR agenda.

Discussion points

There are expectations across the political spectrum that big business has the power and responsibility to benefit society. There are also fears across the spectrum that big business is a 'monster'.

- Does 'big business' have different responsibilities to those of other types of business?
- How does limited liability influence how companies view their relationships with society?
- Find examples, at the national and provincial levels, of ways in which company law makes companies responsible to stakeholders other than shareholders.

The globalization era

The relationship of business with society has changed again with globalization, the phenomenon that has affected social, political, economic, and business life since the 1980s. Globalization is often portrayed as a new era, bringing changes that are as momentous as those of the Industrial Revolution. It is certainly an era during which business's place in society is being transformed and, for that reason alone, it is important that we understand its meaning and consequences.

But we can go further than this. Writers such as Crane and Mattan (2004), Pedersen and Huniche (2006), and Wood et al. (2006) tie CSR to the social, political, and environmental challenges of globalization. In fact, to some degree, its success may influence the direction of globalization overall.[7] This is because globalization is associated, on the one hand, with a limited set of global governance mechanisms and weakened national governments, and on the other, with unprecedented private sector wealth, power, and impact. Thus CSR has become an important means for addressing what Stiglitz (2002) sees as the fundamental problem with contemporary globalization—a system of global governance without global government.

However, there is a lot of confusion about what is meant by globalization. In CSR literature, the term is often used in its narrowest sense to mean the worldwide flows of data, capital, goods, and services. Indeed, some aspects of globalization highlighted by certain corporate observers were already features of previous eras. For example, globalization critic Naomi Klein (1999) talks about global colonization by brands—what she calls 'McDonaldization'—and a wider process as part of which Western norms and values wipe out diversity and local cultures. Yet generations earlier, in his travels between South Africa, England, and India, Mahatma Gandhi would have found it as easy to buy a packet of Player's cigarettes as we would find it to buy a Big Mac today.

Many economists use globalization to mean the global spread of liberal economic ideas, notably the creation of a global market built on free trade. This kind of liberal globalization is essentially the realization of the economic relations explained by economists such as Smith, Ricardo, or Marx, and the socio-economic system described by Mises and Hayek. Some political economists, on the other hand, argue that we should think more broadly than just economics—that we should see globalization as a social condition that also includes politics, culture, ethics, ecology, and all the other facets that affect human life. What separates globalization today from any previous historical period is that a combination of technological innovation, policy shifts, power relations, and values has meant that physical space and time have become much less important determinants of economic and social activity and of social identity. Alluding to Fukuyama's (1989) idea that globalization marks the end of history, Virilio (2000) concludes that globalization is really the end of geography.

Understandably, the economic dimension to globalization is attractive to many in business, but it is worthwhile understanding the perspective of political economists—what has been called 'globalization as deterritorialization'.[8] In our business lives, we witness many symptoms of globalization, such as the offshoring of jobs, rapid growth in international trade, and international capital flows. Deterritorialization theorists say that all of this reflects more fundamental changes in our social condition (e.g. new social orders transcending traditional political and geographical boundaries; powerful companies and other organizations not strongly linked to a specific place; intense rapid interaction between groups allowing events in one region to trigger reactions anywhere in the world), and is part of a growing consciousness of our interconnectedness and interdependence.[9] This is important for companies to understand because on the one hand they are often criticized for exerting excessive power in this new global order, and on the other they can fall victims to it such as when people connected through cyberspace form an alliance to hold a company to account for its behaviour. This is what the chocolate industry experienced when journalists found slave labour on cocoa farms in West Africa (see Case study 2), or what Monsanto still experiences because of some people's objections to genetically modified organisms. Moreover, while not all such alliances survive for long, some do, as Nestlé will vouch for after three decades of fighting allegations about its infant milk formula.

Business in the modern globalization era is fundamental to understanding contemporary CSR, and we discuss it in far more depth in Chapter 4. It accounts for many of the issues companies are being held responsible for, the growth in wealth, poverty, and inequality that has accompanied unprecedented private-sector activity, and the recognition of the values and materiality dimensions of issues such as global poverty and sustainability that business is being asked to address. It also accounts for the changing nature of corporate governance, investment, public scrutiny, and social expectation that affect companies' licence to operate and the very definition of success. However, before we flesh out these statements, let us explore the evolution of CSR theory that shapes some of our thinking today.

Theories of CSR

The preceding sections describe the historical landscape that has influenced CSR theory and practice. It feels at times that there is an archaeological quest to discover the earliest instance of CSR, with examples reported as long ago as Mesopotamian and Roman times.[10] If by theory we mean something that is written down, CSR theory is relatively new, but if we mean the ideas that underpin business practice, then any enterprise at any moment in history has had to establish what Donaldson and Dunfee (1999) call its 'licence to operate' because without the support of those in power or the wider public it cannot prosper. The different histories and cultures of CSR are a fascinating area of enquiry, but for purely practical reasons the following discussion of CSR theory's evolution takes as its starting point business in the West (see Snapshot 2.2).

Evolution of CSR theory

Before CSR had a name, philosophy and theology were already informing the thinking of entrepreneurs. Carnegie's *Gospel of wealth* (1889) sets out the duties wealthy capitalists have to society. The Lever Brothers, the Clarks, and the Cadburys were not only successful industrialists but also Quakers who found it contrary to their faith to ignore worker well-being, or to leave people's fates to the market. They differed from Carnegie in their belief that responsibility was not just about how one used one's wealth, but how that wealth was created in the first place. Early academic writers on CSR, such as Berle and Means (1932), focused on the responsibilities of the individual business leader rather than the company, reflecting a widely held view in the USA that success and responsibility go hand in hand. Davis called this the 'Iron Law of Responsibility' which states that the social responsibilities of business leaders need to be commensurate with their social power[11] (Figure 2.2).

Snapshot 2.2 Trafigura takes on global civil society

Trafigura is a Singapore commodity trading company that was formerly based in the Netherlands. How it came to move its headquarters is a story of CSR. That story is also the reason why Trafigura has a twenty-four-hour grievance hotline on its website and became the first oil commodity trader to join the Extractive Industries Transparency Initiative, a voluntary body trying to reduce corruption in oil, gas, and other extractives.

Traditionally, dealing in base metals and energy, it is not the kind of company that gets much public attention. However, search on the web for Trafigura and one will typically find the word 'scandal' come up alongside the company's name. In countries such as Malta, Zambia, Nigeria, Jamaica, and Thailand it has been involved in high-level corruption, smuggling, and collusion that has brought down government ministers and led to international enquiries and legal proceedings. During the Saddam Hussein era, the company was accused of sanctions busting and smuggling 500,000 barrels of oil out of Iraq, according to a UN report. It pleaded guilty in the USA and forfeited $20 million. Even in 2017, it was singled out by the *Financial Times* for continuing dubious trading practices.[12]

(*continued . . .*)

However, its highest-profile scandal occurred off the waters of Côte d'Ivoire, and came to public attention not because of government officials or the traditional media, but due to a concerted campaign that is typical of the kinds of pressures companies can find themselves under today. In 2006, Trafigura chartered the *Probo Koala* to transport its toxic waste. Its first port of call was the Netherlands, which had the facilities to dispose of the waste safely. However, the costs were high, and instead the *Probo Koala* sailed towards Africa. Shipping this waste outside of Europe was illegal because few countries have the facilities to process it properly; but the company made a deal with another company for $15,000 that would lead to the waste being put in landfill sites in Côte d'Ivoire. Within a month, the people of Abidjan were finding foul-smelling toxic waste that had been dumped in numerous places around their city. According to an NGO report:

> Tens of thousands of people suffered from nausea, headaches, breathing difficulties, stinging eyes and burning skin. They did not know what was happening; they were terrified. Health centres and hospitals were soon overwhelmed. International agencies were drafted in to help overstretched local medical staff. More than 100,000 people were treated, according to official records, but it is likely that the number affected was higher as records are incomplete. The authorities reported that between 15 and 17 people died.[13]

Trafigura vigorously denied any wrongdoing, claimed it was not responsible for its subcontractor's behaviour, and won a high court injunction in the UK to stifle coverage of the story by the media. However, if it thought that the story would go away, it was wrong. Human rights and environmental organizations were outraged at the impact the waste had had in Côte d'Ivoire. Newspapers were angry about the use of a court order to stop what they saw as coverage of a legitimate news story. Together they whipped up a worldwide storm among concerned citizens linked by social media. A thousand Ivorians filed suit against the company. The network of politicians that the company seems to have nurtured to ensure local support were powerless when it came to the global onslaught. Legal teams found that the loopholes the company was accused of exploiting in its global operations were now working in favour of the company's critics.

As the story snowballed, the company was forced into various agreements, although it always denied liability. It was found guilty of illegal exports in the Dutch courts and fined €1 million, while its CEO had to pay a €67,000 fine. In Côte d'Ivoire, although the case never went to court, the company paid $160 million to the government and $50 million in individual settlements. The head of the subcontractors was given a twenty-year jail term. Trafigura employee Naeem Ahmed, who was involved in the ship's operation in Amsterdam, was fined €25,000 and the captain of the *Probo Koala* was sentenced to a five-year suspended jail term. Trafigura denies responsibility for the dumping of the waste and any deaths or injuries caused.

(*Sources:* http://jamaica-gleaner.com, 5 December 2012; Onzivu, 2013; http://www.bbc.co.uk/news/world-africa-10735255, 5 September 2018; https://www.timesofmalta.com/articles/view/20130221/local/Trafigura-and-Total-are-barred-from-fuel-tenders.458549, 21 February 2013 (accessed 21 September 2018); https://www.trafigura.com; http://www.ft.com/content/9a75ed17-a46c-3006-9fa0-ec72b0eddb0a, 22 November 2017 (accessed 15 January 2018))

Quick questions

1 Are companies more susceptible now than in the past to worldwide campaigns criticizing their behaviour?

2 What could Trafigura have done differently?

3 What other examples can you think of where companies have had trouble protecting their reputations against community and NGO attacks?

Key concept: Licence to operate

Licence to operate refers to the public's acceptance of a company's impact on wider society. It is an idea rooted in theories of the social contract that exists between a government and the people proposed by philosophers such as Hobbes and Locke. Just as in a democracy the electorate can grant and remove a government's permission to govern, so a company's constituents (e.g. consumers, investors, customers, communities) grant tacit or explicit approval to companies to conduct their business.

The right to extract profit from commercial activities is one part of the licence to operate, but the company's constituents can dictate what is a legitimate profit-seeking activity. For example, human trafficking might be profitable, but the criminal networks that are involved cannot claim to have a licence to operate. The tobacco industry is an example of where companies have had their licence to operate severely restricted, not least because of their role in hiding the connection between smoking and cancer. An alternative energy company such as Vestas can claim to have a strong licence to operate because of the positive relationship it seems to have with tackling climate change, whereas a company such as EDF may have to invest more in building its licence because of its association with coal-fired and nuclear power.

There are numerous ways companies can strengthen their licence, including stakeholder engagement, transparency, and CSR reporting. Such approaches may help companies to build better relations with their constituents, but they should not regard the licence as irrevocable as it will be under continual scrutiny and re-evaluation.

However, Davis (1973) was also one of the first CSR theorists to argue that social responsibility was more than the acts of individuals—that CSR should refer to the company as an institution. The shift in focus from the individual to the company led to a new discussion of responsibilities. Some saw CSR as a way of utilizing company resources towards broad social ends rather than to serve only narrow private interests.[14] In addition to linking responsibility to power, Davis himself held that the social responsibility of business demanded that companies should be open to public input and scrutiny, that social costs and benefits should be factored into their business decisions and also priced into products, and that, where it has the necessary competencies, the company as a citizen should be involved in social affairs.[15] He also noted that there might be long-term economic gain from behaving responsibly.

All of these issues are relevant to CSR today. So too are some of the dilemmas raised. Should companies take actions beyond what is legally required (see Chapter 1)? Should a company's assets be used for purposes other than maximizing shareholder value (see Chapter 13)? Are the fiduciary duties of executives and directors too narrowly defined (see Chapter 7)? However, since the 1990s, the theory and practice of CSR has evolved more rapidly than ever before, raising questions and possibilities that Davis could not have imagined. CSR in the 1990s and beyond dominates most of the discussion in this book; but it is interesting and worthwhile to look at its earlier forms because Davis and his peers spurred thinking about how companies could demonstrate their contribution to social goals such as economic justice, stability, and freedom,[16] and the ways in which this can be accomplished, asking three questions that are still as pertinent today.

1 How can business be responsible?

2 For what is it responsible?

3 To whom is it responsible?

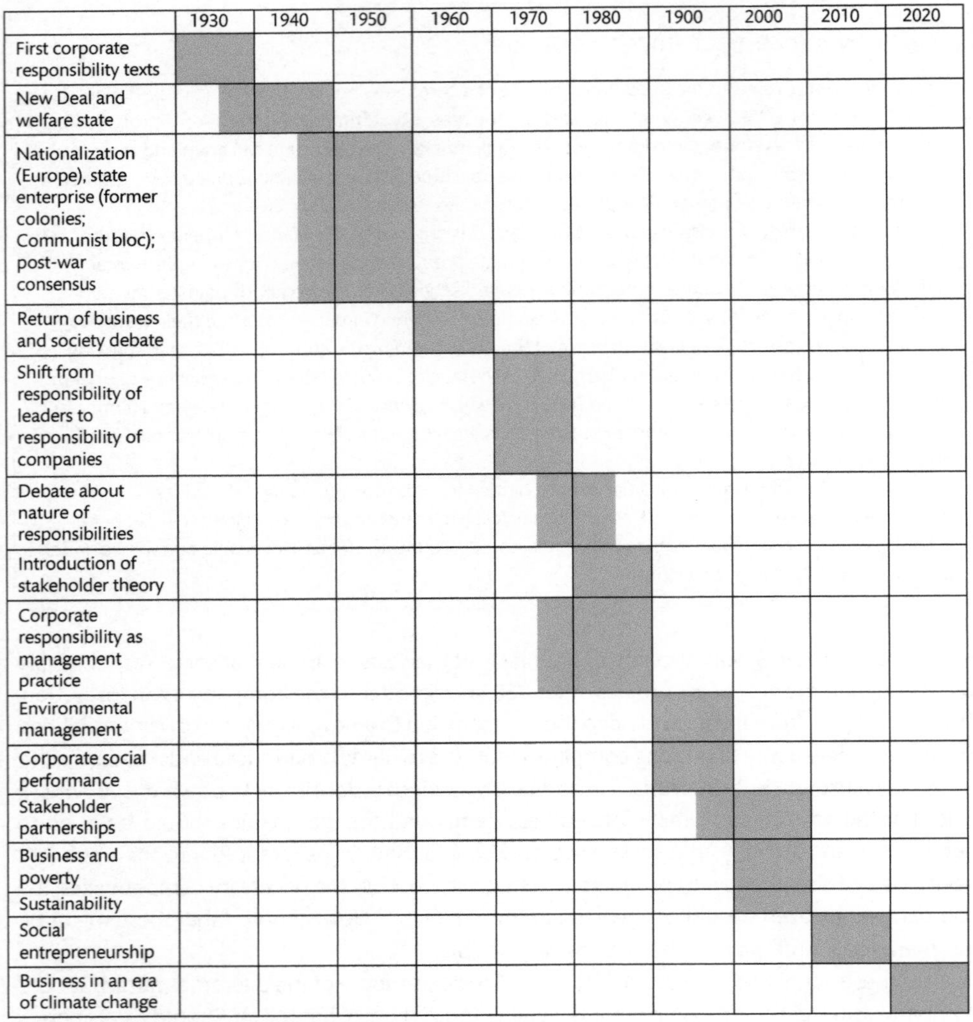

	1930	1940	1950	1960	1970	1980	1900	2000	2010	2020
First corporate responsibility texts										
New Deal and welfare state										
Nationalization (Europe), state enterprise (former colonies; Communist bloc); post-war consensus										
Return of business and society debate										
Shift from responsibility of leaders to responsibility of companies										
Debate about nature of responsibilities										
Introduction of stakeholder theory										
Corporate responsibility as management practice										
Environmental management										
Corporate social performance										
Stakeholder partnerships										
Business and poverty										
Sustainability										
Social entrepreneurship										
Business in an era of climate change										

Figure 2.2 Timeline of CSR

It is to these questions that we now turn.

Defining the responsible enterprise

How can business be responsible?

Identifying the enterprise as the focus of CSR led theorists to question when and how companies should exhibit responsibility. Manne and Wallich (1972) said that CSR refers to actions for which the company is under no legal compulsion. If CSR begins where the law ends, however, what does this mean? Manne claimed that true CSR expenditure, as well as being voluntary, was that which:

1 generates marginal returns less than those available from alternative courses of action;
2 is an actual corporate expenditure, not a conduit for individual largesse.[17]

This raises two interesting questions. First, should CSR be limited to what companies do to generate a profit? Second, should companies be denied moral credit for actions taken for commercial reasons? The Committee for Economic Development, comprising US corporate leaders, identified three concentric circles of responsibility which blurred Manne and Wallich's distinctions:

1 creating products, jobs, economic growth;
2 sensitivity to changing social values;
3 emerging responsibilities such as poverty and urban blight.[18]

These circles embrace both core business activity and how the company manages its relationship with society more widely, but, again, the emphasis is on voluntary actions and in no case is the company required to be accountable for failing to carry out these responsibilities.

Debates about voluntary versus mandatory approaches to CSR continue to this day. They are further complicated because companies may feel they have to take particular actions even without legal compulsion (e.g. because of civil society pressure—see Chapter 9). We explore these issues elsewhere and so, for now, limit ourselves to flagging voluntarism as a recurring theme in this book.

Discussion points

George Soros, the American financial speculator, stock investor, philanthropist, and political activist, has said: 'We can have a market economy, but we cannot have a market society.'[19]

- What distinction is he making between 'economy' and 'society'?
- Does CSR help the market economy to become a market society?
- Describe how a company from the former Eastern Bloc might use CSR to establish its licence to operate in the European Union.

For what is business responsible?

Defining CSR as voluntary action does little to explain for what business should take responsibility. In Chapter 1, we set out various perspectives on this, including Carroll's (1979) multidimensional model of CSR, which has proved one of the most widely referenced frameworks because it makes clear important principles and spheres of responsibility (i.e. economic, legal, ethical, and discretionary responsibilities—see Figure 1.2). Its strength is that it draws together different types of responsibility that had tended to be treated as mutually exclusive or otherwise problematic. It does this by identifying separate categories, and any action that falls under one category or another can be considered part of CSR. But this, in itself, can cause problems. For example, does a company accept responsibility for any issue that fits into one of the categories? If not, how does it prioritize its response? Equally, how does the company go about deciding what is ethical, or what discretionary actions it should take?[20] Consequently, at least as important as what companies are responsible for is how those responsibilities are defined.

CSR, as already noted, is dynamic and changes according to time, industry, and location. Much of academic CSR theory originates from the USA, and therefore reflects social conditions that are different even in similarly advanced capitalist economies. For example, an American employee often has the legal status of 'at-will employment', meaning that worker and employee can break their relationship without liability to either party. In Europe, a worker may have a three-month notice period before their relationship with the company ends; in the USA, as anyone who watches American TV knows, a worker can walk out the same day, taking their box of personal effects with them. Therefore, in Europe severance pay and dismissal may not be spelled out as a CSR issue because the responsibilities are set out in legal statute. In the USA, on the other hand, CSR might offer a counterbalance to relatively limited legal protections.

The nature of the American free enterprise system—its financial and governance systems, its culture, its education and labour systems, the institution of the firm, etc.—is unique, and different in important ways from that in Europe and elsewhere.[21] This may account for the differences in CSR between the USA and elsewhere, with the USA adopting what has been called 'explicit' CSR (i.e. the company carries out certain activities with the explicit intent of serving social interests) and Europe concentrating on 'implicit' CSR (i.e. business is one of many institutions that are expected to serve the social good and must conform with the social consensus about its role).[22] It may also explain why business in the USA has been what Drucker (1946) called 'the representative institution', responsible for representing and upholding American society's basic values and beliefs, whereas in Europe, for example, companies have been viewed more as supplicants to the social good.

The Atlantic Ocean is not the only CSR fault line; claims about the geographical distinctions in what companies are responsible for have been made about India, Japan, China, Brazil, and Africa and Asia in general. We will touch on these differences, as well as dissimilarities in responsibility between industries in later chapters. But it is important to consider some of the consequences of thinking in terms of disparities in responsibilities. It may be that an area of behaviour has to be spelled out as an explicit responsibility in one region but not in another because of different laws. But to what extent can something be acceptable in one country and not in another? If violence on the factory floor is commonplace in one country, should a French multinational such as Carrefour accept that behaviour among its suppliers when it would not be able to do so in France?

This is the area of ethical relativism. There may be good reasons to define the responsibilities of corporations in the context of where they are being applied, but there is also a risk of turning a blind eye to unacceptable actions on the grounds that something is a cultural convention. For example, when abuse of workers in global supply chains first hit the headlines in the late 1980s, companies and politicians argued that European consumers had no right to dictate what was tolerable in developing countries. Relativism is a topic of much discussion in business ethics,[23] reflecting wider philosophical debates about whether or not morals are universal or culturally contingent. And if they are not applicable everywhere, are there value systems originating in one part of the world that are universalizable to all parts in much the same way that the economic system we know as capitalism, originating in Europe, has been introduced throughout much of the world?

Underpinning these debates are quite different philosophical traditions (see the online resources for a more detailed overview). For example, justice is defined quite differently by the Utilitarian school than it is by non-consequentialists such as Kant. The former believe that justice is whatever benefits the majority; the latter believe that justice is not a popularity contest, and the good of the many cannot be achieved at the expense of the few. These are contradictory schools of thought. Likewise, Aristotle's belief in absolute values is at odds with Habermas's notion of discourse ethics two millennia later, whereby values are the result of public consensus. This is not a book on business ethics, and therefore we are not going to unpack how different ethical schools influence ideas of responsibility. That is not to dismiss them as unimportant; on the contrary, business ethics is a vital subset of CSR with its own body of literature—Oxford University's Bodleian Library alone contains 265 business ethics titles.

There are various management studies texts on how to incorporate the ideas of Mill, Aristotle, Jesus, Kant, and others, and there are many books offering ethical advice to the individual manager. But rather than repeat much of what has already been written, our focus is on filling two gaps that affect the defining of CSR. First, instead of studying what companies ought to do, we want to emphasize what they actually do and why they make some of the choices they make. Second, mirroring Davis's accomplishment in moving the wider debate about CSR from the role of the individual to the role of the company, we want to explore how companies as entities manage their responsibilities. In doing this, we are not only going beyond the scope of conventional business ethics, we are building a bridge between what Scherer and Palazzo (2007) call positivist and deliberative CSR—the former concentrating on actual business practice without much reflection on the wider context that affects what companies do and do not do, and the latter concerned primarily with theories of responsibility and not how these are actually enacted.

To whom is business responsible?

For economist Milton Friedman, it was straightforward that companies were responsible to the law and their investors, and nobody else. Some still defend this position, some say it was never accurate, and some say that it may have been right once but not any longer (see Chapter 1). Investors' interests may conflict with those of wider society, especially when they want rapid or high-yield returns on their capital. Irrespective of the behaviour of business, the law is never a comprehensive code, and for every Bernie Madoff or Ernest Saunders who goes to jail there is a Dick Fuld or Bruno 'the London Whale' Iksil, who seriously harm their companies with seeming impunity despite public outrage.[24] Moreover, legal responsibilities differ from jurisdiction to jurisdiction, and multinational companies can, to a degree, choose which laws they like or not by relocating their operations. There may be no legal distinction between someone who invests for the short run and one who does so for longer, but their interests and what they would like the company to do may be quite different.

According to ex-IBM CEO Sam Palmisano, the biggest shift in recent business history is that from shareholder to stakeholder companies.[25] The idea that business has responsibility to a variety of stakeholders has been an important element of CSR theory, at least since Preston and Post's 1975 book on how host environments affect corporate behaviour. As we explore in Chapters 6 and 9, stakeholder theory suggests a way of explaining why and with whom corporations should engage. It is based on the notion that many people (and groups of people) have a stake in any corporation and that, in order for a company to achieve its objectives effectively, it must consider them all, not only the shareholders to whom corporations have long discharged accountability. In this regard it is not only distinct from previous ideas of the responsibility of companies, but echoes the discourse ethics of Habermas (see earlier at 'For what is business responsible?') and the idea that duties and responsibilities are fluid, defined as part of a social consensus that itself depends on the free and informed participation of the populous in democratic processes.

Stakeholder theory promises a way in which companies can learn what is needed to establish and maintain the aforementioned 'licence to operate', i.e. the idea that business requires the approval of others in society in order to function effectively. It provides a potentially stronger rationale than Carroll's framework for choosing certain courses of action by implying that a company should do whatever is necessary to maintain its legitimacy, but that it is under no obligation to go further than that.

The licence to operate is central to legitimacy theory and posits that an organization can only continue to exist if its core values are aligned with the core values of the society in which it operates. The fate of accounting firm Arthur Andersen, in the wake of the 2001 Enron scandal, brought this into stark relief when the company's integrity was so badly damaged that it went out of business. Legitimacy theory offers a method of managing stakeholders in the face of various threats through, for example, educating them about the company's intentions, changing their perceptions of events, diverting their attention, and altering their expectations.[26] Such strategies are evident in the actions taken by Shell in response to Brent Spar or the treatment of the Ogoni people in Nigeria, or by BP after the Deepwater Horizon disaster.

Important though theories such as those described above are in their own right, one of their major contributions is that they have made management practice part of CSR enquiry. Early CSR theory was primarily concerned with the normative behaviour of companies, but, since the 1970s, there has been at least equal emphasis given to CSR as management practice.[27] For example, Ackerman and Bauer's (1976) theory of 'corporate social responsiveness' put the emphasis on what companies *can* do to respond to societal expectations (i.e. capacity), in contrast with more theoretical ideas of what they *should* do. Social responsiveness shunned the idea of philosophy in favour of a managerial approach and, in many ways, helped CSR to get out of academia and into day-to-day business. By the 1990s, managerial approaches to CSR were evolving rapidly and measurement had become an integral part of this, summed up in MacGillivray and Zadek's phrase: 'If you want it to count, count it.'[28]

We take a closer look at CSR as management practice in Chapter 6 and later chapters. But we would not pretend that responsiveness to society is an unproblematic way of resolving what business should take responsibility for; on the contrary, as later discussions of stakeholder theory reveal (see Chapter 9), it can leave companies without clear moral guidance of the kind promised by ethical theory.

Discussion points

A number of companies publicize the amounts they donate to philanthropic causes. Indeed, it is one of the measures used by some rating agencies when scoring CSR points.

- To what extent do philanthropic donations act as a measure of CSR?
- What arguments can you put forward against using this criterion as a measure of CSR?
- Using other companies as benchmarks, present a case to the board for adopting a particular philanthropic strategy.

Case study 2 CSR in different eras: Cadbury

In 1909, the *London Evening Standard* accused the confectionery company Cadbury of knowingly profiting from the widespread use of slaves on cocoa plantations in the Portuguese colony of São Tomé. The public was shocked: the company was not only one of the most famous brands in the British Empire, but also an exemplar of compassionate capitalism founded in the Quaker religious tradition.

Cadbury sued the *Evening Standard* for libel. The company won the case, but over the course of the trial Charles Cadbury, joint head of the firm and a figurehead of virtuous capitalism, was forced to admit that he not only knew slaves were being used, but actually regarded it as essential to his company's prosperity. Despite the court's ruling in Cadbury's favour, it lost in the court of public opinion, and the reputation of the firm was damaged.

A century later, in 2000, the company found itself once again accused of buying slave-farmed cocoa beans from West Africa in a media assault by the full spectrum of the British press, from the *Daily Mirror* to the *Financial Times*. Acting with others in the industry, Cadbury (by then Cadbury Schweppes) denied the allegations. In contrast with the 1909 case, this time the industry condemned the use of slavery outright, but to no avail because it was unable to prove that it really knew what was happening on cocoa farms. The human rights advocates seemed to know little more; their early allegations of slavery soon switched to ones about child labour as it became apparent that slavery was not prevalent on cocoa farms. But that did not matter—these groups held the moral high ground and the industry could do nothing to displace them.

The news headlines could not have come at a worse time, appearing on the front pages in the run-up to Easter, a peak time for chocolate sales. Schoolchildren around Britain wrote in to Cadbury saying they would not be buying Easter eggs that year. In the USA, two congressmen persuaded the industry to sign up to the Harkin-Engel Protocol, an industry-wide certification standard to eliminate the worst forms of child labour. Cadbury had once again lost in the court of public opinion. The company's share price was not hurt, but its reputation was. The question was whether it needed to take action, and if so what?

Across the industry, companies pondered whether to be defensive and protect their reputations, or to become more proactive and see if there was a value-adding dimension to the cocoa labour problem. Cadbury supported a 2002 study by the International Institute of Tropical Agriculture to investigate the extent of child labour and forced labour. It also joined the International Cocoa Initiative, a partnership of business, NGO, and government representatives committed to getting rid of unacceptable labour practices in cocoa production. In 2006 it asked consultants to map out what sustainable production would mean for the company.

These activities helped the company realize that it had lost touch with its supply base. Not only was it blind to human rights issues in the supply chain, it was ignorant of the production issues affecting

(*continued . . .*)

the millions of small independent farmers it depended on. If anything, the risk of being out of touch was greater now than in 2000. In 2005, Cadbury had acquired Green & Black's, the organic chocolate company with a loyal ethical consumer base. This was one of Cadbury's fastest-growing business areas, a brand built on product quality and ethical credibility. Any criticism of the Cadbury supply chain now would damage Green & Black's reputation as well.

But another problem came to light as Cadbury started to re-acquaint itself with its supply base: various farmers were growing less cocoa, and if the situation continued Cadbury risked not having enough beans to meet demand. Cadbury-commissioned academic research had shown that the average production for smallholder cocoa farmers in Ghana had dropped to just 40% of potential yield, and that cocoa farming was becoming less and less appealing to the next generation of farmers, despite rising prices. In January 2008, Cadbury launched its £44 million Cocoa Partnership 'to secure the economic, social and environmental sustainability of around a million cocoa farmers and their communities in Ghana, India, Indonesia and the Caribbean'. Furthermore, in 2009 Cadbury announced that all cocoa used in its top-selling Dairy Milk brand would be sourced from Fairtrade-certified farms, with the hope that farmers would benefit from the stable prices and community investment that Fairtrade promises.

(*Sources:* Original research; Du Cann, 1993; IITA and ILO, 2002; Satre, 2005; http://www.cadbury.com/ourresponsibilities/cadburycocoapartnership/Pages/mappingsustainableproduction.aspx; http://www.cadbury.com/ourresponsibilities/cadburycocoapartnership/Pages/cadburycocoapartnership.aspx)

Questions

1 The events of 1909 and 2000 had few major commercial ramifications for Cadbury, and until the 2010 takeover by Kraft (now Mendelez), the company was a long-time member of the Fortune Global 500 list of leading businesses.

a Did the company overreact by stopping its sourcing of 'slave-produced' cocoa?

b Why did the company feel the need to act at all?

c Is it not the role of government to regulate how industries are run and to prevent these practices from recurring?

2 Cadbury faced similar issues in 1909 and 2000, and in both cases had to mount a defence of its reputation and practices.

a Are companies more responsible today than they were in the past?

b Are Cadbury's responsibilities different today than they were in the early twentieth century?

c Why do you think companies' responsibilities have changed in the last hundred years?

3 In CSR theory, a distinction is sometimes made between actions taken to reduce risks, such as protecting reputation, and those taken to add value, such as using ethical values to promote a brand.

a Which of Cadbury's actions do you think were done to protect its reputation?

b Why do you think Cadbury purchased Green & Black's?

c How would you persuade senior management to support the Cocoa Partnership?

Summary

CSR did not spring out of nowhere. What we think of as the responsibilities of business and how these are acted upon reflect some of the main debates about social justice going far back in time. Nowhere is this more apparent than in theories about how private enterprise impacts upon economic well-being and how the economy itself relates to society. In this chapter we have discussed how different types of economy affect what we mean by 'justice' and 'well-being'. We have also compared different theories of how business and free markets can best contribute to the good of society in capitalist societies. What emerges is a set of questions on issues such as the relationship between private self-interest and the public good, and how the rewards of enterprise are distributed—things that lie at the heart of contemporary CSR.

Tackling these questions has occupied politicians, academics, company managers, and community leaders since the earliest days of capitalism. We have explored how CSR theory developed as one way of finding answers about what business should be responsible for and to whom. We have also examined the way in which different approaches to thinking about responsibility can lead to quite different conclusions about what companies should be responsible for.

However, the origins of CSR are not only to be found in theory. The evolution of modern business, and, in particular, the emergence of limited liability and the corporation, have all affected business's relationship with society and expectations about companies' responsibilities. Equally, the specific aspects of business activity that society addresses have, paradoxically, both changed and remained constant over time. What the exploration of aspects of CSR over three eras does show, however, is how the role of business in resolving these issues has changed. In fact, the unintended consequence of the market liberalization that was central to economic globalization is that business is being expected, as never before, to take action to rectify perceived weaknesses in markets on issues such as social justice and sustainability. It is how globalization has affected CSR in developing countries to which we turn in Chapter 3.

Further reading

Historical context

Bakan, J. 2004, *The corporation: the pathological pursuit of profit and power*, Free Press, New York.

Stachowicz-Stanusch, A., Amann, W., and Mangia, G. (eds) 2017, *Corporate social irresponsibility: individual behaviors and organizational practices*, Information Age Publishing Inc., Charlotte, NC.

Readable and provocative critiques of the dominance of corporations.

Kenneally, T. 1982, *Schindler's ark*, Hodder and Stoughton, London.

Novel based on the true story of a businessman's struggle to do good in Nazi Germany. The Spielberg film adaptation is called *Schindler's* List.

Robins, N. 2012, *The corporation that changed the world: how the East India Company shaped the modern multinational*, Pluto Press, London.

A lively look at one of the earliest multinational companies, and what it tells us about modern-day business.

Thompson, E.P. 1963, *The making of the English working class*, Victor Gollancz, London.
Comprehensive study of workers, working conditions, and worker protest in nineteenth-century England.

Theoretical context

Carroll, A.B. 1999, 'Corporate social responsibility: evolution of a definitional construct', *Business and Society*, vol. 38, no. 3, pp 268–95.
Widely cited overview of CSR theory.

Drucker, P.F. 1946, *Concept of the corporation*, John Day, New York.
Early work by leading management thinker on the nature of the corporation.

Koch, C.G. 2015, *Good profit: how creating value for others built one of the world's most successful companies*, Piatkus, London.

Mackey, J. and Sisodia, R. 2013, *Conscious capitalism: liberating the heroic spirit of business*, Harvard Business Review Press, Boston, MA.
Prominent US entrepreneurs set out their views on values-driven business.

Marx, K. 1865, *Value, price, and profit: an introduction to the theory of capitalism*, abridged by P. Zarembka, 2000, JAI/Elsevier Science, Amsterdam, New York, online at https://www.marxists.org/archive/marx/works/download/pdf/value-price-profit.pdf.

http://www.oup.com/uk/blowfield-murray4e

Visit the online resources that accompany this book to enrich your understanding of this chapter. Among the resources available are web links, exercises, and additional case studies.

Endnotes

1. Du Cann, 1993.
2. Kennedy, 1987; Evans, 1983.
3. Carney, 1998, p 662.
4. McQuaid, 1977.
5. Sennett, 2007.
6. Frederick, 2006.
7. See e.g. Blowfield 2005a; Demirag, 2005.
8. The term comes from Scholte, 2000, but a similar conceptualization of globalization has been set out by many theorists (e.g. Gray, Mittelman, Held) and has evolved from early work on interdependence (e.g. Giddens, 1990; Robertson, 1992).
9. Steger, 2003.
10. Asongu, 2007.
11. Cited in Carroll, 1999, p 271.
12. https://www.ft.com/content/9a75ed17-a46c-3006-9fa0-ec72b0eddb0a (subscription access), accessed 24 November 2018.
13. https://www.amnestyusa.org/files/afr310022012eng.pdf, accessed 6 December 2018.
14. Frederick, 1960, cited in Carroll, 1999, p 271.
15. Birch, 2003, pp 7–8.

16. See the discussion of the work on corporate social performance by Anshen and Johnson in Birch, 2003.
17. Cited in Carroll, 1999, p 276.
18. Cited in Carroll, 1999, p 278.
19. Soros, 2009.
20. Carroll is not unaware of these types of question and revisited his model in Schwartz and Carroll, 2003.
21. Matten and Moon, 2008.
22. Matten and Moon, 2008.
23. See Donaldson, 2003; Beauchamp et al. 2008.
24. http://www.fnlondon.com/articles/the-london-whale-resurfaces-bruno-iksil-speaks-out-20170306 (accessed December 2017).
25. Blowfield, 2007.
26. Lindblom, 1994.
27. Tinker, 1985; see also: Sethi, 1975; Wartick and Cochran, 1985.
28. MacGillivray and Zadek, 1995; see also Gray, 1996.

Sustainable development

Chapter overview

In this chapter we explore the concept of 'sustainable development', tracking its enduring importance in the business context, made more challenging as evidence that climate change is inexorably linked to industrial activity becomes stronger and more forceful with each report from the Intergovernmental Panel on Climate Change (IPCC). In particular, we will:

- consider what is meant by the term 'sustainable development';
- examine the evolution of sustainability;
- assess the evidence provided by scientific reports into issues of climate change;
- identify the challenges that climate change poses for 'business as usual';
- examine the capital market implications of sustainable development;
- explore recent thinking about 'social' aspects of sustainability.

Main topics

Key terms

Brundtland Commission

Climate change

Financing sustainability

Global warming

Sustainable development

Introduction

In the first two chapters of this book we examined the meaning and origins of CSR, but in practice very little of this is of any relevance unless, as a collection of societies around the world, we protect precious resources to ensure that succeeding generations can also enjoy economic development while at the same time being able to sustain themselves.

This presents business and policy-makers alike with a number of challenges. The neoclassical theory of the firm places the maximization of shareholder returns central to the business model adopted by the overwhelming majority of 'for profit' companies. In addition, this model assumes a pattern of continued growth. Read any corporate annual report and you soon realize how important growth is to the financial stakeholders in the business.

Key concept: Sustainable development

Sustainable development means 'development that meets the needs of the current generation without compromising the ability of future generations to meet their own needs' (WCED, 1987). At the same time, government policies around the world demand continued economic growth to fund social infrastructure projects and welfare benefits, and governments depend on business to fuel patterns of economic growth.

Of course, we all benefit in some way from this activity, especially in the West. Whether it results from a wider and cheaper range of consumer goods to choose from, a more efficient and effective health-care service, or a generally more comfortable lifestyle, over the past fifty years standards of living in the West have improved immensely.

However, as noted in Chapter 4, these improvements have not been universal, and in many developing countries large sections of the population continue to live in poverty. Large numbers of people are still living on $1.25 a day or less, the commonly accepted measure of 'extreme poverty',[1] and since the WCED definition of sustainable development, there have been repeated reminders that the term has social as well as environmental dimensions to it.

Moreover, scientific findings suggest that the resources available to the human species on this planet are being consumed at a rate which is not sustainable. These findings are available from a number of sources and all point to the same trend.[2] In the quest for growth, natural resources are being exploited in an unprecedented manner, leading to an increase in commodity prices (in real terms) beginning around 1950, but increasing particularly in the past decade.[3]

The push for greener fuels has also had negative effects in many parts of the world. The demand for palm oil, for example, has led to a scale of deforestation in Indonesia that has resulted in the loss of indigenous lands, the threat of species extinction, and a pall of pollution extending far beyond its borders, into Singapore and Malaysia, creating a level of greenhouse gas emission third only to the USA and China. In the developed world too, we are witnessing the conversion of agricultural land to the production of alternative fuels for traditionally fuelled power stations, which potentially reduces the food-producing capacity within any given country. And as Snapshot 3.1 shows, oil itself as a carbon fuel is highly problematic.

Of equal significance is the recent scientific evidence of human influence on climate change caused by global warming. There is no longer any widespread scientific dispute that '... the wealth of attribution studies ... show that there is an increasingly remote possibility that climate change is dominated by natural rather than anthropogenic factors'.[4]

These findings, which will be augmented with additional evidence later in the chapter, point to a pressing need to respond to the challenges presented by climate change and sustainable development.

Snapshot 3.1 Is there a green energy future?

Government policies to combat climate change around the world hinge on transitioning out of oil- and coal-based energy to greener types of energy such as renewables and nuclear. Countries such as China and Germany have set ambitious renewable energy targets, as indeed have certain large companies such as IKEA. Renewables are an increasingly important part of the energy mix, and the UK has proudly announced that on certain days in 2018 it was able to supply the energy demands of the National Grid without resorting to hydro-carbons at all.

Yet the real picture of this energy transition is more complex. In 1980, the price of crude oil was just under $40 per barrel and production was about 50,000 million barrels a day. If the energy transition was in full swing, one would expect that either prices or production would have fallen. However, except for troughs in 2008 and early 2016, prices have been rising year on year while production is greater than ever (81m bpd in 2017). In other words, oil production and consumption are continuing to rise.

There are two main reasons for this. First, the increase in clean energy from less than 10% of oil and gas in 2015 to approaching 15% today, has taken place against a backdrop of growing overall energy demand. In other words, oil and gas may be slightly less important in terms of total energy demand, but demand for energy as a whole is still rising. Second, any fall in non-renewable fuels is accounted for by the drop in coal price and production, while the growth in renewables is largely accounted for by changes in electricity generation. We can see this in the arrival of electric cars, solar panels on houses, and the attention given to renewable energy by retailers and offices. However, there are large and growing areas of demand where renewable energy is not yet an option such as manufacturing, chemicals and aviation, and marine transportation. BP, a major oil and gas company, predicts that total energy demand will reach over 17 billion toe (tonnes of oil equivalent) by 2040, and 5 billion of that will be hydro, nuclear, and renewables. But oil and gas itself will be over 8 toe, about 1 billion tonnes more than today.

(*Source:* International Monetary Fund's International Financial Statistics; International Energy Agency data; BP statistics)

Quick questions

1. What steps can companies, and individuals, take to mitigate the effects of higher oil prices?
2. What can companies in specific sectors such as retail, tourism, and manufacturing do to reduce oil demand?
3. Can technology come to the rescue and deliver a cleaner energy mix?

Meanings of 'sustainability' and 'sustainable development'

A brief examination of how these terms are defined by various organizations offers a bewildering series of options to researchers and students of the subject. For example, for BP sustainability means 'a safe leader in our industry, a world calss operator, a responsible corporate citixen and a good employer';[5] and for Shell, 'working with governments, partners, communities and others to deliver more energy in economically, socially and environmentally responsible ways'.[6]

But there are also international definitions of sustainability that do not represent the views of business but rather society as a whole. The most famous of these is that of the UN World

Commission on Economic Development (see the following section). Furthermore, as the UN's Sustainable Development Goals make clear, sustainability is not limited to environmental issues: it includes social justice, workers' rights, women's rights, health, and various other themes that might be considered social issues. Many of these are covered in other chapters of this book (e.g. poverty in Chapter 4; strong institutions in Chapters 7, 8, and 9; gender equality in Chapters 12 and 13). However, when it comes to major global issues, it is hard to unpack them and treat them as unconnected or unrelated. As this chapter shows, when it comes to climate change, for instance, the social and environmental issues are largely intertwined.

The UN World Commission on Economic Development

It is now over thirty years since the World Commission on Economic Development (WCED), more commonly known as the Brundtland Commission, deliberated on, among other things, 'environmental strategies for achieving sustainable development by the year 2000 and beyond'. Having sat for almost three years, the Commission finally agreed a definition of 'sustainable development', which, although intended more as a challenge to governments, is widely referred to in debates about the role of business.

How effective and sufficient the progress has been since the Brundtland Report was published is a matter of continuing debate. The contributors to the report may well be further alarmed by the escalation of the threat to the environment posed by the effect of industrial activity on climate change. Yet in order to appreciate fully the difficulty of linking corporate activity to notions of sustainable development, it is useful to review the processes that led to the Report's publication.

The Commission was established by the United Nations in 1983 as the result of a process that can be traced back to the 1960s, at which time environmental concerns became the focus of various pressure groups. Rachel Carson's *Silent spring* (1962) had raised popular consciousness about the dangers of excessive pesticide use, and some progress had been made in improving air and water quality in industrialized areas through 'Clean Air' Acts and similar laws. By the early 1970s, NGOs such as Friends of the Earth and Greenpeace had been established in response to the perceived dangers posed to the planet by such phenomena as nuclear testing and the flooding of vast areas as a result of dam building.

However, the calls for a UN conference on the environment originated from the Swedish ambassador to the UN, who was particularly concerned with the effects of 'acid rain' and the general acidification of the water systems in Scandinavia, which was largely due to the emission by coal-fired power stations of excessive quantities of sulphur dioxide. In 1971, a UN-sponsored meeting of experts in pollution in Founex, Switzerland, had, for the first time, made the explicit connection between industrial development—a perceived desire of developing nations—and environmental degradation, which was seen as the price the nation had to pay. By the time the full conference took place in Stockholm in 1972, the issue of pollution had been widened to include the problems being experienced by developing countries. Indeed, environmental protection was seen as one of the limiting factors to development,[7] and in the years since, increasing emphasis has been placed on the social as well as environmental dimensions to sustainable development as evidenced for instance by the United Nations' Sustainable Development Goals launched in 2015, which bring together economic, social, and environmental targets.

In this chapter, our focus is more on the environmental side of sustainable development because many of the social aspects are covered elsewhere, notably Chapter 4. However, the conundrum of whether environmental issues can be tackled without jeopardizing economic growth remains central to sustainable development debates today. For example, the 2007 Stern Review for the UK government argued that not only was there not a contradiction, but that tackling climate change was a prerequisite for long-term prosperity. Certainly, the debate was not settled at Stockholm, but, in many ways, the conference was of greater international significance than is often reported. It involved the participation of not only more than 100 countries, but also of over 400 intergovernmental organizations and NGOs. It ended with the *Stockholm declaration on human environment* and the *Action plan for the human environment*.[8] In sum, it not only raised the environment to national consciousness, but also placed it firmly on the international agenda. Indeed, within twenty years of the end of the conference, over 100 countries had a government department dealing with the environment. Also, the principles of the sovereign right to exploit national resources and the responsibility for transboundary pollution became explicit, and were subsequently ratified in international agreements such as the UN Framework Convention on Climate Change (see later). It also led to the establishment of the United Nations Environment Program (UNEP) a year later.[9]

In addition, throughout the 1970s, there was continuing concern about a number of issues that impacted on notions of justice and fairness. The oil supply crisis in 1973 caused oil prices to rise to their highest-ever levels (after inflation adjustment). While the debt of developing countries was already rising, this enormous rise in oil prices brought debt to crisis levels, not only because of the increased costs of oil (from which some developing nations benefited), but because lending institutions, awash with oil money, encouraged such countries to take on more debt than they could afford—something that has only started to be resolved in recent years, with debt relief programmes. Equally, a number of projects designed to aid prosperity in the developing world, particularly huge hydroelectric schemes involving dam building and population relocation, were criticized for their adverse social and environmental ramifications.

In 1982, a special session of UNEP's governing council was convened to discuss Stockholm *'ten years on'*. It was here that it was decided that something far more radical and wide-ranging was needed to look much further forward. It was felt that, while the world economy had grown considerably, the least developed countries had made little ground and, in fact, many had seen a fall in per capita production during the 1980s.[10] It was at this point that the UN convened the World Commission on Environment and Development under Gro Harlem Brundtland 'at a time of unprecedented growth in pressures on the global environment, with grave predictions about the human future becoming commonplace'.[11] Its aim was to build a future that would be *'more prosperous, more just, and more secure'*, resting on ecologically sound policies and practices. Even at the outset, however, there was an overwhelming conviction that, in order to attain this goal, *'significant changes in current approaches'* would have to be confronted, which would involve changes in individual attitudes and lifestyles, and, more crucially, 'changes in certain critical policies . . . and the nature of co-operation between governments, business, science and people'.[12]

The significantly different approach that this Commission took was to try to conceptualize the relationship between the environment and development, in light of the continuing disparity between levels of prosperity in the northern and southern hemispheres, and the sentiments expressed at Founex in 1971. During its sitting, which lasted two-and-a-half years, a number of unprecedented events occurred.

A major famine in Ethiopia, which led to the death of over 1 million people, was broadcast to the West in graphic detail. It led to the 'Band Aid' concerts in London and Philadelphia, transmitted on television non-stop for over sixteen hours. At a policy level, the role of the government of Ethiopia, in terms of its willingness and ability to help its own peoples, was questioned amid accusations of corruption and ineptitude.[13]

Additionally, Farman, Gardiner, and Shanklin discovered the 'hole' in the ozone layer over Antarctica.[14] The importance of this discovery was not fully understood at the time and was met with some scepticism, because US monitoring satellites did not immediately corroborate the discovery. However, once the monitoring parameters were adjusted to access the data and the phenomenon was confirmed, the implications began to impact on policy-makers.

As these events unfolded, another tragedy struck—this time in Bhopal, India, in 1984. In what has become an iconic study of corporate social responsibility or irresponsibility, Union Carbide, which had established a site in Bhopal in 1969 to manufacture pesticides, initially imported one of the key ingredients, methyl isocyanate (MIC), before developing its onsite manufacturing facility in 1979. It seems clear from subsequent investigations that the level of maintenance was seriously short of the required standards. In November 1984, a leak of MIC caused the deaths of some 20,000 people. The health of over 120,000 people remains affected and the site is still not considered safe.

In late April 1986, a nuclear reactor at Chernobyl in the USSR (now Ukraine) exploded; thirty-one people died within three months and 237 were diagnosed with acute radiation sickness. Again, lack of maintenance was cited as the main cause and, like Bhopal, the legacy remains.[15]

The developed world did not escape either. In November 1986, agricultural chemicals and solvents leaked into the River Rhine following a chemical spill that was the result of a fire at a factory operated by Sandoz, a pharmaceutical conglomerate, in Basel, Switzerland. The Swiss government failed to act quickly enough to contain the spill, and, as a result, the drinking water of millions of people was affected and fish stocks were seriously depleted.

The WCED definition of sustainable development

Some of these events are acknowledged as having had an impact on the Commission,[16] and what emerged was a vision for a sustainable future that was dependent on some fundamental changes to what, in the West, had become an accepted way of life, with standards of living measured in terms of capital accumulation, levels of technological application, travel options, etc. In this new vision, the environment was to be placed at the centre of strategic decision-making. Rather than being seen as a limiting factor in the cause of continued development, the environment was to be seen as an '*aspect of policy*' if growth was to be sustained.[17] It also articulated notions of justice and fairness to the peoples of the developing world, in terms of fair shares of the world's resources and redistribution of wealth to improve the standards of living of the world's worst off.

> Humanity has the ability to make development sustainable—to ensure that it meets the needs of the present generation without compromising the ability of future generations to meet their own needs. The concept of sustainable development does imply limits—not absolute limits, but limitations imposed by the present state of technology and social organization on environmental resources and by the ability of the biosphere to absorb the effect of human activities.
>
> (WCED, 1987, p 8)

This definition of sustainable development—*'meeting the needs of the present generation without compromising the ability of future generations to meet their own needs'*, as it is commonly paraphrased—carries with it a number of implications and a number of challenges to the business world. This definition requires companies to act in *'three time zones'*.

1. Actions will have been taken in the lives of most existing companies that may have created liabilities due to the practice of 'externalizing' costs. This means, for example, that before legislation is passed to prevent companies discharging effluent into rivers and streams, it is clearly in the company's interest to dispose of as much waste as possible, and the more difficult the material is to purify, the greater the benefit. In most developed countries this is now against the law, but there are many companies whose sites are contaminated with chemicals, oils, and other toxic materials which require remediation. Indeed, there have been recent instances of companies which have gone into liquidation, leaving disputes over who picks up the cost for remediation.[18]
2. There is an expectation that companies not only demonstrate an awareness of their environmental responsibilities, but are able to show that they are meeting the benchmarks of today's citizens and consumers, and that the company will be a responsible citizen.
3. There is an expectation that companies consider the interests and rights of future generations.

This challenge is discussed further in the following sections, where we explore the definition of sustainable development and consider the implications within each part of it. First, we look at the implications of the needs of this generation ('intra-generational' equity), and the needs of this generation together with those of the next generation ('inter-generational' equity).

Intra-generational equity and inter-generational equity

If we break down the definition and look at its component parts, we begin to unravel the complexity of the idea and to understand why it poses such a potential challenge to current commercial activity. 'Development that meets the needs of the present generation' suggests fair distribution across the present population of the world, in terms of quality of life, measured, perhaps, by comparative standards of living or benefits from sharing the resources of the planet. There is some evidence that this is not happening at the present time. If we reflect on living standards in terms of Western developed societies and think of the comforts that the majority of the population enjoy, we can still observe that there are levels of inequality many find unacceptable and which, in extreme cases, have resulted in civil unrest.[19] If we then reflect on the developing world, we need little reminder that poverty and famine still blight many peoples of the world. For example, more than 40% of Africa's population live in arid, semi-arid, and dry sub-humid areas, meaning that millions in Africa suffer water shortages throughout the year. Perhaps more disturbingly, women bear the overwhelming responsibility for collecting water by a huge proportion.[20] Therefore it can be argued that we are not achieving the first of the tenets of sustainable development and, if that is the case and we are not meeting the needs of the present generation, it is logical to ask whether the next generation will fare any better. The balance of evidence from researchers who have looked into this suggests, rather pessimistically, that we are unlikely to perform any better in the future.[21]

The problem that this offers business relates to the tension which arises when the traditional profit-maximizing objective of the company is challenged by the need to reduce inputs, emissions, and waste.

We discuss the business case for adopting some of the strategies for sustainability elsewhere (see Chapter 6), but most of that case involves identifying opportunities for business, whether in terms of market niche, efficiencies, or tackling issues of risk and reputation. Putting environmental or social issues at the heart of business strategy is a more challenging proposition, and if these strategies seriously seek to address social justice issues, the challenges become even more profound.

Eco-justice and eco-efficiency

Also wrapped up in the WCED definition are notions of 'eco-justice' and 'eco-efficiency'. By 'eco-justice', we mean that some fairness is applied to the distribution of benefits that accrue from the development of the world's resources. To read the history of the colonial past of various European nations, for example, is to read how single countries sought to exploit the resources of many other countries without considering the needs of the indigenous peoples. Robins (2012) draws parallels between the companies that led the colonial charge and today's multinationals. He is not alone in believing that commercial exploitation continues to ignore the needs of local communities, and that the profits from such activities are often expatriated from the host country to benefit shareholders and investors who are far removed from the theatres of activity.

Eco-justice is often interpreted as laying the blame at business's door for impacts that may not have been anticipated at the time, or which may not even be substantiated by the evidence. 'Eco-efficiency', on the other hand, is a concept that has an appeal to the commercially minded. The idea that one should 'get more from less' is the sort of challenge to which a company can rise, and there is ample evidence that industrial processes are becoming more efficient. As noted in Chapter 6, in the discussion of the business case, it is in this area that we see most innovation. There are good commercial reasons for this, but there are also drivers from outside the economic sphere. Most of these stem from an increasing recognition that industrial activity poses specific threats to the world's environmental health.

However, it is important not to conflate notions of eco-efficiency with those of sustainable development. Eco-efficiency may well become the goal of each commercial entity, but, in itself, this might not prevent overall world resources from becoming depleted. So far, we have reviewed the development and challenges of sustainable development in terms of the Brundtland Commission's remit; we now move on to look at what has now been identified as the greatest threat to modern society—climate change.

 **Discussion Points**

In the 1970s and 1980s, there were many dire predictions of ecological collapse that did not materialize, and many natural systems have proved to be less fragile and faster to mend than once thought.

- Why are forecasts relating to natural systems so difficult to predict?
- Does the fact that some predictions were not borne out undermine or strengthen current arguments about climate change and other aspects of sustainable development?
- Which industries have most to win, and which have most to lose, from adopting a 'business as usual' attitude to sustainable development?

Climate change and global warming—a case of business and sustainable development

One of the constants of business's interest in its relationship with wider society this century has been its concern with climate change, which in many ways exemplifies the business-sustainable development interaction. We know that the Earth's climate is changing—humans are changing it—and it will continue to do so unless forceful action is taken. Moreover, this action needs to take place within a fairly well-known period of time—there is a strong scientific consensus that the period until the 2040s is crucial (Allen et al., 2014). There are many possible actions, some of which are in train: some will enable people to combat climate change; others will lead to society being transformed by climate change.

We also know that climate change will affect some of society's most fundamental principles and institutions. This chapter emphasizes the consequences for business, but climate change also has implications for international governance (achieving binding international agreements has been at the heart of climate negotiations since the 1990s), economics (in particular the centrality of growth to mainstream economic policy), and consumption (the globalization of consumption as a social norm and economic right). In each case, the implications of climate change are not trivial: as we will see, they strike at the heart of some of society's most basic and unquestioned assumptions about what is a good life (see Snapshot 3.2).

There are also things we do not know. Climate change deniers are wrong about the changing climate (there is no compelling evidence that it is anything but a real phenomenon); but they are right on one thing: there are many aspects of climate change about which we are ignorant. We do not know, for instance, all of the actions that should or can be taken in relation to climate change, either because the necessary innovation has yet to happen, or because we do not know what actions will be effective and plausible in a world filled with competing demands (e.g. the demand for economic growth versus the need to reduce carbon emissions). Also, we do not know how long some key initiatives will take to implement—an important knowledge gap given that in many instances one of the things that determines if an action is effective or not is when it is undertaken. For example, a 5-metre-high flood wall to combat rising sea levels could be very effective if built by 2020, but useless if built by 2040, when sea surges might require a higher wall.

Of course, we are not completely blind nor ignorant. Many actions have already been taken. The 2016 Paris Agreement, part of the United Nations Framework Convention on Climate Change, which countries ratified in record time, commits governments to action to combat climate change. Carbon emissions trading has spread from Europe to China, South Korea, New Zealand, and beyond. The Carbon Disclosure Project provides investors with unparalleled information on the carbon emissions of companies, cities, and states. Some might even argue that there are too many initiatives, evident for instance in the setting up of the Task Force on Climate-related Financial Disclosures to move from the current 400 or so disclosure regimes to a consistent model.

However, we do not know how effective these actions will be. We do not know because they are new or have long-term goals. After years of gradual acceptance that global warming is a real phenomenon and one caused by human activity, major economies, notably the USA, have backtracked. In 2017, the US government withdrew from the Paris Agreement, the President has spoken forcefully in favour of regenerating the coal industry, and the Environmental Protection Agency is led by climate change deniers. We also do not know if these actions are comprehensive enough, and what will happen if, for instance, there is innovation in financial disclosures in the major commercial centres of the world, but nothing is done to address the challenges of the majority of businesses in the world, i.e. the vast number of enterprises that are small and often in the unregulated, informal economy (Chapter 9). We also know that some initiatives are not working properly. For example, of the \$14.1 billion approved climate finance, only 3% is allocated to decentralized energy, even though this is the most important source of energy for 15% of the world's population (Rai et al., 2016).

In summary, we know that climate change requires transformation, and we know some of the actions needed. But we also know that the actions being undertaken are insufficient either to prevent rises in global average temperatures by more than 1.5°C or to deal with the social consequences of rises beyond 2°C, the point at which catastrophic climate change is reckoned to become a reality.[22] Furthermore, we do not know with any certainty whether the current initiatives will work, and we are ignorant as to what approaches will be most effective.

Snapshot 3.2 Aviation and climate change

Most of us who read this book will have benefited from cheap air travel, whether for holiday travel or business trips. Flights from Europe to the USA are on offer for under £500, and from Europe to the Far East and Australasia may be at little over £600. How can some airline companies offer flights so cheaply, and does this activity contribute to global warming?

The increase in greenhouse gas emissions from international aviation is the highest of any industrial sector in Europe. An individual taking a return flight between London and New York generates about the same quantity of emissions as they do from their home in an entire year. If global aviation was a country, it would rank in the top ten emitters. Aviation was included in the EU Emissions Trading Scheme (ETS) in 2009, but at present it only applies to flights wholly within the union, and because of overseas protests will not include all international flights until 2023.

(*Source*: https://ec.europa.eu/clima/policies/transport/aviation_en)

(*continued . . .*)

Quick questions

1. What is the purpose of an ETS?
2. Why have non-European airlines rejected ETS rules so far?
3. Is it possible to have a sustainable airline industry at the present scale?

Discussion Points

Climate change is a very important and high-profile aspect of sustainable development, but it is not the only one.

- What other aspects of sustainable development should business consider?
- Are there contradictions and dichotomies between some of these aspects?
- Which of these aspects are beyond the concerns of CSR at the present time?

The challenge to business

We opened this chapter with examples of how three businesses defined sustainability in the context of their own business operations. To our knowledge, the only business that has openly acknowledged that it is not environmentally sustainable, and has taken positive steps to correct this, is Interface Inc., the global floor coverings company (see Case study 3). As noted earlier, the weight of evidence suggests that organizations operating under the traditional business model work within a framework where externalizing costs is seen as good practice. Equally, investors expect returns on their investments, and returns are obtained by growing the profits of the business. The challenge is that growth of the business has invariably meant increasing resource usage, which both depletes the Earth's stock of resources and leads to increased emissions.

The above uncertainties are very important for business because our current models of management, governance, and finance all have their roots in the pre-climate-change era. If one dates modern business back to the Industrial Revolution, then value has been created by taking a raw material and incrementally adding value to it through processing, manufacturing, marketing, etc. The only limits to creating value were the capacity to extract raw materials and the size of the consumer market. Business-related legislation from ownership to labour laws to investment were all built around assumptions about infinite production, consumption, and growth.

That era may well have passed. We say 'may' because the thrust of climate change policies worldwide is that society can combat climate change with a modified 'business as usual' approach (BAU). Two core elements of modified BAU policies are to do with energy and economic growth. It is assumed that climate change can be addressed if fossil fuels are replaced with low carbon or renewable energy. If this is achieved, moreover, business and economic life in general can go on as before without the need for changes in consumption patterns, stringent limits on resource use, and other types of interference with the market. The market is part of the second core element to modified BAU policies. The bulk of economists hold as an axiomatic truth that markets allocate finite resources most efficiently, hence the emergence of carbon markets around the world (Bowen and Hepburn, 2014).

The advantage of framing climate change as an energy or economic challenge is that it does not require radical change to established business or economic models. The disadvantage, though, is that the framing is not working. There have been significant and rapid changes in energy generation. Renewable energy has experienced rises in terms of annual growth rates and annual capacity additions since 2005, and now accounts for nearly 20% of global energy consumption (REN21, 2016). However, this is not significantly different to the percentage in 2012 because global growth in energy consumption overall has been greater than the additions from renewables (Rapier, 2016). Yet, despite increased demand for energy, the growth-dependent neoliberal economy is struggling to deliver sustained prosperity and has come under increasing criticism for creating inequality and exclusion (Atkinson and Morelli, 2011; Beinhocker and Hanauer, 2014).

Therefore, unless the energy and economic responses to climate change improve significantly in a short space of time, there is good reason to think that business in an era defined by climate change will be different to what we have grown used to. For instance, as the stranded assets movement in accounting has highlighted, the value of booked assets of companies may change. Notably, the valuation of publicly traded oil companies has been shown to include reserves they could not exploit without causing hazardous levels of carbon emissions (HSBC Global Research, 2012). Climate change will require new forms of accounting so that environmentally damaging aspects of business practice are not dismissed as externalities for which a company has no responsibility. Accounting will need to recognize that what in a previous era were assets, in a climate-changed era are liabilities. However, it will require a raft of other changes as well. For example, risk managers at banks are currently not mandated to include climate change risk in their assessments. This is because their risk horizon is limited to five, at most seven, years. As yet, climate change does not represent a risk to banks over that period. By the time it does, it will probably be too late for the industry to take any meaningful action. Indeed, the Chair of the Bank of England, Mark Carney, has suggested that the finance industry may be reaching its 'Minsky moment', i.e. the moment at which financial exposure to a risk is so great that a collapse is inevitable (Carney, 2016).

There are many examples of where climate change poses a risk (recognized or not) to business, or requires new ways of doing business. This latter refers not only to alternative management practices or finance (although both are important): it also concerns the purpose of business, the meaning of value, and the role business plays in society (Blowfield, 2018), aspects of which are explored in Chapter 7.

Discussion Points

One of the most controversial areas is whether economic growth and sustainable development are compatible.

- Is the Stern Review right to say that sustainable development is essential for economic growth?
- Is it possible to run a business that will grow within the limits of the Earth's ecosystem?
- Is it possible to grow a business while shrinking its environmental footprint?

Capital markets and sustainable development

Despite these initiatives to find new models of sustainable business, there are those who believe that the most fundamental challenge to sustainable practices is that posed by the way in which capital markets reward and punish participants. Although the tension between sustainability and the capital market has been acknowledged for some time, the debate was widened in the 1990s with the work of Stephan Schmidheiny (*Changing course*, 1992), and Schmidheiny with Federico Zorraquin (*Financing change*, 1996). Both these authors are industrialists who depend upon the capital market system for their business success, yet have tackled problematic questions regarding the role that capital market activity might play in either helping or hindering the development of sustainable practices.

Elsewhere in this book, we look at some of the mechanisms that govern the ways in which companies operate, and equally at the notion of responsible investing, which considers social and environmental impacts on a par with financial returns (see Chapter 6.) But it might be useful to review briefly the mechanisms of the capital market system, to illustrate the dilemmas that they reveal.

First and foremost, only in the initial public offering do capital markets transfer funds from those who wish to invest to those who wish to apply these funds to means of producing goods or services. Thereafter investors in the stock market trade on an expectation of either dividend returns or share returns. In most cases success in the market is calculated by rather short-term returns. Bonus schemes for capital market participants, including bankers, are calculated, in the main, on short-term measures of success. The problem, in relation to the connection between capital market investment practices and sustainable development, arises in the way in which companies are rewarded, or punished, by the market.

Signals to the market

It is acknowledged in the finance literature that markets respond to 'signals'. These signals are interpreted from information about company activity that is obtained from diverse sources. For example, if a company is thought to be underperforming, a good signal to the market might be an announcement of a change in top management; reducing declared dividends is seen as a bad signal. These signals are interpreted by financial analysts in terms of potential future cash flows and are reflected in patterns of investment, or disinvestment. They contribute to some of the changes that we witness in share price movements over time. Traditionally, the information that tends to move share prices is normally financial, relating to earnings forecasts, dividend policy, investment policy, etc. Indeed, the nature of the investments that a company makes in the course of its operations is central to the way in which the future performance of a company may be assessed. These strategies are disclosed in the course of both formal and informal discussions with analysts, and the concern here is that the fear of communicating the wrong signal may act to inhibit companies from undertaking innovative or experimental investments, which may be necessary if a sustainable development agenda is to be adopted.[23]

Schmidheiny and Zorraquin (1996, p 8) list several 'worrying' assumptions about sustainable development that might convey the wrong signal to markets. They include the following:

- there is a common perception that sustainability requires longer-term investments, where payback times might not fall in the 'good signal' time span;
- a concerted effort to innovate may reduce present earnings;
- for global companies, investment in sustainable development initiatives in developing countries brings with it additional high-risk premiums;
- accounting and reporting systems do not adequately reflect risks and opportunities.

Another issue that companies try to avoid signalling to the market is the threat of regulation. The idea that governments are about to intervene in a particular sector creates uncertainty, which is interpreted as a bad signal. This helps to explain why companies combine to form strong associations aimed at helping to persuade governments that there is no need to regulate. If they can demonstrate that they are handling thorny issues, the hope is that governments will accept that industry is capable of regulating itself. The World Business Council for Sustainable Development (WBCSD) is one such organization, boasting a large number of major corporations worldwide within its membership. The Global Reporting Initiative (GRI) is another example, and adoption of its guidelines (see Chapter 8) has been used to demonstrate that serious efforts are being made to address previously perceived reporting imperfections. These examples and countless others, at professional, industry, national, or supranational levels, are all designed to counter the possibility of the adverse market effect of announcements of regulation.

However, those in favour of a more regulated approach remain sceptical of the motives behind this lobbying process. Their argument is that if regulation only represents the lowest level of acceptable behaviour beyond which it is deemed illegal, and that as CSR programmes are supposed to go beyond this point in any case, what is the issue with regulation?

As judged by markets, however, operating to the minimum standards allowed by law is usually seen as a positive signal. It also gives rise to the acronyms that are taken as a guide to much commercial activity in the area of environmental management systems, such as BATNEEC and CATNIP.[24] The question is, what will it take for the market to reward behaviour that goes beyond regulation, even if that involves expenditure that might have an adverse impact on short-term earnings? At what stage, for example, might markets see initiatives such as switching away from biomass back to coal in the production of electricity as a bad signal?

Discussion Points

The accountancy profession is seen by some as an essential element in encouraging companies to tackle sustainable development.

- What can the accountancy profession bring to sustainable development that will help companies to change their business models, enabling them to operate with less of an environmental impact?
- To what extent does the accountancy profession lock companies into outdated business models?
- What can the accountancy profession do to remove the barriers to client behaviour change?

Rewarding financial intermediaries

Since the global financial crisis in 2007–2008 which led to national governments 'bailing out' many global financial institutions, the award of bonuses to employees by banks has become a discussion about CSR in itself. Those involved in the investment process as financial intermediaries work within a bonus system, which can represent a large percentage of an individual's salary and which, collectively in the City of London in 2006, amounted to some £8bn, a figure equivalent to the GDP of some developing countries. As the depth of the financial crisis began to emerge and allegations of imprudent trading products and practices emerged, focus turned to those senior executives in the banks at the point of collapse. In a move that further enraged the public, many of those who were accused of being involved in the bad practice that led to the collapse left their posts on very generous terms, a move which seemed to many to epitomize the problems that brought about the crisis in the first place. The global recession which followed the financial meltdown meant that bonuses in 2008 and 2009 were lower than previously, but 2010 saw a return to a figure in the region of £6bn, although some high-profile CEOs of banks declined to take their bonuses, and continued pressure on the UK government, especially, has seen continued calls for bonuses to be capped at a salary level, or deferred to a point where recklessness or malpractice can be ruled out.

In Joel Barkan's documentary film *The Corporation* (2004), a Wall Street trader enthuses over the profits made from trading in gold on 11 September 2001 as the twin towers descended to dust. When discussing the possibility of disease affecting the pig population, the trader talks of the opportunities that the news presents: 'It's almost ludicrous not to jump on board.' Other interviewees talk of the market as *'amoral'*, suggesting that issues of morality and ethics should have been negotiated before the trading process began—that is, it is not the trader's job to think about morality. These are important questions that are not fully acknowledged by market participants. There is nothing in corporate governance guidelines that gives companies any direction or reassurance should they consider any such strategy, and shareholder return remains the main driver of market activity.

However, there are attempts to engage analysts in considering social and environmental impacts. The Enhanced Analytics Initiative, the UN Principles for Responsible Investment, the London Accord, and the Marathon Club, which have all enjoyed the backing of major financial institutions, have all over time worked in different ways to get financial intermediaries to take sustainability seriously. The Institute of Chartered Accountants in England and Wales, in association with the World Wildlife Fund (WWF), has also launched the Finance Innovation Laboratory, a broad multi-stakeholder initiative that aims to activate solutions for change in financial systems. These emerging trends are discussed further in Chapter 10.

Discussion Points

Some believe that business can only go so far in addressing sustainable development without the support of other members of society.

- Do markets incentivize short-term and continued-cost externalization of the kind cited as a threat to sustainable development?
- Are consumers motivated as much by encouraging good performance in sustainability as they are by punishing poor performance?
- Would NGOs be likely to criticize a company more or less if it were to take on sustainable development issues?

Case study 3 Interface Inc.

From modest beginnings in 1973, Interface has risen in stature to become the world's largest manufacturer of floor tiles, selling products in 110 countries, with sales approaching $1bn and over 3,000 employees. What singles out Interface from other companies in an industry which typically relies on petrochemicals in the manufacturing process is its commitment to become environmentally neutral. Until 1994, like its competitors, Interface used an accepted business model to grow the company, complying with laws and regulations as required.

However, in 1994 Ray Anderson, the founder of the company and then CEO, was asked to make a presentation on the company's environmental plans. In preparation for this he was given a copy of Paul Hawken's book *The ecology of commerce* (1993). The effect, in Anderson's words, was like 'a spear to the chest'. From that point Anderson determined to change the way the company interacted with nature and set about its journey to conquer 'Mount Sustainability'.

The journey of Interface towards sustainability has marked a considerable shift in the way the company both operates and designs its products. The company was faced with the considerable challenge of reimagining its business model and then redesigning all of its processes, as well as moving away from its dependency on petrochemicals. It developed a vision to become 'the first company that, by its deeds, shows the entire industrial world what sustainability is in all its dimensions: people, process, product, place and profits—by 2020'.

The journey is characterized by addressing 'the seven fronts of Mount Sustainability':

1 eliminate waste;
2 benign emissions;
3 renewable energy;
4 closing the loop;
5 resource-efficient transportation;
6 sensitizing stakeholders;
7 redesigning commerce.

Each of these approaches is developed and explained with practical advice on how to approach the challenges offered.

Equally, the company was open to taking advice and guidance from a number of partners to help it achieve its aims, including the World Resources Institute, the Forum for the Future, the US Environmental Protection Agency, and the National Minority Supplier Development Council. It also has an 'Eco Dream Team' comprising leading thinkers, architects, and engineers to maintain the momentum. Far from costing money, Interface sees its move to a sustainable business model as a positive benefit. As Ray Anderson puts it:

> Costs are down, not up, dispelling a myth and exposing the false choice between the economy and the environment, products are the best they have ever been, because sustainable design has provided an unexpected wellspring of innovation, people are galvanized around a shared higher purpose, better people are applying, the best people are staying and working with a purpose, the goodwill in the marketplace generated by our focus on sustainability far exceeds that which any amount of advertising or marketing expenditure could have generated—this company believes it has found a better way to a bigger and more legitimate profit—a better business model.

(*Source:* http://www.interfaceglobal.com)

(*continued . . .*)

Questions

1. Sustainable development is often seen as an insurmountable objective for many companies.
   a. How might a company approach this challenge, and where might it look for help?
   b. How can companies involve NGOs in this process?
   c. To what extent does collaboration pose a threat to a company's competitive advantage, and how should that threat be managed?
2. Sustainable development, in the Brundtland definition, encompasses notions of social justice across and between generations.
   a. How can notions of social justice be assimilated into the neoclassical theory of the firm which places the emphasis on maximizing shareholder wealth?
   b. What responsibilities do transnational corporations have to their employees in different locations?
   c. To what extent is product re-engineering a viable strategy to address sustainability?
3. Interface embarked on a twenty-five-year journey towards 'mission zero', where it will eliminate any negative impact on the environment.
   a. What other sectors might follow this example?
   b. What are the major obstacles to achieving this mission for other companies?
   c. How important is it to have top-level support for this kind of initiative?

Summary

This chapter began and ended with looking at how companies portray their activities in terms of sustainability. In between, we examined how concepts of sustainable development emerged and were defined, how that definition conceals subtle notions of equity and fairness, and how these notions present challenges to the 'business as usual' model of corporate behaviour. Although there are broadly accepted definitions of sustainable development, individual companies still choose to define the concept in their own ways. As will be discussed in relation to the impact of CSR (see Chapter 13), companies are, at best, only starting to understand that they must take responsibility for some of their most significant sustainability consequences. This is evident in the sustainability reports that many companies are producing and, as we have illustrated, some companies approach this task by redefining sustainable development in ways that can be addressed while leaving out the issues that present the greatest challenges. This also relates to the accountability framework within which reporting sits (see Chapter 8).

If, initially, such reports were dismissed as a public relations exercise, the seriousness with which issues such as climate change and sustainable energy are being taken by both governments and the private sector strongly suggests that sustainability will become an increasingly important part of the business agenda. In some ways, this makes getting the management and reporting frameworks right even more important. This and other aspects of sustainable development, such as demographic change, may also be among the most crucial business questions and with equally significant prizes at stake. Although questions remain about the exact science of climate change (as they do in relation to most areas of scientific enquiry), there is an overwhelming consensus—and one that is increasingly endorsed by business—that it poses a real risk and is related to human activity. As the different dimensions of sustainable development become more apparent in everyday life, so people will turn to major institutions to take a lead in controlling harmful emissions. Business is clearly one such institution and its role is likely to become more prominent, not least because the conventional command-and-control regulatory model of government is being tested by the social and political realities of globalization.

Further Reading

Gregoriou, G.N., Micocci, M., and Masala, G.B. (eds) 2017, *Pension fund risk management: financial and actuarial modeling*, Chapman and Hall/CRC Finance Series.

The importance of sustainable development from a financial and actuarial perspective.

Anderson, R.C. 1998, *Mid-course correction: toward a sustainable enterprise: the Interface model*, Peregrinzilla Press, Atlanta, GA.

An early but fascinating analysis of the significance of environmental management and sustainability to corporations by the head of a multinational company.

Gardetti, M.Á., and Torres, A.L. (eds) 2014, *Sustainable luxury: managing social and environmental performance in iconic brands*, Greenleaf, Sheffield.

Insights into how to approach sustainable consumption in a brand-conscious society.

Gore, A. 2006, *An inconvenient truth*, Bloomsbury, London.

The book accompanying the Oscar-winning film about the importance of climate change.

Raworth, K. 2017, *Doughnut economics: seven ways to think like a 21st-century economist*, Random House, London.

An alternative perspective on the economics that will help transform companies and societies to a sustainable world.

Robertson, M. 2017, *Sustainability principles and practice*, Routledge.

Interdisciplinary overview of sustainability that links practices to the workplace.

http://www.oup.com/uk/blowfield_murray4e/

Visit the online resources that accompany this book to enrich your understanding of this chapter. Among the resources available are web links, exercises, and additional case studies.

Endnotes

1. For a detailed analysis, the Oxford Poverty and Human Development Initiative analyses poverty across 104 countries—see http://www.ophi.org.uk, accessed 24 November 2018
2. E.g. http://web.unep.org/geo/assessments/global, accessed 24 November 2018.
3. Jacks, 2013.

4. Stott et al., 2010.
5. BP Sustainability Review, 2012, p 5, available at https://www.bp.com/content/dam/bp/pdf/sustainability/group-reports/BP_Sustainability_Review_2012.pdf, accessed 6 December 2018.
6. See https://www.shell.com/sustainability/our-approach/sustainability-at-shell.html, accessed 24 November 2018.
7. Grubb et al., 1993.
8. http://www.unep.org, accessed 24 November 2018
9. UNEP was established with its headquarters in Nairobi under the Executive Directorship of Maurice Strong, who had been appointed Secretary-General of the Stockholm Conference in 1972.
10. Tolba and El-Kholy, 1992.
11. WCED, 1987; see http://www.un-documents.net/ocf-a2.htm, accessed 24 November 2018.
12. WCED, 1987, p 356; see http://www.un-documents.net/ocf-a2.htm, accessed 24 November 2018.
13. Since then, and despite massive amounts of aid raised in the West for the starving of Africa, famines still occur and continuing allegations of malpractice are laid at the feet of host governments, with new roles being defined for NGOs to administer aid programmes.
14. Farman et al., 1985.
15. Incidences of thyroid cancer in children of up to fifteen years old increased tenfold between 1986 and 1997, and it is feared that many others may have died as a consequence of the accident.
16. Tolba and El-Kholy, 1992.
17. Grubb et al., 1993.
18. Vass, 2013.
19. The Guardian reported on riots in Sweden in May 2013: 'as inequality and segregation start to rise, the spread of youth disorder has shaken ethnic Swedes and older immigrants alike. These riots follow major disturbances in Paris in 2005, and in other European cities in between' (Orange, 2013).
20. UNEP, 2010.
21. See e.g.: Hawken, 1993; Gray et al., 1995a; Elkington, 1998; Birken, 2000; Gray and Bebbington, 2000; Suranyi, 2000; Bebbington et al., 2004; Gray 2006 a, b.
22. There are many sources for this claim, such as Gao et al., 2017.
23. Murray et al., 2006.
24. BATNEEC, 'Best Available Technology Not Entailing Excessive Cost'; CATNIP, 'Currently Available Technology Not Involving Prosecution'.

Corporate social responsibility in developing economies

Chapter overview

In this chapter, we discuss the role of business in developing economies, and whether and how business can be an agent of poverty reduction.[1] In particular, we will:

- review the role of business in social and economic development;
- review what it means for business to be an agent of development;
- examine under what circumstances business takes on a developmental role;
- explore the limitations of business as a force for development.

Main topics

Key terms

International development
Poverty
Business as development agent
Bottom of the pyramid
Fairtrade
Microfinance

Introduction

Since the mid-2000s, there has been a flurry of activity around the role of business in advancing social and economic development in what are variously called emerging or developing economies. There are diverse arguments for putting business and development towards the top of theoretical and practical CSR agendas. Companies have great wealth; by some measures greater than that of many poor nations. Companies have a significant, sometimes negative, impact on developing economies. Governments cannot always be trusted to deliver the social and economic benefits that the poor and marginalized have a right to expect. Business activity is essential to economic growth. Certain types of enterprise are well suited to meeting the needs of the poor. The gap between rich and poor is a threat to political and economic stability. According to philosophers such as Singer (1972), it is morally indefensible to allow suffering on the grounds that it happens in far off places, and, as part of this ethical debate, it could be argued that companies have a responsibility not just for the harms they produce but equally for the ones they fail to prevent.

Typically, in considering these perspectives the emphasis is on the role of multinational companies, and sometimes one can forget that many developing economies have a vibrant private sector, especially at the level of small and medium-sized enterprises, often located in the informal rather than formal economy. We examine CSR in the context of small and medium-sized companies in Chapter 11, but their role in developing economies should not be overlooked, as some of the examples in this chapter remind us.

Nonetheless, much more is known about the responsibilities and practices of larger companies, but as we shall see there are many views about when, where, and how they should act in developing economies. This has become more complicated in recent years because of the entry of companies headquartered in emerging economies, notably China and India. Chinese companies operating in Africa, for example, have developed their own definition of CSR, often in conjunction with the Chinese government, which funds a wide array of projects across that continent.[2] Moreover, the rapid rise in business activity by companies from India and especially China in Africa has introduced a new dimension to CSR. A company's relationship to poverty is a major determinant of how it behaves in this environment (e.g. whether it is a cause or victim of poverty), and understanding this relationship is very useful in assessing what a company can and should be doing. As the following sections reveal, it is possible to build a framework for understanding what can and cannot be expected of business in the development context.

Development agent or development tool?

The array of viewpoints on why business is important to the prosperity of developing countries, and vice versa, have given rise to quite different ideas about what business should be doing and why. Liberal economists argue that companies exist to create value for shareholders, subject to legal constraints (see Chapter 2), and by so doing they are a positive force for development—creating jobs, supplying goods and services, and helping to fund necessary social institutions. This thinking underpinned the so-called 'Washington Consensus', the set of private-sector-oriented policies that countries around the world had to adopt if they were to receive assistance from the major international financial institutions in the 1980s and 1990s. The Consensus in its pure form has gone out of fashion, but echoes of it can be heard in discussions about growth-driven development, and in particular the view that as sustainable poverty alleviation depends on economic growth, then business as the primary creator of wealth has a central role to play.

But this gives rise to another question. Should business be regarded as a development agent, consciously striving to deliver and moreover be held to account for developmental outcomes? Or should it be considered a development tool, no more responsible for positive or negative outcomes than a hammer is for a carpenter's thumb? When business acts as a development tool, the outcomes can be positive—creating jobs, generating wealth, meeting people's needs through the provision of goods and services. Two studies, one of Unilever's impact on the poor, and one of its economic footprint in Indonesia and South Africa, show the complex economic outcomes that can result when a multinational produces and markets goods in developing countries.[3]

However, the question is not simply whether business has an impact on poverty, but whether or not it can and should be accountable for causing, preventing, and alleviating poverty. For instance, the development tool might create jobs, but business as development agent takes responsibility for the number of jobs it creates, their location, and the quality. The development tool might make products available in poor countries, but the development agent makes products suited to the needs of and accessible to poor segments of the population. And whereas the business-as-usual approach to development emerges from managerial calculations related to costs, returns, and competition, business as a development agent is also motivated by stakeholder concerns, pressures, and demands.

In this chapter, our main interest is private enterprise as development agent—something that not only affects poverty, but is also the subject of conscious actions undertaken because of poverty. The agent can be a company, an industry, an inter-company alliance, a multi-sector partnership, or any other entity where the actions of the private sector are influenced by an awareness of poverty. Our main focus will be on company actions (e.g. by management or investors), but we will also explore how others, such as international development agencies, have influenced the private sector.

A brief history of business as development agent

There is nothing new about companies being development agents. From the Dutch East India Company in Indonesia to the British South Africa company in 1920s Zambia, private companies have administered vast territories, and performed parallel governmental and commercial functions. The expectations of companies may shift over time, but what these examples and other histories[4] highlight is that while definitions of responsibility change, the idea of companies having responsibility towards society remains constant. Yet despite the evidence that the responsibilities of corporations alter, CSR theory has failed to produce a substantive theory of change. The analyses that other disciplines bring to the relationship of business with society are not widely used in CSR theory. For instance, there is a considerable body of scholarship about business and international development, concerning areas such as corporate imperialism and influence over newly independent post-colonial states,[5] but it has not significantly influenced discussion of CSR and poverty.

There are exceptions such as Ruggie (2003), who draws on Polanyi's theory of embedded and disembedded economies to explain general shifts in the nature of the business–society relationship:

> [CSR] may be seen as a voluntary effort to realign the efficiency of markets with the shared value and purposes that societies demand, and that markets themselves require to survive and thrive.
>
> (Cited in Nelson, 2007, p 58)

But more typically, the responsibilities of companies are presented as ahistorical. Shifts over time are treated as normative, and there is little attempt to explain why, for instance, the radical agendas of the 1930s have been replaced with something much less ambitious in recent times.[6] In other words, the definition of corporate social responsibilities is treated as something divorced from the social, political, and historical context of the locations where business is operating. The consequences of this become apparent when we consider the shifting nature of development as a concept.

Discussion points

International development is increasingly emphasized as an important aspect of CSR.

- Why are social and environmental issues associated with international development important for business?
- Should companies be held to account for the harms they fail to prevent as much as for the ones they cause?
- What can national governments do to encourage companies to be more proactive as development agents?

Theories of development

In the literature on business and development, it is common to concentrate on the type of things that companies are doing, and why they add value to society and the bottom line. However, the potential trap of focusing on a business rationale is that the scope of companies' responsibilities comes to be defined from within the framework of management theory, rather than that of development. Yet what we have labelled the development agent role can be constructed quite differently depending how we think about development. For example, Utting (2007) discusses the relationship between CSR and an equality/equity approach to development. If such an approach were used to inform business strategy, then the responsibilities of business would include aspects of social protection, rights, empowerment, and redistribution.

Key concept: International development

International development refers to efforts to improve standards of living in the poorer countries of the world. It is not a new idea; one of the justifications for colonialism, particularly in its later years, was that it would bring about economic growth and better social conditions. But international development as an idea really took off in the post-colonial era as it became clear that independence alone was not going to end the low levels of health, education, household income, infrastructure development, and other features that seemed characteristics of what are variously called less developed countries, emerging economies, and developing nations.

Since the 1960s, international development has been a distinct aspect of social and economic reform, typically referring to the efforts of wealthier countries to help poor ones. Most rich countries have specific government departments dedicated to funding and promoting international development. Often these were set up to deal with emergency aid (e.g. famine relief), but their remit was soon extended to address such emergencies through longer-term development activities based on the principle that if you give someone a fish they will eat for a day, but if you teach them how to fish they will eat forever.

However, international development is not the preserve of donor governments, and indeed there is considerable frustration that so few rich countries have lived up to their agreement in principle to commit 0.7% of GDP to development spending. Oxfam (short for Oxford Famine Relief) was one of the first of what are now an enormous number of development-oriented NGOs with offices around the world. Some of the largest NGOs, such as BRAC in Bangladesh, were founded in developing countries, but there are also numerous development consultancies such as the USA's 'beltway bandits', so called for their location around Washington, DC, where some of the most significant development funding decisions are made.

In earlier development paradigms, such as those of Frank and Wallerstein, the condition of poor countries was held to be a direct consequence of the wealth of others. Today, however, mainstream international development practice has discarded such structural considerations, and development's core aim is to establish the conditions whereby a country is ready to compete in a capitalist world economy. Business's unique position in that economy is the main reason why in recent years attention has been paid to business as a development agent, and how, for instance, it can contribute to measures of that development, exemplified for instance in the targets of the Sustainable Development Goals.

Different models of development have been favoured over time, ranging from Streeten's theory of basic human needs to Rostow's take-off model to Sen's work on welfare economics. Each model has its implications for what business might do. However, contemporary CSR theory in general does not openly acknowledge these different models. Instead, for the most part it adheres to, and tacitly accepts, what Rodrik (1997) calls the augmented Washington Consensus, a model that dominates current development theory.

Current approaches to CSR as management practice are stronger in some areas than others. For example, for all the widespread adoption of core labour rights into the responsibility discourse, meaningful interventions have proved difficult, especially on issues such as freedom of association and the rights of women. Moreover, the role of business looks different again if one emphasizes the rights-based, empowerment, redistributive, or neoliberal elements of development agendas.[7] However, the distinct responses demanded by such differing ideas of development are often blurred in business–poverty discussions, something that can lead to unwarranted criticism and praise of the private sector's role.[8]

International agencies such as the United Nations Conference on Trade and Development (UNCTAD), the United Nations Development Programme (UNDP), the World Trade Organization (WTO), the World Bank, and the Organisation for Economic Co-operation and Development (OECD) have set out various ways that business can help alleviate poverty.[9] For example, the International Labour Organization (ILO) highlights low wages and vulnerable employment as causes of poverty, OECD stresses the consequences of short-termism among multinational corporations, and their abuse of political and economic muscle, while UNCTAD concentrates on the importance of backward linkages and embedding companies into local economies. The United Nations Industrial Development Organization (UNIDO) distinguishes between the substantive dimension to CSR (i.e. the particular issues that are addressed), and the process dimension (the ways business goes about addressing these issues and identifying the boundaries of accountability) (Nelson, 2007). Various international organizations emphasize the importance of this process dimension as a determinant of the effectiveness of poverty interventions, including support for the self-organization of the poor at community level or workers in factories, a cognizance of local conditions, and cross-sector coordination.[10]

However, there is a mismatch between this kind of aspirational development agenda and what companies are actually doing as development agents (see Snapshot 4.1). The array of substantive issues being addressed is incomplete, but is nonetheless more comprehensive than that of process issues, which may not be included at all.[11] Various questions arise from this observation. Is it the case that business has an ad hoc poverty agenda, and if so how has that come about, and what are the likely outcomes? Can business be more effectively integrated into established agendas, and what would this require? Or is it that business is already part of an alternative poverty agenda, and what are the implications of this? We will explore these questions in the coming sections.

Discussion points

Theorists such as Easterly claim that government aid to developing countries is a failure, and that the private sector offers a better alternative for economic growth.

- Why do you think that the private sector was previously overlooked in some development theories?
- What are the strengths of companies in tackling development issues?
- Are there aspects of development where a private-sector response is inappropriate?

Snapshot 4.1 Clean water for poor communities—P&G PuR

Procter & Gamble (P&G) is the largest consumer goods manufacturer in the world, with net sales of over $65 billion. In 1995, in association with the US Centers for Disease Control and Prevention, it developed PuR packets, which purify dirty water. It invested more than $10 million in R&D, and a similar amount in market testing for bottom-of-the-pyramid markets. However, it eventually shifted the product to its

(continued . . .)

charitable foundation because testing in 2000–2003 found the product take-up to be commercially non-viable. This was because PuR required too much investment in public health education to be profitable, despite its undoubted benefits for consumers, employees, and society. Seeing the social returns on investment, the company shelved plans to end the product and chose instead to explore non-conventional marketing approaches.

Instead of using normal outlets, PuR was sold to NGOs for about 3.5 US cents per sachet. Through P&G's Corporate Sustainable Development unit, the company launched its Live, Learn and Thrive programme, and PuR became an important element in partnerships with community development NGOs such as World Vision, Care, and Save the Children. The alliances cost P&G about $3.5 million to fund donations of product, technical expertise, and marketing expertise. Operating around the world, including in disaster zones such as Haiti, P&G aimed to provide 4 billion litres of clean water by 2012, and now claims to have provided 13 billion litres worldwide. If correct, this would have saved an estimated 10,000 lives, and prevent about 80 million days lost due to diarrhoea annually. PuR sachet sales have increased as a result of the partnership model.

Quick questions

PuR is a market approach to delivering clean water to poor communities, but it was almost dismissed as a commercial failure.

1 Is the current partnership model a genuine viable business model?

2 Why does P&G continue to market PuR despite selling the product at cost?

3 Are there other bottom-of-the-pyramid situations where this type of marketing approach could work?

The business–poverty framework

Irrespective of whether we consider business to be a development tool or a development agent, to have a bit part or the starring role in tackling poverty, we need to understand that there are multiple facets to the business–poverty relationship. One might argue, in line with Kramer and Kania's (2006) model, that CSR is either defensive (protecting a company's reputation) or offensive (burnishing the company's reputation), but from society's perspective such a two-dimensional model does not capture the variety of ways that business affects or is affected by poverty. To do this we need to give equal consideration to three dimensions: business as a cause of poverty, its victim, and a solution (see Figure 4.1).

There is also a fourth dimension which is not explored here, but is worth noting, i.e. that business can be indifferent to poverty, seeing it as neither a threat nor an opportunity, but simply as something that is not factored into decisions. Thus, for instance, decisions about investment are not typically based on their impact on poverty, but what will bring the best return on investment. Sometimes poverty might be appraised as an opportunity in those deliberations (e.g. low labour costs), or it might be a barrier (e.g. weak infrastructure), but in many instances (perhaps in the majority of investment decisions) poverty is not a consideration, and business positions itself as a bystander.

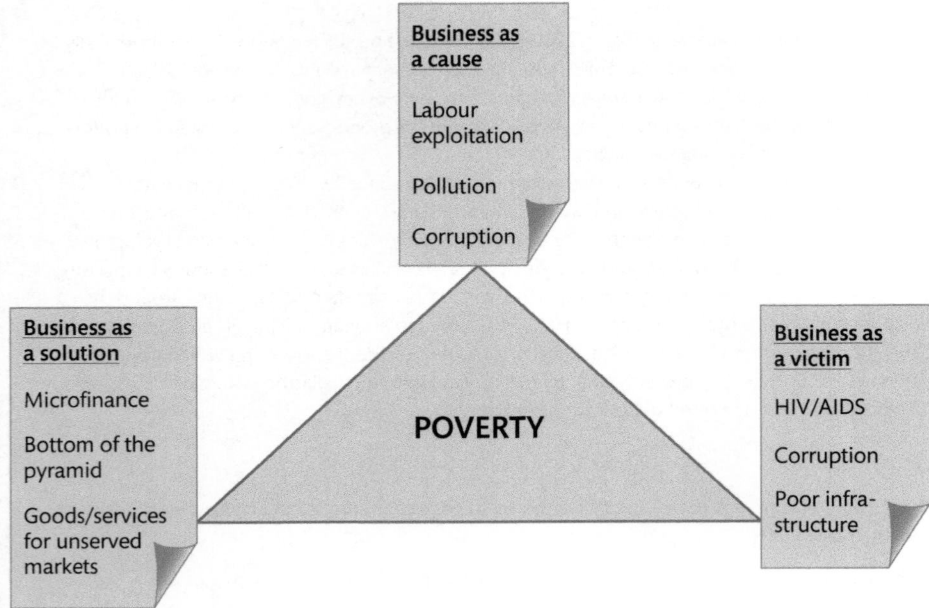

Figure 4.1 Business's relationships to poverty

Business as a cause of poverty

In the free market system, an inefficient company has the potential to cause poverty if it fails to generate wealth, create jobs, and provide goods and services (i.e. when it fails as a development tool). However, it is the way in which seemingly efficient companies can cause or exacerbate poverty that is our interest here. The Tazreen (2012) and Rana Plaza (2013) factory fires in Bangladesh which killed 1,250 workers are just two of many examples over the years of major apparel companies and retailers being linked to unsafe and inhumane working conditions in developing countries. It led to the Accord on Fire and Building Safety in Bangladesh, a safety pact signed by global unions and more than 200 brands, but similar disasters continue to happen.[12] At one level, some argue that the very functioning of international markets may exacerbate poverty, although for reasons too complex to do justice to here. Equally, business and government in developed economies have been accused of protecting parts of their markets from developing economy competition, and also for denying developing economies the kind of protections that some feel are essential for economic development.[13]

Advocates of the assumption that free markets have a singularly important role in economic development make the case that business cannot cause poverty if it acts rationally because the market is the most effective way of determining price and allocating resources. Even if one accepts this, power asymmetries that favour certain business actors mean that there are wide disparities in how the proceeds of trade are distributed, and that poor producers in particular (e.g. marginal smallholder farmers) can find themselves selling their produce for even less than the cost of production.[14] Similarly, the power that some brand-owners hold as gatekeepers to lucrative consumer markets means that some manufacturers have limited bargaining power regarding price or specification, making labour one of the few areas where management can influence profitability. Hence, low wages, long hours, and other abusive labour practices are the norm in places where low-skilled labour is plentiful, the opportunity cost of relocation is low, and law enforcement is lenient.[15]

In the long run, developing economy labour markets may obey the laws of liberal economics, and if so wages will rise with the overall upgrading of a country's economy. But in the short term, wages at less than the cost of survival and reproduction put enormous burdens not only on individual workers, but also on their families and social networks. For example, in a sample of factories in China producing for Walmart, the hourly wage is less than the legal minimum and overtime hours exceed the legal maximum.[16] Only by working excessive overtime can the workers achieve earnings approximating a living wage. Rural to urban migrants often face particularly difficult conditions in terms of stagnating real wages and having to pay for health care and education.[17] Yet, labour continues to migrate, not just within national boundaries but also overseas, where they may also be at risk from exploitation as recurring news coverage about migrant labour used to build the facilities for the football World Cup in Qatar demonstrate.[18]

Sudden injections of wealth, and unequal distribution, can have long-term consequences. For example, the promotion of cocoa production in parts of Sulawesi, Indonesia, in the 1990s, together with weak enforcement of traditional land rights, allowed certain migrant ethnic groups to prosper using land alienated from the indigenous population.[19] Other impacts of private-sector activity are also experienced differently by different sections of the population. For example, labour markets are gendered institutions that impact differently on women than on men, not least because of the former's need to balance productive and reproductive responsibilities. Poverty as experienced by women is not just a matter of unequal wages, but also relates to issues such as child care, maternity leave, and care of the elderly, aspects that are often neglected in the CSR initiatives of companies that either do not understand or are not concerned about the connections between reproductive work or care and both business and societal sustainability.[20]

These are examples of the substantive dimension to business's relationship to poverty, and there are more facts and figures in the online resources. But we should not forget what we earlier called the process dimension including, for example, the issue of empowerment. Poverty is often associated with disenfranchisement, marginalization, and the lack of capacity or opportunity to advocate for one's own interests. Freedom of association and collective bargaining are among the rights business has been accused of interfering with, the absence of which can perpetuate poverty. Companies can also affect the process of poverty alleviation by paying low wages, or avoiding or evading taxes, thereby denying governments essential resources that potentially could be used to invest in the poor.[21] And short-term contracts with suppliers may ultimately limit the opportunity to build up the capacity of poor producers and their communities.[22]

There are other areas where business relates to poverty, if not as the direct cause, then at least as the apparent beneficiary. The poverty that is behind child labour, forced labour, and labour trafficking is something that has benefited business in some circumstances. In an indirect way, business is held responsible for these types of poverty, not just because it is seen as a beneficiary of the global economic system within which such poverty exists, but because it is associated with the changing patterns of governance that are characteristic of that system.

Bad (i.e. corrupt) and weak (i.e. ineffective) government is one cause of poverty, and business has variously supported, tolerated, and resisted such practices. Corporate ambivalence in this regard can be seen from the positions taken by the private sector during the apartheid era in South Africa, where parts of the business community both supported and undermined the government.[23] However, generalizations are difficult to make.

While good public governance is generally accepted as essential to alleviating poverty, it remains to be seen if that is true of the alternative models of governance that business is part of. Companies have played a part in the process of deregulation, and the subsequent emergence of an international regulatory system that is highly skewed towards the protection of capital and non-human corporate assets.[24] For Ruggie (2003), companies must help redress the imbalances of the global governance system, and '*the key governance question before us*' is how much burden companies, and in particular the kind of voluntary efforts associated with CSR management, should bear. Wrapped inside that question are issues of regulatory capture by the private sector, and how well self-regulation and voluntary regulation protect the interests of the poor.

Another dimension of the business–poverty nexus, namely the bias of markets against the poor, in terms of both the difficulties small producers have in accessing international markets and the unequal distribution of value along the trading chain, is addressed by fairtrade (Snapshot 4.2). Elements of the fairtrade model, which involves the payment of a premium price to small producers and the organization of producers into associations, have found their way into the trading practices of large companies, such as Starbucks' Coffee and Farmer Equity (CAFE) Practices.[25]

To date, when business has been accused of causing poverty, if it has not denied the charge (as has typically been the case with regard to disinvestment, relocation, and corporate tax avoidance and evasion), it has for the most part sought to protect its reputation, notably by adopting new regulatory systems such as company, industry, or multi-stakeholder codes of conduct that promise some form of social accountability. The most significant approach in the development context is the use of multi-stakeholder or non-governmental systems of regulation involving multiple actors in new roles and relationships, and new processes of standard-setting, monitoring, benchmarking, and enforcement. Examples include the Fair Wear Foundation (FWF), the Ethical Trading Initiative (ETI), and the Fair Labor Association (FLA).

Snapshot 4.2 Fairtrade: an approach to market redistribution

Fairtrade is concerned with the bias of markets against the poor, in terms of both the difficulties small producers have in accessing international markets, and the unequal distribution of value along the trading chain. Although it initially grew as part of a network of alternative trade producers, buyers, processors, and retailers, the term fairtrade today is mostly associated with a product-labelling initiative that ensures a place for the products of marginalized producers in developed economy markets. While there is tension within the fairtrade movement between those who see it as a tool for radically modifying the dominant economic model for the benefit of the poor, and those who see it as an entry point for products from developing economies,[26] fairtrade-labelled products succeed today because they respect many of the rules, norms, behavioural expectations, and cultural assumptions of the wealthiest markets. As Taylor (2005) observes, the challenge for fairtrade is to be in the market but not of it.

(continued . . .)

Distinguishing features of fairtrade include a focus on the products of small-scale, often family-based, producers (although over time fairtrade buyers have also sourced from plantations and commercial farms), and the organization of producers into politically independent democratic associations such as cooperatives. Fairtrade buyers agree to enter into long-term contracts (more than one harvest cycle) with these organizations, and to pay farmers at least the minimum price that Fairtrade Labelling Organization International has calculated represents a fair return. Buyers also agree to pre-finance farmers so that they can avoid falling into debt, to pay for producer certification, and to pay a portion of all sales to producer organizations as a social premium to help empower and develop the producer community.

Therefore, from a fairtrade perspective, poverty is not only a factor of financial wealth, but also of impersonal commoditized relationships, power asymmetries within trading chains, lack of institutional capacity among poor producers, and the disadvantageous decisions producers make in consequence. Fairtrade challenges liberal economic assumptions that markets are impersonal and fair, and turns trade into a more personal relationship between grower, buyer, retailer, and consumer which requires that a managed distribution of value-added is distributed along the chain (Taylor, 2005). While this model is coming under pressure as mainstream demand for fairtrade products from processors and retailers increases, it is also noticeable that features of the fairtrade system (e.g. long-term contracts, capacity building, and buyer–producer trust) are finding their way into the companies' trading practices of larger companies, such as Starbucks' Coffee and Farmer Equity (CAFE) Practices (Macdonald, 2007).

(*Sources:* Nicholls and Opal, 2005; Macdonald, 2007; Doherty et al., 2013; Raynolds, 2017; Krumbiegel et al., 2018)

Quick questions

1 What weaknesses in conventional trading systems does fairtrade address?

2 Why are consumers attracted to fairtrade?

3 Would the use of fairtrade-certified products help defend a multinational brand from accusations that it is a cause of poverty?

Business as poverty's victim

One only needs to look at the facets of poverty set out in the Sustainable Development Goals (SDGs) to see how business can be a victim of poverty. The seventeen goals are indicators of sustainable development, and the majority are directly related to poverty. Failure to achieve them is indicative of the insufficiencies that can hamper business in developing economies. For example, the fact that half the world lives on less than $2 a day, and 1.1 billion people live in 'extreme poverty'—less $0.5 a day—shows how much greater the market for goods and services could be if only people had more income. The number of children who do not finish primary school is a warning of how difficult it can be for companies to fill even relatively low-skilled positions. Women are less likely to receive education, more likely to work at home, and less likely to obtain full-time salaried positions than men, and gender inequality and disempowerment can harm companies that need educated and independent workers and consumers.

Goals 2 and 3 of the SDGs concern health and hunger, and high morbidity, failing health-care systems, malnutrition, and disabling or terminal diseases can all harm business. Companies such as SABMiller (now Anheuser-Busch InBev) in South Africa have invested in programmes to prevent AIDS and provide antiretroviral drugs because of the attrition the disease was causing among experienced personnel. Wall (2007) shows how oil companies in Kazakhstan are having to compensate for the declining quality of state health-care provision. Indeed, authors such as Banerjee and Duflo (2011) argue that business is essential to radical solutions for tackling poverty.

Weak public governance and the failure of governments as development agents are underlying themes of the SDGs. They are equally factors in business being a victim of poverty. Though not explicit in the goals themselves, the idea that the private sector can compensate for weak government is evident in crucial agreements and policies surrounding the SDGs. The goals address some of the weaknesses of their predecessor, the Millennium Development Goals (MDGs). For example, a criticism of the MDGs was that they were silent on certain important dimensions of global poverty.[27] Rising inequality, for example, is something that poses particular threats for business. This situation creates all manner of uncertainties that risk-averse companies might rather not face, such as mass migration, conflict over natural resources, and political unrest. It is now included in the SDGs (e.g. gender equality and decent work). However, there is a gap between recognizing a problem and tackling it, and it should not be forgotten that an earlier era of economic globalization in the 1900s came to a halt because of a political backlash against globalization's distributional effects.[28]

There are innumerable examples of companies addressing issues which could affect their long-term prospects, particularly in relation to education. Mining companies in Africa, such as Anglo American, have had to engage seriously with the issue of HIV/AIDS. In addition to investing in human capital, companies respond to other weaknesses in their value chain. The Forest Stewardship Council (FSC), for example, has enabled companies to reduce reputational and supply risks arising from weak governance of forest resources.[29] Cadbury launched its Cocoa Partnership to address the risk of long-term shortages of cocoa should the lack of investment by farmers continue (see Chapter 2). And one of the UN Global Compact's aims is to increase business's commitment to achieving the SDGs.

Discussion points

Evidence that poverty negatively affects business prospects has attracted many companies to consider CSR as a management approach.

- Is it more important for companies to tackle issues where they cause poverty or where they are its victims?
- What are some of the main areas where business can justify its investment in tackling poverty on the grounds that it would otherwise be a victim?
- How are small and medium-sized enterprises in developing countries affected by poverty?

Business as a solution

Increasing attention is being paid to the idea of business as a solution to poverty. This is not simply a restatement of the centrality of business to the capitalist economy as the source of employment, goods and services, and wealth. Rather, it is the belief that business can consciously invest in ways that are simultaneously commercially viable and beneficial to the poor. This relates to and overlaps with ideas of social entrepreneurship, a concept with many definitions, but where typically business methods are employed for social development ends (see Chapter 11). In contrast, Hammond, Hart, and Prahalad in their influential work on the 'fortune at the bottom of the pyramid' (BOP) emphasize that there are genuine commercial market-based opportunities to be had by targeting the poor.[30] They argue that whereas the richest 0.8 billion people represent a largely saturated and overserved market, and despite there being significant opportunities to serve the 1.5 billion members of the emerging middle classes, the greatest unexplored opportunity is the 5 trillion dollar market of 4 billion people who individually or as households have low incomes, but as a group account for a significant percentage of national income and expenditure.

While these figures are controversial, given the varying income thresholds that have been suggested,[31] the insight that the poor control considerable wealth is important because it suggests that what is considered the untapped purchasing power at the BOP provides an opportunity for companies to profit by selling to these unserved or underserved markets.

If that was the extent of the BOP model's proposition, it would have little direct relevance to the idea that business can be a development agent because all it would imply is that the poor represent a rational, if overlooked, business opportunity. However, BOP advocates say that by meeting the needs of the poor, business can increase their productivity and incomes, and be an engine of empowerment, not least by allowing them to enter the formal economy. In other words, by selling to the poor, companies can help eradicate poverty. Prahalad (2005), in particular, emphasizes the role multinationals can play in this by allowing the poor to benefit from both the quality of their products and the efficiencies of their systems.

A large number of companies invest in building the capacity of local entrepreneurs—for example, in response to government policy such as the Black Economic Empowerment (BEE) programme in South Africa or as a result of business initiatives such as Business Action for Africa—and creating markets for their produce. In a different way, the consultancy Accenture is giving the private sector in developing economies access to management and technological expertise through its Accenture Development Partnerships programme.

Microfinance is perhaps the most widespread example of business providing a solution to the problems of the poor. Put simply, it is a system that enables poor people without conventional collateral to access loans at affordable rates of interest, making them less dependent on traditional moneylenders and providing them with a form of savings, insurance, and investment. In recent years, several commercial banks, including Citigroup, and Deutsche Bank, have offered microfinance services, and multinational companies such as Telenor have developed finance for the poor product offerings. There are a number of examples, such as ICICI Prudential, Hindustan Lever Limited (HLL), and Grameen Phone, where the infrastructure developed for microfinance has been used to develop other services such as retail and distribution.

Microfinance and other examples of BOP have encouraged thinking about other entrepreneurial approaches to development problems. Social enterprise has developed rapidly, and can be defined as market-based ways of addressing unmet social needs. Many of these are small enterprises (Chapter 11) but there are examples of large companies engaged in social entrepreneurship. For example, in Bangladesh, Danone has entered into co-ownership agreements with the Grameen Foundation and CARE to run a nutritious yoghurt factory (Grameen Danone Foods) and a yoghurt-selling network (JITA), respectively.

A major criticism of the BOP theory is that it places too much emphasis on integrating the poor into consumer markets and treating them as consumers, when in fact they might be better served if they had better jobs or access to markets as producers.[32] It is inaccurate to say that BOP theory entirely ignores the role of the poor as producers. Indeed, organizations such as the Shell Foundation (e.g. through its collaboration with the retailer Marks & Spencer to promote flower-growing groups on the Agulhas Plain, South Africa) and others involved in Business Action for Africa are focused on the production opportunities for the poor, and especially the promotion of entrepreneurship.

However, within BOP theory and practice the role of the poor as consumers is very important. Many companies that identify with the BOP approach emphasize precisely this aspect. Companies such as Coca-Cola and Procter & Gamble have invested in making their products available to the poor, and organizations such as KickStart (capital equipment), D.Light (sustainable energy), and Aravind (health care) specialize in serving poor communities. Vodafone is among the telecommunication companies that have recognized the need of migrant workers to remit money home, and operates its mobile-phone-based M-PESA remittance system in Kenya. Companies as diverse as Philips, Intel, Infosys, and Godrej have also developed new products tailored to the needs of poor communities.

To understand the theory behind this 'consumerist' dimension of BOP, one needs to consider the situation facing many poor people. Not only do they have low incomes, but also (a) they have significant unmet needs; (b) they are typically part of an informal or subsistence economy (the ILO estimates that 70% of the workforce in developing economies is in the informal sector); (c) they are part of high-cost microeconomic systems where they pay more for goods and services (e.g. water is more expensive in a Nairobi slum than in central New York); (d) they are often 'prisoners' of local monopolies (e.g. moneylenders); and (e) they lack access to quality products. Therefore, according to Prahalad, if companies compete to serve the poor, the upshot will be lower living costs (e.g. because interest rates will fall), increased productivity (e.g. because if medicines are more affordable, people will be healthier), and new employment opportunities (e.g. from selling the products).

One of the issues in relation to this model as a conscious approach to tackling poverty is the degree to which, having identified the opportunity, the market alone will deliver developmental benefits. The difference between certain proponents and critics of BOP is to a degree a moral one, with the former reluctant to make choices about what the poor should have access to, and the latter arguing that high spending by some poor people on tobacco, alcohol, and gambling suggests that they do not always make 'wise' purchasing decisions. This tension is evident in case studies of the BOP,[33] but if we are thinking of business as a development agent, then it is important to distinguish between companies that serve the poor, and companies that factor poverty alleviation outcomes into their decisions and strategies. This is not straightforward. For example, at first glance it may seem that HLL's supply of shampoo to rural women is less beneficial than Aravind's provision of low-cost cataract surgery, yet this conclusion ignores the increase in rural women's incomes arising from new opportunities to sell shampoo and other household items. However, in the business–poverty context, the key point is that ultimately financial performance should be less important an indicator than social outcomes.

This is not to say that companies should approach poverty as a social enterprise where profits are unimportant,[34] although successful examples of targeting the poor such as Aravind, HealthStore Foundation, and the Grameen Bank have been run on a not-for-profit basis, or involve some form of subsidy or alternative funding. However, to be profitable can require unconventional business models, not only in terms of understanding the market or designing products, but equally in the collaborations that are required. There are various examples of companies collaborating with NGOs to identify needs and deliver products; these include the collaboration of Telenor and Grameen to create Grameen Phone, and ICICI Prudential's collaboration with women's groups in India on insurance products. Brugmann and Prahalad (2007) and, more recently, Verhoef et al. (2013) view these collaborations as part of a trend towards 'co-creation' where business and NGOs or grassroots organizations create hybrid business models suited to the very different conditions for commercial and social success when dealing with poverty.

To a degree, these collaborations are about scaling up the success of NGO innovations as witnessed by the entrance of mainstream banks into the world of microfinance. However, companies such as Standard Chartered are bringing new capacities to existing sectors (e.g. raising capital for microfinance on international markets), while partnerships such as that between World Diagnostics and Ugandan NGOs allow existing networks to be used to provide new types of health service. This is not without its problems. For instance, ICICI's collaboration with women's self-help groups in India was criticized by some NGOs for undermining their wider social development goals, and there will be fundamental shifts in relationships as collaborations require NGOs to privilege task-driven partnerships with companies over ideology-driven dialogues.[35] Moreover, such partnerships are becoming a defining (and perhaps legitimating) feature of initiatives affecting the poor's access to, and control over, essential resources such as water privatization, projects associated with the Clean Development Mechanism, and now forest management in the context of voluntary emissions trading. We discuss the implications of this kind of change later, but we should recognize that in stressing partnerships with large companies, we risk further marginalizing the contribution that local small and medium-sized companies make, and the local partnerships that they have historically been part of.

Discussion points

Commercial opportunities linked to poverty have attracted a great deal of attention in the business community.

- Are companies justified in saying that they are benefiting the poor when they are pursuing a profit motive?
- Do you agree with Prahalad that the poor benefit as much from being seen as consumers as from becoming producers?
- What advantages do microfinance organizations have compared with conventional banks?

Assessing the business response

The previous discussion of business acting as a development agent provides a framework for the different types of interaction (i.e. based on cause, solution, and victimhood). What it does not reveal is (a) the conditions under which business will actively manage its relationship with poverty; and (b) the effectiveness of its taking on a development role. It is this we turn to now.

Features of managing poverty

The business–poverty relationship can be the focus of different spheres of business activity, such as core business operations, social investment, and philanthropy, as well as policy dialogue and advocacy.[36] As we have also seen, the actions taken may assume a variety of forms. In some instances, such as creating or destroying jobs, or choosing where to locate factories, business clearly impacts economic and social development, but does so as a development tool, not as a development agent consciously negotiating its relationship with poverty. Under what conditions might companies act as development agents?

The examples in the previous section suggest that there are three basic conditions that dictate the circumstances under which business can take on the development agent role. These are set out in Table 4.1.

Any of the initiatives undertaken by business as a development agent mentioned in this chapter can be explained by appeal to one or other of those three conditions. Likewise, dimensions to development that lie outside the scope of these conditions are unlikely to be addressed by business overtly. For example, redistributive elements such as corporate taxation, though part of debates about development economics, are not normally incorporated into normative debates about the responsibilities of business. Neither is there any thorough consideration of power and conflict, even though some of the areas where business affects development are historically the sites of dispute and tension (e.g. relations between buyers

Table 4.1 The three conditions of business's engagement in poverty

Condition	Examples
Condition 1: Business is more likely to act when poverty is associated with an identifiable risk to a company or industry, including risks to reputation, to the availability of commodities, to production, etc. This condition accounts for genuine innovations with respect to supply chain governance, and responsibility towards producing communities. It also accounts for some of the links created between companies and development organizations.	FWF, ETI, Worldwide Responsible Apparel Production, FLA, CAFE Practices, FSC, Cadbury's Cocoa Partnership
Condition 2: Business is more likely to act when poverty offers a favourable return on investment (ROI). This accounts for services to underserved markets, new market opportunities for the poor, and in some cases a re-engineering of the benefits of trade in favour of the poor. Initiatives that seek to deliver what might be thought of as a social return on investment (SROI) in addition to ROI can position the poor as producer or consumer.	Fairtrade, microfinance, enterprises such as D.Light, M-PESA, or the Shakti Project, and Merrill Lynch's investment in Ulu Masen
Condition 3: Business is more likely to act when poverty is associated with inefficiency. This accounts for initiatives to combat corruption, enhance the poor's productive capacity, increase health and safety standards, invest in education, and improve living environments.	Extractive Industry Transparency Initiative, investment in AIDS prevention by firms such as SABMiller and L'Oréal, and the education programmes of companies such as Anglo American and Cisco Systems

and small contract farmers or outgrowers). The gender dimensions to poverty are frequently ignored, and this is part of a general pattern of preferencing, where the individual good is preferred to the communal, financial wealth is favoured over non-financial, and issues such as class, ethnicity, sexuality, and other determinants of privilege are discounted or isolated from their wider context. It is not that these dimensions are absent from debates about development; indeed, it is their importance to development theory that makes their absence from CSR in the development context so noticeable. These and other types of exclusion will be more apparent when we look at the impact of CSR (see Chapter 12).

Discussion points

Risk, profitability, and inefficiency are the conditions that underpin any business investment as a development agent.

- Can you imagine a situation where business would make such an investment even though these conditions were not met?
- What sorts of inefficiency in developing countries are significant for business?
- What issues in developing countries will business tackle in 2020 that they are not addressing today?

Business's impact on development

Despite the many examples of business seeking to act as a development agent, there remains criticism that not enough is being done, or that the impact of what is being done is unclear. Blowfield and Dolan (2014) argue that business does not yet fulfil the criteria for being a proper development agent, not least because it does not hold itself up to account for its development impacts. They argue that even though companies are acting voluntarily, there is a case to be made that they are renegotiating their social and environmental responsibilities in ways that meet the requirements of commercial competitiveness rather than societal good. Certainly the three conditions of business acting as a development agent set out in the previous section are all rooted in business self-interest. It is evidence of this kind of shift (e.g. in relation to pensions, labour relations, and taxation) that make some people fearful of companies acting as development agents because ultimately they might pick and choose what constitutes societal good and co-opt the development process. Private sector involvement can be seen as part of a process of neoconstitutionalism, whereby those involved in managing the global economy see their rights being secured in law, but are increasingly isolated from popular scrutiny.[37]

There is certainly evidence that business interacts with development in particular ways, and reason to be concerned that it constricts the meaning of development itself. As the business-poverty framework shows, it is something that can lead companies to rethink their relationships, but does not fundamentally alter them. Ponte et al. (2011) and Schwittay (2011) make the case that the standards used to improve social and environmental performance in supply chains or the theory behind BOP have resulted in poverty being reconstructed around a business logic. However, elements of the business response (e.g. the adaptation of conventional management tools and concepts for development purposes, the depoliticization of economic opportunity, and the reduction of complex social, cultural, and economic factors to technical problems) are characteristic of contemporary development itself.[38] Therefore, it may be harder to argue that business co-opts development than to make the case that business as a development agent mirrors the established norms of the predominant development discourse.

Rather than examining business's role as development agent as subversive either to business or to development, we have concentrated on the possibilities and limitations of business's current and likely contribution. In much of the mainstream literature on business and development there is a tendency to stress the generic strengths of private enterprise to explain the significance of the role of business in development (e.g. client focus, ability to raise capital, and specific skills, tools, and competencies). However, the role that any single company or industry can play is greatly affected by the type of relationship it has with poverty (e.g. victim or cause), whether offensive or defensive strategies are pursued (see section 'The business–poverty framework'), and the location and context (e.g. whether or not there is a functioning civil society and state regulatory capacity). Too often, in making the case for business to act as a development agent, advocates overlook the context-specific variables and complexities that can ultimately influence outcomes in a given situation as much as flaws in execution can.

Yet even such contextual variables are of secondary importance to the three conditions that predicate any corporate engagement in development, i.e. the association of poverty with risk, opportunity, and inefficiency. The examples of business responses in this chapter demonstrate that at least one of these conditions needs to be met for companies to act as development agents. However, knowledge of how the conditions influence development is far from complete, and to date success has been measured in terms of the instrumental benefit for companies, not the developmental benefit for communities. Various recent studies have raised doubts about the empirical benefits of fairtrade, microfinance, and the bottom of the pyramid.[39] While the poor may participate, they do not have the means to hold others to account for the outcomes. Similarly, while a positive association between poverty and ROI can stimulate companies to deliver an SROI, there can be a tension between developmental outcomes and commercial imperatives, evident, for example, in how the demand for certified timber has been met largely by sourcing from developed rather than developing nations, and concerns that the expansion of fairtrade is weakening the relationships between producers, buyers, and consumers. The emphasis on the financial success of initiatives of this kind, and the limited information on the social impacts, suggest that developmental consequences can be lost or overlooked once ROI attracts more attention than SROI.

Recognizing these conditions is an important step in understanding the parameters of possibility for business as a development agent, and in particular what dimensions of poverty are likely to be included or excluded. However, we should not treat these parameters as static, and it may be too early to pass judgement on what is possible given instances such as the recent change in emphasis from simply expecting suppliers to comply with standards, to major brands working with supplier management and workers to increase local capacity, including creating spaces in oppressive regimes where workers can organize and collaborate. This offers the promise of a more effective way of dealing with reputational issues arising from allegations of exploitation.

At the same time, certain aspects of social development that complement the interests of business are being normalized, and this could explain why they appear less likely to be critiqued. These include, for instance, flexible labour markets in contrast to the emphasis on secure employment in previous eras, private ownership of natural resources, and the free flow of capital. While it is hard to claim that business's role in development exacerbates such trends in a significant way, there are issues of legitimization and delegitimization that need to be addressed. CSR plays an important role in framing our understanding of poverty and development. For example, modern management rationalism has been incorporated into the way poverty is understood and approached. Similarly, there are examples where a term such as empowerment has come to be associated with a business quality such as entrepreneurship, thereby imbuing business behaviour with a new moral creditworthiness.[40] This is problematic morally if notions of good come to be reassessed using commercial criteria,[41] but also from a technical developmental perspective, where a distinction has to be drawn between very different types of entrepreneurs, some of whom play an essential role in growth and innovation that is conducive to poverty reduction, while others create few jobs and have little security.

Nonetheless, there are examples of issues that are developmentally important being accommodated, even though this means challenging conventional business wisdom, as we have seen with the accommodation of practices with their roots in fairtrade. London and Hart (2010) highlight how initiatives are becoming more sophisticated over time, and similar trends are evident in the overview of multinational labour standards by Mosley (2011). As Kolk and Van Tulder (2006) show in the context of voluntary standards, a variety of pressures contribute to what is ultimately legitimized or ignored, and often what emerges is a 'sector-conditioned morality' that reflects a minimum level of expectation from civil society on the one hand, and a ceiling level acceptable to an industry on the other.

The experience of CSR and business as a development agent suggests that development ends can best be served when there is genuine collaboration whereby different sectors pursue shared or complementary poverty objectives. This conclusion can be challenged on the grounds that it relies on evidence about large companies, and says nothing about the smaller firms and informal sector that are such an important feature of developing economies. It also disregards changes associated with the new influx of foreign direct investment from countries such as China and India, and the different types of relationship that may emerge as a result, just as it ignores the role that large domestic companies played in the development of countries such as Singapore, Taiwan, and South Korea. However, even if consideration of these dimensions to business in developing economies revealed very different features of managing the relationship with society, a significant part of the business community would still be looking to employ collaborative models.

Nevertheless, based on the current pattern of corporate engagement in development, there are reasons to think that increasingly sophisticated models of partnership will be appealing (see Chapter 9). However, a stumbling block could be the unwillingness of companies to be accountable for development objectives in any rigorous way. A test of how far this can be overcome may be the recent wave of socially oriented entrepreneurs claiming a blend of social and commercial vision (see Chapter 11). If these find viable ways to demonstrate social returns, they may influence other companies that recognize a role as development agent, but limit their accountability to internal rationalization.

Case study 4 Poverty as a business opportunity: M-PESA

Mobile telephony is having a huge impact in Africa, where the relatively cheap infrastructure is helping to bridge the gap caused by poor transport and communications infrastructure. In Kenya, for example, one in three adults carries a mobile phone, and in five years the number of mobiles in Kenya grew from 1 million to 6.5 million, compared with 300,000 landlines. One driver of the boom is the large population of economic migrants eager to stay in touch with their home communities. Migrant workers are a main source of income in many rural areas, but one challenge is how to remit money home given the lack of banks and unsafe roads.

Vodafone is the world's second-largest wireless phone services carrier with more than 200 million customers and sales of $50 billion. Although most of its business is in Europe, it has interests in companies worldwide, including Safaricom in Kenya, and is increasingly looking to penetrate developing markets. In Africa, when M-PESA was launches, there were only sixteen mobile phones for every hundred people, compared with Europe where there is more than one phone per head. Recognition of this market potential and the unique contribution that mobile phones could play in meeting consumer needs led to the introduction of M-PESA.

At first glance, there is nothing spectacular about M-PESA. For the user, it is simply an extra line on their mobile phone menu that says 'Send Money'. The subscriber goes to a shop, adds funds to their phone account, and then sends them to friends, family, or anyone else with a mobile. The recipient goes to a similar shop, shows the code on the mobile and some ID, and collects the money.

Yet in Kenya where bank accounts and plastic money are scarce, and carrying cash on journeys can leave you prey to robbers, the M-PESA money transfer system is a genuine innovation. It is not the brainchild of the conventional banking system, but an entirely new product, developed by Vodafone and Safaricom, part-funded by the British government's Department for International Development (DFID), and piloted with the help of the Kenyan microfinance institution Faulu.

M-PESA was launched commercially in March 2007 after a two-year trial period, and Safaricom CEO Michael Joseph says that there are over 2 million active users: 'We also know that it channels over Kenyan Shillings (KSh) 100 million in a day . . . I see it getting to three or four million customers very soon.'

According to M-PESA pioneer Nick Hughes, the idea came about at the 2002 World Summit on Sustainable Development in a conversation with someone from DFID about what Vodafone could do to address the Millennium Development Goals. One area where he thought Vodafone could play a role was making it easier to move money around so that entrepreneurs and others had better access to finance. Returns on investment would not be great, and it was likely that, as with many ideas linked to social development, this one would lose out to others in the internal competition to allocate project funding. However, DFID ran a challenge fund offering capital to help ideas that were useful to developing countries circumvent the constraints of company product development processes. With the government offering 50% matching funding, what would otherwise have been seen as a low-yield, low-priority project started to look like an interesting idea. However, making the idea a reality presented a variety of challenges ranging from new software to the systems and capabilities of Safaricom, introducing the product to Safaricom's staff and distributors, and working with the Faulu savings groups on product testing.

None of these hurdles has proved insurmountable, and overcoming them may have put M-PESA in a stronger position in the long run because the internal support and external relations are much stronger than before. Soon after its launch, M-PESA was being talked about as a serious competitor to existing money transfer agencies, and Safaricom has started an aggressive campaign to extend the number of subscribers by partnering with established financial institutions such as Equity Bank and Post Bank.

An unintended consequence of M-PESA is how it has spawned new enterprises. M-PESA is no longer just about sending money—the brand has grown organically, taking on a life of its own. Pioneer Nick

(continued . . .)

Hughes, has launched M-KOPA, a solar energy company that allows M-PESA account-holders to buy solar-powered electricity in instalments. Rural customers can use their accounts to buy crop insurance and their phones to check on the weather and market prices. Such initiatives have created an appetite in rural areas for further innovation that is building the conditions for markets for local entrepreneurs such as KickStart, a manufacturer of low-cost irrigation. The service is also being expanded beyond Kenya. Vodafone set up M-PAISA in Afghanistan, and its Vodacom subsidiary has launched M-PESA in Tanzania, and other companies such as Telenor have developed similar systems across Africa and in Pakistan.

(*Sources:* Original research; Hughes and Lonie, 2007; Akumu, 2008; Wenner et al., 2017)

Questions

1 M-PESA was part-funded by the British government, which saw its potential to contribute to its goals of poverty alleviation.

   a How does M-PESA contribute towards the Millennium Development Goals?

   b Is M-PESA an example of business acting as a development agent?

   c Do you think expansion of M-PESA will depend on continuing government support?

2 M-PESA is a product aimed at poor and marginalized consumers.

   a Is it a good example of a company identifying commercial opportunities at the 'bottom of the pyramid'?

   b Is it a financially viable business model?

   c What impacts has it had on poor consumers?

3 M-PESA's funding model allowed it to compete for internal resources.

   a Do you think that the service's success will have a significant impact on either Vodafone or Safaricom in the future?

   b How might their behaviour change?

   c How might Safaricom build on this success as it attempts to expand its services in East Africa?

Summary

When we examine the role of business as a development agent today, what we are witnessing is part of a constantly shifting debate about business's contribution to society that plays out differently according to place, time, and culture, but is ultimately about how the norms and values of capitalism, as embodied in modern enterprise, can be accommodated, harnessed, and utilized for societal good. The framework of business's interactions with poverty used in this chapter shows that, even if a company focuses on its financial mission, there can be good reasons to consciously manage the relationship with society. Consequently, there are companies that are mindful of poverty, and are showing a degree of innovation in how they respond. But they have a narrow perspective on what to be accountable for and to whom, and the incentives to be more rigorous about this are lacking. At present, the conditions under which business engages in poverty alleviation are rooted in self-interest, even if responses differ depending on what is meant by that term. What are often called countervailing agents have made some progress in expanding this definition of self-interest, but these government and non-government actors have had more success in getting companies to commit to development objectives than they have in holding them to account for delivering on them. By clarifying how business relates to poverty, and under what conditions it chooses to act as a development agent, it might be easier to hold companies to account and make it in their interests to be more accountable. Without this accountability there is likely to be a randomness and unpredictability to business's interpretation of its responsibilities, leaving open the possibility that for all the justification for business to be a development agent, it will remain a development maverick.

Further reading

Ali, W., Frynas, J.G., and Mahmood, Z. 2017, 'Determinants of corporate social responsibility (CSR) disclosure in developed and developing countries: a literature review', *Corporate Social Responsibility and Environmental Management*, vol. 24, no. 4, pp. 273–294.

A review of academic literature focused on CSR as practised in developing countries.

Banerjee, A.V. and Duflo, E. 2011, *Poor economics*, Public Affairs, New York.

An engaging look at economics from the poor's perspective.

Jamali, D., Karam, C., and Blowfield, M. (eds) 2015, *Development-oriented corporate social responsibility*, Vols 1–2, Greenleaf, Sheffield.

Two volumes of contributions from international CSR and development thinkers looking at CSR in large and small companies in different industries and countries.

Prahalad, C.K. and Hart, S.L. 2002, 'The fortune at the bottom of the pyramid', *Strategy & Business*, no. 26, pp 2–14.

The initial exposition of an idea of business and poverty that has captured the imagination of people around the world.

Rajak, D. 2011, *In good company: an anatomy of corporate social responsibility*, Stanford, CA, Stanford University Press.

An anthropologist's take on the role of business in development.

http://www.oup.com/uk/blowfield_murray4e

Visit the online resources that accompany this book to enrich your understanding of this chapter. Among the resources available are web links, exercises, and additional case studies.

Endnotes

1. This chapter draws heavily on Blowfield and Dolan, 2014; Jamali et al., 2015.
2. Weng and Buckley, 2016.
3. See e.g., Newell and muro, 2006; Fig, 2007; Glover, 2007; Robins, 2007
4. Clay, 2005; Kapstein, 2008.

5. Newell and Frynas, 2007.
6. Ireland and Pillay, 2009.
7. Utting, 2007.
8. Bond, 2006.
9. Kolk and Van Tulder, 2006.
10. Kolk and Van Tulder, 2006.
11. Kolk and Van Tulder, 2006.
12. Prentice and De Neve, 2017.
13. Chang, 2002.
14. Raynolds et al., 2004.
15. Graham and Woods, 2006.
16. Chan and Siu, 2007.
17. Pearson, 2007.
18. Chaudhury, 2017.
19. Blowfield, 2004.
20. Pearson, 2007.
21. Jenkins, 2005.
22. Macdonald, 2007.
23. Fig, 2007.
24. Graham and Woods, 2006.
25. Macdonald, 2007.
26. Raynolds et al., 2004.
27. Saith, 2006.
28. O'Rourke and Williamson, 1999.
29. Taylor, 2005.
30. Prahalad and Hart, 2002; Hart, 2005; Prahalad, 2005; Hammond et al., 2007.
31. Hammond et al., 2007; Karnani, 2007.
32. Karnani, 2007.
33. See, e.g., contributions to Rangan et al., 2007.
34. Contrast with Karnani, 2007.
35. Brugmann and Prahalad, 2007.
36. Brainard, 2006.
37. Sum, 2009.
38. Ferguson, 1990.
39. Hermes and Lensink, 2011; Elyachar, 2012; Ansari et al., 2012.
40. Rajak, 2006.
41. Blowfield and Dolan, 2008.

Globalization and corporate social responsibility

Chapter overview

In this chapter, we explore the importance of globalization for CSR, and how it accounts for some of the ways that CSR has evolved. In particular, we will:

- discuss different meanings of globalization;
- identify the main areas in which globalization has had an impact;
- discuss the ways in which globalization has altered employment, trade, production, and investment;
- consider how globalization influences governance and the implications of this for CSR;
- explore CSR as a business response to the challenges of globalization, identifying what it addresses and examining why some feel it is inadequate;
- examine industry responses to aspects of globalization.

Main topics

Key terms

Globalization
Deterritorialization
Liberal economics
Global governance
Civil society
Employment
Self-regulation
Stakeholder partnerships

Globalization and CSR

In Chapter 2, we saw how the relationship of business with society has altered during different historical periods. Globalization is the latest of these periods and has brought with it changes that are as momentous as those of the Industrial Revolution. Various writers have linked CSR to the social, political, and environmental challenges of globalization.[1] In fact, to some degree, the success or failure of CSR may influence the direction of globalization overall.[2] This is because globalization is associated, on the one hand, with a limited set of global governance mechanisms and weakened national governments, and, on the other, with unprecedented private-sector wealth, power, and impact. Since the 1990s, CSR has been an important means for addressing what Stiglitz (2002) sees as the fundamental problem with contemporary globalization—a system of global governance without global government.

In this chapter, we examine the implications of globalization for CSR, and how that accounts for particular aspects of CSR such as the stakeholder partnerships developed in several industries. We also consider how over the past decade or more globalization has affected what constitutes CSR, not least in terms of the changing nature of employment. But to put that in context, we need first to reflect on the meaning of globalization itself.

The meaning of 'globalization'

We touched on different meanings of globalization in Chapter 2, in particular the distinction between globalization as an economic construct, and as a social condition called deterritorialization. To clarify this more it can help to think of ice cream. Growing up in the UK, we remember summers consuming Wall's ice creams, and it was a shock to go to France and Spain to find that there were brands called Miko and Frigo, with very different ideas about what an ice cream should be. Travel to far-off Indonesia and one did not find any ice cream brands, only locally produced, garishly coloured lollies, sold from home-made insulated boxes. Today, Walls, Miko, and Frigo are all part of Unilever: they all market identically tasting, identically packaged Magnums and Cornettos; the products are developed at a single Unilever laboratory, and a shop in Toronto will sell the same products as the teams of bicycle-riding sellers in Indonesian villages.

These changes are emblematic not of the power of brands so much as what some theorists believe constitutes a fundamental change in our social conditions, particularly:

1. new or intensified social networks, leading to the creation of new social orders that transcend traditional political, cultural, economic, and geographical boundaries;
2. stretched and expanded social relations, activities, and interdependencies, leading to the emergence of powerful organizations that are not linked to a specific place (e.g. global corporations, international NGOs, and international crime syndicates and terrorists);
3. intensified and accelerated interaction between these networks and organizations, so that what happens in one area can be shaped by events anywhere in the world;
4. a growing consciousness of our interconnectedness and interdependence, so that people do not simply observe globalization—it is something that is shaping who we are and how we act in the world.[3]

Instagrams from friends in Thailand, blogging and tweeting, and commercial transactions with people we never meet are all manifestations of this shift. Snapshot 5.1 shows the consequences of these four phenomena and how they have at once allowed an industry to prosper, but also subjected it to unprecedented public scrutiny. It also shows some of the ways in which globalization is interpreted as both beneficial and damaging. It is to the merits and criticisms of globalization that we now turn.

Snapshot 5.1 Sexual and reproductive health in Pakistan's football manufacturing industry

When Messi or Ronaldo make the perfect run or smash in another amazing goal, it is hard to imagine that the ball at their feet may have come from a small area in north-eastern Pakistan called Sialkot. Yet since the 1970s, footballs for international markets have been sourced from this city and its surrounding villages. They are made in three types of manufacturing facility: factories in the city that make complete footballs; smaller factories that outsource parts of manufacturing to subcontractors in villages; and home-based stitchers who produce for independent contractors. The last of these types once dominated the Sialkot football industry, but after child labour was discovered to be rife in the late 1990s, international brands, NGOs, the International Labour Organization, and the UN Children Fund have introduced standards called the 'Atlanta Agreement' to enforce tougher labour standards.

The Atlanta Agreement, the CSR demands of the large international brands, and the greater use of machine stitching have led to a centralization of production for the export market, not least because these are easier to monitor. Women are a particularly important part of football manufacturing. Women's participation in such global supply chains can provide more income generation opportunities that in turn give them more influence in their lives. But women's jobs tend to be less secure and precarious than men's ones. Such work can also affect women's sexual and productive health by, for instance, having an impact on young women's nutrition and hygiene, their reproductive choices, their access to birth attendants, and mortality (pregnant women in Pakistan have the highest risk of mortality of any South Asian country).

Although international 'ethical trade' agreements and standards such as the Atlanta Agreement recognize the need to treat women equally to men, they do not normally pay special attention to the specific needs of women in areas such as reproductive health. In Sialkot, this accounts for the wide variation in treatment of women at export-oriented factories. For instance, some factories operate what they call a 'home-grown' CSR model that offers workers access to private health care, and education on issues such as hygiene, mother and child health, and family planning. In factories that strictly adhere to international voluntary labour standards, medical benefits were less gender-specific and the quality of service was lower. Furthermore, women are not given time off to use these facilities, and because there is no paid maternity leave, women may work up to a day before their due date and return to work soon after.

Women's health campaigners point out that there are other opportunities for the industry to improve sexual and reproductive health. For instance, factories are where large numbers of women spend a lot of their time during a six-day work-week, and therefore have the potential to be centres of health education. Closely spaced, unwanted, and ill-timed pregnancies are an important cause of women's death, and could be prevented by contraception and better general knowledge. However, it is only a small minority of male and female managers and factory owners who are paying attention to this.

(*Sources:* Lund-Thomsen and Coe, 2013; Husain and Lund-Thomsen, 2015; Lund-Thomsen and Lindgreen, 2018)

(*continued . . .*)

Quick questions

1. Should stitching factories take responsibility for women's sexual and reproductive health? Why?
2. How do working conditions in the factories affect women's sexual and reproductive health?
3. Should women have paid maternity leave?

Globalization—a tale of the glass half-full

Few would deny that globalization is problematic. The free flow of goods, services, and capital has helped to reduce the percentage of people in developing countries living in extreme poverty from 52% in 1981 to under 20% today. Yet, because of population growth, the number of extremely poor people worldwide has only fallen by 0.19 billion in that time.[4] Even globalization's supporters refer to the unavoidable pain involved and the need to have faith that it is ultimately for the good. Some of that good we experience today. Since 1990, the volume of international trade has increased enormously, and even during the recent recession has continued to grow by an average 3% a year.[5] This has created jobs in many countries, allowed new industries to emerge, encouraged the transfer of technology, increased the flow of capital, and, for the well educated at least, has allowed people to pursue opportunities across the world. It has also meant that until the 2000s, at least, international competitiveness kept prices stable, and this has been an important factor underlying low inflation in advanced economies.

Moreover, growth has not been confined to the major industrialized countries, as shown by the phenomenal expansion of the Chinese and Indian economies. And while China and India account for a disproportionate amount of foreign direct investment, other developing countries have entered the global economy as suppliers of everything from flipflops to flowers and, increasingly, as consumer markets themselves. Moreover, economic recession in the West has not stopped these trends, in part because inter-regional trade between developing countries is increasing.

What is good for business is meant to be good for society as a whole, and many have benefited from new opportunities, new technology, and the cultural shifts that phenomena such as urbanization have brought. Whether because of class, educational opportunity, or entrepreneurship, many people have seen their life expectations expand by virtue of the new types of skilled employment that have been created. The most fortunate have been able to pursue opportunities in stable, prosperous economies as multinational companies increasingly embark on a global war for talent.

Economists and politicians agree that, in a capitalist or free enterprise system, economic growth is essential for long-term prosperity, and international free trade is held to be vital for sustainable growth and equity. Therefore, for many policy-makers and politicians, globalization is nothing short of essential for global prosperity, demanding the removal of government-imposed trade and investment barriers, increased integration of markets across national boundaries, and the spread of market-oriented policies around the world.[6] These elements were characteristics of the first era of liberal globalization that started in the nineteenth century, the end of which is blamed on a revival of government controls and the closing down of economic interdependence which ultimately ushered in decades of conflict and instability in the twentieth century. For Martin Wolf, the significance of liberal globalization is not only that it fosters economic growth: 'Liberalism is . . . far more than a purely economic creed. It is the bedrock of democracy at home and peaceful relations abroad.'[7] As Friedman (2005) has observed, no two countries with McDonald's franchises have ever gone to war.

Wolf's belief, therefore, goes further than those who say globalization is simply about economics. In the traditions of Adam Smith and Hayek, he treats the rights to freedom and property, democratic government, the rule of law, and a supportive values system as being as important as liberalizing markets. Although individual elements may develop at different speeds, ultimately this is the full package that globalization both depends upon and promises. Therefore the benefits of globalization are not simply economic growth, but the particular cultural, political, and ethical model associated with the liberal democracies of Europe, North America, and other 'Western' societies. All of this leads Wolf to conclude that, for all of globalization's shortcomings, 'the world needs more globalization, not less'.[8]

Globalization—a tale of the glass half-empty

Wolf's view has become more contentious in recent years for reasons that can seem more to do with politics than business. The populist and nationalist political movements that have sprung up in various parts of the world, not least the USA and the UK, are in part a response to globalization's effects such as low pay and job insecurity. Equally, ISIS and other terrorist movements have positioned themselves as opponents of globalization and the values of the West. Authors such as Chang (2002), Gordon (2016), and Piketty (2017) have written best-selling academic books on the worsening consequences of globalization, and Rodrik (2017) argues that rather than see it as an inevitable force, society should recognize that a very different form of globalization is possible to the one we have experienced in the past few decades.

These critiques of the consequences of economic globalization present new challenges for CSR. Modern CSR is, to some degree, a response to globalization's excesses, and it will be judged on how effective it is at mitigating them. However, it is also one of the methods that companies and others have used to navigate the new terrain associated with globalization that is not necessarily good or bad, but simply different from preceding eras. We look at two areas of globalization criticism, as follows:

1 wealth, poverty, and equity;
2 universalization of norms, values, and culture.

Wealth, poverty, and equity

In 2002, Joseph Stiglitz provided a wake-up call to those who felt that criticism of globalization was misguided. It was one thing for what Wolf labels 'antiglobalization.com' to protest about injustice, poverty, and environmental degradation; it was quite another when a one-time chief economist of the World Bank appeared to be joining their ranks. Yet Stiglitz's conclusion was that, for millions, globalization is a failure: 'Many have actually been made worse off, as they have seen their jobs destroyed and their lives become more insecure.'[9]

He argues that the policies that have created the conditions for overseas companies to set up factories, or source from suppliers in countries that hitherto had adopted policies of protectionism and import substitution, have led to the promotion of market solutions to the challenges of welfare and equity. Hardt and Negri (2000), for example, argue that globalization needs to be understood as a 'grid of power', informed by the ways in which capitalism copes with the overproduction, high labour costs, and devaluation that block the capitalist process once markets become saturated. For Stiglitz (2002), however, the issue is not the intractable logic of capitalism, but the way in which globalization is implemented and how rich countries use their power to their advantage in institutions such as the World Bank, the International Monetary Fund, and the World Trade Organization. He counters those opposed to government intervention and restrictions on the free market, arguing that the countries that have benefited most from globalization are those, such as China and India, in which governments have challenged the notion of self-regulating markets and taken charge of their own destiny. As Chang (2010) has argued forcefully, successful developing economies have typically been the ones that have not adopted neoliberal free market prescriptions.

However, globalization affects all countries, not just emerging economies. In developed economies, industries that were once major such as steel production have shrunk, if not vanished, and the number of manufacturing jobs has declined. The offshoring of certain types of blue-collar job has been followed by that of white-collar jobs, such as data processing, computer programming, and research and development. There is public anxiety as to whether new jobs—and especially well-paying jobs—will be created in their place.[10] As predicted by early globalization theorists such as Beck et al. (1994), the nature of employment is changing. Repeatedly, surveys in the richest countries point to longer working days, stress, job insecurity, and difficulties in balancing working lives with personal lives as causes of public concern.

The 2013 *Great British Class Survey* identified a new class that it called the 'precariat', people whose daily lives are the most precarious and insecure, not least because of globalization's impacts.[11] It highlighted that as important as traditional divisions between skilled and unskilled, white collar and blue collar, are the distinctions between those of classes in secure employment and underclasses, such as illegal migrants and 'guest workers', without secure employment. Across Europe and North America, there has been an upsurge in new types of employment contract. The 'gig economy', where workers are regarded as self-employed but are tied into 'zero-hour' contracts with specific companies, has caused controversy because workers are not guaranteed paid work but are expected to be available regardless of whether they are being paid or not. Home-carers, delivery drivers, taxi drivers, restaurant workers, and others fall into this category, and are denied paid sick leave, holiday leave, and other rights that employees are often guaranteed under law (see Snapshot 5.2).[12]

Universalization of norms, values, and culture

Globalization is often portrayed in terms of how it affects society and culture, and, in particular, how some see it as spreading the values, ethics, and institutions of the West. Dating back to the 1990s, authors have examined globalization as a socio-political force. MacLean (1999) argues that a key feature of globalization that distinguishes it from its historical antecedents is that it fosters, legitimizes, and universalizes a transcending form of knowledge, especially in respect to political, economic, ethical, and social ideas. For Wolf (2004), this is one of its benefits; for Klein (1999), it is one of its dangers. Whatever stance one takes, the idea that globalization alters the world in this way is a powerful one.

There are many empirical studies of how particular industries and companies have affected local populations, especially those of indigenous peoples who, by definition, live in non-capitalist societies. Logging, mining, oil and gas drilling and pipelines, tourism, and industrial agriculture have all been in the spotlight for the ways in which they affect indigenous people's land, livelihoods, and lifestyles.[13] The impact is not necessarily as simple as appropriating resources or putting people out of work. It can also involve changes in basic social institutions so that, for example, communal land becomes privately owned, or diverse economic livelihoods are replaced with daily-waged labour.[14]

Such examples can be seen as evidence of more fundamental assertions of power. Various authors have argued that, in addition to understanding how organizations and individuals operate in the new networks and alliances that globalization is producing, we need to understand the underlying biases that favour particular norms and values,[15] and how the technologies and techniques that we use to analyse, control, and regulate globalization extend or limit the possibilities for change as much as the actions of any actor.

One of the reasons for considering specific industry partnerships in the context of globalization later in this chapter is because what they reveal about this distinction between overt actors and underlying agency has a significant impact on CSR, and helps to explain some of its successes and failures. It also helps to explain why CSR is sometimes accused of spreading particular values, or of failing to accommodate others' world views.[16] In terms of understanding the meaning of globalization, it alerts us to the fact that even seemingly neutral views can be charged with norms, values, and meanings that legitimate and advance specific interests. Indeed, building on Gramsci's political theory, Levy and Newell (2005) argue that the moral and intellectual leadership role exhibited by business in areas such as CSR is a contemporary example of how, throughout history, powerful forces rule through consensus and hegemony.

Discussion points

Liberal globalization theorists, such as Wolf and Henderson, take umbrage with companies and others that support CSR.

- What are the main reasons for their hostility?
- Do you think that there are shifts within CSR thinking that address their concerns?
- Referring to examples such as Unilever's work with Oxfam in Indonesia and theorists such as Stiglitz and Porritt, how would you refute Wolf and Henderson's arguments to a business audience?

Influence of globalization on business

Business is often portrayed as a beneficiary of globalization, but there is truth, falsehood, and myth in such a belief. Under globalization, many of the norms and values suited to private enterprise have been given preferential status, but commerce has prospered under all manner of different political and economic regimes—to say that business benefits from globalization is no more or less true than to say that enterprise flourished under mercantile capitalism or protectionism. However, the nature of business has undoubtedly changed in ways that have special significance for CSR.

Global capital, production, and trade

For business, the most important outcome of globalization has been the enormous increases in international trade and investment. Between 2006 and 2016 world exports of manufactured goods rose from $8 trillion to $11 trillion, and over the same period the value of commercial service exports went from $2.9 trillion to $4.8 trillion.[17] The value of world trade is approximately $16.5 trillion, according to the World Trade Organization. This has gone hand in glove with the liberalization of financial transactions, whereby a combination of technological advances and policies to remove credit controls, deregulate interest rates, and privatize banking has created much greater investment opportunities. Today, global business-to-business transactions are worth about $6 trillion, and the world's financial markets are becoming more like networks in cyberspace that can relay billions of trades almost instantaneously.[18] Furthermore, this does not accurately reflect the value of new economic systems such as the blockchain and cryptocurrencies such as bitcoins.

This does not mean that what happens globally is divorced from the local. The consequence of over-zealous selling of mortgages to poor Americans—while in some ways promoted as a socially beneficial act—ricocheted around the world, and in turn exposed corruption and incompetence from Bear Sterns to BayernLB to Dubai's Sovereign Wealth Fund. Perhaps more important in the long term, the unprecedentedly high levels of household and corporate debt in developed economies are only affordable because of the willingness of emerging economies to buy it, marking a historic shift from when developed economies bailed out poorer countries during economic crises to a new era when weak economies come to the aid of stronger ones.[19]

Speculative investment has increased due to the ease of conducting fast, low-cost transactions. Global investment has also led to industry consolidation and increased foreign ownership, not least of formerly state-owned companies. Indeed, globalization challenges the very idea of an American or European company given how shares are owned around the world. What unites many globalization sceptics is what is viewed as an unhealthy growth in corporate power and alarm at facts such as that one-third of world trade occurs between multinational corporations, or that five companies control the global market for consumer durables.[20] At times, the growing presence of multinationals has been highly contentious (e.g. the privatization of utilities in Latin America). It has also provoked fears about security, the global power balance, and other national imperatives. The flood of foreign direct investment from China into Africa to acquire natural resource rights, the rise of sovereign wealth funds buying swathes of land and water resources, and 'foreign ownership' of strategic assets from ports to power plants have all generated controversy. Yet this is just a continuation of a trend started by freeing up trade and capital flows which created the conditions necessary for shifting certain aspects of production to new locations. As countries, such as Malaysia, Indonesia, and, later, China, removed barriers to foreign investment, companies from developed economies rushed to them, either to invest directly or to source from new vendors. Today, we take it for granted that goods and services, from training shoes to banking, can be delivered from around the world, but it is important not to overstate the degree to which poorer countries have succeeded in attracting capital and accessing markets.[21] For all of the focus on multinational firms in India and China, the bulk of investment remains within developed economies and there are still significant barriers in some industries for developing countries to access wealthy markets.[22] Moreover, investment in developing countries is often centred on export processing zones (EPZs) offering financial incentives to investors, and even labour and environmental regulations and enforcement policies that are different to those that are available elsewhere in the country.

Claims about the wealth of corporations being on a par with that of many governments may be exaggerated,[23] and CSR is full of examples demonstrating that wealth and power are not always synonymous. Nonetheless, the behaviour of multinational companies on a global stage is an important part of CSR's story and, as we examine later in the chapter (see section 'CSR as a response to globalization'), sets important parameters for what CSR addresses and how.

Snapshot 5.2 New jobs, new responsibilities—zero-hour contracts and the gig economy

In 2016, New Zealand abolished 'zero-hours contracts' which demand full-time availability seven days a week without any guarantee of actual paid work. The practice, which had been used by Starbucks, KFC, McDonald's, and other famous brands, was seen as a cause of low pay, discrimination, and insecurity. Now workers have minimum fixed hours. But they do not have the same statutory rights as traditional employment contracts such as a fixed working week, sick leave, holiday leave, pension rights, and so on. The outlawing of zero-hour contracts was heralded as a victory, but the fact the battle ever needed fighting sheds light on the changing nature of work for many people.

Events in New Zealand reflect similar protests, legal disputes, and social movements elsewhere. In the UK, the number of self-employed has swelled by 45% since 2000, and on average they are earning less than they were twenty years ago. 'Taxi firm' Uber failed to defend its position that it did not employ its drivers, and an employment tribunal ruled it had to pay the minimum wage and holiday pay. Bicycle courier, CitySprint, was adjudged to employ its couriers. But even seemingly established companies such as Royal Mail and DPD have been accused of taking advantage of the 'gig economy', charging self-employed drivers a penalty if they are off sick.

The situation with the gig economy and zero-hours contracts also has a knock-on effect for other workers. Sports Direct and Walmart are among the companies regularly in the news for low pay, even breaching minimum wage laws. The possibility of losing their job and having to join the gig economy if they protest or try to join a trade union limits the action they can take when faced with workplace bullying, unpaid overtime, compulsory searches, and other behaviour that was deemed unacceptable for much of the twentieth century. In the late twentieth century, CSR, through ethical trade and fairtrade, focused on working conditions in developing countries, but now there is a case to be made that companies have changed the rules of employment in developed countries as well, and that one of the consequences of globalization has been the growth of the precariat worldwide.

(*Sources:* BBC, 2015b; Ainge Roy, 2016; O'Connor, 2017)

(*continued . . .*)

Quick questions

1 Why do some companies advertise opportunities in the gig economy as a benefit to workers?

2 Are people on zero-hours contracts employees or self-employed?

3 Why do some companies prefer workers of this type?

The changing nature of governance and enforcement

Mention of the different, often more lenient, regulatory regimes enjoyed by companies in EPZs is an example of how globalization is connected to changes in how society is governed. In part, this is because liberal globalization depends on the slew of policy changes described earlier. At the same time, deterritorialization creates a new space that cannot readily be governed by existing governance structures, such as national governments, or even the international mechanisms housed within the United Nations. For example, a national government can legislate on toxic emissions, but once those emissions affect the global commons, a multinational solution is required.

There are a few long-established institutions with an international regulatory mandate—notably the International Labour Organization (ILO) which, since the end of World War I, has brought national governments, the business community, and international trade unions together to set and enforce international labour standards. There are also national laws applying to actions overseas, such as the US Alien Tort Claims Act 1789, which has been used to hold US companies to account for human rights violations around the world. More noticeable since the 1970s, however, has been a trend away from seeing government as the sole, or even primary, solution to both regulation and social welfare.

This trend may have reached its peak on 11 September 2001,[24] and in banking in particular light-touch regulation is now being criticized by politicians, investors, and the public alike. But for anyone born before the 1970s, the changes in the roles and expectations of government have already been enormous. They continue to be at the heart of debates about how society responds to globalization and attitudes towards CSR worldwide.[25]

There are four main interpretations of what has happened.

1 National government has seen its power eroded by globalization.

As a condition of joining the global market, national governments surrender much of their power to create policy autonomously, and poor countries, in particular, have had policies forced upon them. Some of those policies have undermined state sovereignty, not only in areas of macroeconomic policy, but also in areas such as taxation, social welfare, and human development. Even in rich countries, governments not only no longer try and control exchange rates, but they are also afraid to raise corporate taxes or the minimum wage, for fear of driving business overseas.

2 There is a governance vacuum at the global level.

There is no clear responsibility or accountability for issues such as human rights and poverty, for which the forces of economic globalization may have unacceptable consequences that cannot be resolved by market forces. Equally, there are new challenges, such as the management of the global commons, that cannot be solved through conventional governance mechanisms. As Bell puts it: 'The nation-state is becoming too small for the big problems of life, and too big for the small problems of life.'[26]

3 Government has deliberately chosen where and where not to exert influence.

There are many examples in which national governments have exerted influence on the governance of globalization. For example, the World Trade Organization is a direct result of national government negotiation and agreement, and has been criticized for being too influenced by the interests of the wealthiest economies (e.g. its slowness in tackling agriculture subsidies).[27] As Braithwaite and Drahos (2000) observe, what we are witnessing may not be deregulation but *'re-regulation'*, with state rollback in some areas, such as capital and trade, and a strengthening of regulation to protect other rights. Migration is another issue relating to which governments have been accused of hypocrisy because, while they have removed barriers to trade and investment, they have put up barriers to allowing most people to pursue job opportunities through international migration.

4 Governments still maintain power.

As Ward (2003) emphasizes, it is important not to dismiss the regulatory role of government. National laws, such as the US Foreign Corrupt Practices Act 1977 and Alien Tort Claims Act 1789, can affect the behaviour of multinational companies around the world. Bilateral trade agreements, for example, are one way in which the poor in developing nations can benefit from global trade and, in some instances, these agreements have created favourable environments for CSR.[28]

Whatever one's interpretation of governance in this era of globalization, one noticeable change is the prominence of non-government actors in governance processes. From Occupy and the Arab Spring, to LGBT (lesbian, gay, bisexual, and transgender), civil society movements have been at the heart of major issues in recent years. While it would be flying in the face of history to deny the influence that owners and managers of capital or public protest have had on government over time, nonetheless new forms of governance are emerging. There is a growing element of self-regulation by business and, in particular, of business being used by government as the initial enforcer (e.g. in the UK, supermarkets are liable for enforcing food safety standards in their supply chains). There is also widespread outsourcing of the policing of business behaviour, building on approaches originating in financial auditing, and quasi-independent bodies, notably the International Organization for Standardization (ISO), have had a significant impact on environmental management and have tried to develop systems for CSR more broadly.

Civil society organizations are increasingly involved in both 'street regulation', through campaigns, watchdog activities, and 'naming and shaming' of particular companies, and participation in new regulatory systems, such as international standards and multi-stakeholder partnerships.[29] These different views of public governance are all relevant to the relationship between notions of CSR and globalization, and the changing nature of governance is especially important in the CSR context, as we discuss in the next section. Business has gone from dealing with a handful of government regulators to wrestling with innumerable informal regulators.[30]

Discussion points

CSR has been variously described as a 'response' to globalization and as its 'reflection'.

- What distinction is being made here?
- Do companies' policies and programmes appear to reflect one of these views more than the other?
- Selecting the ideological framework of a particular political party, how would you make the case that CSR complements its policy objectives?

CSR as a response to globalization

Understanding the phenomenon of globalization is a necessary part of comprehending the context within which contemporary CSR has emerged. Ruggie (2003) treats it as a manifestation of Polanyi's notion of the embedded economy (see Chapter 2)—an attempt to contain and share the social adjustment costs that open markets inevitably produce. Criticisms of business, and of big business in particular, as reaping the benefits of globalization without taking responsibility for its negative consequences have become an important driver of contemporary CSR as a whole. Moreover, specific initiatives, such as codes of labour practice or participation in the environmental agenda that first emerged from the 1992 Rio Earth Summit, address the perceived mismatch of regulatory scope and actual economic structure that is a consequence of expanding global trade. Even if 2012's Rio Plus 20 Summit was downbeat overall about Rio's achievements, business-civil society initiatives that began in 1992, such as the Forest Stewardship Council, continue to flourish.

This does not mean that CSR is a comprehensive response to business-society issues related to globalization. For example, tax avoidance by companies, though legal, arguably deprives countries of resources that could be used to tackle environmental, social, and governance issues, yet is overlooked in CSR practice and much of the theory. Equally, it does not mean that the issues that CSR addresses are necessarily the consequences of globalization. For example, slavery, deforestation, child labour, and over-fishing all took place before globalization. In some cases (e.g. slavery), it may not even be the case that what is happening is worse than that which occurred in the past.[31] But globalization exaggerates and exacerbates by making things quicker, larger, and more visible than before, and this has increased the pressure on companies to act responsibly. For some, CSR is about making the benefits of globalization accessible to more people, by either limiting the need for government intervention[32] or making new resources available for human development. It can also be seen as a reflection of the interdependence of government and business, under which the former looks to the latter to create wealth in order to retain power, while the latter looks to the former to develop human capital and maintain stability.[33] What is more, reflecting the general widespread growth in self-regulation and voluntary agreements by business, CSR can be regarded as an element of a new system of global governance that sits alongside the democratic model of national government that is promoted by the most powerful countries.[34]

Discussion points

If we compare the issues raised in the sections above on globalization: 'Globalization—a tale of the glass half-empty' and 'CSR as a response to globalization', there are clearly gaps between the consequences of globalization and the concerns of CSR.

- What are the main aspects of globalization that CSR does not address?
- What are the reasons for these gaps?
- Which of these gaps will CSR attempt to bridge in the future and why?

How CSR addresses the challenges of globalization

Some of contemporary CSR's earliest initiatives were related to globalization. The Rio Earth Summit, for example, brought together different sectors of society to address global environmental challenges. It succeeded in sending the message that business could and should act, and indirectly encouraged business and environmental groups to work together on initiatives such as sustainable forest management. It also lit a flame in the oil industry that influenced Shell's early CSR reporting and eventually led to BP rebranding itself as Beyond Petroleum, as its then CEO, John Browne, began to speak out on the importance of business addressing greenhouse gases and other threats to the environment.[35]

In a different way, early initiatives intended to rethink the nature of working lives were a response to the ways in which globalization had influenced the workplace. In the UK, Business in the Community was started as a response to urban decay and industrial decline during the 1980s, and the lack of government action. The Prince of Wales Business Leaders' Forum was a tentative step to encourage UK business executives to think about their role in the world. At that stage, these organizations were still firmly rooted in traditions of giving back to communities through, for instance, philanthropy, community investment, and volunteering.

At the same time, the fairtrade movement was establishing itself as a way of dealing with what were seen as inequitable trading relations with poor producers in developing countries. Trade union and NGO campaigns raised public awareness about labour conditions in the apparel and sporting goods industries, which had been early movers in globalizing production. This, in turn, led to a number of companies, primarily in the UK and USA, adopting codes of labour practice and partnering with civil society organizations to implement them. This interest spilled over into parts of agriculture, which was already becoming more global, and which, in Europe, was increasingly interested in improved environmental management and product safety.

Other industries that were, perhaps, more removed from globalization were nonetheless feeling the consequences of rapid information exchange and the power of civil society alliances. Mining companies in Papua, or oil companies in Burma, came under the spotlight because of allegations about human rights, environmental damage, and corruption. Such criticisms, in turn, raised questions about the funding of major private-sector projects, such as the Chad-Cameroon oil pipeline, and public- and private-sector finance bodies, such as the International Finance Corporation and Citigroup, began to pay more attention to the non-financial aspects of their investments. This eventually led, in 2003, to the Equator Principles—a framework promoting environmental and social responsibility in project financing.

In 1999, the UN announced its Global Compact to bring companies together with UN agencies, labour organizations, and civil society to promote responsible corporate practices and to help business be part of the solution to the challenges of globalization. It has paid particular attention to business in developing countries and the private sector's role in meeting the aforementioned Sustainable Development Goals (see Chapter 4). The World Economic Forum's (WEF's) Centre for Public–Private Partnership has also stressed that these goals cannot be met by governments, business, or civil society alone. Its mission highlights that, in addition to the role of business in upholding and advancing principles on human rights, labour, environmental, and anti-corruption practices in countries with weak regulatory capacity, business competencies can improve the effectiveness of development programmes (e.g. technology development, providing essential goods and services, and managing large-scale operations).

In Chapter 4, we offered various examples of CSR as a response to poverty in developing countries. Several of these are partnerships between organizations and groups, reflecting the belief that poverty, global governance, imbalances in power, and other features linked to globalization are best met through collaboration. We turn to this now.

Partnerships

One consequence of economic globalization and the changed nature of governance is that it has created the space where business impacts upon and is influenced by a more geographically dispersed body of stakeholders than ever before. The exact nature of stakeholder is something we explore in Chapter 9, but in terms of globalization, it is not just that business has to manage stakeholders, which is important, but partnering with them has become a significant element of business's relationship with wider society.

Business has long run on networks—the labyrinth of personal relationships and long- or short-term alliances that comprise the web of the day-to-day functioning of business. At various historical moments, collaborations of this kind have met with a political and public backlash when they become the backbone of collusion, oligopoly, and other practices that run against the principles of free market capitalism. As Adam Smith pointed out,

> People of the same trade seldom meet together, even for merriment and diversion, but the conversation ends in a conspiracy against the public, or in some contrivance to raise prices.
>
> (Smith, 1776)

Despite this, alliances and collaborations of one form or another have thrived, especially in recent years, often with the full support of governments. Competitive clusters of complementary businesses in a given geographical area are often seen as essential to competitive advantage,[36] and public-private-sector partnerships have gained traction in some countries as a way in which to deliver public services, from schooling to incarceration. Civil society groups which might historically have been expected to be wary of business alliances have come to favour what are called multi-stakeholder partnerships, i.e. alliances between actors from the private, public, and civil society sectors. As we shall see, there are many types of partnership, but the United Nations, which has taken a great deal of interest in alliances with business, offers a broad working definition, describing partnerships as

> voluntary and collaborative relationships between various parties . . . in which all participants agree to work together to achieve a common purpose or undertake a specific task, and to share risks, responsibilities, competencies and benefits.
>
> (Cited in Mouan, 2010, p 368)

The aims of partnerships range from the broad and grand, to the narrow and specific. For example, the aforementioned Rio Summit on Sustainable Development, which is attributed with stimulating various partnerships between government and civil society, placed business at the centre of international efforts to reduce poverty. In contrast, a partnership might be formed between airport authorities, local government, local community groups, and environmental NGOs, with the specific purpose of negotiating a runway extension. Equally, as we shall discuss further, partnerships involve different levels of participation and involvement, ranging from a company promising to report on social and environmental performance to stakeholders or to fund a specific project, to civil society, business, and government groups collaborating together to achieve certain ends. It is not that one type of partnership is necessarily better than another—the question is what is fit for purpose—but it must be recognized that there are different types, each with implications for goals, design, and implementation.

The principle of partnership has been widely lauded both within and outside the business community. It has been called the 'collaboration paradigm of the twenty-first century' that allows actors to exceed their individual capabilities, the 'development approach of our time', and 'the last remedy to the stresses [of] intense globalization'.[37] A large number of companies have spoken out in favour of partnerships. Hershey acknowledges that

> corporations cannot address the challenges of ensuring a truly sustainable supply chain without working in partnership with [our] particular industry and, increasingly, without the help of outside nongovernmental organizations.
>
> (Cited in Long, 2008, p 317)

Accenture sees business-NGO partnerships as essential to improving the performance of civil society organizations.[38] The International Council on Mining and Metals (ICMM) says that a partnership approach is essential in establishing and strengthening sustainable development approaches in mining areas.[39] As Warner and Sullivan describe it:

> Tri-sector partnerships are, in essence, a new form of strategic alliance . . . [A] voluntary collaboration to promote sustainable development based on the most efficient allocation of complementary resources across business, civil society and government.
>
> (Warner and Sullivan, 2004, p 17)

Discussion points

Managers often want to see the financial value of partnerships.

- Is it possible to demonstrate how a partnership contributes to the bottom line?
- What are the most convincing non-financial arguments for partnerships?
- As the director of an NGO, how would you demonstrate the financial added value of a partnership to a South African mineral company?

Partnership as ideology?

There are examples of partnership, particularly of the multi-stakeholder variety, around the world, and these are being discussed and replicated not just as a methodology, but as an ideology—what Bendell et al. (2010) term the ideology of 'partnerism'. In the 1990s, partnerships such as the Ethical Trading Initiative were considered radical, but now partnering of some kind has not only entered into mainstream corporate thinking, it is an indicator of a company's commitment to good governance, social responsibility, and sustainability, and it has become an indicator of good performance in these fields in its own right.

There are some widely accepted reasons as to why this has come about. Stakeholders in their broadest sense are putting pressure on companies to act on environmental, social, and governance (ESG) issues. Some companies will react to stakeholders as a threat, and seek to manage them accordingly. However, other companies might see them as groups to engage with in order to help them navigate the uncertainties that confront modern business.[40] This reflects a fundamental philosophical difference in stakeholder management theory that we explore in Chapter 9. However, the role of stakeholders, including how they have been empowered by the social interconnectedness and opportunities for transparency that are features of contemporary globalization, is an important factor in the evolution of partnerships. Other factors discussed elsewhere in this book also shed light on the emergence of partnerism. There is a sense that governments are less able than before to regulate business, and certain partnerships have arisen to fill this governance vacuum. The perceived diminishing power of governments is often linked to the drop in government overseas development assistance as a percentage of capital flows into developing economies, and partnerships have to a degree been a response to this shift.[41] There are also various instrumental benefits that companies associate with partnership, such as employee satisfaction and morale, effective risk management, and above all brand image, which in one survey was rated as three times more important than other benefits.[42]

A challenge to convention?

Given the enthusiasm for, and proliferation of, partnerships and other variations on collaboration in the broad ESG arena, it is easy to forget that partnering of the kind relevant to CSR is recent and is a significant change from conventional business models. For example, mainstream management theory still promotes a corporation perspective model of the firm in which the primary goal is to create values for shareholders. An exemplar of this is Porter's 'five forces' framework which seeks to limit the number of competitors by putting one's company in a dominant position and optimizing outcomes for shareholders (and typically executives) over those for suppliers, customers, employees, and regulators.[43] Stakeholder engagement is not precluded by such a model, but its purpose is always to benefit the company (i.e. its shareholders and executives) rather than society as a whole.

The ideological value awarded to partnerships is that they offer an alternative to the corporation perspective model, but, in examining and evaluating partnerships in practice, we should always remember the power of well-established conventions, and therefore be wary of the distinction between collaborations that mark a radical shift away from the status quo and those that are a refurbishment of existing structures. In particular, we should be aware of the differences in sustainability outcome that result from these distinctions. If partnerships that reinforce the aims of the corporation perspective model deliver real benefits from a CSR perspective, then it would be mistaken to criticize them. However, as the discussion of impact in Chapter 4 shows, demonstrating the benefits is no easy task. The reality is that much of the coverage of partnerships exists in order to promote the ideology of partnering, and there is a dearth of reliable empirical evidence to show the benefits of partnership beyond the many individual case studies that tell interesting stories but do not comprise a comparable analysable data set.[44]

Discussion points

Partnerships have become one of the ways that companies manage sustainability issues.

- Why do companies think that partnerships are well suited to sustainability challenges?
- What specific advantages do multi-stakeholder partnerships offer?
- Why is the five forces framework at odds with the intentions of partnership approaches?

Types of partnership

There are various ways of categorizing partnerships (Table 5.1). We have already mentioned multi-stakeholder partnerships which, in contrast with business-to-business partnerships, bring together actors from different sectors of society to achieve an agreed set of goals. The Forest Stewardship Council (FSC) is an example of business partnering with social development and environmental NGOs to further the goal of responsible forest management. It stands out from other partnerships created in the 1990s in that it includes organizations from developing as well as developed economies. It is a voluntary partnership in that there are no legally enforceable elements bringing the organizations together, in contrast with most conventional business-to-business or business-to-other-party relationships. It also does not include government or its agencies, although in common with some other pioneering international collaborations, it has received direct or indirect government funding.

Table 5.1 Examples and types of partnership

	Business-to-business	Multi-stakeholder
Rule-setting partnership	EUREPGAP/GLOBALGAP International Council on Mining and Metals	RSPO FSC MSC
Service/implementation partnership	Sustainable Agriculture Initiative Platform	Better Cotton Initiative Cadbury Cocoa Partnership
Resourcing partnership	Connected Urban Development	Accenture Development Partnership

Rule-setting, implementation, and resource partnerships

The FSC operates a certification standard that is applied to well-managed forests, and compliance is recognized by the FSC logo applied to certified products using the output of those forests (e.g. paper, wooden furniture, sawn timber). As such, it is an example of a *rule-setting partnership*, along with the Marine Stewardship Council (MSC), and the IFOAM organic agriculture standard. Not all such partnerships are multi-stakeholder in nature; for example, EUREPGAP is a partnership of retailers and producers that develops certifiable criteria for good agricultural practice.

The World Wildlife Fund (WWF), the environmental NGO, played an important part in creating the FSC and the MSC, and that experience was carried over into the creation of the Roundtable on Sustainable Palm Oil (RSPO). The RSPO is a collaboration of companies throughout the palm oil value chain and NGOs, and it oversees a standard for the cultivation of socially and environmentally acceptable oil palm at the plantation and smallholder levels. However, as well as a rule-setting function, the RSPO is involved in creating a market for sustainable palm oil, and in improving cultivation standards. As such, it can also be seen as an *implementation or service partnership* which fulfils not only a governance function, but also a pastoral one with regard to oil palm growers. There are a large number of service partnerships, and they are often found in developing countries, where they offer distinct models for increasing the capability of local producers to meet sustainable production best practice.[45] The Cadbury Cocoa Partnership brings NGO and government partners together to improve the livelihoods of cacao farmers and their communities, and the Sustainable Agriculture Initiative Platform is a food-industry-wide initiative to promote sustainable agriculture practices.

Roundtables such as RSPO have become a popular partnership model; there are roundtables on sustainable sugar cane, soy, and biofuels, and such is the momentum behind this approach that the International Cocoa Organization, a traditional industry body, is now imitating it in its industry–government collaboration, the Roundtable for a Sustainable Cocoa Economy. They are examples of 'co-regulation' in which civil society and business representatives jointly regulate business policies and practices.[46]

Another attraction of roundtables is that they offer the potential to provide resources that might otherwise be unavailable. The RSPO generates revenue from the sale of certified palm oil and this is available to build up the capacity of growers, but resources need not just be financial; rule-setting partnerships such as the Fair Labor Association have given companies access to the grassroots-level knowledge of NGOs about working conditions, and a service partnership such as the Better Cotton Initiative has made available the competencies of agriculturalists, manufacturers, and designers for the common goal of more environmentally acceptable cotton cultivation. *Resourcing partnerships* are considered by some a separate type of partnership, especially when their primary aim is to provide particular groups with additional competencies. For example, Accenture Development Partnerships, which makes the skills of management consultants available to NGOs, is a resourcing partnership. This category also includes partnerships to conduct systematic dialogues, i.e. forums that allow business and other stakeholders to come together to discuss particular aspects of sustainability, including sharing best practice.[47] The UN Global Compact and the UN Principles for Responsible Investment (see Case study 5) can be seen as resourcing partnerships because although they set out criteria for best practice, these do not constitute rules comparable to the certifiable standards of the FSC or the MSC, and their contribution is probably best measured in terms of the process of dialogue than improved governance.

There are various subtypes of partnership that fall under the preceding three broad headings (Table 5.2). Employee volunteering, for example, is a common form of resourcing partnership, as is company sponsorship, and short-term business–NGO consultations. Philanthropy is often dismissed as a lesser form of partnership, in part because it does not imply a substantive change in company behaviour. However, from a company's perspective, philanthropy can be a prized form of partnership because of its demonstrable impact on employee morale, and its measurable effects on reputation and brand value. For example, the Finnish forest products company Stora Enso engages in rule-setting partnerships and systematic dialogues about sustainability, but its support of children's charities is still a key part of its partnership approach.[48]

Table 5.2 Partnership outcomes for different stakeholders—examples from mining

Outcomes for business	
Enhanced licence to operate, because communities affected by operations will be satisfied that the business unit is responsive to their concerns	Availability of new social capital for the business
Reduced community dependency on the business unit (e.g. owing to empowerment of communities to manage their own development)	Becoming 'company of choice' in the eyes of governmental authorizing agencies and removing political objections to future ventures
Basis for resolving local disputes that might delay financial approval or operations	Reduced risk to marketing, sales, and share price associated with negative image of social and environmental performance
Outcomes for local communities	
Additional resources for community development	Ensuring that those impacted by operations have an equal or greater level of welfare, income, subsistence, and security
Fairer settlement/compensation for community assets	Access to the technology, finance, and markets that are necessary for new assets, and skill sets that can be transformed into sustainable livelihoods
Improved infrastructure and capacity to manage it	
Outcomes for the public sector	
Agreed revenue distribution mechanisms before commencing operations	Increased legitimacy with local populations
More equitable distribution of revenues across government, and between government and communities	Exposure to new ways of working and international good practice
Enhanced tax and skills base	Empowerment of local communities

(*Source:* Adapted from Warner and Sullivan, 2004; Seitanidi, 2010)

Partnerships and globalization

Five different cases can be made for promoting partnering:

1. It is a better way of doing business.
2. It is a new way of regulating business.
3. It is an alternative way of harnessing the power and resources of business, and of redistributing benefits.
4. It is a more effective way of dealing with the realities of global governance.
5. It is an entirely new way of thinking about business.

In each case, the promise of partnership resonates with the challenges of globalization. For instance, we have discussed the changing nature of governance, and partnerships that can harness the respective competencies of different sectors domestically and internationally might provide an effective alternative approach to regulation. We have seen too that business has unique competencies and resources, and partnerships provide a way of leveraging these for the public good, not least in developing countries. The acquisition of TXU by two major private equity firms using a partnership with environmental NGOs, or Unilever's partnership with local women's organizations and microfinance groups for its Shakti programme are just two examples of how new business models are linked to partnering.

However, we should be cautious about uncritical faith in the actual benefits that partnerships deliver. As Windsor, and Svansson and Kalmansson highlight (in Stachowicz-Stanusch, 2015), partnerships are context dependent and complex. Caplan (2003) claims that the literature on partnerships too often promotes the idea that they are, by their very nature, harmonious and built on trust, common vision, and voluntary commitment. He argues that there are various myths and half-truths behind this belief.

First, multi-sector partnerships are rarely built on a common vision because stakeholders have different reference points and, if they focus too much on what they have in common, their aspirations become diluted or masked. The partnership then ends up with a mission statement for which nobody feels ownership. He points out that stakeholders can appear to share values when what is actually happening is that they are using the same words to mean different things. For example, for a company, 'sustainability' has some relationship to cost recovery; for the public sector, it means something that is technically sound that can sustain itself in the future; for a development NGO, it is to do with empowerment and giving communities a voice.

Second, while trust is a much-vaunted element of partnerships, it might be more accurate to say that individuals within the partnership build a mutual respect for that which people and organizations can offer. Trust is most likely when organizations can choose with whom to partner, but this rarely happens and most partners are thrust upon each other. Consequently, more important than trust can be creating an understanding of what the various partners can and cannot do. Indeed, more significant than genuine trust can be knowing partners well enough to predict how they will behave within the partnership.

Increasingly, the lessons of partnership seem to be that it is not a panacea for CSR challenges arising from globalization, and that organizations need to enter into partnerships with their eyes open to both their strengths and their weaknesses. There are many views on why partnerships are important and how to engage in them, and perhaps insufficient information on what is appropriate in different situations. But, overall, there is little argument about the importance attached to partnerships as part of CSR's armoury.

Unmet challenges

CSR faces three main criticisms about how it addresses the challenges and impacts of globalization. The first of these—not least from within the business community itself—is that business can, and should, do more to find new solutions to meet the challenges that globalization presents. There is general consensus that governments cannot meet these challenges alone—hence the formation of alliances with non-state actors, such as the private sector, is essential.[49]

This criticism takes different forms; for example, it underpins the calls for action from Business Action for Africa and WEF's Centre for Public–Private Partnership. It takes a different shape in the concept that Wood et al. (2006) call 'global business citizenship', which seeks to develop a new framework for CSR within which its boundaries are not prescribed by the competitive pressures of globalization. And it appears again in authors, such as Hart (2005), who recognize business as part of the solution to creating a sustainable environment, but push it to go beyond the business-case-related thinking of the triple bottom line. What is common to all of them, however, is the acceptance of business as a crucial actor, not simply because it does harm, but because it has unique resources, scope, and competencies that need to be harnessed for society's good. As Wettstein (2005) notes, if multinational companies are as powerful as they are portrayed, perhaps they should not be allowed to stay out of political debate or to ignore global problems, but rather should be thought of as quasi-governmental institutions with an inherent responsibility for global well-being.

The second criticism is more accusatory. An Accenture analysis highlights what it calls 'pilot paralysis', referring to the limited replication of seemingly successful initiatives.[50] It acknowledges that business has tried to address society's concerns through certification schemes, adoption of global framework agreements, standard setting and monitoring, and dialogues with other sectors and its critics, but deems all of these approaches to voluntary regulation inadequate. Utting's (2005) analysis concludes the following: too many companies have not participated; there has been limited penetration of CSR ideas across the corporate structure; compliance procedures are often weak; initiatives, such as codes of conduct, are often top-down and technocratic, and, while focusing on particular named issues, they do not examine the impact of CSR, especially in developing countries. There are some signs of change,[51] but Reich (2007) concludes that, ultimately, CSR demonstrates the limitations of self-regulation and the need for government to assert its regulatory role, or, as Utting argues, a more robust approach to 'articulated regulation', under which different regulatory approaches and agents would come together in ways that are complementary, mutually reinforcing, and synergistic.

The final criticism of CSR as a response to globalization builds on these debates about self-regulation and centres on CSR's capacity to alter perceptions of corporate self-interest. It holds that many of globalization's shortcomings are exacerbated, or at least overlooked, by companies pursuing their narrow self-interest. For example, lay-offs and plant closures make sense in terms of global competitiveness, but can be devastating for individuals and communities. Indeed, as Visser (2006) has argued in an African context, accepted CSR frameworks, such as Carroll's pyramid (see Chapter 2), can appear simplistic and static when applied in developing countries, and may not recognize that conflicts and contradictions should be anticipated as the norm rather than treated as the shocking exception. In recent years, companies such as Amazon, Google, and Starbucks have all been ridiculed for their tax avoidance policies. In the USA and the UK, zero-hours contracts, which require workers to be available without paying them, have become the latest in a line of practices that harm rather than improve people's standards of living.

One strand of this critique holds that companies do not try to understand the consequences of their behaviour and focus only on those issues that they feel will affect their reputation, or that will serve their self-interest in other ways (e.g. investing in maintaining a healthy, educated workforce and protecting their image).[52] There are indications that companies committed to CSR are more sensitive to these issues. The collaboration between Unilever and Oxfam to examine ways that the behaviour of a multinational affects poverty in Indonesia is an example of how partnerships are beginning to wrestle with the complexity of international development.[53]

Oxfam's attempts to use what it calls its 'poverty footprint' methodology with other companies has had a limited impact, and only two others (cut flowers in Kenya, and the impact of Coca-Cola and SABMiller in Zambia and Ecuador) have been published. A similar approach by other companies has also met with limited success, and PPR (the holding company of Puma), a leader in environmental profit-and-loss accounting, abandoned its social profit-and-loss exercise.[54] A critical dimension to this in future will be how far companies can align around a CSR sensibility so that they are not, for example, claiming improved environmental practices, while at the same time aggressively marketing high-risk products to ill-educated consumers,[55] or not promoting better labour conditions, while using just-in-time contracting that can exacerbate labour exploitation.

The second strand of the same critique argues that aspects of trading and other contractual relationships are inherently unfair and biased towards the interests of the most powerful companies, but mainstream CSR has done little to address this. For example, as Oxfam's Make Trade Fair campaign asks, to what extent will CSR push for fairness in trading relations, both between countries and within specific supply chains?[56] And as Jenkins (2005) has noted, there are many areas that might be important for long-term development in which business seems to be silent or hostile (e.g. corporate taxation and tort reform), and CSR has done little to influence corporate investment in countries with the least foreign direct investment.

Finally, it is argued that the mindset and tools of CSR are so deeply embedded in the normative frameworks of business that CSR theory and practice ends up taking for granted, reproducing, and legitimizing, rather than providing an alternative to, the values and priorities associated with free enterprise. We saw earlier how some believe that globalization universalizes certain values; it has been argued that CSR is one way in which this is done, not only by what is included or excluded from standards of acceptable social and environmental performance, but also by the way in which those tools are used.[57] Current approaches, such as ethical sourcing, have been criticized for ignoring the priorities of workers, and failing to consider the broader impacts of initiatives on other producers and neighbouring communities;[58] as case studies from Fig (2005) and Newell (2005) have shown, initiatives driven from the bottom up run the risk of being ignored or discounted by CSR. Such case studies reveal how important voices are missing from CSR partnerships and other initiatives that claim to engage with stakeholders, but often end up doing so on a selective basis.

Discussion points

Since the 1990s, worries about the global environment have been an important driver of CSR, although some believe that social issues are now more prominent.

- What environmental challenges are most clearly associated with globalization?
- To what extent can, and should, business seek to tackle the major global environmental challenges?
- Nearly thirty years since the Rio Earth Summit, what are the main overall achievements of the environmental initiatives in which business has been involved?

Case study 5 The United Nations Global Compact

The United Nations Global Compact is one of the most well-known CSR partnerships, and has been called 'an excellent source of inspiration' for companies thinking about their relationship with society. It was established in 2000 as a direct result of the call of the then UN Secretary-General, Kofi Annan, for business leaders to partner with UN agencies, and for civil society to support universal environmental and social principles. The partnership was in part a response to the neglect of social and environmental protections in the promotion of economic globalization, and also the failure of UN agencies to engage effectively with the business community. It is based on the premise that the longevity of globalization and the international economic order depends as much on such protections as it does on free markets and economic inclusivity.

The Compact was never intended to resolve all of global capitalism's deficiencies, but rather to lay a foundation of shared values, as embodied in various UN conventions and declarations, and to attempt to harness the skills and resources of the private sector to uphold those values. Although sometimes mistaken for a certification standard, its main aim is to foster a dialogue among actors from the private, public, and civil society sectors. However, to make that dialogue effective and transparent, companies are expected to report on their progress and actions in implementing the Compact's ten principles (Table 5.3).

Table 5.3 The ten principles of the Global Compact

Businesses should:
1 support and respect the protection of internationally proclaimed human rights within their sphere of influence;
2 ensure that their own operations are not complicit in human rights abuses;
3 uphold the freedom of association and the effective recognition of the right to collective bargaining;
4 uphold the elimination of all forms of forced and compulsory labour;
5 uphold the effective abolition of child labour;
6 eliminate discrimination in respect of employment and occupation;
7 support a precautionary approach to environmental challenges;

(continued . . .)

Businesses should:
8 undertake initiatives to promote greater environmental responsibility;
9 encourage the development and diffusion of environmentally friendly technologies;
10 work against corruption in all its forms, including extortion and bribery.

(*Source:* http://www.unglobalcompact.org)

> The ultimate measure of success for the initiative is the degree to which it promotes concrete and sustained action by its varied participants, especially the private sector, in alignment with broad UN objectives, the [Compact's] principles, and the international Millennium Development Goals. It does not substitute for effective action by governments, nor does it present a regulatory framework or code of conduct for companies. Rather the Global Compact is conceived as a value-based platform designed to promote institutional learning with few formalities and no rigid bureaucratic structures.
>
> (Kell and Levin, 2003, p 152)

The Principles mirror the commitments of UN member states under the Universal Declaration of Human Rights, the 1992 Rio Declaration on the Environment and Development, the 1998 ILO Fundamental Principles and Rights at Work, and the 2003 Convention against Corruption. In other words, they already have a degree of legitimacy with national governments. Companies that sign up to the Compact make a clear statement of support for the Principles, signed by the CEO and endorsed by the board, and they agree to report publicly on progress towards meeting this commitment. From this stem the Compact's three stated goals:

1 to build consensus and inspire recognition of social and environmental concerns in the global marketplace, especially around problematic areas;

2 to develop a learning bank of corporate best practices, and to integrate the Compact's ten principles into business strategies and operations;

3 to generate concrete sustained implementation of the Millennium/Sustainable Development Goals.

Partnering is an important way of achieving these, and activities include: (a) learning forums to analyse case studies and examples of good practice; (b) global policy dialogues on the challenges of globalization; (c) multi-stakeholder collaborative development projects to further the Sustainable Development Goals; (d) supporting the creation of new national networks. An important part of the Compact has been local networks that serve as forums within which companies can exchange experiences in a particular region.

The Compact now has about 9,500 corporate members in 160 countries, a rapid rise that includes commitments from over 20% of the world's 500 largest companies. There is a large under-representation of US companies, partly because they fear litigation based on any alleged failure to comply with the Principles. Although there are over a thousand companies each from Latin America and Asia, these regions are underrepresented in terms of their population size and economic importance, while Africa and the Middle East, where many important CSR governance challenges lie, are poorly represented. Equally, 9,400 companies divided into seventy-six local networks around the world is a less impressive number when one considers that there are 4.8 million companies in the UK alone.[59]

More important, though, are the achievements of the signatories. Are they leaders in the different areas of CSR the Principles embrace, or is being part of the Compact an insurance policy against closer

(*continued . . .*)

scrutiny? The Compact may not be a regulatory body, but it does require that companies engage in continual improvement, and this has grown in emphasis since the launch in 2010 of its Differentiation Framework (to allow companies at different levels of progress to explain their achievements) and its Blueprint for Corporate Sustainability Leadership.

Ultimately, the Compact will be assessed on its contribution to realizing the UN's social and environmental goals, although the Compact and commentators are at pains to stress that it is only one part of the solution and depends heavily on other efforts towards the same end. However, it is natural to want to know more about the direct impact of the Compact itself, and moreover to want to learn about its achievements in the social and environmental spheres. At present, it is much easier to find out about the number of signatories, and the meetings they have had, than to discover whether a company such as G4S, with a well-documented reputation for human rights abuses in prisons and poor employment conditions,[60] has improved its employment practices as a result of Compact membership. Hamann et al. (2009a) and Runhaar and Lafferty (2009) argue that there is little evidence on the ground that participating in the Compact improves companies' CSR efforts, although Woo (2010) states that it has improved the management of initiatives in some companies.

However, even at the broader level for which information about participation is more readily available, the signs of success are hazy. For the Compact's 2017 progress report, less than 25% of companies responded, and of these the majority were European firms, including many defining rather than fully implementing programmes.

(*Sources:* Kell and Levin, 2003; Hamann et al., 2009; Woo 2010, cited in Rasche and Kell, 2010; Kell, 2013; Rasche et al., 2017; Ruggie, 2017; UNGC, 2017)

Questions

For the Compact to be successful, it needs to be a credible partnership tackling important issues.

1 How well aligned are the ten principles to the main issues that business is being asked to address globally by governments and civil society?

2 What are the advantages and disadvantages of striving for a large but less active membership compared with a small but very active one?

3 What can the Compact do to encourage more active involvement from companies?

Summary

Globalization is a specific historical era in which the role of business in the world is being redefined. The human and environmental consequences of globalization are causing us to rethink CSR. Yet there are competing definitions of globalization and these, in turn, affect what we think the responsibilities of business are, and how we believe companies should approach them.

There are various definitions of globalization that variously emphasize its economic and wider social characteristics. The meaning that we give to 'globalization' affects how we look at its impacts. For some, these impacts are synonymous with 'liberalism', whether we mean by that the benefits of free trade, comparative advantage, and enlightened self-interest, or the exploitation of workers, social inequality, and the externalization of industry's ecological costs. Others may not deny these impacts, but instead highlight that what is distinctive about globalization is how it affects social networks, generates new types of organization, and creates the need for new approaches to governance, in particular the various types of rule-setting and resourcing partnerships that straddle nations, sectionrs, and industries. These different views are highly evident in debates about CSR. Some treat it as either a hindrance or a palliative to economic liberalization; others see it as related to the new organizations and alliances that globalization has spawned, and as part of the response to the challenges of global governance.

Further reading

Cairns, G. and Sliwa, M. 2017, *A very short, fairly interesting and reasonably cheap book about international business*, Sage.
Short overview of business in an era of globalization.

Chang, H. J. 2010, *23 things they don't tell you about capitalism*, Allen Lane, London.
Lively look at the effects of globalization around the world.

Porritt, J. 2005, *Capitalism: as if the world matters*, Earthscan, London.
An alternative view of capitalism's future from an important sustainability thinker and activist.

Rodrik, D. 2017, *Straight talk on trade: ideas for a sane world economy*, Princeton University Press, Princeton, NJ.
Reasons why economic globalization should not be accepted as 'end of history'.

Stiglitz, J.E. 2005, *Fair trade for all: how trade can promote development*, Oxford University Press, Oxford.
An influential economist's view on the shortcomings of liberal economic globalization.

http://www.oup.com/uk/blowfield_murray4e
Visit the online resources that accompany this book to enrich your understanding of this chapter. Among the resources available are web links, exercises, and additional case studies.

Endnotes

1. 2006; Pedersen and Huniche, 2006; Wood et al., 2006; Crane et al., 2013.
2. See, e.g., Blowfield, 2005a; Demirag, 2005.
3. Steger, 2003.
4. World Bank data, accessed 25 April 2018. The actual figures are a little unclear at present because the last comprehensive household study was done in 2013, and since then the poverty line has shifted from \$1.5 to £1.9/day. The next full analysis is due in late 2018.
5. WTO data, accessed 9 October 2013.
6. Henderson, 2001; Lindsey, 2002.
7. Wolf, 2004, p 36.
8. Wolf, 2004, p 320.
9. Stiglitz, 2002, p 248.
10. Johnston, 2003; Johnson, 2004.
11. http://www.bbc.co.uk/science/0/21970879, accessed 6 April 2018.
12. Standing, 2016.

13. Caufield, 1996; Gardetti et al., 2014; Legrand et al., 2016.
14. See, e.g., Blowfield, 2004.
15. For example, MacLean (1999), Germain (2000), and Levy and Newell (2005) build on theories of power from writers such as Lukes, Gramsci, and Foucault to examine how exertions of power are not necessarily overt or attributable to recognizable actors.
16. Blowfield and Frynas, 2005.
17. https://www.wto.org/english/res_e/statis_e/wts2017_e/wts17_toc_e.htm, accessed 24 November 2018.
18. Waters, 2001; Steger 2003.
19. According to IMF data, household debt in the USA in 2009 was over 90% of GDP, in the UK it was nearly 120%, and in the Eurozone it was over 60%. Corporate debt for the same countries was 80%, 120%, and 100% respectively. In the seven richest economies, government debt guarantees (sovereign debt) are nearly 120%, the same as in the period immediately after World War II.
20. Bendell, 2004a.
21. World Bank, 2005.
22. Wolf, 2004.
23. This is Wolf's position: he says that corporate wealth has been exaggerated by dubious arithmetic. The merits of different claims about the power and influence of multinational companies is examined in Chandler and Mazlish, 2005.
24. Ring et al., 2005.
25. McMurtry, 2002.
26. Cited in Waters, 2001, p 123.
27. See, e.g., Stiglitz, 2002; Wolf, 2004; Watkins and Fowler, 2005.
28. Elliott and Freeman, 2003. Abrami (2003) discusses the US-Cambodia bilateral textile agreement, which was lauded for linking increased market access to the USA to improvements in workers' rights.
29. Utting, 2005.
30. Blowfield and Johnson, 2013.
31. For an overview of modern slavery, see Bales (2004).
32. Block and Barnett, 2005.
33. Stopford et al., 1991.
34. Blowfield, 2005a.
35. Browne, 2004.
36. Porter, 1990.
37. Austin, cited in Kolk and Pinkse, 2010; Kjaer et al. and Rochlin et al., cited in Mouan, 2010.
38. Bulloch, 2009; https://www.icmm.com/en-gb/about-us, accessed 24 November 2018.
39. McPhail, 2008.
40. Berns et al., 2009.
41. Nelson, 2007.
42. Berns et al., 2009.
43. Harris and Twomey, 2010.
44. Mouan, 2010.
45. Hamann and Boulogne, 2008.
46. Albareda, 2008.
47. Kourula and Halme, 2008.
48. Kourula and Halme, 2008.
49. See, e.g., Nelson, 1996; Fox and Prescott, 2004; Pedersen, 2005.

50. WEF and Accenture, 2012.
51. See, e.g., UN, 2005; World Bank, 2005.
52. See. e.g., the shift from policing suppliers to engaging suppliers and workers in labour monitoring (CCC, 2005a; ETI, 2005a).
53. Maitland, 2005.
54. PPR is now called Kering, which ironically means 'dry' or 'drought' in Indonesian and Malay.
55. Clay, 2005.
56. Christian Aid (2004) and Utting (2005) provide examples of this kind of non-alignment.
57. Materials on Make Trade Fair are available at http://www.oxfam.org, accessed 24 November 2018.
58. Blowfield, 2004; Mosley, 2011.
59. http://www.fsb.org.uk/stats, accessed 24 November 2018.
60. See, for instance, media coverage in 2013 of Mangaung Correctional Centre (Gauteng, South Africa) in which G4S was accused of using unskilled staff who were involved in violence against prisoners. Also, see coverage of G4S's use of unskilled low-wage non-permanent workers at the London Olympics in 2012, which resulted in the police and army having to provide security.

Part 2

Managing and implementing corporate social responsibility

How corporate social responsibility is managed

Chapter overview

In this chapter, we begin to examine the way in which CSR is being managed within companies, and whether or not there is a business case. In particular, we will:

- discuss the different goals that companies are trying to achieve;
- identify the types and levels of CSR that companies exhibit;
- examine the shared lessons and common elements of CSR management;
- look at how CSR is managed inside companies;
- explore evidence of a business case for CSR.

Main topics

Key terms

Change management
Defensive CSR
Integrated business strategy
Offensive CSR
Business case
Leadership

Understanding what companies want from CSR

CSR management is typically described in terms of organizational change and transformation, and therefore distinguishes between:

1 the purpose and results (the why and the what);
2 the principles and processes (the how);
3 the leadership (the who).

The next sections broadly follow these distinctions, and therefore we begin with a discussion of the way in which companies decide whether to adopt CSR. The exception would be companies founded with the specific goal of achieving social or environmental outcomes, and which are discussed in Chapter 11 under 'Social Entrepreneurship'.

The most basic questions that any company thinking about CSR must answer are as follows.

1 What is our purpose in doing this—i.e. what Holliday et al. (2002) call the 'corporate magnetic north'?
2 What do we need to do to achieve it?

The wide range of definitions, approaches, and issues related to CSR mean that these basic questions do not necessarily have simple answers (see Chapter 1). Should a company focus on things that affect its financial bottom line? If so, what exactly are those things? Threats to the company's reputation; risks to the supply of materials; attempts to undermine the share price; harm to the company's ability to recruit or retain top-quality personnel; acts that expose the firm to costly lawsuits—all of these can affect financial performance and require that significant attention be given to CSR. But should the company define its CSR more in terms of addressing social issues, such as access to education, support for the arts, or reducing inequality? Must it try to do both and, if so, is there a point at which the company's social mission overwhelms the conventional business purpose?

Immediately, we see what one study of approaches to CSR concludes is the distinction between operational responsibilities and citizenship responsibilities.[1] Companies are not limited to focusing on one set of responsibilities to the exclusion of the other, but the resource implications of any decision mean that even the largest corporation has to choose what to prioritize. Yet the same study also makes clear that it is not only the company that decides what responsibilities to act upon. Consumers, for example, have their own priorities, and may reward or punish a company in the marketplace if its values do not concord with their own. For the reasons spelled out in Chapter 5 and elsewhere, the contemporary capitalist has to make sense of a cacophony of voices which have little, if any, acknowledged interest in business's wants or needs.

Defining the company's CSR purpose is further complicated by the fact that perceptions of responsibility differ from country to country.[2] For example, in Germany, it is a priority that companies provide secure employment; in South Africa, it is a priority that companies improve health, education, and other elements of social welfare; in Australia, the emphasis is on environmental protection. These priorities shift and often reflect recent local crises, so that in Argentina, for example, the main expectation that people have of business is job creation because of the unemployment and financial loss caused by the recent economic collapse. In China, the main expectation is for safe, high-quality products because of recent incidents of fire and serious injury caused by shoddy electrical goods. In countries characterized by a strong legally explicit framework defining the social contract within which business operates (e.g. Sweden, Japan, Austra), CSR issues look quite different from those built on a laissez-faire economy (e.g. Australia, USA, UK). Considerable effort has gone into identifying national distinctions about CSR,[3] and these are particularly valid when thinking about national or regional companies, as van Tilburg et al. (2013) show in their extensive study of Dutch companies pursuing the goal of becoming sustainable enterprises. What is less explored, however, is whether multinational companies (MNCs) reproduce the social contract from their place of origin. On the admittedly limited evidence available, it seems that while some attention is paid to the national setting, the frameworks used by MNCs to manage CSR are imported, meaning that while different CSR issues might receive attention, there is an orthodoxy in how they are managed. Furthermore, that orthodoxy reproduces many of the features of laissez-faire economics, even when the company concerned originates from one with different sociopolitical conditions (e.g. IKEA, VW, Toyota).

Other factors and actors also influence the purpose of CSR. For example, the European Commission has defined CSR in a way that is intended to reflect what it calls the unique European social model, under which employers and other stakeholders, such as trade unions, function together to shape society and the economy. Reflecting the ideal that companies should not focus solely on profit, but also on the welfare of the workforce, consumers, and the environment, the model sets out the purpose of CSR in terms of the benefits to workers, customers, communities, and the wider society. Acknowledging the importance of different types of company across Europe, it requires that CSR be relevant to small and medium-sized enterprises. Reflecting the need to establish European competitive advantage in the global economy, it also requires that CSR finds ways of demonstrating that responsible business attracts investment and builds a skilled workforce.[4]

Similarly, an industry or a multi-industry collaboration can influence a company's CSR purpose. For example, the Global Social Compliance Programme, comprising companies such as Walmart, Bata, Carrefour, and the Walt Disney company, aims to improve working and environmental conditions in global supply chains. The programme not only sets out areas in which member companies should take action, but seeks to build a consensus on best practice that would apply across companies by, for example, requiring them to report their progress against individually determined timelines and goals.[5]

The increase in the range of organizations, individuals, and sectors of society that seek to influence business behaviour is one trend that needs to be understood in terms of thinking about a company's CSR purpose; how companies consider other trends is also an influencing factor. For example, what significance does the company attach to changing patterns of demand for (and often shrinking supplies of) natural resources, or the challenge of demographic change (see Chapters 4 and 12)? Is the threat of climate change so great that it overwhelms other aspects of the business–society relationship? How will the growing number of tangible and intangible financial factors that might affect the way business is valued and its success measured influence the way in which the company is managed, and in what it invests? Or does the company need to respond to the growing role of international institutions, and the continued acceleration in the speed of policy and behavioural change caused by the global media?[6] Each of these trends has relevance for CSR, whether in terms of the need to change energy use, or to invest in new building technology because of the natural resource situation, or the financial case for investing in innovative technologies to solve social problems, or the challenges of participating in new models of global governance.

Basic distinctions in CSR purpose

Given this array of issues, are there common frameworks to help understand a company's CSR purpose? One way of thinking about what the company aims to achieve through CSR management is to distinguish between what Kramer and Kania (2006) call 'defensive' and 'offensive' CSR. In their view, most companies view CSR in terms of vulnerability, i.e. as an external risk that needs to be managed with minimal investment. Thus, for example, an NGO will raise an issue and the company will seek to find the least costly way to defuse attention, through actions such as lobbying, public relations, and advertising. The defensive approach can also be used to maintain the company's reputation and to avoid legal liabilities, and is generally employed when companies are seeking to resolve problems of their own making.

In contrast, the offensive approach can involve companies offering themselves as the solution even if they had no part in creating the problem. It requires companies to exploit their full capabilities to find and implement solutions, and requires them to do four key things.

1 Pick the right issue—one that is important, timely, and leverages the company's core competencies.
2 Establish concrete goals and report on progress both inside the company and externally.
3 Deploy the company's key assets in addressing the issue including, for example, its products and services, the relevant skills of its employees, industry expertise, and its infrastructure.
4 Work in partnership with other sectors.

BP is a widely cited example of a company that decided early on to adopt an offensive approach, because the company chose the single issue of global warming, confronted it squarely before others in its industry did so, publicly announced quantitative targets and deadlines, and provided objectively verified reports of its progress.

As Nike's approach to CSR demonstrates, defensive and offensive approaches are not mutually exclusive, but the two bring different results. For example, a defensive approach allows the company to make short-term gains when it has to respond to specific charges (e.g. child labour in supplier factories), but the gains flatten out as the company meets its critics' expectations. Meanwhile, a company might see little tangible benefit from initial social investments, but, as these become more focused, they can have a significant impact in differentiating the company from its peers.[7] Put simply, as Kramer and Kania conclude:

> offensive [CSR] can distinguish a company's reputation but cannot protect it; defensive [CSR] can protect a reputation but cannot distinguish it.
>
> (Kramer and Kania, 2006, p 25)

This is an instrumental framework that presents a business rationale for acting, but does not provide much guidance on the intrinsic value of those actions. In contrast, Martin (2002) distinguishes between acts that are instrumental because they maintain or enhance shareholder value, and those that are done for their own sake, which are therefore regarded as having an intrinsic value. In what he calls the 'virtue matrix', he divides instrumental acts between those that are done because they conform to norms and customs, and those that are necessitated by legal compliance. He divides intrinsically valuable acts between those that create social and shareholder value, and those that benefit society but not shareholders. This distinction between instrumental and intrinsic value brings us back to the discussion of the meaning of CSR in Chapter 1 (and the debates about impact in Chapters 13 and 14). Is a company's purpose less admirable if the business rationale is strong, or vice versa, as some business ethicists maintain? Is a strong business case a signal that a company will remain committed to delivering extra-financial outcomes? What is an acceptable balance between return on investment and social return on investment? People may have strong opinions about which is the right set of questions to ask, but in today's business world each is a valid way to think about purpose, and decisions are highly subjective.

Advocates of CSR as management reform largely favour the more innovative forward-looking agendas implicit in the concepts of intrinsic value and offensive CSR. These people see CSR, to paraphrase Paul Tebo of DuPont, as the right to operate and grow, because products that make lives better and reach more people equate with expanded markets and new customers.[8] But, as we shall see, for many companies the instrumental/defensive approach to CSR better defines what they want to achieve. Moreover, Waddock (2007) has argued that the defensive-offensive distinction is not comprehensive enough. She accepts that CSR can be a defensive response to crises and scandals, or a way in which to harness the power of business to meet societal needs. But she adds a third distinction, under which the company's CSR purpose is to respond to concerns in society that arise from the very success of the company's strategy. This arises when public expectations about the behaviour of business are neither the result of particular abuses, such as forced labour or oil spills, nor linked to demands that companies fill societal needs. Rather, the expectations (or criticisms) are directly related to the consequences of business implementing a system within which success is equated with:

1 continual growth and expansion;
2 a focus on efficiency and externalizing costs wherever possible;
3 corporate control or influence over resources, markets, customer preferences, and employees.

In other words, whether it be outrage at the bonuses paid by Goldman Sachs or disquiet among independent booksellers at the competing low-cost volunteer-based business model of Oxfam bookshops,[9] success creates a set of expectations which do not fit comfortably within the two-approach model, but which, as noted earlier, clearly inform public perceptions of responsibility, such as fair competition, job security, workforce prosperity, and aspects of environmental stewardship.

Stages of CSR

Several theorists use the analogy of a journey when explaining how companies define, and then develop, their CSR goals. This is a convenient way of exploring why companies' policies, processes, and programmes change, and also of discussing to what companies should aspire. The idea of responsibility as a journey was used by Post and Altman (1992) to describe the evolution of environmental management, and is the subject of numerous case studies of corporate transformation that set out the steps and mis-steps taken by individual companies.[10] Clarkson (1995), building on others, developed the RDAP framework that separates the 'reactive', 'defensive', 'accommodative', and 'proactive' stages of CSR. Zadek (2000) identified four types of CSR (defence of reputation, cost-benefit orientation, the strategic business case, and the 'new economy' case, in which CSR is seen as part of new approaches to learning, innovation, and risk management). He has developed this idea to analyse the experience of Nike in moving from being what he calls a 'stubborn resister' to the idea it was responsible for the consequences of its products, into what he regards as an active citizen and what Nike itself describes as a stage at which sustainability is a core attribute of Nike product innovation.[11]

Mirvis and Googins (2006) warn that there is no single developmental pathway, but believe that there is a natural progression. Their model builds on ideas of behavioural psychology and posits that companies, like individuals, exhibit distinct patterns of behaviour at different stages of development, with their activities becoming more complex and sophisticated as they mature. We can tell the level of maturity by the company's actions in seven areas of management (see Figure 6.1):

1 how CSR is defined and the comprehensiveness of the definition (what they call the 'citizenship concept');
2 the purpose of the company's CSR ('strategic intent');
3 the support given by company managers ('leadership');
4 the day-to-day management of CSR within the firm ('structure');
5 responses to social, environmental, and other relevant issues ('issues management');
6 managing the relationship with key constituencies within and outside the company ('stakeholder relationships');
7 openness, transparency, and disclosure about different aspects of CSR performance ('transparency').

Thus, for instance, a company at the 'elementary' stage might define CSR in terms of the creation of profits and jobs, and payment of corporate taxes (its citizenship concept), it might see its CSR purpose as complying with the law (strategic intent), and it might adopt a defensive approach to issues management. In contrast, a company at the 'engaged' stage might in addition conceptualize CSR in terms of philanthropy or environmental protection, see its purpose as maintaining a licence to operate, and begin to develop policies that allow it to predict what issues it will need to manage. Meanwhile, a company at the 'integrated' stage might be thinking in terms of the triple bottom line, be using CSR as a way to inform its product development, and have in place management systems that allow it to predict societal trends (see Figure 6.1).

Both Zadek and Mirvis and Googins feel that companies have yet to reach the most developed stage of CSR (what they respectively call the 'new economy' and 'transforming' stages). As the overview of criticisms of CSR in Chapter 13 shows, there are good reasons for doubting whether companies, especially large corporations, can ever have the kind of game-changing purpose some would like them to have. However, authors and business people, such as Mackey, Senge, and McInnes, continue to press the importance of striving for this level of transformation. Their calls for more radical change are in part recognition of the way major external events such as climate change require companies in some industries to leapfrog to an advanced evolutionary stage. Nonetheless, as a whole, the stages provide a framework for

Dimensions	Stage 1 Elementary	Stage 2 Engaged	Stage 3 Innovative	Stage 4 Integrated	Stage 5 Transforming
Citizenship concept	Jobs; profits; taxes	Philanthropy; environment protection	Stakeholder management	Sustainability/ triple bottom line	Change the game
Strategic intent	Legal compliance	Maintain licence to operate	Make business case	Integration of value and values	Create new markets/social change
Leadership	Minimal	Supportive	On top of the issues	Ahead of the curve	Visionary
Structure	Marginal	Functional ownership	Cross-functional coordination	Organizational alignment	Integrated into mainstream
Issues management	Defensive	Reactive	Responsive	Proactive	Defines the issues
Stakeholder relationships	Unilateral	Interactive	Mutual influence	Alliances and partnerships	Multi-organizational
Transparency	Enough to protect flanks	Public relations	Public reporting	Assurance	Full disclosure

Figure 6.1 Stages of CSR
(*Source:* Adapted from Mirvis and Googins, 2006)

understanding the different purposes that companies are pursuing. Equally, as we consider in the next section, they reveal some of the key dimensions to CSR management.

Discussion points

CSR is often presented as an evolutionary journey.

- Does it help managers to think of CSR in this way?
- Are the criteria used to measure progression adequate and appropriate?
- What companies would you put at Mirvis and Googins' stages 3 and 4, and which would you say have reached or are approaching stage 5?

Qualities of good CSR management

Following the three critical areas of organizational change mentioned earlier, we move now from the company's purpose in managing CSR to a discussion of its implementation (the 'how'). There is a large number of books about how to manage CSR, aimed largely at existing managers. Peters's *Waltzing with the raptors* (1999) was one of the first of these, promising a practical roadmap to protecting a company's reputation, and since then further titles have concentrated on particular advantages of CSR (e.g. risk management, the business case, enhanced strategy) and/or the needs of particular business functions (e.g. CSR for PR professionals; marketing).

A glance at the contents of these books reveals the central elements of CSR management today. For example, the *Guide to best practices in corporate social responsibility*,[12] a book targeted at mid-level PR managers, features chapters on communicating CSR, building an integrated CSR strategy, demonstrating its value to senior management, working with stakeholders, managing crises, CSR reporting, and measuring CSR performance. Such books reveal a managerial orthodoxy that embraces much of CSR today and is reflected in various assessments of best practice.[13] This orthodoxy comprises:

1 particular tools and approaches—the ingredients of good CSR management;

2 advice on execution—the qualities of that management.

We now discuss these two dimensions and also take a more in-depth look at some of the ingredients in coming chapters.

One of the things that distinguishes CSR today from that of the past is that it is becoming an identifiable area of management expertise. As we discuss later in this chapter (see section 'Structuring the CSR function'), this expertise is housed in a variety of organizational structures, but there is also a large amount of general advice that is presented as best practice which draws on analysis of diverse corporate experiences and case studies. This ranges from identifying broad areas to which the company should pay attention (e.g. integrating strategies into the corporate culture, adhering to declared values and standards, and communicating what the company is doing, including both achievements and challenges)[14] to more specific steps. Some of the most common advice that can be offered to a company once its purpose is clear is set out in Box 6.1.

Box 6.1 Common advice on introducing CSR into management

- Get started—don't take too long before getting under way with the first activities.
- Pay attention to terminology—for example, a term such as 'sustainable growth' may have more resonance with company managers than 'sustainability', 'sustainable development', or 'social responsibility', because the latter terms can be interpreted as discarding the idea of economic growth with which managers are most familiar.
- Be frank and transparent—this is the best way to get staff attention, and winning their attention makes it easier to change the corporate ethos.
- Instil a company ethic of education and learning around issues of responsibility.
- Find useful partners and CSR champions across the company.
- Get to know the community within which the company exists, including understanding its norms, values, cultures, traditions, and, of course, applicable laws.

(continued...)

- Establish dialogues and debates with stakeholders from different sectors and sections of society, and make these transparent and honest, not least in terms of agreeing realistic expectations.
- Form 'smart partnerships' with stakeholders to achieve genuine CSR goals, rather than only public relations imperatives.
- Measure and account for what the company does in areas of CSR.
- Report to the public and key constituencies on what the company is doing and make these reports accessible to all who have an interest.

(*Sources*: Adapted from Peters, 1999; SustainAbility/UNEP, 2001; Olsen, 2004; CCC, 2005a)

Much of this advice relates to the initial stages of adopting CSR and, as, we discuss in Chapter 9 in relation to stakeholder engagement, for example, some aspects of CSR management ultimately involve many layers of skill and complexity. This is also true of making the business case for CSR, which some consultants and theorists stress needs to be established as early as possible within the company (see section 'The business case for CSR'). However, returning to our earlier discussion about instrumental and intrinsic value, Hemingway and MacLagan (2004) argue that the commercial imperative is only part of effective CSR management and that it should also be linked to the personal values of individual managers. They point out that individual discretion allows personnel to introduce their values into CSR policies, whether through officially sanctioned actions, the unintended consequences of an individual resolving a problem by drawing on personal beliefs, or an individual's entrepreneurship in bringing values into the workplace.

Leaders—or, perhaps more accurately, 'initiators' or what Pinchot (1985) calls 'intrapreneurs'—can come from almost any part of the company and a key ingredient is what Arnold and Hartman (2003) call 'moral imagination', a theme that Grayson and Nelson (2013) develop in their overview of corporate partnerships. For example, at BAT, some of the early enthusiasm for CSR is said to have come from middle managers in corporate affairs, while at The Body Shop and Timberland it stemmed from the moral imagination of CEOs from the outset. Regardless of how it begins, however, there comes a stage at which senior management needs to give legitimacy to the CSR agenda, so that it is valued across the company. Part of this legitimization is the creation of relevant systems to develop policies, processes, indicators, and targets, so that the full range of CSR-related activities are managed. Companies such as Anglo American and the ICT firms involved in the Global e-Sustainability Initiative (GeSI) have made a point of sharing their learning in such areas.[15]

In CSR literature, there is much more discussion of the aims of these systems (e.g. that they be inclusive, responsive, and engaged with stakeholders),[16] than there is of what they look like in practice. We examine the structuring of the CSR function in more detail in the next section, but it is typical for systems to evolve and change as the company becomes more familiar with CSR as a management area. Part of this is the creation of CSR capacity, and comparative research of company practices shows that systems can include capacity building both within the company (e.g. to understand CSR issues, or to engage with stakeholders) and among stakeholders themselves, so that they can interact more effectively with firms.[17] For example, through its Leadership Development initiative, 3M has taken the idea of ethics programmes a step further than many companies by having executives give examples of where opportunities for business advantage did not concord with the company's values, and then debating and undertaking role play based on how others would react in that situation. Some companies, such as Levi Strauss and Nike, are investing in building the capacity of suppliers to manage their human resources more effectively so as to avert the need for abusive labour practices, and others, such as Tesco, are training their buyers so that procurement practices do not exacerbate such problems.[18]

However, any single idea of how to manage CSR reflects received wisdom; it should not be treated as infallible truth. Research with managers from several leading companies has shown that following received wisdom can assist the CSR effort, but, at the same time, can lay potential traps.[19] For example, making the business case can help to explain why a company should take CSR seriously and legitimate the topic inside the business—but managers' experiences also show that it can cause companies or individuals to promise more than they can actually deliver or demonstrate, given the available data. In the long run, this makes it more difficult to make a compelling non-financial case. Moreover, the business case tends to be demonstrated using lagging indicators that only explain what happened in the past and do not necessarily help in deciding about future investments.

Structuring the CSR function

One area in which more detailed information about the actual management of CSR has emerged is the structuring of CSR management within companies. Some of this information takes the form of consultancy advice to individual firms and is not in the public domain, but what is available (both officially and unofficially) provides a reasonably detailed picture of actual CSR management practice.

A relatively early management guide on this topic identified what it considered to be nine essential steps for designing a CSR structure:[20]

1 understanding the drivers of CSR within the firm;
2 identifying the key CSR issues;
3 identifying and evaluating stakeholders;
4 identifying functions within the company that support CSR efforts;
5 analysing company systems, culture, and impending changes;
6 evaluating structural options;
7 developing a staff plan;
8 creating a structure for cross-functional interaction;
9 assessing the process and framework for budget and resource allocation.

At first glance, this can appear to be an unwieldy list of actions, but the steps can be divided between four main areas of activity:

1 understanding the drivers (step 1);
2 mapping what is already happening inside and outside the company (steps 2, 3, and 4);
3 coming to grips with existing systems (step 5);
4 designing a specific CSR management structure (steps 6, 7, 8, and 9).

Nobody knows how often this type of methodical approach is followed in real life, but it does highlight aspects of CSR structuring that have engendered debate within companies. These include the importance, or otherwise, of cross-functional interaction within the firm, decisions about resource allocation, staffing the CSR function, and, perhaps most significantly, deciding what is the most appropriate structure for a specific company. What has emerged is an array of structures. For example, at Pfizer there is a long-standing tradition of the full board of directors making major decisions rather than specific committees, and as a result, while some firms have brought specialists in at the non-executive director level, the company has sought to diversify the full board with CSR expertise. Another approach is to place formal responsibility for CSR issues in the hands of existing executives; for example, at Novartis the heads of legal affairs and human resources have formal responsibility for CSR issues inside the executive committee. CSR can also be placed in other parts of the organization: at IBM, it comes under the executive vice-president for innovation and technology; at Groupe Danone, the head of sustainable development and social responsibility reports to the company general secretary; at Telefónica, a stand-alone department was created, reporting to the head of corporate communications.

A survey of 254 managers and directors, who saw CSR as part of their role, found that they had twenty-three job titles.[21] Anecdotally, it seems likely that many companies have renamed their CSR function as 'sustainability'.[22] Another survey of 580 company structures worldwide found that, in 30% of cases, CSR was managed by an existing department, such as communications or HR, without staff who have CSR as their primary function.[23] Ten per cent of companies had set up non-departmental working committees to manage CSR and 4% had outsourced CSR activities to an external consultancy. However, in the majority of companies (56%) there were designated CSR personnel of some kind. The majority of these were either part of a stand-alone CSR department or team in the corporate centre (22%), or part of another department, such as corporate communications (24%). The remaining companies had several teams dispersed across the organization, either as stand-alone entities (9%), or as part of a number of different departments (10%).

These statistics tell us something about how far companies have moved towards the kind of idealized structure and systems that are depicted as CSR best practice. The fact that only 10% of companies have dedicated CSR managers in the regions or business lines suggests that there is a long way to go before the ideal of embedding CSR into business operations is realized. This is in marked contrast to the areas of knowledge management and quality management, in which specialists are less likely to be located in the corporate centre and more likely to be found in teams dispersed across the business. It also contrasts with the situation in companies acknowledged by their peers as CSR innovators. In Marks & Spencer and Unilever, for instance, CSR is embedded throughout the company. This has happened because those firms have evolved from a CSR focus to a sustainability focus in which issues such as waste, energy, and natural capital management are seen as essential to the future of the business.

There are strong arguments for structuring CSR in different ways. Some argue that it needs to be at the locus of internal power, so that CSR factors influence business decisions (e.g. housing it where prices and deadlines are negotiated with suppliers rather than in public affairs). Some believe that it should be at the nodes where key business areas connect, so as to build cross-functional influence. There is a widely felt sentiment that as important as a knowledge of CSR is an understanding of what affects company performance (e.g. operations, investors, sourcing) and, related to that, there is a desire among many external commentators for CSR issues to be dealt with in the operational functions to which they belong (e.g. employee issues to be addressed by HR; sourcing issues by buying; customer issues by sales and marketing).

However, as already noted, this kind of integrated CSR function is a long way from being realized in most firms. Furthermore, some management theorists argue that CSR managers are unlikely to have the complete range of organizational elements at their disposal (e.g. hierarchy, sanctions, rules), and more typically rely on 'partial' organization in which only sporadic conventional management elements are at the manager's disposal.[24]

Alongside the question of where to situate the CSR function lies that of how to resource it. Early movers in the field, such as The Body Shop, tended to establish separate well-resourced CSR departments that were a statement of serious commitment. Now, it is less certain how large a CSR department should be, or even if there should be such a thing. In a company such as GlaxoSmithKline, a small team is said to have made significant progress because it gained the attention and commitment of multiple departments, encouraging them to deploy their own resources and to incorporate CSR into their own practices. In other companies, such as Gap Inc., relatively large teams have been created because of the challenges faced in managing global supply chains; procurement is an increasingly important aspect of CSR management in both private- and public-sector organizations.[25] Moreover, none of these structures are static, as demonstrated by the evolution of CSR at Marks & Spencer described in Case study 6.

Discussion points

The structure of CSR functions is often seen as an indication of how serious a company is about realizing its CSR vision.

- Do you think structure is an important indicator of a company's attitude to CSR?
- Why have some companies rebranded CSR as sustainability?
- How would you structure the CSR function in a sports shoe or apparel company?

CSR as strategy

Underlying questions about how to locate the CSR function is the issue of an integrated strategy that makes CSR part of the corporate DNA.[26]

As early as 1973, Andrews recognized that:

> the overriding master problem . . . impeding the further progress of corporate responsibility is the difficulty of making credible and effective, throughout a large organization, the social component of a corporate strategy . . .
>
> (Andrews, 1973, p 57)

There is now widespread agreement with Andrews' subsequent point that a company's social policy should be as much a function of strategic planning as is its choice of products and marketing, or its establishment of profit and growth objectives. Indeed, numerous authors have explored CSR from the perspective of conventional management disciplines such as marketing and organizational behaviour.[27] As already noted, there is a widely held belief among CSR thinkers that companies should develop management approaches that establish CSR as a core driver of business performance, thereby fully aligning it with the firm's strategic operations.

This kind of belief is reflected in the definitions of the more evolved forms of CSR that we described earlier (see section 'Stages of CSR'), but there is often frustration among theorists that current CSR scorecards, standards, reports, and other widely used management tools fail to support strategic alignment or planning.[28] Subsequently, there is a stark contrast between conventional business management excellence and CSR management excellence. The former involves building a strategy that creates competitive advantage and then reinforcing that strategy with high-quality operational processes that lead to best quality and productivity. In contrast, CSR often creates programmes to tackle specific issues, and then puts in place systems to enforce and sustain what it considers to be ethical practices, finally producing a report reviewing its commitments and practices. In other words, there is a strong tendency to define excellence as the production of a report about programmes and systems, begging the question: is there any other area of business management in which this would be considered acceptable, let alone 'excellent'?

In contrast, the strategic integration of CSR means that CSR is seen as a business driver. It involves CSR creating value within the company and the company creating value for wider society. An example of this type of integration is when GE began to see spiralling health costs and difficulties in accessing health care as both a social problem and a business opportunity. It responded by investing in products that were tailored to the needs of specific markets around the world, instead of focusing purely on the best technology accessible only to the wealthy.[29] Moreover, as the quote in Snapshot 6.1 shows, serving emerging markets through this kind of approach has become central to the company's strategy for growth.

The GE case is an example of a strategy for offensive CSR, but strategic integration can also be applied to more defensive objectives. For example, it is already common for companies to use CSR as part of a strategy to protect their reputations, as was the case when leading IT companies, such as IBM, HP, and Dell, established the Electronics Industry Code of Conduct as a common approach to monitoring the CSR issues in their suppliers' operations. Similarly, Fedex applied integrated thinking in its collaboration with the Alliance for Environmental Innovation, with the aim of developing trucks that are 50% more fuel-efficient and less harmful to the environment than those it previously operated.

The examples given earlier imply that integrating CSR into business strategy is another way of making the business case for improved social and environmental performance. But true integration requires that there are processes to ensure that CSR imperatives are considered on their own merits in strategic planning, regardless of the financial implications. What proponents of integration claim is that the distinction between business imperative and responsibility imperative will become irrelevant, pointing for comparison to quality management, for which poor quality came to be seen as symptomatic of unproductive systems, just as waste, emissions, and environmental impacts are seen today. In this way, CSR ceases to be a contained entity, and becomes an inseparable part of a larger complex and changing system which, as van Tulder (2006) says, needs to influence different levels (at which it will take different forms) and functions such as marketing, quality control, financial management, and research and development.

Discussion points

Integration of CSR into mainstream business strategy is a widely touted ambition among both theorists and practitioners.

- What arguments might managers make to persuade a company of the advantages of the integration of CSR?
- If integration does not happen more widely than at present, how will this affect future developments in CSR?
- What examples are there of companies successfully integrating CSR into business management decisions?

Snapshot 6.1 General Electric—integrating CSR as a business driver

Edison once said, 'Vision without execution is hallucination.' Yet much of the information on managing CSR deals with aims, expectations, and general principles, and not with the detail of its implementation. Part of what is missing is the connection between the why, the what, and the how of transformation management, i.e. the rationale, the expected results, and the way in which these will be achieved.

GE, founded by Edison, which owns businesses in industries as diverse as aviation, transportation, energy, and health care, has been trying to make this connection since the mid-2000s, when it launched what it called 'Ecomagination'. Managers consulted across the company and with what were sometimes hostile external groups, and came up with a list of social and environmental issues in relation to which it could employ its assets to bring about change. They then created a business plan that committed company resources to set output targets which, not least, promised to double company revenues to $2,000 million by 2010 by developing products offering environmental advantage to customers. Nearly twenty years later, Ecomagination continues to drive business thinking across the company and since its launch, GE has invested $20 billion in cleaner technology solutions that have returned $270 billion in revenue. It has also reduced its greenhouse gas emissions by 42%. To put this in perspective, this investment is double what it predicted at the launch of Ecomagination, and emissions reduction is 10% more than expected in 2010.

According to GE, Ecomagination's achievements have hinged on moving clean technology and emissions out of a sustainability silo to making it part of their DNA. Managers point to five lessons from the Ecomagination experience:

1 Start with your own house: in order to succeed, GE began by finding ways to improve sustainability internally such as refurbishing lighting, installing solar panels, and energy efficiency. Learning from these internal projects is shared with the company's businesses to help them demonstrate or improve products for customers.

2 Figure out where you can make the biggest impact: no company can tackle every sustainability issue. GE is heavily involved in electricity generation and distribution, hence Ecomagination's focus on technologies in these areas.

3 Tap into your collective brain power: 'Never underestimate the power of your own people. We launched Ecomagination by inviting every department to submit its best project ideas.' Internal stakeholder engagement of this kind led to what the company calls 'a treasure trove of innovative projects'.

4 Stoke the flames of innovation: ecomagination began in the 2000s, and it has been vital to maintain long-term enthusiasm. GE has done this through employee engagement campaigns such as EcoAwards to recognize unsung heroes making a difference within GE.

(continued . . .)

5 Continue to stretch: the original Ecomagination targets set in 2005 have now been replaced by two more ambitious rounds of goals. Initially, the goal of reducing emissions by 1% in five to seven years seemed very ambitious, but that stretch target resulted in a 32% reduction in seven years. In 2015, the company said it would reduce greenhouse gas emissions and water usage by 20% by 2020, and is already close to achieving this ahead of schedule, with greenhouse emissions down 18% and water use down 29%.

(*Sources:* GE, 2005; Stewart and Immelt, 2006; Reed and Neubert, 2012; GE, 2017)[30]

Quick questions

Under long-time CEO Jack Welch, GE was widely admired by investors but repeatedly criticized for its environmental performance.

1. What evidence is there that GE has acted on the Ecomagination promise of putting CSR issues at the core of business strategy?
2. Are the reasons that GE gives for integrating CSR convincing from a shareholder's perspective?
3. What is the business case for Ecomagination?

The business case for CSR

Launching Creating Shared Value, Nestlé's business response to nutrition, water, and rural development challenges, Chairman Peter Brabeck-Letmathe said, 'The financial crisis . . . revealed once more a basic business axiom: if you fail to work on behalf of public interest and take short cuts that put the public at risk, you will also fail your shareholders.'[31] The term 'shared value' is also used by Porter and Kramer (2011). It refers to a resetting of the boundaries of capitalism by reconceiving products and markets so that they focus on social and environmental impact, redefining productivity, and embedding business activities more in local communities (e.g. through cluster development). The significance of a long-time advocate of business competitiveness and free market capitalism revisiting the purpose of business in this way has meant that shared value has gained attention even if it reflects well-established thinking in the CSR field. But Porter and Kramer argue that shared value is still driven by the profit motive: the difference is that not all profit is equal, and commercial activities with a social purpose represent a 'higher form of capitalism'.

Pick up any book on CSR, browse the session themes of conferences, or look at companies' social or environmental reports, and you will soon discern how important the business case has become to contemporary CSR. For business managers, government officials, academics, consultants, to name but a few, making the business case has become the Holy Grail. There is a simple reason for this—demonstrating a positive correlation between CSR and business performance is seen as giving social and environmental issues legitimacy in the world of mainstream business. In this way, it greatly increases the likelihood that CSR practices will be adopted. Consequently, information, such as that 91% of executives believe that CSR creates shareholder value, or that 80% say that non-financial indicators are essential to characterize future financial performance, is widely cited as proof positive of CSR's importance, not as the nice thing to do, but as part of good management practice.[32]

Making the business case has grown in importance as the focus of CSR has moved from philanthropy and generally giving a proportion of revenues back to society, to the function of CSR in core business activities, and the role of business in tackling major societal challenges.[33] Showing how CSR relates to business performance is intended to help managers to understand why they should be paying attention and to what they should be attending. It is also meant to help companies to explain the importance of social and environmental performance to investors, and vice versa. Meanwhile, away from the company-specific level, it provides a basis for CSR's advocates to demonstrate to mainstream management theorists and economists that CSR can add to shareholder value, or at least will not damage it.[34]

There are, then, good reasons why the business case has become so important to CSR. But the gravitas that it has accrued gives rise to further questions: What evidence is there of a business case? How does its presence or absence affect CSR now and in the future? Neither question is easy to answer and there is good reason to consider what the consequences are for CSR if the business case continues to be brought to the fore. But we will begin with some examples.

Examples of the benefits to business

When BP met its target of reducing greenhouse gas emissions at twice the rate specified in the Kyoto Protocol nine years ahead of schedule, the reductions were the equivalent of 9.6 million tonnes and the company achieved operational savings of $250 million. In 2012, Walmart's investment in fleet efficiency saved it almost $130 million and avoided emitting almost 103,000 tonnes of carbon dioxide, equal to taking 20,000 cars off the road. Dow Chemical estimates that if it could make its water filtration technologies available to the 1.2 billion poorest people in the world, it could generate $300 million in sales. When 3M pre-empted new government regulations by abandoning the use of solvent-based coatings in favour of water-soluble ones, it benefited commercially from having an early mover advantage, and operationally from reductions in downtime, product loss, and waste related to the new technology. Staving off regulation and repairing a severely damaged reputation were key motivations for financial institutions to set up the Equator Principles to combat corruption in overseas projects.[35] Gap Inc. has found that purchasing decisions that negatively impact working conditions also undermine quality, on-time delivery, and cost.[36] Major DIY and furniture stores, such as Home Depot, Ikea, and B&Q, have made sourcing from sustainably managed resources part of their buying policy. Even if there is not a clear financial case, as REWE claims about its commitment to sourcing all of its energy from renewable sources, a strong position can increase the company's leverage with government and civil society.[37]

Different industries; different countries; different dimensions of CSR—all suggesting that a link can be made between social and environmental performance, and business performance. According to the investment group Innovest, 85% of studies show a positive correlation between environmental governance and financial performance.[38] According to UK-based telecommunications company BT, the benefits of CSR to a company's reputation, and the money that can be saved through efficient environmental planning and the identification of new market opportunities, 'often amount to a convincing financial reason for why business should engage with such issues'.[39] According to one former executive, strategies built around the triple bottom line can yield a 46% increase in profit over five years, fully costed.[40]

Meanings of the 'business case'

Examples such as those in the previous section have generated considerable excitement about the business case, but they also highlight some of the problems in making that case. The case is more than just shareholder value or return on investment; equally, it can be the indirect benefits of creating a favourable business environment (e.g. maintaining reputation, innovation, licence to operate). It is not immediately clear which dimensions of CSR have the strongest or weakest links to business performance. It is also not always apparent what type of relationship exists between CSR and business performance, i.e. whether the one causes the other and under what circumstances.

Preston and O'Bannon (1997) divide the business case into three types of relationship:

1 that within which CSR relates to financial performance;

2 that within which financial performance relates to CSR;

3 that within which CSR and financial performance are synergistic.

In all three types, the relationship can be positive, neutral, or negative, so that according to Friedman (1962), for example, there is a negative relationship between CSR and financial performance because the former misuses company assets (see Chapter 1). According to Cornell and Shapiro (1987), there is a positive relationship because meeting the needs of stakeholders other than shareholders enhances financial performance. Case studies and other analyses exist for each type of relationship; for example, Waddock and Graves (1997) study how the strength of performance affects the amount that a company invests in CSR.

To make sense of the business performance–CSR relationship, we need to know what each term refers to. There are many different definitions available,[41] but Boxes 6.2 and 6.3 offer a generic set of possibilities applicable to a variety of industries.

Box 6.2 Dimensions of CSR

1 The influence of *ethics, values, and principles* on a company's actions, as evident, for example, in business principles, decisions, and legal actions.

2 A company's *accountability and transparency* for its CSR performance, as evident, for example, in its reporting and management systems.

3 A company's overall commitment and performance in social, economic, and environmental areas (i.e. the *triple bottom line*).

4 A company's record on *eco-efficiency*, evident, for example, in its minimization of adverse environmental impacts associated with product processes.

5 The *environmental product focus* of a company, as seen, for example, in its redesign of products to reduce their environmental impact (e.g. cradle-to-grave product stewardship).

6 The use of a company's resources to support the *social and economic development* of communities.

7 A company's respect for, and protection of, *human rights*.

8 Efforts by a company to foster a high-quality *work environment*, including health-and-safety issues, but also those such as work–life balance.

(continued . . .)

9 Involvement of the company's *business stakeholders* (e.g. suppliers, partners, contractors, shareholders) in implementing its CSR strategy.

10 The quantity and quality of a company's engagement with *external stakeholders* (e.g. civil society organizations, government) in relation to CSR.[42]

Box 6.3 Measures of business performance

1 **Shareholder value** Changes in a company's stock price and dividend.

2 **Revenue** Changes in a company's revenues due to pricing, market share, new markets, etc.

3 **Operational efficiency** A company's cost-effectiveness in turning inputs into productive outputs.

4 **Access to capital** A company's access to equity and debt capital.

5 **Customer attraction** A company's ability to attract and retain customers.

6 **Brand value and reputation** The value assigned to a company and its brands due to their reputation.

7 **Human capital** The knowledge and skills of a company's employees, resulting from the ability to attract, develop, and retain a workforce.

8 **Risk management** Exposure of a company's assets to short- and long-term risks.

9 **Innovation** A company's ability to maintain its competitive advantage through better products, services, and business models.

10 **Licence to operate** A company's ability to maintain a level of acceptance among its stakeholders that allows it to operate effectively.

The application of these measures is affected by several variables. First, each audience requires information to meet its specific needs. For example, business managers may want information that will help to convince their superiors or colleagues, while shareholders will want to know whether CSR pays, and governments will want information that will test whether CSR is a viable basis for delivering social and environmental benefits.[43]

Second, the business case differs from industry to industry. For a mining company, such as BHP Billiton, CSR might result in preferred access in future gold-mining projects, whereas for Aldi, the supermarket company, it might help the company to relate better to consumers in fiercely competitive mature markets, especially when the company owns low-end outlets in Europe but high-end ones such as Trader Joe's in the USA.

Third, the business case partly depends on how CSR is viewed within a company and on how developed that company's approach to CSR is. For example, since disasters such as the Texas refinery explosions and the Deepwater Horizon oil spill, BP has had to shift its focus from blue-sky thinking about a world 'beyond petroleum' (its slogan in the late 1990s) to safety, reputation management, and licence to operate. Shell, by contrast, which was once caught up in scandals about drilling rig decommissioning and its impact on local communities in Nigeria, is now able to exhibit leadership through its energy scenario planning work.[44]

Finally, studies of the business case tend to overlook how the local, national, or regional contexts affect the business case.[45] For example, there might be quite different arguments to be made for eco-efficiency in a country with a tough regulatory regime and a strong utilities infrastructure, compared with that in a country in which environmental regulations are weak, but the cost of energy or clean water is relatively high. Just as CSR can look different from country to country (see Chapter 5), so, too, can the business case (see Snapshot 6.2).

Discussion points

One reason for making the business case is that it helps to make CSR more comprehensible to senior executives and operational managers.

- Choose a particular company or industry with which you are familiar. How would you go about making the business case to the executive team?
- Is there a distinct financial performance case? What do you think are the strongest and weakest areas of that case?
- Pick a company you know that is working on CSR. Apply conventional marketing and entrepreneurship analysis tools such as Mullins' seven domains (Mullins, 2006) or Chan Kim's value curves (Chan Kim and Mauborgne, 2005) to understand the business case for one of its products addressing social or environmental issues.

Snapshot 6.2 Facebook: about face

The business case is not simply a question of economics; it also depends on the environment within which business operates. Everybody loves Facebook, right? It brings friends and families together. It is a shining example of how a giant corporation can emerge from a student's bedroom. It has a share price that leaves investors beaming. And yet since 2017 it has faced government investigations around the world, been accused of helping to rig elections, been fined for data protection violations. In July, during the football World Cup, it launched a series of adverts admitting that it had let customers down, lost their trust, and needed a new approach. Essentially, it was forced to admit very publicly what it had tried to deny for the previous twelve months: it had acted irresponsibly by building a business model that depended on selling customer data without their meaningful consent, and at times to companies whose activities were legally dubious.

But from a CSR perspective, what, if anything, did Facebook do wrong? From some angles, Facebook was a positive role model of a successful, technology-driven social service. Its product was free to users, who benefited from new ways to hook up and stay in touch with people around the world, and arguably learn about new products and services. Facebook had also grown into a platform for news content and information, allowing, for instance, political and other groups to network more easily. Above all, it was user-driven: Facebook has consistently denied that, unlike newspapers and television channels, it is not a content provider, and should not be governed by media laws.

From other perspectives, however, what Facebook did was irresponsible. Most famously, data given by users for a particular service (e.g. purchasing insurance), were then sold by Facebook to third parties who proceeded to harvest the data for their own purposes. In the USA, this generated data on tens of millions of people that companies such as Cambridge Analytica could use in its work for political parties, notably the campaign to elect Donald Trump as president. In the UK, Cambridge Analytica (which is no longer in business) is the subject of a criminal prosecution, and Facebook was fined for lack of transparency and failure to comply with data protection laws. It is also being blamed for making data available that was used to influence the UK's referendum on leaving the European Union.

(*Sources:* Ram, 2018; Ram and Thompson, 2018)

(*continued . . .*)

Quick questions

1 Has Facebook been irresponsible?

2 Is Facebook right to say it isn't subject to normal media laws because it is not a traditional publisher?

3 What can Facebook do to make itself more responsible in the public's eyes?

Evidence of a business case

The trouble with the business case is that, apart from individual company case studies that are difficult to compare, the evidence is patchy and confusing. Carroll and Shabana (2010) agree with the earlier findings by Margolis and Walsh (2003) that it is impossible to draw the conclusion that CSR helps or harms a company. Frustratingly, a decade after Margolis and Walsh, most articles about the business case for CSR (and more recently sustainability) discuss possible frameworks for analysis rather than attempting a systematic review of the evidence.[46] Alternatively, they try to identify a direct correlation between corporate social performance and financial performance as measured by share price, which is probably too narrow a definition of the business case.[47] It is probably more useful to consider business's justification and rationale for CSR in terms of the specific benefits to businesses in an economic and financial ('bottom-line') sense that would flow from CSR activities and initiatives.[48]

The consultancy company SustainAbility developed a matrix to review multiple reports, case studies, and academic analyses pertaining to the business case for sustainable development. Although not meeting the criteria of academic rigour required by business studies journals, it is a useful way of comparing the information about the business case found in very diverse sources. The matrix links the business measures of success with the different dimensions of CSR (see Boxes 6.1 and 6.2). For example, one could look at whether eco-efficiency affects a company's operational efficiency, or if there is a correlation between the firm's licence to operate and its attention to human rights.

The original SustainAbility reports identified twenty-one areas in which there was strong evidence that CSR positively affects business performance (see Figure 6.2).[49] The most demonstrable contribution was in the area of eco-efficiency, in which changes in the use of raw materials, recycling and reuse, reductions in emissions, and other new practices had tangible benefits in terms of shareholder value, operational efficiency, access to capital, reputation, risk management, and innovation. Eco-efficiency has become so prevalent in industries such as chemicals, energy, and electrical goods that it could be seen as nothing more than rational profit maximization, i.e. common-sense management practice. But it is relatively recently that pollution has come to be seen not as the inevitable by-product of economic prosperity, but as a form of economic waste,[50] and this change has occurred because of, not despite, the kind of transformation associated with CSR (see also Chapter 3).

There was also strong evidence that other dimensions of CSR are linked to better business performance, including protection of human rights, high-quality working conditions, relationships with external stakeholders, and transparency and accountability around CSR performance. What also stands out is that, whereas eco-efficiency delivers a wide variety of benefits, these other dimensions affect a much narrower selection of business performance measures. By far the greatest impact was on brand value and reputation, for which there is evidence of a strong positive impact from six different dimensions of CSR, although in emerging and developing economies revenue and operational efficiency are also important. The next most frequent area of impact was risk management, for which dimensions such as eco-efficiency, the development of environmental products, protection of human rights, and a commitment to values and principles all have a strong positive impact. In other words, CSR is most likely to have a strong positive impact on intangible, rather than tangible, aspects of business performance.

Figure 6.2 also shows that there are as many areas on which CSR has a neutral or negative impact on business performance as there are those on which there is a strong positive impact. Notably, the business case for engaging with business stakeholders appears weak, and engaging with non-business stakeholders cannot be justified in terms of financial

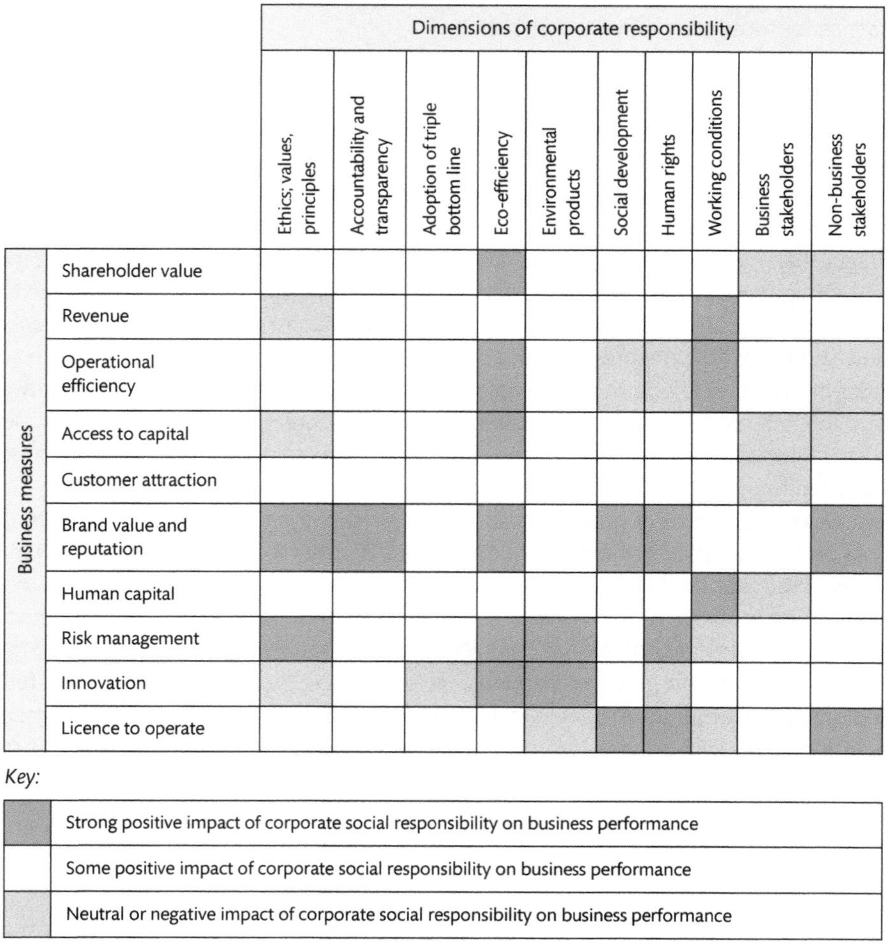

		Dimensions of corporate responsibility									
		Ethics; values, principles	Accountability and transparency	Adoption of triple bottom line	Eco-efficiency	Environmental products	Social development	Human rights	Working conditions	Business stakeholders	Non-business stakeholders
Business measures	Shareholder value										
	Revenue										
	Operational efficiency										
	Access to capital										
	Customer attraction										
	Brand value and reputation										
	Human capital										
	Risk management										
	Innovation										
	Licence to operate										

Key:

	Strong positive impact of corporate social responsibility on business performance
	Some positive impact of corporate social responsibility on business performance
	Neutral or negative impact of corporate social responsibility on business performance

Figure 6.2 Sustainability matrix

(*Sources:* Adapted from SustainAbility, IFC, & Ethos, 2002)

performance. Important dimensions of CSR, such as ethics and values and protecting human rights, also have a neutral or negative relationship to financial performance measures, such as revenue, access to capital, and operational efficiency.

The SustainAbility research is dated now but many of its findings are borne out by more recent work, and, as subsequent authors have emphasized, in assessing the business case, we are often using data that are difficult to compare, drawn from a mixture of case studies and quantitative surveys covering different industries and countries, and often focused on different dimensions of both CSR and business performance.[51] Salzmann et al. (2005) conclude that making the business case encounters two stumbling blocks:

1 the complex web of parameters (e.g. technology, regulatory regime, company visibility) and variables (e.g. location, industry, country, time) that can affect outcomes;
2 the difficulty of detecting the impact of CSR because, except in a small number of areas—notably, eco-efficiency and brand reputation—it tends to be marginal to business practice for most companies and industries.

As Margolis and Walsh (2003) conclude, in their extensive study of corporate social performance, there is little evidence to suggest that paying attention to societal impact damages shareholder value, although companies should not expect to be handsomely rewarded (Margolis et al., 2008). Some argue that, given how little evidence there is of damage to profitability, we should not be asking 'Does CSR pay?', but rather 'Under what conditions does CSR pay?'[52] This might mean explaining the specific conditions within a company or industry, but, more broadly, it might mean asking under what market conditions companies will maximize total value by taking account of stakeholder expectations.[53] In relation to the former issue, there are very few studies of how the business case drives CSR management, and most research concentrates on how CSR affects business success. Regarding the latter, the relationship between CSR and the four conditions of perfect competition (i.e. a large number of buyers and sellers, complete information, homogeneity of products, and free entry to and exit from the market), while alluded to by both advocates and critics of CSR,[54] has not been studied in depth.

It is a weakness in current business case literature that ways in which CSR might damage business performance are not properly explored. CSR's critics like to make the case that it is anti-growth and therefore that it deprives people of the benefits of economic growth which, for example, have raised living standards in successful economies. There is no evidence that CSR is inherently anti-growth; on the contrary, some advocates of sustainable development say that serious economic growth is needed if we are to meet the needs of current and future generations, and some companies clearly see that addressing social and environmental issues in the future will provide growth opportunities. But some companies, such as low-cost air carriers, would clearly suffer under tougher environmental norms, because air travel results in significantly higher greenhouse gas emissions than does travel by rail or sea.[55] Similarly, despite the instances of increased wages having been offset by productivity gains, it is counter-intuitive (and therefore demands further examination) that increased labour costs due to CSR will never affect company growth.

As important, though, is that most current studies are unidirectional, focusing on how CSR affects business performance and ignoring the ways in which business performance may impact on CSR. For example, few companies have followed Patagonia's lead in disclosing the pros and cons of the social and environmental footprint of its products, and providing the kind of information that consumers would require to make informed decisions about the performance-responsibility relationship.[56] This leaves unanswered questions such as the extent to which successful pursuit of revenue growth has a positive or negative effect on human rights or environmental management. As is explored further later in the text, in relation to criticisms of CSR (see Chapter 13), the implicit primacy given to the benefits for business is one of the concerns of some observers.

Not surprisingly, therefore, the evidence we have on the business case treats CSR as an instrumental benefit that can be divided into three types:[57]

1 CSR as a means of avoiding financial loss (e.g. by defending a company's reputation);
2 CSR as a driver of tangible financial gains (e.g. by improving the quality of the workforce, or by driving product innovation);
3 CSR as an integral element of the company's strategic approach to long-term business performance (e.g. by prompting a move away from dependence on non-renewable natural resources).[58]

Referring back to Martin's virtue matrix (see section 'Basic distinctions in CSR purpose'), some believe that a fourth type of business case is emerging, within which CSR is intrinsic to how companies learn, innovate, and manage risk in ever more dynamic and complex business environments (see Chapter 14). However, there is limited evidence of a direct correlation between CSR and financial performance. In one study, News International had the worst CSR performance but the best share price, while The Body Shop's good CSR reputation did not protect its share price when it suffered from poor management and may even have made it more susceptible to public criticism when it was exposed for making false claims about helping developing country suppliers.[59] Furthermore, the quest for a business case could hide the fact that other factors are at least as influential on CSR management decisions. For example, it has been argued that the widespread adoption of CSR reporting (see Chapter 12) is because of the readily recognizable analogies it has with financial reporting rather than demonstrable instrumental benefits.[60] Nonetheless, some companies, such as Monsanto, have suffered financially partly because of CSR failings, while others, such as Shell, have used CSR to rebuild a damaged image.[61] Perhaps the difficulty again lies in how the problem is framed and, rather than trying to demonstrate that CSR is a predictor or guarantee of certain outcomes, we should view it, for example, as an approach to strategy and management practice.[62]

Discussion points

Eco-efficiency is the main area in which a strong business case has been made, while reputation management is an important aspect of business performance.

- Can the success of eco-efficiency be attributed to CSR, or is it a case of rational profit maximization?
- In which industries do you think reputation is the main management driver of CSR?
- How would you make the case that CSR promises benefits to risk management?

Case study 6 Marks & Spencer's Plan A–The evolution of a CSR strategy

Marks & Spencer was founded in 1884 in Leeds, England. A long-time fixture of British and Irish high streets, it has over 1,000 stores around the world and is the 43rd largest retailer. Its UK stores have 35,000 product lines and it employs 82,000 people, serving 21 million customers weekly. Ninety-nine per cent of its products are own-brand, sourced from 2,000 independently owned factories and 20,000 farms which between them employ over 1 million workers.

In 2018, M&S announced a series of store closures and other cut backs due to a decline in sales, especially in its non-food lines. It said it was being hit by the general decline of the British high street and competition from online retailers. Yet despite this, the company maintains its commitment to a social and environmental responsibility initiative launched in the mid-2000s called Plan A. Then CEO, Stuart Rose, said that sustainability 'will shape everything about the way we do business', and this commitment was continued by his successor, Marc Bolland, who said that 'Plan A is now delivering more for our customers than ever before. It is creating great products with eco and ethical benefits'. Current CEO, Steve Rowe, has carried on the tradition of top-level support for Plan A. Announcing new targets for the period until 2025, he wrote, 'Business needs to find a new way to satisfy customer needs, one that is good for the individual but also equally good for the planet and communities too.'

With Plan A now in its second decade, there are two important aspects to consider. First, why has the company chosen to continue its support despite an adverse trading environment? Second, why has Plan A lasted this long and what lessons does it offer others interested in managing CSR?

According to M&S, Plan A is not a luxury: it feels companies must redefine the role of business in society, and this involves addressing issues that the company has an influence over so that it improves human well-being, transforms people's lives, and takes responsibility for its impact on the planet. If this sounds vague, one of the early innovations of Plan A was to announce 100 headline targets that it would be accountable for. The latest targets[63] include the percentage of global food sales coming from healthier products, supporting the worldwide workforce to provide 1 million hours of work-time community volunteering, and halving net food waste relative to sales. There is a financial aspect to this (£750 million in cost savings to date) and a reputational one (Plan A has won 240 awards), but given M&S's poor trading performance in recent years, it is hard to argue that Plan A's survival is due to revenues or public image. What else, then, accounts for the company's commitment?

An important reason for Plan A's longevity is that throughout its existence it has delivered conventional business benefits while changing internal and external perceptions of the firm. The commitment to Plan A was not an overnight decision; it was the result of a long journey. As long ago as 2000, M&S was experimenting with various ways to restore its company's reputation among consumers, investors, and the media after a chain of marketing and reputation failures. Among these were scandals involving genetically modified foods and pesticide residues, and although there was no question of illegality, M&S found it hard to defend itself in the court of public opinion.

The company's financial position was perilous, and although the need for change was apparent, high-profile radical action was out of the question. Instead, in keeping with the spirit of what some managers have since called a guerrilla war, a number of low-profile or off-the-radar actions were taken, such as building internal alliances among people in the company with shared CSR concerns, and building external alliances with organizations such as Greenpeace, Friends of the Earth, and WWF. These did nothing to lift the company out of its financial plight, but they did generate some much-needed positive news, and shareholders applauded in 2004 when it was announced that M&S had been chosen as the most responsible company in Britain.

(continued . . .)

Buoyed by this, the company began more coordinated initiatives that would eventually evolve into Plan A. Its commitment to fairtrade and non-GM food, as well as moves to cut salt and fat in foods, promote sustainability, recycle packaging, and protect animal welfare met with public approval. This became the spur for Plan A, which directly involved the CEO, the directors of technology and communications, as well as the head of marketing. They decided the first 100 priorities based on the company's impact, estimates of the cost of taking action, and an assessment of what the competition was doing about these issues. In many instances, nobody knew what the solution would look like, but insiders felt that the risk-taking culture they saw as part of the retail culture meant that it was more important to know what needed to be done than to know if it could be done. Plan A was formally launched in January 2007 with enormous media and public attention. In part, this was because in addition to full-page adverts and in-store promotion, Stuart Rose was willing to tell the Plan A story to anyone who would listen—that M&S was committed to becoming—'The greenest—genuinely the greenest—retailer in the UK'.

One can compare those initial 100 commitments with the state of play today by looking at Figure 6.3 and the 2025 targets on the M&S website. What has not changed is that the company is willing to be accountable, and each year it reveals its progress. As Mike Barry, now Director of Plan A and Sustainable Business, said early on the aim has always been to set benchmarks for the retail sector: '[Competitors] will have to take the same pillars and try to better our performance. But the 100 targets are already challenging enough; going beyond them right now would be commercial suicide.'

Climate change	Waste	Sustainable raw materials	Fair partner	Health
Making our operations in the UK and Republic of Ireland carbon neutral and helping customers and suppliers reduce their emissions too	Stoping sending waste to landfill from our UK and Irish stores, offices, and warehouses; reduce our use of packaging and carrier bags	Ensuring our key raw materials come from the most sustainable sources available to us	Improving the lives of hundreds of thousands of people in our supply chain and local communities	Helping thousands of customers and employees choose a healthier lifestyle

Figure 6.3 Plan A headline commitments

Another part of Plan A's evolution is the way it is managed. Responsibility for it was originally split between two teams: one, under the Director of Communications and CSR, focused on policy and was responsible for engagement, strategic direction, problem-solving, and communications support; the other, comprising successful M&S line managers, focused on delivery and was responsible for project management, integration, and making the business case (see Figure 6.4). Their focus, and one that continues today, was making sure that Plan A was implemented throughout the business lines, not by the team members themselves, but as part of everyday operations so that it became treated not as a sustainability strategy, but as a business plan and part of a five-pronged business strategy.

In terms of understanding how CSR is managed, it is informative to see how this has changed and what has remained the same. The continuing policy of integration means that much of Plan A does not sit outside other parts of company management. There is now a Plan A Committee that meets

(continued . . .)

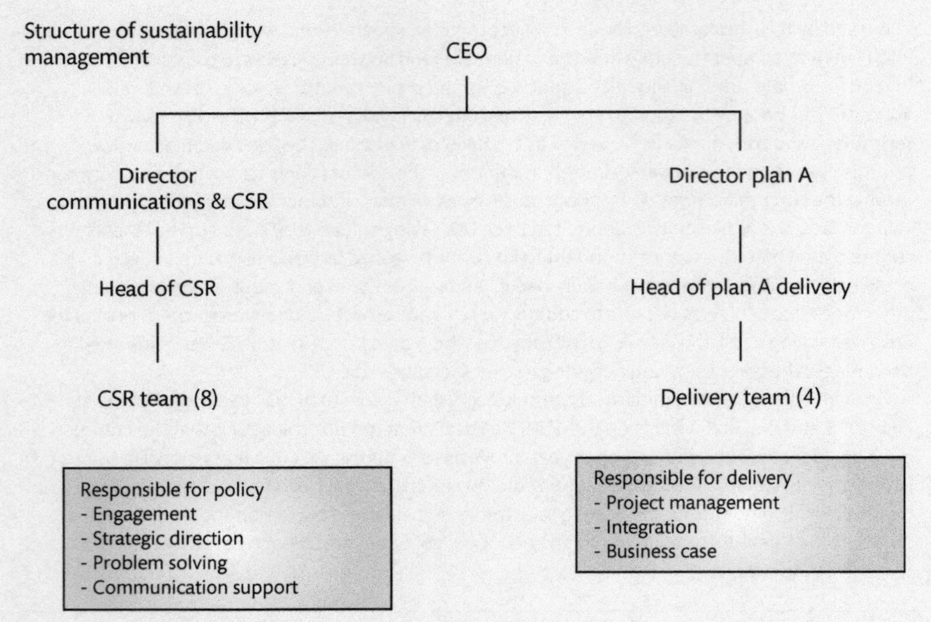

Figure 6.4 Early CSR management structure at Marks & Spencer
(*Source:* Marks & Spencer plc)

quarterly to ensure this integration is taking place, and reviews the company's progress against commitments as well as risk management. Senior management representatives from key parts of the business sit on the committee as well as the Director of Sustainable Business and the Corporate Head of Human Rights. The Committee chair reports to the CEO annually. The Committee also interacts with the Sustainable Retail Advisory Board, effectively a group of non-executive directors that meets every six months to provide guidance and insights.

(*Sources:* Rose, 2007b; https://corporate.marksandspencer.com/plan-a/delivering-plan-a#e53cfce7a74346158a8a06239c6f2971; https://corporate.marksandspencer.com/documents/plan-a/plan-a-2025-commitments.pdf; author interviews)

Questions

1. M&S provides insight into how CSR evolves within a company.
   a. What are the major changes in the M&S approach since the company first paid attention to CSR issues?
   b. Why do you think M&S continues its commitment to Plan A?
   c. What does the evolving Plan A management structure indicate about M&S's commitment to embedding CSR in the company?
2. Plan A has been described as setting the bar on CSR for retailing.
   a. What evidence is there that Plan A is more than a PR exercise?
   b. Are there responsibility issues in retailing that Plan A does not address?
   c. What evidence is there for a business case for Plan A?

(*continued*...)

3. Plan A was originally meant to end in 2012 but has now been extended until at least 2025.
   a. What are the key management lessons to learn from implementing Plan A?
   b. How do you think M&S's commitments are likely to change after 2025?
   c. Using the framework in Figure 6.4 and information on the M&S website, where do you think the different elements of Plan A have benefited aspects of business performance?

Summary

Managing CSR in companies is a form of change management, and, like other types of corporate transformation, CSR management activity is divided between identifying the purpose and intended results, establishing the principles and processes to achieve the end goal, and allocating responsibility for its execution.

Companies find themselves at different stages of CSR, which affects what the company wants to achieve and how to go about it. There are important distinctions to be made between *defensive* approaches to CSR, which are focused on reducing risks, protecting the company's reputation, and ensuring that it stays within the law, and *offensive* approaches, which employ corporate assets in finding solutions to societal problems. These approaches can be broken down further into evolutionary levels of responsibility, beginning with a focus on creating jobs, paying taxes, and abiding by the law, and eventually reaching a stage at which values are clearly at the heart of business decisions, the company is transparent about what it is doing, not doing, and hoping to do, and sees part of its role as standing out as a leader in tackling societal issues.

The further one gets from starting to implement CSR, the more difficult it becomes to state hard-and-fast rules for execution. While there is a consensus that good practice involves elements such as consulting internally and externally to decide the purpose, engaging with those upon whom the company impacts or by whom it is influenced as part of the management process, and communicating what the company is trying to achieve and the progress it is making, structuring the management function, building awareness and capacity, and deciding what actions to take will vary according to the company's culture, its industry, the regions it operates in, and the resources available. Another set of challenges emerges when companies take responsibility for the behaviour of their suppliers and others in their value chains, requiring the development of additional management styles and approaches, as companies committed to CSR seek out ways of improving others' performance, not least by exerting their own power as customers.

Further reading

Diehl, S., Karmasin, M., Mueller, B., Terlutter, R., and Weder, F. 2017, *Handbook of integrated CSR communication*, Springer, Basel, Switzerland.
Multiple articles on how to communicate CSR internally and externally.

Epstein, M.J. 2018, *Making sustainability work: best practices in managing and measuring corporate social, environmental and economic impacts*, Routledge, London.
New edition of this business academic's take on CSR management.

Holliday, C.O., Schmidheiny, S., and Watts, P. 2002, *Walking the talk: the business case for sustainable development*, Greenleaf, Sheffield.
Influential early argument by European executives emphasizing the importance of sustainable development to business success.

Schwartz, M.S. 2017, *Corporate social responsibility*, Routledge, London.
A comparison of the nature and roles of CSR officers in top management teams in different companies.

Werther, W.B., 2016, *Strategic corporate social responsibility: sustainable value creation*, Sage, Thousand Oaks, CA.
Aspects of the business case for stakeholder engagement and other CSR management practices.

http://www.oup.com/uk/blowfield-murray4e

Visit the online resources that accompany this book to enrich your understanding of this chapter. Among the resources available are web links, exercises, and additional case studies.

Endnotes

1. Maitland, 2006.
2. For a detailed comparison of country differences in Europe, see http://www.csreurope.org, accessed 26 November 2018.
3. See, e.g., Visser and Tolhurst, 2010.
4. European Commission, 2002.
5. http://supply-chain.unglobalcompact.org/site/article/126, accessed 26 November 2018.
6. PWC, 2006.
7. Cited in Kramer and Kania, 2006.
8. Holliday et al., 2002, p 27.
9. Hale, 2009; Quinn, 2009.
10. See, e.g., Schwartz and Gibb, 1999; Holliday et al., 2002, pp 142–49; Jackson and Nelson, 2004; Werther and Chandler, 2011.
11. https://www.nike.com/gb/en_gb/c/sustainability, accessed 26 November 2018.
12. PR News, 2006.
13. Ethical Performance, 2008.
14. PWC, 2006.
15. See, e.g., http://www.angloamerican.com/sustainability, accessed 26 November 2018.
16. BSR, 2002.
17. CCC, 2005a.
18. CCC, 2005a.
19. CCC, 2005b.
20. CCC, 2005c.
21. BSR, 2002.
22. See also van Tulder et al., 2013.
23. Melcrum, 2005.
24. Rasche et al., 2013a.
25. Harwood and Humby, 2008.

26. PWC, 2006.
27. Bowd et al., 2006; Jahdi and Acikdilli 2009; Weybrecht, 2009.
28. This section draws on Holliday et al., 2002; Olsen, 2004; Werther and Chandler, 2011. The authors are also very grateful to Steve Rochlin at AccountAbility for his ideas on this topic.
29. Stewart and Immelt, 2006.
30. https://www.ge.com/reports/5-ways-companies-can-weave-sustainability-dna, accessed 18 July 2018, accessed 26 November 2018.
31. Email announcing launch of Creating Shared Value, sent from webmaster@nestle.com, accessed 26 November 2018.
32. Ethical Corporation and Nima Hunter Inc., 2003.
33. See, e.g., Pinkse and Kolk, 2009, pp 79–85, on the business case for disclosing information relevant to climate change.
34. See, e.g., Hawkins, 2006.
35. Heal, 2008.
36. Fitzpatrick, 2004;http://www.corporatewatch.org, accessed 26 November 2018; Porter and van der Linde, 1995; Vogel, 2005, http://www.gapincsustainability.com/people/improving factory-working conditions, accessed 26 November 2018.
37. REWE, 2012.
38. Innovest and Environment Agency, 2004.
39. http://www.bt.co.uk, accessed 26 November 2018.
40. Willard, 2002.
41. See, e.g., Margolis and Walsh, 2003; Salzmann et al., 2005; Schuler and Cording, 2006.
42. Zadek, 2000.
43. Zadek, 2000.
44. Based on categories in Zadek, 2000; SustainAbility and UNEP, 2001; Zadek et al., 2003.
45. Salzmann, et al., 2005.
46. See e.g. Searcy, 2012; Schaltegger et al., 2012; Calabrese et al., 2013.
47. Schreck, 2011; Aguinis and Glavas, 2012; Barnett and Salomon, 2012.
48. Carroll and Shabana, 2010.
49. See SustainAbility and UNEP, 2002, p 31 for specific figures on developing economies.
50. Porter and van der Linde, 1995.
51. Barnett, 2007; Lim and Tsutsui, 2012; Servaes and Tamayo, 2013.
52. Amalric and Hauaser, 2005; Zadek et al., 2005.
53. Amalric and Hauser, 2005.
54. See e.g. Henderson, 2001; Holliday et al., 2002.
55. Holliday et al., 2002.
56. Zadek et al., 2005.
57. Zadek et al., 2003.
58. Zadek, 2000.
59. Zadek, 2000; Hopkins, 2003.
60. Etzion and Ferraro, 2010.
61. ABI, 2001.
62. Zadek et al., 2005.
63. For a full list of the 1,000 targets, see https://corporate.marksandspencer.com/documents/plan-a/plan-a-2025-commitments.pdf, accessed 26 November 2018.

Corporate social responsibility and governance

Chapter overview

In this chapter, we explore two main aspects of governance. First, we look at the connection between governance and responsibility by tracing the development of corporate governance frameworks as they evolved, prompted in no small way by reaction to previous scandals. Second, we examine how the governance challenges are affected by global issues at a time when the former are typically regulated under national law and the latter by their very nature are trans-boundary.

We consider some of the fundamental tensions that exist between governance frameworks and calls for greater societal accountability by examining traditional approaches to corporate governance which always place the shareholder, as the 'owner' of the business, at the centre of the accountability relationship, and protection of investment as the primary goal. We examine this model and then consider how and whether it might be adapted to offer greater levels of accountability to a wider group of stakeholders, and how CSR links to wider aspects of governance in a global context. We also explore how business challenges such as Sustainability (Chapter 3) may affect governance. In particular, we will:

- examine what is meant by 'corporate governance';
- explore the theories of corporate governance;
- trace the development of the UK corporate governance framework;
- examine international developments in corporate governance;
- look at how sustainability, and especially climate change, could affect governance.

Main topics

Key terms

- Accountability
- Auditing
- Stakeholder engagement
- Corporate governance framework
- Corporate malfeasance
- Governance and climate change
- Governing the gig economy

Introduction

In Chapter 2, we discussed the reasons for the move away from proprietor-run businesses to the limited company form of enterprise. We noted that this practice became the favoured route as businesses became larger and greater capital was required than could be easily raised by an individual, or even in a partnership. The issuing of shares made it possible to reach a much wider investment community and therefore easier to raise larger amounts of money.

In turn, however, the investor, whether an individual or an institution such as a bank or a pension fund, will expect that their funds are handled with care and invested in such a way that, in due course, they will receive a return on their investment. But this raises some serious issues for an investor. How can they be sure that their investments are going to be handled with the required levels of stewardship? What structures are there in place to ensure that managers do not invest in risky projects, or simply squander the investors' money on generous salaries and perks? Above all, in the context of CSR, how does corporate governance relate to the behaviour of companies and serve to encourage, restrict, or otherwise shape their relationship with wider society? In a corporate world in which optimum profit is the measure of success and reward, is there room for any notion of social responsibility?

In this chapter, corporate governance will be examined from the perspective of both the shareholders and their *agents* (i.e. company directors and managers). How frameworks of corporate governance have developed will be contrasted with the continuing scandal of corporate collapse and fraud. The role of the auditor will also be examined, to see if there is more that the audit process can contribute to good corporate governance in the face of persistent criticism from some quarters.

Key concept: Corporate Governance

Corporate governance 'deals with the ways in which suppliers of finance to corporations assure themselves of getting a return on their investment'.[1]

Our primary focus initially is on corporate governance as it applies to listed companies, and we have especially highlighted the situation in the UK. We have made this choice because the Anglo-Saxon notion of the firm, with the primacy it grants to investors and the role of capital markets, while not universal, has come to epitomize the efficiency and hazard of the modern company. It is also the case that the UK model of governance structures has been replicated in many other countries. However, we shall examine international guidelines developed to aid countries seeking to bring their own systems in line with international norms, and we recognise that not only have countries such as India, South Africa, and China developed their own governance systems, but also countries such as Germany have a governance tradition that is different to the Anglo-Saxon model.

Theories of corporate governance

Although there are exceptions, most large companies are not run by their shareholders, as would be the case in smaller enterprises; rather, they are run on behalf of the owners by *agents*, a board of directors, and a management structure that is intended to best serve the interests of the owners. Definitions of corporate governance invariably reflect this owner-agent relationship, and focus on issues of control and accountability in this context.

In the corporate governance literature, 'agency theory' articulates some of the conflicts of interest that must exist between an agent and an owner if agents cannot be readily held to account for their actions or are, perhaps, predisposed to act in a self-interested manner. It is easy to imagine how this might manifest itself in actual situations in which a manager might pursue policies that owners may not consider to be in their best interests. What, then, can shareholders do to ensure that managers return some of the profits and manage their investments carefully?

One frequently quoted definition of corporate governance states simply that it 'deals with the ways in which suppliers of finance to corporations assure themselves of getting a return on their investment'.[2] This very narrow definition predicates a huge volume of research in the field of accounting and finance, and is vigorously defended when the criticism is made that, for example, it omits the interests of all other stakeholder groups.[3] This shareholder emphasis is shared in many other influential definitions and discussions. Even the most recent version of the UK guidelines, *The UK corporate governance code* (FRC, 2016), relies on the 1992 Cadbury Commission definition:[4]

> Corporate governance is the system by which companies are directed and controlled. Boards of directors are responsible for the governance of their companies. The shareholders' role in governance is to appoint the directors and the auditors and to satisfy themselves that an appropriate governance structure is in place. The responsibilities of the board include setting the company's strategic aims, providing the leadership to put them into effect, supervising the management of the business and reporting to shareholders on their stewardship. The board's actions are subject to laws, regulations and the shareholders in general meeting.
>
> (Cadbury, 1992, p 4)

In an international context, the OECD, for example, broadens the scope slightly, but still maintains a strong shareholder/investment focus:

> Good corporate governance is not an end in itself. It is a means to create market confidence and business integrity, which in turn is essential for companies that need access to equity capital for long term investment. Access to equity capital is particularly important for future oriented growth companies and to balance any increase in leveraging.
>
> (OECD/G20, 2015, p 3)

Although some theorists argue that it is enough to recognize and manage stakeholder groups, others believe that companies need to be accountable to them even though they may have no financial interest in the firm. Stakeholder accountability is highly contentious and its position in CSR is contested (Chapter 9), but to understand how it has won a place in the development of governance structures, we need to consider the events that have brought calls for changes in corporate governance during the past few decades.

Discussion points

Directors of companies owe certain fiduciary duties to the owners of the companies.

- How far should a 'duty of care' include social and environmental responsibilities?
- What steps can directors take to demonstrate that they are taking their fiduciary duties seriously with respect to ethical issues?
- Referring to work such as that of Mallen (2012) and Corporation 2020 (https://www.corporation2020.org), what key features would you want to see in an alternative governance framework?

The 'drivers' of corporate governance reform

Two drivers of reform have been the changing nature of the beneficial owner and therefore whose interests are represented, and instances of corporate malfeasance.

Changing ownership structure

Like many countries that host major stock exchanges, the UK attracts investors from all over the world. Table 7.1 shows how the type of owner has changed over time. Notably, there has been a significant shift to foreign ownership, which now accounts for more than half of the shares traded in the FTSE 100. There has also been a decline in individual share ownership, which once accounted for over half of shares and is now down to less than 10%. These changes in share ownership have a number of implications for the governance of companies. First, it is not always clear who the beneficial owner is, and therefore transparency with regard to ownership of shares may be obfuscated for any number of reasons, most of which have governance implications. Second, we might assume that foreign owners may not be as keen as UK owners to curb activities seen as damaging to the UK, perhaps in terms of social or environmental stewardship. It may also be the case that foreign owners may not be as aware as UK nationals of the potential role for stakeholders in governance structures. What is clear, however, is that the increase in both foreign ownership of UK companies and, we might expect, UK ownership of foreign-based companies casts focus on structures of governance which transcend borders and bring notions of global governance to the fore.

Corporate collapse and malfeasance

There was no formal code of corporate governance until 1992, only guidelines on financial auditing, and nothing on such issues as the separation of the duties of the Chairman

Table 7.1 Summary of FTSE 100 company share ownership in the UK, 1963–2016 (%)

Category of investor	1963	1990	1998	2010	2016
Rest of the world	7.0	11.8	30.7	43.4	56.0
Insurance companies	10.0	20.4	21.6	8.8	5.0
Pension funds	6.4	31.7	21.7	5.6	3.0
Individuals	54.0	20.3	16.7	10.2	9.5
Unit trusts	1.3	6.1	2.0	8.8	9.1
Investment trusts	0.0	1.6	1.3	2.1	2.0
Financial institutions	11.3	1.1	2.7	12.3	8.1
Charities	2.1	2.3	1.4	0.8	1.1
Non-financial institutions	5.1	3.8	1.4	2.3	2.6
Public sector	1.5	2.0	0.1	3.1	1.5
Banks	1.3	0.7	0.6	2.5	2.0

(*Source:* The Office for National Statistics, http://www.ons.gov.uk)
NB At the time of writing, data post-2016 were not yet available.

and CEO, directors' remuneration, the role of non-executive directors, and so on. This all changed in the late 1980s and early 1990s as two massive frauds—Maxwell (Snapshot 7.1) and the Bank of Credit and Commerce International (BCCI)—which revealed failings of corporate governance contributed to the ability of individuals to steal company assets for their own enrichment.

Snapshot 7.1 The legacy of Robert Maxwell

In recent years, the UK, along with many other countries has been afflicted by mismanagement and corruption of employee pension funds. The British Steel pension fund scandal discovered in 2017 (deficit £2 billion) follows hot on the heels of the one at BHS (deficit £571 million). However, the scandal associated with Robert Maxwell, a publishing tycoon, who pillaged his companies' pension funds and left them with a deficit that about thirty years later has still to be paid off, helps explain the governance system that exists today.

Maxwell was a publishing tycoon whose empire included Mirror Group Newspapers (MGN). When he purchased MGN, he was plunged into debt that he could only finance by shifting money between his 800-plus companies. It was only after his death that the full story began to unravel. Failures were identified in the abilities of the existing regulatory bodies to draw connections between all of Maxwell's various companies and in the abilities of the regulators to instigate investigations. Non-executive directors were also accused of failing to inform the boards of those cash transfers which they knew about. The pension fund trustees were blamed for inaction, the Stock Exchange was blamed for failing to supervise the conduct of his listed companies, and the Serious Fraud Office was blamed for failing to start an investigation until pressured by a Swiss bank. In addition, in common with other fatal examples

(*continued* . . .)

of governance failure such as Carillion and Lehmann Brothers, each company had received a clean audit report from its auditors.

(*Sources:* Department of Trade and Industry, 1971; Bower, 1988, 1996; Clarke, 1993)

Quick questions

1. Would the separation of the CEO and Chairman roles have prevented this scandal?
2. Would following the Corporate Governance Code have prevented this?
3. Could the intervention of institutional investors have prevented this?

The development of the UK corporate governance framework

The ability of Robert Maxwell to appropriate the pension fund assets for his own use, depriving many Maxwell Group pensioners of their savings, caused outrage. However, similar scandals involving pension funds continue to this day (e.g. British Steel in 2017, Carillion in 2018[5]) despite more rigorous attention from the London Stock Exchange, the Financial Reporting Council, and the accountancy profession beginning with the Cadbury Committee, which started a trend for looking into corporate governance, and particularly the financial implications of poor governance.

The steps taken by relevant agencies since the Cadbury Committee are discussed below. They are part of an ongoing process that continues to evolve (a new Financial Reporting Council code is currently being developed and is due in 2019). The early initiatives were responses to specific 'shocks' to the financial systems, but later on in the process there appears to have been a much more coordinated approach to the codes of conduct that were developed, and this trend continues.

The Cadbury Report (1992)

In response to the grave concerns about the general sinking confidence in financial reporting, auditing, and corporate governance, the Financial Reporting Council (FRC), the London Stock Exchange (LSE), and the Consultative Committee of Accountancy Bodies (CCAB) convened a committee to consider 'the financial aspects of corporate governance'. It first met in May 1991 and was charged to consider:

> aspects of corporate governance . . . the way in which boards set financial policy and oversee its implementation, including the use of financial controls, and the processes whereby they report on the activities and progress of the company to the shareholders.
>
> (Cadbury, 1992, p 13)

It took the form of a 'code of conduct' for companies. It recommended that company boardrooms be constituted in such a way that they would feature appropriate sub-committees dealing with matters of remuneration, audit, and nomination, with independent non-executive directors and, more crucially, a separation in the roles and functions of the CEO and the chairman. At the time, there was some debate about whether to make the recommendations compulsory but, in a trend that continues today, companies were eventually asked to comply with the recommendations in a voluntary way. Indeed, the Cadbury Report is widely regarded as the pioneer of the voluntary approach that has become the model for other internationally recognized governance codes.[6]

In the following five years new committees were formed in response to continuing criticism of corporate behaviour addressing issues such as the setting and disclosure of directors' salaries, and the influence of institutional investors on company policy wherever possible. The recommendations of the three main committees were tabulated in a Combined Code (1998), which lists the responsibilities of companies and institutional investors. All of the issues of remuneration, audit, shareholder relations, etc., are covered. From now on, companies listed on the London Stock Exchange would have to either comply with the code or explain why they were not doing so, thereby giving some teeth to something that was ultimately voluntary.

All of this activity led the 1990s to be referred to by commentators, such as Charkham (2005), as 'the decade of corporate governance'. Yet despite this concerted effort on the part of interested parties, from the stock exchanges to the accountancy profession, to improve systems and thus avoid further criticism, corporate scandals continued. The fall of Barings Bank in 1995 had sent further shock waves through the financial world, but it was the collapse of Enron and Worldcom in the USA that, again, led to calls for further attention. The once dormant proposal of two US legislators became the most far-reaching (and hastily passed) piece of governance legislation—the Sarbanes-Oxley Act 2002. It was felt that the role being played by non-executive directors was not robust enough in terms of ensuring good practice and governance. Additionally, further criticism was levelled at the accountancy profession for what appeared to be a continuing inability to uncover signals of underlying corporate distress or malfeasance. This led to a flurry of activity to try, once again, to develop systems of governance that would be sufficient to prevent further scandals.

Three more committees sat in the UK before a revised Combined Code was published in 2003 which, depending on one's perspective, shows the rigorous or painful nature of any governance reform. These saw recommendations to increase the number and influence of non-executive directors, the relationship between internal and external auditors, which some saw as too cosy, and the role of the audit committee within the overall board structure. There was also discussion of diversity on boards, an issue that began to attract attention in the USA but not so much in Britain.

The financial crisis 2007-2008

The aforementioned Combined Code was always intended to be revised on a regular basis, but the 2008 iteration was particularly important given how the events of the preceding nine months were beginning to impact on the regulatory framework, most especially in the UK and the USA. In the late 1990s and early 2000s banks had rapidly increased their dealings in financial products derived from asset-backed securities. In simple terms, banks bundled investments and sold them on, making commission and profits as they went. The ultimate assets that backed these products were real estate assets, and as long as the value of property continued to rise, there seemed to be no long-term problem. Bank profits continued to rise, and although bonuses paid within the financial services sector drew criticism in some quarters, governments seemed loathe to intervene. However, in the summer of 2007 a train of events began to unfurl which cast doubt on the true values of these products, which included 'structured investment vehicles' (SIVs) and collateralized debt obligations (CDOs). Initially the stress on financial markets began to impact on securities backed by sub-prime mortgage lending, and the inherent difficulty of allocating exact valuations to these products.

On 9 August 2007 BNP Paribas froze three of its funds based on their concerns that they were unable to properly value their CDOs, fearing that they were underwritten by sub-prime loans. That action signalled to global capital markets that the bubble had burst. On 14 September, the British Bank Northern Rock, which had famously offered mortgages at 25% above valuation, needed to sell its securitized debts into international capital markets to maintain its liquidity. However, nervousness in the markets following BNP's actions created problems for Northern Rock, which was then forced to approach the British government to seek assistance. As news of the bank's predicament was made public by the BBC's then Business Editor, Robert Peston,[7] customers began queuing to withdraw their savings. In the months following, unsuccessful attempts were made to sell Northern Rock, finally prompting the UK government to nationalize the bank. House prices in both the USA and the UK fell, creating yet more pressure on these financial derivatives. In March 2008, the investment bank Bear Stearns was bought out by J.P. Morgan, and in September the US administration had to step in to give financial support to its main sub-prime lenders Fannie Mae and Freddie Mac. The next major shock came when the US merchant bank Lehman Bros filed for bankruptcy on 15 September, and two days later, in the UK, HBOS was rescued by Lloyds TSB.

The autumn of 2008 saw US and UK stock market falls and, in addition to individual banks coming under pressure, the effect began to impact on nation states, initially in Ireland and Iceland. In response, on 8 October 2008, UK, European, and US central banks cut interest rates to 0.5%. On 13 October the UK government took major stakes in the Royal Bank of Scotland (RBS) and Lloyds TSB, where undisclosed liabilities relating to the takeover of HBOS had been unsupportable.

The financial crisis created another shock to the financial system, to date the most serious since the Wall Street Crash in 1929, and like that crash which brought about the Great Depression that lasted for about ten years, the financial crisis continues to have ramifications in what European countries have tended to call a period of austerity leading to stagnation and cutbacks in health, police, military, welfare benefits, and education services. In part, this austerity has occurred because governments stepped in to prevent (most) financial institutions from failing, and the borrowing required to do so has resulted in a severe reduction in public-sector services.

Another long-term consequence has been the reluctance of capital markets to support corporate activity, especially in the banking sector, which has important implications in discussions about CSR and governance. Correct valuation of assets and liabilities lies at the heart of sound financial regulation, and the trust we can place on financial statements as a 'fair, balanced, and understandable' view of a company's state of affairs (value) is central to the advice given by the bodies that issue guidance on financial regulation (the FRC in the UK, and the Financial Accounting Standards Board (FASB) in the USA).

The financial crisis and the fragile state in which many banks found themselves prompted yet another review into the governance and stewardship of financial assets, known as 'The

Walker Review', which was published in July 2009. It was subsequently updated and blended into the Combined Code to become the UK Corporate Governance Code.

The UK Corporate Governance Code 2010 (revised September 2016)

This code consolidates the guides to governance and stewardship that have developed since the Cadbury Report. Indeed, they are at pains to stress that the definition of corporate governance is still the 'classic' definition:[8]

> Corporate governance is the system by which companies are directed and controlled. Boards of directors are responsible for the governance of their companies. The shareholders' role in governance is to appoint the directors and the auditors and to satisfy themselves that an appropriate governance structure is in place. The responsibilities of the board include setting the company's strategic aims, providing the leadership to put them into effect, supervising the management of the business and reporting to shareholders on their stewardship. The board's actions are subject to laws, regulations and the shareholders in general meeting.
>
> (FRC, 2012, p 1)

What comes through in reading the code is the emphasis that the FRC place on companies abiding by the 'spirit' of the code. They urge boards to 'think deeply, thoroughly, and on a continuing basis' (FRC, 2012, p 2) on their responsibilities and the implications of their actions. Indeed, the preface to the code is a call to directors to face the challenges of being responsible stewards of investors' funds, and also a reminder that mere compliance with the code 'cannot guarantee' effective governance.

This seems to impact on the 'comply or explain' principle which is described as 'the trademark' of corporate governance in the UK (FRC, 2012, p 4). This is at the heart of what is, after all, a voluntary code, although most companies abide by its provisions and markets see compliance as an issue of risk reduction and confidence. However, it means that if a company decides not to comply with the provisions of any part of the code, it should fully explain to shareholders the reasons and circumstances which give rise to the non-compliance.

The Code itself is split into five sections, covering leadership, effectiveness, accountability, remuneration, and relations with shareholders. In these sections each of these topics is broken down and guidance is given relating to duties and responsibilities of boards of directors to shareholders. A discussion on wider accountability and stakeholder relations is given in the following sections.

Discussion points

Codes of corporate governance have developed to include supervision of audit procedures.

- How effective can an audit committee be in supervising the audit procedure within a major corporation?
- Can part-time non-executive directors ever be effective?
- Using the example of a FTSE 100 company, how would you modify the workings of the audit committee to incorporate CSR issues?

International developments in corporate governance

On the international front there has been a convergence of international codes to mirror the needs of companies which are increasingly operating across boundaries and in many different corporate formations. The accounting bodies developed International Financial Reporting Standards (IFRSs), and an examination of some of the international corporate governance guidelines suggests a similar trend. East European countries, which previously conformed to Soviet accounting rules, first established their own 'Accounting Acts' but as time passes so the influence of IFRSs grows, and homogenization of corporate governance rules seems also to be the trend. However, in so far as it is expected that companies will observe the somewhat prescriptive nature of the IFRSs, all corporate governance codes follow the UK model and are explicitly 'guidelines'. Indeed, the preamble to the OECD *Principles of Corporate Governance*, states that:

> The Principles are non-binding and do not aim at detailed prescriptions for national legislation. Rather, they seek to identify objectives and suggest various means for achieving them. Their purpose is to serve as a reference point.
>
> (OECD/G20, 2015, p 11)

In keeping with the discussions we have had on the development of UK guidelines, so the OECD principles are concerned with 'transparent and efficient markets', 'protecting and facilitating the exercise of shareholder rights', 'timely and accurate disclosure', etc. However, the OECD does explicitly recognize the rights of stakeholders when they have been 'established by law or through mutual agreements', and 'encourage active co-operation between corporations and stakeholders in creating wealth, jobs, and the sustainability of financially sound enterprises' (OECD/G20, 2015).

In 2009, the International Corporate Governance Network (ICGN) revised its *Global corporate governance principles* (ICGN, 2009), with a view that they should be of 'general application around the world, irrespective of legislative background or listing rules'.[9] The ICGN is a global membership organization comprising, in the main, institutional investors who clearly have an interest in good governance. Their Principles, while in essence espousing similar approaches to corporate governance as the other codes we have described, also provide additional practical help and direction to those wanting to implement best practice.

As emerging economies seek to develop capital markets to encourage inward investment and joint venture arrangements, so corporate governance structures increasingly come under examination. In countries like China, where there is also a conflict between the traditional command economy model and the new free market approach, transition to that model is problematic, and many institutional obstacles still exist. There is also scrutiny of new employment contracts, exemplified by zero-hours contracts and other aspects of the 'gig economy'. These new arrangements are in part attributable to the power employers can exert as a result of being able to shift production to where wages are lower and corporate governance more lax (see Case study 7).

Discussion points

Corporate governance frameworks are not drawn up with CSR as a guiding structure.

- How would they differ if CSR were to become a major consideration?
- What changes would need to be made to the legal framework to incorporate CSR issues?
- What examples can you find from around the world (historical and contemporary) of legislative attempts to incorporate CSR into governance frameworks?

Commentary from a CSR perspective

In Chapter 3, we noted that some of the biggest changes to business could arise because of the challenges from sustainability, in particular climate change. Climate change exemplifies many of the global governance challenges that are testing the limits of nation-based governance regimes. There are four ways that climate change could affect business (Blowfield, 2018), and each presents particular problems from a governance perspective.

Type 1–The cause of companies' rise or demise

Kodak collapsed because digital photography swept away its film business. Olivetti, one of the Europe's largest companies, was the object for repeated buy-outs once the personal computer pushed the typewriter off office desks. Climate change could be an equally great threat to some firms and sectors. Industries dependent on fossil fuels might seem the most obvious example, although as the cases of oil and mining show there is little chance that hydrocarbons will vanish from the economy any time soon. However, companies producing gas boilers might want to look over their shoulders at the rise of heating and cooking systems based on renewable energy, and ones vested in centralized electricity grids should be cognizant of the disruptive potential of local grids (Bridge et al., 2013).

Equally, there will be climate change equivalents of Intel and Asus during the ICT era, companies who thrived at incumbent companies' expense because of disruptive change. In relation to the green economy, much was made early on of the potential of renewable energy to create new jobs and wealth, and China is now the world leader in this area (Fankhauser et al., 2013). Looking ahead, industries that can take advantage of low-emission manufacturing techniques, distributed production, reuse of materials, and the use of new compounds are all ones that could prosper in a climate-changed era.

The low-hanging fruit in transforming to a prosperous climate-changed society is found when a high-emissions, resource-intensive industry can be readily substituted with one that is more efficient in terms of energy and other inputs, and yet able to produce equally desirable products and financial returns. The difficulty at present is that the fruit meeting these criteria, such as LED lighting, are rare. There is no shortage of industries such as steel-making or cement, where the emissions gains of finding alternatives are obvious. (Cement facilities produce one tonne of carbon emissions for every tonne of cement.[10]) However, there are no readily available products that fulfil the same function.

Although this type of transformation does not have a direct governance dimension, it will result in company owners looking at different facets of business value to see where the firm is at risk. This is already apparent in company reporting, which often includes sustainability (Chapter 8), and this is only likely to increase if it becomes apparent that climate change is not being controlled effectively.

Type 2—The consumption challenge

The lack of low-hanging fruit where a high-carbon industry can be readily displaced by a low-carbon one in the way that typewriters were once supplanted by personal computers is an important reason why business often adopts an efficiency-based approach to climate change. This means that they treat emissions, water use, energy use, and other factors as inputs that can be reduced, recycled, or reused. Walmart is an example of this type of approach: over the past decade it has reduced emissions from its vehicle fleet and its stores, and has worked with its suppliers to reduce packaging and improve recycling. Marks & Spencer has taken this a step further with its 100 Plan A commitments setting out what it will achieve by 2020 in order to move in the direction of thinking what a sustainable retail firm will look like. The airline industry has made gains of about one-third by reducing aircraft emissions through the use of design, traffic control, and fuel innovations (Blowfield and Johnson, 2013). However, in each case, the company/industry itself is promising growth at a rate that means aggregate emissions will increase. The airline industry predicts that total emissions will be higher in 2020 than they were in 2005 even though the emissions per flight will be much lower (Blowfield and Johnson, 2013). This is because the industry is promising investors a growth in passenger numbers that outstrips its efficiency savings.

Of the publicly listed multinational companies, only Unilever has committed itself to decoupling growth in its business from increases in its environmental impact. It is rare for multinational companies to ignore climate change entirely, but many firms adopt flagship initiatives such as powering their stores with renewable energy (IKEA) or cradle-to-cradle product design (Timberland). There is little or no attempt to address the link between climate change and consumption (e.g. by reducing sales), and instead the assumption is that either carbon efficiency gains will offset any emissions increases from increased sales, or any rise in aggregate emissions can be offset by investments in reforestation, geoengineering, and similar carbon-extraction initiatives. Just as there are few low-hanging fruit because society wants to green what it has rather than radically rethink commercial enterprise in an era of climate change, so too is there a lack of appetite—despite the contradictions inherent to current prominent initiatives—to consider how one might transform business to be congruent with the demands of that era.

The consumption/over-consumption aspect of sustainability is the focus of many civil society campaigns and green-leaning political parties (e.g. Klein, 2015), and Case study 3 shows how some companies have addressed this. However, there is a general lack of appetite among law-makers in particular to guide companies on what they can produce. Procurement codes and similar guidance such as that used by organizations such as the British National Health Service represent a form of voluntary governance, just as ethical trade has done by using leverage opportunities within supply chains. Governments currently favour 'nudge' approaches such as the introduction of a tax on plastic bags in Ireland and the UK, or the use of incentives (e.g. subsidies for alternative energy). But given how important consumption is to national economic growth, market-based rather than governance solutions to production and consumption are likely to be favoured.

Type 3—Unpopular views and actions

There are schools of thought that argue that the obvious conclusion from the examples above is that capitalism, economic growth, and business are each to a greater or lesser degree the main barrier to achieving prosperity in an era of climate change. Klein (2015), Jackson (2011), and Bulkeley and Newell (2015) respectively make these arguments, which are very compelling for some people. However, they are also flawed ones. For example, declaring that climate change represents a crisis of capitalism, as Klein does, may or may not be true, but it does not point towards a practical way of addressing the consequences of climate change for society or the natural environment. Her theme that capitalism can be replaced with something better is an ideological one that requires us to believe that major ideological shifts equivalent to the one from feudal society to capitalism can be carried out in the few decades that climate change modellers have shown are crucial for meaningful action to prevent catastrophic change. Historically, there are no examples of such rapid fundamental change except as a consequence of natural disasters or war, and equally little evidence that governance measures have been employed (or are effective) to initiate such change.

Similarly, those who make the case for prosperity without economic growth do not seriously address how the transformation from a growth-based system to a steady-state economy would take place. How, for example, would existing debts be repaid, and if there was no borrowing with interest (something that is only made possible by growth) how would new hospitals, schools, and the new infrastructure of a green economy be funded? According to the Office of National Statistics, UK government debt is £1.6 trillion (84% of GDP). Household and corporate debt are both at a similar percentage of GDP, and financial-sector debt is nearly 200%.[11] None of this could be paid off without economic growth or unprecedented levels of deflation. When UK debt stood at 200% after World War II, it took over five decades to repay loans to the USA, and this was only possible because of a historically high compounded growth rate of 2.6%. It is hard to see how these kinds of growth rates can be achieved in advanced economies in future (Gordon, 2016).

In highlighting the difficulties of tackling climate change through the putting in place of fundamentally different economic systems, we are not trying to defend the status quo. However, we are making the serious point that the economic, business, and political status quo cannot be discounted as a force that has to be taken into consideration when tackling climate change, and as the contributors to Boeger and Villiers (2018) show, governance actions in this regard are severely lacking.

The same is true when it comes to looking at individual industries. For example, there is a strong ideological and indeed scientific case to outlaw fossil fuels as a source of energy and as a raw material. But how would this be achieved without causing a level of disruption that would jeopardize the political and economic feasibility of tackling climate change? Even if there were sufficient renewable and nuclear energy available—something that is unlikely to happen until the second half of this century at the earliest (Nelson et al., 2014)—it would not fully replace fossil fuels.

Fear that support of fossil fuels as part of a climate-changed economy will be met with a backlash, not least from those who think business is a main cause of the climate change problem, means that it can be difficult for business to develop coherent policies. It can also mean that investors are reluctant to put money into important but seemingly perverse technologies, such as carbon capture and storage, for fear that they will be criticized for being supporters of fossil fuels (Richter, 2014).

Type 4—New business

As an alternative to new approaches to governance by law-makers, it has been argued that legislation should support new types of business suited to the needs of sustainable societies. Within companies such as Renault and Caterpillar, remanufacturing has been introduced to enable the same materials to be used multiple times in line with the principles of a 'circular economy', i.e. a development cycle that preserves and enhances natural capital, optimizes resource yields, and minimizes system risks by managing finite stocks and renewable flows. The circular economy is also at the heart of new companies such as Cirkle, a Belgian food-processing and food-waste firm, and Riversimple, the UK car producer. It builds on principles already familiar to companies that have embraced cradle-to-cradle manufacturing (e.g. Herman Miller) and the Natural Step (e.g. Interface; Case study 3). Similar principles have also been adopted within companies such as Nike and Philips. Common to all such initiatives is that products are designed to reduce material usage, to increase the opportunities for reuse, and to enable the management of the product's post-production life.

There are other technological innovations that enable new types of business to emerge. Additive manufacturing, for instance, promises less waste compared to traditional lathes and mills, but is also well-suited to local production of products designed almost anywhere in the world with adequate internet connectivity. Mason (2015) describes new business/economic models in a theory he calls 'postcapitalism'. He points to three features of a new economic system: collaborative production divorced from traditional business structures and ownership models; the replacement of markets built on resource scarcity with a system that creates value from the abundance of information readily available to almost anyone; and the changing nature of work, particularly because of automation.

Postcapitalism is a theory, glimmers of which can be seen in the current economy. There are examples under the broad umbrella of social entrepreneurship that show how new business is being created within the parameters of the existing economic system (e.g. ITC's e-Choupal initiative for farmers in India; KickStart which is developing locally made tools for farmers in Kenya). Companies such as Selco and M-Kopa, providers of off-grid solar energy in India and Kenya, respectively, have developed new business models that specifically meet the needs of rural communities, and the poor and marginalized (Jack and Suri, 2011).

A feature of these initiatives is that they link technological and financial innovation, something that Perez (2002) says is a characteristic of any major transformation in the capitalist era. What is less obvious is any governance innovation. Social enterprises are typically small, privately owned businesses, and typically do not offer the opportunities for joint ownership and long-term benefit that have long been a feature of cooperatives (Nicholls and Teasdale, 2017). This is a significant work-in-progress at the present time because it means that a value proposition framed in terms of climate change impact is always subservient to conventional laws on ownership, accountability, labour, and other aspects of corporate governance.

Discussion points

A number of governance initiatives offer companies the opportunity to adopt voluntarily certain standards of conduct.

- How effective can voluntary codes ever be?
- Why are market-based solutions to climate change preferred to regulatory ones?
- How can more individuals from minority and hitherto marginalized groups gain representation on company boards?

Snapshot 7.2 Company law reform—the Companies Act 2006

The Companies Act came into effect in 2006 and remains the primary legislation affecting corporate governance in the UK. For many who had campaigned for wider changes in company law reform the early signs were encouraging, but on publication there was criticism that social and environmental responsibilities had been relegated to no more than 'a consideration'. Parts of the Act are reproduced below.

s. 172 Duty to promote the success of the company

> **(1)** A director of a company must act in the way he considers, in good faith, would be most likely to promote the success of the company for the benefit of its members as a whole, and in doing so have regard (amongst other matters) to—
>
> - the need to foster the company's business relationships with suppliers, customers and others,
> - the impact of the company's operations on the community and the environment . . .

We can note here that the directors owe a duty 'to promote the success of the company' for the benefit of 'its members' (shareholders) and 'have regard' to the company's impact in social and environmental terms. However, a closer examination of s. 417 of the Act, which deals with the 'Directors Report: Business Review', reveals that in the case of quoted companies the following applies:

> **(5)** In the case of a quoted company the business review must, to the extent necessary for an understanding of the development, performance or position of the company's business, include information about—
>
> - environmental matters (including the impact of the company's business on the environment),
> - social and community issues, including information about any policies of the company in relation to those matters and the effectiveness of those policies . . .

(*Source:* http://www.legislation.gov.uk/ukpga/2006/46/contents)

Quick questions

1 How does company law relate to corporate governance structures, and which has precedence?

2 Taking the climate change example, how might the impacts affect the 'development, performance or position of the company's business'?

3 Where can a company find guidance or a framework which would help it to comply with the provisions of s. 417 of the Act?

Discussion points

Most codes of corporate governance stress the importance of shareholders over other stakeholders.

- What groups of stakeholders might have particular interests in issues of corporate governance?
- Is it useful and possible to consider the natural environment as a stakeholder?
- Imagining that you are an activist shareholder, how would you argue for greater stakeholder representation in the company's governance structures?

Case study 7 Uber

Uber operates in over 600 cities in the world. It calls itself a developer, marketer, and distributor of apps to organize car transportation and food delivery. And therein lies one of this fast-expanding company's problems. Is Uber simply in the app business, or is it an employer of drivers? The company, and especially its co-founder and long-term CEO, Travis Kalanick, argued that drivers were contractors and were not entitled to any of the protections and rights granted to employees under employment law. Others, including competitors in the traditional taxi business, as well as some Uber drivers themselves, said that the company—by requiring drivers to be available at certain times, be on call for long periods, and accept any jobs the company sent their way, was using drivers as employees, not self-employed, as Uber claimed.

Uber, despite being less than ten years old, is already at the centre of various controversies. Traditional competitors said Uber bypassed local licensing and safety laws and amounted to unfair competition. Drivers protested in Berlin, London, Paris, and Madrid in 2014, and in 2016 in Jakarta, thousands of local taxi drivers mounted a mass protest against Uber. Many of these protests were dismissed as a typical reaction to a new technology usurping an old one, just as had happened throughout history. But there were also complaints from other quarters that Uber's drivers were unsafe, and that the company should be held accountable for their actions. There were allegations of sexual assault and other crimes against passengers. Moreover, senior management faced repeated allegations of sexual harassment, and Kalanick himself had to apologize when he was caught on video for berating an Uber driver, who accused the company of making him bankrupt.

In legal terms, things started to come to a head in 2015 when the South Korea government introduced legislation to outlaw unregistered drivers 'working for' Uber. The company had to suspend its service in Seoul. Then in 2016 two Uber drivers took the company to court, claiming they were being denied their rights as employees. This case was critical, not just for Uber, but for the numerous other gig economy companies whose business model critically depended on a workforce categorized as self-employed contractors rather than the more expensive 'employee'. Such people could number over 450,000 across the UK (at least ten times more than work in the steel industry), costing up to £314 million a year in lost tax and employer national insurance contributions. Uber argued that it was a technology firm, not a transport business, and that its drivers were independent self-employed, who could choose where and when they worked. However, evidence from the drivers suggested this was not the case, and that they were treated as employees, without the right to decide where and when they worked.

The drivers won the case. In a landmark decision for the gig economy as a whole, the judges said:

> The notion that Uber in London is a mosaic of 30,000 small businesses linked by a common 'platform' is to our minds faintly ridiculous. Drivers do not and cannot negotiate with passengers . . . They are offered and accept trips strictly on Uber's terms.

(continued . . .)

Kalanick hit back and said the judges were denying consumers the right to the high-quality, affordable service that Uber offered. In media stories, members of the public interviewed seemed to agree, saying how much they appreciated the effect Uber had on their lives. As had happened in Seoul and Seattle, Kalanick tried to portray the authorities as being out of touch with the public's wants.

It was, therefore, a surprise when Transport for London (TfL), the executive responsible for all public transport in the city, said it was suspending Uber's operating licence. This was not because of the court ruling, but the company's approach to reporting serious criminal offences, its approach to how driver medical certificates and police checks are obtained, and the use of software that TfL feels could be used to block regulators from gaining full access to the app to undertake regulatory or law enforcement duties. Kalanick again hit back, saying London's mayor was out of touch. An online petition to 'save' the Uber service got nearly 750,000 signatures. However, TfL refused to budge, and in fact won sympathy from governments around the world, who were sick of what they saw as Kalanick's bullying behaviour.

It seemed others were also tired of Kalanick after the various lawsuits, protests, and allegations. In 2017, he was ousted as CEO by the company's largest shareholders, and replaced by Dara Khosrowshahi, who immediately set off on a worldwide fence-mending tour, including meeting the London mayor and giving a personal apology for how Uber had behaved. He also accepted that the status of drivers would be revisited, something that may have sent shivers down the spines of other pioneers of the gig economy, but could be interpreted as a step up in the maturity of this innovative but contentious model of business.

(*Sources:* https://www.change.org/p/save-your-uber-in-london-saveyouruber; https://www.theguardian.com/technology/2016/oct/28/uber-uk-tribunal-self-employed-status; http://www.independent.co.uk/news/business/news/uber-petition-london-ban-730000-signatures-tfl-sadiq-khan-taxi-licence-expire-not-renew-a7965331.html; https://en.wikipedia.org/wiki/Uber_(company))

Questions

1. Uber has argued that it is not a taxi company but a technology one.
   a. Why does it want to make this distinction?
   b. Does calling drivers self-employed contractors change the CSR of the company?
   c. Were the two London drivers justified in taking Uber to court?
2. The Uber online petition says that the company is defending the livelihoods of 40,000 drivers—and the consumer choice of millions of Londoners.
   a. Do you agree with this statement?
   b. If 40,000 drivers depend on Uber for their living, why did the drivers take Uber to court?
   c. How much importance should be attached to consumer rights and needs when thinking about CSR?
3. Uber is an example of how conventional employment law struggles to deal with issues in new industries such as the ones inhabited by Uber, Deliveroo, Just Eat, and Yodel.
   a. Is there a role for CSR to fill this governance vacuum?
   b. Did corporate governance play a role in ousting the original CEO?
   c. What key features should any new legislation dealing with Uber's troubles contain?

Summary

Increasingly, the connection between CSR and corporate governance is being made by commentators and policy-makers who stand outside the rather specialized field of corporate governance itself. That field has a firm background in and connection with the accounting profession and those involved in regulating capital markets. It is one largely controlled and influenced by the accounting profession, and the main organ of governance in the UK, the Financial Reporting Council, is largely populated by members of this profession. What seems clear in studying these bodies is that the primacy of the shareholder remains, and whatever pressure is brought to bear to widen the responsibility of corporations to be accountable to a wider range of stakeholders than at present seems remote at the present time.

This might not be surprising. Any move away from this model would have huge implications for markets around the world, and there would be a natural reluctance for any single jurisdiction to make the first move in widening accountability. The fear of a market backlash or actions by companies to move operations in advance of any change would be sufficient to deter policy-makers from pressing for change.

Yet we also know that things are still not ideal. The aftermath of the financial crisis of 2007–2008 has left some banks, to a greater or lesser extent, still in public ownership, and debates about splitting such institutions into 'good' and 'bad banks' continues. Ten years on, the amount of public funds used to support these institutions continues to impact on the lives of the populations of many countries, with unemployment rates in several European countries, in particular, creating public unrest. As if that were not bad enough, we know that, in many cases, the manner in which large corporations consume resources is unsustainable, yet there is no place for sustainability to be part of any governance regime to date.

As companies have become more flexible in their operations and, owing to a number of factors, more are able to move spheres of operations to respond to economic and commercial opportunities, so governance becomes more problematic. Furthermore, the nature of work itself is changing—evident, for example, in the emergence of zero-hours contracts, and the stagnation of average wages in many industrialized countries. As discussed in Case study 7, a new wave of automation as the result of advances in Artificial Intelligence also means that a growing number of workers are competing for jobs with machines (Frank et al., 2017).

It is not just that companies can move production elsewhere; they can also choose their domicile for taxation purposes. We have not looked specifically at taxation as a governance issue, but a case can easily be made that it is an issue of CSR. On the one hand, it can be argued that companies have a moral obligation to pay taxes where they fall due. On the other, companies who obey national laws and who structure their corporate activities to manufacture in one location, and have marketing, administrative, and sales functions in other locations, will, and do, claim that they are breaking no laws. (See also Chapter 5.)

As years go by and the scientific evidence strengthens the case for greater regulation in the areas of emissions and consumption, so the governance of companies, in the widest sense, will remain a focus of discussion among many sectors of society. The challenges in this area are exemplified by the global nature of climate change governance. The next potential milestone in this process may be the introduction of 'integrated reporting' by companies.

This is an international initiative being developed by the International Integrated Reporting Committee (IIRC), which has already published consultation documents and is piloting the project with 100 global businesses. The basic premise on which integrated reporting is based is related to the need for reports to be forward-looking and to address the complexity that running a group of large companies involves. It will cover issues of organization, operations, strategic objectives, performance, future outlook, and governance.[12]

Further reading

Boeger, N. and Villiers, C. (eds) 2018, *Shaping the corporate landscape: towards corporate reform and enterprise diversity*, 1st edn, Hart Publishing, Oxford.
Insights from different perspectives on the challenges confronting corporate governance from the perspectives of CSR and sustainability.

Charkham, J. 2008, *Keeping better company*, Oxford University Press, Oxford.
Comparison of governance strategies in five different countries.

Mallen, C.A. 2012, *Corporate governance*, Oxford University Press, New York.
Internationally focused textbook on corporate governance.

Solomon, J. 2013, *Corporate governance and accountability*, John Wiley, Chichester.
Latest edition of an overview of governance and accountability issues.

http://www.oup.com/uk/blowfield_murray4e

Visit the online resources that accompany this book to enrich your understanding of this chapter. Among the resources available are web links, exercises, and additional case studies.

Endnotes

1 Shleifer and Vishney, 1997.
2. Shleifer and Vishney, 1997.
3. See, e.g., Sternberg, 1996; Jensen, 2001.
4. At the time of writing, the UK's Financial Reporting Council is undertaking a comprehensive review of the Corporate Governance Board with the intention that this be presented in 2019.
5. https://www.ft.com/content/01d4ad66-11b1-11e8-8cb6-b9ccc4c4dbbb; https://www.ft.com/content/c9f0e038-04f2-11e8-9650-9c0ad2d7c5b5, both accessed 20 July 2018 (subscription only).
6. http://www.icgn.org, accessed 26 November 2018.
7. Afterwards Economics Editor for BBC News.
8. FRC, 2012.
9. http://www.icgn.org, accessed 26 November 2018.
10. http://blogs.ei.columbia.edu/2012/05/09/emissions-from-the-cement-industry, accessed 26 April 2018.
11. https://www.ons.gov.uk/peoplepopulationandcommunity/personalandhouseholdfinances/incomeandwealth/bulletins/householddisposableincomeandinequality/financialyearending2017, accessed 6 December 2018.
12. For more information, see http://www.theiirc.org and http://www.icaew.com, accessed 26 November 2018.

Corporate social responsibility reporting

Chapter overview

For many years companies have been issuing CSR reports—not that they were called corporate responsibility reports in the early days, any more than the activities that we now count as CSR were thought of as such. The first reports that appeared were normally included as a section in the annual report. Only latterly have companies begun to issue 'free-standing' environmental, sustainability, or other types of report, now grouped under the term 'CSR'. In this chapter we look at the development of CSR reporting through an examination of social reporting practice dating back to the 1980s and before—an activity which has invariably involved companies making voluntary disclosures about their activities, only very rarely driven by a statutory requirement. We examine some of the enduring issues that have created difficulties for companies who take the decision to make such reports, such as:

- Who is the intended audience?
- What do we include or leave out?
- How do we account for the contents?
- Who should write the report?
- Is there a PR element to all of this?

We question the subtleties that exist between the reasons why companies might wish to develop CSR initiatives, and the (sometimes very different) reasons why they might wish to report on these practices. We look at the focus of such practices on issues such as accountability, transparency, and also sustainability, as many reports now encompass a company's engagement with the sustainable development agenda. This aspect has been given greater impetus, first, in the wake of suggested failures in conventional financial reporting practice in the financial crisis of 2007–2008 and, second, in the scientific evidence relating to resource depletion and climate change in the same period.[1] We also plot the rise in the practice of surveying such reporting activity and review longitudinally some of the better-known initiatives that have continued since the early 1990s, most easily illustrated by examining the KPMG surveys which have been conducted since 1993, initially focusing on environmental reports,[2] then on sustainability reports,[3] and latterly on CSR reports.[4] Thereafter, we look at how CSR reporting is likely to develop in the coming decade as the world of work changes due to automation and new types of employment grow, and as new evidence is presented on environmental degradation and climate destabilization. In particular, we will:

- trace the emergence and development of CSR (social) reporting;
- discuss the voluntary nature of the reports and the issues that surround this feature;
- examine the theories which might help explain the practice of CSR and CSR reporting;
- explore surveys of CSR reporting and discuss their findings;
- look forward to new forms of reporting in the coming decade.

Main topics

Key terms

CSR reporting
Integrated reporting
Social accounting
Social reporting
Third-party verification statements

What is CSR reporting?

Financial reporting is acknowledged to be central to the corporate function. There are many reasons for this, not least the statutory requirement in most countries for directors to report to their shareholders. However, over the past forty years or so, an increasing proportion of companies in most countries have chosen to report on a range of activities that go beyond imparting purely financial information and include disclosures relating to issues about the wider business environment in which they operate. Systematic research on this phenomenon can be traced back to the 1970s, and a series of studies[5] using a database of social disclosure identifying categories of disclosure typically reported upon under the general headings of 'community', 'product', 'employees', and 'environment'. Later in this chapter we look at how this form of reporting has increased in terms of volume, geographic coverage, and industry sector, and how the topics covered have developed in equal measure. For example, reporting on the environment may now include reporting on sustainability issues, resource scarcity, and climate change, and in some cases at some depth. So, when researchers look for measures of CSR (or social performance, as it is often referred to in research papers), a company disclosure under these categories is still examined and is often used as a proxy in academic studies.[6]

Key concept: Social accounting

Accounting for the non-financial aspects of a company's performance; extending accountability to a wider range of stakeholders within society.

Since the reporting of a company's activities traditionally falls to the accounting department within an organization, it is not surprising that reporting of the non-financial aspects of the organization's activities creates some conceptual problems. Conventional definitions of accounting emphasize that its purpose is to provide financial information that should be useful for decision-makers. This is the starting point for most academic courses in accounting, and throughout their training accountants are directed to concentrate their focus on 'the entity'—the business for which they are preparing the accounts. This means that accounting information tends to be built on data of relevance only to that entity, ignoring external events if they do not explicitly affect the entity.

Financial accounting and reporting are, essentially, for external stakeholders. Reports of past activity and measures of historic performance are produced both as a legal obligation and as an exercise of accountability to the owners of the business—the shareholders. They are produced using accounting conventions, policies, and standards that have developed over time and which are referred to as the generally accepted accounting principles (GAAP). Recent developments in the internationalization of accounting standards are aimed at bringing consistency across national boundaries as companies adopt global perspectives in their operations. These are the results against which analysts' forecasts are measured, and against which anticipated company performance is compared and management competence assessed in terms of market performance.

Traditionally, these measures of performance have focused exclusively on financial issues. Implicitly, as discussed elsewhere in the book, profit maximization is the goal against which performance is assessed, and the only items that are applied to this equation are those to which, in the past, accountants have ascribed this privileged status. Thus, measures of profit omit to take account of the by-products of commercial activity for which others have to pay, such as pollution, emissions, road use, etc., which economists refer to as 'externalities'. Therefore for companies it is logical to externalize as much of their activities as possible, as this will help keep profits higher and prices more competitive. Yet it seems equally illogical that taxpayers who have no interest in a particular company's products or activities have to pay the cost of cleaning up after it. This might be serious enough where an externality can be identified and a company called to account—for example, where it is found that a river has been polluted or a site contaminated with some substance or other. But now that we are aware of the damaging effects of greenhouse gas emissions, and know that the solution is extremely expensive and there are calls for worldwide cooperation to find a solution, dealing with externalities is an issue of even more importance. In the past, it has been suggested that the reason why externalities have never been included in financial statements is to do with difficulties in putting a value on them in financial terms because these issues are 'intangible'; but that argument is losing support in many quarters. If it is possible to assess the value of other 'intangibles', as accountants have been doing for years, this argument seems difficult to sustain. It is more that taking note of externalities is seen as an obstacle to commercial activity, affecting profits and competitiveness.

We have already mentioned that CSR reporting created challenges for those charged with creating the reports. One of the problems is with the language traditionally used in financial reports. Indeed, those used to reading financial reports expect to find 'accounting language' in the text. In many respects accounting provides the accepted language of business—a language that even non-accountants are keen to adopt to instil elements of what are perceived as essential components of strategic arguments in a business framework. This language and the underlying notions that drive corporate activity, such as year-on-year growth and market positioning, shape the context of corporate activity and help to explain both the power of accounting generally, and how easily thereby it might act against longer-term initiatives that have been designed to take account of sets of more responsible objectives.

Additionally, there is an implicit assumption about the nature of accounting that is shared by the public as well as by many accountants, i.e. that it is a 'neutral' or 'objective' activity. We have already explained that accounting is subject to GAAP and some other conventions that have been agreed by particular interest groups. Thus accountants apply their subjective judgements to the application of such principles—judgements that are values-based, and which often have social and environmental consequences that do not appear in subsequent financial statements. A number of studies have examined the complicity of accounting in such issues as environmental pollution, foreign exploitation,[7] plant closures,[8] and social conflict.[9] The perceived partisan nature of accounting informs a more critical approach that motivates much of the research output in such journals as *Critical Perspectives on Accounting*, *Accounting, Organizations and Society*, and the *Accounting, Auditing and Accountability Journal*. It can also be said that it is in this context that social accounting acts as a critique of conventional accounting practices.

The nature of CSR reporting

We have already explained that financial reporting is traditionally understood as the reporting of the financial results of a company's past activities to external stakeholders. The requirement for such reports is now part of company law in most countries, but, as in the UK and USA, the requirements almost invariably cover only the financial activities and commonly call for the directors' report, the profit-and-loss account, and the balance sheet to be reported to the members of the company. These reports are often augmented by various other requirements of GAAP but, with the exception of a few European countries, all of these requirements—either by law or quasi-law—relate to financial aspects of performance. Reporting of the non-financial aspects of a company's performance is largely voluntary (although changes in corporate governance guidelines have led to increased disclosures relating to directors' contractual details in recent decades).[10] It is the voluntary nature of this form of reporting that has attracted the interest of a growing subset of accounting researchers since the genesis of social accounting. But before we look back at the emergence of social reporting, we should be clear about what it means. The social accounting project in the UK dates back to the mid-1980s, and one of the earliest definitions of corporate social reporting, which still stands up today, states that it is:

> the process of communicating the social and environmental effects of the organisations' economic actions to particular interest groups within society, and society at large. As such, it involves extending the accountability of organisations (particularly companies) beyond the traditional role of providing a financial account to the owners of capital, in particular, shareholders. Such an extension is predicated upon the assumption that companies do have wider responsibilities than to simply make money for their shareholders.
>
> (Gray et al., 1987)[11]

Immediately, this definition challenges the taken-for-granted objectives of financial reporting which are to discharge accountability to the members of the company—the shareholders. In this sense, social accounting research may be regarded as offering a critique of mainstream accounting practice, and social accounting researchers have long called for reforms to company law and corporate governance frameworks to broaden the accountability framework to include a wider range of stakeholders.

What is immediately obvious from the statement above, and unavoidable in any subsequent discussion, is the debate about what is meant by 'accountability'. We examined this issue in the previous chapter in the context of corporate governance, but, at this stage, it might be useful to consider how 'accountability' can be interpreted differently by different constituents, and how, within its meaning, there is an implicit relationship of unequal power between the person or body requiring an account and that which is giving the account. This unequal power relationship is evident in the use of phrases such as being 'called to account' or being asked to 'account for one's actions'. Of course, the word 'account' is not always related to finance, but in the corporate context it invariably has this financial emphasis, and the power relationship here lies in the requirement laid down in law and custom for the directors of a company (the agents) to supply (financial) accounts to the owners (principals).[12] However, the same legal obligation to be called to account for responsibilities that go beyond the financial is largely absent from the CSR sphere and any such reporting is undertaken largely as a voluntary act, and it is this aspect which is the focus of much social accounting research. Social accounting theorists both challenge the primacy of the shareholder group and recognize an explicit obligation for companies to be accountable to wider society.

In the context of this book, the connection between a company's social performance and social reporting is obvious. In many ways, social reporting is the first insight into the social performance of the company, and certainly it is the easiest way in which a company can explain its approach and operationalization of its CSR strategy to interested parties external to the company. Indeed, in research studies, social disclosures have frequently been used as a proxy for social performance.[13] However, the information a company reports will largely depend on how it defines its activities in terms of CSR, and the activities upon which it chooses *not* to report are often as significant as the activities on which it does report. Indeed, many studies looking into the reporting activities of corporations comment on the way in which some companies appear to 'cherry pick' the activities on which they can report favourably, while ignoring those issues towards which criticism may be directed. Equally, many companies report on various issues that come within a broad CSR remit, while failing to address major issues at the core of the business activity. Thus, banks may extol the virtues of CSR within the corporate framework in the same period as being fined by regulators for malpractice in core activities such as fixing LIBOR rates, etc. Equally, an energy company may stress how it promotes its staff development to improve leadership qualities in its employees, but may not detail how it aims to tackle the challenges of climate change. Indeed, the inability of boards of directors to join up what they hold out to be responsible conduct throughout the organization remains a real challenge for many companies.

The challenges of CSR reporting

In the introduction to this chapter, we mentioned that CSR reporting presented challenges to those compiling the reports. One of the challenges mentioned above is in the fact that traditional accounting terminology is not always either appropriate or sufficient to describe some CSR issues. But there is an even more fundamental problem facing companies, and that relates to the perceived audience for CSR reports. Company directors know who the audience for quarterly and annual financial reports is, and this audience sits squarely in the 'investor/analyst' category. They know the information that this audience wants, and prepare financial ratios and further information to anticipate their needs. The disclosures are guided by GAAP and companies, largely, disclose the same sets of financial information.

However, there is no shortage of guidelines for companies who wish to report on a wider set of information. Indeed, there is the Global Reporting Initiative (GRI), which emerged from the earlier activities of the Coalition for Environmentally Responsible Economies (CERES) and the CERES Principles. The initiative was founded in Boston in 1997 and the first version of the Guidelines was published in 2000; since then it has developed through three further 'generations', providing us now with version G4.[14] The GRI guidelines feature elsewhere in this volume, but in terms of offering an approach to CSR reporting they warrant a special mention in this chapter, and we shall return to them later to see how they have become the predominant model for reporting by the major corporations of the world.

However, despite this and other initiatives, there is still a degree of uncertainty about who the reports are aimed at. Indeed, it could be conjectured that the potential audience is so wide that it would be impossible to supply sufficient information to satisfy all potential readers. This means that compilers of the reports have to make judgements not only about who the report is to be aimed at, but also about what should be included or left out. Additionally, unlike financial reports, there is no accepted format in which the information should be presented. Because the whole procedure is voluntary, companies can disclose whatever they want. Equally, if the company is actually a group of companies, as most listed companies tend to be, the question arises about which sets of activities in which locations should be reported on. All of these variables suggest that companies are faced with a vast array of possibilities, helping to explain why it is so difficult to compare social performance among similar companies. Equally, it makes it difficult to gauge the actual CSR performance of the company in question since the information disclosed is always likely to be partial and, whether consciously or unconsciously, likely to reflect the positive rather than the negative aspects of a company's performance.

This raises the question of how we might judge not just the veracity of the reports, given the complex nature of the reporting process, but also the veracity of the CSR performance of the company in question. We know that the technology exists for communication between companies and stakeholders to take place in a meaningful way. Social media is already extensively used by companies seeking to attract customers and in their advertising. Maybe there is scope to rethink how accountability might be demonstrated and discharged. It may take time to reconsider the relationship that business has with society, but many believe that that process is already under way.

If we accept the notion that society assigns control of its economic assets to business for its ultimate benefit, how can it hold corporate management accountable for the use of these assets? In discussing this issue, Dillard and Murray (2012) suggest that an 'ethic of accountability' which would ideally be possessed by members of boards of public companies, would impart the responsibility on corporate boards to provide relevant, timely, and understandable information adequate for being held accountable through rendering actions transparent.

They continue:

> Conceptually, an ethic of accountability requires an ongoing conversation among all affected parties. Instantiating an ethic of accountability does not seek 'the good' in a utilitarian sense or 'the right' in a deontological sense, though both are consistent with the ideal. The good and the right are delineated as part of the process of determining the appropriate action within the context of the ongoing community. Fitting action as well as the act of holding, and being held, accountable depends upon open and trustworthy communication between the actor and the community members as well as among the community members themselves.
>
> (Dillard and Murray, 2012, p 15)

What is being discussed, and suggested, here is that to be accountable, companies need to envision their reporting as a more engaged practice based on accountability and transparency. Some of the more innovative and forward-looking companies may already suggest that they are doing this, but, for the others, we still rely largely on NGOs to call major corporations to account.

Discussion points

In attempting to assess a company's commitment to CSR, the volume and content of company disclosures play an important part.

1. To what extent can a company's CSR performance be judged from the various reports that it publishes throughout the year?
2. Where can independent evidence of behaviour be found?
3. How can we gauge whether NGO reports, which are often critical of company activity, are objective and verifiable?

The emergence of CSR reporting

Research in the 1980s demonstrated that some US and Australian companies were reporting on social issues before World War I.[15] Likewise, in the European context, a similar pattern was observed in the early days of Shell.[16] These studies suggest that company managers have always been concerned, to some degree, with considering non-financial issues that are relevant.

Hogner (1982) suggests that US Steel's disclosures were motivated by the need to respond to perceived societal pressures of the period. But it was, perhaps, as societal awareness of environmental issues grew in the 1960s, and as concerns over corporate behaviour were prompted by various company collapses and scandals in the 1970s, that companies responded by including more non-financial information in their annual reports. It was also in the 1970s that, in various countries, new laws required companies to report on aspects of performance relating to, inter alia, employment practices, pollution expenditure, and the like.[17]

There was also interest in the subject in the UK accounting profession and, in 1975, the publication of *The corporate report* (ASSC, 1975) represented a radical rethink of the role of reporting to external stakeholders.[18] It emphasized how the traditional role of the annual report could be made more relevant by the inclusion of social and environmental information. In the USA, the American Institute of Certified Public Accountants entered the debate, offering guidance on the measurement of social performance in a 1977 publication,[19] and the atmosphere was one of examining the role of reporting, in general, and the purpose of reports, in particular. The traditional reason that companies report an account of their activities is for the benefit of the 'users' of accounts. This would normally be thought to be the shareholders, but, in the case of social reporting, traditional theory (i.e. that this information is useful for the purpose of decision-making) does not seem to stand up.

As interesting as its emergence in the 1970s might have been, however, so too was the decline in social reporting in the 1980s and its subsequent re-emergence in the 1990s. The decline is largely attributed to the political shifts in the USA and UK that came with the elections of Ronald Reagan and Margaret Thatcher, respectively, and the renewed focus on free market economics. *The corporate report* largely failed to bring about any major changes and disappeared from the accounting agenda until memories of its recommendations were stirred, in the 1990s, with the initiatives pioneered by such organizations as the Institute of Social and Ethical Accountability, the Council on Economic Priorities, and the World Business Council for Sustainable Development.[20]

The upsurge in CSR reporting since the early 1990s

Despite the varying pattern of corporate reporting of social and environmental issues, a very clear upward trend in CSR reporting began to emerge in the 1990s and this can be readily observed from the triennial surveys conducted by the accountancy firm KPMG. Apart from minor changes in corporate governance recommendations, a number of factors began to influence change within companies. These included action at a number of levels, from initiatives within professions and industries to UN and EU initiatives, all encouraging greater detail in the reporting of social and environmental issues.

For example, the UNEP/SustainAbility 'Engaging Stakeholders' programme was launched in 1994. Initially, it served to raise awareness among companies of environmental reporting and, although its current status as a set of guidelines is unclear, the guidance on offer continues to stress the business case for wider reporting.[21] The programme has clearly encouraged participation by widely publicizing the results of the survey and the benefits of participation. The EU Eco-Management and Audit Scheme also promoted the introduction and reporting of environmental management systems, following the introduction of BS 7750 in 1992 and, thereafter, the ISO 14000 series.

At a national level, the UK government's DEFRA/DTI Environmental Reporting Guidelines were published in 2001, and France followed Denmark, Norway, Sweden, and The Netherlands in introducing mandatory reporting requirements. At a business-to-business level, the International Chamber of Commerce published its first *Business Charter for Sustainable Development* in 1991 (ICC, 2000), featuring a sixteen-point guide to environmental reporting. In 1995, the World Business Council for Sustainable Development (WBCSD) was established through a merger of the Business Council for Sustainable Development and the World Industry Council for the Environment, the two organizations that responded on behalf of business to the challenges arising from the Rio Summit in 1992. The WBCSD maintains an influential voice for business and boasts a membership comprising major corporations worldwide.[22]

Around the same time, various industries began to look at how environmental issues affected the perceptions of activities within their sectors. A good example of this is the initiative by the European Chemical Industry Council (CEFIC). Founded in 1972, it has, over the years, expanded and developed its approaches to various aspects of concern within the industry. It is now closely allied to the International Council of Chemical Associations (ICCA) which, in 2006, launched its Responsible Care Global Charter, a development of CEFIC's Responsible Care Programme's reporting guidelines.

At the level of the professions, the Fédération des Experts Compatibles Européens (FEE)—the coordinating organization for the European accounting professions—has been involved in developing reporting guidelines and making representations to the European Parliament on connected issues. In the UK, the initiative taken by the Association of Certified Chartered Accountants (ACCA) in 1991 in establishing the Environmental Reporting Awards did much to encourage and improve social reporting over the years (see Snapshot 8.2). It broadened its remit in 2002, and until 2005 ran a European Sustainability Reporting Award Scheme, but now appears to no longer be active in this area.

Each of these initiatives, or a combination of more than one, served to increase the incidence and volume of environmental reporting (see Snapshot 8.1). In the early stages of this development, the reports bore little resemblance to the best reports we see today. In general, reporting on environmental issues comprised a section in the annual report and was largely qualitative in nature. Even when the first stand-alone reports began to appear, they seemed to be, as Owen (2003) suggested, 'rather crude exercises in public relations'.

Snapshot 8.1 Sustainability at Fujitsu

Fujitsu has long been aware of the environmental impacts created by multinational firms. For many years it has taken steps to examine its ecological footprint and today is an exemplar in both the understanding and reporting of its sustainability strategies.

It was in 1993 that Fujitsu established its first Environmental Protection Program, which outlined the company's approach to environmental activities around four key areas—products, factories, solutions, and people. It was one of the first companies to consider the environmental impacts of its products throughout their life cycle, from the acquisition of materials used in manufacture, to their disposal at end of life. It now sets goals and monitors its performance in each successive report.

As with earlier reports, the company's 2017 Environmental Report clearly outlines its approach to sustainability by arranging sections of the report to mirror their analysis of the priorities in this area: global environmental challenges, food and energy demand, social impacts of urbanization, global population ageing, the digital divide, and cyber attacks and cyber crime.

It is interesting to reflect on these categories and how, in comparison with some other sustainability reports, their first four categories do not intuitively relate to their products yet are seen to be the most important, and where their products may have positive impacts. Against each heading the company suggests how ICT can meet the challenges presented.

(continued . . .)

For example, acknowledging that in a world with a growing population and depleting resources our planet is probably already operating beyond its carrying capacity, Fujitsu sees the power of computing as an essential part of any solution to greenhouse gas (GHG) reduction. In the case of food shortage they see innovative ICT in fields of supply/demand management in areas lacking in this approach to date as an essential part of the solution.

Quick questions

1. Why is it important to be clear about global issues?
2. Why is it essential to measure performance against indicators?
3. In what respect can non-financial information inform the business case?

Researching the practice of CSR reporting—KPMG surveys

In 1993, KPMG Peat Marwick Thorne, as it then was known, conducted its first 'International Survey of Environmental Reporting', where it notes that there was 'a growing need for more and superior environmental information'. It sent questionnaires to the top 100 companies in the UK, Canada, The Netherlands, France, and Belgium, together with a smaller sample of the largest companies in Germany, Denmark, Portugal, and Ireland—690 companies responded. From this modest beginning has grown an enduring and expanding survey of CSR reporting practice around the world. Over the years it has evolved and developed in scope and geographical coverage, and continues to do so, to include, for instance, water, supply chain, and regulatory optimization. It is interesting to note that an examination of the trail of surveys mirrors the development of the field in general. The 1993 survey was entitled 'An International Survey of Environmental Reporting', reflecting the nature of the first 'stand-alone' environmental reports that had begun to appear in the late 1980s. In 2002 the title was changed to a survey of 'Corporate Sustainability Reporting', and since 2005 there have been surveys of 'Corporate Responsibility Reporting', the last one in 2017 analysing some 4,900 reports from around the world.

Because of the nature of the changes made in the focus and methodologies used in constructing the reports it is not so easy to compare results, but the last three have adopted an almost uniform approach, highlighting the fact that CSR reporting is now an almost universal corporate activity among large corporations, with 95% of the 250 largest companies in the world reporting on their CSR activities (KPMG, 2017). The survey on which the report is based has changed emphasis over time, reflecting shifts in CSR concerns. In 2017, the focus was on: reporting on climate-related financial risk; reporting on the UN Sustainable Development Goals (SDGs); reporting on human rights; and reporting on carbon reduction targets. In some reports KPMG has also surveyed the potential reasons why companies choose to report, and these seem to be in line with academic research in the area, with companies citing reputation (67%), ethical considerations (58%), employee motivation (44%), and innovation and learning (44%) as the four leading drivers.[23]

What is clear and irrevocable is that the practice shows no sign of reversing the trend, and it is likely that within a decade CSR reporting will be almost universal among listed companies in most developed countries.

Snapshot 8.2 Is social information of use to investors?

The Association of Chartered Certified Accountants (ACCA), which ran an award scheme for environmental reports in the UK and elsewhere from 1991 to 2008 with the overall aim of improving the quality of non-financial reporting, has recently published a report in response to the European Commission's proposed new requirements that all large EU companies report on the environmental, social, and governance (ESG) aspects of their businesses, with investors as the primary focus.

It has been a feature of most research to date that investors take an ambivalent view of non-financial information, and therefore it was timely that an organization with the reach of the ACCA should collaborate with the European Sustainable Investment Forum (Eurosif) to examine the sort of information that might be of interest to investors. To do this, the authors conducted a survey of analysts and investors in eighteen countries and based the report on the responses of ninety-four participants. They examined the sources of information used by investors and scrutinized its adequacy, content, and form; they also looked at what accountability mechanisms might be applied to ensure the veracity of the information contained in the reports. They also considered what sorts of company should have to report and the implications for policy-makers.

The key findings suggest that investors:

i) do refer to the CSR/SustainAbility reports;
ii) do not believe that sufficient information is supplied to assess financial materiality;
iii) find that reporting is not comparable across companies;
iv) find a lack of quantitative key performance indicators;
v) believe that third-party assurance statements are important.

(*Source:* ACCA, 2013)

Quick questions

1. Is there a case for statutory standards to cover sustainability reporting, in the same way as there are standards for financial reporting?
2. If a voluntary approach is to continue, how might companies be persuaded to take note of the criticisms levelled at current reporting practice?
3. What are the main reasons for non-financial information to be integrated with financial information?

Trends in social reporting

Two other trends emerged in the 1990s that, to some extent, still continue today. First, there was the separation of the 'environmental' from the 'social'. Whereas the reports in the 1970s had, in many ways, a shared focus, the trend in the 1990s was to separate the two and to place a greater emphasis on the environmental aspects of company performance. This is significant because CSR, as a field, is not concerned solely with issues of environmental management;

indeed, at the core of the Brundtland definition of sustainability (see Chapter 3) is the notion of social justice. Second, criticism started to be levelled at companies for failing to embed social and environmental policies into the strategy and 'real' purpose of the business (see Chapter 6).

We can conjecture over the reasons for both trends. In the case of the environmental focus, it is worth remembering that there had been a spate of very significant environmental disasters in the mid- and late-1980s including, for example, Bhopal in 1984, Chernobyl in 1986, *Piper Alpha* in 1988, and *Exxon Valdez* in 1989. For obvious reasons, media coverage of these events was concentrated and prolonged, and the events themselves led to many changes in the way in which companies operated and reported. Indeed, each of these events had a lasting impact within their respective industries that is felt even today. Therefore it is probably unsurprising that companies opted for more of an environmental focus in their activities and reports. If we examine the response of BP to the 2010 Deepwater Horizon incident we see a similar pattern. In many ways, if this conclusion is correct, it also explains why the strategy may be easily criticized as an 'add-on', because, at least initially, that is what it was. It would have been a reaction, most likely of companies within the affected industry sectors, to how they perceived they should act.

Research into social reporting

Although there is evidence of companies reporting non-financial aspects of their businesses going back over a hundred years, a genuine body of research only really began to emerge in the 1970s.[24] During the period 1970–1980, this mainly consisted of empirical (statistical) studies which, while focusing on some aspects of social and environmental information, still had a clear instrumental rationale aimed at discovering the usefulness of this information to investors.[25] Some discursive work began to appear towards the end of the 1970s,[26] however, and this widened the debate to include more philosophical issues, with the phrase 'social responsibility' appearing in many studies.[27]

Research gained momentum from the mid-1980s, at which time a number of authors, principally in the UK and Australia, began to explore the social dimensions of corporate activity. Influential journals, sympathetic to this subject matter, were also founded in this period; *Critical Perspectives on Accounting* (established 1990), *Accounting, Auditing and Accountability Journal* (1988), and *Journal of Accounting and Public Policy* (1982), joined *Accounting, Organizations and Society* (1975) to provide a wide forum through which to engage academics and broaden the terms of the debate.

These works presaged the increase in social reporting of the early 1990s, and heralded a social and environmental accounting project that has continued, and grown in strength, scope, and reach, ever since. Indeed, from modest beginnings, with only a handful of researchers worldwide, social and environmental accounting research is now conducted by hundreds of researchers in many countries and features in many international accounting conferences each year, as well as having a number of its own dedicated conferences.[28]

Such evidence as there is from research studies looking at the value that investors place on such information is no more than suggestive of 'possible' relevance to investment decisions.[29] Indeed, despite the huge amount of research in the late 1970s and early 1980s into the link between social performance and financial performance, the results tend to be contradictory, largely owing to the variety of measures used to determine both financial and social performance. Taking a moment to consider all the different possible measures of 'financial performance', we are left with choices among profit (whatever that might look like), returns on earning, investment, assets, capital employed, and so on, or market measures relating to share returns, earnings per share, etc., and we soon realize that it is difficult to compare studies. Researchers continuing to seek definitive proof one way or the other might like first to refer to the review by Griffin and Mahon (1997) encompassing 'twenty-five years of incomparable research'. For a comprehensive summary, others may refer to Margolis and Walsh (2001) to explore the complexities.

Theories of social reporting

Researchers responded to Ullmann's (1985) call for new theories to be explored to explain the phenomenon of increasing voluntary reporting and a number of studies followed. Roberts (1992) discussed stakeholder theory in an empirical context and, subsequently, Gray et al. (1996a), also prompted by evidence of increasing volumes of social disclosure, reviewed theories of disclosure that might explain the phenomenon. Traditional accounting theories of disclosure aimed at informing market participants were largely discounted and alternative theories focusing on political economy were considered. One of the theories identified—'legitimacy theory'—has since become one of the most discussed in the literature. The notion of a company existing only with the sanction of society, with connotations of a 'public interest' element to its continued existence, may have seemed somewhat fanciful, but the events surrounding Enron and the collapse of Arthur Andersen, one of the world's largest and, at the time, most respected firms of accountants, demonstrated that it is indeed possible to lose the licence to operate if one's actions are seen to go beyond what society deems acceptable. That companies might choose a strategy to support or enhance their legitimacy in these terms is something that has formed a strand of research since 1990. Indeed, many researchers suggest that rather than exercising the discharge of accountability in reporting their social activities, they are actually engaged in a process of legitimation of their operations. Legitimacy theory suggests that company disclosures may be a reaction to the perception that companies have of how they are viewed by different stakeholder groups within society. Therefore the company needs to disclose details about its activities to achieve this objective and to reassure society about them. Lindblom (1994) sparked a long-running debate on legitimacy theory by positing four alternative strategies which might be employed by companies when deciding whether and why to publish. She suggests that companies may seek to 'align activities with expectations', 'educate and inform', 'change perceptions', or 'alter expectations'. We may surmise that each and all of these strategies are connected with the way that the company wishes to communicate with stakeholders, and that they *may* also be connected to its actual performance.

A related theory linked to disclosure strategy concerns the manner in which a company manages its reputation. There is an increasing literature on management of reputation and the risks attaching to events which can damage it.[30] The relationship between social disclosure and social performance seems critical if we are to do anything but discount social reports as some form of public relations exercise. Unless we are able to align reports with performance, we are always likely to be left with this dilemma.

Conventional financial reporting and CSR reporting

The major difference between conventional financial reporting and social reporting hinges on the approach taken to the use of the information reported upon. Traditionally, financial reports contain both aggregated data, which may conceal much of the underlying activity, and analyses that focus on very narrow performance measures. We can only imagine the range of activity that is represented by the income statements of BP or Walmart and, in looking at the earning per share figure or other performance ratios, no consideration is given to the wider implications of the plethora of undertakings that led to the derivation of that measure. Indeed, in the application of many accounting techniques, little attention is paid to any factors outside the concern of the entity, and ratios of liquidity, profitability, and solvency, for example, are often used only to compare performance against historic or other data. The same figures are also often used to compare performance of one company with another (this type of comparison is frequently requested in degree and professional accounting courses dealing with 'financial statement analysis'). Equally, what Chua (1986) calls 'mainstream accounting research' tends to have a similar narrow focus, and research questions regularly focus around issues of market efficiency and the usefulness of certain categories of information to investors. It is little wonder, therefore, that the bigger picture is often overlooked in an effort to examine the minutiae of procedure or practice.

On the other hand, CSR reporting, at a theoretical level, is concerned with how commercial activity links into other social systems and presents an alternative ontological approach to how one views the role of corporations. 'Systems theory', explained in more detail in Gray et al. (1996b), is an approach that is 'designed to reverse the tendency in scientific thought towards reductionist reasoning'. Systems theory has its origins in the natural sciences and can be explained as follows.

> 1 An attempt to study a part without understanding the whole from which the part comes (reductionism) was bound to lead to misunderstandings. The part can only be understood in its context.
>
> 2 Understanding tends to be directed by and limited to one's own discipline. Natural phenomena are complex and cannot be successfully studied by artificially bounded modes of thought.
>
> (Gray et al., 1996b, p 13)

The essence of systems thinking demands that we think about all our activities in the context of how they affect other systems, with what Birkin (2000) calls, 'an ontology of interconnected events'. This concept is particularly relevant when considering sustainability, and is discussed in more detail in Chapter 3.

Reporting issues for corporate management

From the management perspective, there are a number of problems in making the decision to disclose non-financial information. First, who is the intended audience? Traditionally, as we have mentioned already, corporate reports are released for the benefit of the analyst/investor group. That constituency is relatively homogenous and easy to define; their needs have been the focus of investor relations departments and boardroom discussions for decades, and are backed by numerous research studies. However, the audience for reports on CSR issues is much more diverse. These users do not form a homogenous group and are likely to have widely diverging interests. Equally, their desire for information may not always have the company's best interests at heart. Indeed, it is easy to make an argument that few investors take any interest in the non-financial aspects of corporate activity, except if it impinges on issues of risk or governance. Certainly, there is little evidence from research that investors are swayed by social and environmental disclosures. Thus, management must form an opinion on the purpose and scope of the report, and this may pose many challenges.

It is relatively straightforward to make statements along the lines of 'within this company we make every effort to maintain the highest standards of social and environmental practice'. Indeed, statements such as this peppered annual reports throughout the late 1990s as companies became aware that they were expected to address additional non-financial issues, but were unsure how to position themselves in that regard. What is more difficult to do is to explain how any particular programme is to be rolled out and the effect that it might have on profit figures. At that point, conflict will almost inevitably arise within organizations, and one can see the kind of compromises that are reached by examining such reports, many of which fill the list of criticisms by awards judges (see Snapshot 8.2).

If one looks at it from outside the company, the picture is entirely different. As a member of society, concerned about aspects of corporate activity that affect you, you may view the issue as one of accountability. Companies and policy-makers often talk about 'transparency', but on close examination it is sometimes difficult to uncover the level of detail that we require in order to be satisfied on any particular issue. On the other hand, how does the company know the level of detail that any single individual or group might want? These issues reveal that company managers involved in the reporting process are better placed to report effectively if they have knowledge of the theories and functions of social reporting which enables them to position the company effectively in terms of its CSR profile and reputation management.

Key concept: External verification statement

An external verification statement is an opinion regarding the quality and verifiability of the social reports. Unlike financial audits, which are carried out by registered auditors following comprehensive auditing standards, external verification statements on social reports have no such authority.

The trend towards external verification

We know that the initial choice of whether to report at all is made by the company as part of a strategy by the management and motivated for any number of reasons. It is a largely voluntary act and may have much to do with the activity of competitors, perceptions of stakeholder expectation, or other strategies to obtain 'managerial advantage'.[31] As companies embrace a global perspective, many will view both the mandatory requirements of some countries and the recommendations under the Global Reporting Initiative sustainability reporting guidelines, which make specific reference to verification as an opportunity to review and to implement external assurance practices. The trend has been observed to be growing steadily and, in its most recent international survey, KPMG (2011) found that the number of companies in the Global 250 with a formal assurance statement had increased to 46% (from 40% in 2008); for the top 100 national companies, it had slightly dipped to 38% (from 39%). The overriding motivation is probably to build trust between company management and external stakeholders over the implementation and maintenance of CSR strategies. In an ideal world, the verification process should achieve this and reassure the relevant audience, thereby adding value for the company.

However, this motivation is easily contrasted with the theoretical purpose of such accounts—the idea that with transparency comes accountability. There is a real concern, expressed by a number of researchers, that the upsurge in reporting is part of a process whereby the accountability agenda is 'captured' by corporate management, who react to calls for greater accountability and transparency by artefacts aimed at taking control of the agenda, and at taking equal control of the nature and extent of the information reported upon.[32] The idea that such reports only contain information that management wants released adds to criticisms that reports lack completeness and credibility.[33] This notion continues to motivate social accounting researchers to examine the verification process, and to press for the imposition of strict and robust assurance processes.[34] The KPMG (2011) Report devoted a full chapter to the question of assurance statements. Not too surprisingly it notes that:

> . . . of the assurance providers, the market continues to be dominated by major accountancy organizations that currently hold 71 percent of the G250 market and 64 percent of the N100. Market shares of other provider types appear to have grown slightly at the expense of the technical expert firms who lost market share.
>
> (KPMG, 2011, p 30)

Emergence of integrated reporting

CSR reporting is a dynamic field, as can be seen from the evolution described above. Not only has there been a trend to blend CSR with sustainability reporting, but a new approach to reporting known as integrated reporting has been pioneered by academics and accountants. Integrated reporting claims to be a broad-based framework for business and investment decisions that are long-term, inclusive, and with purpose. An important organization in this field is the International Integrated Reporting Council (Chapter 7), which describes itself as a worldwide coalition with the mission to mainstream integrated thinking and reporting and to change the corporate reporting system so that integrated reporting becomes the norm.

The field is relatively recent and objective assessments are only just starting to appear (e.g. Damle et al., 2017; Mervelskemper and Streit, 2017; Rupley et al., 2017). However, it seems to have a certain momentum, not least because the corporate and academic support it is receiving.

Discussion points

There is now strong evidence from recent surveys that a high number of companies in all sectors in all countries are reporting on CSR issues.

1 What theories can you suggest that might help to explain this trend?
2 What theories lie behind the notion that statements should be independently verified by third parties?
3 Given that there are no statutory standards against which to audit third-party verification statements, how is it possible to compare their value between companies?

Case study 8 Environmental reporting at PUMA

Traditionally, accounting information has concentrated exclusively on the valuation of assets and liabilities judged by the accounting bodies, which set the standards, as having an impact on the financial standing of the entity in question. Researchers in social and environmental accounting have always criticized this partial view of corporate activity which excludes the valuation of 'externalities'—the damaging effects of pollution, emissions, and waste which are passed to external agencies to remedy, and the cost of which ultimately falls to the taxpayer. Logically, the larger the company and the longer the supply chains feeding into the product ranges of large companies, the greater the impact will be and the more complex the measurement of such impact becomes. Most corporations have avoided such investigations.

However, in 2011, luxury and sports lifestyle company Kering (formerly PPR), the parent company of PUMA, announced that it was to implement a group environmental profit-and-loss (P&L) account by 2016, and set out on a mission to place values on the GHG emissions, water use, land use, air pollution, and waste caused by their operations worldwide.

The initiative was designed as a three-stage process, which sought to address some of the issues relating to externalities mentioned above, and which may act as a catalyst for other companies with complex supply chains to adopt similar approaches when the full costs are better understood. It was conducted in consultation with PricewaterhouseCoopers and Trucost.[35]

Stage 1 To gather data on 'GHG emissions, water consumption, air pollution, waste, and impacts on land-use'.

Stage 2 It was envisaged that measurement of some of the more problematic elements of sustainability will be included to gauge social impacts and could include:

> decent/fair wages, health and safety, working conditions, standard of living, security and stability, empowerment, community cohesion, human capital, diversity and gender equality, health and well-being, and cultural heritage.

(continued . . .)

It is worth noting that PUMA acknowledged that:

> the development of this stage requires the collaboration with other corporate and civil society stakeholders in tackling the complexities of the social issues.

Stage 3 This stage will complete the other side of the equation, focusing on some of the beneficiaries of the economic impacts from PUMA's operations. This could include:

> the creation of jobs, wages, total tax contributions, indirect tax payments, indirect and induced employment, indirect and induced output, productivity and efficiency gains, and business creation and growth.

Only data relating to stage 1 were published for reasons given below, but they revealed that:

> following an economic valuation of €94 million of GHG emissions and water consumption in May 2011, PUMA has finalised its 2010 E P&L by adding €51 million caused by land use change for the production of raw materials, air pollution and waste along its value chain. Only €8 million of the €145 million total derive from PUMA's core operations such as offices, warehouses, stores and logistics while the remaining €137 million fall upon PUMA's supply chain.

They further report:

> - Over half (57% or €83 million) of all environmental impacts are associated with the production of raw materials (including leather, cotton and rubber) in Tier 4 of PUMA's supply chain.
> - Only 6% or €8 million derive from PUMA's core operations such as offices, warehouses, stores and logistics; a further 9% (€13 million) occur in Tier 1, with the remaining 85% (€124 million) in Tiers 2–4.
> - GHGs make up 90% of the total impact of PUMA's offices, stores and warehouses.
>
> These costs, which will not affect PUMA's net earnings, will serve as an initial metric for the company when aiming to mitigate the footprint of PUMA's operations and all supply chain levels.

This initiative represented an ambitious commitment to reveal the impact that the company was making in terms not only of the cost to the environment, but also of the benefits to society. Changes in the parent company meant it was not taken much further, which in itself raises interesting questions about what allows CSR initiatives to flourish or fail. However, the individuals who pioneered the work and other companies have continued to develop PUMA's ideas. For example, it represented a challenge to traditional accounting approaches and seems to encompass the two tenets of social and environmental accounting: to use proven accounting techniques to measure different things, and to develop new techniques to measure non-traditional costs and benefits. This has been picked up by the Integrated Reporting movement (Chapter 7).

(*Sources:* http://about.puma.com/puma-completes-first-environmental-profit-and-loss-account-which-values-impacts-at-e-145-million (a number of PDFs which explain valuation methodology, etc. are also available on this page); http://www.kering.com/en/sustainability; Epstein and Buhovac, 2017; Gröschl et al., 2017)

Questions

1 PUMA has received much attention for its environmental P&L initiative.

a. What features of its reporting practice put PUMA ahead of its rivals?

b. To what extent does PUMA use targets to monitor emissions reductions?

c. What does PUMA identify as the major issue relating to supply chains?

(continued...)

2 Social and environmental reports are often used by researchers as a proxy for actual social performance.

a. What indicators can we use from PUMA's environmental reports to measure its actual social performance?

b. What are the main elements of PUMA's environmental profit and loss calculations?

c. What does PUMA see as the main benefit for the company in preparing an environmental P&L?

3 PUMA has identified that much of the negative environmental impacts relate to supply chains operating in many countries in the developing world.

a. What difficulties are PUMA likely to face when trying to gather data for stages 2 and 3 of the environmental P&L programme?

b. What benefits to developing nations can environmental P&L data provide?

c. How effectively does PUMA presently cover sustainability issues in its annual reports?

Summary

In this chapter, we have examined how companies report CSR to audiences outside the company. This, we discovered, encompasses a complex series of issues that pose some serious challenges for management, especially if the process is designed to be more than an exercise in corporate communication, marketing, or public relations. This process developed through extending the financial reporting function, and, until relatively recently, the annual report was the usual medium through which such disclosures were made.

This posed a number of problems for companies as it became clear that stakeholder groups were scrutinizing the information contained in these social and environmental accounts with different intentions than those of the traditional audience of annual reports, i.e. the shareholders. Academics also began scrutinizing these social disclosures, offering varying levels of critique and, as the reporting medium moved to the internet, so pressure groups were now using the same medium to counter some of the claims made in corporate releases. Even when companies enter reporting award schemes, they rarely emerge without criticism.

There are various reasons for the dramatic increase in the incidence and volume of CSR reporting, and a large number of contributory factors, a combination of which is most likely to offer explanation. But with this increase has come criticism from certain quarters that the reports are more akin to public relations initiatives. Indeed, even as the incidence and volume of CSR reports has increased, criticism of corporate behaviour does not seem to have abated, not least because the material is accused of being incomplete or inadequate, as attested to by successive judging panels of environmental and similar awards. For example, the banking sector, initially ambivalent to issues of CSR as it saw itself as having less environmental impact than like-sized corporations, became very active in the 1990s and 2000s, with many banks branding themselves as model corporate citizens while their core activities were undermining trust in the financial system worldwide. Even after the financial crash of 2007–2008 and all the stinging criticism levelled against their irresponsible behaviour, new scandals of interest rate fixing and mis-selling of financial products still proliferate.

We noted that accounting plays an important part in this process of improving the credibility of CSR performance. Accounting for an activity is the essence of discharging accountability to the appropriate body. Impacts and effects need to be measured in order to gauge accurately whether particular strategies are worthwhile and effective. The design and implementation of appropriate information systems and reporting structures play an essential part of this process. Therefore there are strong arguments to be made that accountants become aware of the social, environmental, and sustainability issues that are challenging the 'business as usual' approach. These professionals will then be better placed to devise accounting systems that can capture non-financial activity in a more meaningful way. Equally, there are new forms of accounting that might be developed, looking to measure different things than those that are traditionally associated with accounting systems.

What this chapter sets out to demonstrate is that accounting plays a central role in the CSR process and has the potential to play an even greater role. Social, environmental, CSR, and sustainability reports have emerged from the financial reporting function within companies. But, whereas financial reporting procedures are highly regulated and controlled, there seems to be no appetite to impose such controls on non-financial reporting. If that situation continues, despite continued criticism over the format and content of such reports, then these reports will continue to require careful analysis and critical judgement.

Further reading

Ali, W., Frynas, J.G., and Mahmood, Z. 2017, 'Determinants of corporate social responsibility (CSR) disclosure in developed and developing countries: a literature review', *Corporate Social Responsibility and Environmental Management*, vol. 24, issue 4, July/August, pp 273–294.
Overview of corporate reporting comparing developed and developing countries.

Corkery, J., Mikalsen, M., and Allan, K. 2017, *Corporate social responsibility: the good corporation*, Centre for Commercial Law, Bond University, Queensland.
Recent overview of the development of CSR and reporting.

Gray, R.H. 2006b, 'Social, environmental and sustainability reporting and organizational value creation? Whose value? Whose creation?', *Accounting, Auditing and Accountability Journal*, vol. 19, no. 6, pp 793–819.
Revisiting and updating the debate on reporting on the social and environmental dimensions of business.

Gray, R.H., Owen, D., and Adams, C. 1996b, *Accounting and accountability: changes and challenges in corporate social and environmental reporting*, Prentice Hall, London.
An important early work making the case for social and environmental reporting.

Hasseldine, J., Salama, A.I., and Toms, J.S., 2005, 'Quantity versus quality: the impact of environmental disclosures on the reputations of UK PLCs', *British Accounting Review*, vol. 37, no. 2, pp 231–248.
Evaluation of reporting's impact.

http://www.oup.com/uk/blowfield_murray4e

Visit the online resources that accompany this book to enrich your understanding of this chapter. Among the resources available are web links, exercises, and additional case studies.

Endnotes

1. IPCC, 2007; WWF, 2012.
2. KPMG, 1993, 1996, 1999.
3. KPMG, 2002.
4. KPMG, 2005, 2008, 2011, 2017.
5. Beresford, 1973, 1975, 1976.
6. Gray et al., 1995a,b, 2001; Murray et al., 2006.
7. Tinker, 1985.
8. Berry et al., 1985.
9. Lehman, 1992.
10. Changing corporate governance guidelines have increased the amount of recommended disclosure, categorized as social disclosure, relating to the remuneration of directors following the Cadbury and Greenbury Reports in the mid-1990s (see Chapter 7).
11. For a more recent discussion of the definition, see Gray et al., 1996a.
12. This 'agency' relationship lies at the heart of modern corporate activity and is further explored in Chapter 9.
13. There are a number of examples in which disclosure is used when no other measure of performance is available (see e.g. Belkaoui, 1976; Ingram, 1978; Mahapatra, 1984; Belkaoui and Karpic, 1989).
14. http://www.globalreporting.org, accessed 26 November 2018.
15. Hogner, 1982; Lewis et al., 1984; Guthrie and Parker, 1989.
16. Unerman, 2003.
17. Gray, 2002a,b.
18. ASSC, 1975.
19. AICPA, 1977.
20. Deegan, 2002.
21. http://web.unep.org/about/majorgroups/stakeholder-engagement-handbook, accessed 26 November 2018.
22. It also has an extensive website covering issues of climate change, international development, ecosystems, and the business role. There is a section on projects in progress and there are a large number of case studies for reference. See http://www.wbcsd.org, accessed 26 November 2018.
23. KPMG, 2011.
24. See Mathews (1996) for a detailed discussion of the development of social accounting research in different time periods.
25. See, e.g., Bowman, 1973; Belkaoui, 1976; Bowman and Haire, 1976.
26. See, e.g., R.W. Estes, 1975, 1976; Ramanathan, 1976.
27. See, e.g., Jacoby, 1973; Browne and Haas, 1974; Feldberg, 1974; Parket and Eilbirt, 1975; J. Estes, 1976.
28. The Centre for Social and Environmental Accounting Research (CSEAR) at the University of St Andrews boasts a membership in excess of 500 people from over thirty countries and holds an annual conference for researchers each September (see http://www.st-andrews.ac.uk/csear, accessed 26 November 2018).
29. Bowman, 1973; Chenall and Juchau, 1977; Ingram, 1978; Stewart and Konieczny, 1996; Chan and Milne, 1999; Milne and Chan, 1999; Friedman and Miles, 2001.
30. Friedman and Miles, 2001; Toms, 2002; Hasseldine et al., 2005.
31. Owen et al., 2000.
32. See, e.g., Owen et al., 2000; O'Dwyer and Owen, 2005.
33. Dando and Swift, 2003; Adams, 2004; Adams and Evans, 2004.
34. O'Dwyer and Owen, 2005.
35. See https://glasaaward.org/wp-content/uploads/2014/01/EPL080212final.pdf, accessed 26 November 2018.

Stakeholder management and engagement

Chapter overview

In this chapter, we explore the significance of stakeholders and how they relate to the way in which CSR is perceived and managed through partnerships, alliances, and voluntary standards. In particular, we will:

- examine stakeholders as a managerial concept;
- identify the different types of stakeholder and difficulties with the 'stakeholder' construct;
- explore the role of stakeholders in defining and implementing voluntary codes of CSR practice and standards;
- review experiences of stakeholder management.

Main topics

Key terms

Stakeholder	Voluntary standard
Code of conduct	Engagement
Partnership	Developing countries

Meaning and origins of stakeholder

The theme of this chapter is stakeholders: what they are, how they can be managed, how they influence the management of the company, and the validity of the very concept. We have raised the idea of stakeholders in Chapter 5 when we discussed the partnerships companies are creating with stakeholders as a feature of the business–society relationship that has come to the fore during the current era of globalization. As we touched on then, partnerships are not always straightforward affairs, and one of the reasons for this is the complexity of the stakeholder concept. In the early 2000s, prominent CEOs such as IBM's Sam Palmisano called the shift in business from shareholder companies to stakeholder companies as a defining element of the modern corporation,[1] and now the term is so widely used, it might seem there is no need for an explanation. But there is plenty of disagreement about what it implies in terms of definition, management practice, and consequences.

Companies have always had stakeholders. There have always been investors, employees, business customers, consumers, and local communities that are affected by and have an influence on the organization called the company. They can be subdivided so that, for instance, employees comprise managers, supervisors, skilled workers, labourers, and so on, all with their own vested interests. Indeed, although much of CSR literature uses the term 'company' to refer to a homogenous entity, companies often need to be understood as the locus of multiple, frequently competing, contracts between individuals and their alliances. There is a long history of viewing companies in this way, but it is no longer commonplace. In fact, critics of stakeholder theory might argue that replacing unsympathetic terms such as worker–management relations with the seemingly more neutral, inclusive 'stakeholder' is a victory for normative modern management theory. Companies often advertise for 'team members' rather than workers, and talk about 'partnerships' when what they mean are suppliers or customers. We shall return to the ideational nature of stakeholder theory later, but first it is worth considering, if stakeholders have always been part of the business landscape, why we need a special term now, and why that term has gained particular popularity in CSR literature.

Key concept: Stakeholder

A stakeholder is any person or organization affected by or with the power to influence a company's decisions and actions. Because of the company's impact or their influence, stakeholders are deemed to have a stake in the company. In the shareholder theory of the firm which began to dominate the Anglo-Saxon debate about the purpose of business in the 1960s, the outcome that executives are accountable for is shareholder value. Stakeholder theory of the firm offers an alternative to this by making it explicit that the firm has material and/or moral reasons to consider its relationship with more than just investors. In countries such as Austria, stakeholder participation in corporate governance is enshrined in law, but elsewhere, such as the USA and Australia, it is a voluntary aspect of management that is being accepted as at worst prudent and at best performance-enhancing.

In Chapter 5, we talked about contemporary CSR practice as the product of a particular sociopolitical discourse—one where companies are responding to certain features of globalization such as the changing nature of governance and the multi-tiered values framework that shapes expectations of business. Stakeholder, in part, has gained its prominence because of such changes. A company might legally have a primary duty to its shareholders, and senior managers might feel more comfortable exercising that responsibility rather than a more loosely defined one to society, but examples throughout this book demonstrate how companies are affected in a material sense by a range of organizations, individuals, and alliances built around common interests that typically position the company's behaviour as something they want to influence. Equally, there have been numerous examples of how the company affects others, such as workers in supplier factories, consumers reliant on product safety for their well-being, communities dependent on a company for employment creation, former employees living off of company pensions, and so on. Into an already tangled web, rising concern about sustainable development (see Chapter 3) has added non-human stakeholders such as the natural environment, the global commons, and climate.

As awareness of the social and political consequences of globalization increased from the 1970s onwards, stakeholder as an analytical construct became widely used, for example in the influential work of Giddens (1991, 1994) and Ackerman and Alstott (1999). The term had been used in business literature since the 1930s[2] as a way of distinguishing between the main groups towards which companies have different kinds of duty—in particular, shareholders, customers, consumers, and employees. In 1984, however, Freeman's *Strategic management: a stakeholder approach* presented stakeholders as something more extensive, complex, and nuanced than this. What is more, they were not simply to be viewed as a convenient taxonomic device; for Freeman, managing stakeholders effectively was essential to the very survival and prosperity of the enterprise. In what he calls 'radical externalism', Freeman proposes that managers pay attention to stakeholders as a matter of course by adopting integrative strategic management processes.

In light of the very significant impact that Freeman's book has had on management theory, there are two points to note. First, as Walsh (2005) observes, Freeman wrote at a time when business was seen as weak and 'on the ropes'. As discussed in Chapters 2 and 5, stagflation was undermining major capitalist economies, US business in particular was under threat from Japanese competitors, there were unprecedented levels of mergers and acquisitions, and companies were increasingly targets of consumer and environmentalist advocacy. Ironically, given how, today, stakeholder engagement is portrayed by some as a way of harnessing or reducing the power of corporations, the business world that Freeman sought to help was something fragile and troubled.

Second, in contrast with some later authors, Freeman is not positing stakeholder theory as an attack on the shareholder-centric theory of the firm that is central to liberal economics. On the contrary, he adopts a very instrumental approach to stakeholder theory, under which companies choose who their stakeholders are, based on the potential of those stakeholders to jeopardize the firm's survival. This is an important point to note because, subsequently, others have presented the shareholder and stakeholder theories of the firm as something mutually opposed. But as Walsh notes, Freeman only raises this possibility right at the end of his book when he asks (and leaves unanswered):

> Can the notion that managers bear a fiduciary relationship to stockholders . . . be replaced by a concept of management whereby they must act in the interests of the stakeholders of the organization?
>
> (Freeman, 1984; cited in Walsh, 2005, p 249)

Despite writing over three decades ago, Freeman is still respected as a founder of stakeholder theory. But even more recent writers have followed him in subsuming stakeholder management to the purpose of wealth creation,[3] and his work is widely cited by those who have a quite different view of stakeholder engagement. Rather than sets of discrete, typically bilateral, relationships upon which the company chooses to embark with stakeholder groups, more recent stakeholder theory treats the firm as an organism that is embedded in a complex web of relationships, and requires the company to see these other organisms not as objects of managerial action, as was often the case hitherto, but as subjects with their own objectives and purposes. Therefore the stakeholder management model involves the company being aware of, and responsive to, the demands of its constituents, including employees, customers, investors, suppliers, and local communities. In contrast with Freeman, an important consequence of this is that shareholders are no longer regarded as the most important constituents, and shareholder value is not the sole criterion for assessing the company's performance.

This pluralist notion of the company's responsibilities clearly runs counter to the liberal economic model of the firm which postulates that business contributes to the public good by pursuing its narrow economic goals and, hence, that managers should concentrate on maximizing the market value of their companies. It is predicated on the belief that, in real life, the distinction between economic and social ends is seldom as clear as liberal economists pretend, because economic decisions have social consequences and vice versa, and the very idea of separate social and economic worlds is seen by some as mistaken.[4] Although perhaps not what Freeman intended, the stakeholder model has become the dominant framework for seeing companies as integrated in, rather than separated from, the rest of society.

Discussion points

Stakeholder has become a common term in corporate and government parlance.

- What is attractive about the term?
- Is Freeman right to emphasize the importance of knowing one's stakeholders?
- Think of a company. Who are its stakeholders?

Management or engagement?

According to authors such as Barnett et al. (2018), stakeholder thinking today concerns the interactive, mutually engaged, and responsive relationships that establish the very context of doing business and create the groundwork for transparency and accountability.[5] From this perspective, Freeman's stakeholder management is one that is too business-centric, but one reason that managers have accepted the stakeholder concept may be that it complements management thinking. In Chapters 1 and 2, we discuss the difficulty of defining what the responsibilities of business are, and often managers are faced with sets of issues that beg the questions: 'What am I responsible for?' and 'To whom am I responsible?' For managers who have been trained to manage processes such as marketing, production, or finance, it can be easier to understand responsibility in the context of such functional disciplines, and therefore responsibilities to defined constituencies may have more resonance than long, seemingly ad hoc, lists of normative social and environmental issues.[6]

In other words, for stakeholder theorists at least, the value of an issue for a manager derives from the fact that a stakeholder has legitimized it. As Rasche and Esser (2006) point out, this is in line with social theorist Habermas's notion of discourse ethics, wherein ethical norms are justified not by reference to a priori principles, but because all members of society can reach a consensus around them. In contrast with ethicists such as Mill, Kant, Nozick, or Rawls, who offer universal ethical principles (see Chapter 2), Habermas claims that ethical norms can vary according to differences in context. Thus, what is ethical in one situation can change, provided that it is tested and justified through a context-specific discourse involving members of society. Moreover, although the norms can change, what must remain constant and universal are the rules under which the discourse itself is carried out.

CSR theory offers a great deal of advice on how to conduct a consistent, robust, and credible discourse with stakeholders (see Table 9.1). There were attempts to formalize this: for example, the AA1000 Series of the late 1990s and early 2000s was an attempt to spell out the universal rules for reaching an ethical consensus through stakeholder participation. It comprises four main elements underpinned by the principle of stakeholder engagement: (a) company commitment to social and ethical accounting, auditing, and reporting, with stakeholders playing a key role; (b) defining and accounting for the company's actions through stakeholder consultation that identifies issues relating to social and ethical performance, the scope of the social audit, relevant indicators, and the collection and analyses of information; (c) preparation of a CSR report to be audited by an external group, and subjected to external feedback; and (d) embedding social accountability systems into mainstream management practice.[7]

However, the support of some companies and accountancy firms did not guarantee AA1000's success. Although a revised standard was scheduled for 2018, this is ten years after the last revision, suggesting that there has been little progress in the interim.[8] One can conjecture that AA1000's troubles lie in the widely documented problems involved in applying stakeholder theory in everyday management. First, it can be difficult to identify who stakeholders are. At the broadest level, they are individuals, groups, or entities (including, some would argue, the natural environment) that claim rights or interests in a company and in its past, present, and future activities. To narrow this down, Freeman (1984) drew a distinction between 'primary' and 'secondary' stakeholders. Primary stakeholders are those without whose participation a

Table 9.1 Commonly cited phases and factors in engaging with stakeholders

Phases of managing stakeholder dialogue
Selection of stakeholders
Stakeholder dialogue
Interpretation of information from dialogue
Decisions about company actions
Response to the dialogue through activities
Key factors in acting on stakeholder dialogue
Awareness that an issue exists
Commitment to prioritize and resource an issue
Capacity/availability of resources to tackle an issue
Consensus among the company and its stakeholders over the issues and relevance of stakeholder dialogue in general

(*Sources*: Andriof et al., 2017; adapted from Pedersen, 2006)

company cannot survive (e.g. investors, employees, suppliers, customers, and the governments and communities that provide infrastructure and markets). Secondary stakeholders are those that influence the company or are affected by it, but are not essential to its survival, although they may be able to help or harm the company (e.g. the media, terrorists). Therefore the manager's duty is to create sufficient wealth, value, or satisfaction for primary stakeholders to ensure that they remain part of the stakeholder system. He/she may pay attention to secondary stakeholders as well, but there may often be circumstances under which the interests of primary stakeholders are pursued at the expense of those who are secondary (e.g. taking a money-losing product sold to poor communities off the market).

Stakeholders include groups with quite different expectations. One common distinction made is that between those who are influenced by the company's actions and those who have an interest in what the company does. In order to understand the nature of a particular stakeholder and to assess what priority to give its expectations, managers are often advised to make judgements about which they have significant or insignificant degrees of interest, and about those over whom the company has high or low degrees of influence (see Figure 9.1). However, this type of approach does little to help managers to make decisions based on a stakeholder's moral claim and has led to a situation in which companies are accused of responding to stakeholders with the loudest voices or most power, rather than to those with the greatest need or strongest entitlement. Some of these criticisms were expressed in the early 2000s. For instance, Phillips (2003) criticized stakeholder theory for failing to distinguish between, and prioritize, stakeholders based on a moral rather than a business obligation. For Goodpaster (2002), stakeholder analysis was incomplete if it did not weigh the significance of the identified options for the different stakeholder groups and make a normative judgement that integrates this information into a decision. As Gibson (2000) argued, if we do not accept this ethical dimension to the notion of stakeholder, the term itself becomes meaningless, with its use limited to a form of shorthand for referring to a, possibly ad hoc, group of individuals. Similar voices echo today: for example, Moratis and Brandt (2017) highlight the continuing problem of who is excluded from stakeholder engagement, while Elson and Goossen (2017) discuss how the complexities of implementing stakeholder accountability are too great for modern company law to grapple with.

Partly because of this, Freeman abandoned the primary–secondary stakeholder distinction, although it remains widely used by CSR practitioners. Freeman continues to provide a vibrant critique of his own work (e.g. the challenges facing stakeholder theory (Freeman, 2017)). Some of these issues he recognized early on. One outcome he saw was that stakeholders were being treated as the means to corporate ends, rather than as entities whose interests should be served by the company.[9] This is certainly evident in much of what is called 'stakeholder engagement' today, in which consultation and dialogue are carried out with the aim of gathering important input and ideas, anticipating and managing conflicts, improving decision-making, building consensus among diverse views, and strengthening the company's relationships and reputation. There can be a strong business case for stakeholder engagement, including reduced costs, opening new markets, and protecting the company against activism. But this leaves companies open to criticism that they are picking and choosing who to call a stakeholder, and hence whom to listen to, and some managers feel that they are under pressure to respond to some stakeholders rather than others, based on who corporate headquarters regards as important rather than who the company affects.[10]

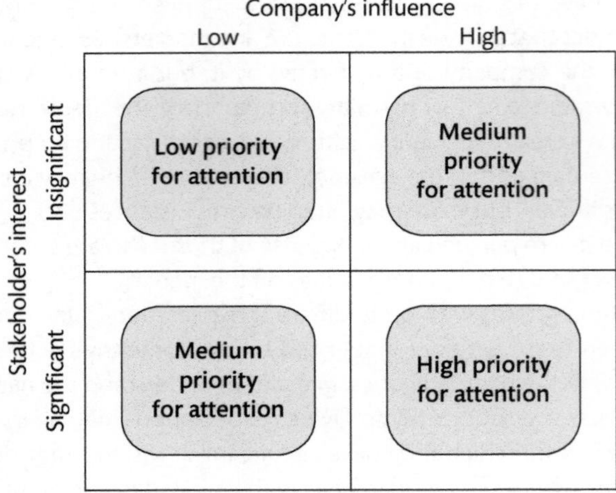

Figure 9.1 How stakeholders' influence and interests affect corporate prioritization

These tensions are highlighted in some of the examples of partnership discussed in Chapter 5, but it is worth reiterating that there is an important distinction to be made between the promise of the stakeholder model, as described by some CSR theorists, and the way in which it is actually being used by companies at the present time. In theory, stakeholder dialogue, engagement, and participation are at the heart of a more democratic form of corporate accountability. As an early advocate of stakeholder approaches to CSR described it:

> Corporate accountability, especially when based on stakeholder engagement . . . is all about learning and change: learning about the organization itself, about those who have a relationship with it, and learning about its place in the larger scheme of things.
>
> (AccountAbility, 2002, p 5)

In practice, the stakeholder model is more typically applied so that a company can manage its stakeholders in the sense of influence and control. It is noticeable, for instance, that many recent studies approach stakeholder engagement from a marketing perspective, and there has been much less interest in applying stakeholder theory in terms of worker or investor relations.[11] This is not to say that stakeholders are taken advantage of, or experience no benefit from this approach; at the very least, companies that participate in extensive stakeholder dialogue have become more sensitized and sensitive to stakeholder concerns. But it is also becoming clear that, if the stakeholder model is to become part of a new way of managing the business–society relationship, companies will need to give up some of their power and influence in order to become accountable to, rather than simply be in discussion with, the wider stakeholder community.[12] One arena of CSR management where this would need to be evident is in the partnerships between a company and other organizations. We have discussed these in general in Chapter 5; now we turn to the particular type of partnership created through voluntary CSR standards.

 Discussion points

The list of a company's stakeholders is potentially enormous.

- Is the distinction between primary and secondary stakeholders valid and useful?
- What are the strengths and weaknesses of using stakeholders to decide the responsibilities of a company?
- Should companies be accountable to stakeholders?

CSR standards

CSR standards are an area of collaboration in a world of harsh corporate competitiveness. The Ethical Trading Initiative (ETI), the Forest Stewardship Council (FSC), the Roundtable on Sustainable Palm Oil (RSPO), the Extractive Industries Transparency Initiative (EITI), and the UN Principles for Responsible Investment are some of the standards, guidelines, and codes that bring together companies from a host of industries. Stakeholder partnerships are frequently presented as an approach to CSR well suited to companies wrestling with the challenges of globalization. Advocates often cite them as a way to hold companies to account in an era when the limits of traditional governance structures are being tested (see Chapter 5). This is taken a step further in the idea of voluntary multi-stakeholder standards or codes of practice. Voluntary standards are a particular approach to managing the effects of business on stakeholders. We begin by discussing this approach in general, but will then highlight the stakeholder dimension to it.

Features of standards

Standards, guidelines, and codes of conduct or practice are largely synonymous terms for an important tool in the management of CSR. The terms might be interchangeable, but there are many types and to say that a company has adopted a standard says little, in itself, about the performance, policies, or strategies of that company. Over half of the 200 largest companies have business codes of some fashion, yet there are enormous differences between businesses in terms of what aspects of corporate behaviour are covered and the extent to which they influence what the company does.[13] Paine et al. (2005), in work that continues to be cited,[14] tried to make sense of this by identifying eight principles that cover the statements, commitments, and requirements found in business codes (see Box 9.1). These show that the codes go beyond much of what is included in CSR today. Many of the issues in contemporary CSR fall under their principles of 'dignity' (e.g. labour rights, workplace health and safety), 'citizenship' (e.g. environmental management, community involvement), and 'responsiveness' (e.g. stakeholder engagement). As is evident in the discussion of CSR in the global value chain (see Chapter 5), there are some who would like CSR to do more to address the principles of transparency and fairness (e.g. treating suppliers fairly and ensuring fair competition). There are also those in the business community who argue that it is hypocritical for companies to talk about CSR if they disregard the principles of property and reliability.

Box 9.1 Underlying principles of business codes

1. Fiduciary principle—aspects of a code that define the responsibilities of directors and management to the company and its investors
2. Property principle—concerning respect for the property rights and assets of the company and its competitors
3. Reliability principle—concerning the honouring of commitments
4. Transparency principle—concerning the conduct of business in a truthful and open manner
5. Dignity principle—concerning respect for people's dignity, including health and safety, human rights, freedom from coercion, and human development
6. Fairness principle—aspects to do with engaging in free and fair competition
7. Citizenship principle—aspects requiring the company to act as a responsible citizen of the community, including legal compliance, environmental responsibility, and non-involvement in politics
8. Responsiveness principle—aspects requiring the company to be responsive to parties with legitimate claims and concerns about its activities

(*Sources*: Adapted from Paine et al., 2005; Carroll and Buckholtz, 2006; Rasche, 2010)

Box 9.2 Johnson & Johnson's credo

We believe our first responsibility is to the doctors, nurses and patients, to mothers and fathers and others who use our products and services. In meeting their needs everything we do must be of high quality. We must constantly strive to reduce our costs in order to maintain reasonable prices. Customers' orders must be serviced promptly and accurately. Our suppliers and distributors must have an opportunity to make a fair profit.

We are responsible to our employees, the men and women who work with us throughout the world. Everyone must be considered as an individual. We must respect their dignity and recognize their merit. They must have a sense of security in their jobs. Compensation must be fair and adequate, and working conditions clean, orderly and safe. We must be mindful of ways to help our employees fulfil their family responsibilities. Employees must feel free to make suggestions and complaints. There must be equal opportunity for employment, development and advancement for those qualified. We must provide competent management, and their actions must be just and ethical.

We are responsible to the communities in which we live and work and to the world community as well. We must be good citizens, support good works and charities and bear our fair share of taxes. We must encourage civic improvements and better health and education. We must maintain in good order the property we are privileged to use, protecting the environment and natural resources.

Our final responsibility is to our stockholders. Business must make a sound profit. We must experiment with new ideas. Research must be carried on, innovative programmes developed and mistakes paid for. New equipment must be purchased, new facilities provided and new products launched. Reserves must be created to provide for adverse times. When we operate according to these principles, the stockholders should realize a fair return.

(*Source*: http://www.jnj.com/connect/about-jnj/?flash=true)

Broad business codes can provide a context for managing CSR, as is the case, for example, with Johnson & Johnson's statement of principles (see Box 9.2). For the most part, however, modern CSR has more narrowly defined concerns. Typical broad issues covered in codes are:[15]

1. the natural environment;
2. labour;
3. corporate governance;
4. money laundering;
5. bribery and corruption;
6. human rights;
7. CSR reporting principles (see Table 9.2).

Table 9.2 Examples of CSR standards

Issue covered	Examples of standards
Environmental	CERES principles ISO14000 environmental management series Kyoto Protocol
Labour	Fair Labor Association workplace code of conduct ETI base code Fair Wear Foundation
Corporate governance	OECD principles of corporate governance Principles for corporate governance in the Commonwealth Toronto Stock Exchange guidelines for improved corporate governance
Money laundering	Wolfsberg anti-money laundering principles Basel Committee on banking supervision
Bribery and corruption	OECD convention combating bribery of foreign public officials in international business transactions International Chamber of Commerce rules of conduct to combat extortion and bribery Extractive Industry Transparency Initiative
Human rights	Amnesty International human rights principles for companies UN draft norms on the responsibilities of transnational corporations and other business enterprises with regard to human rights Voluntary principles on security and human rights
Corporate reporting	AA1000 series Global Reporting Initiative guidelines on social, economic, and environmental reporting
Comprehensive	UN Global Compact principles OECD guidelines for multinational enterprises ISO 26000 CSR standard

In some instances, these issues are addressed in individual company standards which, despite sometimes involving a degree of stakeholder consultation, fall short of what might be considered a stakeholder partnership. However, they can also form part of comprehensive industry-specific or general business standards, such as the FSC's principles of sustainable forest management and the Equator Principles for the financial industry.

The distinctions between standards have become important as interest has grown in assessing the effectiveness of so-called 'voluntary' standards.[16] Particular attention has been paid to the way in which standards are developed, as a determinant of their robustness, effectiveness, and credibility, and the following types are common.

1. Company standards developed within a company for its own use, perhaps with some external consultation, and with reference to relevant international norms and standards (e.g. on human rights, emissions, or corruption).
2. Company standards built on consultation with relevant stakeholders and making explicit reference to international standards.
3. Industry standards developed by a peer group of companies, perhaps with external consultation, and with differing degrees of reference to international norms and standards.
4. Multi-stakeholder standards developed for an industry, or a wider range of companies, built on a consensus among business, non-government, and trade union organizations.
5. Independent standards made available to an industry, or wider range of companies, but developed by non-business groups, such as trade unions and NGOs.
6. Framework agreements between a company and trade unions.

Some argue that standards developed by companies, separately or with their peers, are more likely to reflect the concerns of Northern consumers than the full breadth of social or environmental issues relevant to a company, and that standards developed independently of business are more comprehensive.[17] In the late 1990s, Kolk et al. (1999) claimed that certain types of standard were likely to have a greater impact than others; for example, those developed by international organizations, such as the OECD and the ILO, or those developed by civil society organizations, such as the Clean Clothes Campaign and Social Accountability International, will be more rigorous than those developed by individual companies or industries, such as Levi Strauss, Nike, and the Apparel Industry Partnership. However, there is less difference in content between company and independent standards today than there was a few years ago, although it has been argued that the distinction is still valid in areas such as taxation.[18]

The criteria for assessing codes were set early on. For example, Ranganathan (1998) said that a standard should meet the '3 Cs' used in financial auditing; that is, they must be:

1. *comprehensive*, or complete enough to cover the issues that are most pertinent or material to the company;
2. *comparable*, to allow inter-company assessment of performance;

3. *credible* enough to allow business and other stakeholders to trust their integrity and to use them in making informed judgements.

This last requirement is also sometimes called 'materiality'. Various additional characteristics of a credible standard have been identified, as follows.[19]

1. Content that is relevant to the industry, but not simply a reflection of the most publicized problems.
2. Clarity and conciseness in terms of language, style, and format.
3. Explicit reference made to relevant international standards and conventions.
4. Inclusivity, requiring the participation of all key stakeholders who have a legitimate interest in what the standard is measuring.
5. Continual improvement of the criteria against which performance is assessed.
6. A commitment regarding to whom the results of any assessment will be disclosed.
7. Suitability of the standard for implementation, including setting out indicators that are measurable and trackable over time.
8. Availability of the standard in the main languages of the locations within which it will be used.

Discussion points

Stakeholder standards are often portrayed as the most robust way of implementing voluntary regulation.

- What roles do you think stakeholders can play in implementing standards?
- Should stakeholders ignore the law when deciding standards?
- How can it be ensured that all stakeholder voices are heard?

Multi-stakeholder standards

There are many standards, and a common complaint heard from managers is that they are required to comply with too many standards, many of which address the same issues (see Snapshot 9.1). The Global Social Compliance initiative, originally pioneered by Walmart and now in the hands of the business-backed Consumer Goods Forum, has sought to harmonize the implementation of labour and environmental standards, and attempts to address this concern through a process called 'equivalence'. However, it remains an issue, especially among suppliers of Western retailers and brands which at times have received up to forty audits in a month. Only a relatively small number of standards can show extensive stakeholder participation in their development, implementation, and accountability. But even those that can have their distinct characteristics, as the following three examples show.

Snapshot 9.1 The Global Reporting Initiative

The Global Reporting Initiative (GRI) guidelines serve as a framework for reporting on social, economic, and environmental performance. Launched in 2000, they are now in their fourth iteration (G4) and have undergone a process of integration to create a consolidated set of GRI Sustainability Reporting Standards announced in June 2018. They are neither a performance standard nor a management system, although they can be useful to the development of both. Their primary purpose is to provide a common benchmark to encourage companies to communicate what actions they are taking to improve non-financial performance, the outcomes of these actions, and the future strategies for improving performance.

The guidelines, which are freely available at http://www.globalreporting.org, represent what GRI has identified as the most relevant reporting content. There are also supplements for industries, such as mining and banking, and technical protocols on specific indicators, such as child labour and energy. Companies can choose whether to produce reports 'in accordance with' or more loosely 'with reference to' the guidelines, and 90% of those that cite the guidelines choose the latter. This figure may change as GRI introduces more levels of reporting, but questions about how many and how fast new levels should be introduced are indicative of a wider issue that GRI faces in balancing prescription and flexibility.

Despite any shortcomings, proponents say that the guidelines have provided the signposts that have led many companies away from producing reports consisting of what critics call photos of happy smiling children and not much else to those that at least begin to recognize the array of social, economic, and environmental issues with which the company is involved. Furthermore, by retaining the support of business and non-business constituencies while undertaking three major revisions, the guidelines have become a testing ground for global stakeholder engagement.

(*Sources*: GRI, 2002; Hale and Held, 2018; http://www.globalreporting.org)

Quick questions

The GRI guidelines are intended to provide a common framework for company reporting on sustainability issues.

1. Why is this kind of common framework necessary?
2. Why has the GRI focused on guidelines rather than on a certifiable standard?
3. What are the strengths and weaknesses of this kind of approach?

SA8000—the independent code

In 1998, the Council on Economic Priorities, now Social Accountability International (SAI), created SA8000 with advice from representatives of business, trade unions, and NGOs.[20] It is a verifiable standard, focusing on labour rights and worker welfare, and is intended to be applicable to any industry and in any country. It combines elements of ILO labour conventions with ISO management systems, and has been revised and extended to include more detailed provisions for specific industries, such as agriculture. SAI and its panel of companies, civil society organizations, and academics certify companies that comply with its provisions. This means that conditions in their facilities have been verified by independent accredited SA8000 auditors, and that the auditors' findings have been ratified by SAI.

SA8000 is different from many standards in that it has both performance and process elements, prescribing not only the labour criteria with which a company must comply, but also acceptable systems for embedding the standard into daily management practice. Over 1,000 facilities in fifty-five countries have been certified to date. A bone of contention is that these facilities bear the cost of auditing, even though certification is typically a buyer's requirement. But this is not fundamentally different from other costs relating to management systems, such as ISO certification.

Forest Stewardship Council—a stakeholder-owned standard

The Forest Stewardship Council (FSC) was first mooted as an idea in 1990 in response to the failure of traditional approaches to arrest the decline of the world's forest resources.[21] The organization, which is managed by a secretariat and overseen by a partnership comprising business, indigenous rights organizations, community groups, and environmental NGOs, acts as custodian to a certification standard that sets out key principles and criteria for forest stewardship. The standard provides a basis for assessing if a forest is being responsibly managed in relation to silviculture practices, environmental impact, working conditions, workers' and community rights, and indigenous people's rights. Certification of a forest involves a fairly extensive four-stage auditing process, including pre-assessments, field visits, peer review, and ratification. A certificate is valid for five years, although there may be interim inspections.

A feature of the FSC is that it is not only a standard, but also a partnership. As an organization, it draws support from a wide membership base around the world. Moreover, its governance structure is designed to limit the influence of any single member, or category of member. The FSC board features representatives of those with a commercial interest, those with an environmental interest, and those with a social interest in forests, and these groups all have a say in major decisions at the general assembly. This structure is an interesting example of global democracy in action and, although it has been criticized for being slow and unwieldy, the FSC standard is widely regarded as the benchmark for forest certification.

The Equator Principles—an industry-wide stakeholder code

The Equator Principles[22] stipulate how financial institutions should consider environmental and social issues in their project finance operations. The signatories are primarily European and North American banks, and the standard clearly reflects reputational concerns about their portfolios of lending to developing countries. These arise from the potentially high risk of adverse social and environmental impacts that are attached to the infrastructure, energy, extractive, and other projects financed in this way (e.g. relocation, ecological damage, impact on communities). The Principles commit banks to formulating environmental and social policies and processes against which individual projects can be assessed for compliance. Their provisions are based on the social and environmental policies and procedures of the International Finance Corporation, and, among other things, require banks to screen proposed projects according to their potential social and environmental impacts. The outcome of the screening process, in turn, triggers a range of follow-up activities, and the most dangerous projects are subjected to more rigorous assessment, public consultation, and information disclosure requirements.

While signatory banks agree to adopt these policies and procedures, implementation is left to the individual bank and, in contrast with the FSC or SA8000, there is no requirement that companies independently verify how they are implementing the standard. Indeed, the Principles explicitly state that they are a benchmark for use in the development of each member company's policies. However, there is an implicit assumption that, by involving large project finance banks, the Principles will create an environment within which good social and environmental policies are the norm, and will encourage industry-wide improvements. There has been no publicly available assessment of achievement, but an EP report in 2018 said it was on target to meet its goals. However, at present, success is being measured in terms of the number and size of the signatory companies, with over ninety financial institutions signed up to the third version of the Principles, and a fourth version currently under discussion.

Stakeholder consensus: deviance and uniformity

A promise of stakeholder engagement is that it will allow companies to better understand and respond to the expectations of society. Standards are a way of establishing a widely applicable benchmark for measuring corporate responsibilities, but one should be careful not to overestimate the feasibility or desirability of universal norms and practices. It is possible to portray the stakeholder role in applying standards as a mere embellishment of the uniformity and standardization found in conventional quality or financial management. But the additionality of stakeholder engagement is if it helps to meet the specific challenges of non-conventional performance management. An example of this is the defining and securing of good performance in diverse locations. Cannon (1994) identifies five types of community in which business might have a role to play to ameliorate the effect of economic downturns. The first is high-stress environments, in which the community has endured a long period of economic disadvantage, and has consequently suffered economically and psychologically. The second is structurally disadvantaged areas, such as remote islands or towns, which have lost their physical competitive advantage, as, for example, happened in Liverpool when UK trade shifted from having a transatlantic to a more European focus. Another type is the crisis zone, within which a dominant company or industry in a region collapses, as has happened with the automotive industry in the UK's Midlands. A different type of community is that of the transitional area, within which the important industries for the local economy are changing, as has happened in the German Ruhr. Finally, there are communities in which powerhouse industries that have been the catalyst for local growth (e.g. California's software industry) find themselves buffeted by competition from elsewhere and have to adjust accordingly.

A comparison of regional studies of CSR by authors such as Jamali and Carroll (2017) and Cantino and Cortese (2017) show the importance of understanding CSR in a local context. Hamann et al. (2005) and Egbon et al. (2018) have pointed out, in the African context, CSR needs to take into account realities specific to individual countries. For example, in South Africa, there is the historical legacy of poverty and inequality that is reflected today in the 55% of the population living in poverty, in over 30% unemployment, in chronic housing and sanitation shortages, and in high HIV prevalence. Second, CSR needs to recognize, and be rigorous enough to combat, the distrust of certain companies and industries arising from their complicity in exploitation and the apartheid regime. Third, there are established traditions of CSR in South Africa, particularly community social investment, and now black economic empowerment, through which black entrepreneurship is being encouraged. Fourth, the struggle against apartheid and the consequent emphasis put on legislation to ensure social justice, fundamental human rights, and democracy mean that government has a crucial role to play in CSR. Finally, small and medium-sized companies in the formal and informal sectors make up 95% of South African business and their role, capacity, and needs are all relevant for CSR.

These issues are not only pertinent to Africa more widely. The particular issues that are high on the African CSR agenda may not be identical to those of other regions (see Table 9.3), but, more significantly, they are often different to, or at least more nuanced than, the CSR agendas that many multinational companies think of as globally relevant. Often these agendas are built on what Western-based multinationals and, more significantly, Western-oriented stakeholders think should be the priorities of Africa or elsewhere. Thus, for example, Western stakeholder priorities for Africa might be to combat corruption, improve governance and transparency, and improve infrastructure, while local priorities might be to improve the

Table 9.3 Comparison of priority social and environmental issues across selected countries and regions

Country/region	Social and environmental issue
European Union	Decoupling growth from consumption Sustaining welfare, health, and labour standards in a global economy Clean air and emissions trading Marine environment and fisheries
USA	Energy security, including renewed calls for nuclear power Climate change policy Public health accessibility Social security Corporate governance
Latin America	Rich–poor divide Basic environmental management Good public governance and fighting corruption Infrastructure Competitiveness and security of small farmers
Africa	Good public governance and fighting corruption Terms of trading Infrastructure Conflict Managerial capacity
Japan	Nuclear power Air pollution Exploitation of offshore fisheries and foreign tropical forests Urban environment Foreign workers

(*Sources*: Ethical Corporation, 2006; PWC, 2006)

terms of trading, create good jobs, and transfer technology. Such issues may not be mutually exclusive, but it can be questioned how far CSR can progress if both sets of priorities are not recognized, and there remain serious questions about the effectiveness of stakeholder participation in getting multinationals, in particular, to tackle local priorities. As Rajak's work on CSR in the mining industry shows (Rajak, 2006), companies may not deliberately seek to rule out local priorities, but their decisions about what to support have the effect of legitimizing or delegitimizing particular issues.

Different perspectives on what CSR's priorities are have also been noted in Latin America, where advocates in the West may focus on rainforest conservation and biodiversity, while local people may be more concerned about poverty, poor education, bad housing, and scarce health care.[23] According to Schmidheiny:

> the key [CSR] challenges for these regions . . . have to do not so much with the number of companies talking about [CSR], but with creating a home-grown, meaningful form of [CSR] that addresses local issues and improves society, while also strengthening government's capacity.
>
> (Schmidheiny, 2006, p 22)

Discussion points

The responsibilities of companies can vary according to location and circumstance.

1. Why do some stakeholders misunderstand local priorities?
2. Is it useful for a company to have a universal vision of its responsibilities of the kind developed by Johnson & Johnson (see Box 9.2)?
3. What are the difficulties companies face in recognizing regional differences?

Government and governance

As Visser and Tolhurst pointed out in 2010, what makes CSR important in the context of any developing country is that it embodies many of the dilemmas that business faces in trying to be responsible, sustainable, and ethical (see Snapshot 9.2). For example, it raises questions about when local traditions take precedence over international standards, about how far a company's responsibilities extend in providing public services, and about when business's involvement in local governance enhances a weak governance infrastructure and when it constitutes an unhealthy intrusion into the political process. Are, for instance, multinationals culpable for the deaths of over 200 workers in factories producing clothes for export, or should responsibility rest with the local government and Bangladeshi factory-owners? This last question reflects a wider theme that marks out discussions about CSR in developing economies, i.e. the role of government. While the European Union, for example, has chosen to emphasize CSR as a voluntary approach that places no extra legislative burden on business, the role of government and the links between CSR and regulation are central to debates in developing nations.

There are various explanations for this. For example, in China, the government has defined CSR in terms of its own priority of ensuring social stability and uses the term to mean government regulation.[24] In parts of Latin America, Asia, and Africa, an important element of the CSR agenda concerns fighting corruption and improving public governance, and therefore includes activities to build government capacity and the rule of law. Also, companies do not want to be saddled with an unsustainable burden of providing public goods, and therefore would prefer to partner with government and others. In general, it seems to come down to the fact that the business community is reasonably satisfied that, in countries with developed economies and democracies, government is able to maintain social stability; it is more concerned that business will be over-regulated. In developing economies, however, especially those in which governments are either weak or dictatorial, the business community is more concerned about the rule of law, and the creation of social stability and a favourable business environment, and therefore under- rather than overregulation is the issue.

Snapshot 9.2 Multi-stakeholder governance—Extractive Industries Transparency Initiative

EITI is an example of a strategic multi-stakeholder partnership with an explicit governance function. It was launched by the British government at the 2002 Johannesburg Summit, and after many years of encouraging companies in the extractive industries to disclose their payments to governments (e.g. mining royalties), it launched the EITI Standard in 2016. Although it is primarily an inter-firm partnership, it has always enjoyed strong political support from OECD governments. Furthermore, its successful implementation depends on active civil society organizations, not least at the national level.

EITI is based on the idea that greater transparency and accountability in countries that depend on revenues from oil, gas, and mining will help those countries avoid the 'resource curse', which in the past has been blamed for the mismanagement of finances and corruption in resource-rich but economically poor countries. Relief of the resource curse, it is argued, will enable the revenues from extractive industries to become an engine for sustainable development. The EITI Standard formalized a number of practices that the organization has tried to encourage since its founding. These include disclosure requirements on beneficial ownership, ensuring that the identity of the real owners of the oil, gas, and mining companies operating in EITI countries are public (target for 2020); and a validation system to better recognize efforts to exceed the EITI Requirements while setting out fairer consequences for EITI countries that are not yet EITI-compliant.

At the international level, EITI is based on a set of twelve principles that were developed under the stewardship of the British government through discussions involving multinational extractive companies, NGOs, institutional investors, and international institutions such as the World Bank Group. At this level, companies agree to disclose what they pay to governments in resource-rich countries. At the national level, the EITI is a government-led initiative, and governments agree to publish the revenues they receive from extractive industries. But it is also recognized that for this information to be used effectively, there has to be a formal role for other stakeholders from the private sector and civil society. In this way, not only is the information on payments and revenues disclosed in a transparent, accessible, and comprehensible manner, but it can be acted upon, for instance by exploring whether the revenues are being used for development programmes.

The initiative has earned itself a mix of praise and criticism, often for the same reasons. For example, its narrow focus on financial transparency means that it does nothing about many other sustainability issues in the extractive industry value chain, and depending on one's point of view this is a strength or a

(*continued*...)

weakness. It has also been accused of omitting stakeholders that have historically helped local people tackle the resource curse (e.g. trade unions), and of shifting power to community-level government officials regardless of whether they have local people's trust or not.

A recurring criticism is that EITI is a Western-led initiative that not only has failed to gain the support of the increasingly important extractive industries from emerging economies, but may promote values that are not aligned with the culture, philosophy, and business interests of those economies. For example, China's national oil companies have not supported EITI even though they have pursued a programme of rapid international expansion since 2002. This expansion is paid for through the 'Angola' model of investment in which development aid, debt relief, low-interest loans, and infrastructure development are given to the host country in return for access to its resources. This type of barter relationship is not suited to the EITI system, which assumes a much more Western capitalist model of exchange.

(*Sources*: EITI, 2005; Klein, 2017; Rustad et al., 2017; http://www.EITI.org/history)

Quick questions

EITI is a widely acknowledged example of an international multi-stakeholder partnership.

1. What category of partnership does it represent?
2. Is its narrow focus a strength or a weakness?
3. Are extractive companies from emerging economies right not to join EITI?

When CSR was becoming an increasing part of mainstream management in the mid- and late 2000s, authors such as Reich (2007) and Vogel (2012) were critical of the dumbing-down of regulation that they believe corporate self-regulation permits. It is certainly true that some companies have, over the years, thrived in oppressive regimes, and many are prepared to do business in countries, such as Burma and China, that are openly resistant to Western ideals of public governance. But there is evidence that companies operating in such countries at times use CSR not simply as a substitute for good public governance, but as a way of introducing good governance norms in the hope that they will shape public institutions in the future.[25] This, in turn, reflects a belief that if ever there was a business case for taking advantage of unstable oppressive political conditions, for multinational companies and industries in a global economy these conditions represent an undesirable risk—one that, if it cannot be avoided entirely (e.g. because of the physical location of natural resources, or the competitive advantage of low-waged labour), must be reduced, and CSR offers a means of achieving that end.

These are compelling arguments, especially if one believes that Western prosperity is a consequence of democracy as much as of capitalism.[26] It is also worth noting that, in countries such as Morocco, governments have used CSR as a framework within which to promote a renewed commitment to better labour practices, controlling child labour, and new legislation to combat corruption, and to improve workplace rights of women and the disabled, and the rights of trade unions. Indeed, seeing this as a way of complying with trade agreements and attracting businesses in competition with lower-waged competitors, the government has made CSR part of its strategy to win foreign investment.

Yet many still resent or resist CSR and see it as an outsiders' imposition. This is not simply a case of the status quo resisting reform. Developing countries can be victims of the subsidies and protections that the USA, European, and other countries give to industries such as agriculture and defence—policies that, in turn, are related to poverty and lack of economic opportunity. Moreover, poverty and exploitation are seen by some as the hallmark of colonial and post-war entrepreneurs, and this sudden conversion to responsibility is seen as hypocrisy, at best, and commercial gamesmanship, at worst.[27] As multinationals headquartered in countries such as India, China, Brazil, and Mexico gain prominence, and foreign direct investment from such countries grows (see Chapter 4), so speculation has mounted that this will undermine the efforts of Western multinationals to raise standards. Such views reflect a somewhat rose-tinted view of Western corporate behaviour in developing countries over the years, and may at times be inflected with racial prejudice. At the very least, such assumptions need more sophisticated analysis than they have received to date. In countries such as India, where some conglomerates date back to the nineteenth century, there is resentment of the implication that they are irresponsible, or have not built a relationship with the society. Tata, for example, has established various institutes that invest in social and environmental innovation, and has a long tradition of giving back to communities. In 1998, it formalized the Tata Code of Conduct, which includes areas such as involvement with communities, ethical conduct for company officers, and a commitment not to support any political party or political activity. This, in turn, is backed up with whistle-blower protections, and sanctions such as demotion and dismissal for anyone breaching the code. Conversely, Scandinavian countries are often admired for their strong worker rights and environmental standards, but the voluntary standards that Scandinavian companies promote in developing countries seem little different from those of multinational companies headquartered elsewhere.

Discussion points

Stakeholder participation has been described as more inclusive than the conventional government system.

1. Is stakeholder participation democratic?
2. Is the role of companies in tackling governance issues in developing and developed economies different?
3. Will companies headquartered in emerging economies have different ideas of responsibility to their Western counterparts?

One response to disquiet at the imposition of CSR from overseas has been the creation of local CSR organizations. While many individual companies have started to produce CSR reports, these are often aimed at overseas audiences, not least the US or European stock markets, on which some of these companies are now listed. CSR organizations, however, have more flexibility in terms of developing a locally relevant CSR agenda. They include the Malawi-based African Institute for Corporate Citizenship and the Forum EMPRESA network of CSR organizations in seventeen Latin American countries.[28] However, they are not always successful, and the Chinese Association for Corporate Social Responsibility, established by foreign and domestic companies in 2006, seems to have disappeared without a trace.

Case study 9 Roundtable on Sustainable Palm Oil—two decades of international multi-stakeholder partnerships across the value chain

The Roundtable on Sustainable Palm Oil (RSPO) was formed in 2002 and has been operating around the world for over two decades, making it one of the oldest stakeholder partnerships in existence alongside the Marine Stewardship Council, the Forest Stewardship Council, and the Ethical Trading Initiative.

Palm oil is a major global commodity used in foodstuffs, soaps, cosmetics, and now biofuels. It is produced from the fruit of oil palms that grow in tropical regions on plantations and smallholdings. Production has escalated rapidly since the 1980s, most notably in Malaysia and Indonesia. This expansion has often resulted in the deforestation of tropical forests. This has negative consequences for biodiversity, and conservationists were among the loudest early protesters against oil palm; but when it also involves deforestation of forests in areas of peat, it results in the release of large amounts of what was previously sequestered CO_2.

RSPO was launched as a joint initiative of NGOs, palm oil processors and traders, financiers, retailers, food manufacturers, and industry bodies such as the Malaysian Palm Oil Association. After two years of negotiation, it was formally established as a not-for-profit association in Switzerland, although its head offices are now in Kuala Lumpur and Jakarta. It was intended to be a demand-side coalition creating a demand for sustainable palm oil, much as the FSC had created a market for certified timber. Unilever and Migros had already set standards for sustainable palm oil, but it was felt that retailers and manufacturers working together would be able to put more pressure on producers to conform to the new standards. Moreover, by involving NGOs, it was felt that the demand side could build consumer awareness and support, and reduce what sometimes felt like ill-informed campaigns by advocacy groups.

Not all NGOs accepted this offer and some, such as Greenpeace, have continued to mount anti-palm-oil campaigns since RSPO's launch. There was also disagreement between companies and the participating NGOs, notably on how much the supply side should be involved, and whether the primary focus should be on oil palms as a cause of deforestation. For example, Unilever, which was the most influential of the initial companies, did not think that the causal link between oil palms and deforestation was as strong as NGOs claimed, and moreover did not believe that simply using buyer strength was sufficient to bring about substantial changes in producer practices. Disagreement about this latter point was keeping producers away from the initiative, but after the first roundtable meeting in 2003 it was agreed that producers, NGOs, and buyers would all have equal representation.

Achieving an acceptable balance between different sectors, and different parts of the value chain, was a major step in RSPO's evolution, and while there continued to be disagreements, there was also a sense of common ownership. In 2005, RSPO members adopted the 'principles and criteria for sustainable palm oil production', comprising eight principles and thirty-nine criteria on economic, environmental, and social aspects of palm oil production. Thus, RSPO had evolved from being a partnership for systematic dialogue to one that included rule-setting as a central focus. However, in doing so, it developed standards that its multiple stakeholders could agree on, and the elaborate governance structures and procedures emphasized consensus rather than coercion—common positions rather than differences.

(continued . . .)

This approach, which was also time-consuming, was frustrating for some outside the process who wanted rapid change and interpreted the symptoms of consensus-building as evidence of failure. Greenpeace published a report, *Cooking the climate*, and sent people in orang-utan costumes up the outside of Unilever's HQ. Nonetheless, certification began in 2008 with 106,000 hectares of productive area, and now covers 2.5 million hectares. Over 11.9 million metric tonnes of certified palm oil has been sold on the international market, accounting for 19% of global production. Despite this significant rise, and the support of some of the largest palm-oil producers such as Sime Darby and Wilmar, there are major energy and food markets where non-certified oil can still be sold (e.g. China and India). Because growing units, not companies, are certified, plantation owners can benefit from the certified and non-certified markets, and continue deforestation. Certified palm oil can attract a premium; the organization emphasizes other advantages to certification such as better relations with NGOs and access to certain markets where buyers are committed to only purchasing certified palm oil.

Nonetheless, RSPO has demonstrated the adaptability of its partnership model over time. RSPO now has an office in Beijing and believes it is making positive progress in China, India, the USA, and Australia. Early on, its challenge was to bring together powerful organizations to create an immediate legitimacy, but this led to problems in engaging with some parts of the value chain, not least the smaller producers, who saw RSPO as a threat, a cost, or an irrelevance. RSPO changed from a demand-based to a supply-demand orientation, and also accepted a role for NGOs. It achieved consensus around a sustainable production standard, but members found that the standard itself, rather than protecting their image, became a target for civil society criticism. Producer unease has been partly offset by the growth in the market for certified oil, but the challenge now is to get yet more of the cultivated area certified even if global demand is uncertain.

(*Sources*: Blowfield, 2012; Kadarusman and Herabadi, 2018; http://www.rspo.org)

Quick questions

1. RSPO is an example of a rule-setting partnership and what has been called private or partnered governance.
   - a How does this approach to governance differ from conventional governance mechanisms?
   - b What are the key elements of its governance system?
   - c What are the strengths and weaknesses of multi-stakeholder partnerships as an approach to governance?
2. The partnership challenges of RSPO have evolved over time.
   - a Why were NGOs attracted to a demand-side-led approach to begin with?
   - b Why did retailers and manufacturers doubt that this would work?
   - c Should NGO partners protect the palm-oil industry from criticism by other civil society organizations?
3. RSPO has created a market for certified sustainable palm oil.
   - a How can it expand this market in emerging economies?
   - b Can it expand the area under cultivation for certified oil to more than 20% of total production?
   - c What role can the different stakeholders play in increasing RSPO's legitimacy?

Summary

The notion of a stakeholder and the evolution of stakeholder management and engagement are pivotal in contemporary CSR practice. While stakeholder management theory regards stakeholders as entities to be recognized but ultimately controlled, stakeholder engagement views companies as parts of complex interdependent webs, within which many groups claim a stake (i.e. a right) in the company by virtue of the impact that the company has on them, or their power to influence the company in some way. Voluntary standards, codes of conduct, and guidelines are one concrete outcome of stakeholder engagement. However, there are many examples of standards being designed and implemented without any real stakeholder engagement, and some advocates of stakeholder management believe that normative instruments such as standards run counter to the emphasis of stakeholder theory on continual dialogue and responsiveness.

There are many kinds of standard and a variety of institutional arrangements for developing them. It is in the area of implementation that stakeholder engagement is widely seen as good practice, although, in reality, many companies remain reluctant about how far to go in involving others in what are seen as management decisions. Nonetheless, the stakeholder model has clearly affected the way in which many companies see the world and their role within it, and there is widespread acceptance that, in addition to any responsibility to shareholders, there are also responsibilities to employees, consumers, customers and suppliers, and communities. The location from which a company is engaging with stakeholders has a significant effect on how these processes are managed. In fact, one of the features of CSR that distinguishes it from many other areas of management, such as quality control, is that good practice can vary by country or region. And herein lies the challenge of managing CSR—not only the balancing of the expectations and values of diverse, often globally dispersed, stakeholders, and the demonstration of one's accomplishments in concrete terms, but also the accommodation of the fact that these expectations and values are subject to continual change.

Further reading

Bowie, N. 2018, *Business ethics in the 21st century (issues in business ethics)*, Springer, Dordrecht, The Netherlands.

Discussion of normative and practical approaches to business and its stakeholders.

Freeman, R.E. 2010, *Strategic management: a stakeholder approach*, Cambridge University Press, Cambridge.

A reprint and update of Freeman's seminal book that introduced stakeholder theory to business.

Husted, B. 2011, *Corporate social strategy: stakeholder engagement and competitive advantage*, Cambridge University Press, Cambridge.

An exploration of the business reasons to adopt a stakeholder approach to strategic thinking.

Lindgreen, A., Maon, L., Vanhamme, J., Palacios Florencio, B., Strong, C., and Vallaster, C., eds 2018, *Engaging with stakeholders: a relational perspective on responsible business*, Routledge, London.

An overview of current thinking about stakeholder management theory.

Seitanidi, M.M. 2010, *The politics of partnerships: a critical examination of nonprofit-business partnerships*, Springer, Dordrecht, The Netherlands.
A discussion of the nature of stakeholder partnerships based on in-depth studies of two major business-NGO collaborations.

Steger, U. 2009, *Sustainability partnerships: the manager's handbook*, Palgrave Macmillan, Basingstoke.
Guidance on how to implement partnerships.

http://www.oup.com/uk/blowfield_murray4e

Visit the online resources that accompany this book to enrich your understanding of this chapter. Among the resources available are web links, exercises, and additional case studies.

Endnotes

1. Blowfield and Googins, 2007.
2. Preston and Sapienza, 1990.
3. See, e.g., Andriof et al, 2017; Miles, 2017.
4. See, e.g., the discussion of the work of Karl Polanyi in Chapter 4.
5. Andriof et al., 2017.
6. Clarkson, 1995.
7. AccountAbility, 2006; Leipziger, 2010.
8. Bendell, 2017.
9. Evan and Freeman, 1988.
10. CCC, 2005a.
11. See, e.g., Grappi et al., 2013; Deng and Xu, 2017; Gangi and d'Angelo, 2017.
12. CCC, 2005a; Rasche and Esser, 2006.
13. Kaptein, 2004.
14. See, e.g., Blok, 2017.
15. Cragg and McKague, 2003.
16. Utting and Marques, 2010.
17. See, e.g., Varley et al., 1998; Kolk et al., 1999; Ascoly et al., 2001.
18. Huang et al., 2017.
19. See, e.g., MacGillivray and Zadek, 1995; ISEA, 1999; Mamic, 2004; Leipziger, 2010.
20. Leipziger, 2001.
21. Bartley, 2003.
22. Wright and Rwabizambuga, 2006.
23. Svendsen and Laberge, 2005.
24. CCC, 2005c. L.E. Mitchell (2005) seems to agree with this: out of six benefits cited in the case study, four are given as intangible, i.e. with no assigned monetary value.
25. Sabapathy et al., 2002.
26. For a counter-argument to this viewpoint, see Chang, 2007, 2010.
27. Svendsen and Laberge, 2005.
28. See CSR360 for a comprehensive list of national and regional CSR organizations: http://www.csr360gpn.org, accessed 26 November 2018.

Socially responsible investment

Chapter overview

In this chapter, we examine socially responsible investment (SRI). We outline why the need for SRI exists, the origins and development of SRI and recent developments such as impacting investing and blended value, and address the impact that these investment strategies can have. In particular, we will:

- look at the crisis of mainstream investment;
- review the evolution of SRI;
- describe the main approaches used in SRI decision-making;
- examine the performance of SRI funds;
- provide an overview of the international market for SRI and its development in different regional contexts;
- examine emerging trends in SRI.

Main topics

Key terms

Finance
Socially responsible investment (SRI)
Negative screening
Positive screening
Sustainable investing
Engagement
Cleantech
Venture capital

The problems of mainstream investment

SRI emerged as a reaction against the mainstream investment industry. Initially, that industry was criticized for a blinkered approach to investments so that stocks in arms companies and tobacco were seen no differently to ones in health or environmental safety: all that mattered was a company's performance, not its products. More recently, high pay among financial executives, repeated instances of financial mismanagement and criminality, and the abuse of power (e.g. bullying practices against small businesses) have increased the demand for alternative investments that are more ethical and more reliable, especially if they offer competitive rates of return.

The origins and development of SRI

In Chapter 7, we addressed the place of CSR in the corporate governance framework and how companies shape their relationships with a wider society. That discussion included consideration of the structures that are in place to ensure that managers do not invest in risky projects. This chapter looks at the structures in place to ensure that investors—individual investors, institutional investors, and fund managers—consider carefully the social, environmental, and ethical consequences of their investments. This kind of investment is known as 'socially responsible investment' (SRI). Yet, as we shall see, SRI encompasses different styles of investment decisions and investor behaviour such as 'ethical investing', 'values-based investing', 'cleantech investing', 'impact investing', 'sustainable investing', and simply 'responsible investing' (see Table 10.1). These styles share a degree of overlap, but are not semantic synonyms; in fact, the points of differentiation can be hotly contested. However, what they share is the incorporation of extra-financial factors into investment decision-making. This includes all manner of asset classes (although listed equity predominates) and applies to all regions. It also has relevance along the investment chain—asset owner, consultant, asset manager, investment researcher, asset—and each of these stages is a potential point of breakthrough or blockage depending on the levels of awareness, incentive, requirements, and opportunities on offer.

Key concept: Performance

Performance is a major aspect of an investment decision. But what is the real meaning of performance? The word 'performance' comes from the English 'to perform' which itself comes from the French '*parformer*'. Therefore the real meaning of performance is achievement. And the achievement of an investment cannot depend on return and risk alone. This would be a very limited approach. The investor has to think about a third dimension—the meaning.

(*Source:* Xavier de Bayser of Integral Development Asset Management, cited in Bellagio Forum for Sustainable Development and Eurosif, 2006, p 11)

Table 10.1 Different styles of socially responsible investment

Style	Overview
Negative screening–ethical	Avoiding companies/industries on moral grounds
Negative screening–environmental or social	Avoiding companies/industries because of their social or environmental practices
Norms-based screening	Avoiding companies because of non-compliance with international standards
Positive screening	Active inclusion of companies because of social and environmental factors
Extra-financial best in class	Active inclusion of companies that lead their sectors in social/environmental performance
Financially weighted best in class	Active inclusion of companies that outperform their sector peers on financially material social/environmental criteria
Community investing	Allocating capital directly to enterprises and projects based on their societal contributions
Sustainability themes	Selecting companies on the basis of sustainability factors (e.g. renewable energy)
Impact investing	Investments made in order to generate measurable social and environmental impact
Blended value investing	Active allocation based on a blend of financial and social/environmental return on investment
Engagement	Dialogue between investors and company management to improve management of environmental, social, and governance issues
Shareholder activism	Using shareholder rights to pressure companies to change environmental, social, and governance practices
Integrated analysis	Active inclusion of environmental and social factors within conventional fund management

(*Source:* Adapted from Krosinsky, 2008; Lydenberg, 2005; Sparkes, 2002; Bugg-Levine and Emerson, 2011)

We begin by setting out the historical development of SRI and the evolving interests of investors. Pre- and post-investment strategies regarding publicly traded companies and funds are addressed, including the screening methods that are used in assessing a company's products, services, or business practices. We examine how investors are contributing to social and environmental impact through their investment activities and, subsequently, how the role of fund managers is evolving. The provision of alternative investment opportunities is also discussed, including social and environmental venture capital. We look at different geographies and, in relation to the international SRI marketplace, at the investment options that address the unique social, environmental, and economic factors of those regions.

The origins of ethical investment

The principles of socially responsible investing are rooted in the Judaeo-Christian and Islamic traditions, which embrace peace and avoid business practices designed to harm fellow human beings. In the USA, the Religious Society of Friends (also known as the Quakers) is credited with planting the seeds of modern SRI as early as the seventeenth century by following strategies that adhered to their principles of non-violence and human equality. Early Methodist stock market investment strategies purposely avoided companies that were involved with alcohol or gambling and this, in essence, created some of the first 'screens' or frameworks under which investors could evaluate business practices.

Some churches and charities with sufficient capital were able to persuade individual financial institutions to establish ethical funds, eliminating those companies that were engaging in business practices that they perceived as unethical. However, it was not until the mid-1960s that retail funds were available to private investors, with the first such fund being established in Sweden in 1965. The Vietnam War marked another milestone in SRI, when certain investors started screening their investments to identify companies that supported the war; in 1971, the Pax World Fund, which responded to the demand for investment options that excluded companies benefiting from that war, was launched in the USA.

In the 1980s, concerns grew among investors about supporting businesses with operations in South Africa, thereby supporting apartheid and the poor treatment of employees. Stocks were removed from portfolios, based mainly on ethical or non-financial reasons, and a divestiture movement in South Africa by US corporations emerged. While the public statement was also significant, there is some evidence that institutional shareholdings increased when companies divested.[1] Attention also shifted to domestic business practices, including the use of child labour.

As discussed in Chapter 7, awareness of corporate conduct and responsibility increased during the 1980s and 1990s. In 1983, the Ethical Investment Research Service (EIRIS) was established, providing research on company activities and, subsequently, informing the development and analysis of more investment vehicles for both institutional and private investors. The first UK ethical fund—the Friends Provident Stewardship Unit Trust—was set up in 1984, while the US Social Investment Forum conducted the first industry-wide survey and identified $40 billion of assets managed under SRI principles. Funds addressing concerns about the environment were also established, including the Merlin Ecology Fund (renamed the Jupiter Ecology Fund).

In the early 2000s, the end of the equities boom plus a series of major corporate failures linked to egregious governance practices made pension funds in particular aware of the need to behave as real owners of companies, and to take a longer-term view of investing (see Chapter 7). Consequently, traditionally conservative pension funds began to be innovators in integrating social, environmental, and governance issues into decision-making. In 2001, FTSE launched the FTSE4Good family of social indices, which will be discussed later in this chapter (see section 'Fund indices'). This sent a strong signal to investors that SRI was indeed becoming mainstream.

Since 2003, SRI funds and other offerings have emerged to meet the needs and interests of most investors with offerings in large-cap funds, US domestic equity index funds, international funds, and small-cap offerings (see Glossary). In 2005, the first socially screened exchange traded funds (ETFs) were launched. New funds are being developed continually, and in 2004, having seen the success of Islamic banks in the Middle East and Indonesia, HSBC launched its Amanah Pension Fund, which was designed to comply with Shari'ah law, obeying special rules according to, and avoiding certain investments that are contrary to, Islamic teaching.

At the political level, the year 2000 signalled the mainstreaming of SRI in Europe, and the beginning of a more international and coordinated approach towards the disclosure of social, environmental, and ethical practices. The EU heads of state agreed to the Lisbon Agenda, in which CSR and measures promoting sustainability were core to achieving the agenda's goal of 3% average economic growth and the creation of 20 million jobs by 2010. The first Global Reporting Initiative (GRI) Sustainability Guidelines were also released, setting out a framework for reporting (see Chapter 8).

In 2001, the European Sustainable and Responsible Investment Forum (Eurosif) was launched with the support of national European social investment forums and the European Commission. Also in the UK, the Myners Review of Institutional Investment published its final report, a shortlist of non-mandatory principles for investment decision-making that applied to all pension funds and institutional investors. In the same way as the Cadbury Code addressed corporate governance (see Chapter 7), the Myners Review addressed investment, helping to set a new standard advocating shareholder activism.[2] In 2002, at the World Summit on Sustainable Development in Johannesburg, the 'London Principles' were announced to address how the financial sector, specifically, could contribute to sustainable development (see Box 10.1). Also in that year, a second version of the GRI Guidelines was published.

Box 10.1 The 'London Principles' on the financial sector's role in sustainable development

Economic prosperity

Principle 1 Provide access to finance and risk management products for investment, innovation, and the most efficient use of existing assets.

Principle 2 Promote transparency and high standards of corporate governance in themselves, and in the activities being financed.

Environmental protection

Principle 3 Reflect the cost of environmental and social risks in the pricing of financial and risk management products.

Principle 4 Exercise equity ownership to promote efficient and sustainable asset use, and risk management.

Principle 5 Provide access to finance for the development of environmentally beneficial technologies.

Social development

Principle 6 Exercise equity ownership to promote high standards of CSR by the activities being financed.

Principle 7 Provide access to market finance and risk management products to businesses in disadvantaged communities and developing economies.

(*Source:* Adapted from http://www.environmental-finance.com)

Large-scale global SRI initiatives have continued. In 2004, Kofi Annan, then Secretary General of the United Nations, issued *Who cares wins*, drafted in conjunction with several leading international financial institutions, outlining roles and responsibilities for different groups, including cooperation, working towards the goals of better investment markets, and working towards more sustainable societies. In 2006, the UN Global Compact and United Nations Environment Programme's Finance Initiative (UNEP-FI) coordinated the creation of the Principles for Responsible Investment (see Box 10.2). Initially, twenty mainstream investors worth $2 trillion signed on to the agreement. By 2016, the number of signatories had risen to over 14,000 and the assets under management were about $60 trillion.[3] An initiative that emerged from UNEP-FI was the Inquiry into the Design of a Sustainable Financial System. In contrast to the investor oriented approach of SRI, the Inquiry focused on the effectiveness of financial systems in moving capital towards sustainable development. One example is the 'sustainable financial system' work in Indonesia which examined the current and necessary conditions for different types of lender to finance green investments. This represents a very different level and type of engagement than SRI, but nonetheless one with similar ultimate goals in terms of finance and sustainability.

The G8 declaration from the 2007 meeting in Germany highlighted investment decisions, transparency, and sustainable development.[4] The latest iteration of the GRI—called the G4—has been touted as a standard for performance analysis, although the investor-driven Climate Disclosure Project may be more influential. However, it must be remembered that all of these initiatives, including GRI and the Global Compact, are non-binding and voluntary. And while, arguably, significant progress has been made in the past decade, it can be contended that more is needed. Disturbingly, the *Review of UK equity markets and long-term decision making* (Kay, 2012) raised similar points to the Myners Report a decade and one global financial crisis later, and work by Piketty (2017) and others has shown that capital had grown stronger throughout the 2000s. Indeed, one of the greatest criticisms of CSR's effectiveness is that it did nothing to pre-empt, predict, or avert one of the largest corporate failures in capitalism's history when $2 trillion or 25% of the value of a single asset class—mortgages—was wiped out. In the context of this chapter, this raises basic questions about what it would take, or indeed if it is possible, for SRI to become an investment norm. The answers to these questions will be taken up in later sections of the chapter.

Box 10.2 UN Principles for Responsible Investment

1 We will incorporate ESG (environmental, social, and corporate governance) issues into investment analysis and decision-making processes.

2 We will be active owners and incorporate ESG issues into our ownership policies and practices.

3 We will seek appropriate disclosure on ESG issues by the entities in which we invest.

4 We will promote acceptance and implementation of the Principles within the investment industry.

5 We will work together to enhance our effectiveness in implementing the Principles.

6 We will each report on our activities and progress towards implementing the Principles.

(*Source:* http://www.unpri.org)

Sustainable investing

In the evolution of SRI, one can discern a shift from concerns about tainted money (i.e. capital allocated to unethical or socially and environmentally harmful businesses) to finding ways of deploying capital to address major societal challenges. The most noticeable of these in recent years has been the growth of cleantech investment focused on renewable alternative energy and other technologies suited to the demands of a low-carbon economy; however, issues such as sustainable forestry, water, and natural resource conservation have also attracted investors' attention. Investment specialists with a background in SRI have identified large quantities of what they call 'stranded assets', the value of which would be at risk if climate change and other sustainability issues had the impact that many scientists predict.[5] Important figures within the SRI field are pushing to redefine SRI as 'sustainable investing' (or to preserve the original abbreviation, 'sustainable and responsible investing').

Sustainable investing recognizes the social, environmental, and governance goals of SRI generally, but stresses the need for patterns of finance and investment focused on long-term value creation, sustaining natural as well as financial assets, and a needs-based orientation to financial innovation that would serve the poor. Underlying sustainable investing are two claims: first, that fully incorporating long-term social and environmental trends will deliver superior risk-adjusted returns; second, that global sustainability of the kind discussed in Chapter 3 requires the mobilization and recasting of the world capital markets. For some it is entirely distinct from SRI[6] because, while the behaviour of ethically motivated investors is affected by the societal consequences of business, sustainable investment is built on the premise that sustainably managed enterprises are better able to add value over the long term. The former is highly subjective (i.e. what values are given priority), and taken to its logical conclusion could be an argument for business as usual if one felt (as many do) that 'the business of business is business' was a strong moral position. Values-derived SRI may be profoundly attractive to some for ethical reasons, but it is not underpinned by an encompassing financial discipline or universal logic.[7] Moreover, it is often defensive—the avoidance of certain companies and industries as if to demonstrate that, in defiance of modern portfolio theory, it is possible to build efficient investment portfolios despite excluding parts of the investment universe.

In contrast, it is argued, sustainable investing positively seeks to invest in companies with practices and policies aligned with sustainability goals, not because of ideological reasons, but because the best investments are companies that adhere to long-term drivers of performance, i.e. companies that exhibit superior sustainability. This is a powerful argument (although its persuasiveness hinges in part on an investor's beliefs), and one that gains force from: (a) the uncertainty about conventional financial analysis and innovation that is the fallout from the 2007–2008 financial crisis; and (b) the apparent flood of investment opportunities emerging from addressing climate change (e.g. alternative energy, energy reduction, low-carbon construction, geoengineering). However, as we shall return to later, there is a need for caution, both because of the interpretation and reliability of the historical data produced to support the thesis that sustainable investing outperforms conventional investment, and because the analytical and predictive tools needed to deal with sustainability are only in their infancy. Without a stronger basis for accounting for the past, and for predicting the future, extrapolating too much from a narrow range of companies and industries associated with tackling climate change could be as mistaken as the over-investment that SRI fund managers made in IT and health stocks in the late 1990s, when their funds slumped and underperformed the market.

Discussion points

This chapter reviews the chronology and spread of SRI initiatives throughout the world, particularly since the 1980s.

- What has driven consumer demand for responsible investment offerings and what are likely drivers for the next decade?
- What are some of the various pre-investment and post-investment SRI strategies?
- What are some of the initiatives that have helped to encourage the international expansion of SRI?

Types of SRI analysis and practice

Table 10.1 summarizes the types of SRI strategy, the main ones of which we review in this section. Screening is the longest established strategy. Religious groups have long limited their investment universe by avoiding industries and activities that offend their moral principles. Screening is a pre-investment stage question that asks if a company is engaging in business practices that support or go against the investor's social, ethical, or environmental principles. Individual and institutional investors take different approaches to answering this question, and to determining which companies are therefore 'socially responsible'. Here, we review the different types of screen that are used, and introduce some of the funds and fund indices that employ screens.

Negative screening

'Negative' screening eliminates from an investment portfolio companies that are engaging in what are perceived to be negative business or environmental practices. In a survey of 201 socially screened funds in the USA, the Social Investment Forum (SIF) found that tobacco is the most commonly applied social screen, affecting more than 88% of the total assets in the socially screened fund universe. Alcohol affects 75% and gambling affects roughly 23%.[8] Other negative screens include weapons, pornography, nuclear energy, poor employment practices, the manufacture of hazardous or ozone-depleting substances, genetic engineering, and animal testing.

Shari'ah-compliant funds based on Islamic principles are an important form of negative screening, and are offered in many countries by specialist and mainstream financial institutions. As of 2014, these funds held $60 billion of assets under management, but they have been criticized for being overly dependent on markets with a large demand for Shari'ah-compliant capital (e.g. Iran and Saudi Arabia), which helps explain why investments in such funds fell by 75% from 2014 to 2015.[9]

The potential risk associated with negative screening is the possibility of biasing the geographic or sector allocation of the investment portfolio. As noted earlier, screened SRI funds appeared to outperform conventional funds in the late 1990s, but this was because they were over-exposed to IT and health stocks, which subsequently dropped in value at the turn of the decade. Equally, anti-ethically screened funds such as the Vice Fund (VICEX) outperformed the S&P for significant periods in the early 2000s, but struggled after the 2007–2008 financial crisis. Since 2014, VICEX has traded at significantly less than the S&P 500, and as of 2018 had a load-adjusted return of about 8%, thereby underperforming the S&P 500 average.[10] We discuss performance later in this chapter, but one needs to be cautious about leaping to conclusions on screened fund performance.

'Norms-based' screening is a variation on negative screening, requiring monitoring corporate compliance with internationally accepted norms, such as the Sustainable Development Goals, the ILO core conventions, or the UN Global Compact.[11] Like other negative screening it is used to eliminate specific risks to the portfolio, and to communicate with the general public and corporate members on the ethics of the organization. Because the screen itself makes an ethical statement, it might also be used to guard the reputation of the investor.

Positive screening

Unlike negative screening, a particular industry is not excluded from positively screened portfolios. Rather, 'positive' screening is the selection of investments that perform best against corporate governance, social, environmental, or ethical criteria, and which support sustainability. Positive screening is associated with a 'triple-bottom-line' investment approach, ensuring that a company performs well according to financial, social, and environmental criteria. 'Best-in-class' screening, which selects the best-performing companies within a given sector of investments, is one such strategy, while 'pioneer' screening chooses the best-performing company against one specific criterion.

Examples of positive screens might include improvement of health-and-safety conditions, integration of environmental criteria into the purchasing process, prevention of corruption, elimination of child labour, and promotion of social and economic development.[12] Such screens have the advantage of encouraging companies to improve extra-financial performance irrespective of their industry, but they can be problematic. There is the challenge of how to measure performance in a robust replicable manner, and professional organizations such as the Certified Financial Analysts Institute are only starting to find ways to incorporate this into their certification and career development programmes. More fundamentally, there is the question of whether such screens result in significantly different investment portfolios. Benson et al. (2006) found that SRI mutual funds were virtually no different to mainstream funds, reinforcing Hawken's (2004) conclusion that SRI fund managers were no less likely than conventional managers to put financial returns ahead of trying to combat social injustice or environmental degradation.

In practice, funds may offer a mix of positive and negative screens. BankInvest Global Emerging Markets SRI, an emerging market equity fund, was one of the pioneers. Its negative screen excludes companies that have continuing violations of human rights, the environment, and labour rights, and those that derive more than 10% of turnover from war material, alcoholic beverages, gambling, tobacco, or more than 3% from pornography. The positive screen rewards the best and fastest movers, and companies that have a high score in supporting human rights, labour standards, the environment, and corporate governance. The first investor in this fund was Mistra, the foundation for strategic environmental research that is based in Sweden, which manages its assets in a socially responsible way. Some 80% of its capital of SEK3.6 billion is invested on the basis of environmental and ethical criteria.

Discussion points

SRI strategies require consideration of ethical, moral, environmental, social, and governance issues.

- How would you go about identifying SRI investment opportunities?
- What are some initiatives that try to ensure that companies are disclosing their social or environmental business practices, so that investors can make an accurate assessment?
- What do investors expect from their SRI investments and how might their expectations differ from those of traditional investments?

Fund indices

One way of addressing the need for reliable performance measurement is the use of specialist fund indices. Three of the major SRI indices are MSCI, the Dow Jones Sustainability Group Indexes, and the FTSE4Good Index. Each of the indices uses a different weighting system for financial and non-financial performance.

In May 1990, the Domini 400 Social Index (now the MSCI KLD 400 Social Index) was launched by Amy Domini, Peter Kinder, Steve Lydenberg, and Lloyd Kurtz. The index removed 200 of the 500 stocks in the S&P 500[13] through the application of social screens and then added another one hundred stocks to balance out the new index by sector. The goal of the index was to set a benchmark for SRI fund managers, similar to the S&P 500 but subject to social and environmental screens. Today, it includes small, medium, and large cap companies chosen for what it considers their 'exemplary' records of environmental, social, and corporate governance practices.

The Dow Jones Sustainability Indices (DJSIs) were established in 1999 as the first indices to track sustainability-driven companies on a global basis. They were launched together by the Dow Jones Indices, STOXX Limited (a European index provider), and SAM Group (a pioneer in SRI). There are over $8 billion assets in DJSI-based investment vehicles. The DJSI uses a rules-based methodology and focuses on best-in-class companies. Assessment criteria include corporate governance, risk and crisis management, codes of conduct (including anti-corruption), labour practices, human capital development, sustainability and project finance (for banks), climate strategy (including eco-efficiency and protection of biodiversity), and emerging markets strategy.[14]

The FTSE4Good Index was launched in July 2001 and is derived from the FTSE Global Equity Index Series as an initiative of FTSE, in association with EIRIS and the United Nations Children's Fund (UNICEF). Today, there are two series: a benchmark index and a tradable index. The initial screening process looks at the starting universe—FTSE All-Share Index, FTSE Developed Europe Index, FTSE US Index, and FTSE Developed Index—and screens against tobacco producers, companies providing parts, services, or manufacturing for whole nuclear weapon systems, weapons manufacturers, and owners or operators of nuclear power stations that mine or produce uranium. Positive screens are applied on the subsets of companies, corresponding to each of the original indices, to include companies that are working towards environmental sustainability, have positive relations with stakeholders, and uphold and support universal human rights. The inclusion criteria 'originate from globally recognized codes of conduct such as the UN Global Compact and the Universal Declaration of Human Rights'.[15] Since 2004, FTSE4Good (now Russell FTSE4Good) has run a series of regional indices including ones for Japan, Australia, the USA, South Africa, Malaysia, Taiwan and emerging economies. Yahoo! Finance, the widely used investment price comparison site, has also introduced a special section on sustainability.[16]

Other indices and initiatives

While the KLD's Domini 400, DJSI, and FTSE4Good remain the flagship indices, other initiatives have emerged to address newer dimensions of the SRI market. In 2003, Dutch asset management companies Kempen Capital Management and SNS Asset Management launched an SRI index comprising only smaller companies. USA-based Kenmar hedge firm launched its SRI fund of funds in 2007. SRI indices are also spreading to emerging markets, with the Johannesburg Stock Exchange SRI Index (South Africa) and OWW Consulting's Responsibility Malaysia SRI Index, which applies criteria to the FTSE Bursa 100 Index to determine whether the companies are deemed socially responsible. One of the six groups of criteria in the Malaysian index is community, including Rakyat policies based on Islamic banking principles and Halal accreditation.

Brazil's stock exchange BP took the concept one step further by creating a 'social and environmental stock exchange' called Bolsa de Valores Socioambientais (BVSA). It replicates the stock market environment for non-profit organizations. Similar exchanges were subsequently established in Kenya and in South Africa where SASIX (South African Social Investment Exchange) was launched in June 2006 with the support of the Johannesburg Stock Exchange. The current focus in Brazil is on educational projects that benefit children between the ages of seven and twenty-five who live in poor communities.[17] Education specialists recommend the best NGO projects to the board of BP in Brazil, which then approves a list to become the portfolio of projects presented to investors by BP and its brokerage firms. Individuals or organizations can buy 'social shares' in the projects, which are transferred entirely to the listed organizations without commissions, fees, or deductions. In 2017, BVSA aimed to distribute about $500,000 for twenty social projects, and since its inception has raised $500 million for 500 organizations.[18]

SSEs are intended to solve the liquidity problem facing investors wanting to allocate capital in social enterprises or societally beneficial projects, but concerned about exiting the investment. However, the concept of a 'social stock exchange' is, arguably, too alien for most investors. When the idea of an SSE was presented to other exchanges in Latin America and Europe, it was met with resistance by those who think that SRI is anathema to shareholder interests.

Engagement

While one set of questions posed by SRI investors arise at the pre-investment stage, another set arises at the post-investment stage: is the company *continuing* to engage in socially responsible business practices? Engagement is the process by means of which investors become involved with the business to influence its activities, behaviours, and operations. This section discusses some of these engagement strategies, including shareholder activism, proxy voting, policy statements, and engaging at different levels.

Engagement occurs in response to the company's approach to CSR, or to a change in ethical and social practices. Other issues that might cause concern include the company's overall performance, internal controls, compliance, or general business practices, and responsible investors may raise these matters. Both private and institutional investors may raise the issues, although, typically, it is fund managers who play the largest role in the process.

ESG investments of any kind are only as good as the tools that analysts and investors have at their disposal to make decisions. Influencing these tools is one route to influencing new thinking into the investment world. For example, 'stranded assets', which was proposed as a way accountants could apply additional rigour to assessing company assets, has been taken up by some analysts. There have been various attempts over the years to develop systems for social and environmental accounting, and in addition to the aforementioned Principles for Responsible Investment, there is the Accounting for Sustainability project and the work of the Global Reporting Initiative. GRI has long championed the idea of sustainability reporting, and today accountancy firms and academics are getting behind integrated reporting as a way for companies to present a more holistic account of their assets and value.[19]

Shareholder activism

Shareholder activism includes activities that are undertaken in the belief that investors and shareholders can work together with management to change course and to improve financial performance over time. These activities can be conducted privately or publicly. Private methods might include letters to other shareholders, or to company management, to raise concerns. Institutional investors might raise issues during their routine meetings with company managers, or communicate their concerns to other investors to build pressure on the company; they might even join forces with other like-minded investors to take subsequent public actions. Public mechanisms for shareholder advocacy include raising questions during annual general meetings, or calling an extraordinary general meeting to propose shareholder resolutions. Investors might also issue press statements, or arrange briefings to make their reservations known to the wider international community of investors.

The mix of public and private facets to shareholder activism means that it is difficult to quantify. There are examples, such as the nuns who threatened a shareholder resolution at a GE AGM about pollution of the Hudson River, where activists have affected corporate behaviour. There are also famous individual and institutional activists such as the pension fund CalPERS, Robert Monks, and John Bogle who have fought for more shareholder power, not least in the arena of governance (see Chapter 7). But overall, given the primacy allocated to shareholders by law, company owners have not had the huge influence on extra financial issues that one might have expected. Even companies with a strong stance on particular social or environmental issues may lack a clear responsible investment policy, although there are signs that this is changing in some markets (e.g. 80% of UK pension funds in one survey now have such a policy[20]). Moreover, public-sector pension funds such as CalPERS, the Norwegian Sovereign Wealth Fund, and the Korean National Pension Fund have formed the P8 Group with a focus on getting pension funds to exert leadership in the shift to a low-carbon economy.

Proxy voting

There is, though, a surprising lack of shareholder activism overall. One reason often repeated is that many shareholders have the mentality of traders rather than owners, and hence take a short-term view on company performance.[21] Another reason is that institutional investors have to hold shares in certain companies to balance their portfolios, and therefore have limited room to manoeuvre. To understand the relative paucity of shareholder activism, one only needs to look at proxy voting. At a company's annual general meeting, shareholders are given the opportunity to vote on a number of issues on the agenda. More shareholders are beginning to understand the importance and relevance of their voting and active participation, although this is not happening as quickly as might have been expected given the array of corporate scandals throughout the 2000s. Usually, proxy voting applies to issues of corporate governance and, by voting against the mandatory approval of annual accounts and reports, investors register their protest against company practices. Leading SRI issues that are likely to be the focus of attention include climate change, environmental reporting, sustainability, global labour standards, the HIV/AIDS pandemic, corporate political contributions, and equal employment opportunity.

Voting practices vary from country to country, and Table 10.2 highlights some of the international resources and guidelines available. The Institutional Shareholders' Committee (ISC) Statement of Principles recommends that:

> Institutional shareholders and/or agents should vote all shares held directly on behalf of clients wherever practicable to do so.

It further recommends that institutional shareholders should:

> not automatically support the Board; if they have been unable to reach a satisfactory outcome through active dialogue then they will register an abstention or vote against the resolution. In both instances it is good practice to inform the company in advance of their intention and the reasons why.
>
> (Institutional Shareholders' Committee, 2005, p 20)

Table 10.2 Resources on voting guidelines

Organization	Code
Commissie Tabaksblat (Tabaksblat Commission—The Netherlands)	Concept Code on Corporate Governance (*Concept-Code voor Corporate Governance*)
International Corporate Governance Network (ICGN)	Global Share Voting Principles
Mouvement des Entreprises de France (MEDEF—France)	Bouton Report (*Rapport Bouton*), Promoting Better Governance in Listed Companies
National Association of Pension Funds (NAPF—UK)	Corporate Governance Policy and Voting Guidelines for Investment Companies
Organisation for Economic Co-operation and Development (OECD)	Guide for Multinational Enterprises
Swiss Stock Exchange (SWX—Switzerland)	SWX Code

Quarterly reporting to clients is standard; at this point the fund managers could also report how they voted and any shareholder resolutions. More and more, voting details are made available on fund websites, which could list resolutions, issues, and companies for any given period.

Discussion points

Please review the preceding section on 'Engagement'.

- As a private investor, what are some of the ways in which you might make others aware of your concerns about a company's SRI practices?
- As a fund manager, how might you communicate to the company your concerns about its business practices?
- What are some of the ways in which you think that international investors might better coordinate their engagement efforts, either as institutional members or as members of organizations such as the UN Global Compact?

Snapshot 10.1 Conservation trust funds

Conservation trust funds (CTFs) are a source of sustainable financing for long-term biodiversity conservation, in particular for managing protected areas. More than seventy CTFs have been established to date. For example, the Mexican Fund for the Conservation of Nature was established in 1994 as a non-profit civil association, following a three-year participatory consultation process funded by US government agencies and a number of philanthropic organizations. It is one of the largest CTFs in the world, both in terms of revenues available and number of projects supported. The Fund now manages an endowment of US$120 million, which is complemented by a stream of earmarked sinking funds raised from diverse sources at a rate of US$3–4 million per year. Reviews of the Fund have highlighted two main areas of accomplishment. First, it is an example of how diversified revenue sources can complement each other's deficiencies and become a source of strength. Second, its role in encouraging stakeholder participation, particularly that of communities around the protection areas, shows how a CTF can strengthen civil society engagement in conservation.

Banc d'Arguin Coastal and Marine Biodiversity Trust Fund (BACoMaB) in Mauritania is another example of a fund investing in conservation efforts, in this case those of local fishing communities. A further example is the Moringa Fund: an investment vehicle of €100m, which invests in profitable larger-scale agroforestry projects with high environmental and social impacts in Latin America and sub-Saharan Africa via equity and quasi-equity investments of €4–10 million.

Finding sustainable financial resources for long-term conservation efforts is a major challenge, particularly in developing countries. Although the pool of funds potentially available is enormous, traditional conservation organizations are failing to tap into them at the scale required, and governments bear the main responsibility for investment and related action. Efforts to address the shortage in conservation funding also tend to focus on revenue generation rather than on capacity building. CTFs provide sustainable financing for biodiversity conservation at regional and national level (e.g. protected area management) using diverse financing mechanisms. With good design and management, CTFs can provide the institutional capacity at local and national level for transparent and accountable fund generation and allocation. As legally independent grant-making institutions, they

(continued . . .)

are designed to mobilize and invest funds from a range of sectors, thereby initiating and strengthening inter-sectoral collaboration.

(*Sources:* https://fmcn.org/?lang=en; http://www.moringapartnership.com; http://www.totalgiving.co.uk/charity/banc-darguin-and-coastal-and-marine-biodiversity-trust-fund-limited, all accessed 4 January 2018)

Quick questions

1 How do financial institutions diffuse the US model of corporate governance?

2 What was it about the local Japanese context that brought about a change in strategy?

3 What are the advantages and disadvantages of adopting a partnership strategy to foster change?

Other SRI approaches

One does not need to invest in publicly listed companies to engage in SRI, or indeed trade in stocks (cf. SRI property portfolios). There are a variety of other SRI options, including venture philanthropy, social and environmental venture capital, community investment, and micro-credit. We discuss each of these in the following sections.

Venture philanthropy

'Venture philanthropy' refers to the application of the venture capital model, principles of entrepreneurial business, and the deployment of private equity to charities and other social purpose organizations. On the heels of the technology boom over the past two decades and the economic success of innovative technology entrepreneurs, there is a broad range of initiatives applying the strategies of venture capital within the social sector. Rather than expect a financial return, venture philanthropists are looking for 'social returns' from the project in receipt of the investment. They recognize that capital is necessary for growth and to cover cash-flow difficulties, but this can be difficult for social purpose organizations to access. Grant-makers or banks may be unwilling to provide finance in these situations, creating a space where venture philanthropy alone or co-investing with grant-making trusts offers solutions.

The term venture philanthropy is not new (it was used by John D. Rockefeller III as early as 1969), but its use and its definition are evolving and spreading internationally, embodying the following:

1 a long-term investment in organizations;

2 a partnership between the donor and the recipient (usually a charitable or non-profit organization);

3 provision of finance;

4 provision of expertise, skills, and/or resources that add value to the development of the organization and/or entrepreneur (which often includes access to the venture philanthropist's network of partners, who might be able to provide services such as accounting, marketing, or strategic consulting);

5 a view towards maximizing a 'social return on investment', or the bottom line leaning towards outcome-based solutions to the underlying problem;

6 a focus on accountability, because venture philanthropists hope to understand the cause of the social problem in order to develop effective solutions;

7 an exit strategy, making the organization self-sustaining and financially independent after a few years of support.

Much has been written about the pioneering venture philanthropy organizations, largely based in the USA, which embraced these principles to support local social innovation (e.g. Venture Philanthropy Partners, REDF—creator of the 'Social Return on Investment' Index—Acumen Fund, and Social Venture Partners, to name but a few). In the past few years, these principles have been embraced by philanthropists throughout the world to drive social innovation in both industrialized and developing countries, including traditional foundations (e.g. Rockefeller), newer foundations (e.g. Bill and Melinda Gates, Google.org), and individuals charting their own course in the social sector (e.g. the USA's Pierre Omidyar and South Africa's Mark Shuttleworth).

What is called the 'blended value approach' to investing has also been attractive to foundations looking to align the guidelines set in their programmes with their investment strategies. Typically, 95% of a foundation's resources are used to generate income; this is called the asset 'corpus' and normally leaves 5% to support payouts, administration costs, and grant-making activities. But if the asset corpus is invested only to maximize financial return (sometimes without any consideration of the make-up of the portfolio), only 5% of the resources are driving 100% of the social mission of the foundation. An idea put forward by some scholars and foundations is that, if the 95% of the foundation's resources could be used to maximize the financial, social, and environmental impacts—i.e. the 'blended value' approach—the benefits generated by the investments could be exponentially greater than the impact of grants alone.

Environmental venture capital

Concern about sustainability, and in particular the transformation to a low-carbon economy as a response to climate change (see Chapter 3), has created a significant demand for capital in areas such as alternative energy, geoengineering, and green buildings. One aspect of this is 'environmental venture capital', or 'cleantech', which looks at investment opportunities in entrepreneurial environmental projects and companies that will reap financial, social, and environmental rewards for the investors (see Snapshot 10.1). Opportunities for these investments include sustainable energy technologies, such as renewable energy, transportation, and distributed generation of power. The size of some of these initiatives means that much of the capital will have to be raised from conventional financial markets and government-backed bonds. Certainly, some of the immediate investment needs, such as nuclear power and an energy distribution system matched to the specifics of alternative energy, are not suited to venture capital. Moreover, after years of growth since 2008, alternative energy investment fell by 33% in 2016 to $116.6 billion. Mexico, Chile, Uruguay, South Africa, and Morocco all saw falls in investment of 60% or more, and there was a marked slowdown in financings in China, which hitherto had been held up as a race-leader in renewables[22] (see Case study 10). There are various reasons for this (e.g. the renewable energy sector may need less investment), but it represents the possible end of a boom period. For example, in 2012–2013 venture investors put $6.4 billion into the cleantech energy sector in North America, Europe, China, and India, marking year-on-year improvements since 2008.[23] Furthermore, green technology was an important part of the post-2008 economic stimulus packages in some countries. For example, in the late 2000s, the USA and South Korea, the European Union, and China allocated 81%, 59%, and 31% of their respective stimulus packages to green investment ($31 billion, $23 billion, and $221 billion).[24]

Emerging economies such as China, India, and South Africa are fossil-fuel-dependent nations, and need to take actions to safeguard a reliable stream of fossil fuels, to identify alternative sources of energy, and to pursue greater energy efficiency through technology and innovation. China has already taken significant steps in this regard, although the challenge is enormous (see Case study 10). India has not attracted the same amount of international scrutiny, but in many ways faces equal challenges, and by some accounts lags far behind where it should be on environmental issues.[25] South Africa, which obtains 95% of its electricity from coal-fired power stations, faces significant difficulties in making the transition to low-carbon energy without jeopardizing political stability and economic growth.

The social significance of climate change and the 'energy revolution' it seems to demand (Chapter 3) has stimulated a lot of debate about green investment. The need for investment in clean technologies, alternative energy, and climate-change innovation has led to this revolution being portrayed as a huge investment opportunity. Moreover, this comes at a time when institutional investors in particular are looking for asset classes that can deliver steady inflation-linked income streams that do not imitate the performance or cycles of other classes. By some estimates, $2 trillion of investment is needed a year (equivalent to 2% of GDP) to fund green growth and decarbonization. However, OECD analysis suggests that only half of that sum is being raised at present, and over one-third is coming from company balance sheets rather than the financial markets.[26] What is more, the amount of project finance has dropped because of banks pulling out of the project finance market owing to the restrictions placed by Basel III (see Snapshot 10.2).[27]

The appetite for green investment has also been damaged by a consolidation process in industries such as solar photovoltaic power equipment, which has turned an innovative product into a cheap, low-return commodity leading to the high-profile collapse of companies such as Solyndra and retrenchment by others such as Vestas. In addition, institutional investors, who are often highlighted as a potential source of green investment capital, face fiduciary constraints that under the most optimistic scenarios would see them meet less than half of project debt need and a quarter of project equity investment.[28]

Snapshot 10.2 Irresponsible banks or just rewards—events in mainstream finance

In 2014, board members of Dutch banks were told to take the following oath: 'I swear that I will do my utmost to preserve and enhance confidence in the financial-services industry. So help me God.' The oath, the first of its kind in Europe, is binding on board members, and all 90,000 bank employees. The chair of the Banking Association in Amsterdam said the oath was binding and bankers would be punished if they breached the new ethical rules.

(continued . . .)

Given that words like 'trust' and 'bank' had long been synonymous with stability and prosperity (e.g. 'You can bank on her being a good worker'), how had it become necessary to take a binding oath to rein in the industry? Long-running concerns that bankers were over-compensated and too powerful came to a head in 2008 when the Netherlands government had to spend more than $128 million in capital and guarantees to bail out its banks. Rabobank alone was fined almost £1 billion and its chief financial officer was among the first to take the oath. And of course this was not just a Dutch problem, even if the government's response was more direct than, say, that in Britain or Germany. Three senior executives at Anglo Irish Bank were put on trial because of events that almost bankrupted Ireland in 2014 (although the cases collapsed in 2017 due to legal technicalities); Barclays and Credit Suisse settled regulator investigations in 2016 by paying $154 million, two years after Lloyds Banking Group paid £370 million to settle claims about rate-rigging which may or may not have played a part in its laying off 9,000 workers in the same year. German Deutsche Bank was fined $2.5 billion by US and UK regulators for manipulating interest rates, while attempts to rig foreign exchange markets—a practice forex traders called 'making free money'—resulted in fines of over £2 billion for banks such as RBS, HSBC, and UBS.

Yet in many of these cases, the fines on banks were not accompanied by charges against individuals and in the UK and USA regulators were accused of 'going soft' on financial institutions. In fact, the UK has been accused of refusing to get tough on banks because it fears they will leave London as a result of the country's departure from the European Union. Despite two decades of campaigning to increase shareholder power, executive pay has continued to rise by 6%. PwC, which itself has been accused of promoting tax avoidance, points out that pay includes a lot of performance-based remuneration, and executive salaries have only risen by 2%. However, public-sector workers such as nurses and teachers have had several years of pay freezes, and salary increases as a whole have struggled to keep up with inflation. Consequently, hostility towards what is viewed as on overpaid and untrustworthy finance services industry shows no signs of abating.

(*Sources:* BBC, 2014, 2015a,b; Colchester, 2014; van Gaal, 2014; Milligan, 2015; Bennison, 2016; Howard, 2016; Monaghan, 2016; Sikka, 2016)

Quick questions

1 What aspects of bank irresponsibility does SRI address.?

2 Is SRI an effective response to the problems in mainstream finance?

3 How can mainstream institutions rebuild public and investor trust?

Community development investment funds

Community investing is defined by the Social Investment Forum as:

> direct investments into poor communities via community development banks, credit unions, loan fund and microfinance institutions. Community investing is closely tied to socially responsible investing and focuses on economically improving disadvantaged communities by offering banking services and small loans to fund businesses, non-profit groups and affordable housing initiatives.
>
> (Investopedia, nd)

Community development investment funds deploy equity and equity-like investments into small businesses in geographic areas that are traditionally overlooked by traditional venture capital and private equity funds. Typically, the businesses are located in disadvantaged communities and will increase the entrepreneurial capacity of the area and create jobs, resulting in what is termed 'high social impact'. Other development investment funds pool together investors, such as banks, corporations, insurers, foundations, and public pension funds, to provide support that can enable the provision of affordable housing, education, community centres, and small businesses.

Microcredit

'Microcredit' is the making of very small loans (or 'microloans') to individuals. The fundamental idea is to make money available to the poor, based on terms and conditions that are appropriate and reasonable. The concept emerged out of initiatives in the 1970s by organizations, such as Accion International and the Grameen Bank, which wanted to provide economic opportunity to poor people looking to start small businesses. Traditional banks were not interested in making small loans to what were considered 'the unbankable' (i.e. people without collateral), so a system of community banking was set up, under which small, informal groups (called 'solidarity groups' within the Grameen Bank) were formed. Their collateral was the social networks that these savers and borrowers formed so that loans were effectively guaranteed by a combination of peer pressure and social cohesion. Women's groups in particular proved successful, and loan repayment far exceeded the normal percentage in traditional banking.

We discuss aspects of microcredit (also called microfinance) elsewhere (Chapters 4 and 12). It has spread rapidly, and not only in developing economies. Originally, the brainchild of NGOs, it is now offered by mainstream banks such as Deutsche Bank and Standard Chartered. However, it is not an unalloyed success. A little money can support the development of a one-person business or the beginnings of a small shop, for example, but scaling up the business to the next level is not always easy when further financial support is needed. If one looks at a country such as Bangladesh, where microcredit is the main form of banking, the signs that it has lifted people out of poverty (e.g. growth in incomes or GDP) are not obvious. This may be due to the entrenched nature of poverty, and microcredit could be as much a strategy for survival as a means of growth. But while the largest bank in Bangladesh is now the microcredit NGO BRAAC, the impact of microcredit on the poor is only starting to be measured systematically (see Chapter 13). In the drive to scale-up microcredit, there is evidence from around the world that the solidarity-group-based model has been increasingly bypassed in favour of direct loans to borrowers. Also, interest rates are often very high compared with other formal money-lending. This may make the lending organizations more viable, but it raises questions about the social impact and how microcredit is ultimately different from traditional banks other than the size of their loans.

Impact investing

Impact investing is social investing that actively seeks to have a positive social or environmental impact. It comprises investments for financial return in companies or projects that have social and/or environmental benefit as their core goal. It includes blended value investment which seeks social/environmental and financial returns. Thus, investments that promote energy efficiency, provide credit to rural farmers, or develop drugs that would mainly benefit the poor exemplify blended value.

Impact investments inhabit a space between philanthropy, where no financial return is expected, and pure financial investments, where social considerations are not a factor and financial profit is maximized. Individual examples occupy a spectrum between 'Below Market Financial Return with High Social Return' and 'Full Market Financial Return with Some Social Return' investment philosophies. It is, by definition, a market-based approach to addressing many of the challenges facing the global community and seeks to engage capital in creating sustainable, long-term solutions to those same challenges. Such strategies are defined as 'blended value' and not 'double bottom line' because they view the value being created as neither solely economic nor solely social, but a blend of both. This approach recognizes that economic value can create various forms of social and environmental impact and cannot be viewed as a separate component of the value proposition found within any given investment.

Large foundations are among the institutional investors that have shown interest in impact investing because it offers a range of investments that provide a blended return and gives foundations the opportunity to vary approaches to risk by choosing the nature of the organization to be supported and the terms of the investment. They can invest through a variety of means, including cash, structured notes, securities (debt and equity), funds, and venture capital. They can also invest in a range of sectors where it is possible to measure social impact, including clean technology, microfinance, global health, and SME-oriented job creation in developing economies.

Impact investing is not expected to be a huge part of the investment world. One report estimated that it could potentially reach $500 billion out of a $50 trillion of managed assets globally.[29] However, it is estimated that, at present, at least $114 trillion of funds are committed to impact investment, a significant rise since 2012.[30]

SRI performance

Although there is a philanthropic type of SRI, most investors want to see a reasonable financial as well as a social or environmental return on their investment, and many want to know how SRI performs compared with traditional full-universe funds. A company may engage in socially, ethically, and environmentally sound business practice, but the financial performance, or potential for return on investment, is undoubtedly an important factor driving the investment decision. As Statman (2000) found, socially responsible investors do not want to sacrifice return for social responsibility. To a degree, this is because of the way some SRI funds have been promoted, promising that they can outperform the mainstream indices in defiance of conventional investor wisdom that screening out part of the investment universe puts investors at a disadvantage.

SRI index performance

One way to compare SRI performance with mainstream investment vehicles is to look at the various indices available. An early analysis of 29 SRI indices (not investment funds), Schröder (2005), found that they did not exhibit a different risk-adjusted return to that of conventional benchmarks. In other words, there was no significant difference between SRI and conventional index performance. This conclusion is supported by more recent work such as Revelli and Viviani (2015), and Friede et al. (2015).

A closer look at the performance of the KLD DS400, DJSI, and FTSE4Good indices provides a clearer picture of the overall performance of the SRI industry in comparison with overall market performance. A critical point was 2007, which was the watershed moment between the investment fever of the early 2000s and the global financial crisis of 2007–2008. Comparing the performance of the then ground-breaking KLD DS400 Index with the S&P 500 prior to the financial crisis, the former outperformed the latter from its inception in 1990 (12.28% compared with 11.71%). Annualized returns over a ten-year period were equal, with 7.78% returns. Looking at the five-year, three-year, and one-year periods, however, the picture is slightly different, showing an underperforming DS400 Index. Equally, analyses of the FTSE4Good indices, conducted over different time periods, found that investors would not necessarily be worse off by investing in a fund that tracks the FTSE4Good index. An important factor to consider is the risk of the market sectors and individual stocks that are included in the index.

Krosinsky's (2008) comparison of different types of SRI with mainstream indices suggests that there is a difference in performance between general SRI funds (values-based ethical investing) and sustainable investing (see Figure 10.1).[31] The former underperform, or at best are comparable to, mainstream indices, depending on what time horizon one uses; the latter outperform the mainstream irrespective of the time period being compared. A study of ninety ethical funds over ten years in the UK concluded that annual returns were 0.1% less than the FTSE All Share Index.[32] However, sustainable investing funds have not only outperformed ethical investing funds, but also even the best of the mainstream indices (18.7% versus 17% for

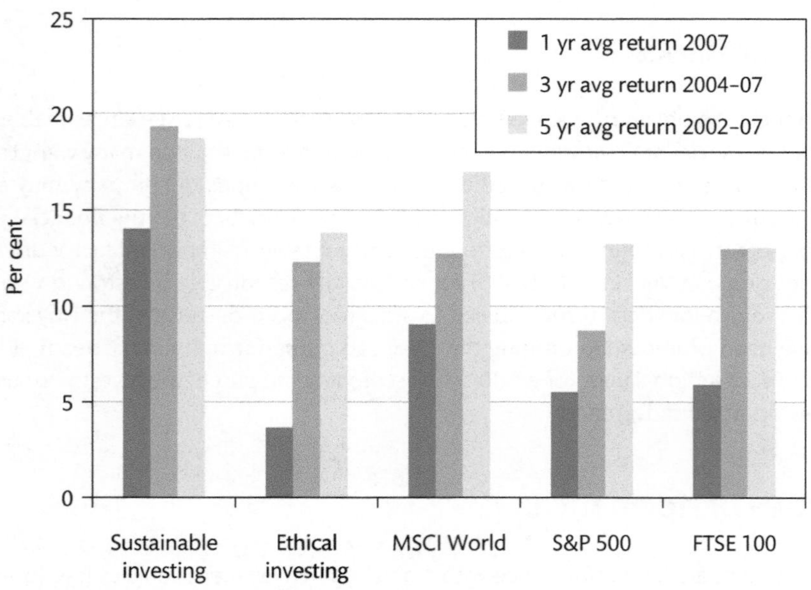

Figure 10.1 SRI returns compared with mainstream indices until 2007
(*Source:* Data from Krosinsky, 2008)

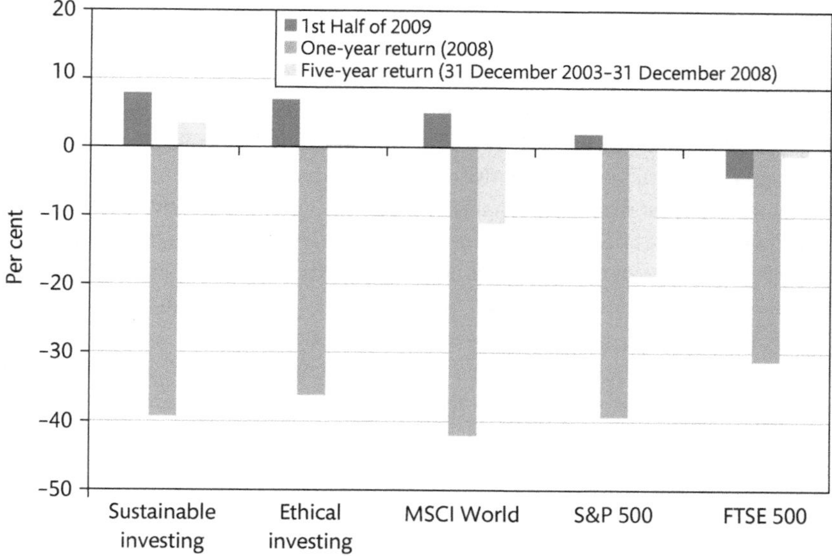

Figure 10.2 Sustainable investing—updated performance analysis
(*Source:* Krosinsky and Robins, 2010, personal communication)

2002–2007). An important period for comparing performance was the post-2008 one after the financial crisis. Comparison of indices shows that sustainable investing funds lost slightly less of their value in 2008, produced net positive returns over the period 2003–2008 (compared with a net loss on the mainstream indices), and outperformed mainstream indices in the first half of 2009 (see Figure 10.2).

Discussion points

- The figures in the sections on performance are from 2014 or earlier. Pick one of the SRI indices discussed in this chapter and say how it has performed since then.
- Pick one of the SRI funds and assess how it has performed in recent years.
- If you were to apply an Islamic screen to this SRI index, what companies would you remove and why?

SRI fund performance

There are an estimated $50 trillion of managed assets worldwide, and just under $7 trillion of these are affected by some form of social screening and shareholder advocacy.[33] For some advocates of SRI, in view of the fact that SRI index performance is broadly comparable to mainstream indices, and in some circumstances offers superior performance, it is a mystery why investors are not more keen. Several academic studies that have compared the performance of ethical and non-ethical funds have found no difference in financial performance,[34] and a review of sixteen academic and broker studies concluded that there was a positive correlation between fund performance and attention to extra-financial issues in 38% of cases, and a neutral correlation in 44%.[35]

Accompanying the success stories, however, is continuing criticism of SRI funds. While there are some funds with five-year returns of 50% or 60%, the shorter-term returns for one year might only be 3% or lower.[36] SRI advocates are keen to emphasize the importance of time horizons in evaluating fund performance and investment strategies. In part, this is because the high turnover of stocks in mainstream funds is blamed for investors' lack of interest in the extra-financial dimensions of business performance, and the disconnect between corporations and their owners. But there is also evidence that sustainable investing funds, for example, that have a low turnover (i.e. their portfolios change every three to five years) exhibit stronger performance.[37] However, one needs to be cautious about the period one is considering. For example, a comparison in late 2007 of the Winslow Green Growth Fund (WGGF), a Morningstar five-star rated fund with an aggressive growth policy focused on small-growth companies that have a positive or neutral environmental impact, with Berkshire Hathaway (BRK-A), investment sage Warren Buffett's holding company, would have found that the latter grew by 100% in the preceding five years, but the sustainable investing fund grew by 200%.[38] However, from 2008 onwards, BRK-A consistently outperformed WGGF; as of October 2012 it had delivered roughly 30% growth on 2003, compared with WGGF's approximately 20%, and the Winslow fund was sold to Brown Advisory Funds in September 2012.

There is an inherent bias in some SRI funds towards particular sectors such as stocks, and the overall volatility of such stocks over a particular period, although some argue that this should be considered another way of diversifying one's overall portfolio. Relative size is another problem when looking at the figures used to portray SRI's success. Although growth rates in percentage terms can be large, the actual amount invested in SRI funds is small when compared, for example, with that invested in hedge funds,[39] and the impact of applying the current SRI strategies on a grander scale would almost certainly affect the value of those assets. Additionally, SRI screening of some kind is being applied beyond the relatively small universe of SRI retail funds, making it increasingly difficult to calculate the exact size of the SRI market.

A further factor is uncertainty about the utility of SRI analysis as a forecasting tool, and the absence of, or analysts' unfamiliarity with, tools to analyse performance. Much of what we know about CSR is about what has happened and why, and therefore falls within the explicative concerns of accounting. Analysis, in contrast, is predictive, so that, for instance, financial analysis—no matter how imperfectly—allows one to forecast future flows in order to obtain the net present value. In the case of sustainable investing, for example, an analyst would want to integrate environmental, social, and governance factors into financial valuation tools, but while, as we have seen throughout this book, there are plenty of ideas about how such factors are material to companies, their incorporation into areas such as risk analysis is not yet commonplace.[40]

Market growth

Throughout the 2000s, the growth of the SRI investment universe has outstripped that of the wider investment market. There is increasing interest in India and China (see Case study 10), and as described earlier Brazil and South Africa were innovators in establishing social stock exchanges. Nonetheless, the main interest has been in developed economies. Australia has experienced enormous growth, going from practically zero in $16.49 billion in 2007 to $52

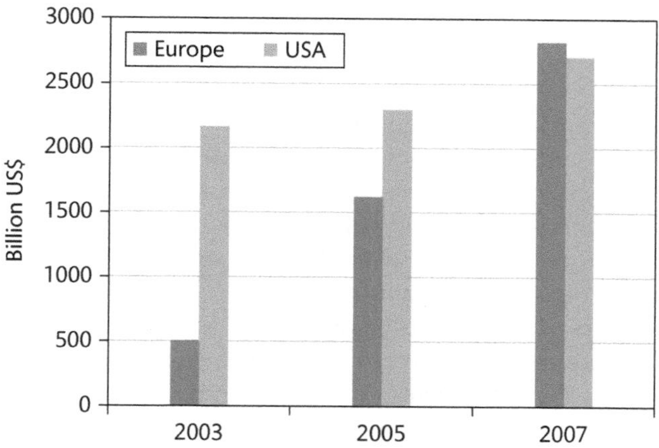

Figure 10.3 Growth of funds under SRI management—comparison of USA and Europe
(*Source:* Data from Robins, 2008)

billion today.[41] Similarly, SRI funds under management in Canada grew from under $49 billion in 2003 to represent 20% of funds under management today.[42] However, the largest markets are the USA and Europe (see Figure 10.3). Mutual funds have been the fastest-growing segment of SRI. About £88 billion in assets are under some kind of impact investing strategy worldwide. This is a small fraction of the $85 trillion in assets under management.[43] Nonetheless, investors in what is still a small market overall, are able to exert influence and shareholder advocacy has become increasingly important.

The European SRI market has overtaken the USA to some degree . This trend began in the mid-2000s, and today according to the Global Sustainable Invesetment Alliance, Europe accounts for over half of the $22.89 trillion in global sustainable invesetment assets, while the USA accounts for 38%. The fastest-growing regions are Japan and Australia/New Zealand. About 65% of the funds are negatively screened.[44] The assets managed under this kind of 'broad' SRI can appear large, but it raises the question of how broad is 'broad'? For example, if companies are screened for little more than pornography or eco-efficiency (one that is largely an illegal activity, and the other a proven business efficiency), SRI may be nothing more than efficient fund management, spurring doubts about the extent to which some of the figures on SRI are useful.

There are a number of developments behind this growth, some of which shed light on the potential of similar trends happening in other markets. One influence was the change in attitude among pension funds following the failure of companies such as Enron in the early 2000s (see section 'The origins of ethical investment'). Coincidentally or consequently, a group of sustainable investing practitioners emerged (e.g. fund managers and rating agencies) who in turn instigated catalytic initiatives such as the establishment of analytics firms Innovest Strategic Value Advisers, Trucost, and Vigeo. Ethical research organizations such as MSCI/KLD and EIRIS emerged, alongside which agencies initially focused on corporate governance, such as PIRC, have evolved to include CSR and sustainability analysis. In other words, in understanding the growth of a market, it is important to look at the enabling infrastructure, and not just the allocation of capital.

Trends in SRI

Whether one is looking at fears about global warming, the opportunities presented by the shift to a low-carbon economy, calls for longer-term investment horizons, the governance lessons from the financial crisis, or the increased interest in products and services for the poor, some long-established concerns of SRI are now higher on political and business agendas than ever before. Kay's report to the UK government (Kay, 2012) shows the limitations to changing the behaviour of mainstream asset managers (e.g. they invest globally, and individually only own a small portion of any particular company), and this situation may generate more interest in SRI that can demonstrate genuine impact. This is not only creating an environment in which SRI can flourish, but is also causing governments and investors to take a closer look at ideas from the SRI world. For example, socially responsible bonds or bond funds have provided an investment vehicle for SRI investors, offering a comparatively low-risk alternative, particularly for endowments and institutional investors looking for safe investment strategies with guarantees. Green bonds for environmental projects have been issued by the US government since 2004, the European Investment Bank issues 'Climate Awareness Bonds', and the Malaysian government issues bonds for reforestation.

The financial crisis drew attention to a long-running concern of the SRI community—the importance of investment for the long term, and the importance of investors acting as genuine owners rather than rent-seekers. Renewed interest in the idea of a Tobin tax to limit speculation reflects another well-established concern among SRI advocates. As noted earlier, the two main premises behind sustainable investing are that incorporating long-term sustainability-related trends will offer superior risk-adjusted growth, and there needs to be a recasting of the world's capital markets. The first of these is in many ways contingent upon the second, and while some have criticized sustainable investing advocates for appearing to say that nothing can be achieved unless everything is changed, there is a far greater appetite for reform than there was just a few years ago.

However, the question remains as to whether the environment for long-term growth upon which much of SRI's superior performance seems to hinge can be created without further major financial, social, or environmental shocks. While segments of SRI, not least offshoot sustainable investing, are booming, the consistent institutional and legal framework necessary to mobilize capital and bring convergence between SRI issues and financial analysis is scarcely happening. SRI might seem large, but set against the size of the world's capital markets, or indeed the scale of transformation some say is necessary to meet the world's social and environmental challenges, it barely casts a shadow. Moreover, this is unlikely to change if the social and environmental costs of business are not internalized. Furthermore, for all the debate about regulation, and the undeniable fact that at a national level banking is an extremely highly regulated industry, it remains that finance enjoys a privileged status—free, for instance, of the kind of regulation applied to many other sectors. Thus, while pharmaceutical companies will spend years getting regulatory approval for new drugs, financial institutions plough ahead with newer and ever more complex products such as derivatives without any accountability or oversight.

Discussion points

In the light of what we have discussed about SRI's origins and future trends, consider the following.

- What new initiatives are likely to emerge or develop between now and 2025?
- Are there issues missing from the current SRI agenda (e.g. gender pay-gaps; work-life balance)? Why?
- Which leading social issues are likely to gain attention in your country in relation to corporate governance and why?

Case study 10 China—SRI's rising star or nemesis?

For many years, SRI funds avoided China and took companies to task for labour standards, human rights, lack of transparency, and environmental conditions in that country. While many multinationals argued that avoiding China would be disastrous to their competitiveness, or that transferring best practice from around the world to an isolated autocracy would open new opportunities for democracy, SRI proponents said that foreign investment would inevitably support and legitimize an unacceptable exploitative form of capitalism.

At first glance, China's emergence as the most polluting nation in 2007 seemed to reinforce the SRI position. Its greenhouse gas emissions exceed those of the USA, 700 million of its people (about half of its population) lack access to safe drinking water, it is home to sixteen of the twenty most-polluted cities in the world, and 68% of its power comes from coal. Yet, while human rights and democratization have provoked enervation among Chinese politicians, the threats of environmental catastrophe have spurred innovation. Since the mid-2000s, there has been a raft of policy and administrative initiatives such as the Eleventh Five Year Plan for Energy Development (2006–2010), the 2006 Renewable Energy Law, the 2008 amendments to the Energy Conservation Law, and the strengthening of the Ministry of Environmental Protection. The government has promised to reduce the nation's energy consumption as a proportion of GDP by 20% through energy efficiency and new technologies. Stretch targets have been set for an increase in renewable energy and enshrined in law (see table in the online resources), and it is expected that by 2025 renewables will make up 16% of total primary energy and 20% of electric power capacity.

The investment opportunities implicit in this redirection of energy policy in what should be one of the world's largest and fastest-growing economies has attracted attention from conventional investment funds, but also from SRI funds, which have been pioneers of cleantech investing. Some predict that reaching China's renewable energy targets will require investments of $174 billion until 2020, and venture capital inflows continue to boom (e.g. $420 million in 2006, rising to over $55 billion in 2016).

China is also home to leading renewable energy companies such as solar panel maker Jiangsu Shunda, and is the largest producer of wind turbines. Thinking about the low-carbon economy is also leading to other innovations such as BYD Auto, producer of electric cars. Its leading green companies such as Goldwind, Shoto, and LDK Solar are listed on foreign exchanges, and the initial public offerings have been profitable.

However, the current state of China's renewable energy investment raises questions about the global shift from carbon-based fuels to alternative energy as a whole. In 2016, the 'big three' developing economies of China, India, and Brazil saw a combined 28% setback in dollar investment in renewable

(continued . . .)

energy to $94.7 billion, with China down by almost one-third. The Chinese solar market decelerated sharply and was one of several up-and-coming renewable energy markets in the developing world that, following record investment figures in 2015, fell sharply in 2016.

It also shows the importance of China to global investment. The world's most populous country committed $78.3 billion to renewables last year, but this was down 32% ($37.1 billion) on 2015's record, reflecting a combination of lower costs per MW and a dip in activity as grids concentrated on integrating capacity already built and after the previous feed-in tariff expired in mid-year. US investment fell 10% in 2016 to $46.4 billion. This was in line with its average for the 'levelized', or all-in, costs of generation from solar panels and wind. In the second half of 2016, levelized costs for photovoltaic cells (the costs of electricity include the costs of capex, finance, operating and maintenance, development, and fuel), and lower total capex costs were responsible for part of the $70.6 billion fall in global renewable energy investment that year.

The long-term significance of this fall in green investment needs to be understood in context. Renewables (excluding large hydro) have gone from being labelled as 'alternative energy' to the majority (55.3% in 2016) of new generating capacity installed worldwide. Wind and solar are undercutting coal or gas—or both—in terms of levelized costs, in an increasing number of countries. But that does not mean cleantech investment in China will be unproblematic. Furthermore, China's green energy industry as a whole will depend on the global competitiveness of the cleantech market, and the consequences of US energy policy in particular. The growth in solar power could also be threatened by the industry's dependence on imported silicon for which Chinese firms are paying a premium, and biodiesel distribution has not yet been incorporated into the main petrol station networks. A combination of these factors means that many Chinese firms face rising costs and shrinking profit margins on top of an unstable demand—a fact reflected in the share price of companies such as Solarfun Power, JA Solar, and China Sunergy, which have failed to achieve the NASDAQ average since late 2009.

Nonetheless, many SRI funds see China's environmental markets as the ideal opportunity to support positive change in this huge economy. The Taida Environmental Index is the country's first social responsibility index, and Chinese institutions have started to create SRI funds such as the Sustainable Growth Equity Fund and the green private equity fund ZheShang Nuohai Low Carbon Fund. Organizations promoting SRI have emerged, such as the Association of Sustainable and Responsible Investment in Asia (ASrIA). Calvert, a leading SRI house in the USA, was among the first partners in the highly profitable cleantech-focused China Environment Fund. For some SRI investors, such as CalPERS, the appeal of environmental investment has meant reversing previous boycott China policies, and led them to wrestle with compromises about the potentially enormous environmental impacts and their principles on human rights and democratic values. Following the argument made by many multinationals, SRI advocates say that the infrastructure for change is being put in place (e.g. an emerging CSR culture, and new SRI vehicles), and that one cannot bring about change without being active in the country. Their expectation is that a vibrant and indigenous SRI industry will be created, expanding beyond cleantech to other CSR issues.

(*Sources:* Frankfurt School-UNEP, 2017; Cheung, 2008; Guo, 2009; http://www.chinacsr.com)

Questions

1 SRI investors were for a long time reluctant to invest in China.

   a What were their main objections to investing in China?

   b Do more recent changes in investment policy reflect an ethical or a business argument?

   c What are the dangers of a narrow focus on environmental industries?

(*continued*...)

2 China's environmental challenges have attracted the attention of SRI investors.
   a Why are companies and the government in China interested in the environment?
   b What investment opportunities are arising as a result of these challenges?
   c Can SRI offer anything to environmental investment that mainstream investors cannot?

3 'Buyer beware' is an adage often applied to doing business in China.
   a What investment infrastructure needs to be in place to establish a viable indigenous SRI industry?
   b What might be the role of foreign SRI organizations in establishing SRI in China?
   c What are the advantages for Chinese companies of attracting stable, long-term investors of the kind identified with SRI?

Summary

In this chapter, we have looked at the development of SRI and at its appeal to investors as a way in which to maximize financial, social, and environmental returns in the long term. We have looked at both pre-investment and post-investment strategies used to identify SRI opportunities—namely, screening and engagement. In reviewing the comparative performance of SRI and traditional vehicles, we learned that, on the whole, there is no evidence that SRI indices or funds underperform, and that some SRI-related strategies offer better returns, particularly if one takes a longer-term perspective.

While there are those who think that SRI and traditional investment are diametrically opposed, it can be argued that we are in the midst of a convergence. Cleantech, for example, is at the intersection—appealing to both conventional investors and SRI investors. This convergence may continue as reporting mechanisms become more transparent, analytical methods become more sophisticated, established SRI issues become of increasing concern to companies and investors, and SRI offerings continue to grow. But this is not to predict that SRI will radically transform the investment world, and the importance of SRI needs to be considered in the context of the other business, governance, and investment trends that are discussed elsewhere in this book.

Further reading

Baker, H.K. and Nofsinger, J.R. (eds) 2012, *Socially responsible finance and investing: financial institutions, corporations, investors, and activists*, Wiley, London.
A far-reaching study of SRI from academics and practitioners.

Barker, R.M. and Chiu, I.H. 2017, *Corporate governance and investment management: the promises and limitations of the new financial economy*, Edward Elgar Publishing, Cheltenham.
Assessment of how investment management is affecting changes in finance.

Bugg-Levine, A. and Emerson, J. 2011, 'Impact investing: transforming how we make money while making a difference', *Innovations*, vol. 6, no. 3, pp 9–18.
Introduction to impact investing.

Krosinsky, C. and Robins, N. (eds) 2008, *Sustainable investing: the art of long-term performance*, Earthscan, London.
Prominent professionals from the sustainable investment world examine the case for sustainable investing, and how it differs from SRI.

Louche, C. and Lydenberg, S.D. 2011, *Dilemmas in responsible investment*, Greenleaf, Sheffield.
Practical examples of the issues that arise when trying to invest responsibly.

Maas, K. and Grieco, C. 2017, 'Distinguishing game changers from boastful charlatans: which social enterprises measure their impact?', *Journal of Social Entrepreneurship*, vol. 8, no. 1, pp 110–128.
Insightful look at the different ways social enterprises measure impact.

http://www.oup.com/uk/blowfield_murray4e

Visit the online resources that accompany this book to enrich your understanding of this chapter. Among the resources available are web links, exercises, and additional case studies.

Endnotes

1. Teoh et al., 1995.
2. More detailed information can be found online at http://www.hm-treasury.gov.uk, accessed 27 November 2018.
3. Odell, 2007; http://www.unpri.org/about, accessed 4 January 2018.
4. Keefe, 2007.
5. See, e.g., Gore and Blood, 2012; HSBC Global Research, 2012.
6. Krosinsky and Robins, 2008.
7. Global Reporting Initiative, 2007.
8. Social Investment Forum, 2006, pp 6–7.
9. Mooney, 2016.
10. Data from Yahoo! Finance, April 2018.
11. More information can be found about the Millennium Development Goals online at http://www.un.org/millenniumgoals and about the ILO core conventions at http://www.labourstart.org/rights, accessed 27 November 2018.
12. See extensive lists available at http://www.eurosif.org, accessed 27 November 2018.
13. The Standard and Poor's 500 is an index of 500 large-cap companies and is often used as a baseline for comparison. Stocks are chosen using S&P's methodology. Detailed guidelines can be found at https://www.indices.standardandpoors.com, accessed 28 November 2018.
14. See http://www.sustainability-index.com for a summary of indices and screening criteria.
15. https://www.ftse4good.com, accessed 27 November 2018.
16. See for instance https://finance.yahoo.com/quote/VICEX/sustainability?p=VICEX, accessed 24 April 2018.
17. Grecco, 2007, p 131.
18. http://brazilfoundation.org/impact/#menu-overview, accessed 4 January 2017.
19. Eccles and Krzus, 2014; Rezaee, 2015.
20. UKSIF, 2009.
21. Kay, 2012.
22. Frankfurt School-UNEP Centre, 2017.
23. Data from Cleantech Group.

24. Cobb et al., 2005; Collison et al., 2008.
25. Reddy, 2008.
26. Kaminker and Stewart, 2012.
27. Basel III is the latest standard on bank capital adequacy, stress-testing, and risk.
28. WEF and Deloitte, 2011.
29. Monitor, 2009.
30. J.P. Morgan figures, https://www.jpmorgan.com/global/research/esg, accessed 6 December 2018; GIIN, 2017.
31. Although this work is now dated, it remains the most comprehensive analysis of CSR-related investment.
32. Jewson Associates, 2008.
33. Monitor, 2009.
34. See, e.g., Gregory et al., 1997; Kreander et al., 2002, 2005; Bauer et al., 2005.
35. UNEP FI and Mercer, 2007.
36. See historical data on Ave Maria Catholic Values fund, or Calvert Large Cap Growth, as examples of this.
37. Krosinsky, 2008.
38. Krosinsky, 2008.
39. Total money in SRI Funds 2005 = £6.1 billion; total money in hedge funds 2006 = $1.786 trillion. Based on figures from EIRIS and HedgeFund.net.
40. Lucas-Leclin and Nahal, 2008.
41. http://www.afr.com/personal-finance/shares/ethical-investing-comes-of-age-20170518-gw7kuc, accessed 24 April 2018.
42. http://funds.rbcgam.com/beta/investment-solutions/socially-responsible-investments/index.html, accessed 24 April 2018.
43. https://www.cnbc.com/2017/10/30/global-assets-under-management-to-double-by-2025-as-the-world-population-ages-study-says.html, accessed 24 April 2018.
44. https://www.forbes.com/sites/dinamedland/2017/03/27/europe-accounts-for-over-half-of-22-89-tn-global-sri-assets-as-sustainable-investing-takes-off/#6dd0848b64f1, accessed 30 November 2018.

Corporate social responsibility in smaller enterprises

Chapter overview

In this chapter, we look at CSR as an aspect of business theory and management practice as it applies to small and medium-sized enterprises (SMEs). As part of this, we include the field of social entrepreneurship. In particular, we will:

- discuss what is unique about SMEs in the CSR context;
- explore the distinctions between SMEs, and how these affect their behaviour;
- consider CSR as an area of opportunity and competitive advantage for SMEs;
- examine how CSR is being managed in practice;
- discuss those SMEs that are categorized as social entrepreneurs.

Main topics

Key terms

Small and medium-sized enterprise (SME)
Supply chains
Social enterprise
Lifestyle enterprises
Corporate social opportunity

The small business 'problem'

The vast majority of businesses in the world are SMEs. Many of these, especially in developing economies, are in the informal sector (sometimes called the 'grey economy'), which means it is not directly taxed and often outside of legal regulation. Therefore, if CSR is to have an impact on business, it is important that it is relevant to smaller enterprises.

However, for a long time in CSR literature smaller businesses were considered either irrelevant or problematic. Normative CSR theory was typically portrayed as something universal with application to all companies, irrespective of their size.[1] CSR practice was depicted as something that could be fairly easily transferred from multinational enterprises to smaller companies.[2] However, as the notion of CSR as a managerial construct gained hold, its application to smaller businesses—not least in developing countries—began to receive more attention.[3] There was increasing recognition that contemporary ideas of CSR needed special consideration in the small business context, whether because they were seen as irresponsible, or because they were at risk for failing to meet CSR performance standards.

The role of smaller businesses, particularly entrepreneurs, earned further attention with the rise of new business concepts focused on societal outcomes such as the bottom of the pyramid (see Chapter 4) and social entrepreneurship (see section 'Why now?'). Smaller business was no longer just seen as irrelevant or problematic, but was increasingly talked about as having unique contributions to make. Today, there is a significant body of research and innovation built around the theme of CSR and smaller businesses. This ranges from the types of business involved to the quantity and quality of corporate-responsibility-related activity, the business case, and what constitutes best practice.[4]

In this chapter, we focus primarily on smaller businesses which, for the most part, would not see themselves as having an overt societal mission. We will leave until later in this chapter discussion of social enterprise and those organizations that treat social and environmental outcomes as at least as important as financial results.

The meaning and significance of smaller business

Smaller businesses are typically lumped together under the abbreviation SME—small and medium-sized enterprise. The meaning of SME is explained in the Key concept box, which highlights how firms in this sector are defined primarily by number of workers, size of turnover, and ownership. Although relatively small individually, collectively, SMEs are the largest employers worldwide and comprise the vast majority of businesses (90% by some measurements). Moreover, they cannot be defined by quantitative measures alone. As a sector, SMEs exhibit management features that mark them out from larger businesses (e.g. the influence of the entrepreneur/founder/leader, greater informality in management practices, narrower strategic vision, and weak capacity to influence the wider business environment), but it is also a mistake to treat such businesses as homogenous. For example, despite being grouped into the same sector, the owner of rickshaws rented out to forty drivers in Jogjakarta, Indonesia, is likely to have little in common with a software engineering start-up in Iceland, even if the number of workers is about the same. Indeed, SMEs often appear to be defined as much by what they are not (i.e. they are not multinational enterprises) as what they share in common.

Key concept: Small and medium-sized enterprises (SME)

SMEs may account for 50–60% of employment worldwide. In countries such as Russia and Kenya they are the major job creators, and even in more developed capitalist economies, such as the UK, they account for nearly half of all jobs. In the EU, an SME has less than 250 workers, an annual turnover of less than €40 million (or a balance sheet not exceeding €27 million), and is an independent enterprise where no more than 25% of capital or voting rights belong to larger enterprises. The World Bank separates out SMEs, classifying small enterprises as those with 10–50 workers, total assets of $100,000–$3 million, and total sales of $100,000–$3 million. It further defines micro-enterprises as those with less than ten workers, assets of less than $100,000, and annual sales of less than $100,000.

However, as authors such as Jenkins (2006) and Burns (2001) point out, there are many less quantifiable characteristics of SMEs such as less formal management structures, the role of individual personality, and difficulties in diversifying risk. Furthermore, it can be misleading to treat SMEs as homogenous because factors such as industry, ownership, location, and position in the supply chain can all significantly affect how an SME behaves. It is also misleading to treat SMEs as marginal to economic life. In economies such as Italy and Ghana they have always been major sources of employment, and now, with shifting patterns of work in economies such as northern Europe and the USA, the SME sector has grown broader and more complex than ever before.[5]

One reason that SMEs are not homogenous is that they represent different types of entrepreneurship. Much of the excitement about the potential of SMEs in a CSR context stems from the fact that all innovators start small, and that is true of sustainability innovation and green entrepreneurs. However, these entrepreneurs are a specific type, called variously 'opportunity entrepreneurs' and 'gazelles'.[6] They are often the serial entrepreneurs who derive enormous satisfaction from establishing new businesses, and whom it is hoped will be attracted by the opportunities found in tackling major societal challenges.

Thus, it could be Stephan Schmidheiny, who got out of asbestos, bought Swatch, and now runs the triple-bottom-line conglomerate GrupoNuevo; or it could be Kresse Wesling, the young entrepreneur behind Elvis and Kresse, which creates fashion items from recycled materials.

The opportunities that are arising connected with mega-trends such as demographic change and global warming (see Chapter 14) are already being seized on by such people. It has been argued that they are far more likely to be receptive to ideas and practices associated with CSR, and therefore should get preferential treatment in the allocation of resources (e.g. government funding to foster CSR).[7] Over the past few years, new concepts of business such as the 'benefit corporation' focused on the social and environmental contributions a company makes, have been adopted by SMEs. Yet, even if their products do not have a societal orientation, they will have a growth orientation that provides an added incentive to be aware of their social and environmental footprint, increases the importance of a robust and more complex approach to stakeholder management, and opens the door to new sources of capital (e.g. venture philanthropy). Innocent, the drinks company, and Green & Black's are examples of this type of company, that have subsequently been merged into multinational corporations.

However, when we talk about CSR and SMEs, the gazelles are only one part of the conversation. There are 25 million SMEs in Europe, and most of them are 'lifestyle' businesses, run by people who have chosen to work for themselves or have been left little choice, given the changing nature of employment in wealthier economies. They have little desire or indeed potential to grow, and they may regard running an SME not as an exciting springboard to business success, but more as a trade-off between factors such as independence, income, employment, and other lifestyle-related decisions.[8] Most of them serve local markets. They may be heavily engaged in their local communities, and have particular passions such as education or conservation, but they are likely to be unaware or suspicious of terms such as CSR and sustainability. When Napoleon described England as 'a nation of shopkeepers', he was talking about a nation of lifestyle SMEs. Often it is a lifestyle chosen by immigrants who may lack the education and social networks to enter other strands of economic life, and therefore includes people such as Iranian refugee Kazem Ariaiwand, who owns the Red Polar Bear, the world's most northerly kebab van on Spitsbergen, Sweden; German émigré Frederick Drumpf, who ran the Arctic Restaurant, serving gold prospectors in late nineteenth-century Canada and was to be the grandfather of Donald Trump; and the Bell family from Scotland, whose Canadian farm housed the first workshop of telephone inventor Alexander Graham Bell.

Lifestyle SMEs have a different relationship with CSR than the gazelles, as we will discuss. On the one hand, there is a perception that they have poor employment practices akin to Charles Dickens' portrayal of 'Bleak House'.[9] On the other hand, they may feel that they have a closer bond with workers and local communities, and treat formal CSR requirements on issues from freedom of association to child labour to pesticide management as unwarranted interference. For instance, Ghana's small commercial pineapple growers identified a list of areas which could be considered part of CSR practice (e.g. skill transfer, strengthening property claims, job creation, stimulating local economies, investing in local infrastructure) but are not recognized in the CSR requirements of their overseas buyers.[10]

As part of a shift in ideas of economic development assistance, fostering of entrepreneurship in developing economies has gained increasing attention.[11] There is a tendency in this context to mix up gazelle and lifestyle SMEs, and, as important, to overlook the specific features of what have been called 'necessity entrepreneurs', i.e. small operations (often in the informal economy) where own-account enterprise is the option of last resort, and where the opportunities and incomes are typically worse than in formal employment.[12] Examples include the female small market traders in Nairobi, food hawkers in Jakarta, and the laid-off Detroit car worker who is trying to run his own machine shop. The taxi firm Uber has found itself embroiled in legal disputes because it considered its drivers to be exactly this kind of entrepreneur, while imposing conditions that the courts interpreted were more akin to traditional employer–employee relations.[13] This type of SME presents yet different challenges in a CSR context; the owners may see the venture as a temporary occupation until something better comes along, there will be little capital to invest in anything that does not show an immediate return, and the very existence of such entrepreneurs may cause tension with local authorities and residents. Moreover, in so far as these enterprises are recognized in a CSR context, they are more likely to be described as potential recipients of acts of responsibility from larger operations (e.g. preferential contracts, donations) than as actors in their own right.

Discussion points

People have very different motivations for setting up SMEs.

- Why might 'gazelles' be more interested in CSR than other types of SME?
- Why did necessity entrepreneurs increase in number in North America and Europe in 2008–2009?
- Are SMEs from ethnic minorities likely to have different notions of responsibility than others?

Local, national, and regional differences between SMEs

In addition to the above, there are other differentiators of SMEs relevant in a CSR context. We have mentioned that immigrants are an important part of the lifestyle SME group. In developed economies these have a particular importance in poorer communities because they often provide a range of services where other businesses are reluctant to go.[14] Interestingly, these are often more growth-oriented than other lifestyle SMEs, notably once the business has been passed on to second or later generations. They are major employers among ethnic minorities, and often have a high local multiplier effect as their customers, owners, and workers typically live within a small radius of the business. Furthermore, depending on the ethnic group concerned, there can be a high degree of female ownership of the businesses (e.g. 75% of African and Caribbean businesses in the UK are owned or co-owned by women).[15] Indeed, no matter what sort of SME we are talking about, we should not overlook the importance of women in this sector, whether it be the female traders who are the backbone of West Africa's fish trade, the women's savings groups that were behind the growth of microfinance in Bangladesh, or waste trader Zhang Yin, the richest woman in China.

Figure 11.1 shows the types of social impact that these businesses have, although one needs to be careful not to exaggerate their role in tackling issues such as economic regeneration and social exclusion.[16] In some ways, the close association that such businesses have with local communities is both a strength and a weakness in terms of responsibility, as case studies by the European Commission highlight.[17] The need to build a strong licence to operate is an important driver of responsible behaviour, but it also means that what constitutes responsibility will

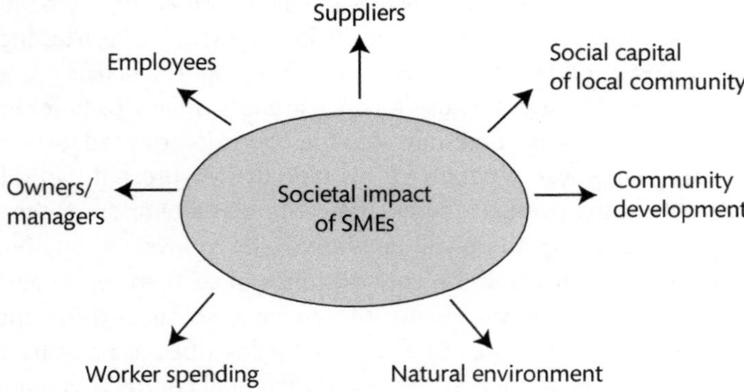

Figure 11.1 Types of social and environmental impact that SMEs can have

be locally determined. Thus, for example, the relationships that SMEs in Tuscany build, involving trade unions, local authorities, and other established stakeholders, are quite different to those that SMEs in Uzbekistan seek to create where 'responsibility' is to a degree defined by Islamic norms of philanthropy and tithing.[18] Equally, these relationships are affected by the sociopolitical context. For example, while much attention has been paid to the role of multinationals such as oil companies in regional conflicts, SMEs can also be a flashpoint. Race riots that periodically erupt in Indonesia are often focused on Chinese-owned SMEs because they are an easy target for unrest. In Nigeria, markets have been flashpoints for ethnic conflict, although conversely they can serve as spaces to bring together conflicting groups. The example of SMEs in Russia (see Snapshot 11.1) highlights the significance of political context.

Snapshot 11.1 SMEs in Russia—unique challenges and common ground

Many of the private enterprises that have arisen in Russia since the end of communism are SMEs. Their situation is interesting in that they have emerged out of an economy that did not recognize private enterprise, and now exist in one where there is enormous suspicion of business. In the 1990s, American economist Jeffrey Sachs and others encouraged 'shock therapy' to the Russian system, which not only left many in greater poverty than before, but through the USA-funded Russian Privatization Center, positioned the private sector as the main engine of economic reform. But instead of allowing a million SME stars to shine, the largest part of the new economic pie seemed to go to a new class of private-sector oligarchs, including Lisin (steel), Prokhorov (mining), and Abramovich (oil). The way that these people acquired and managed their resources as well as their close relationship with the state has led many locally to feel that big business is detrimental to Russia's interests, and caused others to wonder how business's legitimacy can be improved.

Vladimir Putin, Russia's current president, has initiated efforts to reassure the public that business will be mindful of general welfare, and this has been a driver behind the government's promotion of CSR, including requirements about CSR policies and transparency. This has been accepted by many larger companies as the quid pro quo for protecting their assets and independent management. However, SMEs do not have this kind of relationship with the state, and moreover often do not want to be seen as aligned with government. Their concerns are corruption, insecure property rights, arbitrary law enforcement, and bureaucratic inconsistencies.

Thus, there are two tiers of CSR in Russia: one involving the largest companies concerned about their international reputation and the success of initial public offerings; the other involving SMEs worried about local sociopolitical conditions and often resentful of the state. The former are often eager to be involved in international initiatives such as the UN Global Compact, but although the Compact advertises advice to SMEs on its Russian website, there is little mention of the issues that smaller businesses want to see addressed, or how to go about tackling them.

(*Sources:* Original research; Smith, 2016; Sauka and Chepurenko, 2017; http://www.undp.ru)

Quick questions

In Russia, CSR is treated as irrelevant by most SMEs.

1 What issues should CSR practice include to make it of interest to SMEs?

2 Why are SMEs reluctant to be involved in state-backed initiatives?

3 How could the Global Compact's SME guidelines be improved in a Russian context? (downloaded from http://www.unglobalcompact.org/docs/news_events/8.1/Operational_guide_ME.pdf)

SMEs as society members

It is widely held that SMEs often practice CSR without knowing it. This is because if they are visible members of local communities, they need to build a strong licence to operate, whether that be through sponsorship of local sports teams, charitable donations, or involvement in community activities. Moreover, as they typically lack the influence over local authorities and other local leaders that bigger companies have, individually or collectively they need to find alternative ways to remain effective. For example, the Rotary and Lions Clubs found around the world are primarily made up of smaller entrepreneurs, and, as well as networking, are used as a means of contributing funds to the local community.

Historically, the need to maintain a licence to operate stems from the particular role entrepreneurs, such as traders, have played in society. Those engaged in trade were often treated with suspicion by local communities concerned about profiteering, and at the same time were relied upon to get the best deal for local products traded with outsiders.[19] It is no coincidence that groups who came to dominate trade were often immigrants or other types of outsider, sometimes differentiated by religion; these were already stigmatized to some degree, and being a trader did not lower their status in the way that it might for indigenous citizens.

Whether it be Arabs in coastal Java, Chinese in Malaysia, or Lebanese in West Africa, suspicion of traders has led them to invest heavily in their own and their adopted communities, often in very visible prestige projects ranging from temples to schools. Some of this suspicion can be explained sociologically, but other perceptions have more to do with business reality. Employment conditions in SMEs are often considered poor, characterized by long hours, low wages, poor working conditions, and few protections. Women working in sweatshop conditions, be it in London or Manila, are emblematic of SME exploitation. Some of the criticism of labour rights in the production of popular apparel is about the conditions among second- and third-tier suppliers who are often SMEs. Indeed, to strangers there can appear to be a contradiction between the desire of certain SMEs to retain a respectable external face, and their internal neglect.

Not all SMEs can be tarred with the same brush, and poor working conditions are much less prevalent than they once were in some parts of the world, not least because of greater regulatory oversight and the need to attract good employees.[20] A small hardware store may not be able to compete with the big box stores on price, for instance, but if it has knowledgeable staff it can be a more attractive consumer destination. In industries from tourism to coffee bars, the quality of staff can be essential in wooing customers away from large companies. All of this amounts to a concern with stakeholder management and engagement (see Chapter 9), even if it is done informally and unconsciously. In fact, when SMEs have been approached about CSR, owners frequently feel that in terms of both issues and approaches, much of what is discussed is what SMEs have historically engaged in.[21]

SME perspectives on CSR

Confronted directly with the question 'Should SMEs do CSR?', the response is often negative. Some typical answers are captured in Box 11.1, and the SME attitudes can be summarized as too hard, too expensive, irrelevant, and unwarranted. Some of these attitudes hardened in the rush to formalize CSR management practices in the late 1990s, especially in the supply chains of large companies, when SMEs came to be treated as 'little big companies', where practices simply needed scaling down to be effective.[22] As already noted, SMEs are not homogenous, and even if they were, they still exhibit quite different managerial, operational, and ownership features to large listed firms.[23] These features tended to be overlooked early on, not least in developing countries, where listed firms felt most at risk from the possibility of poor social and environmental performance by SMEs. For example, in Kenya and Zimbabwe, major supermarkets, in collaboration with NGOs and trade unions, sent delegations to encourage SME suppliers to adopt labour codes of practice. This often came across as heavy-handed, especially early on, and was worsened by the seeming lack of coordination between technical staff responsible for the codes of conduct and supermarket buyers who continued to focus solely on price, quality, and delivery times.[24] In one instance, a supplier in Kenya had its contract terminated despite investing heavily in meeting supermarket J. Sainsbury's ethical standards (Dolan and Humphrey, 2004). Such examples reinforced existing tensions in supply chains, and hardened SME attitudes to CSR, which was seen by some as yet another way for large firms to exert control over their suppliers.

Box 11.1 SME objections to CSR

- It is too costly (e.g. the cost of verifying performance).
- Outsiders mistakenly think CSR strategies from big companies can simply be scaled down for SMEs.
- There aren't any real business benefits.
- It takes up too many financial and human resources.
- There are more immediate concerns to deal with to survive.
- SMEs don't have the expertise to manage CSR.
- SMEs typically don't seek external help until late in the day.
- It is yet another way that customers can exert power over SMEs.

(*Sources:* Quayle, 2003; Jenkins, 2009; Testa et al, 2016; Wu, 2017)

That situation has changed over time, not least because multinational companies now see their role less as policing suppliers than aiding them for mutual benefit. Nonetheless, many SMEs still wrestle with CSR, especially in countries struggling to compete in global markets.[25] One reason is that terms such CSR and sustainability appear vague, too general, and not especially business-related. When the terms are explained or substituted by others, SME managers may start to see managing the business-society relationship not so much as a cost burden but as a source of competitive advantage[26] (see Box 11.2). Furthermore, it has started to be recognized that many SMEs are already 'doing CSR'; that it is a natural part of running a successful business to engage with local communities, manage stakeholders, create a good working environment, and preserve local natural resources. If this is so, it begs the question whether, rather than see SMEs at fault, one should revisit the question 'Should SMEs do CSR?' Jenkins (2009) argues that it is the CSR debate that is the problem because it fails to engage

SMEs. But this remark in itself treats CSR as a fixed management approach, and not as a sphere of business concern where the theory (what are the responsibilities of business?) and management practice (how are those responsibilities managed?) are continually evolving as part of the shifting nature of the role of business in society.

Box 11.2 Reasons for SMEs to adopt CSR management practices

- SMEs are often already 'doing' CSR even if they don't know it.
- Social and environmental performance is already a common part of supply chain management requirements.
- CSR provides SMEs with a way to attract and retain good-quality personnel.
- Young people often seem attracted to values-driven organizations.
- The modern networked economy attaches a premium to reputation and relationships, and CSR is a way of contributing to this.
- Early adoption of CSR issues helps SMEs anticipate future legislation.
- There is a growing number of 'lohas' consumers (lifestyles of health and sustainability).
- CSR can be a business opportunity to create new platforms for competitiveness.

(*Sources:* Morsing and Perrini, 2009; Spence, 2016)

One can argue with some of the reasons proposed for SMEs to take CSR seriously (see Box 11.2). Some, such as attracting good personnel, anticipating legislation, and the growth in 'lohas', are the same reasons given for why large companies should 'adopt CSR'. Others seem vague or dubious. For instance, are young people more value-driven than in the past, or is it a feature of youth that values play a particular part in decision-making, and if so for how long will values be an advantage to the SME? Equally, how generalizable is the evidence that a premium is being put on relationships and reputation, particularly given the global spread of the debate about SMEs, and the continuing promiscuity of producer–buyer relations at the second and third tier of global supply chains?

The idea that CSR can be a business opportunity may also seem inexact, but it is one that has attracted considerable attention. Authors such as Grayson and Hodges (2017) use terms such as 'corporate social opportunity' to describe how companies can look for innovation in non-conventional areas such as those that are a part of the current CSR agenda. Comparative case studies of European SMEs, such as that by Lamberti and Noci (2012) in Italy, suggest that many smaller firms are well placed to take advantage of these opportunities, even if it is in a field requiring more investment (see Box 11.3).[27]

Box 11.3 SME vantage points on CSR

Your outlook on CSR depends on where you sit in the universe of SMEs. Three types of SME viewpoint stand out.

(*continued . . .*)

First, there is the 'responsibility innovator', most often seen in social enterprises and among entrepreneurs who regard for-profit and not-for-profit, private-sector mechanisms as an important way of achieving social and environmental benefits. But these innovators are also behind for-profit companies that are trying to balance social, financial, and environmental outcomes, building on the concept of the triple bottom line (Chapter 3). A recent manifestation of this in the USA is B Corporation (where B stands for beneficial), a set of companies that are certified for their social and environmental performance, but it would also include companies such as Seventh Generation, technology firm Linden Lab, and craft seller Etsy.[28]

Second, there are 'supply chain victims'—SMEs that are pressured into adopting certain social and environmental standards as a requirement of doing business with large customers such as retailers. While for some the word 'victim' may describe an early passing disgruntlement that evaporates when the relationship with the customer improves, there are still examples of SMEs that feel that their customers' commitment to CSR brings little tangible benefit.[29]

Third, there are the 'unconscious agents'—SMEs that in order to maintain their licence to operate, or because of the values of the owner or manager, are already engaging in activities that help manage the company's relationship with society, and are not intended to have a direct impact on the financial bottom line. This accounts for much of the CSR activity associated with SMEs but is typically considered informal.

Discussion points

CSR is often portrayed as a burden on SMEs.

- Which do you think are the strongest and weakest reasons for SMEs to take CSR seriously?
- What are some examples of corporate social opportunity that could be attractive to SMEs?
- Are some SMEs right to see CSR as an extension of supply-chain bullying by larger companies?

Responsibility issues for SMEs

As mentioned earlier, SMEs often practice aspects of CSR management without recognizing it. Given that many SMEs recruit locally, and produce, buy, and sell locally, it would be hard for them to escape the consequences of poor stakeholder engagement. In Tuscany, for instance, SMEs exist within sophisticated networks involving trade unions, competitors, and local authorities, as well as the public, without which they could not operate effectively.[30] In developing economies, the creation of stakeholder partnerships is reckoned by some to be a key element in gaining competitive advantage.[31] Philanthropy and involvement in community development are long-established traditions for many SMEs, reflecting the pragmatic reasoning behind maintaining a licence to operate, or the values-based orientation of an SME owner/manager.

The relatively greater influence an owner's values can have on SME behaviour compared with other types of business has been widely held up as a unique advantage that such companies can have.[32] Because the company is seen as an extension of the owner's sense of self, and because he/she has more control over how to distribute the benefits of the enterprise among stakeholders, there may be greater opportunity to use the company as an instrument for realizing personal virtue (see Snapshot 11.2). However, we should not get carried away with this viewpoint as, for various reasons (e.g. inadequate regulatory oversight, struggle for financial survival, lack of transparency, indifference), SMEs may have poor employment practices, inadequate health-and-safety provisions, and so on. This is evident, for instance, in slave labour on cocoa farms, employer lobbying against maternity and paternity rights in Europe, and the various instances of workers trapped inside blazing sweatshops with locked fire doors. While it may well be true that attention to working conditions is essential to SMEs in skill-intensive sectors where there is a battle for good employees, it would be counter-intuitive to expect the same degree of care to be valued as central to business survival in labour-intensive sectors where there is significant unemployment. Moreover, in the latter case, an SME might have an active external-facing programme to secure its reputation among the community, while exploiting its workforce with impunity. For example, in Uzbekistan, as already noted, SMEs abide by religious norms about charity and other matters that enhance their public reputation, but they do not proscribe workplace discrimination and unequal employment opportunities.[33]

Again, it is difficult to generalize about SMEs, even if there is a tendency so to do in some CSR literature. However, there are other features of employment in SMEs that deserve attention. SMEs can offer opportunities to people who would find it difficult to work in larger companies. This could be because of their educational background, their race or ethnicity, their gender, the need to balance household and income-generating activities, or accommodating physical or mental disorders. While in the worst instance, the willingness of SMEs to be employers of last resort for disadvantaged people can lead to exploitation, in societies where there is sufficient impetus to control abuses an SME's flexibility can benefit those who might otherwise be low down in the employability pecking order.

Snapshot 11.2 Wallsend Boys Club—bigger than football

What do footballers Michael Carrick (former Manchester United captain), Alan Shearer (record Premier League goal scorer), Steve Bruce (triple Premier League champion and FA cup winner), and Peter Beardsley (two-times league champion with Liverpool) have in common? They all started at Wallsend Boys Club in Newcastle upon Tyne. Since 1904, the club has not only produced famous professionals, but has also been at the heart of young boys' (and now girls') education. Although it is most famous for football, and has nine pitches spread across the site of a former colliery, it runs a range of youth activities including sailing, kayaking, and outdoor adventure camps.

Despite being over 100 years old, the club exemplifies the kind of community-based enterprise that the UK government is promoting through legal instruments such as community-investment companies (CICs). Oxford City Athletics Club, the Isle of Skye Ferry, and Belfast's Skills for Life Learning Centre are examples of CICs which have expanded the meaning of small enterprise. What unites them is that they have a social purpose that is not only core to their vision, but is a legal requirement. If Oxford City Athletics Club stopped promoting athletics for the local community, it would lose its legal status. Just like the chartered companies set up with a specific purpose in the nineteenth century (e.g. to build railways and operate turnpikes), CICs have to serve their communities through defined activities.

In Wallsend, this kind of purpose is well established. Chair Steve Dale says:

(continued . . .)

> [The club doesn't] single-mindedly churn out professional footballers. More importantly, it touches the local community, it brings young boys and girls out ready to face the world positively, and it improves their lives and those of their families in the process.

One area where this applies is racism. Racism has been a hot issue in professional football (although not on that gets much coverage in 'CSR') with fans' abuse of non-white players and the lack of non-white managers getting plenty of media attention. At Wallsend, the senior figures stress that part of their role is to ensure that their youngsters are steered away from negative elements of the game, be it sexism, racism, or attacks on referees. 'In youth football there's always the temptation with youngsters in their formative years to mimic . . . their heroes', explains Dale. It might be boots and goal celebrations, but it also includes arguing with referees, hitting an opponent, or other things they see at the highest levels. 'It's an image that's in their mind. If their hero did it, why can't they?'

Wallsend Boys Club does not tolerate something just because professionals do it. This has a wider impact that exemplifies the importance of values in small enterprises. The club may have produced over sixty professional players, but it has also produced many football managers.

> Many of our players have gone on to management. And it's not an accident. Every time you interview one of those ex-players and ask them about [the club], the same word comes out—discipline.

In other words, the club's values-driven system has a long-term knock-on effect among many of its stakeholders, past and present. As a BBC article about the club concluded, the heart of the club is not an echo chamber of the Premier League but a leading example of the positive role that football can bring into the lives of those who engage with it. And it is exactly this kind of role that small enterprises anywhere could bring: not mimics of big business, but a more purposeful version of the company.

(*Sources:* http://www.bbc.co.uk/sport/football/20170270; http://wallsendboysclub.org.uk/history; https://www.gov.uk/goernment/organisations/office-of-the-regulator-of-community-interest-companies)

Quick questions

Wallsend Boys Club is an example of a community-based organization that shows one of the different forms small enterprise takes.

1 What is the Club's social purpose?

2 What lessons does the Club have for SMEs generally?

3 Are community interest companies and community-based organizations 'real' businesses?

SMEs and CSR management

Introducing CSR to an SME

There are some who hold that SMEs are by their very nature more responsible than other types of company because of aspects such as their close relationship to communities, long-term family ownership of the enterprise, paternalism towards workers, and less pressure to maximize shareholder value.[34] If this were always true, then it would be relatively straightforward to enhance management performance to improve social and environmental outcomes. To a degree this is what has been tried in initiatives such as People and Profit in Denmark, where 12,000 SME personnel were trained to understand CSR as a way of enhancing competitiveness.

However, as the earlier comparison of gazelles and lifestyle enterprises makes clear, not all SMEs are equally responsive to CSR ideas, from which we can infer that something more sophisticated is required to engage and then enhance the impacts from SMEs.

Grayson and Dodd (2007) highlight five factors that can affect SME receptiveness toward CSR ideas.

- Using acceptable understandable terminology: a term such as CSR could have a very different impact than one such as sustainable enterprise or good citizen.
- Targeting: given the sheer number of SMEs and the fact that some are likely to be more receptive to ideas of CSR than others, prioritizing which companies are involved in awareness-raising and capacity-building initiatives seems crucial.
- The messenger: support for improving SME CSR management may have to come from government, but this does not mean that the public sector is best placed to deliver the message. There is evidence that anything that makes CSR issues seem part of a political agenda generates indifference or even hostility, and that organizations known and respected by SMEs such as chambers of commerce and trade associations are better conduits.
- An evolutionary journey: in Chapter 6 we explore the idea that CSR management is an evolutionary journey, and this is as true of SMEs as of other companies. Because of the diverse nature of SMEs and the effect that this has on the company's orientation towards or away from CSR management, the journey may actually be more complex, but comprehending that 'CSR' is not a state to achieve but a definitional construct and managerial process is essential to understand direction and progress.
- Think of SMEs as people: following the theory that SMEs are different in character as well as size from larger companies, some argue that they exhibit more 'human' traits. For example, while larger firms value orderliness, formal systems, planning/strategy, and accountability, SMEs might be as comfortable with informality, intuitiveness, and trust. Recognition of such characteristics would in turn affect how SMEs were introduced to CSR as a concept.

Managing CSR

Despite the arguments about why CSR means something different in the SME sector, the advice to SME on CSR management has much in common with that given to other types of company. The Danish People and Profit project mentioned previously was one of the most extensive attempts to reach out to SME managers, but no longer functions. However, its practical guide to CSR management shows some of the recurring problems of linking SMEs and formal CSR.[35] For example, the aspects of management it highlights are very similar to those for multinational companies whether this be broad areas of suggested managerial activity (see Figure 11.2), or the more detailed advice on areas from communication to innovation to customer relations (e.g. the reference to the ISO 14001 environmental management system or the EU Eco-management and Audit Scheme [EMAS]). It provides a checklist for assessing current performance, and advises the use of a think-plan-do-check model of continual improvement. Such advice may be practical for a Danish SME, but despite the numerous claims made that SMEs are not scaled-down versions of large companies, the advice offered is not significantly different to what might be given to any business.

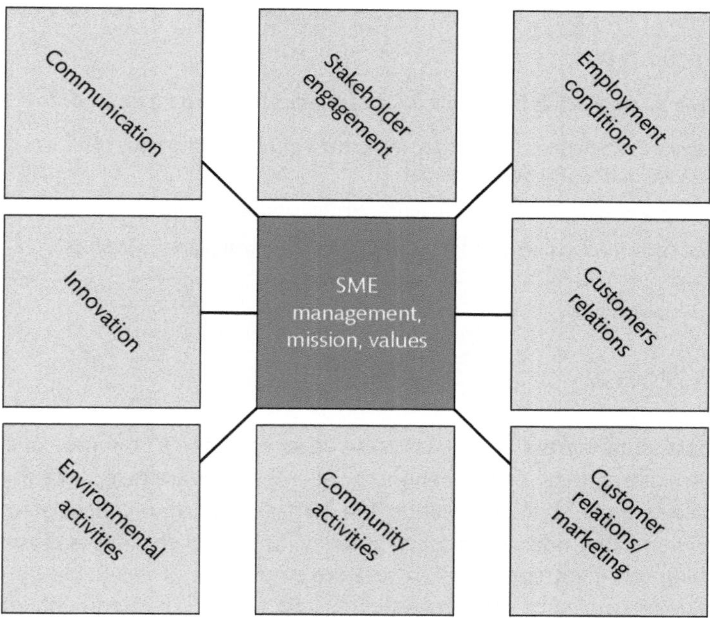

Figure 11.2 Areas of SME management where CSR issues are relevant
(*Source:* Adapted from People and Profit Project, 2007)

This would not matter except for the evidence that SMEs are unwilling to manage social and environmental issues because of their specific managerial circumstances and constraints.[36] Even in the area of innovation, highlighted already as an aspect of particular interest to SMEs (or at least to the growth-oriented gazelles), the models proposed rely heavily on conventional consultancy and academic models of innovation. If other constraints are not overwhelming, this may not be a bad thing in that framing CSR issues within established management models could improve their acceptability, but the limits on transferability of such models set out throughout this chapter do beg questions that current literature does not seem able to answer.

Exceptions to this are work on social enterprises (see next section) and the attention given to the SME dimension to certain aspects of mainstream CSR management approaches such as stakeholder engagement (Jenkins, 2006; Soundararajan et al., 2016), the distinction between formal and informal aspects of management in SMEs (Russo and Tencati, 2009), and supply chain management, although in the last case most guidance is aimed at multinationals and how to deal with SME suppliers (ETI, 2006; Pedersen, 2009; Spence, 2016;), and the difficulties that can arise (Tencati et al., 2008; DeGhetto et al., 2016;). Therefore we are left with the sense that although there are unique responsibility dimensions to which SMEs should pay attention, an array of areas where SMEs are already active, and good reasons for some SMEs to consider CSR issues as part of their competitive advantage, nonetheless the specifics of CSR as a distinct element of SME management are not well understood.

Discussion points

SMEs are frequently described as having unique characteristics that affect their attitude to CSR issues.

- Given the above characteristics, why do you think that a comprehensive body of distinct management approaches has yet to emerge?
- Why have SMEs in supply chains received more attention than most others?
- What role can government play in encouraging CSR management practices in SMEs?

Social enterprise

One of the most vibrant areas of CSR in recent years has been in the field of social entrepreneurship. An international phenomenon, social enterprises are being established around the world, applying much of the innovation and management theory associated with entrepreneurship in general to addressing social and environmental challenges. Business schools are now teaching social entrepreneurship, and the emergence of this field of private-sector activity is also being studied by disciplines such as international development, anthropology, and environmental studies. Universities such as Oxford, Harvard, and Alberta have centres for social enterprise, and it can be studied in institutes from Argentina and Belgium to Switzerland and Spain. In addition, there are a host of networks and support organizations for social entrepreneurs such as Ashoka (worldwide), NESsT (Latin America and Eastern Europe), and the Skoll Foundation (international). One can call on specialist consultancies such as Bridgespan, and trade bodies such as the Social Enterprise Alliance, and one can seek funding from dedicated sources such as the European Venture Philanthropy Association (EVPA) and the Acumen Fund.

By some measures, start-up rates and employment growth in social enterprises are outstripping those in conventional commercial enterprises, and they are having an impact on significant numbers of people; for example, Grameen Bank has 2.4 million microcredit customers in Bangladesh and Afghanistan, and the Bangladesh Rural Advancement Committee is the country's second-largest employer after the government.[37] The size of these organizations raises questions about what is meant by social enterprise, and certainly why it is part of a chapter on SMEs. For some, size is not a determining factor, and therefore GE's ecomagination initiative (Chapter 6) or the retail company Whole Foods deserve the label social entrepreneurship as much as Fairtrade's web of small producers or Andrew Mawson's Bromley-by-Bow Centre, a focal centre for enterprise in one London community.[38] Zopa, the peer-to-peer money-lending company, is sometimes depicted as a socially oriented enterprise, but is its value proposition of lending out money at competitive rates any more socially oriented than those of other lending institutions? Moreover, as the examples of fraud at A4e, one of the British government's favoured social enterprises, and the death from neglect of five people at Southern Cross's Orchid View care home demonstrate, social enterprises are at risk from the same ethical and mismanagement pathologies that can affect any firm.

By blurring the definitions of social enterprise, advocates are able to make major claims about its impact. For example, classifying all not-for-profit organizations as social enterprises allows proponents to claim that the sector is worth over 1 trillion dollars, and subsuming the long-standing credit union sector within social enterprise enables the claim that 25% of the US population is affected by social enterprise.[39] As noted in other chapters, there is a tendency in certain areas of CSR for advocates of a particular approach or idea to use self-serving data, but it can lead to the conclusion that almost any business activity that feasibly has a positive social or environmental outcome is worthy of the mantle 'social enterprise', or that any socially or environmentally oriented activity is an enterprise. In other words, it can become harder to identify what a social enterprise is not than what one is.

Meanings of social enterprise

Definition

From the outset, 'social entrepreneurship' has been used to embrace a wide range of entrepreneurial activity. A collection of fourteen academic articles on social enterprise used ten different definitions of the term, including basic disagreements about whether it applied to individual entrepreneurs or to organizations, whether trade and financial objectives were an essential element, or if it were as likely to be found in public and non-profit sectors as the private sector, and whether the defining characteristics are the goals and outcomes (e.g. tackling social problems) or the process (e.g. employing ideas of innovation to create new social value).[40]

In a field where practitioners and theorists can often appear intoxicated by the excitement of their endeavours, it is not surprising that many define social enterprise in terms of its ambition and intent. The Skoll World Forum attracts 1,000 attendees each year, and companies such as Selco and Boma Investments describe genuinely innovative business models. The entrepreneurs at such events are called 'disruptive change agents' and 'sectoral iconoclasts', and their enterprises have been described as 'social justice in motion' and world-changers. As a social entrepreneur explains:

> the real measure of social entrepreneurship should be 'direct action that generates a paradigm shift in the way a societal need is met'. What such people do, in effect, is to identify and attack an 'unsatisfactory equilibrium'. Their endeavors are transformative, not palliative, with the power to catalyze and shape the future.
>
> (Elkington and Hartigan, 2008, p 6)

In what remains an important introduction to the field, Dees (1998) sets out a continuum of social entrepreneurship organizations defined by the way they are funded. On one side are organizations with a social or environmental mission that are run and largely funded by volunteers; at the other end are socially oriented ventures conducted within commercial private-sector organizations. In between, lie an array of not-for-profit and for-profit enterprises that are variously funded through grants, capital investments, and revenues. As Leadbeater (1997) points out, these enterprises can be found in the public, private, and civil sectors, and one thing that marks them out is how the competencies associated with one sector are transferred to another. For example, a public-sector social enterprise may be marked out by its adoption of business skills to pursue its social and environmental remit; businesses may choose social or environmental returns/outcomes ahead of financial ones; and NGOs may adopt entrepreneurial solutions.

With this in mind, social entrepreneurship could be defined as the innovative use of combinations of resources to build organizations and practices that yield and sustain social and environmental benefits.[41] However, this would still leave us with a large range of only tangentially related initiatives, some of which we have discussed in other chapters (e.g. Ecomagination, M-Pesa, and Whole Foods).[42] It would also draw us into a discussion of the roles of government and third-sector welfare provision, both of which largely fall outside the scope of this book. Therefore, Haugh's (2006) definition is broad enough, yet not too inclusive, to act as a working definition of social enterprise in this chapter (see Key concept). It needs to be expanded to explicitly include environmental benefits, but it does emphasize the importance of business-led solutions in pursuit of social (and environmental) outcomes. While some would contest this as too narrow, it fits the purposes of this chapter, and also chimes with an important strand of business-focused (though not necessarily for-profit) social enterprise.[43]

Key concept: Social enterprise

Social enterprise is a collective term for a range of organizations that trade for a social purpose. They adopt one of a variety of different legal formats but have in common the principles of pursuing business-led solutions to achieve social aims, and the reinvestment of surplus for community benefit. Their objectives focus on socially desired, non-financial goals and their outcomes are the non-financial measures of the implied demand for and supply of services.

(*Source:* Haugh, 2006, p 183)

Social and environmental mission and process

Haugh's definition also helps highlight that even if social enterprises are run at a profit, this is not their primary purpose. For many, what is special about social enterprise is the primacy attached to the social or environmental mission. This means identifying and addressing an unmet need or value-creation opportunity. For example, La Fageda in Spain was established to provide meaningful work for the mentally ill, shifting them from producing ashtrays and trinkets to being the core personnel in a dairy business; the Population and Community Development Association in Thailand exists to tackle overpopulation as a cause of poverty, and does this by funding its birth-control programmes from its social business ventures. In such enterprises, financial returns are not an indicator of business performance; rather, they are a means to a non-financial end, where what matters is social or environmental impact.

However, measuring this performance is not straightforward, especially as the goods and services produced may be only one form of social enterprise output. For example, in some social ventures, creating employment, engaging community members, empowering individuals, attracting government services, and achieving the social integration of marginalized people may be more significant benefits than the actual delivery of tangible products such as potable water, schools, or trading opportunities—a lesson learned from international development (see Chapter 4). These process benefits are widely accepted as being essential to the kinds of sustainable transformational social change that social enterprise aspires to achieve, but they can be difficult to measure and realize, especially compared with more concrete, but perhaps short-term, outcomes such as a wage, a playground, or a surgery. The case study of

Fairtrade in Chapter 12 highlights this, and in-depth studies of the impact of social enterprise, such as that by Lyon and Moberg (2010), show the complexity of understanding benefits.

Therefore, one finds some who consider social enterprise primarily in terms of the field of social endeavour (e.g. poverty alleviation, health care, education, community development, advocacy), and others who concentrate more on the operational features of the enterprise (e.g. decision-making not based on capital ownership, beneficiaries of the venture are participants not just recipients, limitations on profit distribution, social goals). Neither of these is mutually exclusive, but they might be reflected in the workings of the enterprise. For example, social enterprises are often closely identified with their founders, and the strengths of such single-minded visionaries (e.g. their self-assurance, their emotion, their 'insane ambition' (Elkington and Hartigan, 2008)) can create institutional weaknesses (e.g. unwillingness to delegate or build organizational capacity, reluctance to recognize criticism or fault, inability to think strategically or objectively), and these in turn can prove a barrier to achieving goals such as genuine empowerment, democratization, and indeed the scaling up of the enterprise.

A further feature is the context within which social enterprises develop. If a social need were being met adequately by other means (e.g. state welfare services), arguably social enterprises would be redundant, and some of the criticisms of social entrepreneurship focus on the extent to which they represent an ideologically motivated privatization of public services rather than a genuine innovation.[44] Emerson (2003) stresses that social entrepreneurs typically work in dysfunctional markets where there might be high transaction costs, a lack of innovation, or no credible information on performance. Enterprises working at what has come to be called the bottom of the pyramid[45] (see Chapter 4) are among those working in underserved markets, but the rationale of initiatives such as Hindu Lever's Shakti is to generate a profit by serving poor markets. By contrast, social enterprises are more concerned with the social impact of working in areas of market failure. Moreover, there are examples of 'critical social entrepreneurship' (Nicholls, 2008) that challenge existing institutional structures and aim to build alternatives, and there is a historical continuity between the Rochdale cooperative movement in nineteenth-century England and Fairtrade cooperatives set up to counter price monopsony in certain commodity chains.

Examples

There are examples of what might be categorized as social entrepreneurship throughout this book, including Vodafone's M-Pesa (see Case study 4), Merrill Lynch's investment in Ulu Masen (see online resources), and Fynsa (see online resources). Another example of the many that have been written about is Witness, a non-profit enterprise that helps human-rights activists and others to film human-rights abuses. It began by giving cameras to victims and witnesses of abuses, and was funded by the Reebok Human Rights Foundation. It then progressed to building better technical and tactical (i.e. advocacy) capabilities, and is now operating in about sixty countries, serving as a watchful eye on public- and private-sector abuses.

Despite Witness's radical social goals, it is a fairly conventional social organization, relying on grants in the same way as most NGOs have done since the 1960s. Lifeline Energy (formerly the Freeplay Foundation) is somewhat different. It was born out of Freeplay Energy, a producer of wind-up radios and other electronic devices. Its main markets are in North America and Europe, where emergency workers, outdoor enthusiasts, and emergency response teams use the company's torches, radios, generators, and medical instruments. For several years, profits from Freeplay Energy were used to subsidize the supply of the same robust products to poor nations through the Freeplay Foundation, creating a hybrid of for-profit and non-profit elements.

This situation changed in 2008 when—a year after winning *Time* magazine's Heroes of the Environment award—Freeplay Energy was bought out by the Narang Group following financial difficulties.[46] The new owners severed links with the Foundation, and the hybrid model ceased. However, the Foundation continued and now operates as Lifeline Energy, developing technology through its for-profit arm, Lifeline Technologies Trading, in a reworking of the hybrid model that has proven more robust.

Recycla Chile deals with electronics in a different way: it tackles end-of-product life-cycle issues to do with computers, televisions, mobile phones, and other electronic goods. Recycla recognized 'e-waste' as a business opportunity, and employs ex-convicts to dismantle appliances and prepare the parts for export. However, income is reinvested in Recycla's greater social mission—to raise awareness of the need to recycle e-waste, and to create a legislative framework to support this. Within four years, the social enterprise was profitable, and it is now the preferred recycling outlet for many companies.

These examples demonstrate quite different funding and business models. The degree of long-term viability of each example is debatable, as is its scalability, although scale and replication are not defining characteristics of social enterprise. What they have in common is that they seek to serve dysfunctional or under-served markets through innovative ideas, and give primacy to their social/environmental impacts.

Why now?

One effect of the wide variety of definitions of social enterprise is that the term can be applied to all manner of historical examples, including the Quaker family enterprises of Victorian capitalism, the gilded age philanthropy of Andrew Carnegie (see Chapter 1), and the Rochdale cooperative movement. Yet, placing contemporary social entrepreneurship in a long historical tradition goes against some of the claims that it is a new and unique response to a particular set of events and circumstances. For example, it has been portrayed as a response to the market dysfunctions associated with global poverty (see Chapter 4), leveraging the overall rise in global wealth, the spread of capitalist democracies, and the rising crises in health and the environment, income inequality, and inefficient public service delivery.[47] It also complements the 'third way' political paradigm that seeks to balance the free market bias of conventional democratic right-wing parties, and the state-control bias of their left-wing opponents. The third-way, which for a time dominated much European and North American political policy after the early 1990s, treats economic development as an apolitical good that can be achieved through technological development, education, and competitive mechanisms. Entrepreneurship and social inclusion are important parts of this narrative, and social enterprise is often seen as uniquely placed to bridge them.

Social enterprise can also be portrayed as part of a more overt political paradigm, where the values of the free market are transferred to arenas that hitherto were the sphere of the public sector. Thus, not only are social entrepreneurs filling roles that in the government agencies of previous decades were the duty of government (even if the entrepreneurs often remain dependent on government funding), the frameworks and language of business come to dominate the poverty alleviation and environmental management discourse. For example, the poor are considered 'dynamic', the 'solutions' to poverty are to be found in 'entrepreneurship' and 'innovation', and even sustainability of the planet is described in terms of natural 'capital'.

As discussed in Chapters 4 and 14, an aspect of CSR that needs consideration is the extent to which it causes us to translate social and environmental issues into the norms and metaphors of business. However, it is misleading to think of a golden age when government was the sole purveyor of social goods. In some countries during a particular period, as the result of particular social and political upheavals, the state took on a role unprecedented in history. But whether it be mosques and churches, mutual societies and cooperatives, or guilds and masons, there has long been a private social sector that has often been at least as active as government in spawning innovative solutions to meet social and environmental needs.

One new feature of contemporary social enterprise, however, is the widening sources of funding. Our earlier example of Witness shows how conventional grant giving remains important, and Orlando Rincón Bonilla, the Colombian social entrepreneur, is similar in many ways to Carnegie and Rowntree, wealthy businessmen who decided to spend their wealth on tackling social needs. But, as explored further as part of socially responsible investing (see Chapter 10), alternative and increasingly sophisticated capital markets focused on social entrepreneurs are emerging. There are mentor organizations such as UnLtd that provide incremental seed capital as well as advice; there are networks that bring together angel investors and social entrepreneurs; and there are market brokers such as Investing for Good linking investors interested in a blend of social and financial returns on investment with social enterprises. This last group is focused on what is variously called impact investing, programme-related investing, or blended-value investing.[48] These investments inhabit a space between philanthropy (where no financial return is expected) and pure financial investments (where social/environmental considerations are only a factor in so far as they affect profit maximization). The impact investing market is estimated to reach $500 billion by 2020.[49]

Impact

Much of the analysis of the impact of CSR in Chapter 12 is applicable to the particular field of social enterprise. In general terms, there are a large number of case studies that show social entrepreneurship in action, but these tend to be written by advocates of the field and consequently the cases themselves are weak on objectivity and rigour, and highlight successes rather than the inevitable large number of failures that are typical of entrepreneurship generally.[50] Systematic impact assessment is still at an early stage, even in well-established areas of social entrepreneurship such as fairtrade and microfinance. Moreover, there is a growing body of analysis (again, often reliant on individual case studies) that challenges the effectiveness of social entrepreneurship.[51]

It seems likely that a more rigorous approach to understanding impact will be an inevitable consequence of the impact investing market where investors (perhaps unlike philanthropists) will be more concerned with evidence of social returns on investment. Yet, even if a significant number of social enterprises prosper and have a distinctively strong impact in dysfunctional markets, there may be limits on the change they can bring about. Muhammad Yunus, founder of the Grameen Group of social enterprises, says that the

> future of the world lies in the hands of market-based social entrepreneurs. The more we can move in the direction of business, the better off we are—in the sense that we are free.
>
> (Elkington and Hartigan, 2008, p 17)

There are echoes in his words of the Hungarian school of business thinkers and economists such as Hayek and Mises (see Chapter 2), who interpreted free markets as an escape from dictatorial governments, but there is also an assumption that entrepreneurship is an abundant quality that simply needs to be harnessed. However, most entrepreneurs are 'necessity entrepreneurs' of the kind discussed in section 'The meaning and significance of smaller businesses' rather than the 'gazelles' that advocates of social entrepreneurship idealize. As one social entrepreneur puts it, 'One does not decide to be an entrepreneur. One is an entrepreneur [from birth].'[52] If this is true, then social entrepreneurs may never be sufficient in number to make a significant impact on the social and environmental challenges of the twenty-first century. But if what is meant are the hordes of necessity entrepreneurs who would rather not be entrepreneurs at all, then it seems unlikely that the innovation hoped for from social enterprises will ever be realized.

Case study 11 SELCO-India—bringing energy to the rural poor

Like many of the largest emerging economies, India is fuelling its economic growth with high-carbon energy plus nuclear power. The country has substantial coal reserves, and in international forums it is at pains to assert its right to exploit these just as OECD countries have done in the past. Yet, according to SELCO founder Harish Hande, coal and nuclear—the backbone of India's electricity grid—are irrelevant to vast sections of the population: 44% of Indians lack mains electricity, and for many more the supply is erratic.

Hande established SELCO in 1995. It is based in Bangalore and employs nearly 200 people at its HQ and twenty-one branch offices across South India. SELCO's purpose is to provide sustainable energy services to photovoltaic (PV) solar home systems for low-income households and businesses. It has served over 150,000 customers, and in the process developed a unique business model that makes solar energy available at an affordable price to underserved markets.

SELCO's success hinges on two types of innovation that are welded together in the company's business model. The first type is technological innovation. SELCO designs and sells photovoltaic energy systems for the home. These are primarily to provide lighting that is cleaner, more reliable, and more affordable than the kerosene lamps found in most rural homes. A typical unit is sufficient to power four 7W compact fluorescent lights, although consumers also use electricity for radios and fans. SELCO's engineers install the systems, which typically comprise a 35W PV module on the roof and a lead-acid battery to store the power inside. Both the cells and the batteries have been specifically designed to meet the needs of their users so that, for example, the batteries can cope with daily discharge in a way that would destabilize conventional car batteries.

Technological innovation is not limited to PV and batteries. SELCO helps customers to modify their homes to get the most use out of their installations. For example, a lamp installed in a corner can serve several rooms if parts of the dividing walls are removed, or bulbs can be moved from one room to another if sufficient wiring and sockets are installed. Whether it be the hardware, the installation, or the subsequent service contract that forms part of the package, SELCO sources as locally as possible. Its PV modules are made in India, although the success of the Indian solar energy industry

(*continued . . .*)

has resulted in one supplier ceasing manufacture of the smaller units that SELCO needs. SELCO has developed a network of local installers in what has become a new trade in the areas where the company operates.

Installations typically cost about Rs.18,000: a significant outlay for customers whose daily income could be Rs.400 (under £5) a day. However, energy is a significant outlay for poorer people, and while SELCO's target market could not afford Rs.18,000 in one payment, paying in instalments of about Rs.400 a month over five years is an attractive proposition. Moreover, in many cases the extra productivity resulting from a steady supply of light throughout the day is more than sufficient to pay for the installation and maintenance. PV modules might be too expensive for street traders, but a battery and a fluorescent lamp are within their means, so SELCO has encouraged a network of PV battery-charging businesses. To pay the initial deposit and to organize monthly payments, potential customers can go to the local development banks that India's state-owned banks were compelled to set up in the 1980s. The government also supported SELCO's expansion with 33% subsidies on installations, but this agreement has now ended.

SELCO itself says that its model is sustainable. It has a long-term financing partnership with E+Co, a non-profit organization that provides debt and equity investments in clean energy businesses in developing countries. More recently, it has received support from the Lemelson Foundation (USA) and Good Energies (Switzerland). Among its proudest claims is that its success has demonstrated that clean energy need not be expensive, and that a low-carbon economy does not have to deprive poor people of electricity. The next step in innovation will be making better use of the power to which people have access. For example, many women would like to use electric sewing machines, but the PV modules do not generate enough power. However, on further investigation, the problem is that the sewing machines on the market are over-powered for what rural women need them to do, and if a less powerful machine were available it could run off the current modules and still meet the women's aspirations.

(*Sources:* Conversation with Harish Hande, Oxford, 29 October 2011; Goyal et al., 2017; http://www.selco-india.com)

Questions

1 SELCO-India is an example of innovation by a social enterprise.

a What are the essential elements in the company's success so far?

b Is the SELCO model replicable in other countries?

c Is the SELCO model only applicable in rural areas?

2 The company has won various awards for creating a viable business model that addresses social and environmental issues.

a What are the main sustainability impacts that the company delivers?

b Could a mainstream energy company adopt a similar approach?

c What will the company need to do differently in order to increase its impact?

3 SELCO-India is an example of technological and financial innovation.

a Under what conditions is PV technology more affordable than coal-based energy?

b How could you develop a similarly innovative approach to a different sustainability challenge, such as clean water?

c Are there other examples of clean energy being provided to poor communities? How are they similar to and how are they different from SELCO?

Summary

SMEs have often been overlooked in discussions of CSR. For a long time they were viewed as either smaller versions of larger companies, or a threat to large companies because of their perceived poor social and environmental standards in global supply chains. Nowadays, SMEs are more likely to be considered as worthy of special attention. Not just in terms of size, they are fundamentally different from other types of business (e.g. their close relationship to local communities, their resource constraints, their style of management, and their different measures of success).

However, it is misleading to think that SMEs are more naturally responsible, or indeed irresponsible, than other firms. The SME sector is not homogenous, and an SME's attitude towards CSR is affected by its attitude to growth, the values and goals of the owner/manager, and the reasons why the company was established in the first place. There are SMEs that were established in part to achieve social and/or environmental goals, and for small firms keen on growth 'corporate social opportunity' can help identify profitable openings. However, most SMEs are better seen as 'lifestyle enterprises', or indeed 'necessity enterprises', where the reason for establishing the business is personal preference or lack of other choices. CSR is less immediately attractive for these types of SME, and is typically greeted as a burden. Yet often such SMEs are practising CSR of a kind in order to maintain their licence to operate in their communities, or to achieve business objectives such as attracting and retaining staff.

The difficulty in these instances is that CSR practices can be too selective (e.g. an emphasis on charitable giving but a failure to attend to working conditions), or they may be ignored (e.g. when a large customer imposes its own standards on SME suppliers irrespective of what they are already doing). For many SMEs, CSR management is seen as an additional bureaucratic burden or another instance of large companies exerting power over small ones. However, there are examples of companies in the supply chain working together to achieve common CSR objectives that have demonstrable business benefits. There is also growing private- and public-sector investment in improving SME CSR management. What is still missing, though, is a detailed understanding of CSR management practice as something distinct from the approaches adopted in larger firms.

Further reading

Bugg-Levine, A., Kogut, B., and Kulatilaka, N. 2012, 'A new approach to funding social enterprises', *Harvard Business Review*, vol. 90, no. 1/2, pp 118–123.

A look at the problem of social enterprise financing, including the challenges of liquidity and exiting.

Elkington, J., and Hartigan, P. 2008, *The power of unreasonable people: how social entrepreneurs create markets that change the world*, Harvard Business School Press, Boston, MA.

Wide range of examples of social entrepreneurship assembled and discussed by two strong advocates in the field.

Epstein, M.J., and Yuthas, K. 2017. *Measuring and improving social impacts: a guide for nonprofits, companies and impact investors*, Routledge, New York.

Overview of ways to measure the impacts of social enterprise.

Jamali, D., Karam, C., and Blowfield, M. (eds) 2017. *Development-oriented corporate social responsibility: volume 2: locally led initiatives in developing economies*, Routledge, London.
Collection of articles and cases looking at CSR and SMEs in developing economies.

Jenkins, H. 2009, 'A "business opportunity" model of corporate social responsibility for small and medium-sized enterprises', *Business Ethics*, vol. 18, no. 1, pp 21–36.
Theoretical framework for understanding when SMEs are most and least likely to overtly address CSR issues.

Kechiche, A. and Soparnot, R. 2012, 'CSR within SMEs: literature review', *International Business Research*, vol. 5, no. 7, p 97.
Useful overview of research into CSR in the SME context.

http://www.oup.com/uk/blowfield-murray4e

Visit the online resources that accompany this book to enrich your understanding of this chapter. Among the resources available are web links, exercises, and additional case studies.

Endnotes

1. See, e.g., Carroll, 1999; Crane and Matten, 2015.
2. See, e.g., Bennett et al., 1999; Hennigfeld et al., 2006.
3. See, e.g., NRET, 1999; Lyon, 2003.
4. See, e.g., Spence, 2007; Jamali et al., 2009; Pedersen, 2009.
5. Sources: Burns, 2001; UNIDO, 2002; Jenkins, 2006.
6. Patricof and Sunderland, 2006; Grayson and Dodd, 2007.
7. Grayson and Dodd, 2007.
8. Jamali et al., 2015; Soundararajan et al., 2016.
9. Jenkins, 2006.
10. Blowfield, 2010.
11. Brainard, 2006; Wilson, 2006; Nelson, 2007.
12. Patricof and Sunderland, 2006.
13. Smith and McCormick, 2019.
14. Lyon and Bertotti, 2007.
15. Lyon, personal communication, March 2010.
16. Southern, 2009.
17. https://www.business-humanrights.org/en/eu-commission-launches-guide-to-human-rights-for-smes-at-un-forum-on-business-human-rights, accessed 1 April 2018.
18. Battaglia et al., 2010; Stevens et al., 2008.
19. Evers and Schrader, 1994.
20. Jenkins, 2006.
21. Jenkins, 2006; Perrini et al., 2007; Jamali et al., 2009.
22. Tilley, 2000.
23. See, e.g., Goffee and Scase, 1995; Spence and Rutherfoord, 2001.
24. Blowfield, 2010.

25. See, e.g., Lund-Thomsen and Lindgreen, 2013; Lund-Thomsen et al., 2012.
26. Jones and Tilley, 2003.
27. Jenkins, 2009; Murillo and Lozano, 2006.
28. See also Hollender and Breen, 2010.
29. Tencati et al., 2008; Ballinger, 2010.
30. Battaglia et al., 2010.
31. Nelson, 2007.
32. See, e.g., Enderle, 2004; Jenkins, 2006; Hamann et al., 2009b.
33. Stevens et al., 2008.
34. Murillo and Lozano, 2006; Grayson and Dodd, 2007; Morsing and Perrini, 2009.
35. The guide is available at http://csrgov.dk/file/318759/people_profit_practical_guide_april_2008.pdf, accessed 18 July 2018.
36. Thankappan et al., 2004; Lyon and Vickers, 2009; Lund-Thomsen et al., 2016.
37. See Nicholls, 2008, p 3.
38. Elkington and Hartigan, 2008; Mawson, 2008.
39. Salamon, 2003; Smallbone et al., 2001, cited in Nicholls, 2008, p 3.
40. See the contributions collected in Mair et al., 2006.
41. Mair and Noboa, 2006.
42. Kanter (1999) provides an overview of social innovation in major companies, and Weiser et al. (2006) offer numerous examples.
43. Dees et al., 2002; Drayton, 2002.
44. Leadbeater, 2004.
45. Prahalad and Hart, 2002; Hart, 2005; Prahalad, 2005; Hammond et al., 2007.
46. The company's debt reached over $13 million on less than $8 million of revenue, apparently due to problems in assimilating an acquisition made in 2006.
47. Ridley-Duff, 2015.
48. See e.g. Emerson, 2003; Nicholls, 2010.
49. Monitor, 2009.
50. For examples of cases, see Elkington and Hartigan, 2008; Mawson, 2008; and Hollender and Breen, 2010.
51. See, e.g., Ridley-Duff, 2015; Lyon and Moberg, 2010; Epstein and Yuthas, 2017.
52. Elkington and Hartigan, 2008, p 22.

Part 3

Impact, critics, and future of corporate social responsibility

The impact of corporate social responsibility

Chapter overview

In this chapter, we examine the impact that the practice of CSR has had. In particular, we will:

- consider the importance of understanding impact;
- look at the ways we learn about impact and the ways it is assessed;
- establish a framework for understanding the different dimensions to impact;
- provide an overview of the impact of CSR to date;
- discuss the challenges of assessing impact.

Main topics

Key terms

Impact

Non-financial performance

CSR reports

Ratings indices

CSR awards

Understanding impact

What does CSR do? Does it help to make the Earth more sustainable? Does it restore trust in corporations? Does it reduce poverty? Uphold international human rights? Reduce corporate malfeasance? Increase business profitability? Lessen corruption and improve public governance? End illegal activity such as smuggling and human trafficking?

These are some of the areas in which CSR is intended to have an impact. In this chapter, we look at the evidence to support these claims. In business or any area of life, understanding the impact is essential for making decisions, justifying courses of action, and recognizing the point at which we stand on particular journeys. In the CSR context, impact is essential if CSR is to defy its critics and move from being a 'feel-good thing' to being recognized as a 'good thing'. Whether one looks at the theoretical work on corporate social performance in the 1970s and 1980s, or at that on social accountability since the 1990s, the importance of measurement is apparent. Yet, given the emphasis put on 'if you want it to count, count it', or the rooting of important CSR tools and methods in financial accounting, it is surprising how patchy attempts to measure CSR have been and that we do not know more about the overall impact of CSR management.

CSR embraces big goals, such as contributing to sustainable economic development, improving the lives of workers and their communities, and accelerating progress towards the Sustainable Development Goals. Moreover, these contributions are often linked to conventional ones of corporate growth and profitability. Part of this chapter is concerned with finding out what evidence there is to show how far CSR has met these goals and, as importantly, the extent to which the evidence itself is being gathered. As we shall see, the information is fragmentary and, to make sense of it, we offer a framework that clarifies the different types of impact about which we do know something (see section 'A framework for understanding impact'). We use this framework in an overview of the current state of play in the section 'Different dimensions of the impact of CSR', and conclude the chapter with a section discussing 'The challenges of determining impact' and what might happen in the future.

The meaning of 'impact'

In its most general sense, 'impact' refers to outcomes associated with particular actions. Although this is too simple a definition, it draws attention, first, to the importance of outcomes and, second, to the significance of causality. As examples in this chapter reveal, discussion of impact often confuses 'outputs' with 'outcomes'. But although the two words overlap in some contexts, the former is narrower in meaning, referring to the specific actions that are needed to achieve a larger result, whereas the latter is the larger result itself. (For example, degrees are an *output* of university that have the *outcome* of creating a better-educated population.) Thus, in the CSR context, a CSR report is an output, not an outcome, if our aim is to enable business to manage its relationship with society better.

However, demonstrating a causal relationship between inputs, outputs, and outcomes is far from straightforward. A company might be clear about what it wants to achieve (e.g. to remove child labour from its supply chain), but even if this happens, can it be sure that the outcome was the result of its own actions rather than, for example, a concerted enforcement effort by the police? Roche (1999) argues that one should not place too much emphasis on causality, defining impact assessment as the systematic analysis of lasting or significant changes—*positive or negative*, intended or unintended—in people's lives brought about by an action or series of actions' (emphasis added).

This definition also highlights how, for many, impact refers to the outcomes for people although, as we shall see, the beneficiary of CSR may also be a company or a particular stakeholder group.

The discussion of impact in this chapter stretches back to the 1990s when CSR became a distinct part of management practice (Chapter 1). Since then, one of the achievements of CSR has been to expand the horizons of what business can and should take responsibility for. It can take credit for introducing new areas of management practice, and some of contemporary management that is taken for granted today, would have been considered beyond the pale and even deviant as little as fifteen years ago.

CSR is also significant because mainstream business—particularly large companies but also smaller ones—make extensive use of the concepts and management techniques it has fostered. However, even if it has altered the way people inside and outside of companies think about business, it has not always spawned ideas or models attuned to the most difficult challenges surrounding sustainable development (e.g. decent jobs, economic growth in an era of climate change (Chapters 4 and 5)). CSR theorists and practitioners—along with other strands of management practice—notably failed to see the corporate practices that led to the global financial crisis in the mid-to-late 2000s, and moreover have not taken a leadership role in the rethinking of business that crisis and its consequences demand.

Discussion points

Some people claim that, when we talk about CSR's 'impact', what we are actually referring to are its 'actions' or 'outputs'.

- What are examples of the distinction between 'actions' and 'outputs', and 'outcomes' and 'impacts'?
- What is the significance of thinking in terms of actions rather than outcomes?
- Taking a real company's CSR report as the basis, how would you modify it to focus on outcomes?

How we learn about impact and the limits of our knowledge

There are three readily available sources of information relating to the impact of CSR: CSR reports (including social, environmental, and sustainability reports); ratings of companies such as FTSE4Good, the Ethibel Sustainability Index, the MSCI-KLD Indexes, and the Dow Jones Sustainability Indices; and case studies of companies undertaken by companies, CSR organizations, and others.

There are also case studies of companies and industries that are undertaken by a variety of organizations monitoring corporate behaviour (e.g. RobecoSam, CorpWatch, Stichting Onderzoek Multinationale Ondernemingen (SOMO)—the Centre for Research on Multinational Corporations). These have been very influential in the overall development of CSR and, in important ways, have set out benchmarks against which the CSR practices of firms can be assessed. There are reports documenting the progress of companies within particular partnerships, such as the annual reports on compliance with labour standards by the Ethical Trading Initiative or the Fair Labor Association. There are also publicly available reports about the certification of particular resources in accordance with the criteria of bodies such as the Marine Stewardship Council, or, in some cases, of facilities such as those adopting the ISO 14000 series (although often the information most pertinent for assessing the impact of these is considered proprietary and not in the public domain).

What is notable about all of the above is that they have been in existence for nearly two decades, suggesting that the demand for independently verified, voluntary information on aspects of CSR is strong. This can be seen, for instance in 'trend-tracking' reports, focused on particular aspects of CSR (see Box 12.1). There has been a well-documented rise in the number of

CSR reports and, according to the 2017 edition of KPMG's International Survey of Corporate Responsibility Reporting (itself established in the 1990s), at least 60% of companies in every business sector produce CSR reports, and 93% of the 250 largest public companies in the world issue reports containing a mix of environmental, social, and governance (ESG) information. The framework of the report, and how that is used over a number of years, is an important factor in showing impact. Seventy-five per cent of the companies in the KPMG survey used the GRI Sustainability Reporting Guidelines described in Chapter 8. Various company reports also refer to the UN Global Compact, the ILO's core labour standards, the UN Declaration on Human Rights, and other agreements which, while not binding on business, are often used in defining CSR performance. As we shall discuss later, a significant area of impact is how CSR's success has impacted its own behaviour (see section 'The impact of CSR on itself'), and the adoption of common standards that facilitate comparison between companies is an important aspect of this.

Box 12.1 Surveys and reports on CSR performance

- *Business in the Community's* CSR Index
- *State of Corporate Citizenship*—a biennial annual report highlighting trends and corporate attitudes to CSR among US companies
- *Corporate Responsibility's* 100 Best Corporate Citizens list
- *Covalence's* Ethical Quote—a reputation index of the largest market capitalizations in the Dow Jones Index, based on their contributions to human development
- *Business Week/Climate Group's* Climate Change Rankings—multinational companies by their total reduction of greenhouse gases
- *Sustainability Reporting Survey* (Germany)—an overview of company reporting
- Fortune 100 *Accountability Rating*—scoring Global 100 companies on how seriously their future decisions will consider non-financial matters
- *GMI's* Corporate Governance Ratings—3,200 global companies
- Transparency International's *Global Corruption Barometer*—public opinion of corporations

The limitations of the information

Before we look at the types of impact that the above sources of information reveal, it is worth noting some of the comments that have been made, particularly about reports, ratings, and case studies (Table 12.1). The 2017 KPMG survey observes a trend towards the majority of companies in all sectors providing reports, a significant shift from the situation ten years ago when industries with the greatest environmental impact had the highest levels of reporting (e.g. 80% of electronics and computers, utilities, automotive, and oil and gas companies produce reports). The range of topics is increasing so that, now, about two-thirds of reports have sections on corporate governance and nearly 70% set climate-change targets. Nonetheless, certain issues are seldom reported upon, such as economic impacts (25% of reports), and, in general, environmental impacts are better reported on than social ones. Furthermore, while GRI guidelines are the most commonly used framework, stakeholder consultation to identify the issues that the reporting company should be addressing is still not common.

Table 12.1 Strong and weak areas of CSR reports

Strengths	Weaknesses
• Comprehensibility; appropriateness of report length	• Lack of a clear and credible articulation of the meaning of sustainable development, consideration of the implications of its pursuit, and any tensions that emerge
• Identification of key social, environmental, and economic impacts and business issues as a basis for credible reporting	• Lack of description of risk identification and management processes, including disclosure of actual risks identified and opportunities resulting from them
• Explanation of the process behind decisions on key impacts and issues for the business and report indicators	• Identification of, and accounting for, social and environmental externalities is rare
• Identification of key stakeholders, including rationale for their selection	• Need for more demonstration that sustainability is integrated into core business strategy
• Explanation of the governance structure in place to manage sustainability performance (e.g. existence of named board director)	• Few reports provide description of how incentives for staff and managers are linked to sustainability performance and achievements of targets

(*Source:* Summarized from ACCA, 2008)

The use of particular standards, even if well regarded, tells us only so much about impact. As Clarke (2005) shows, CSR is being undermined by such practices as the falsification of records and the training of workers in how to respond to auditor questioning. The UK consultancy firm Impactt Ltd says that 95% of the factories it visits in China probably falsify records and that managers can buy software to help with this. In response, some have called for stronger independent assurance and, in 2005, 30% of reports were independently assured in some way, mostly by the large accounting firms, even though there are questions about the objectivity of such organizations (see Chapter 8). However, in 2002, the *Trust Us* report[1] pointed out that there are major questions about how far such companies had restored public trust in their own integrity, and this remains an area of uncertainty. On the one hand, a company with codes of labour practice, such as Primark, is widely criticized for factory disasters such as that in Bangladesh in 2013, but it can also point out that in part because of its experience of CSR initiatives it was able to respond by paying affected workers nine months' wages. There is also evidence that competition between firms and the need for credibility has improved the market for standards.[2] What is interesting as well is that criticisms dating back to the early 2000s remain relevant today, as a review of the KPMG and UN Global Compact annual reports over the past decade show.

Ratings, inasmuch as they derive data from corporate reports, will reflect the above limitations to some degree. The situation is also confused by the heterogeneous methods they use. Schafer (2005) distinguishes between ratings systems that are economically oriented (i.e. those that focus on the economic impact of ethical, environmental, and social criteria on the company) and those that are normatively oriented, within which evaluation criteria are dominated by what he calls 'ethical' motivations. Among the economically oriented systems (which he says predominate), there are four groups:

1 risk assessment approaches (how the company deals with its social or environmental risks);
2 efficiency models (how management strategies relate to sustainability, on the assumption that sustainability offers competitive advantage);
3 industries of the future (identifying the above-average growth companies inside what are considered to be the hot sectors of tomorrow);
4 best-practice CSR management (identifying companies with the best approaches to CSR management).

For Margolis and Walsh (2003), this focus on the economic consequences for the company is a basic weakness in our understanding. Echoing some of what we have discussed regarding the business case (see Chapter 6), they say:

> if corporate responses to social misery are evaluated only in terms of their instrumental benefits for the firm and its shareholders, we never learn about their impact on society.[3]

Indeed, they argue that the emphasis on instrumental benefits is so great that there is little attempt to examine when it is permissible or necessary to act on other stakeholders' interests if they are not consistent with those of shareholders. Their focus was particularly on corporate social performance (Chapter 1), and more recent work in that field suggests their remarks remain valid.[4]

Work on impact by the UN Development Programme (focusing on developing countries) and the Overseas Development Institute (focusing on tourism) stresses the instrumental benefits of CSR, and the World Business Council for Sustainable Development's impact assessment framework begins by stating that it was 'built by business for business and thus, begins with the business perspective'.[5] The consequences of an economic orientation in reporting and ratings will become apparent in the next section, when we look at what we do and do not know about the actual impact of CSR. Moreover, we should not be surprised at this orientation, given the degree to which CSR has sought legitimacy by rooting important elements of its methods and approaches in the norms and instruments of financial management, accounting, and managerial efficiency. However, anyone looking for a clear correlation between CSR and financial performance is likely to be disappointed, as even at the most simplistic level of analysis a company's prestige among shareholders and among non-financial stakeholders can be widely at odds.[6]

Finally, we need to note the limitations of case studies as a way in which to assess impact. These have proved important in terms of drawing attention to particular issues and examples of company behaviour. The best known early assessments were by civil society organizations, such as the Clean Clothes Campaign's case study of an Indonesian factory producing for Fila, or SOMO's 2005 investigation of labour rights violations in computer factories (Schipper and de Haan, 2005). More recently, there have been numerous academic case studies such as Lee Shabib and Ganguli (2017) and Lee et al. (2018). There are also interesting examples commissioned by companies, dating back to the 2005 study by Impactt Ltd of overtime in Chinese factories. But by their very nature, case studies tend to use differing methodologies and a meta-analysis of findings is all but impossible.[7] Moreover, as Elliott and Freeman (2003) note, the organizations that produce many of the case studies typically only need to understand the situation on the ground in order to start a campaign; from that point on, the main dynamics happen away from the site of the problem, i.e. through the media, company responses, consumer reaction, and government action.

A framework for understanding impact

If we think about the possible answers to the question posed at the start of this chapter—'What does CSR do?'—it is readily apparent that 'impact' has a different meaning if we are talking, for example, about helping to make the Earth more sustainable than if we are referring to reducing corporate malfeasance, or to improving business profitability. What is recognized as impact also differs if one is looking at instrumental or normative dimensions of performance.

To help to make sense of these different dimensions, we offer a framework that captures the different ways in which impact is being interpreted. It is based on what others have written about the impact of CSR and measuring corporate social performance,[8] and also the different aspects of impact included in a selection of award-winning CSR reports.[9] What emerges are five dimensions on which CSR practice is held to have an impact.

1 **The social, environmental, and governance 'big picture'** This refers to large social and environmental issues, including global warming, human rights, economic growth, and poverty reduction.
2 **Instrumental benefits** This covers the connection between financial performance and ESG performance, including the impact of making the business case for CSR.
3 **Business attitudes, awareness, and practices** These refer to the impact that CSR is having on the way in which companies think about the non-financial aspects of business operations and the way that they operate.
4 **Non-business stakeholders** This refers to the impact of CSR on other stakeholders, including the critics who advocate for greater ESG responsibility.
5 **The impact of CSR on itself** This area covers the way in which CSR's evolution and growth has affected how we think about and practise CSR today.

We use this framework throughout the following section.

Different dimensions of the impact of CSR

The impact of CSR on the 'big picture'

One only has to think of the US$65 billion Bernie Madoff scandal, the $13 billion fine paid by J.P. Morgan for its role in the sub-prime lending crisis, or the Montara oil spill in the Timor Sea to realize that business remains a highly problematic element of society. It would be very unrealistic to expect CSR to eradicate the abuses and excesses that have always dogged human economic activity. Moreover, one would need an unprecedented belief in industry self-regulation to think that CSR initiatives could have a fundamental impact on financing, given the disparity that lies between the uniquely high level of regulation applied to banks nationally in the largest economies and the absence of regulation at a global level (see Chapter 10). Nonetheless, CSR is increasingly being linked to many of the biggest challenges around the world. These include how we:

1 respond to climate change;
2 address the consequences of globalization;

3 increase the effectiveness of internal corporate governance;
4 uphold international human rights;
5 increase justice and equity, especially in the poorest countries;
6 fight corruption and poor governance;
7 achieve stable and sustainable economic growth.

Although some CSR initiatives have been framed in terms of these big-picture issues, it is impossible to show attributable impact at this level. Instead, we can only understand pieces of the mosaic. The GRI Sustainability Reporting Guidelines, the ISO 26000 international standard on CSR, and various other standards used internationally are attempts to break these overarching goals down into addressable pieces. Unfortunately, a comprehensive review of the impact of standards conducted by the Natural Resources Institute for the British government had not produced its final report at the time of publishing, but should shed more light in this area when it comes out, probably by early 2019.

In this section, we examine what is known about the impact of CSR on some of these issues. Areas such as corruption are inherently unsuited to measurement of external outcomes, at least in the short term, and have largely been viewed in terms of changes in business attitudes and practices (see section 'Impact and the business case'). Therefore, we will look at the broad areas of environmental, social, and economic impact.

Environmental impact

Environmental management has been central to CSR thinking since the 1980s and it is not surprising that we know more about the impact of CSR in this area compared with others. The term embraces such aspects as natural resource management, waste management, recycling, marketing of green products, and pollution prevention and control. There are a number of well-developed initiatives that can demonstrate their impact over a period of several years. For example, in 1995, the Forest Stewardship Council had certified less than 5 million hectares of responsibly managed forest, but that figure had grown to over 182 million hectares by 2013.[10]

Many companies, such as Diageo, Procter & Gamble, and Unilever, have successfully reduced their water use. For example, Unilever has lowered its own worldwide usage per tonne of production by 38% over ten years.[11] Unilever is often cited as a leader in terms of environmental reporting, and other areas of impact are also worth noting. Before selling on its Birds Eye brand, the company estimated that by 2006 it would source 60% of the fish it sold within Europe from sustainably managed fish stocks; it has increased its paper-based packaging by 28%; it has reduced diesel fuel usage for transportation; and it has lowered carbon dioxide emissions per tonne of production by 43%. It demonstrates year-on-year reductions in units per tonne of production in what it recognizes as seven key areas of eco-efficiency, including energy, hazardous waste, and improvements in the management of ozone-depleting gases.

In some instances, companies' management of the environment is basically in compliance with national laws. Therefore it can be difficult to conclude what is an impact of CSR and what is the result of government regulation. In fact, unlike social impacts, most environmental information seems to concern developed, rather than developing, economies, even though government regulation in the latter seems likely to be weaker.[12] In the USA, however, where federal government was not at the forefront on environmental issues such as global warming, companies such as DuPont, Procter & Gamble, and Coca-Cola have adopted targets for reducing greenhouse gas emissions that broadly reflect the spirit of the Kyoto Protocol.

BP, one of the three largest oil- and gas-sector companies, positioned itself at the forefront of thinking about how business can contribute to sustainability when, in 1996, it became the first energy firm to withdraw from the Global Climate Change Coalition, which challenged scientific arguments for climate change. It said that it would reduce its greenhouse gas emissions at twice the rate specified in the Kyoto Protocol and met those targets nine years ahead of schedule, reducing emissions by the equivalent of 9.6 million tonnes and bringing operational savings of $250 million.[13] Walmart has now positioned itself in a similar leadership position on the environmental impacts of retail supply chains, achieving, for instance, a worldwide reduction of waste going to landfill by over 70%, and sourcing 20% of the energy used in stores from renewable sources.[14] Public investment in variations of what Barack Obama called the Green New Deal led to more scrutiny of the impact of corporate environmental actions, and the importance attached to taking environmental issues seriously is evident in companies such as Johnson & Johnson, Pacific Gas and Electric, and Exelon withdrawing from the US Chamber of Commerce because of the latter's policy on climate change.

Figures on individual company performance in important areas of environmental management are available for most major oil and gas companies, automotive companies, utilities, and other industries with high levels of environmental impact. But commentaries on ratings and reporting continue to emphasize that too many companies have not identified what their key sustainability issues are, or how they most affect the environment.[15] The information available is synthesized by ratings organizations, but there has been little attempt to assess the overall impact of CSR on key areas of environmental management. Furthermore, the data highlight trends (e.g. the year-on-year percentage change in a particular performance area), but do little to show what is the 'right' number, such as the level of carbon dioxide emissions that is ultimately acceptable or the amount of water usage needed to maintain a certain ecosystem. Indeed, companies have tended to shy away from this type of claim. Failure to gauge systemic impact will become a more important issue as certain approaches are accepted as best practice, something that is already evident in the questions being posed about carbon trading.[16]

Discussion points

Companies seem to have made most progress in demonstrating their environmental impact.

- How far do you think the experience with environmental impact is a forerunner for what we will see with social and economic impact? What do you think the possible differences are?
- What are the weaknesses in our understanding of environmental impact at present?
- What is the most important thing that a company can do to have a positive impact on public trust in its environmental performance?

Social impact

Social impact includes such issues as human rights, working conditions, labour rights, the impact on indigenous peoples, and the impact on local communities. As already noted, this is a more recent development than that of environmental management and, not surprisingly, there are fewer data on impact. But the different ways that companies have a social impact are also less well understood, and certainly less comprehensively reported on. In an industry such as horticulture, for example, extended production times, piecework, short-term contracts, and job insecurity have all come to be seen as necessary for competitiveness and, in so far as these are poorly addressed, CSR protections can appear as a shield for deflecting attention from the most profound social impacts.

Although companies such as Anglo American, with its Socio-Economic Assessment Toolbox (SEAT), have been lauded for developing tools designed to fully understand their social impact, overall there has been a focus on particular aspects, with the adoption of labour standards in supply chains becoming a significant component of CSR. Vogel's (2005) comprehensive review of the literature concluded that there had been little systematic analysis of the impact on workers and their families, but a study of 800 suppliers in fifty-one countries concluded that if monitoring of labour conditions were to be accompanied by other interventions (e.g. improved factory management), there would be significant improvements for workers.[17] A multi-country empirical study of the impact of monitoring a voluntary labour standard endorsed by major companies in the UK showed that conditions in some places had improved (especially with regard to health and safety, and child labour), but there had been little effect on wages or freedom of association, and some improvements had even left workers worse off (e.g. a decline in take-home pay because of reduced working hours).[18] However, the study by Nelson et al. (2007) of South African wine producers and Kenyan cut-flower producers, in which firms that had adopted voluntary labour codes of practice were compared with those that had not, shows that working conditions and standards of living were higher among workers in the former than in the latter. The apparel industry, in particular, has made significant advances in driving out child labour, and the ILO says that child labour fell by 11% during the period 2000–2004. However, there is also evidence that removing children from an export-oriented factory can be a mixed benefit if other opportunities are worse, or if opportunities for education decrease. In fact, the net impact can be that Western consumers have their demand for goods produced by adult labour fulfilled, but there is no change in the numbers of working children.[19]

Exploring labour conditions in Indonesia, Harrison and Scorse (2004) conclude that codes of labour conduct, together with anti-sweatshop campaigns, were responsible for increasing wages in export-oriented factories during the 1990s and, moreover, that this was achieved without reducing employment opportunities. This finding is interesting because of the large dataset with which they had to work, but smaller studies can also be insightful. For example, data from 142 southern Chinese factories audited by Verité in 2002–2003 revealed excessive overtime in 93% of cases, supporting the findings of Impactt Ltd that compliance-focused auditing of labour conditions has had little impact on improving working hours. As ETI remarked in its 2003/2004 report, improved compliance with codes is not necessarily a sign of sustained improvements in labour practice and may only mean that suppliers are becoming better at passing audits. A glance at the most recent ETI report bears this out, stressing as it does the importance of worker training and capacity building among suppliers in order for codes of conduct to be effective.[20]

This is probably truer for some aspects of social performance than it is for others. For example, although there may be little sign that workers are receiving true living wages because of CSR, Vogel (2005) concludes that there are attributable signs of improvements in working conditions, and ETI's annual reports consistently show that the majority of non-compliances detected and addressed relate to workplace health and safety. Although this has been derided for being a simple target in terms of the greater CSR challenge, when one considers that, in 2005 in China, based only on official figures, there were 250,000 workplace accidents and over 126,000 deaths,[21] advances in working conditions are a significant achievement.

But companies are frequently not making data about social impact available. According to Ruggie et al. (2006), only one company—BP—has made public the findings of a human rights impact assessment. Likewise, companies may admit to the need for public reporting on all material aspects of their performance, but this does not mean that they are consistently reporting on the benefits of programmes with potentially significant social impact, such as those in the pharmaceutical industry to combat HIV/AIDS in poor countries.[22] This reinforces the impression noted earlier that many companies are not systematically identifying key issues.

The picture is not necessarily clearer when one examines niche areas of CSR with explicit social objectives. A series of case studies comparing the social impact of fairtrade, organic farming, and forest certification projects found that they increased livelihood opportunities and income levels for many participants, and provided access to new markets and the opportunity to develop human and social capital.[23] However, the studies also showed that certain groups of people can be excluded, projects can have negative impacts on those not participating in them, and, ultimately, that the most significant long-term determinants of success are factors that are not normally considered to be part of CSR, such as building the capacity to run a business, overcoming trade barriers, and lowering entry barriers to new markets. Similar findings emerged from a meta-analysis of fairtrade case studies (Nelson and Pound, 2009).[24]

The insights offered by case studies, such as those available on Rio Tinto's website, suggest that individual company programmes are having positive impacts for local communities. However, in areas such as human rights and security, the consequences for local communities of voluntary principles and other CSR approaches will always be difficult to measure, while the outcomes of actions such as investing or disinvesting, which may even be a consequence of CSR policies, are not normally being addressed. Moreover, as Rajak's (2008) study of CSR among mining communities reveals, companies may redefine what they mean by CSR and hence what they consider to be legitimate impacts.

Finally, one should not overlook the social impact of CSR on different demographics. For example, the evidence that companies with strong CSR credentials are attractive to millennials has moved from the anecdotal to the empirically demonstrated.[25] This applies to that demographic's attitudes as employees and as consumers, and is not confined to Europe or North America.[26]

Economic impact

The distinction between social and economic impact is to some degree artificial; after all, what is the economy if it is not part of society, and hence a social institution? Polanyi (1944) argued that a well-functioning society is one where economic activity aligns with that of society, and Ruggie (2003) believes that embedding the economy in this way is something that companies and governments should strive for, not least through CSR. Nonetheless, CSR practice and theory still often make a distinction between the social and the economic.[27] There are case studies that seek to test models for defining the meaning of economic impact,[28] and companies such as Unilever and SAB Miller have commissioned studies to examine the economic impact of their operations.[29] Mining companies such as Anglo American and Rio Tinto have also begun to examine the economic impacts of their investments in local communities.[30]

Mainstream companies tend to think of economic impact as the consequences of the conduct of their normal business operations. In contrast, there are alternative business models where the rationale for the operation itself is that it is an effective means for contributing to the social good. Among the best-known examples of this are fairtrade and microfinance, as well as a large number of organizations that fall under the social entrepreneurship umbrella (see Chapter 11). Such enterprises are looking further afield than before to raise capital, and new investor interest in knowing about impact has led to the creation of impact analysis tools such as GOODadviser. Nonetheless, social and environmentally focused enterprises are still at the experimental stage of impact assessment. An early overview of microfinance found that to the extent that the impact was known, the poor benefited, but to a limited extent,[31] and according to the latest studies this situation has not changed.[32] Awareness that social goals are not being managed has led to the belated creation of the Imp-Act Consortium to promote social performance measurement in the microfinance community.

The situation is similar with the equally well-established approach called fairtrade. Fairtrade is often held up as a clear example of the kind of economic impact that CSR has brought, particularly relating to the economic condition of producers in poor countries. In impact assessments, a number of proxies for economic benefit for such producers are used. These include the growth in the volume of fairtrade produce, the increase in the number of producer groups, sales outlets, and importing organizations, and the ability of fairtrade to maintain a floor price that is equivalent to the cost of production.[33] For example, the fairtrade price for coffee in 2003 was $1.26 per pound compared with $0.82 per pound on the world market. However, as the fairtrade company Traidcraft recognizes, sales volume and market growth are not necessarily synonymous with the benefit brought to poor producers, and in its award-winning social accounts it looks at the value of purchases, the sales of goods from developing countries, and the percentage of cost of sales spent in developing countries' volume of sales, revealing, for example, that not only have sales of products from developing countries increased, but that the money spent there has risen from £2 million in 2001 to £3.4 million in 2005.

Case studies of producer groups around the world show that the fairtrade price for farmers can be significantly higher than that available on conventional markets. For example, a study of seven cooperatives found that the price to farmers was twice the world price and three times that paid by local traders, while in Ethiopia fairtrade producers receive 70% of the export price compared with 30% for coffee sold on conventional markets.[34] And even when fairtrade only results in modest increases in per capita incomes, this can be the difference between destitution and survival.[35] However, overall information on the actual impact that fairtrade has on individual producers is scarce,[36] and may be funded by the fairtrade industry.[37] Independent studies have shown that Fairtrade's tag line, 'Guarantees a better deal for third world producers', is hard to substantiate on the ground, with some people excluded and certain types of priority projects for communities not being delivered.[38] Furthermore, the main case study in this chapter draws out some of the difficulties of measuring fairtrade's impact, and how impact on the intended beneficiaries can be overlooked (see Case study 12). Filling this kind of information gap will be a challenge for CSR more widely in the coming years.

Discussion points

Economic impact is something that has started to appear in some CSR reports.

- What distinguishes 'economic impact' from financial performance?
- What are the ways in which a company has an economic impact?
- Using the Unilever–Oxfam study of impact in Indonesia as a basis (Clay, 2005), how would you develop this into a framework for understanding economic impact in another industry?

Impact and the business case

The majority of impact studies since the 1970s have concentrated on CSR's relationship with financial performance, and major studies conclude that there is not a strong correlation between doing well financially and doing good for society.[39] But making the business case for CSR has remained relevant (see Chapter 6), setting CSR apart from other areas of management[40] even though the rationale for expecting investments in CSR demonstrably to create shareholder value when other business investments are not held to the same standard is certainly questionable.

This is not the result of any conspiracy by the anti-corporate-responsibility groupings. In fact it as much as anything a result of developments within CSR. The socially responsible investment movement, in order to distinguish itself from the conventional investment world, has sought to establish a link between wealth creation and the way in which companies address social and environmental issues. SRI performance is discussed in Chapter 10, but overall it is hard to conclude that many firms have been rewarded or punished by investors for their social/environmental performance.[41]

There are other ways of examining CSR's outcomes from a business case perspective, as we explore in Chapter 6. There is a fair amount of anecdotal evidence that employees and prospective applicants value CSR and a company's overall image, although there has not yet been a definitive analysis of this. At times, it becomes personal and there is some evidence that employees of companies such as Nike and Dow decided to change attitudes inside their companies after too many taunts about their companies' reputations made over the barbecue grill.[42]

The financial return on CSR can also be seen, to some degree, in its impact on consumer behaviour. Smith (2003) argues that CSR has helped companies to avert boycotts of brands and has increased consumer loyalty. We have already mentioned the emergence of CSR labelling, such as FSC, Rugmark, and Fairtrade, and reputation surveys such as Covalence's EthicalQuote.com demonstrate how companies such as Marks & Spencer can gain global reputation advantages through successful CSR initiatives.

As described in Chapter 6, the strongest link between financial and non-financial performance is probably the impact of CSR on environmental management. The often significant improvements in eco-efficiency environmental management that we cited earlier are largely attributed to their neutral or positive impact on the financial bottom line. Company reports provide a wealth of case study material in this area, although, as noted earlier, many companies are not rigorous when it comes to identifying the most material issues for their business and therefore it can be hard to conclude if they are addressing genuine priorities, or simply those that are the most financially advantageous. Walmart is one company that has tried to identify its major environmental impact and develop actions to tangibly reduce them, in the process making considerable savings from waste reduction, less energy consumption, and more efficient management processes. Furthermore, Walmart has had a considerable impact on its supply chain, forcing suppliers to rethink their environmental practices as a condition of continued business.

There is a question as to whether this same kind of positive financial link can be made for areas of social performance. There are numerous individual cases in which companies have stressed that there is money to be made from tackling social needs (e.g. from Vodafone's targeting of the migrant remittance market, valued at $270 billion, to Innocent's growth to become an £80 million business in ethical smoothies, now wholly owned by Coca-Cola).[43] Vogel (2008) says that there are noteworthy examples of US-based companies with a good reputation for CSR that have fared poorly in leveraging this for improving financial performance (e.g. Starbucks, Gap, Timberland). Collinson has developed and tested a methodology for assessing the business costs of ethical supply chain management, and some consultancy firms, such as Cost Benefit Systems, have product offerings that claim to demonstrate the return on investment of CSR activities.[44] In general, however, this remains an unexplored area.

While most companies emphasize the financial-ethical win-win outcomes brought by CSR, Cooperative Financial Services in the UK is exceptional in that it reports on the business opportunities foregone as a result of applying its ethical principles. Although this is widely admired, it might also only be possible because of the organization's cooperative status, and a publicly held company might face legal action if it appeared to be breaking its fiduciary obligations by disclosing this type of business decision.

Discussion points

Margolis and Walsh (2003) say that, because companies are so focused on understanding the instrumental benefits, they may never tackle some of the key impacts they have on society.

- Do you think that this argument is valid?
- Give examples in which society in general might want a company to have an impact, although there may not be a clear business case.
- Under what conditions do you think companies will take action if there is not a business case?

Impact on business attitudes, awareness, and practices

CSR has served as the seed bed of many of what are now considered new, alternative approaches to business worldwide. Pioneers of new business models, such as Roddick's

The Body Shop, used CSR as an umbrella term to include the company's innovative work on ethical supply chains, ethical product development, alternative marketing, and pro-poor job creation. The European Union defines CSR as 'the responsibility of enterprises for their impact on society'.[45] Initiatives to do with ethical trading, social and environmental certification, and voluntary governance in sectors such as mining, forestry, and fisheries—all of which are a core business function—are attempts by companies to be responsible for their societal impacts.

What unites an admittedly eclectic array of initiatives is that as well as tackling important social and/or environmental issues, they are non-compulsory and entirely dependent on business's participation and often leadership. They include company programmes, company-company collaborations, and multi-stakeholder partnerships. There is always a benefit to the company even if this is not always easy to measure. They can be triggered by external stakeholder pressure, and often rely on individual leadership within the company. From the early 1990s until the mid-2000s, the most visible and often highly innovative approaches to do with reimagining business's responsibilities to society (or at least the parts of society business recognizes as its stakeholders) fell under CSR.

Yet now, the term CSR is often used derisively: one hears statements such as 'Oh, that's just CSR' to dismiss a company's efforts, or 'We used to just do CSR, but now we've moved on' to show that a company is at the cutting edge. How has this happened, and is it justified to say CSR is no longer useful when thinking about deviating from conventional business?

CSR was a victim of its own success

CSR had existed as an area of academic study since at least the 1930s, but gained little traction in the world of business. For a variety of reasons, not least the emergence of global supply chains, the growing power of multinational corporations, the effectiveness of civil society activism, and technologies to enable interconnectedness, both the demand for and the means to tackle what was seen as irresponsible corporate behaviour shifted CSR out of the classroom and into business management. The more attention CSR got—and the more corporate buy-in initiatives won—the more social and environmental issues linked to company behaviour were identified. Organic agriculture, child labour, conflict diamonds, sustainable forestry, developing country corruption, slavery, climate change, biodiversity conservation, responsible investment . . . the list of issues grew and grew. Moreover, tools for managing these issues emerged involving companies and also their erstwhile critics such as NGOs and trade unions.

As other parts of this report show, many of these issues such as responsible investing, partnerships, and purposive businesses have become large enough to be considered focus areas in their own right. What's more, some of the people who are thought leaders in these areas cut their teeth working on CSR (e.g. Nick Robins of the UNEP Finance Initiative and formerly of HSBC began as head of CSR at IIED). In other words, as the idea that companies should be accountable to society took hold, CSR became too broad a term to be meaningful. Indeed, as an overview of business and sustainability explains, one-time champions of CSR such as Marks & Spencer now describe CSR as a phase in their journey towards sustainability.

CSR was a victim of its failures

The biggest failing of CSR was that it neither pre-empted nor subsequently took meaningful action over the global financial crisis of 2007–2008. This was a business-driven crisis, and for critics of CSR such as Vogel and Reich, who had long argued for more government intervention, it revealed the shortcomings of business self-governance. One-time CSR thought-leaders such as Zadek have shifted their attention to finance but mostly viewed through a sustainability lens, including examining what selected poorer nations need to do to transition to a green economy.

Perhaps it is overly ambitious to expect CSR to have come up with a solution to the financial crisis (after all, institutions far closer to the problem were more culpable), but there have also been cases closer to the core CSR agenda where systemic failures have occurred. For example, workplace auditing and product certification emerged in the late 1990s as an area of CSR practice. But abuses have continued despite workplaces being audited and products certified (e.g. Rana Plaza's collapse in Bangladesh, sexual harassment in Kenyan agriculture, and slavery in Thai seafood).

The financial crisis has exposed many pathologies of contemporary global capitalism, and these too are often areas that CSR ignored. For example, despite the attention paid to workers in supply chains, there seems to have been a tacit agreement that treatment of a company's own workers was not part of the CSR agenda. Yet, a key issue for the workforce in OECD nations, for instance, is employment instability, not just because jobs are shipped overseas but due to casualization and worsening terms and conditions. There is little evidence that companies with a good CSR reputation perform any better than their competitors in this regard. This is not because better performance is impossible: examples such as Lincoln Electric (which has refused to make people redundant during recessions), suggest that firms can succeed despite tackling areas of stakeholder relations that CSR has treated as too difficult (e.g. respecting workers' rights to employment and to be treated as an asset, not an expense).

Devaluing the CSR brand

If one looks at the work of a CSR champion such as Tata or a major US corporation such as Verizon, one is struck by how different the meaning of the CSR term is from what Roddick had in mind. For them, CSR is about corporate philanthropy, and in the USA in particular CSR is managed through company foundations. Furthermore, this interpretation of CSR as being synonymous with what might be better termed corporate philanthropy or corporate citizenship has spread to Europe, which at one stage seemed to be developing an alternative to the North American model. Business in the Community (UK) and CSR Europe are examples of the shift to (or perhaps more accurately re-emergence of) the 'giving back to society' model of CSR.

This shift is reinforced in some countries by legislation. India's Companies Act requires firms to spend 2% of profits on CSR; in the USA corporate philanthropic activity is tax deductible; in South Africa, which is prominent among developing nations for its pioneering work on a more holistic approach to corporate governance, CSR is characterized in the post-apartheid era by community development activities. However, not all foundations are the same. The Ikea Foundation, for instance, has a more comprehensive approach than most to tackling specific development challenges such as women's empowerment and the position of refugees. It is also worth noting that many of the largest companies in Asia are family-controlled, and the foundations of business leaders such as Ciputra (Indonesia) and Godrej (India) are strongly identified with their businesses just as foundations such as Ford, Kellogg, and Rowntree were in their early days. This link between the family business and the family's reputation expressed in part through its philanthropy is as strong as ever and, as is discussed further in Chapters 1, 2, and 14, is one reason why philanthropy will continue to be important in business transformation.

CSR's continuing importance

Does CSR serve any purpose from an Oxfam perspective in terms of fostering deviant business or thinking about business governance? Given that some of its most successful offspring are building lives of their own, and that it proved a poor parent in relation to some of the main events in the history of C21 business, it might seem to be a dead end. However, there are four main aspects of CSR to consider moving forwards.

First, CSR is still a term with resonance in parts of the world and among many companies. KPMG's latest review of CSR reporting highlights that companies in India, Indonesia, Malaysia, and South Africa are among the countries with the highest rates of reporting, and it would be mistaken to be dismissive of a term that is recognized around the world. Chinese companies operating in Africa, for example, have created a complex governance matrix built around CSR which influences these firms' social and environmental performance. A recent study of Chinese companies operating overseas concludes that this CSR matrix seems to have far more influence on company behaviour than the formal policies and guidelines set out by the Chinese government on the conduct of Chinese state and privately owned businesses overseas.[46]

Second, many of the initiatives that emerged out of CSR in the 1990s are now embedded into corporate management practice. The fact that there are no longer many CSR teams or specific managers outside of company foundations is in some ways a positive sign that elements of CSR are now part of corporate culture. There are now numerous examples of voluntary governance, for example, and although this field may not be cutting edge any more, it is something that can have an impact. Moreover, it is always worth remembering that most companies are uncomfortable with being at the cutting-edge: they like the tried and trusted.

Third, within companies active in CSR there has been a tangible increase in awareness of a host of social and environmental issues, and also where they can seek external expertise (e.g. from the third sector and business peers). This is an important foundation for tackling such issues, and is noticeably absent in middle-income country companies (e.g. the Foxconn labour conditions and suicide incidents in China), not least in their operations in sub-Saharan Africa.

Finally, it can be difficult to know where philanthropic CSR ends and business-oriented CSR begins. Unilever's involvement in the African water and sanitation enterprise, WSUP, originated in part as a CSR partnership, but is now connected to important product streams. WSUP is also an example of the frequent overlap between CSR and multi-stakeholder partnerships, involving as it does Thames Water, Mott Macdonald, Water Aid, and CARE, among other organizations.[47]

Snapshot 12.1 The impact of ethical trading on workers

When some people say that CSR is a fad that companies are only interested for the short-term, their attention can be steered towards key initiatives that have lasted for far longer than most corporate programmes, many CEOs, and even high-profile companies such as Yahoo! (now part of Verizon) and Napster, the forerunner of Spotify, which was shut down after two years.

The Ethical Trading Initiative was a pioneer in using multi-sector partnerships and supply-chain governance to improve worker conditions in global value chains. Established in the late 1990s, it continues to thrive. Recognizing early on that the impact of the ETI alliance was crucial to all stakeholders, in 2002, it commissioned a three-year, three-country impact assessment study that remains seminal today as one of the first and still rare in-depth empirical studies of how voluntary labour codes affect the lives of workers and their communities. The findings on the impact of the codes at the worker level were mixed, as can be seen from the comparison of workplaces in three countries (see Table 12.2).

Table 12.2 Summary of impacts by ETI Base Code principle at Country Study supply sites

Base Code principle	South Africa (6 worksites)		Vietnam (6 worksites)		India (6 worksites)	
	Mgmt	Mgmt	Wkrs	Mgmt	Wkrs	Wkrs
Freedom of employment	None	None	None	None	None	None
Freedom of association	None	None	None	Minor	None	None
Health and safety	Minor	Minor	Major	Major	Major	Major
Child labour	Minor*	Minor*	Minor*	Minor	Minor	None
Living wage	Minor	None	Minor	Minor	Minor	Minor
Working hours	None	None	Major	Major*	Minor	Minor*
Discrimination	Minor	None	Minor	Minor	Minor	None
Regular employment	None	None	Minor	None	Minor	Minor
Harsh treatment	Minor	None	None	None	Minor	Minor

Mgmt, Management; Wkrs, Workers
*Impacts that were considered negative by some respondents.
(*Source:* Adapted from Barrientos and Smith, 2007).

Table 12.2 shows the mix of outcomes. For instance, reduction in working hours or the introduction of health-and-safety precautions at over half the sites constitutes a major change, whereas the introduction of age documentation or the correct payment of annual leave observed at a few sites is a minor change. In some instances, seemingly positive impacts were viewed as negative by at least some workers (e.g. because a reduction in working hours resulted in a decrease in take-home pay).

Overall, the assessment shows that ETI has brought demonstrable impacts, notably under the provisions on health and safety, and on legal employment entitlements such as the minimum wage, working hours, and deductions for employment benefits such as health insurance and pensions. At most

(*continued...*)

workplaces, workers' physical and social well-being has been enhanced through health-and-safety improvements and reductions in working hours. Other improvements may have occurred prior to the study; for instance, the assessment did not discover any child labour. Some improvements were limited to certain types of worker, so that, for example, there was evidence of improvement in the treatment of permanent and regular workers, but contract labour was still poorly treated in most countries.

However, there were other areas where the impact was either mixed or unclear. For example, the ETI has not led to a substantial increase in income in terms of guaranteeing a living wage, and there are workplaces where use of an ETI-based code of conduct has led to a reduction in working hours and a resultant decrease in take-home pay (although this is not necessarily considered a negative outcome if there are other benefits such as more leisure time). Also, ETI has not had an impact on underlying patterns of employment related to gender, ethnicity, caste, and religion, although there is evidence of a connection to certain changes in relation to discrimination in some locations (e.g. employment benefits to women, access to training and promotion). There is an emerging awareness in the ETI that these and other apparently intractable issues ultimately depend on achieving a balance between company power over suppliers, and empowerment of workers to have greater control over their lives. Hence, it is not enough to enforce codes; instead, there is a parallel need to help build the capacity of workers and other local agents to implement a sustainable system of monitoring, enforcement, and remediation.

(*Sources:* Barrientos and Smith, 2007; Blowfield, 2007; ETI, 2009)

Quick questions

1 What are the most important impacts of ETI?

2 What are the major areas of disappointment?

3 How can ETI improve its impact in the future?

Examples of how CSR has affected attitudes and behaviour are to be found throughout this book, even if the recent safety scandals affecting BP and Toyota show that positive change in one area may not be repeated in another. What we want to emphasize here is that this is an important element of CSR's impact. Overall, CSR has increased awareness of, and spawned initiatives to address, issues as diverse as corruption, international development, labour rights, global warming, human rights, environmental management, and sustainable resourcing (see Snapshot 12.2). It has raised the profile of long-established concerns, such as workplace health and safety, diversity, and discrimination, especially in suppliers' facilities. It has turned these issues into ones of legitimate business interest, even if it has not always found effective ways of addressing them (or, as importantly, has not yet been able to demonstrate its effectiveness). Its impact has been recognized in countries such as China, where CSR has become something of a buzzword.[48] In recent years, the appearance in CSR discussions of corporate taxation, company valuation, responsibilities to women, the role of small producers, the place of local suppliers and small retailers, the terms of trading, and other topics has shown that new issues continue to be recognized, even if it is less clear if and how they can be addressed from within a CSR framework.

However, it is also important to acknowledge the limits of this impact (see Snapshot 12.2). Some companies are clearly very responsive, others are less so, and some hardly at all. Despite CSR reporting becoming the norm among major companies, the geographical spread is inconsistent, and, as noted, FTSE4Good has expressed concern about the lack of uptake in the USA, other than by its leading multinational companies. The relationship between CSR as management practice in medium-sized firms remains problematic (see Chapter 11). Equally, most social and environmental standards apply to export-oriented production, and the impact of CSR on the behaviour of producers for domestic markets (the majority) is unknown. Moreover, it might remain difficult to implement standards effectively, even in export sectors, because auditing capacity is not keeping up with demand[49] and its quality has been criticized, not least by companies.[50]

Snapshot 12.2 Levi's and global trade wars

In 2018, the USA announced it was imposing trade sanctions on a number of trading partners, including the EU and China, which it claimed was depriving US workers of jobs and forcing American companies out of business. One of the companies mentioned was Levi Strauss, producer of Levi's jeans and Dockers, which sources much of its product from China. However, Levi's was also hit by the threat of sanctions from the EU, which said it would put tariffs on the company's products in retaliation for tariffs imposed on European companies by the US.

There are various ironies in this story. Is Levi Strauss a Chinese company that should be sanctioned for selling imports into the USA, or is it a US company that should be punished as part of a tit-for-tat war between two of the world's largest markets? Is Levi Strauss being responsible or irresponsible by developing a worldwide manufacturing base, and not making any of its clothes where the majority of its consumers live?

Levi's has a long history of offshoring manufacturing. In the early 1990s, it was one of the first companies to explore sourcing from China's emergent garment sector. Low-cost labour, favourable tax and excise regimes, and reliable infrastructure were among the attractions. But politically China was a closed country; a single-party state with a poor record on human rights. On issues from freedom of speech to the death penalty to forced pregnancy testing of workers, Chinese practices seemed to jar with Levi's commitment to being a values-centred business. It had a big manufacturing base in the USA, where its factories were held to be among the best employers in their sector, but the tariffs that helped make domestic production competitive were being phased out.

In 1993, Levi Strauss phased out its China operations, blaming 'pervasive human rights abuses' that were taking place. But five years later it announced it would be expanding output in China once again, declaring it was 'not in the human rights business'. Since then it has been a target for US labour activists, but has justified its stance by saying that its presence in China raises labour and environmental standards. Moreover, it claims much of its product made in China is for the booming domestic market.

However, perhaps the biggest irony is that since 2017, the company has indeed moved part of its manufacturing back to the USA, but this time not creating many jobs but rather employing lasers to do the once labour-intensive finishing work. According to CEO Chip Bergh, 'This is the future of jeans manufacturing.'

(*Sources:* Colwell, 2002; Donnan, 2018; FT Reporters, 2018)

Quick questions

1 What does the Levi Strauss case tell us about future CSR issues?

2 Would keeping production in the USA be more 'responsible'?

3 Should companies be in the 'human rights business'?

Companies that are well ranked in CSR awards may be open to criticism for particular aspects of their performance. For example, MITIE, a company that has prospered from undermining workers' pay and conditions, was a top category winner in the 2013 Business in the Community responsible business awards, and Citigroup, which was at the heart of funding the sub-prime mortgages that forced many poor people into bankruptcy, won an award for its work on poverty alleviation. Earlier, Fortis NV, Royal Bank of Scotland, Citigroup, and HBOS had been recognized as 'sustainability leaders' but were either out of business or dependent on government bail-outs a year later.[51] BP was long held up as a leader in the area of sustainability because of its work on rethinking energy, but its slogan 'Bringing oil to American shores' took on a very different meaning when the Deepwater Horizon rig caused human and environmental devastation in the Gulf of Mexico.

Such examples raise major questions about analysis of CSR information, and the usefulness of the data companies provide. Many companies do not make available the information that would help others to assess the degree and effectiveness of their commitment. Similarly, belonging to a partnership means very little if the quality and nature of that partnership is unclear. There is some evidence that partnerships with members from different sectors of society are associated with stronger CSR performance, compared with those that only involve business, although the latter are still more effective than when companies work on their own. As Chapter 9 explores in more detail, however, it is still uncertain what constitutes a successful partnership and how this can be evaluated.

Overall, therefore, although there have been changes in company behaviour, we are still a long way from understanding, or being able to compare, the relative effectiveness of companies' different approaches. Perhaps this is nowhere more evident than in the extent that success in non-financial performance is a feature of individual performance reviews. Fifty FTSE 100 companies now use a non-financial measure in their annual bonus schemes, but none of them uses more than one measure, and only 7% factor such measures into long-term incentive plans.[52]

Impact on other stakeholders

A further way to look at the impact of CSR is to look at its outcomes for others in society. For example, we mentioned earlier the growing number of framework agreements between international trade unions and multinational companies that, at least indirectly, seem to relate to a rising awareness of CSR. Furthermore, after years of declining union strength, particularly in developed economies, union recognition agreements are part of the criteria used in ratings indices such as FTSE4Good.

Discussion points

One area of CSR in which there appears to have been significant changes is in terms of management awareness and attitude.

- Is it valid to regard these changes as indicators that CSR is bringing about wider changes?
- Is it more important to understand this type of change in the context of some companies rather than that of others?
- How would you set about measuring and communicating this type of change to external stakeholders?

There is mixed evidence about the impact that CSR has had on consumers, with some citing evidence of their willingness to pay higher prices for improved working conditions, while others suggest that attributes unrelated to CSR, such as customer satisfaction and financial performance, ultimately have more influence on a company's reputation.[53] Environmental and health issues have affected branding, even if there are differences of opinion about what an 'ethical brand' is. A positive relationship between CSR and purchasing decisions might be expected, but measuring the related benefits seems difficult and a company's reputation can vary greatly from country to country (see Table 12.3). Moreover, when consumers become suspicious about the benefits of ethical consumption, they may change their behaviour, as seems to have happened with the hitherto high-flying sales of organic foods in the UK, which fell by 5% in 2008–2009.[54]

CSR has an impact on the investment community, as evidenced by the growth in socially responsible investment (see Chapter 10) and the appointment of ESG specialists by banks such as UBS. It has also had some success in persuading students to think more critically about the role of business, rather than simply criticizing companies. For example, NetImpact claims a 15,000-strong network of members, primarily MBA and graduate students seeking to use the power of business to improve the world, and it will be interesting to see whether this less aggressive approach will prove more sustainable than, for example, the Workers' Rights Consortium, which, despite having used college campuses to affect corporate behaviour, has struggled to maintain more than a handful of its 140 college chapters.[55] Business-oriented web-based resources, such as GreenBiz, and less structured web-based networks, such as the 1,300-member CSR Chicks listserv, have also become ways in which CSR both influences people and is sustained.

Table 12.3 Country variations in ratings of brand reputation

France	UK
1 Danone	**1** Co-op
2 adidas	**2** Body Shop
3 Nike	**3** Marks & Spencer
4 Nestlé	**4** Traidcraft
5 Renault	**5** Cafédirect and Ecover
Germany	**USA**
1 adidas	**1** Nike
2 Nike	**2** PepsiCo
3 Puma	**3** Procter and Gamble
4 BMW	**4** Prudential Insurance
5 Demeter	**5** Sony Playstation

(*Sources:* Werther and Chandler, 2011; Grande, 2007)

The impact of CSR can also be seen in aspects of government. The UK briefly had a minister for CSR, and CSR has been recognized in legislation in both France and the UK. In Brazil, the government officials who have played a major role in that country's relatively effective approach to slowing deforestation often came out of the FSC organization there. CSR's impact is felt in the EU Accounts Modernisation Directive, which requires that directors' reports contain a business review including information that is material to the well-being of the environment, communities, and employees.

The impact of CSR on itself

Over the past few years, there have been significant changes in how we conceive of, and conduct, CSR and, in any discussion of impact, we should not ignore how the experience of addressing CSR has affected the evolution of CSR itself. Earlier, we mentioned an expansion in the range of issues that fall within the, at least theoretical, purview of CSR. By comparing the initial GRI Guidelines with its two subsequent iterations in 2002 and 2006, we can see how the range of criteria for reporting on sustainability has been extended, the indicators used in measurement have become more sophisticated, and the advice on using the guidelines has expanded (e.g. the guidance on sustainability reporting for small and medium-sized enterprises). Similarly, the AA1000 series relating to stakeholder engagement has been through several modifications since its launch in 1999, incorporating the experiences of its users and others.

Moreover, the experience of one initiative affects others. For example, national social and environment standards, such as those of the Wine Industry Ethical Trade Association in South Africa or the Agricultural Ethics Assurance Association of Zimbabwe, have been strongly influenced by European initiatives. It is interesting to note how what were once contentious issues have been adopted, even to the point of being considered CSR best practice. There were concerns that codes of labour practice would be more likely to address issues that damaged a company's reputation (e.g. child labour, health and safety) than those that were opposed by management (e.g. freedom of association, collective bargaining), but while some rights have proved easier to address than others, in general the most credible and influential initiatives have proved to be those that set the bar relatively high. This has remained the case even when companies have collaborated to reduce the costs of implementing standards, such as the Global Social Compliance Programme involving Migros, Ikea, Tesco, and others. Even issues that were once regarded as leading edge or contentious, have started to filter into the mainstream. For example, advocates of more local involvement and capacity building in implementing social and environmental standards have seen some of their demands begin to be accommodated, as have groups wanting attention paid to the specific conditions of homeworkers.

This is not to say that there is a virtuous race to the top. Some projects seeking to extend the boundaries of CSR, such as the Sigma Project in the UK to benchmark sustainability, have failed despite their close links with other CSR actors and initiatives. The Race to the Top project, coordinated by the International Institute for Environment and Development, brought together NGOs, trade unions, and UK retailers to track what supermarkets are doing to promote a greener and fairer food system, but ended in 2003.[56] Beyond the UK, the Global Alliance for Workers and Communities, established by major US companies and NGOs to help empower workers, also withered away after failing to win long-term support.

The challenges of determining impact

The picture that emerges is that measuring CSR's impact is as difficult today as it was in the past. There are three main reasons for this, each of which we examine in this section:

1 the practical challenges of assessing impact;

2 the problem of what to measure;

3 the question of in whose interests it is to understand impact.

There are three main sources of information on impact: ratings indices, corporate reports, and case studies of individual companies, industries, or locations. These are self-referential to a large degree in that, for example, researchers compiling ratings will use corporate reports and case studies, in addition to other sources of information, while the report may allude to the company's rating as a performance indicator. A fundamental difficulty is that the basic data needed to assess impact are often lacking because, for example, the company has not properly identified its key issues, or has not reported on them in a clear and consistent fashion. But ratings indices can exacerbate this problem by the a priori assumption that they make about outcomes and causal relations. For example, they assume that the outcome of a blend of stakeholder participation and rigorous social or environmental standards will be better working conditions, sustainable fisheries, etc. Consequently, what is measured is more likely to be the criteria of the standard and indicators for the partnership, rather than an attempt to examine the contribution that such a combination makes towards those bigger goals.

Mattingly and Berman (2006) argue that some ratings indices make incorrect assumptions about associations between different types of social action and that, because they do not properly recognize the context within which actions take place, they end up rewarding actions that appear to be proactive, but are not especially laudable (e.g. those that are easily solved problems or easily achieved targets). In doing so, they overlook those that may appear weak or reactive, but which are actually impressive if the context is understood (e.g. becoming a pioneer in tackling hazardous waste in an otherwise unresponsive industry).

Ratings indices continue to evolve and some of the above limitations may be overcome. For example, the Enhanced Analytics Initiative seeks to redress some of the current information gaps by encouraging quality long-term research, which considers material extra-financial issues that can be used by sell-side analysts. In 2006, the Center for Sustainable Innovation in Vermont, USA, launched Social Footprint to assess the degree to which CSR contributes to true sustainability. Trucost Ltd, a London financial research firm, has also launched TrueVa (True Valuation) to measure companies' overall value added by subtracting from the firm's operating surplus not only its costs of capital, but also the environmental damage that it imposes elsewhere in the economy.

Nonetheless, ratings indices and other attempts to synthesize company performance are hampered by a strong dependency on case studies, including those from companies, in media stories, and in academic or other reports. There is a tendency for organizations to choose the case study which best tells the story they want to communicate, but even in instances in which that is not true, taken together, case studies do not have the consistency of approach to constitute a systematic body of evidence, or, if taken individually, may not have the necessary depth from which to draw wider conclusions. This is starting to change as impact assessments about particular CSR approaches and initiatives begin to appear. Two early assessments by business and academics observed that increased incomes alone did not prove that people were better off, and that factors that are harder to measure, such as terms of trade and building strong local institutions, were important. Equally, standards did not adequately capture local people's concerns and priorities.[57] Moreover, even if researchers know what information to gather, there are challenges in obtaining it, either because of the risk of false documents and of respondents who are reluctant to talk honestly or openly, or because of the sheer size of company operations.[58] And when the data are reliable, it can still be difficult to demonstrate whether an action or outcome is the result of CSR, or of some other event, such as changes in local laws or improved enforcement.[59]

An alternative approach would be to assign a monetary value to particular outcomes such as generating income for the poor. For example, a dollar paid to someone earning just $2 a day can be predicted to have far greater impact than the same amount paid to someone earning $100 a day. Therefore, one could assign extra value to the dollar paid to the poor person, for example $3. Consequently, $1 million paid to genuinely poor people could be calculated as having a social worth of $3 million. Such figures could be included in income statements in annual reports, which would then include, in addition to total revenues, total costs, and net income, the value of external benefits, the external costs of greenhouse gas emissions, etc. While this would undoubtedly be controversial, it highlights the importance of the issues raised in Chapter 8 about how we account for CSR.

Another challenge is how to measure and assess the effectiveness of initiatives that are intended to encourage learning about how to tackle large issues, rather than to have a direct demonstrable impact on those issues themselves. For example, the UN Global Compact highlights how about half of its signatory companies have changed their policies to reflect the Compact's principles and the high level of managers' recognition of the Compact's role as a catalyst for change (see Chapter 5). But relatively few companies have participated in the Compact's learning forums, raising questions about whether participation in the network is responsible for these outcomes.[60]

Ultimately, it could be that companies are producing the wrong kind of data, focusing on outputs and activities when stakeholders want information on outcomes.[61] Yet the type of information that is required depends on knowing who is really interested in CSR's impact. It is quite possible to argue that it is not in the self-interest of certain stakeholder groups, with a significant influence on CSR, to gain a more sophisticated understanding of the impact of CSR practice. Groups such as worker or environmental activists have particular short-term aims when collecting data and may not be motivated to monitor a particular company over the longer term.[62] Professional monitors, on the other hand, have an interest in building a long-term relationship with a company, but are subject to confidentiality agreements and other restraints on how their data are used. Companies, in turn, may have an interest in selecting what they disclose and to whom, especially when reporting is voluntary or the resource implications of proving a company's impact on societal issues may be too great.[63] Whether from companies or multi-stakeholder partnerships, what is disclosed to the public is often a synthesis of a larger and more complex picture that, according to some, too often requires the public to trust the reporters without providing adequate justification for this trust.[64] Arguably, unless there is a change in how investors value companies, real non-instrumental impact in the sense that Margolis and Walsh (2003) intended is not in the interests of the most influential groups that are engaged in CSR. That kind of impact may only matter to CSR's stated beneficiaries, whether these are the poor, the natural environment, the victims of human rights abuses, or future generations. Yet the outcomes of CSR for this type of stakeholder have still not been thoroughly demonstrated, and it remains an open question whether others are prepared to invest in providing this type of information.

Case study 12 Is CSR different to business?—Danone

Danone, the France-headquartered food company, has a dual commitment to business success and social progress. In 1972, then CEO, Antoine Riboud, said:

> CSR does not end at the factory gate or the office door. The jobs a business creates are central to the lives of employees, and the energy and raw materials we consume change the shape of our planet. Public opinion is there to remind us of our responsibilities in the industrial world of today. It is clear that growth should no longer be an end in itself, but rather a tool used to serve quality of life without ever being detrimental to it.

This is one of the earliest statements committing a major company to address the concerns of modern CSR. Its impact was probably not as great as it might have been (e.g. compared to later statements by Unilever) because some of Danone's products (e.g. bottled water and powdered milk) are controversial in some quarters. Moreover, the so-called 'dual purpose' had less impact on the company in the late 1990s and early 2000s when publicly listed firms had a strong growth and stock price orientation.

The dual purpose came to the fore again after the 2007–2008 financial crisis when Danone returned to the vision set out by Riboud. As part of this rethinking, the company established three funds to invest in social progress. The Ecosystem Fund is intended to strengthen and develop the activities of the partners who make up Danone's ecosystem: farmers, suppliers and subcontractors, transport and logistics operators, distributors, territories, and local authorities. The danone:communities fund is open to Danone shareholders, employees, and other stakeholders, and individual and institutional investors. It places 90% of funds in fixed-income securities, and makes the other 10% available as venture capital. The third fund, the Livelihoods Fund, is a joint venture focused on restoring the natural ecosystems of rural farming communities.

The funds operate in very different ways, but all are oriented towards enterprise in the Global South. The Livelihoods Funds (there are now two) pool investments from different companies such as Michelin, Mars, and Veolia, and rather than financial returns, generate carbon offsets that the companies can use. The Ecosystem Fund has an endowment from Danone that invests through grants in the more marginalized parts of Danone's current and prospective value chain. An example of an Ecosystem funded programme is the Warung Anak Sehat (healthy children food kiosks) in Indonesia, which provides seed capital and training to food vendors that sell what Danone considers to be healthy food to primary school children. The programme currently runs in five locations. It is ultimately managed by Ecosystem, which is not a core business unit, but interestingly any Ecosystem programme has to have a sponsor who is a senior manager from the core business. For example, Warung Anak Sehat is sponsored by the marketing director of one of Danone's two main companies in Indonesia. A programme receives funding for about five years. Although there is a link through senior management involvement to the core business, Ecosystem programmes do not have to have a business measure of success. However, in Indonesia, the aforementioned programme has recently

(continued . . .)

promoted the sale of a particular Danone powdered milk product. It is unclear if this is opportunistic or constitutes a long-term trend for Ecosystem programmes.

The danone:communities fund offers a different approach again. It is most well known through its funding of two 'social businesses' in Bangladesh: Grameen Danone Foods and JITA. Grameen Danone Foods Ltd produce nutritiously beneficial yoghurts at its wholly owned factory. The yoghurt, Shokti Doi, is aimed at poor sections of the rural and urban population. Initially, it was anticipated that investors could take one percent of the company's profits, but now profits are reinvested in the business. It is unclear from public data if the Grameen Danone Foods Ltd financial model is applied across the fund's projects. If it were, this would mean 10% of the fund is available for investees, and 90% is invested for the financial benefit of investors. What is clear though is that within Danone, the danone:communities fund is considered as an example of a new generation of CSR through which the company (by providing a grant) encourages other stakeholders to invest.

The other example from Bangladesh, JITA, began as the NGO CARE's Rural Sales Programme, which engages women in the kind of route-to-market approach described in the Grass Roots Solutions Case. The danone:communities fund made a €1 million investment in this in 2011, about five years after Grameen Danone Foods Ltd (GDFL) was launched. The Rural Sales Programme dated back to 2005, and had previously involved partnerships with BATA and Unilever, both with the intention of creating route to market programmes using small vendors to access rural markets. In neither case had the programmes become commercially viable. However, Danone's investment was made with the explicit intention to move from something part philanthropy, part commercial, to something that could become self-sustaining.

Taken as a whole, these examples show how CSR continues to evolve and in certain situations acts as a catalyst for energizing mainstream corporate action in experimenting with alternative business models. In each of the Danone examples, the company has used its capital and reputation to leverage actions by internal and external stakeholders. It is hard to argue that its investments are anything other than a form of philanthropy because there is no expectation that the financial returns are not put back into the core business (cf. investment in a major production facility), but senior management has made it clear in various forums that there is a positive return for Danone in areas commonly associated with good CSR performance (e.g. company reputation, employee morale, attraction to prospective managers).

(*Sources:* http://www.livelihoods.eu; http://www.danonecommunities.com; http://ecosysteme.danone.com)

Questions

1. Danone is an often overlooked example of early CSR practice.
   a Why do you think Riboud was interested in CSR?
   b Why did the company stop paying attention to it in the 1980s and 1990s?
   c Why did it start paying attention again in the mid-2000s?
2. Several of Danone's programmes involve partnering with other organizations.
   a Why does Danone choose to partner with other companies?
   b Why does Danone choose to partner with NGOs?
   c Does partnership strengthen or diminish Danone's CSR activities?
3. Danone calls itself a 'dual-purpose' company.
   a What does this term mean?
   b Do you think Danone is truly a dual-purpose business?
   c What do you think about Danone's emphasis on self-sustaining CSR?

Summary

Many claims are made about how managing CSR can help business to have a positive impact through its social, environmental, and economic performance. However, the reality is that the data to demonstrate such impact are lacking and, moreover, collecting and collating such data does not appear to be a priority. This is not to deny the numerous case studies of companies addressing important issues, or the efforts of ratings, surveys, and company reports to demonstrate the efficacy of what companies are doing. But there are deficiencies in each of these sources of information.

There are many levels and categories of impact. Most of what we know about relates to the instrumental benefits of CSR, i.e. how it affects the financial bottom line. This can be considered a sign of progress, in that it creates a link between good business management and CSR, but it can also be a cause for concern if it precludes companies from considering actions for which the business case is weak.

Also, much of what we know relates more to activities than it does to outcomes. For example, companies may have environmental policies in place, or may be committed to international standards on corruption, but the actual outcome of these actions is often not known. This is less true of environmental issues than it is of those that are social or economic, and the growing sophistication of some companies' environmental management and reporting is a possible harbinger of the future of CSR more broadly. Even here, however, there is no clear consensus about what acceptable levels of performance look like, or about how to measure impact beyond the level of the individual company.

It remains an open question as to how the current partial understanding of impact will affect CSR in the future. Critics are using the lack of information to conclude that CSR is an inadequate response to tackling the social, governance, and environmental consequences of modern business. There is pressure within CSR for companies to become more rigorous in terms of what they manage and the targets they set themselves. Ultimately, what we know about impact will depend on the demand for information, and the current situation suggests that the various stakeholders are only beginning to understand what it is that they need to know.

Further reading

Barrientos, S., and Smith, S. 2007, 'Do workers benefit from ethical trade? Assessing codes of labour practice in global production systems', *Third World Quarterly*, vol. 28, no. 4, pp 713–729.

Detailed case study of the impact of ethical trade, highlighting the possibilities and difficulties of assessing impact.

Chandler, D. 2016, *Strategic corporate social responsibility: sustainable value creation*, 4th edition, Harvard University Press, Cambridge, MA.

An exploration of the business case for CSR.

Krumbiegel, K., Maertens, M., and Wollni, M. 2018, 'The role of fairtrade certification for wages and job satisfaction of plantation workers', *World Development*, vol. 102, pp. 195–212.

Discussion of the impact of the fairtrade model of business.

Margolis, J.D., and Walsh, J.P. 2003, 'Misery loves companies: rethinking social initiatives by business', *Administrative Science Quarterly*, vol. 48, no. 2, pp 268–305.
Widely cited study of impact from a corporate social performance perspective.

Roodman, D.M. 2012, *Due diligence: an impertinent inquiry into microfinance*, Center for Global Development, Washington, DC.
Examination of the strengths and weaknesses of microfinance.

Stachowicz-Stanusch, A. (ed.) 2017, *Corporate social performance: reflecting on the past and investing in the future*, Information Age Publishing, Charlotte, NC.
Diverse authors' perspectives on the impact of CSR in its various forms.

UN Compact, 2017, *2017 United Nations Global Compact progress report*, United Nations Global Compact, New York.
Report on the progress made by companies signed up to the UN Global Compact.

Vogel, D. 2005, *The market for virtue: the potential and limits of corporate social responsibility*, Brookings Institution Press, Washington, DC.
Detailed critique of CSR's effectiveness as a response to social and environmental challenges.

http://www.oup.com/uk/blowfield_murray4e

Visit the online resources that accompany this book to enrich your understanding of this chapter. Among the resources available are web links, exercises, and additional case studies.

Endnotes

1. SustainAbility and UNEP, 2002.
2. See, e.g., Elliott and Freeman, 2003 on improved labour standards and monitoring.
3. Margolis and Walsh, 2003, p 282.
4. Stachowicz-Stanusch, 2017a.
5. https://docs.wbcsd.org/2017/10/WBCSD_Reporting_matters_2017_interactive.pdf, accessed 27 November 2018.
6. Mahon and Wartick, 2012.
7. Crane et al., 2017.
8. There is a distinction between corporate social performance and CSR. CSP is an ex post measurement of past performance (e.g. assessing if there is a relationship between social impact and corporate reputation), whereas CSR can be ex ante.
9. The main sources for understanding the impact and measurement of CSR and corporate social performance were Sethi (1975), Anshen (1980), Wartick and Cochran (1985), Margolis and Walsh (2003), and the discussion in Birch (2003). The company CSR reports used included the Anglo American 2005 Report, the Unilever 2005 Environmental Report, the Cooperative Financial Services Report 2005, and the Traidcraft Report 2005.
10. https://ic.fsc.org/facts-figures.19.htm, accessed 24 October 2013.
11. http://www.unilever.com/sustainable-living/reducing-environmental-impact/water-use, accessed 12 December 2017.
12. Vogel, 2005, pp 110–111.
13. Vogel, 2005, p 126.

14. https://corporate.walmart.com/2016grr/enhancing-sustainability/reducing-energy-intensity-and-emissions, accessed 12 December 2017.
15. Michael Blowfield, personal observation, 15 November 2000.
16. See, e.g., the BBC news broadcast 13 March 2007 headlined 'BA green scheme fails to take off', http://news.bbc.co.uk/1/hi/uk_politics/6447229.stm, accessed 17 September 2018.
17. Locke et al., 2006.
18. Barrientos and Smith, 2007.
19. Elliott and Freeman, 2003.
20. https://www.ethicaltrade.org/resources/eti-annual-review-2017-18, accessed 6 December 2018.
21. Phylmar Group, 2006.
22. Abbott Laboratories, 2005; http://www.gsk.com. accessed 27 November 2018.
23. Vogel, 2005, p 102.
24. NRET, 1999.
25. See, e.g., Ali et al., 2017; Klimkiewicz and Oltra, 2017.
26. See, e.g., Kuzey, 2017, on impact in Turkey.
27. BSR, 2005; KPMG, 2005.
28. http://www.economicfootprint.org, accessed 27 November 2018, offers economic impact reports for the agriculture, mining, pharmaceutical, and financial services sectors.
29. Clay, 2005; BER, 2008; Kapstein, 2008.
30. Rio Tinto case studies, and its framework for understanding linkages between its investment in communities and their development, can be found at http://www.riotinto.com, accessed 27 November 2018.
31. Economist, 2006.
32. See, e.g., Armendáriz and Morduch, 2010; Hermes and Lensink, 2011; Ansari et al., 2012.
33. See, e.g., Raynolds et al., 2004; Nicholls and Opal, 2005; IFAT, 2006; Nelson and Pound, 2009.
34. Raynolds et al., 2004; Vogel, 2005.
35. Vogel, 2008.
36. Ronchi, 2002.
37. Nelson and Pound, 2009.
38. McMichael, 2009; Kuriyan et al., 2012; Berlan and Nolan, 2014.
39. Margolis and Walsh, 2003; McWilliams and Siegel, 2000.
40. Vogel, 2005.
41. Vogel, 2005, p 73.
42. Vogel, 2005, p 59.
43. UK government data at http://www.financialdeepening.org; http://www.innocentdrinks.co.uk, accessed 27 November 2018.
44. Collinson, 2001; Collinson and Leon, 2000.
45. http://ec.europa.eu/growth/industry/corporate-social-responsibility_en, accessed 25 April 2018.
46. Weng and Buckley, 2016.
47. https://www.wsup.com, accessed 25 April 2015.
48. McGregor, 2007.
49. Ascoly and Zeldenrust, 2003.
50. ETI, 2006.
51. http://www.bitc.org.uk, accessed 6 April 2018; SAM-PWC, 2008.
52. http://www.lapfforum.org, accessed 3 January 2018.
53. Compare, e.g., Brown, 2004 and Elliott and Freeman, 2003 with Vogel, 2005.

54. Industry data cited in Skapkinker, 2009.
55. Kauffman and Chedekel, 2004.
56. Information on Sigma is accessible at http://www.projectsigma.com.
57. DFID, 2002.
58. DFID, 2002; ETI, 2004.
59. ETI, 2004; Vogel, 2005; Barrientos and Smith, 2007.
60. Vogel, 2005, pp 157–158.
61. Mattingly and Berman, 2006; Mitnick, 2000.
62. Elliott and Freeman, 2003.
63. Weiser and Rochlin, 2004.
64. SustainAbility and UNEP, 2002.

Criticisms of corporate social responsibility

Chapter overview

In this chapter, we focus on the most fundamental criticisms of CSR. In particular, we will:

- discuss why some see CSR as being anti-business or anti-free markets;
- examine how some regard CSR as being too pro-business;
- explore why CSR has been criticized for failing to deal with major areas of the interaction of business with society;
- discuss why some feel that CSR needs to become more rigorous and tougher in its approach.

Main topics

Key terms

Civil society organizations
Corporate accountability
Liberal economics
Self-regulation

Introducing critiques of CSR

If CSR came to prominence due to criticisms of business behaviour, it has itself now become the object of criticism. This is not something new. *The Economist* (2005a) and Reich (2007) attacked CSR from different perspectives, and their respective positions about the harm it can cause business and conversely the ways it increases the power of business continue to this day. Advocates of social enterprise or impact investing are at pains to distance themselves from what they pejoratively call the CSR movement.[1] To a degree, this reflects the extent to

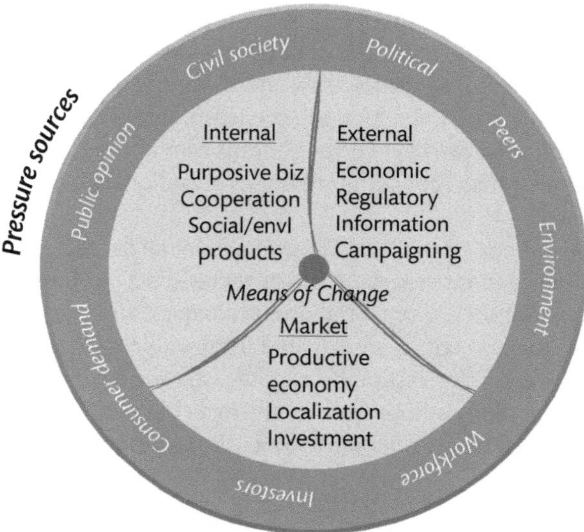

Figure 13.1 The pressures that affect CSR

which ideas of CSR have influenced business thinking, public debate, and public policy in some parts of the world; after all, nobody criticizes what is irrelevant. We have raised some of those criticisms in other chapters (e.g. in Chapter 1, difficulties in defining CSR; in Chapters 7, 8, and 9, the many challenges of implementing CSR), and Figure 13.1 shows the different types and sources of pressure that companies are under.

These criticisms are part of an often lively debate within the field about how to carry out CSR in ways that are efficient, effective, and best able to satisfy the needs of business while recognizing the concerns of other stakeholders. They are largely technical or instrumental in nature, focusing more on 'how to do it' than on 'what it means' and 'why to do it'. For a few, this focus in itself has been the subject of criticism, because it turns CSR into a pursuit of technical excellence and ignores (or stifles discussion of) more fundamental questions about what the responsibilities of business to twenty-first-century society are.[2] This situation is changing and a scan through CSR media such as *CSRwire ethical performance*, and *Ethical corporation* shows that such topics are widely discussed.

CSR theorists and practitioners have raised each of these questions over many years. Doubts about effectiveness stem from a sense that the parameters of CSR have already been set, not least through the ways in which different issues and ideas are assessed and, ultimately, included or excluded. In Chapter 6, we discussed at length the importance of the business case and how this influences CSR. We also showed how certain tools, techniques, and approaches have come to be regarded as best practice in the ways in which CSR is managed and implemented; new areas of responsibility are more likely to be accepted if they can be tackled using such established methods.

Doubts about the desirability of extending the realm of CSR to include a potentially endless array of new issues and expectations stem from a fear that companies will find the demands placed on them overwhelming, and will become more resistant to change.

This itself derives from the experiences of academic CSR theory. As discussed in Chapter 2, there is a rich history of academic debate about what the nature of the corporation's responsibilities should be. But as we also saw, there was frustration, in the past, that academic debate was having little impact on the corporate world and therefore there is now a strong desire not to jeopardize the current enthusiasm among companies for addressing CSR concerns, even if these concerns are not as broad or their address as thorough as some might have liked.

The urge of some to want to 'protect' CSR as a discipline for fear of hindering progress ignores the fact that allegations regarding the negative effects of business behaviour continue to emerge from civil society organizations, academics, and legal actions. Many of the criticisms of CSR discussed so far have emanated from within the loose community of CSR theorists and practitioners. In the rest of this chapter, we want to concentrate on voices that are external to that community—those who, for the most part, either reject CSR, or are waiting for a different approach before they condone it. We have divided their criticisms into four types of accusation.

1 'CSR stifles the primary purpose of business and, ultimately, hampers the functioning of free markets.'
2 'CSR favours the interests of business over the legitimate concerns, demands, and expectations of wider society.'
3 'CSR is too narrow in its focus and does nothing to address the key aspects of the business–society relationship today.'
4 'CSR is failing to achieve its objectives and needs to adopt new approaches if it is to succeed.'

Before exploring these, it is worth noting that each strand of criticism relates back to the theoretical perspectives outlined in Chapters 1 and 2. The argument that CSR stifles the primary purpose of business is rooted in liberal economics, whereas the view that it favours the interests of business is a development of the long-standing critique of free enterprise externalizing its costs onto wider society. Similarly, arguments that CSR is too narrow are part of a wider debate about the role of business in society and contrast with criticisms, rooted in management science, that new approaches are required if CSR is to succeed.

Discussion points

The criticisms of CSR in this chapter are primarily external, i.e. those from outside the world of academics, practitioners, and companies which promote CSR as a legitimate area of business management. Yet we know from other chapters that there have been internal critiques of CSR.

- What are the main differences between the internal and external critiques of CSR?
- To which of the external criticisms should companies respond? Are these the same as those to which they are *likely* to respond?
- Examine the external criticisms made of Berkshire Hathaway's investment in Chinese oil companies operating in Darfur, Sudan, and Warren Buffet's response, and explain which is strongest, and why.[3]

'CSR is anti-business'

As early as 2005, when CSR was making inroads into management practice, *The Economist* attacked it with a series of articles that presented CSR as a threat to the effective functioning of capitalism and free markets, and hence to global prosperity. The core argument of the articles was as follows. The standard of living in Western industrial democracies is higher today than ever before and is at a level that would have been unimaginable 200 years ago: 'In the West today the poor live better lives than all but the nobility enjoyed throughout the course of modern history before capitalism.'[4] This, it says, is largely due to the success of free enterprise, yet we have entered an age in which capitalism is deplored, suspected, and feared by a broad cross-section of society, and even by some business leaders. This anti-capitalist sentiment stems from beliefs that profit has nothing to do with the public good, and that the pursuit of profit drives companies to put crippling burdens on society and the environment. These beliefs have given rise to CSR as a check on business behaviour. Yet they are ill-founded, because they see profit as an unfortunate necessity that can be controlled and muzzled, whereas it is, in fact, the engine that allows business to make its phenomenal contributions to the public good, and restrictions on profit or wealth creation—especially those that come from civil society rather than from governments—will be more harmful to society than anything else.

Many of the themes in those articles continue today. CSR is portrayed as a victory for the concerns of NGOs over the traditional priorities of business; its uptake by mainstream companies can have a serious effect on the ability of business to fulfil its role within the capitalist system. In views still discussed in business schools, Friedman (1962) and Jensen (1986), both have argued that CSR negatively affects the abilities of company agents to maximize profits for investors (see Chapter 7). Management, after all, is not the owner of the company, they are employees, and it is unethical to put the owners' assets to any use other than maximizing long-term value. Ideas such as the triple bottom line (see Chapter 1) distract management from this goal and, by making companies accountable on multiple fronts, threaten to make them accountable for nothing, because they offer no measurable test of business success.

Whole Foods founder, John Mackey, has countered this argument over a number of years, saying that it is only by being accountable to multiple stakeholders that a company can perform optimally.[5] Mackey, a strong libertarian whose company is now owned by Amazon, is not in favour of regulating business, and argues that actions that might be broadly called CSR reduce the need for governmental interference. It is at this point that arguments that CSR is anti-business get a little confusing. Some people believe that it gets in the way of business achieving its primary goal of profit maximization, while others say that they are not arguing for corporate social *ir*responsibility, but rather there needs to be better governance and regulation (Chapter 7). In between sit those who think it can be good business practice to take account of multiple stakeholders (see Chapter 9), but that is quite different to being held accountable to them, unless this is in a formal way such as in Germany, where companies are legally required to have non-shareholders on the board.[6]

We discuss these apparent contradictions in the following sections, but today it is fair to say that few companies argue that CSR is anti-business as evidenced by the CSR or sustainability sections of most major corporations. As we discuss in the next section, this may be because the idea of CSR has been co-opted by business. However, even if that is the case, there have been major developments, not least the use of social media to monitor and protest about company activities, that have made it harder and harder to present a firm as adhering strictly to what Friedman or Jensen considered to be the narrow essence of accountability, as can be seen in Snapshot 13.1.

Snapshot 13.1 Do boycotts work?

Whenever a company gets in trouble because of something it has done socially or environmentally, you can be sure that an early response will be a call for a boycott. The public protested slave-produced cotton in nineteenth-century Britain, and working conditions in Lowell's mills in the USA. There was an outcry about Cadbury in the early twentieth century (Chapter 2), and about Nike eighty years later. Starbucks has been boycotted for its use of plastic cups, Dick's Sporting Goods (USA) was boycotted by the gun lobby after defending gun control, and since its alleged involvement in the 2016 US Presidential elections (Chapter 6) there have been calls for a boycott of Facebook. Yet, do these public actions to demand greater CSR actually work?

Boycotts are by definition a protest against a particular company and can be portrayed as anti-business. But a look at boycotts over time suggests that they are effective when they are not just driven by public outrage. Fox Television has found that the behaviour of its presenters such as Bill O'Reilly and Laura Ingraham not only led to public protests, but also resulted in major brands refusing to advertise on the network. Equally, major brands can be at risk if they have a particular social or environmental weakness. Nike was first attacked for its working conditions in Indonesia in the 1990s, and those events continue to be taught as part of the secondary school curriculum thirty years later. Arguably, the relatively small boycott then became the driving force for Nike's drive to be a sustainability leader today.

What's more, a boycott can be small but it can spread like wildfire through social media, catching the attention not only of the general public but also of investors. Once investors launch their own 'boycott' (Chapter 10), then a company is at further risk, as BP found out after the Deepwater Horizon catastrophe, when investors saw the company's handling of the issue as a sign of weak leadership.

So, is Facebook at risk from the boycott of its sites following its links to various political parties? Individuals such as founding board member Peter Thiel have come under attack for their links to right-wing groups, and he has said he might leave. Apple, Mozilla, and Elon Musk's companies pulled their Facebook pages. Chair and CEO Mark Zuckerberg has faced government committees in Brussels, London, and Washington DC. It is too early to say what the long-term consequences will be, but it is noticeable that Zuckerberg has softened his anti-regulation tone (one typical of many Silicon Valley entrepreneurs) and put out adverts saying the company must rethink its attitude to society.

He is not alone. Google may have been pleased to see its competitor in trouble, but now faces fines in the billions of euros because of its own behaviour. Apple has long had to deal with consumer and media attention about its working conditions, and Elon Musk faces his own public backlash after suggesting one of the divers involved in saving children's lives in a Thailand caving accident was a paedophile. Silicon Valley may have long projected the view that it represents the future, not just for technology but also social organization, but now it finds itself the subject of the same public criticism that has affected business since the dawn of capitalism.

(*Sources:* Watson, 2015; Casey, 2018; http://www.CSRwire.com)

Quick questions

Boycotts are often a knee-jerk reaction to protest about companies we object to.

1 When do you think boycotts are most effective?

2 Why do many boycotts fail?

3 Do you think boycotts will have a lasting impact on Facebook, Google, and other social media firms?

Discussion points

A criticism made by liberal economists is that CSR hinders company financial performance and poses an obstacle to economic growth.

- What evidence do such economists need to present to substantiate this claim?
- Is their argument still valid given the rise of social media and its impact on social activism?
- What evidence can CSR advocates offer to show that it improves company management and makes companies more reliable engines of economic growth?

'CSR is pro-business'

Most current criticism of CSR begins from the position that business is in various ways damaging to the social good, and that neither the theory nor practice developed under the CSR umbrella has remedied this situation. Critics argue that a key element of CSR should be to realign business with the values of society and to optimize its contribution, but that companies will not return to their original purpose without reform of the legislative and economic environment surrounding private companies.

This is a broad school of criticism, ranging from those who believe that CSR is not up to the task of reforming business,[7] to those who regard CSR as a weak countervailing force,[8] to those who see business interests as being opposed to societal ones.[9] Some highlight the role ownership plays in determining a company's impact, arguing that there is nothing inherent in the legal definition of a company that stops it from having a social purpose, and others point to examples of privately held companies that have just that.[10] But, it is argued, once a company is publicly owned, its purpose can only be to maximize profits. This means that no matter how well intentioned CSR practice might be, ultimately it will not serve the common good. Arguments, such as those described earlier, that business serves the common good by creating wealth and goods are refuted with examples of companies that have rigged prices, deceived regulators, caused environmental damage, produced harmful products, and otherwise acted in ways that were intended to create shareholder value (and management rewards) at the expense of public well-being. Moreover, some argue, the larger and more powerful some companies become, owing to the opportunities of economic globalization, the greater is the risk that the public good will be jeopardized by what Bakan (2004) called the 'pathological pursuit of profit'. The Occupy movement which staged long-term protests in major financial capitals adhered to this critique.

It is worth noting that some pro-business thinkers would agree that some of the corporate actions set out above are unethical, and that companies and the public would benefit from better governance, and from greater transparency and disclosure. They might also agree that what is required is better regulation of business, but what they mean by this is only regulations that improve market efficiency. This is in marked contrast to those who are sceptical of business's purpose, who tend to want to see regulation that limits both markets and companies. What both tacitly agree upon, however, is that CSR is not the best way in which to put right the wrongs of corporate behaviour.

One reason for this is that CSR is simply too weak for the task at hand. Nowhere is this more evident than in the case of the 2008 financial crisis and the subsequent fall-out for banks and other financial institutions (Snapshot 13.2). Not only did CSR theory fail to predict or prevent the crisis, the main responses have all come from government, be it in the form of new regulations or large fines such as the £34.5 million imposed on Merrill Lynch International for its failure to report derivative transactions, the £163 million imposed on Deutsche Bank AG for financial crime in the investment sector, and the $246 million of banking fines paid by BNP Paribas for its foreign exchange dealings. All of these fines were imposed in 2017 alone, and the total costs to the world's twenty largest banks for fines, legal fees, and compensation are estimated to be in excess of £264 billion.[11] This criticism focuses on CSR as a voluntary approach, something that is already tainted because self-regulation is seen as the corollary of diminished government capacity or unwillingness to regulate private enterprise, and becomes more damaged by examples of how companies have allegedly used voluntary initiatives to dilute their responsibilities to others. A frequently cited example of this is how companies have become signatories to the UN Global Compact—an action which requires them to uphold the Compact's ten responsibility Principles—and yet, according to critics, many such signatories continue to violate UN Principles, knowing that, until very recently, the Compact was without a disciplinary, or even a complaints, mechanism in relation to these transgressions (see Chapter 9). There are many other examples, including ones of once-lauded CSR practices such as the Chad–Cameroon oil pipeline.[12]

As we shall discuss later, such examples are, for some, evidence that CSR needs to be implemented more effectively; for others, they reveal the fallacy of trying to achieve justice without confronting power. Unless this is recognized, critics claim, engagement with business through CSR initiatives or similar means leads to co-option by business and fosters an illusion that issues, such as global poverty, can be addressed while continuing to do business as usual.[13]

Again, there is an irony here: those who see CSR as anti-business regard it as an imposition of activist agendas onto corporations, while those who see it as pro-business regard it as a co-option and dilution of those agendas by corporate interests. In both cases, CSR is being criticized for failing to meet particular sets of expectations, yet given the centrality of business in most of the modern world, these expectations embrace all aspects of human welfare and values. The array of expectations from those who oppose the behaviour of large corporations is diverse and far more sophisticated than is typically portrayed in the media. Consequently, the issues that CSR is accused of not addressing are equally diverse. For some, it is CSR's failure to tackle what are seen as aspects of corporate behaviour that pose a threat to the functioning of society and democracy that is at issue. This includes corporate lobbying of government, the avoidance of corporation taxation in developing countries and elsewhere, and the consequences for business and wider society of privatization and liberalization. Others highlight the behaviour of particular companies and industries, such as marketing and smuggling in the tobacco industry, the impact of supermarkets on small farmers, and the conditions of workers in computer manufacturing.[14] And then again, there are goods and services that at one stage are lauded for their social benefits (e.g. sub-prime lending to facilitate house buying for the poor), and end up being derided for being exploitative. As an early pioneer of private equity argues, this now widely criticized financial instrument began with the purpose of freeing up business for the good of workers and investors.[15]

There are a vast number of reports and briefings on these and similar issues, and as we shall see in the next section, not everyone sees CSR as being powerless to address them. In fact, a criticism of CSR sometimes heard from within the CSR community is that it has stimulated rather than appeased civil society organizations' demands. This is probably a misplaced sentiment which assumes that there are a finite number of issues in which companies have a role in addressing, or that winning the support of such organizations will end their criticisms of corporate behaviour. Perhaps more significant is to note that, for some, the fact that CSR does not tackle certain issues is a sign of its inherent weakness, while, for others, it is part of the process of mapping out future challenges and directions.

Some who regard CSR as inherently weak are not opposed to business, per se, as is evident from their support for fairtrade and other alternative trading companies, and particularly for ethically oriented firms such as nosweatapparel.com. Some also support the new agendas for engaging with companies. But none of this detracts from the repeated call for government intervention and legislative frameworks that prescribe business activity.

Governance experts have claimed that CSR can only succeed if there is a well-developed conceptualization of corporate law that exposes human responsibility and accountability.[16] Arguing that companies are nothing but their individual members, they suggest that the law, companies, and markets need to be structured so as to encourage responsible behaviour and to discourage the irresponsible. It has long been argued that CSR has come to the fore at the same time as executive pay has spiralled; corporate governance reforms have too often been about making it easier to conduct mergers and acquisitions, and shareholders—not least, institutional investors—have pressured companies into producing quicker and higher returns. Thus, we see two distinct trends happening: one called 'CSR', under which companies are reconsidering their duties to society, and the other wherein what critics see as irresponsible behaviour is increasingly considered to be acceptable business practice. CSR is not only blamed for failing to mitigate the latter, but also for helping to foster it by putting a gloss on corporate reputations.

A frequently cited example of how CSR has been hijacked in this way is the tobacco industry. For some critics, there are industries, such as tobacco, arms, and gambling, that can never be responsible because of the very nature of their products, and we have already seen how this principle has informed the responsible investment movement (see Chapter 10). There are also those who regard particular companies as egregiously irresponsible, and see it as proof positive of the coercion and co-option of CSR by business's interests when companies such as Nestlé—long criticized for its marketing of infant milk formula in poor countries—are accepted into high-profile CSR initiatives such as the UN Global Compact.

Snapshot 13.2 CSR and the financial crisis of the 2000s

A host of companies and business leaders were blamed for the international financial crisis of 2007–2008: Bernie Madoff—sentenced to 130 years' imprisonment in 2009 for a $64 billion-plus financial fraud. Dick Fuld—Chair and CEO of financial services firm Lehman Brothers, Fred Goodwin—CEO of Royal Bank of Scotland, once the fifth largest bank in the world, which had to be nationalized; Fortis, Landbanski, Anglo Irish, Roskilde, IKB, Shinsei, and many more financial institutions.

Some institutions with a strong record of CSR practice seem to have survived the crisis relatively well—for instance, Standard Chartered and Audur Capital. But institutions like Citigroup, Bank of America, and

(continued . . .)

UBS, all previously acclaimed for their CSR initiatives, were all embroiled in major controversies during the crisis. Moreover, notions of responsibility seem to have played no part in the ensuing allocation of government bail-outs or the rapid frequently engineered acquisitions. Goldman Sachs, which received $31 billion in US government support, was accused of being 'a great vampire squid wrapped around the face of humanity, relentlessly jamming its blood funnel into anything that smells like money'.

Why, then, despite the resurgence of interest in CSR since the late 1990s, was such a conventional financial crisis allowed to happen? What does it tell us about CSR today? One perspective is that business cannot be allowed to self-regulate, and as importantly should be reined in from interfering with regulatory governance. Companies such as Citigroup and ABN Amro burnished their reputations by establishing the Equator Principles and supporting other responsible finance initiatives such as the UN Principles for Responsible Investment. In hindsight, critics say that these acts were a smokescreen.

Another perspective is that, even if much of the heavy lifting to do with financial sector reform is driven by government, CSR ideas will have an important role. The Tobin tax, which some theorists have discussed in a CSR framework, is being seriously considered as part of the reform package. Banking bonuses might be something that self-regulation can address. Understanding the social and environmental impact of investments is an area where CSR practice is starting to develop.

Whatever perspective one adopts, the banking crisis raises fundamental questions about how society manages corporate behaviour. CSR may not have predicted the crisis, but neither did government regulators, despite the fact that banking is probably the most tightly regulated industry, with banks in major markets having to submit daily balance sheets. A different way of looking at the issue is to consider how much can be achieved through banks addressing problems of which they are a part, unless some of the experiences and ideas of contemporary CSR are recognized. The sense of injustice because bailed-out banks damaged their investors and were spared the consequences is something that might be remediated through genuine stakeholder dialogues as well as political intervention. Even if the largest questions, such as whether banks that are too big to fail are also too big to exist, may not be addressed through the kind of approaches associated with contemporary CSR, does this mean that theory and practice have nothing to offer?

(*Sources:* Lewis, 2011; Castells, 2017; Lins et al., 2017)

Quick questions

The crash caused by financial institutions happened at a time when CSR was attracting private-sector attention like never before.

1 Was the crash evidence that CSR management is ineffective?

2 How could CSR initiatives help avert such a crisis in the future?

3 CEO of Goldman Sachs said at the time of the crash that financial institutions have a 'social purpose'. Is he right?

A central question here is whether business is best influenced by engagement (e.g. through stakeholder partnerships) or by confrontation. We have discussed this at length in Chapter 10, and there are many civil society organizations, such as Oxfam and WWF, that engage with companies while keeping up a critique of business in society. For some observers, however, the crucial point is not who takes part in the process of engagement, but rather the norms and conventions that dictate that process, and thereby its possible outcomes. Much of CSR theory treats the participation or exclusion of particular agents as indicative of CSR's efficacy.[17] But it is possible to argue that the very nature of business as an element of the capitalist economy excludes certain values and ideals.[18] This raises questions about how particular social systems influence responsibility, and the parameters of what can be achieved by business within the capitalist system. It has been argued in the wider context of organizational theory that the primacy given to prediction and control in all walks of organizational life not only makes it difficult to introduce ideas that do not directly relate to organizational effectiveness, but also reinforces the notion of knowledge as something value-free and empirically derived.[19] What some critics of contemporary CSR would like to see is business adopting values beyond those justified by an instrumental logic. Therefore the participation of some of the harshest critics of business in a CSR partnership should not be seen as a sign of success, because the discourse (i.e. the language, mechanisms, tools, agendas, etc.) that governs it has already been settled and, moreover, is that which favours the business's interests. Thus, for example, what can be dealt with or not in a CSR initiative, the priority given to an issue in terms of time, expertise, and other resources, the array of possible solutions, and even the very language that is used to discuss the issues are all ultimately a reflection of what benefits or causes no harm to business. Moreover, this is something of which the participants themselves may be unaware, because, as Lukes has noted, 'the most effective and insidious use of power is to prevent . . . conflict arising in the first place' (Lukes, 1974, p 23).

The questions of power—who holds it, what form it takes, how it is exhibited, and what it allows or precludes—are an implicit underlying theme in many of the ongoing critiques of CSR. In fact, the essential criticism set out in this section is that CSR (both theory and management practice) is not able to confront corporate power and therefore that alternative approaches are required. Thus, for example, while CSR has gone some way to challenging both management and neoliberal orthodoxy, it is ultimately an example of how business secures the conditions for the ongoing and long-term accumulation of wealth and power, albeit in more socially and environmentally sensitive ways.[20] However, the critiques outlined in the following sections draw a different conclusion—one under which power can be addressed and dominant institutions reformed, even if this has not been achieved as yet.

Discussion points

In the influential CSR book, *Walking the talk*, Holliday et al. argue that sustainability is best achieved through open, competitive, international markets which promote human progress by encouraging efficiency and innovation.[21]

- Does this claim support or counter the arguments of critics who regard CSR as being too favourable to business?
- What alternatives to market-based solutions are these critics advocating?
- Are such alternatives plausible in today's world?

'The scope of CSR is too narrow'

We have seen that CSR is criticized for not addressing what are seen as important areas of corporate behaviour and that, to a degree, those who are supportive of, and sceptical about, the role of business share this view. We have also seen that critics in both camps regard CSR as not being suited to addressing these larger issues and see government as the proper institution in many cases. This overlooks the fact that, for the time being at least, effective regulatory mechanisms do not exist in many areas of global business activity. Indeed, as pointed out in earlier chapters, CSR is, at least partly, a response to the limited power of national governments in a global economic system.

Consequently, there are some critics who regard CSR as desirable, but who feel that the range of issues it currently addresses is too narrow. We have already mentioned corporate lobbying, tax avoidance, and how practices in specific industries to do with marketing, smuggling, and sourcing are said to affect society adversely, especially in poor countries. Some point out that the CEO of Walmart earns more in three hours than a US worker on the minimum wage does in a year,[22] and therefore not only fair wages, but also broader policies concerning wealth distribution, should be part of the CSR agenda. The total number of female CEOs at FTSE 100 companies is still lower than the number of CEOs called Dave, and women account for just 5% of CEOs in Fortune 500 companies. Gender in general is increasingly discussed in CSR theory but it is typically missing from practice.

Indeed, employment generally needs to be tackled more comprehensively than at present. For example, CSR practice does not typically require companies to address the social costs of moving their production to another location, even though the consequences of such actions can be highly beneficial for the company and potentially devastating for the communities left behind. Also, given the worldwide trend for more flexible labour arrangements, which are said to aid company competitiveness but make employment less secure than it has been in the past, CSR is challenged to address the nature of the employment contract by, for example, giving workers stronger protections.

There is a strong national/regional dimension to this because even in countries where there is limited employment protection, the consequences of redundancy are very different; for example, compare the USA (with weak welfare provisions) with Denmark, where dismissed workers can claim state benefits for up to four years. Flexibilization of the workforce is accused of having particular impact on women. For instance, zero-hour contracts, by which workers must be available for work without being paid, are particularly prevalent in industries with high numbers of female employees, such as retailing and office administration. Moreover, while CSR has had a significant impact on the way in which companies think about labour conditions in developing countries, issues that are central to labour relations in many developed economies, such as gay and disabled rights, have not been part of the mainstream CSR debate in places such as China, India, and Latin America.

Outside the workplace, there are expectations that CSR should do much more to ensure that a company's CSR policies are not at odds with its policies in other areas. Home Depot, the American DIY chain, attracted praise from environmental groups because of its timber-sourcing policies and, as well as being a major corporate philanthropist, it has provided help to communities affected by natural disasters such as the Katrina hurricane in New Orleans. Yet, in marked contrast to its response to civil society organizations, the company has been criticized for its lack of attention to diversity.[23]

Equally, companies that have established strong CSR credentials are criticized for abandoning, or failing to build on, these when they face a crisis. Enron, for a long time the largest bankruptcy in US corporate history, was once a widely cited example of a company that had a strong CSR reputation which did not reveal, but rather masked, the corruption and malfeasance that eventually brought the company down. In more recent times, Lehman Brothers, an important supporter of women's empowerment at the executive level, was embroiled in a similar affair that led to the company's demise. But tarring CSR with the Enron or Lehman Brothers brush is probably unfair, given how that company's officers deceived so many institutions.[24] A more illuminating example is Merck USA, the pharmaceutical company, which had long been held up to be a model of business ethics. It was praised for its response to concerns about its pain reliever Vioxx, which it withdrew from sale—at least in the USA. However, it has since been alleged on numerous occasions that the company vigorously sought out researchers and physicians who would endorse the drug, and tried to intimidate and stifle those who criticized it.[25] Not that this behaviour was unique to Merck USA, as Goldacre's (2012) comprehensive review of practices in the pharmaceutical industry amply demonstrates.

Another area in which companies have been criticized for inconsistency between their CSR policies and their business practices is in their terms of trading and the way in which some companies use their power in the marketplace to drive out small businesses, or to force producers to adopt management practices which, ultimately, exploit workers, communities, and the natural environment. Just-in-time purchasing practices and promiscuous sourcing in search of low costs are examples from the apparel industry of how retailers and major brands are said to exploit their supply chains. These are issues that have started to register in mainstream CSR, and Tesco, for example, has started to train its buyers in understanding responsibility issues.[26] Yet Tesco is an example of the mixed messages a company can send out: training buyers, supporting research on sustainable consumption, and initiating programmes on carbon labelling, for instance, but also getting embroiled in arguments over animal cruelty and stifling press freedom by using its wealth and questionable litigation.[27]

There are many more examples of aspects of business which critics say that CSR could be addressing, but which it is not. But a list of issues does nothing to explain why some things have been included and others not. For some CSR theorists, as touched on in Chapter 2, this is a test of how the nature of business's role in society is defined and hence what we mean by 'corporate citizenship'.[28] At one level, companies are said to choose the limits of their actions. In some cases, they regard CSR as being fairly low down in terms of corporate objectives, and it is allocated too few resources and benefits from little push to have the issues taken up by other agents (e.g. by government service agencies). In fact, it is claimed that CSR can be used to prevent alternative political, economic, and social solutions from being developed—something that has been observed in Nigeria, and also in South Africa, where, critics argue, CSR has had more to do with helping to erase memories of business's role in apartheid than in seriously tackling today's societal challenges.

Critics argue that CSR is more likely to include contentious issues if companies are under pressure from governments and civil society, and therefore that we should not view effective CSR as voluntary. But some take this further and argue that the limits of CSR may have already been reached. Not only may CSR be partially to blame for drawing attention away from certain traditional expectations about the role of business (e.g. payment of taxes to fund public policy initiatives), but many of the issues and conflicts that it is now being asked to address are, ultimately, the result of global economic and political systems that cannot be tackled at the company, industry, or other levels at which most CSR initiatives operate.

Implicit in such criticisms are questionable assumptions about the effectiveness and willingness of even liberal democratic governments to act in the public interest, and especially their acceptance of the need to be accountable and transparent. There is also a tendency to blur the ways business engages with society, failing to distinguish, for instance, between companies as citizens, as governors of citizenship, and as the providers of arenas where stakeholders can interact.[29] Often, those who are most sceptical criticize companies' track record on being citizens, and are fearful of the power they can exert as governors (e.g. influencing government and civil society agendas).

Discussion points

A recurring criticism is that CSR has yet to deliver on its promises and therefore has not proved strong enough to deal with important aspects of the business-society relationship.

- What are the most important areas in which CSR needs to demonstrate progress in order to win public support?
- How would you structure an effective complaints procedure for use in relation to a voluntary set of principles?
- Is imposing informal sanctions on business through actions such as 'naming and shaming' more likely to influence business behaviour than inter-company learning and peer pressure?

'CSR fails to achieve its goals'

For those who see CSR as a whitewash, greenwash, or bluewash, the fact that CSR fails to deliver on its promises is no surprise. On numerous email listservs and blogs, CSR is dismissed as a kind of Faustian pact between business, NGOs, and government that weakens more effective policies. Such criticisms have been levelled at organizations giving awards for CSR performance (e.g. Business in the Community) and ones such as Oxfam that both monitored and collaborated with companies, but has recently found itself in its own corporate behaviour scandal.[30]

It is often these types of organization, as much as companies, which are the focus of critics who claim that CSR has not lived up to people's expectations. They are blamed for focusing too much on CSR's successes and failing to consider its real impact. As of 2018, there are about 9,500 signatories to the UN Global Compact out of an estimated 900,000 multinational companies, meaning that little over 1% of MNCs are members. As far back as 2005, Bennett and Burley asked, 'In what realm of life other than the strange world of [CSR] would a [1%] take-up rate be considered to be a success?,[31] and although Compact membership has grown considerably since then, the under-representation of companies both large and small is still very apparent.

Moreover, some say that being a signatory to the Global Compact has little effect on corporate behaviour. The latest progress report (UNGC, 2017), provides a wealth of information on what signatory companies are doing, but is equally noteworthy because only 22% of 'participants' participated in the report (i.e. submitted information) with European companies representing over half of these. In theory, the information the Compact provides on its website should leave companies open to peer-group and civil-society pressure to improve their performance, but there is no longer a clear grievance procedure, and the sanction of delisting non-compliant companies which led to over 600 companies being barred in 2008, no longer seems to be applied. Furthermore, given the organization's small staff, it is hard to see how a credible process of ensuring members' integrity can be maintained.[32]

Another criticism of the Global Compact is that the high profile granted to a voluntary initiative detracts from broader UN attempts to regulate business behaviour. For example, critics point to the way in which the Compact rose to prominence at the same time as the UN Commission on Human Rights was backtracking on its draft Norms on the Responsibilities of Transnational Companies and Other Business Enterprises with Regard to Human Rights, following pressure from business and the US government. However, independent analysis commissioned by the UN has concluded that although the current system of global rule-making may be imbalanced in favour of markets rather than human rights, there is reason to believe that voluntary human rights initiatives will become the basis for binding standards and that it will be in the interests of business to lobby government for stronger regulations.

Case study 13 Global Business Coalition for Women's Economic Empowerment

The Global Business Coalition for Women's Economic Empowerment is a partnership of twelve multinational companies that has come together to increase the impact of those firms' work on gender issues. It has been a significant presence at the Power Shift conferences that began in 2014 with the aim of promoting women's leadership in driving economic growth. The Coalition includes ExxonMobil, Walmart, MasterCard, and Coca-Cola.

The Coalition is a business-to-business partnership, although at conferences and in meetings NGOs and government agencies have been involved as speakers and participants. The reason for limiting the Coalition to companies is to focus attention for the time being on the lessons of their respective programmes worldwide. For instance, a particular interest of the group is to know more about the impact of the companies' gender programmes (e.g. Walmart's work with women in disadvantaged communities in North America; MasterCard's women's advancement programme in the Asia Pacific region). These programmes are highly diverse in terms of location and goals, and the Coalition represents an opportunity to bring a greater degree of cohesion and mutual learning to the issue of women's economic empowerment that seems to be a growing area of interest for multinational companies (Linda Scott, personal communication, July 2016).

The Coalition was brought together through pump-priming funding from ExxonMobil which enabled two meetings to be held in 2015. There is now a mission statement and a budget, and the fourth meeting was held in May 2016. The companies are represented at senior management level (e.g. partner, executive director, senior vice president). This has advantages in terms of the profile of the group both within members' respective companies and with other firms. However, it means that the time for coalition meetings is limited, and this in turn has reduced the opportunity for engaging with other organizations.

But it is the high-level participation in the Coalition and the fact that the companies want to improve the performance of their gender programmes that makes the grouping most interesting. The Coalition grew out of a common recognition by the companies that they were experiencing similar difficulties and 'pain points' when it came to implementing programmes. Over time, this has led to a more substantive discussion about what women's economic empowerment means, and what the companies should be doing. Ironically, it has often been easier to make progress within companies than with parts of the conventional international aid community. For example, a large UK aid organization was

(continued . . .)

attracted by the fact that large companies were working on development issues, but when it was made clear that the focus of the firms was gender and not development more broadly, the aid organization's representative said it could not work on 'political issues like gender; we are here to deal with poverty'.

Not all of the Coalition members are focused on the Global South: the gender and empowerment focus means that it is just as legitimate in members' eyes to consider disempowerment in the Global North. It is also important to note that most member companies concentrate on women's empowerment outside of their firms, and do not engage with their company's internal gender empowerment. Coca-Cola seems to be an exception to this, but not much information is available to explore this further.

As well as a common interest in impact, members want to build a knowledge base about how others are addressing and thinking about empowerment. Another joint activity that has been mooted is a joint collaboration in a specific region so that firms (and perhaps aid agencies) could develop interventions together. However, it has proved difficult to arrange this kind of collaboration because the members have different regional interests and focuses (e.g. some work with female entrepreneurs, while others are tackling health issues). But this process of working out what is and is not possible within the partnership has helped advance members' thinking about the importance of developing a gendered approach to their programmes. For example, it has become apparent that conventional measures of entrepreneurial success are inappropriate when it comes to measuring impact among female entrepreneurs. This is something new for the companies involved, and is enabling them to understand, for instance, why women do not grow their businesses as rapidly as men do. Previously, this would have been interpreted as an indication that women do not perform as well as men (e.g. as measured by return on investment), but it is now becoming clear that there are gendered restrictions on women's performance. In future, it will not be enough to know that women drop out of enterprise training programmes: the companies are wanting to know if this is due to male influence or other factors.

The Coalition is not a gender thought leader, and many of the things it is coming to recognize would be unsurprising to anyone familiar with gender or women in development work dating back to the 1990s. Nonetheless, it is through partnership that these companies are learning about and acting on these things now. According to Linda Scott, whose organization DoubleXEconomy was funded to assist the Coalition early on, an important lesson is that people have to learn for themselves, and the partnership enables this in ways that would otherwise be difficult for the companies concerned.

(*Sources*: Linda Scott, Oxford University, personal communication, July 2016; https://corporate.walmart.com/_news_/news-archive/2011/03/18/the-walmart-foundation-donates-2-million-to-help-unemployed-women-get-back-to-work; https://www1.mastercard.com//content/intelligence/en.html)

Questions

1 The Coalition is a response to the lack of attention given to women's issues in other CSR initiatives.

a Why is it important to have a women-oriented initiative such as this?

b Are women's issues different in the Global South to the North?

c What are the advantages and disadvantages of having a business-to-business partnership of this kind?

2 Sexual harassment in the workplace has attracted a lot of attention in recent years.

a What do you think the priority issues are for companies to address regarding treatment of women?

(*continued . . .*)

   b Is the Coalition a good forum to address such issues?
   c What role should men play in the Coalition?
3. For many years, issues within the workplace were not a highlight of CSR initiatives.
   a Why have companies been more willing to look at external issues rather than workplace ones?
   b Have male issues been more readily addressed than women's ones?
   c What other issues in the workplace should companies be addressing?

Summary

CSR has come in for increasing criticism, especially from outside the field, perhaps as a reflection of the influence it now has on business life. The criticisms fall into four main areas: (a) CSR is a specific agenda imposed on business by civil society organizations that damages profitability and therefore the ability of business to generate wealth for society; (b) ideas of CSR are now dominated by business, which is able to shape the agenda in its own narrow interests; (c) the current concerns within CSR are too narrow and leave out many of the key issues for which the public expects business to take responsibility; (d) to date, CSR practice has failed to achieve its goals, and needs to be more rigorous and innovative in the future.

The stance taken on these issues is often informed by individuals' responses to two questions. What is the purpose of business? What kind of societal issues can corporate policies rooted in self-regulation, public pressure, and business self-interest adequately address? If one thinks that the primary purpose of business is to make a profit, then CSR will be criticized if it does not support that end. But if one thinks that the purpose is its social function (e.g. producing useful, affordable goods), then CSR will be assessed on a different set of criteria. Similarly, those who see legislation as a barrier to competitiveness will look at CSR in terms of its capacity to remove the regulatory burden, while those who are suspicious of market-based self-regulation will want to know whether CSR is as rigorous and effective as are government interventions.

In consequence, there is neither a dominant critique of CSR, nor even a common definition of what is meant by the term. But the points raised are often insightful, thought-provoking, and deserving of proper consideration, regardless of whether they are accepted or not.

Further reading

Carbo, J.A., Dao, V.T., Haase, S.J., Hargrove, M.B., and Langella, I.M. 2017, *Social sustainability for business*, Routledge, New York.

A recent addition to the literature on critical perspectives of CSR and what the alternatives are.

Dolan, C. and Rajak, D. 2016, *The anthropology of corporate social responsibility*, Berghahn Books, New York.

An alternative, non-business-based critique of CSR.

Fleming, P. and Jones, M.T. 2013, *The end of corporate social responsibility: crisis and critique*, SAGE Publications, London.
No-holds-barred critique of CSR as an extension of business's domination in a globalized economy.

Matten, D., Crane, A., and Moon, J. 2017, 'Corporate power and responsibility: a citizenship perspective' in Conill, J., Schönwälder-Kuntze, T, and Luetge, C. (eds), *Corporate citizenship, contractarianism and ethical theory*, Routledge, pp 19–38.
The latest thinking by three established theorists in the area of corporate citizenship.

http://www.oup.com/uk/blowfield-murray4e

Visit the online resources that accompany this book to enrich your understanding of this chapter. Among the resources available are web links, exercises, and additional case studies.

Endnotes

1. See, e.g., Elkington and Hartigan, 2008.
2. See, e.g., Levy and Newell, 2002; Blowfield, 2005a; Fleming and Jones, 2013
3. As a starting point, see https://www.biznews.com/interviews/2014/12/16/warren-buffett-how-to-make-3-5bn-on-a-500m-investment; https://www.business-humanrights.org/en/shareholders-at-berkshire-hathaway-annual-meeting-press-warren-buffett-to-divest-from-petrochina-over-darfur-berkshire-says-petrochina-has-no-role-in-darfur, accessed 27 November 2018.
4. Economist, 2005c.
5. Mackey and Sisodia, 2013.
6. Boeger and Villiers, 2018.
7. See, e.g., Fransen and Burgoon, 2017.
8. See, e.g., Ballinger, 2010.
9. Carrington et al., 2018.
10. Boeger and Villiers, 2018.
11. Treanor, 2017; FCA data: https://www.fca.org.uk/news/news-stories/2017-fines, accessed 27 November 2018.
12. http://www.columbia.edu/itc/sipa/martin/chad-cam/overview.html, accessed 27 November 2018.
13. Monbiot, 2005.
14. For examples of this, see the cases at *CSRwire*, *Ethical performance*, and *Ethical corporation*.
15. Brooke and Penrice, 2009.
16. See, e.g., articles in Morgan, 2018.
17. Kolk et al., 1999; Neergaard and Pedersen, 2017.
18. See, e.g., Banerjee and Prasad, 2008; Bachmann-Medick, 2017.
19. Alvesson and Willmott, 2002; Newark, 2018.
20. Banerjee, 2018; Windsor, 2017.
21. Holliday et al., 2002.
22. Data from http://www.issproxy.com, accessed 20 June 2006.
23. https://www.bizjournals.com/atlanta/news/2018/05/17/shareholder-proposal-on-diversity-reportreceives.html, accessed 6 December 2018
24. Dempsey, 2017.
25. Ginsberg, 2005; Prakash, 2006; Dempsey, 2017.

26. Pamela Robinson, personal communication, 2014.
27. For a newspaper perspective on this litigation, see Rusbridger, 2009.
28. See, e.g., Moon et al., 2005; Wood et al., 2006.
29. Crane et al., 2013.
30. Ratcliffe and Quinn, 2018.
31. Bennett and Burley, 2005.
32. There is little mention of UNGC staffing in the academic literature, and the organization's own materials devote more space to the institutional structures than the quantity and qualifications of staff. Most staff seem to be based in New York (about twenty people) with small secretariats in local networks. It is unclear how many staff are full-time employees, and anecdotally a lot of the work seems to be done by unpaid interns.

The future of corporate social responsibility

Chapter overview

In this chapter, we focus on the current trends in CSR and consider in what directions the field is moving. In particular, we will:

- look at the different pressures that drive CSR, and the consequences of each for business behaviour;
- examine the major trends that will affect what is meant by 'CSR' over the coming years;
- discuss what is motivating the transformation of business;
- reflect on what CSR reveals about the changing role of business in twenty-first-century society.

Main topics

Key terms

Pressures on business behaviour	Business in society
Social and environmental trends	The purpose of business
Corporate governance	Sustainability

Throughout the previous chapters, we have shown that multiple sources of pressure (e.g. consumer demand, public attitude, political objectives, etc.) create the environment within which the responsibility of companies is occurring, being shaped, and being prevented. Table 14.1 lists some of these, but it is beyond the scope of this book to do a thorough analysis of these kinds of pressure source. What the cases do reveal, however, is that these pressures lead to three main means of change:

- external means that are the purview by parties separate from business (e.g. economic policy-makers, regulators, campaigning groups);
- internal means that are carried out by business itself (e.g. new business models, social/environmental products, alternative governance structures);

- market means whereby different markets exist or are created to provide the opportunity for change (e.g. localization, new forms of investment, the productive economy).

All of the examples in this book fall into one or other of these categories, as Table 14.1 shows. The majority are examples of internal or market means of change, but in terms of considering influencing change in the future, it is important to include external means of change as well, even though the examples given do not necessarily draw on cases.

This categorization applies to the examples in the round, but if one looks just at the Global South the situation is somewhat different. For instance, there is significant growth in the creation of purposive companies and the supply of social and environmental products, but this is only achieving scale in the field of social entrepreneurship or in the much longer established areas of community and cooperative enterprise ownership. CSR is often dismissed in the Global North, but advances in purposive supply chain management, and multinational-supported route-to-market initiatives show that it remains significant in terms of sustainable

Table 14.1 Different drivers of change

External means of change	
Type	Examples
Economic	Environmental taxation; carbon trading; conditional finance
Regulatory	Environmental control; alternative corporate structures; labour law; 3LC legislation; CIC legislation
Campaigning	Beyond GDP; new economic theory
Information	Certification; integrated company reporting; carbon disclosure; ethical indices; quadruple bottom line
Internal and market means of change	
Internal examples	Market examples
Purposive company of various types (e.g. 3LC, Benefit Corporation; coops; bottom-of-the-pyramid enterprises)	Localization
Supply chain relations, route to market initiatives and other aspects of CSR	New forms of purposive finance (e.g. impact investing; blended investing)
Social and environmental products	Sustainable consumption and production
Cooperation through voluntary agreements and standards among peers	Social enterprise (demand side)

development in the South. However, initiatives and movements that are important in the North have yet to gain traction in the South, although the picture isn't always black-and-white. The benefit corporation, for instance, has made progress in parts of Latin America, but India, Bangladesh, and China have only three B. Corps between them, and there are none in Indonesia. We will discuss aspects of this North–South distinction in later sections, but it is worth noting that after periods of strong innovation in the South (e.g. the post-colonial cooperative movement; the creation of microfinance), the flow of innovation has changed, especially with respect to new organizational forms, finance, and even the very notion of empowerment (see Case study 14).

Discussion points

External and internal factors are influencing change in business.

- Of the four types of externally motivated change, which do you think is most important?
- What do the abbreviations CIC and 3LC mean? (You will need to look this up.)
- Why are these types of enterprise called 'purposive companies'?

Snapshot 14.1 When companies lie

In July 2018, car giant Nissan admitted that it had falsified data from car-exhaust emissions tests at most of its Japanese factories. In so doing, it joined other automotive manufacturers such as Fiat Chrysler and Volkswagen that were found to have manipulated emissions data in order to make diesel engines seem cleaner than they were.

Volkswagen was the first such company, its practices coming to light when the US Environmental Protection Agency said it had tampered with emissions controls during testing, so that its turbo direct injection delivered results that it could not achieve on the open road. This led to far-reaching product recalls in the USA, and billions of dollars of fines as well as the sacking, resignation, and arrest of senior VW managers. Investors such as Blackrock have also brought law suits. The scandal, which continues to play out, has also triggered renewed criticism of the health impacts of diesel engines, with countries such as the UK toughening the testing criteria of diesel cars and promising to phase them out in the coming years.

VW was protected to a degree because the major shareholders are the Porsche and Piëch families, who control the company. But Norway's oil fund, the fourth-largest owner of ordinary shares, decided to take legal action against the company, linking the emissions scandal to a wider, long-running critique of the firm's governance structure.

At a time when public ownership of companies is in decline and large corporations are effectively controlled by small groups of investors and financiers, the VW scandal has turned out to be about not just emissions, but how companies are governed and directed. As Yngve Slyngstad, CEO of the company managing Norway's oil wealth, has made clear in unusually public comments, this is not about a single company's attempts to deceive government regulators: there are significant consequences for employment, German politics, and the automotive industry as a whole.

(*Sources:* Milne, 2015; Franks and Mayer, 2017; Thomas, 2017; BBC, 2018)

(*continued . . .*)

Quick questions

The diesel emissions scandal has hit a wide range of companies with different ownership structures.

1 VW's supervisory board comprises 50% workers' representatives and fewer than five members of the Porsche and Piëch families. Why do you think the supervisory board was unable to prevent this costly scandal?

2 What does the VW case tell us about the different drivers of change discussed earlier?

3 Would a different type of ownership structure help avoid this type of scandal happening in future?

How business is changing

The purposive company

The emergence of what can broadly be termed the purposive company is an example of the internal means of change noted above. There are various examples of organizations established with a purpose other than maximizing financial profit and shareholder value, and some of them reflect what White thought of as a wish-list of principles for a new type of corporation in 2005 (Box 14.1). A company built on the principles of the quadruple bottom line asks, 'What kind of business do I want to create or work for that will benefit the common good as its primary purpose?' This is not a new phenomenon—Carl Zeiss, the lens manufacturer, for example, was founded in the 1840s with the dual aim of good engineering and good worker welfare, and Novo Nordisk was established in 1923 with the purpose of combating diabetes—but through social enterprise, the benefit corporation, 3LC and other movements, it has gained a new energy in recent years, in many ways as a response to the idea that the responsibility of business is to create shareholder value.

Discussion points

Charles Handy (2002) asked the question 'What's a business for?'

- Is the role of business different today than it was fifty years ago?
- Do you think business will have changed again in twenty years' time?
- What is a business for in the twenty-first century?

Box 14.1 Principles of the redesigned corporation

1 The purpose of the corporation is to harness private interests in the service of the public good.

2 Corporations shall accrue fair profits for shareholders, but not at the expense of the legitimate interests of other stakeholders.

3 Corporations shall operate sustainably to meet the needs of the present generation without compromising the ability of future generations to meet theirs.

(continued . . .)

4 Corporations shall distribute their wealth equitably among those who contribute to its creation.

5 Corporations shall be governed in a manner that is participatory, transparent, ethical, and accountable.

6 Corporate rights shall not supersede or weaken the rights of natural persons to govern themselves.

(*Source:* White, 2005)

Even among large companies, purpose is attracting interest. Mars, for instance, through its Economics of Mutuality initiative, is trying to answer the question, 'What is a fair profit?' And examples are not limited to for-profit enterprises. Enterprises in the not-for-profit economy offer examples of mission-driven not-for-profit or 'charity' organizations that are generating their own income, and moving away from the traditional non-profit funding approach of depending on grants and donations. These and other purposive enterprises can be guided on their journey by the various supportive organizations gathered by the Economy for the Common Good movement.

There are examples of the purposive company in the Global South, but the majority of recent ones seem to be part of the social enterprise movement. Cooperatives can rightly claim to be 'purposive' but, despite the success of Telapak in Indonesia or the relevance of Spain's Mondragon to developing economies, they are noticeable by their absence from much of the current interest in positive deviants. One can speculate why this is the case (e.g. cooperatives are marginalized because of their association with left-wing political movements; investors are attracted to things that are new, not the old), but a single chapter cannot provide a proper analysis of why this is the case.

There are other facets related to the purposive company that need consideration. First, some of the examples of organizations cited in the case studies highlight objectives that in many ways would not have been considered ambitious or radical a few decades ago. For example, Premium Cola has given ten months' paid sick leave to one worker, but this is not extraordinary among European organizations that have so far not eroded the employment conditions of the 1990s (e.g. universities). Equally, Vaude gives as an example of its progressive attitude the fact that it offers 'most' employees open-ended contracts to provide job security, and yet until the 2000s this would have been the norm for most European organizations.

Second, if business is to contribute to the common good, it needs to be clear who decides what that good is. For example, basic elements of the common good such as equality will look very different if one is in Texas, Copenhagen, or Bandung, which may respectively emphasize equality of opportunity, distribution of national wealth, and the collective rather than the individual good. Even if one believes that there is a meaningful global definition of the common good, many of those engaged in purposive business take for granted that organizations including companies are best placed to uphold that good, when it might be asked whether the common good is not better guaranteed by the law rather than markets. This is not an abstract question. If one follows through the logic of the not-for-profit economy, for instance, organizations could legitimately minimize their tax payments to reinvest surpluses into their own activities and hence their particular definitions of the common good. Is the end result of this in terms of government coffers any different to what happens when big companies offshore their revenues? In parts of the world such as Canada, significant portions of GDP are being attributed to the not-for-profit economy, but we cannot find economic models to show the consequences for national or regional economies if these trends were to accelerate.

Third, if as seems to be the case, the purposive company is with the exceptions noted earlier a dynamic more prevalent in the Global North, one needs to consider if and how it will develop in the Global South. We have shown in case studies that social enterprise has certain Northern biases, and, as has happened time and again in discourses affecting development, the conditions are being created where ideas of the purposive company are being created in the North, and the South's involvement may well end up being contingent on their tacit acceptance of the norms and power relations originating in North America and Europe.

Business practices

There is good evidence of a change in business practices that applies to mainstream as well as the alternative business organizations discussed in the previous section. Shifts in business practice fall mostly into the category of internal means of change and to an extent market means of change (see opening section). However, they are not entirely divorced from external means of change, notably the growth in information available on company behaviour and the use of this in initiatives such as the quadruple bottom line and integrated reporting.

In terms of the Global South, some of the most important innovations in business practice were discussed in Chapter 4. In both instances, we emphasized the importance of not being too dismissive of what has been achieved. The worst thing in terms of transforming business would be metaphorically to disown the older children of the CSR movement in order to lavish attention on the new born. We will return to this in our discussion of transformation and in particular the idea of waves of progress. However, it should be noted that some of the issues addressed and concerns of, for example, a B. Corp such as Cotapaxi are barely distinguishable from those of a mainstream company with strong CSR credentials such as IKEA (e.g. attention to conditions for employees; using profits to work with refugees; taking responsibility for production overseas).

Firms such as Novo Nordisk and Lightning Electrics, with their low staff turnovers, even during periods of recession, demonstrate an implicit belief that employees are an asset to be maintained, not a cost to be reduced, and show that a company does not need to sacrifice conventional business success to achieve a more multi-dimensional form of good performance. This is in contrast with some of the innovative new companies such as Uber (see Case study 7) that are seeking to redefine the employer–employee relationship. However, even among some established companies, the idea that high standards of business practice inside a company should be advocated throughout a company's supply chain has not gained traction. Large companies with a good reputation for paying attention to their supply chains are still more focused on driving out egregious practices than on expecting (or indeed enabling) suppliers to introduce working conditions comparable to even the legal minimum in the countries where they are headquartered. Equally, the kinds of practice that, for instance, the fairtrade movement has established to help suppliers (e.g. forward commitments, short supply chains, price premiums, alternative payment terms) are not readily discernible in these firms. It is possible that such things exist and are not made public because of commercial considerations, but this seems unlikely given the propensity for many companies to publicize their innovations in this area.

Furthermore, there is no sign that this aspect of business practice, which has the potential to be hugely influential in terms of changing norms in the Global South, is central to new approaches to business such as social entrepreneurship, route-to-market initiatives, and bottom of the pyramid. Overall it is fair to say that new models of business that are gaining attention today are less innovative in terms of business-to-business relations than what already exists, for example, in the cooperative movement.

Some of our examples suggest that the greatest area of change in terms of business practices—especially in the Global South—is change relating to products rather than production itself. Social enterprises are delivering a large range of new products in line with notions of the purposive company (see section 'The purposive company'). Technology is being made accessible to previously marginalized groups, and to help improve their well-being and opportunities. Enterprises such as M-KOPA and Selco are not only improving access to technologies but designing their products in such a way as to improve the productivity of poor and marginalized people. Some people might dismiss this as creating new markets among poor people, but there is a fundamental difference between making products available to the bottom of the pyramid, and designing products specifically to address the challenges people face when they are in that segment of the population.

Ownership

Ownership sits at the nexus of the internal and external means of change: people can choose what type of business to form (internal), but this is greatly influenced by company law (external). 'Mainstream business' is undergoing a huge shift. The publicly traded company is in decline as private equity grows and alternative models such as the industrial foundation prosper. Large family companies have long been important in the West (e.g. Mars, Maersk, Miele), and the largest companies in emerging economies are often family firms (e.g. Tata Group, Hutchison Whampoa, Reliance Industries). State-controlled companies, especially in China, are among the largest businesses in low- and middle-income countries, as well as having a sizable presence in certain sectors in Europe (e.g. EDF, Deutsche Bahn). Influencing publicly listed companies is a well-documented means of encouraging transformation of business, but there is little evidence that how to influence privately or state-held firms is being giving equal attention. This is true of movements such as social investment, but also of those who advocate change in company law (Chapters 7 and 10). Thus, in terms of the future, we observe a situation where most effort is being put into an area of business that in parts of the world is shrinking in its significance.

The existing evidence does, however, provide insights into the significance of ownership. There has been a lot of academic analysis of whether one form of company is better than another (see Chapter 7). However, contradicting conventional business theory, there is good evidence that alternatively owned/controlled enterprises do not underperform in financial terms their publicly listed peers, and moreover are likely to have a longer lifespan (sixty years compared to twenty according to Børsting and Thomsen (2016)). Most of these alternative forms of ownership/incorporation have a long history. Employee ownership is on the rise in certain jurisdictions, sometimes because it offers tax advantages, but also because—in line with the principles of the FairShares movement in the UK—it is considered a better way of running enterprise. However, employee ownership also has existed for a long time, as shown by the examples of the John Lewis Partnership (UK), Publix (USA), and Huawei (China).

It is noteworthy given the emphasis placed by many economists and management theorists on the superiority of the Anglo American public company model, that many of the most interesting alternative ownership models exist well away from the Atlantic. There is renewed interest in the industrial foundation model adopted by IKEA, Velux, Carlsberg, and other Scandinavian companies. Cooperatives continue to prosper even if they are often sidelined in discussions about alternative business. (There are 6,797 cooperatives in the UK, with 17.5 million members.) Initiatives such as 3LC may provide guidance so that people from entrepreneurs to investors can understand how cooperatives and related forms such as community trust funds and community interest companies foster the common good, but it would be a mistake to think there is a lack of models already existing through which change could be achieved in future.

Even though there are a variety of legal forms to choose from, and established examples of positive deviance linked to different types of ownership, there are important points to note with regards to ownership. First, family ownership and industrial foundations might allow companies to behave differently (e.g. because they are not subject to shareholder pressure), but this does not mean they will do so. For every example of a Mars exploring what the future firm will look like, there is a Koch Industries that is forcefully advocating for a profit-oriented vision of the firm.

Second, the ownership landscape in the Global South is not populated with a great deal of innovation. Countries such as India have huge cooperatives in certain sectors, notably agriculture, and the case studies give examples of cooperatives and community-based organizations. The picture in China and Vietnam is confused because the actual governance of worker-owned companies such as Huawei has not been fully studied. However, movements such as new kinds of employee ownership are not strong, and the most vibrant areas of transformation (e.g. social entrepreneurship) are happening without any real innovation in terms of ownership or governance (Chapter 7). One can only speculate why this is the case, but entrepreneurship and family ownership are still closely linked in the South, and in countries such as Tanzania and China, common ownership of enterprises cannot be divorced from troubled experiences in living memory.

The ownership situation regarding social enterprise is also important to note. There is no legal definition of a social enterprise, and enterprises have been formed as limited liability companies, not-for-profit enterprises, cooperatives, community interest companies, and charities. In Europe, a common definition of a social enterprise is that it has a primary social objective, has a participatory governance system, and limits profit distribution to prevent profit maximization. In the USA—and this is the definition that seems to be common in the Global South—a social enterprise is an independent entity that has a social purpose, and reinvests its profits into the enterprise. There is no mention of ownership or governance. Thus, while it can be difficult to figure out the ownership/governance structure of some social enterprises, it seems fair to conclude that—in contrast with the cooperative and employee ownership movements—ownership is not central to the advance of social entrepreneurship at this time.

Discussion points

There are three areas affecting business where there are signs of change.

- Which of these do you consider most important?
- What additional examples of the purposive company can you think of?
- In your experience, what are the advantages and disadvantages of common ownership (e.g. cooperatives)?

Snapshot 14.2 UN Principles for Responsible Investment

The UN Principles for Responsible Investment (PRI) is one of several initiatives aiming to persuade investors to think of matters other than the financial bottom line when placing their money. Its backers are investors responsible for 10% of global capital (or more than $4,000 billion of assets), including asset owners and investment managers. By signing up to the PRI, these investors commit to integrating environmental, social, and governance (ESG) issues into conventional investment analysis, to being active, responsible owners by promoting good corporate practice in these areas, and to reporting transparently on what actions have been taken in this area.

What marks out the PRI is that its supporters are major global institutions that are not known for putting their name to frivolous or marginal initiatives. The initiative's principles make explicit that ESG issues, or extra-financial risks, have an effect on the long-term performance of companies. They mark a step towards learning about measuring companies in ways that do not necessarily fit into the normal accounting framework and, ultimately, towards identifying long-term investment drivers.

(*Sources:* http://www.unpri.org; http://www.greenbiz.com)

Quick questions

The PRI has been welcomed as a step towards getting the international investment community to focus on long-term drivers of company value.

1 What is the significance of the PRI?

2 Are its principles genuine ones for responsible investment?

3 How might the PRI influence the development of CSR?

Are we seeing genuine change?

We have seen a variety of sources of pressure that are driving the transformation of business (Figure 13.1). All of these are important, but their respective significance varies from country to country and industry to industry. For example, in countries such as the USA, Denmark, and Germany there is considerable interest in different structures and forms of governance. This is more than a reflection on corporate governance in OECD countries following the 2007–2008 financial crash (although one should not ignore the importance of that event, as Chapter 7 highlights): it is a rethinking of the purpose of business. However, in most countries, not least in the Global South, the emphasis is on new and hopefully more effective ways to deliver goods and services that address sustainable development issues. There are instances where this has been encouraged by legislation (e.g. the UK's Public Services (Social Value) Act 2012, which promotes local government sourcing from social enterprises), but for the most part it seems to be market-driven. At the risk of over-simplification, it is possible to argue that the historically wealthiest countries are more focused on new types of business structure and governance (perhaps because of the failures of mainstream business in the 2000s), while in other economies attention is being paid to the delivery of products (because significant parts of the population are under-served). Put simply, in the wealthiest countries business transformation is a political discourse; elsewhere it is an entrepreneurial discourse. There are, of course, exceptions, notably the enduring presence of cooperatives and other community-owned enterprises, but their principles of solidarity and common cause mark them out from the new kinds of enterprise emerging in the Global South.

Amid a somewhat confused and sometimes contradictory transition picture, two important elements are visible: waves of transformation, and the significance of clusters. As noted, it is mistaken to dismiss the progress made under the broad umbrella of CSR. It is a rare example in recent times of something that arose to a significant degree as a response to public pressure (from NGOs and unions to school children and business schools) and was adopted by the corporate mainstream. It has continued to evolve so that what would have been considered deviant as little as fifteen years ago is now taken for granted. CSR practice provides many lessons about what can and cannot be achieved, and the periods of time required to bring about change. But the history of CSR also shows how transition can take place in waves. CSR in the 1990s was largely defensive (e.g. working conditions in supply chains), but this expanded, with the next generation of CSR focused on companies as a solution to social and environmental challenges, and there were subsequent waves focused on sustainability and other issues. Quadruple bottom line companies are part of the latest wave. The pressure sources that generate each wave are complex and would require a separate chapter to do them justice. However, information (an external means of change) is an interesting component. During each wave, there have been initiatives to audit and verify company performance (e.g. SA8000, GRI, Carbon Disclosure Project), and this is happening again with the B. Lab's activities to register companies.

The growth of ideas is often occurring in particular regions. For instance, industrial foundations are most prevalent in Scandinavia; large agricultural cooperatives are features of parts of India and Ireland; the northwest corner of the contiguous USA is especially vibrant in terms of entrepreneurs working on the purposive business. The individual case studies in this book give some insight as to why this might be the case, but it is probably also an example of the well-established theory that business innovation thrives where there are clusters of like-minded and supportive organizations. What fosters these clusters is beyond the scope of this book, but physical proximity of empathetic people, favourable tax codes and regulatory frameworks, local demography, and local economic conditions all play their part. It is also interesting—though again beyond the scope of this book—that places where deviants are emerging are also in some instances places where other experiments in social organization are occurring. For instance, the alternative bank, Triodos, is based in the UK city of Bristol, which is home not only to a wide array of alternative enterprises, but also innovative community groups. It may not be an accident that companies like Premium

Cola are emerging in Germany at the same time as new forms of political organization such as liquid democracy.

Geography remains important in the creation of these deviant clusters, even though they have emerged in an era of globalized communication and interaction. Even movements that claim to be global, such as the benefit corporation, are only strong in a limited number of jurisdictions. The process of scaling-up beyond a particular region, though, is important in understanding how positive deviants can become more prevalent. The spread of CSR from a handful of companies in the 1990s to something that thousands of companies report on worldwide is an example of how this can happen, and shows that once companies respond to pressure sources such as campaigns, the scaling up of implementation is influenced by inter-company and inter-industry interaction as well as external factors such as legislation and investment.

More informative, though, in terms of deviance outside of mainstream business is the example of social enterprise. Social enterprise is now at a stage where it can be called a self-sustaining business ecosystem. By this we mean that it is not reliant on a particular organization or group of organizations, and has the capacity to continue even if organizations that are part of the ecosystem drop out (e.g. become insolvent). In this sense, it is now much more than a movement. Movements are characterized by their thought leaders, a fairly small group of pioneer enterprises, and a strong element of grant-based funding. This was the situation with social enterprise fifteen years ago; it is the situation examples of alternative corporate structure are in today; and it is the situation that the bottom of the pyramid has struggled to escape from. By contrast, the social enterprise ecosystem comprises innumerable enterprises and consumers dispersed worldwide, various types of business model, think-tanks, university courses, diverse types of investor, and mechanisms for exiting investments. It is still deficient in some areas (e.g. legal framework) and, as noted earlier, its approach to sustainable development is subject to criticism. However, it demonstrates that a deviant model of business can be scaled up and become self-sustaining.

Discussion points

Throughout this book, we have looked at the criticisms, strengths, and limitations of CSR.

- Considering what has been discussed in earlier chapters, which of the trends outlined in this chapter is likely to be most significant in the future?
- Which are those that are likely to be least significant?
- Are there trends that have not been identified?

Case study 14 Google—global struggles and responsibilities

'Don't be evil.' These are the opening words of Google's code of conduct. Founded in 1998, the company behind the world's most-used internet search engine has revenues of over $23 billion. It employs nearly 20,000 people, only 250 of whom are at corporate HQ in Mountain View, California.

(continued . . .)

Google has joined Hoover and Xerox as one of the few brands to become a verb. But as a premier citizen in cyberspace, Google faces unique responsibility challenges. First, there is the conventional problem of market dominance—Google has the world's most-used search engine; the backbone of the advertising business that generates most of the firm's revenue. In this sense, Google shares the same issues of power, responsibility, and reputation that in previous eras faced Standard Oil, De Beers, and the British East India Company. At the same time, Google's rise has been portrayed as a semi-subversive way of undermining the dominance of another information technology giant, Microsoft, and its public acceptance as a brand is evident in places from the blogosphere to *The Simpsons* cartoons.

Google added to its kudos in some quarters by its stand on information access in China. Since 2005, Google and the Chinese government have tussled over the data that Google's search engine provides. The government has demanded that links it has censored, such as the 1989 Tiananmen Square protest, should not appear on Google, and moreover that Google should hand over information about the sites that alleged dissidents are visiting. Early on Google seemed to comply, but in 2009 it threatened to pull out of the Chinese market after large-scale attempts to hack into messages on the company's Gmail service and to steal proprietary code. The hacking was particularly sensitive because in 2006 Yahoo! had handed over personal data from a Chinese journalist who ended up serving a prison sentence. The US government was increasingly insistent that US companies needed to think about the human rights aspects of their businesses.

Google's stand in China brought protests from the Chinese government, but was well received in many other parts of the world, which saw the company as making a stand for freedom of expression despite the business costs. It continued to operate in China, but unlike its main competitors, Baidu and Soso.com, it inserted a warning into searches that the government had censored. However, by 2013 it had removed this function, claiming that it interfered with the users' experience.

Some observers regarded this as unconvincing, especially when seen in the context of other actions by the company. Its Street View service, photographing entire neighbourhoods and making them available on the web, has been criticized as an aid to burglars. The publishing of email accounts on its Buzz social networking service rekindled concerns about the amount of information Google collects and how it is used. The company has also been criticized for its tax avoidance policies which, for instance, saw earnings shifted from its British to its Irish subsidiaries. It has also been embroiled in long-running legal cases about digitizing books in the USA, Germany, and France, and in each case was portrayed as a corporate bully trying to ride roughshod over authors, publishers, and copyright law.

The latest example of Google's seemingly endless struggle to defend its licence to operate is the furore over the role of internet companies in online information accessed by the US security forces. There is no hard evidence that Google or other companies knowingly colluded with the US government in accessing data about phone calls and internet use by millions of private citizens, but at the very least the government seems able to hack in at will to what were once portrayed as secure systems, and there is some evidence that secret trapdoors were deliberately put into software to enable such access. Whatever the truth turns out to be, Google's claim to be empowering people at the expense of the status quo has been weakened, although that has not damaged its share price, which is now over $1,000.

(*Sources:* Darnton, 2009; Watts, 2009; Waters, 2010; Wines, 2010; BBC, 2013; Holpuch, 2013)

Questions

1 Google aspires to provide a new model of business.

a. What are the features of Google's code of conduct, and are they distinct (see http://investor.google.com/conduct.html)?

(*continued . . .*)

   b. What are the challenges for a cyberspace-based company compared, for example, with a conventional retailer or publishing company?
   c. What are the drivers of Google's emphasis on responsibility?
2. Google has developed a strong reputation as a responsible company, but has also been criticized.
   a. What do you think Google is doing that marks it out as a responsible company?
   b. What aspects of the company raise questions about the ethos of 'Don't be evil'?
   c. What should the company do in future to be a CSR pace-setter?
3. In this chapter, we have set out various future trends and directions in CSR.
   a. What does the case of Google tell us about the role of business in society?
   b. What significant contributions is the Google Foundation making to social entrepreneurship and sustainability (see https://google.org)?
   c. What aspects of Google's business have the greatest impact on society and the environment? Is the company addressing these adequately?

Summary

There are many elements to the CSR universe, as we have seen throughout this book. The indications are that this firmament will grow larger in the coming years for three reasons: first, there are pressing social and environmental issues that represent genuine challenges for both sustainability and global justice; second, there is an increasing expectation from different sectors of society that business will help to meet those challenges; third, the relationship between business and society is changing in profound ways, not least the nature of employment in the richest economies.

The future course of CSR will, to a large extent, be determined by how business's obligations to involve itself in major societal issues, such as climate change, demographic change, and global poverty, are defined and realized. No single institution will dictate how business responds; rather, as with other areas of CSR, the trends that emerge will be decided in various arenas of conflict, contestation, and collaboration. The growing power of multinational enterprise will be a significant factor in terms of the resources and influence that major corporations possess, and the way in which they act as a pole star for both public protest and aspiration. Moreover, struggles within the corporate world—not least the changing nature of corporate ownership and the emergence of new kinds of enterprise—will affect how ideas of CSR evolve.

Government responses to both the mega-trends affecting global society and the changing form of the corporation will also significantly influence what happens in the name of CSR. In some areas, such as that of flexible labour markets, it would appear that many governments are comfortable encouraging voluntary approaches and relaxing regulations; however, in other areas, notably that of climate change, some governments appear reluctant to rely on non-mandatory solutions. Given this situation, defining CSR in terms of voluntary actions seems likely to be increasingly less useful. This does not mean that non-mandatory approaches will be unimportant, and there are various ways in which CSR as management practice may be refined and enhanced over the coming years. Equally, there are strong signs of new types of approach gaining prominence, some of which (e.g. social entrepreneurship) will constitute free market responses to societal needs and others (e.g. sustainable consumption and production) that are likely to require significant government intervention.

However, one of the major trends around CSR will be less to do with management practice or government intervention, and more about the way in which we consider the role of business itself. Many of the current criticisms of CSR relate to how the prerogatives of the modern corporation determine its societal role. For some, this severely limits what business can do and, in important instances, causes business to act in ways that are counter to the overall societal good. This will remain the case, it is argued, until the corporate purpose is altered to reflect the rights, duties, and obligations of business as a citizen. There is by no means a consensus that such a radical shift should happen; some argue that this kind of philosophical reflection will divert attention away from the strength of current approaches as pragmatic management responses, while others claim that society should resist the notion of legal entities such as companies being thought of as citizens.

In terms of CSR as a discipline, there is no right or wrong answer to this type of debate. (Indeed, the weakness of recent CSR debates may be that thinkers have been too willing to champion either theory or practice as if they are mutually opposed, and their inability to consider reflexively what underlies this division.) Whether we are thinking about the chartered trading companies of the eighteenth and nineteenth centuries, the corporate philanthropists that emerged during the Industrial Revolution, the European cooperative movement, the place of international companies in twentieth-century banana republics, the sense of social obligation that is central to some of the most successful examples of business in Japan, South Korea, and Germany, or the denial of responsibility to anyone other than shareholders that dictated much of corporate strategy in the 1980s and 1990s, we are constantly reminded that, regardless of what we choose to call it, the role of business in society is fundamental to both business and the world at large. This will not change, regardless of what names we choose to assign to the pantheon of issues, practices, and hypotheses that have relevance to the business–society relationship. Future trends in CSR will not be determined by names, but by the discourse that evolves around the role of business and the relevance of CSR as a discipline, as a profession, as an antagonist, as a protagonist, or as a commentator in relation to that discourse.

Further reading

Accenture and UN Global Compact 2016, *Architects of a better world*, Accenture and UN Global Compact, New York.

A thousand CEOs give their impressions of what sustainability means to their business.

Beinhocker, E. and Hanauer, N. 2014, 'Capitalism redefined: Resolving the tension between a prosperous world and a moral one', *Juncture*, vol. 21, no. 1, pp 12–24.

An adventure capitalist and an economic theorist give their views on the tensions at the heart of contemporary capitalism.

Blowfield, M. and Johnson, L. 2013, *Turnaround challenge: business and the city of the future*, Oxford University Press, Oxford.
A hard look at whether business can succeed given the challenges of global mega-trends.

Branson, R. 2011, *Screw business as usual*, Virgin, London.
Virgin founder's take on business as an institution for the common good.

Green, S. 2009, *Good value: reflections on money, morality and an uncertain world*, Allen Lane, London.
HSBC boss reflects on the role of business and the importance of responsibility. Arguments for a radical overhaul of company law.

Hollender, J. and Breen, B. 2010, *The responsibility revolution: how the next generation of businesses will win*, Jossey-Bass, San Francisco, CA.
Popular CSR entrepreneur provides admittedly US-biased insights into trends in innovation, social entrepreneurship, and investment.

http://www.oup.com/uk/blowfield_murray4e

Visit the online resources that accompany this book to enrich your understanding of this chapter. Among the resources available are web links, exercises, and additional case studies

APPENDIX:

CSR information resources

Here are some of the most well-known newsletters, magazines, and web resources offering regular news, analysis, and thinking on CSR. We have provided dedicated web links where these are available, but you should note that some of these online resources are available only by subscription.

Readers should also check the occasional coverage of CSR issues in management journals (such as the *Harvard Business Review*), development and economics journals (such as the *Third World Quarterly* and *International Affairs*), and the mainstream media (such as the *Financial Times* and *The Economist*).

Accountability Forum Practitioner-oriented journal, focusing on accountability for sustainable development; published by Greenleaf Publishing.

Brooklyn Bridge-TBLI Group E-newsletter comprising articles and features on the triple bottom line and sustainability; online at http://www.tbligroup.com/.

Business Ethics Quarterly academic journal debating issues of business ethics; published by Blackwell Publishing.

Business Ethics Magazine Magazine of Corporate Responsibility Officers, a professional association; online at http://www.business-ethics.com.

Business Ethics Quarterly Academic journal bringing different disciplinary perspectives to bear on the general subject of the application of ethics to the international business community; published by the Society for Business Ethics.

Business and Human Rights Resource Center Web-based resource with links to coverage of discrimination, environment, poverty and development, labour, access to medicines, health and safety, security, and trade; online at https://journals.sagepub.com/loi/bas.

Business and Society Academic journal, focusing on social issues and ethics, and their impact and influence on organizations; published by Sage and sponsored by the International Association for Business and Society; online at http://www.bas.sagepub.com.

CasePlace Collection of CSR-related case studies; online at http://www.caseplace.org.

The Chronicle of Philanthropy Newspaper focusing on corporate philanthropy; online at https://www.philanthropy.com/.

Chronos E-learning tutorial on the business case for sustainable development; online at http://www.sdchronos2.org.

Corporate Citizenship Briefing Magazine for CSR news and analysis; published by Corporate Citizenship Company; online at http://www.ccbriefing.co.uk.

Corporate Governance Academic journal, focusing on international business and society; published by Emerald.

CorporateRegister.com Online collection of CSR reports; online at http://www.corporateregister.com.

Corpwatch.com Online information resource monitoring corporate behaviour and malfeasance; online at https://corpwatch.org/.

Critical Perspectives on International Business Academic journal, presenting social science perspectives on international business and society; published by Emerald.

CSR Asia Online resource offering information on corporate responsibility in Asia; online at http://www.csr-asia.com.

CSRWatch Web-based media service offering criticisms of CSR; online at http://www.csrwatch.com.

CSRWire Web-based resource featuring CSR news and press releases from publicly traded corporations; online at http://www.csrwire.com.

Eldis Information gateway to web-based resources on globalization and international development, including special section on CSR; online at http://www.eldis.org.

Ethical Corporation Monthly magazine featuring CSR news and analysis in both print and online versions; free email newsletter also available; online at http://www.ethicalcorp.com.

Ethical Performance Monthly newsletter on CSR and socially responsible investment; online at http://www.ethicalperformance.com/.

Faith in Business Quarterly Journal relating Christian faith and values to the business world; published by the Ridley Hall Foundation and Industrial Christian Fellowship; online at http://www.fibq.org.

Global Corruption Report Annual report focusing on the consequences of corruption; published by Transparency International; online at http://www.transparency.org/publications/gcr.

Governancefocus.com Web-based resource offering information on worldwide corporate and board governance issues; online at http://www.governancefocus.com.

GreenBiz.com Free web-based resource for companies seeking information on environmental business practices; online at http://www.greenbiz.com.

Green Money Journal Newsletter offering resources and contacts for environmentally and socially responsible investing; online at http://www.greenmoneyjournal.com.

Greener Management International Management journal focusing on strategic environmental and sustainability issues; published by Greenleaf Publishing.

ID21 Online information service featuring links to research on globalization and international development, plus a series of issues Insights papers; online at http://www.id21.org.

Journal of Business Ethics Academic journal, covering ethical issues related to business; published by Kluwer Academic Publishers.

Journal of Corporate Citizenship Quarterly academic journal dedicated to CSR; published by Greenleaf Publishing.

Oneworld.net Web-based community and resource focusing on globalization and development; online at http://www.oneworld.net.

SD Gateway Online resource offering information from members of the Sustainable Development Communications Network; online at http://www.sdgateway.net.

SocialFunds.com Web-based resource for individual socially responsible investors; online at http://www.socialfunds.com.

Socially Responsible Investing Compass Online resource featuring all existing green and ethical retail funds and indices in Europe; online at http://www.sricompass.org.

Society and Business Review Practitioner-oriented journal, aiming to assist businesses in enhancing their commitment to societal purposes; published by Emerald.

Stanford Social Innovation Review Journal focusing on strategies for non-profit organizations, foundations, and socially responsible businesses; online at http://www.ssireview.org.

SustainableBusiness.com Online resource offering information and links for environmentally oriented businesses; hosted by Green Dream Jobs, a sustainable business jobs service; online at http://www.sustainablebusiness.com.

Glossary

accountability The obligation to render an account of one's actions.

auditing The evaluation of an organization in order to establish the validity and reliability of information about that organization. Social auditing relates to the validity and reliability of information about a company's social performance (e.g. its impact on local communities, its relationship with stakeholders); environmental auditing relates to its performance in relation to the environment (e.g. emissions, waste management).

best-in-class screening An approach to positive screening in socially responsible investment that involves selecting the best within a given sector of investments, based on certain criteria.

bottom of the pyramid (also known as base of the pyramid) The potential commercial market provided by the 6 billion people who live on less than US$2 a day. Developed by C.K. Prahalad and Stuart Hart, American business theorists, the concept regards poor people as a seriously under-served market that might be the engine of the next wave of global trade and economic prosperity. Examples include microfinance (the provision of innovative financial services to poor people in ways that help their development), Cemex's affordable housing programme, and Hindustan Lever's marketing of iodized salt to rural communities. Bottom of the pyramid is one of the most discussed areas of social entrepreneurship.

bribery The giving of favour to influence another's action. (*See* corruption.)

Brundtland Commission (formally, the World Commission on Environment and Development) Convened in 1983 by the United Nations and widely known by the name of its chair, Gro Harlem Brundtland, the Commission proved to be a highly influential enquiry into environmental deterioration and the challenge of sustainable development. Its definition of sustainable development—development that meets the needs of the present without compromising the ability of future generations to meet their own needs—is frequently cited in discussions about the role of business in sustainability.

business ethics Typically regarded as a strand of applied ethics, focusing on the ethical issues facing a company and its officers. The US branch of the field, in particular, is primarily concerned with helping individuals to navigate the ethical dilemmas that arise in a commercial context. There is, to a degree, an alternative European approach that is more concerned with the role of business in society, and with the ethical duties and obligations that arise from this. Some would argue that corporate responsibility is a subset of business ethics.

business and society An area of academic enquiry (normally undertaken by social scientists) concerning the relationship between business and wider society. Long established, with its own journals and professional association, the themes of business and society have recently been more widely acknowledged by corporate responsibility scholars and practitioners. The consultancy firm McKinsey & Co. is among those offering services that will help companies to understand business and society issues.

capitalism An economic system under which the means of production are privately owned, and the price of inputs and outputs are determined by markets within which people engage on a free and voluntary basis, and within which goods and services are sold with a view to making a profit. Adam Smith, the eighteenth-century philosopher, was the first to describe comprehensively the free market capitalist system in his books *The theory of moral sentiments* and *The wealth of nations*. He recognized that an economic system could not be treated as something separate from society, and hence had implications for the way we live. Issues relating to the moral dimensions of capitalism—such as the responsibilities, duties, and obligations of business—in many ways underlie corporate responsibility.

capital markets The financial markets on which long-term debt and equity securities are traded. The role of these markets in influencing corporate behaviour is an area of debate within corporate responsibility.

CFO Chief Financial Officer.

change management (also known as transformation management) A systematic approach to managing change within an organization which includes adapting to, controlling, and effecting change. Within management practice, corporate responsibility is often described from a change management perspective.

civil regulation A theory positing that companies are not only regulated by government, but increasingly by the norms and actions of civil society that control a business's licence to operate. This is most evident in the role that civil society organizations play in affecting company behaviour irrespective of legal requirements. In the 1990s, for example, trade unions and non-government organizations were able to pressurize Nike into paying attention to working conditions in its supply chain, despite there having been no government pressure to do so.

civil society Historically, the term has meant private interests that are distinct from those of the state, but in the corporate responsibility context, it tends to refer more specifically to the uncoerced collective action around shared interests, purposes, and values of institutions that are distinct from those of the state and the market (e.g. civil society organizations).

civil society organizations (CSOs) Non-government, non-business organizations with a social function. CSOs include non-government organizations and free trade unions, and are an important constituency both in influencing corporate behaviour (civil regulation) and in conducting partnerships.

climate change Significant change in measures of climate, such as temperature or precipitation, that last for an extended period (i.e. decades or longer). These changes can be the result of natural factors and processes, such as alterations in ocean circulation, or of human activity, such as deforestation and burning fossil fuels. (*See also* global warming.)

code of conduct/practice A set of principles, typically with accompanying criteria, that set out a company's commitment to maintaining a standard in a specific area of its operations. Corporate responsibility codes set standards regarding the natural environment, labour, corporate governance, money laundering, bribery and corruption, human rights, and corporate responsibility reporting principles. While codes may make mention of legal requirements (e.g. minimum wage, toxic emissions), they are themselves voluntary in nature.

COO Chief Operating Officer.

corporate accountability A company's moral or legal obligation to account for its actions and performance to its stakeholders. In the corporate responsibility context, it is also often discussed in terms of the capacity of those stakeholders to influence company actions.

corporate citizenship At times used synonymously with corporate responsibility, CSR, etc., but (in the USA, in particular) can specifically refer to discretionary initiatives undertaken by a company, such as employee volunteering and corporate philanthropy.

corporate governance Conventionally refers to the system by which companies are directed and controlled for the benefit of shareholders. In some jurisdictions, the scope of benefit includes multiple stakeholders, and, in recent years, there has been renewed interest in the balance between economic and social goals, and between individual and communal goals as the object of governance, as per the 2002 Cadbury Report.

corporate governance framework The regulatory structure, designed to safeguard investors' assets, within which the rules for the running of companies are outlined.

corporate malfeasance Misconduct by a company or by an officer of a company.

corporate philanthropy Proportion of corporate revenues donated for philanthropic purposes (in the USA, the amount is typically 1%). Once associated with somewhat arbitrary donations to worthy causes, there is increasing focus on strategic philanthropy, under which donations are targeted towards areas that are synergistic with the company's interests or competencies.

corporate reporting The act of publicly reporting on a company's performance. In the corporate responsibility context, emphasis has been placed on the publishing of social, environmental, and sustainability reports that, in some cases, form part of the company's annual report to shareholders.

corporate responsibility An umbrella term embracing theories and practices relating to how business manages its relationship with society.

corporate social performance The way in which, and degree to which, a business organization's principles of social responsibility and related processes motivate actions on behalf of a company and deliver outcomes of societal benefit.

corporate social responsiveness The response of companies to the demands that they address their social responsibilities. The term was introduced by scholars in the mid-1970s to denote a greater focus on corporate responsibility as an area of management practice, in contrast with more theoretical debates about the meaning of responsibility that had previously dominated academic thinking.

corruption The misuse of power associated with a public or corporate office for the purpose of personal gain. It includes bribery, which is the giving of favour to influence another's action.

defensive corporate responsibility Actions taken by a company or industry to protect its reputation and to reduce its risk in relation to aspects of its non-financial responsibility.

deterritorialization The detachment of social practices from a specific place, so that the relationship between culture and geographical location is no longer paramount. The phenomenon is a consequence of the social and political processes associated with globalization.

developing country A country with low per capita income relative to the world average. In many developing countries, incomes can be less than US$2 a day. (*Compare* emerging economy.)

eco-efficiency Achieving efficiencies through the reduced use of natural resources and energy, fewer harmful emissions, greater recycling and reuse, increased lifespan, and the increased use of renewable resources in the design, manufacture, and consumption/use of products.

economic globalization (also referred to as liberal economic globalization) Increased world integration as a result of free trade, and financial, technology, and labour flows. The term is sometimes treated as synonymous with globalization, but, strictly speaking, refers to only one feature of that phenomenon.

embedded economy Stemming from Polanyi's argument (1944) that a feature of capitalism is the way in which the economy is treated as something separate from society ('*disembedded*'), whereas the interests of justice and prosperity are best served when the economy is interrelated with social, political, and religious institutions ('*embedded*'). Corporate responsibility (theory and practice) can be interpreted as concerned with re-embedding business so that it is more than simply an economic actor.

emerging economy A country that, based on GDP and indicators of human development, is considered to be on a path towards being included among the wealthy/developed nations in the foreseeable future. (*Compare* developing country.)

engagement An approach, used in responsible investment, by which investors become involved with the companies in which they invest in order to influence the activities, behaviours, and operations of those companies.

environmental auditing The evaluation of an organization to ascertain the validity and reliability of information about that organization's claims concerning its performance in relation to the environment (e.g. emissions, waste management).

environmental ethics Enquiry into the ethical relationship of human beings to the environment and non-human entities, and into the value and moral status of these.

environmental impact assessment Assessment of a company or facility's environmental consequences, normally focusing on inputs and outputs within a particular geographical location.

environmental, social, and governance (ESG) Commonly used term that captures the areas of non-financial performance with which corporate responsibility management practice is often concerned.

equity index funds *See* index funds.

ethical sourcing A company's recognition of its responsibilities for the social and environmental conditions under which products are manufactured/grown within its supply chain. Typically, this involves the application of a code of practice as a condition of doing business with suppliers, although it may also involve engaging with suppliers to improve their capacity to meet that standard.

ethical theory Theories of what is right and wrong, based on reason. (*Compare* moral theory.)

ethical trade An umbrella term for a variety of approaches under which companies take responsibility for the conditions under which products are manufactured/grown within their supply chains. Includes ethical sourcing, fairtrade, and sourcing from sustainably managed forests and fisheries.

fairtrade A trading partnership established as a contribution to achieving greater equity in international trade through, for example, ensuring a price paid to the producer that is greater than the cost of production, a surplus paid to the producer group (not the individual) for investing in social development activities, and a long-term relationship between producer and buyer. Originally intended to help small producers in developing countries, larger producers are now included, and, for these, the emphasis is on worker rights. Fairtrade takes different forms, but is most widely associated with the Fairtrade label, which certifies that an item has been produced and traded according to the principles set out by the Fairtrade Labelling Organizations International (FLO International).

fair wage (also called a living wage) A wage sufficient to provide the basic needs (food, shelter, education, health care), with some discretionary income, for a worker and his or her immediate dependents within a reasonable working week (typically, not more than forty hours). It is often a provision in codes of labour practice and workers' rights, although it is sometimes replaced with a minimum wage, which is a legally defined wage that should reflect a fair wage (although, in practice, it may not).

financing sustainability An emerging facet of corporate responsibility, dealing with the interrelationship between companies' corporate responsibility objectives and the behaviour of the finance community (investors, analysts, fund managers, etc.). At its core is the perceived mismatch between the long-term nature of sustainability and the short-term orientation of much investment activity.

free trade union A type of trade union that is able to operate without interference from employers and government.

global commons Natural assets important to human well-being that are outside national jurisdiction (e.g. the oceans, outer space, the atmosphere).

global governance Historically, governance has referred to the exercise of political, economic, and administrative authority in the management of the affairs of a country or other locality. Globalization and accompanying phenomena, such as deterritorialization, present particular challenges for governance, because important areas of life cannot be managed by the nation state alone. Hence, increasing concern is paid to global governance, including the governing of global commons, such as the atmosphere, and the behaviour of multinational companies. The institutions for addressing such issues are, however, still weak and incomplete for the most part, giving rise to what some see as a governance deficit. The emergence of corporate responsibility as an area of business practice can be seen as a contribution to filling that deficit by making companies pay attention to their global social and environmental performance.

globalization A term used to refer to the increasing global connectivity, integration, and interdependence in the economic, social, technological, cultural, and political dimensions of existence. It is often used to focus on particular aspects of the phenomenon (e.g. global cultural homogenization, economic globalization, the spread of particular ideas such as democracy and free markets), but what marks it out as historically unique is the interplay of its different facets, which presents all manner of challenges for global governance, justice, and sustainability.

Global Reporting Initiative The custodian body behind an international effort to create a common framework for the voluntary reporting of the economic, environmental, and social impact of the activities of business and other organizations. This framework is set out in the GRI Guidelines.

global warming The average increase in atmospheric temperature near the Earth's surface and in the troposphere, which can contribute to changes in global climate patterns. (*See also* climate change.)

government A particular group of legitimate representatives of the state.

health and safety (also known as occupational health and safety; workplace health and safety) The dimension of corporate responsibility relating to the health and safety of people at work. Some of the most measurable outcomes of corporate responsibility programmes have been in this area.

human rights Basic entitlements accorded to all human beings. There are significant differences of opinion as to what these rights should be, although the most commonly mentioned ones in a corporate responsibility context concern legal, civil, and political rights, especially those set out in the Universal Declaration of Human Rights.

human rights impact assessment An assessment of the human rights dimensions of a company's operations, including, for example, issues of the rights of indigenous peoples, intimidation of local communities by company security forces, and the fundamental rights of workers in the workplace.

index fund A mutual fund with a portfolio constructed to match or track the components of a particular market index.

Industrial Revolution The historical period, lasting throughout most of the nineteenth century, during which the economies of the USA and many European nations shifted from an agricultural to a manufacturing base, with an accompanying strengthening of the capitalist economic system.

integrated business strategy In a corporate responsibility context, 'integration' refers to the embedding of corporate responsibility issues into mainstream business practice. The consequence of this is that corporate responsibility becomes a business driver that creates value for the company at the same time as the company creates value for wider society. (*Compare* corporate philanthropy.)

international development The policies and programmes undertaken by government and non-government agencies in developed and developing economies, with the intention of alleviating poverty and creating sustainable livelihoods for people in developing countries.

international funds A mutual fund investing in companies located anywhere outside of its investors' country of residence.

large cap funds Investment funds focused on companies with a market capitalization of more than $10 billion.

liberal economic globalization *See* economic globalization.

liberal economics A theory of economics that is rooted in the belief that individuals' economic actions based largely on self-interest ultimately make the greatest contribution to the common good. Some see globalization as synonymous with economic liberalism, particularly its free flow of capital, goods, services, and (more contentiously) labour, with minimal government or other non-market interference.

licence to operate The right granted to a company (or other organization) to carry out its business. In the corporate responsibility context, licence to operate usually refers to the licence granted by a community or other stakeholder group, rather than by a formal regulatory authority.

limited liability Form of incorporation under which the liability of a partner or investor is limited to the value of his or her shares in the company. The introduction of this legal concept in the nineteenth century greatly affected the role of business, the nature of investment, and the notion of risk.

living wage *See* fair wage.

microfinance Financial model that involves making small loans available to help poor people who are denied access through conventional lending channels, typically towards their starting, or expanding, a small business.

Millennium Development Goals (MDGs) A set of eight targets (including eradicating extreme poverty and hunger, improving maternal health, and ensuring environmental sustainability) that were adopted by all countries represented in the UN General Assembly, and which were to be achieved by 2015. The targets commit countries to a particular vision of international development and are widely used as a framework for measuring development progress.

minimum wage A legally defined wage that should reflect a fair wage (although, in practice, it may not). (*See also* fair wage.)

moral theory Theories of right and wrong, based on norms and custom. (*Compare* ethical theory.)

mutual fund An investment vehicle made up of multiple investors for the purpose of investing in securities such as stocks, bonds, money market instruments, and other assets.

Natural Step An approach to sustainability that is based on four systematic principles, relating to people's capacity to meet their needs, and aspects of the interaction between humanity and the earth. Karl-Henrik Robèrt first proposed the approach in 1989, following the publication of the Report of the Brundtland Commission.

negative screening An approach to socially responsible investment that involves the exclusion of certain companies based on their poor performance against corporate governance, social, environmental, or ethical criteria. (*Compare* positive screening.)

New Deal The legislative and administrative programme, established under US President F.D. Roosevelt's administration during the 1930s, which was intended to promote economic recovery and social reform following the Great Depression. It marked the end of a period during which the theories of liberal economics had gone largely unquestioned, particularly in the USA.

non-financial performance Aspects of business performance not normally addressed in financial reporting and auditing, including wider environmental, social, and governance indicators.

non-government organization (NGO) A loose term distinguishing a range of organizations that are concerned with particular social and environmental objectives from profit-making organizations and government agencies. Commonly called 'non-governmental organizations', some actually perform a governmental function by way of their role in influencing the process of governing. (*See also* civil regulation.)

occupational health and safety *See* health and safety.

offensive corporate responsibility Policies, strategies, and programmes undertaken with the specific intention of addressing societal needs in order to gain commercial advantage. (*Compare* defensive corporate responsibility.)

partnership A collaboration between two or more parties conducted with the intention of realizing mutually acceptable or beneficial outcomes that are greater than those which any single party could achieve. Stakeholder partnership has become an important area of corporate responsibility management practice.

performance standard A code of conduct or similar instrument by means of which achievement is largely measured in terms of specific outcomes, such as workers being paid a fair wage, the eradication of workplace discrimination, etc. Codes of labour practice, organic standards, and good agricultural practice guidelines are examples of this type of standard. (*Compare* process standard.)

pioneer screening An approach to positive screening in socially responsible investment that involves choosing the best-performing company against one specific criterion.

positive screening An approach to socially responsible investment, under which companies are chosen based on their performance against corporate governance, social, environmental, or ethical criteria. Positive screening can be subdivided into best-in-class screening and pioneer screening. Conversely, SRI investors can use negative screening.

process standard A code of conduct or similar instrument by means of which achievement is largely measured in terms of the process that an organization undergoes rather than fixed outcomes. The ISO 14000 series on environmental management and the AA1000 series are examples of this type of standard. (*Compare* performance standard.)

proxy voting A method of voting at a company's annual general meeting on environmental, social, and governance issues.

reporting awards Schemes offering awards for the quality of corporate reports.

reputation management The aspect of management practice that is concerned with understanding perceptions of an organization's reputation, and the actions necessary to protect or enhance it. Reputation management has been identified as a significant driver of defensive corporate responsibility.

rights Powers, privileges, or other entitlements that are assured by custom or law.

Rio Earth Summit A meeting, in Rio de Janeiro in June 1992, of over one hundred heads of state plus representatives of non-government organizations, business, and local government, which was the summit of an international discussion of environmental and development issues of the kind raised by the Brundtland Commission. It was the first time that a multi-sectoral dialogue had been conducted to address these issues, and resulted in leaders signing a number of important agreements, including the United Nations Framework Conventions on Climate Change (UNFCCC) and the Convention on Biological Diversity (CBD), the Rio Declaration on Environment and Development, and Agenda 21 (an international plan of action for achieving a more sustainable pattern of development in the twenty-first century). The meeting is highly significant in the history of contemporary corporate responsibility, because it recognized the importance of business–government–civil society cooperation in achieving sustainable development goals—something that was developed further at the 2002 World Summit on Sustainable Development.

risk management The aspect of management practice that is concerned with understanding and acting upon the degree of risk presented to an organization by political, social, environmental, and economic factors. Risk is often seen as a driver of defensive corporate responsibility and is evident, for example, in the support of food companies for sustainable agriculture and fisheries.

screening A strategy used in socially responsible investment. (*See also* positive screening.)

self-regulation This refers to the practice of a company or other organization voluntarily putting constraints on what it does, e.g. through the adoption of a code of practice or adherence to voluntary guidelines, even though the constrained policy or action might be legal. Some see voluntary self-regulation as a defining feature of corporate responsibility.

shareholder activism Actions taken by shareholders with the intention of improving corporate governance.

small cap Companies with a relatively small market capitalization. (*Compare* large cap funds.)

small and medium-sized enterprises (SMEs) A classification of company that is normally based on number of employees (or, occasionally, on turnover). In the EU, a small enterprise employs fewer than fifty people and a medium one, less than 250; in the USA, the figures are higher, but still not more than 100 and 500, respectively. SMEs comprise the vast majority of businesses in the world (99% in the EU) and account for the bulk of private-sector employment generation.

social accounting Accounting for the non-financial aspects of corporate reporting.

social and environmental ratings The rating of companies for investment purposes, according to defined criteria for their social and/or environmental performance. Examples include the Domini 400 Social Index, the KLD Climate Change Index, the FTSE4Good Index series, and the Dow Jones Sustainability Indices.

social auditing The evaluation of an organization to ascertain the validity and reliability of information about that organization's claims concerning its social performance.

social contract The implied agreement between members of a society that defines and puts limits on the duties, responsibilities, and obligations of each member. Social contract theory is associated with the ethical theory of John Locke and underpins ideas about the company's licence to operate.

social entrepreneurship An imprecise term used to refer to a wide range of organizations—both profit-making and non-profit—for which the primary purpose is to deliver social and/or environmental value in contrast with financial value.

social impact assessment Assessment of the social consequences of a company or facility, normally focusing on inputs and outputs within a particular geographical location. (*Compare* environmental impact assessment; human rights impact assessment.)

social reporting The reporting of the social and environmental aspects of corporate activity.

socially responsible investment (SRI) An approach to investing that considers the social, environmental, and ethical consequences of investments within the context of financial analysis.

stakeholder An entity with a stake in another organization, by virtue of the fact he, she, or it is affected by, or has influence over, that organization. In corporate responsibility terms, 'stakeholder' usually refers to the stake that an individual or organization has in a company, and includes employees, local communities, shareholders, customers, and clients.

stakeholder dialogue The convening of a discussion between a company and (all, or some of) its stakeholders.

stakeholder engagement The managed process of interaction between a company and its stakeholders.

stakeholder management The application of stakeholder theory to management practice. It includes stakeholder engagement, stakeholder dialogue, and stakeholder partnership.

stakeholder partnership A partnership between a company and its stakeholders, intended to capitalize on their combined capabilities in pursuit of a particular purpose.

state An organized political community, occupying a definite territory and governed by a sovereign government. In some corporate responsibility literature, the term 'state' is used interchangeably with government—but the terms are distinct.

strategic philanthropy A form of corporate philanthropy under which donations are targeted towards areas that are synergistic with the company's interests or competencies.

sustainability Refers to those forms of human economic and cultural activity that can be conducted without long-term degradation of the resources used. The term is often used interchangeably with sustainable development.

sustainable consumption and production Continuous economic and social progress that respects the limits of the Earth's ecosystems and meets the needs and aspirations of everyone for a better quality of life—now, and for future generations.

sustainable development According to the Brundtland Commission, which is the most widely known definition, this is human development to meet the needs of the present generation without compromising the ability of future generations to meet their own needs.

third-party verification statements Statements made by third parties, verifying the content of corporate reports.

trade union An association of workers in any trade, or allied trades, for the protection and furtherance of their interests with regard to wages, hours, and conditions of labour, and for the provision, from their common funds, of pecuniary assistance to their members during strikes, sickness, unemployment, old age, etc. There is an important distinction between free trade unions and yellow unions. (*Compare* workers' committee.)

transformation management *See* change management.

triple bottom line A framework for measuring company performance and added value in terms of economic, social, and environmental parameters. Triple-bottom-line accounting is an extension of the conventional financial accounting framework to measure these additional areas of performance.

United Nations A supranational organization founded in 1945 with the purposes of: (a) maintaining international peace and security; (b) developing friendly relations among nations; (c) cooperating in solving international economic, social, cultural, and humanitarian problems, and in promoting respect for human rights and fundamental freedoms; (d) acting as a centre through which nations can work jointly to attain those ends. It comprises member states, as well as bodies such as the General Assembly, Security Council, and the International Court of Justice, and it administers programmes to achieve its purpose through agencies such as the UN Development Programme, the UN Environment Programme, and the International Labour Organization.

United Nations Global Compact A UN-convened initiative to promote concrete and sustained action by business participants to align their actions with broad UN social and environmental objectives, the Compact's ten principles, and the international Millennium Development Goals (MDGs). It aims to achieve this through: (a) learning forums to analyse case studies and examples of good practice; (b) global policy dialogues on the challenges of globalization; (c) multi-stakeholder collaborative development projects to further the MDGs; (d) support for new national networks, such as those in India and South Africa.

Universal Declaration of Human Rights A 1948 UN Declaration—signed and ratified by most of the world's countries—that sets out a basic definition of universal human rights. The Declaration is often referred to in human rights and workers' rights codes of conduct.

venture philanthropy Application of the venture capital model of investment and the deployment of private equity to achieve social and environmental outcomes.

Washington Consensus The set of policies that, during the 1980s and 1990s, became a condition of loans to countries from the World Bank. Countries were required to open their domestic markets to foreign competition, to limit state intervention (including income redistribution, public education, and welfare provision), and to establish policies that would promote a favourable business environment. The Consensus encouraged private foreign direct investment and encouraged countries—such as Indonesia and Mexico—to focus on export markets. Some saw it as responsible for creating the exploitative social and environmental conditions that, in turn, led to calls for greater corporate responsibility, especially in relation to multinational corporations.

welfare state A system under which government seeks to provide an economic safety net for the general population (e.g. through unemployment, child, and disability benefits) and the opportunity for individual improvement (e.g. through health care and education). A feature of Communist Bloc countries, it also became widespread in Western Europe (especially after World War II), was mirrored in the US New Deal, and was a feature of many newly independent governments in Africa and Asia. It put a greater tax burden on business, in return for reducing the pressures on companies to take on social responsibilities. Dismantling the welfare state was typically a condition of the Washington Consensus policies adopted by developing countries in the 1980s and 1990s.

workers' committee Sometimes treated as the equivalent of a trade union, but different, in that it brings together employees within a single company (rather than a trade). Some workers' committees are similar to yellow unions.

workplace health and safety *See* health and safety.

World Commission on Environment and Development *See* Brundtland Commission.

yellow union A type of trade union that is tightly controlled by parties other than union members.

Bibliography

Aaronson S.A., Reeves, J.T., and National Policy Association 2002, *Corporate responsibility in the global village: the role of public policy*, National Policy Association, Washington, DC.

Abbott Laboratories 2005, *2004 Corporate citizenship report*, Abbott Laboratories, Chicago, IL.

ABI 2001, *Investing in social responsibility : risks and opportunities*, Association of British Insurers, London.

Abrami, R. 2003, 'Worker rights and global trade: the US-Cambodia bilateral textile trade agreement', *Harvard Business School Case Study 703-034*, Harvard Business Publishing, Boston, MA.

ACCA 2005, *ACCA UK awards for sustainability reporting 2005: report of the judges*, Association of Chartered Certified Accountants, London.

ACCA 2008, *ACCA UK awards for sustainability reporting 2008: report of the judges*, Association of Chartered Certified Accountants, London.

ACCA 2013, *What do investors expect from non-financial reporting?*, Association of Chartered Certified Accountants, London.

Accenture and UN Global Compact 2016, *Architects of a better world: the UN Global Compact-Accenture CEO study on sustainability 2013*, UN Global Compact, New York.

AccountAbility 2002, *AA1000 conversations: lessons from the early years (1999–2001)*, AccountAbility, London.

AccountAbility 2003a, *Redefining materiality: practice and public policy for effective corporate reporting*, AccountAbility, London.

AccountAbility 2003b, *The state of sustainability assurance*, AccountAbility, London.

AccountAbility 2006, *What assures?*, AccountAbility, London.

Ackerman B.A. 1980, *Social justice in the liberal state*, Yale University Press, New Haven, CT.

Ackerman B.A. and Alstott A. 1999, *The stakeholder society*, Yale University Press, New Haven, CT.

Ackerman R.W. and Bauer R.A. 1976, *Corporate social responsiveness: modern dilemma*, Reston Publishing Co., Reston, VA.

ActionAid 2005a, *Power hungry: six reasons to regulate global food corporations*, ActionAid, London.

ActionAid 2005b, *Rotten fruit*, ActionAid, London.

Adams C. 2004, 'The ethical, social and environmental reporting-performance portrayal gap', *Accounting, Auditing and Accountability Journal*, vol. 17, pp 731–757.

Adams C. and Evans R. 2004, 'Accountability, completeness, credibility and the audit expectations gap', *Journal of Corporate Citizenship*, no. 14, Summer, pp 97–115.

Adegbite E., Amaeshi K., and Nakajima C. 2013, 'Multiple influences on corporate governance practice in Nigeria: agents, strategies and implications', *International Business Review*, vol. 22, no. 3, pp 524–538.

Aguinis H. and Glavas A. 2012, 'What we know and don't know about corporate social responsibility: a review and research agenda', *Journal of Management*, vol. 38, no. 4, pp 932–968.

AICPA 1977, *The measurement of corporate social performance: determining the impact of business actions on areas of social concern*, American Institute of Certified Public Accountants, New York.

Aidt T., Tzannatos Z., and World Bank 2002, *Unions and collective bargaining: economic effects in a global environment*, World Bank, Washington, DC.

Ainge-Roy E. 2016, 'Zero-hour contracts banned in New Zealand', *Guardian*, 11 March. Available online at https://www.theguardian.com/world/2016/mar/11/zero-hour-contracts-banned-in-new-zealand, accessed 3 October 2018.

Akumu W. 2008, 'M-PESA turning into a big virtual bank', *Daily Nation*, Nairobi, 8 April. Available online at https://allafrica.com/stories/200804072077.html, accessed 3 October 2018.

Albareda L. 2008, 'Corporate responsibility, governance and accountability: from self-regulation to co-regulation', *Corporate Governance*, vol. 8, no. 4, pp 430–439.

Ali W., Frynas J.G., and Mahmood Z., 2017. 'Determinants of corporate social responsibility (CSR) disclosure in developed and developing countries: a literature review', *Corporate Social Responsibility and Environmental Management*, 6 March. DOI: 10.1002/csr.1410.

Allen M.R., Barros V.R., Broome J., Cramer W., Christ R., Church J.A., Clarke L., Dahe Q., Dasgupta P., and Dubash N.K. 2014, *IPCC Fifth Assessment Synthesis Report—Climate Change 2014 Synthesis Report.*

Alvesson M. and Willmott H. 2002, 'Identity regulation as organizational control: producing the appropriate individual', *Journal of Management Studies*, vol. 39, no. 5, pp 619–644.

Amalric F. and Hauser J. 2005, 'Economic drivers of corporate responsibility activities', *Journal of Corporate Citizenship*, no. 20, Winter, pp 27–38.

Ambachtsheer J. 2005, *SRI: what do investment managers think?*, Mercer Investment Consulting, Toronto.

Amba-Rao S.C. 1993, 'Multinational corporate social responsibility, ethics, interactions and third world governments', *Journal of Business Ethics*, vol. 12, pp 553–572.

Amin S. 1997, *Capitalism in the age of globalization: the management of contemporary society*, Zed Books, London.

Amnesty International 2005, *Contracting out of human rights: the Chad–Cameroon pipeline*, Amnesty International, London. Available online at https://www.amnesty.org/en/documents/pol34/012/2005/en, accessed 28 November 2018.

Anderson R. 2003, 'Ethics ain't rocket science', *Seattle Weekly*, 6 August. Available online at http://www.seattleweekly.com, accessed 28 November 2018.

Anderson R. 2005, 'From CEO to cipher', *Seattle Weekly*, 9 March. Available online at http://www.seattleweekly.com, accessed 28 November 2018.

Anderson R.C. 1998, *Mid-course correction: toward a sustainable enterprise: the interface model*, Peregrinzilla Press, Atlanta, GA.

Andrews K. 1973, 'Can the best corporations be made moral?', *Harvard Business Review*, vol. 51, no. 3, pp 57–64.

Andriof J. and McIntosh M. 2001, *Perspectives on corporate citizenship*, Greenleaf, Sheffield.

Andriof J., Waddock S., Husted B., and Rahman S.S. 2002, *Unfolding stakeholder thinking*, Vol. 1: *Theory, responsibility and engagement*, Greenleaf, Sheffield.

Andriof J., Waddock S.A., Husted B., and Rahman S.S. 2003, *Unfolding stakeholder thinking*, Vol. 2: *Relationships, communication, reporting and performance*, Greenleaf, Sheffield.

Andriof J., Waddock S., Husted B., and Rahman S.S., 2017. *Unfolding stakeholder thinking: theory, responsibility and engagement*. Routledge, Abingdon, Oxfordshire.

Annan K. 2004, *Who cares wins*, UN, Geneva.

Ansari S., Munir K., and Gregg T. 2012, 'Impact at the "bottom of the pyramid": the role of social capital in capability development and community empowerment', *Journal of Management Studies*, vol. 49, no. 4, pp 813–842.

Anshen M. 1980, *Corporate strategies for social performance*, Macmillan, New York.

Aras G. 2011, *Governance and social responsibility [electronic resource]: international perspectives*, Palgrave Macmillan, Houndmills, Basingstoke; New York.

Arce A. and Long N. (eds) 2000, *Anthropology, development, and modernities: exploring discourses, counter-tendencies, and violence*, Routledge, Abingdon, Oxfordshire.

Arlidge J. 2009, 'I'm doing "God's work". Meet Mr Goldman Sachs'. Available online at https://www.thetimes.co.uk/article/im-doing-gods-work-meet-mr-goldman-sachs-zflqc78gqs8, accessed 3 October 2018.

Armendáriz B. and Morduch J. 2010, *The economics of microfinance*. MIT Press, Cambridge, MA.

Arnold D.G. 2003, 'Libertarian theories of corporation and global capitalism', *Journal of Business Ethics*, vol. 48, pp 155–173.

Arnold D.G. and Hartman L.P. 2003, 'Moral imagination and the future of sweatshops', *Business and Society Review*, vol. 108, no. 4, pp 425–461.

Ascoly N. and Zeldenrust I. 2003, *Considering complaints mechanisms*, Centre for Research on Multinational Companies (SOMO), Amsterdam.

Ascoly N., Oldenziel J., and Zeldenrust I. 2001, *Overview of recent developments on monitoring and verification in the garment and sportswear industry in Europe*, Centre for Research on Multinational Companies (SOMO), Amsterdam.

Ashridge Centre for Business and Society 2005, *A catalogue of CSR activities*, Ashridge Centre for Business and Society, Berkhamsted, Hertfordshire.

Asongu J.J. 2007, 'The history of corporate social responsibility', *Journal of Business and Public Policy*, vol. 1, no. 2, pp 1–18.

ASSC 1975, *The corporate report* (Accounting Standards Steering Committee), Institute of Chartered Accountants in England and Wales, London.

Atkinson A.B. and Morelli S. 2011, 'Economic crises and inequality', paper prepared for the *2011 Human Development Report*, United Nations Development Programme. Available online at http://www.nuff.ox.ac.uk/Users/Atkinson/Paper-Economic%20Crises%20and%20Inequality.pdf, accessed 3 October 2018.

Attfield R. 1999, *The ethics of the global environment*, Purdue University Press, West Lafayette, IN.

Attfield R. and Wilkins B. 1992, *International justice and the third world: studies in the philosophy of development*, Routledge, London.

Australian Government 2005, *Corporate social responsibility discussion paper*, Australian Government Corporations and Markets Advisory Committee, Canberra.

Avtonomov V. 2006, 'Balancing state, market and social justice: Russian experiences and lessons to learn', *Journal of Business Ethics*, vol. 66, no. 1, pp 3-9.

Ayres C.E. 1946, *The divine right of capital*, Houghton Mifflin, Boston, MA.

Ayers J.B. and Odergaard M.A. 2008, *Retail supply chain management*, Auerbach Publications, Boca Raton, FL.

Bachmann-Medick D. 2017, 'Cultural turns: a matter of management?', in Küpers, W., Sonnenburg, S., and Zierold, M. (eds), *ReThinking management*, Springer, Wiesbaden, Germany, pp 31-55.

Bagehot W. and Marshall A. 1885, *The postulates of English political economy*, Longmans Green, London.

Baird L., Post J.E. and Mahon J.F. 1990, *Management: functions and responsibilities*, Harper and Row, New York.

Bakan J. 2004, *The corporation: the pathological pursuit of profit and power*, Free Press, New York.

Baker H.K. and Nofsinger J.R. 2012, *Socially responsible finance and investing: financial institutions, corporations, investors, and activists*, John Wiley, Hoboken, NJ.

Baker M. 2002, 'The GRI—the will to succeed is not enough', *Corporate Responsibility News and Resources*. Available online at http://www.mallenbaker.net/csr/CSRfiles/GRI.html, accessed 28 November 2018.

Baker R.W. 2005, *Capitalism's Achilles heel: dirty money and how to renew the free-market system*, John Wiley, Hoboken, NJ.

Bales K. 2004, *Disposable people: new slavery in the global economy* (revised edn), University of California Press, Berkeley, CA.

Ballinger J. 1992, 'The new free trade heel: Nike's profits jump on the backs of Asian workers', *Harper's Magazine*, vol. 285, pp 46-47.

Ballinger J. 2010, 'The threat posed by "corporate social responsibility" to trade union rights', in MacDonald K. and Marshall S. (eds), *Fairtrade, corporate accountability and beyond*, Ashgate, Farnham, Surrey.

Ballinger, J. and Olsson, C. 1997, *Behind the swoosh: the struggle of Indonesians making Nike shoes*, Global Publications Foundation, Uppsala.

Banerjee S.B. 2001, 'Managerial perceptions of corporate environmentalism: interpretations from industry and strategic implications for organizations', *Journal of Management Studies*, vol. 38, no. 4, pp 489-513.

Banerjee S.B. 2007, *Corporate social responsibility: the good, the bad and the ugly*, Edward Elgar, Cheltenham.

Banerjee S.B. 2018, 'Transnational power and translocal governance: the politics of corporate responsibility', *Human Relations*, vol. 71, no. 6, pp 796-821.

Banerjee A.V. and Duflo E. 2011, *Poor economics*, Public Affairs, New York.

Banerjee S.B. and Prasad A. 2008, 'Introduction to the special issue on, "Critical reflections on management and organizations: a postcolonial perspective" ', *Critical Perspectives on International Business*, vol. 4, no. 2/3, pp 90-98.

Bannock G., Baxter R.E., and Davis E. 2003, *Dictionary of economics*, Bloomberg Press/Profile Books, Princeton, NJ.

Barker R.M. and Chiu I.H. 2017, *Corporate governance and investment management: the promises and limitations of the new financial economy*, Edward Elgar, Cheltenham.

Barmann T.C. 2006, 'Glaxo settles Paxil complaint with 46 states', *Providence Journal*, 29 March. Available online at http://www.highbeam.com/doc/1G1-143844591.html, accessed 22 November 2018.

Barnard C.I. 1938, *The functions of the executive*, Harvard University Press, Cambridge, MA.

Barnett M.L. 2007, 'Stakeholder influence capacity and the variability of financial returns to corporate social responsibility', *Academy of Management Review*, vol. 32, no. 3, pp 794-816.

Barnett M.L. and Salomon R.M. 2006, 'Beyond dichotomy: the curvilinear relationship between social responsibility and financial performance', *Strategic Management Journal*, vol. 27, no. 11, pp 1101-1122.

Barnett M.L. and Salomon R.M. 2012, 'Does it pay to be really good? Addressing the shape of the relationship between social and financial performance', *Strategic Management Journal*, vol. 33, no. 11, pp 1304-1320.

Barnett M.L., Henriques I., and Husted B.W. 2018, 'Governing the void between stakeholder management and sustainability', in Dorobantu S., Aguilera R., Luo J., and Milliken F. (eds), *Sustainability, stakeholder governance, and corporate social responsibility*, Emerald Publishing, Bingley, West Yorkshire, pp 121-143.

Baron D.P. 2002, *Business and its environment* (4th edn), Prentice Hall, Upper Saddle River, NJ.

Barrera A. 2000, 'Social principles as a framework for ethical analysis (with an application to the Tobin tax)', *Journal of Business Ethics*, vol. 23, no. 4, pp 377-388.

Barrett R. 1998, *Liberating the corporate soul: building a visionary organization*, Butterworth-Heinemann, Boston, MA.

Barrett R. 2017, *The values-driven organization: cultural health and employee well-being as a pathway to sustainable performance* (2nd edn), Routledge, Abingdon, Oxfordshire.

Barrientos S. and Smith S. 2007, 'Do workers benefit from ethical trade? Assessing codes of labour practice in global production systems', *Third World Quarterly*, vol. 28, no. 4, pp 713–729.

Barrientos S., Dolan C., and Tallontire A. 2001, *Gender and ethical trade: a mapping of the issues in African horticulture*, Natural Resources Institute, University of Greenwich, Chatham, Kent.

Barrientos S., Dolan C., and Tallontire A. 2003, 'A gendered value chain approach to codes of conduct in African horticulture', *World Development*, vol. 31, no. 9, pp 1511–1527.

Barry B.M. 1989a, *Democracy, power, and justice: essays in political theory*, Clarendon Press, Oxford.

Barry B.M. 1989b, *Theories of justice*, University of California Press, Berkeley, CA.

Barry N.P. 1979, *Hayek's social and economic philosophy*, Macmillan, London.

Bartley T. 2003, 'Certifying forests and factories: states, social movements, and the rise of private regulation in the apparel and forest products fields', *Politics and Society*, vol. 31, no. 3, pp 433–464.

Basu K. and Palazzo G. 2005, 'An inductive typology of corporate social responsibility', in *Proceedings of the Academy of Management Conference, Hawaii, 2005*. Available online at http://proceedings.aom.org/content/2005, accessed 22 November 2018.

Batstone D.B. 2003, *Saving the corporate soul—and (who knows?) maybe your own: eight principles for creating and preserving integrity and profitability without selling out*, Jossey-Bass, San Francisco, CA.

Battaglia M., Bianchi L., Frey M., and Iraldo F. 2010, 'An innovative model to promote CSR among SMEs operating in industrial clusters: evidence from an EU project', *Corporate Social Responsibility and Environmental Management*, vol. 17, no. 3, pp 133–141.

Bauer R., Koedijk K., and Otten R. 2005, 'International evidence on ethical mutual fund performance and investment style', *Journal of Banking and Finance*, vol. 29, pp 1751–1767.

Bauman Z. 1998, *Globalization: the human consequences*, Columbia University Press, New York.

BBC 2005, *'Costing the earth': the Kenya flower trade*. Available online at http://www.bbc.co.uk/radio4/science, accessed 22 November 2018.

BBC 2013, 'Google turns off China censorship warning'. Available online at http://www.bbc.co.uk/news, accessed 22 November 2018.

BBC 2014, 'Lloyds Bank confirms 9,000 job losses and branch closures', BBC News, 28 October. Available online at https://www.bbc.co.uk/news/av/business-29798232/lloyds-bank-confirms-9000-job-losses-and-branch-closures, accessed 3 October 2018.

BBC 2015a, 'Deutsche Bank in record $2.5 billion fine over interest rate manipulation', BBC News, 23 April. Available online at https://www.bbc.co.uk/news/business-32430710, accessed 3 October 2018.

BBC 2015b, 'Sports Direct to review worker rights', BBC News, 18 December. Available online at http://www.bbc.co.uk/news/business-35130394, accessed 1 February 2018.

BBC 2018, 'Volkswagen admits it can't cope with new emissions tests', BBC News, 6 June. Available online at https://www.bbc.co.uk/news/business-44383226, accessed 6 June 2018.

Beauchamp T.L., Bowie N.E., and Arnold D. (eds) 2008, *Ethical business and theory* (8th edn), Pearson Education, London.

Beaver W. 1995, 'Levi's is leaving China', *Business Horizons*, vol. 38, no. 2, pp 35–40.

Bebbington J. 2001a, *Sustainability assessment modelling at BP: advances in environmental accounting*, Association of Chartered Certified Accountants, London.

Bebbington J. 2001b, 'Sustainable development: a review of the international development, business and accounting literature', *Accounting Forum*, vol. 25, pp 128–157.

Bebbington J. 2009, 'Measuring sustainable development performance: possibilities and issues', *Accounting Forum*, vol. 33, pp 189–193.

Bebbington J., Larrinaga C., and Moneva J.M. 2008, 'Corporate social reporting and reputation risk management', *Accounting, Auditing and Accountability Journal*, Vol. 21(3), pp 337–361.

Beck U. 1992, *Risk society: towards a new modernity*, SAGE Publications, London.

Beck U. 2000, *What is globalization?* Polity Press, Cambridge.

Beck U., Giddens, A., and Lash, S. 1994, *Reflexive modernization: politics, tradition and aesthetics in the modern social order*, Polity Press, Cambridge.

Beinhocker E. and Hanauer N. 2014, 'Capitalism redefined: Resolving the tension between a prosperous world and a moral one', *Juncture*, vol. 21, no. 1, pp 12–24.

Belkaoui A. 1976, 'The impact of the disclosure of the environmental effects of organizational behaviour on the market', *Financial Management*, vol. 5, no.4, pp 26–31.

Belkaoui A. and Karpic P.G. 1989, 'Determinants of the corporate decision to disclose social information', *Accounting, Auditing and Accountability Journal*, vol. 2, no. 1, pp 36–51.

Bellagio Forum for Sustainable Development and Eurosif 2006, *PRIME toolkit primer for responsible investment management of endowments*, Bellagio Forum for Sustainable Development, Osnabrück, Germany.

Belvedere V.A. and Grando, A. 2017, *Sustainable operations and supply chain management*, Wiley, Chichester.

Bendell J. 2000, *Terms of endearment: business, NGOs and sustainable development*, Greenleaf, Sheffield.

Bendell J. 2004a, *Barricades and boardrooms: a contemporary history of the corporate accountability movement*, UN Research Institute for Social Development, Geneva.

Bendell J. 2004b, *Flags of inconvenience? The Global Compact and the future of the United Nations*, International Centre for Corporate Social Responsibility, University of Nottingham.

Bendell J., 2017. 'Talking for change? Reflections on effective stakeholder dialogue', in Andriof, J., Waddock, S., Husted, B, and Rahman, S.S. (eds), *Unfolding stakeholder thinking 2: relationships, communication, reporting and performance*, Routledge, Abingdon, Oxfordshire, pp 53-69.

Bendell J., Collins E., and Roper J. 2010, 'Beyond partnerism: toward a more expansive research agenda on multi-stakeholder collaboration for responsible business', *Business Strategy and the Environment*, vol. 19, no. 6, pp 351-355.

Bennett C. and Burley H. 2005, 'Corporate accountability: an NGO perspective', in Tully, S. (ed.), *Research handbook on corporate legal responsibility*, Edward Elgar, Cheltenham, pp 372-394.

Bennett M., James P., and Klinkers L. 1999, *Sustainable measures: evaluation and reporting of environmental and social performance*, Greenleaf, Sheffield.

Bennett M., Rikhardsson P.M., and Schaltegger S. 2003, *Environmental management accounting: purpose and progress*, Kluwer Academic, Dordrecht, The Netherlands.

Bennis W.G., Goleman D., and O'Toole J. 2008, *Transparency: how leaders create a culture of candor*, Jossey-Bass, San Francisco, CA.

Bennison, J. 2016, 'Barclays and Credit Suisse agree record $154m "dark pools" settlement', *Financial Times*, London, 1 February.

Benson, K.L., Brailsford, T.J., and Humphrey, J.E. 2006, 'Do socially responsible fund managers really invest differently?', *Journal of Business Ethics*, vol. 65, no. 4, pp 337-357.

Bentham J. 1789, *An introduction to the principles of morals and legislation, etc. MS. notes [by the author]*, T. Payne & Son, London.

BER 2008, *The contribution of South African Breweries Limited to the South African economy*, Bureau for Economic Research, Cape Town.

Beresford,D.R. 1973, *Compilation of social measurement disclosures in Fortune 500 annual reports*, Ernst & Ernst, Cleveland, OH.

Beresford D.R. 1975, *Social responsibility disclosure—1974 survey of Fortune 500 annual reports*, Ernst & Ernst, Cleveland, OH.

Beresford D.R. 1976, *Social responsibility disclosure—1975 survey of Fortune 500 annual reports*, Ernst & Ernst, Cleveland, OH.

Berger F.R. 1984, *Happiness, justice, and freedom: the moral and political philosophy of John Stuart Mill*, University of California Press, Berkeley, CA.

Berlan A. and Dolan C. 2014, 'Of red herrings and immutabilities: rethinking fair trade's ethic of relationality among cocoa producers', in Goodman, M. and Sage, C. (eds), *Food transgressions: making sense of contemporary food politics*, Ashgate, Farnham, Surrey.

Berle A.A., and Means G.C. 1932, *Modern corporation and private property*, Commerce Clearing House, Loose Leaf Service Division of the Corporation Trust Company, New York.

Bernauer T. and Caduff L. 2004, 'In whose interest? Pressure group politics, economic competition and environmental regulation', *Journal of Public Policy*, vol. 24, no. 1, pp 99-126.

Berns M., Townend A., Khayat Z., Balagopal B., Reeves M., et al. 2009, 'The business of sustainability: what it means to managers now', *MIT Sloan Management Review*, vol. 51, no. 1, pp 20-26.

Bernstein P.L. 1996, *Against the gods: the remarkable story of risk*, John Wiley, New York.

Berry A., Capps T., Cooper D., Hopper T., and Lowe E.A. 1985, 'NCB accounts—a mine of disinformation?', *Accountancy*, January, pp 10-12.

Bhagwati J.N. 2004, *In defense of globalization*, Oxford University Press, New York.

Bhattacharya C.B. and Sen S. 2004, 'Doing better at doing good: when, why, and how consumers respond to corporate social initiatives', *California Management Review*, vol. 47, no. 1, pp 9-24.

Billings A.C., Butterworth M.L, and Turman P.D. 2017, *Commuications and sport: surveying the field* (3rd edn), SAGE Publications, Thousand Oaks, CA.

Birch D. 2001, 'Corporate citizenship: rethinking business beyond corporate social responsibility', in Andriof, G. and McIntosh, M. (eds), *Perspectives on corporate citizenship*, Greenleaf, London, pp 53-65.

Birch D. 2003, 'Corporate social responsibility: some key theoretical issues and concepts for new ways of doing business', *Journal of New Business Ideas and Trends*, vol. 1, no. 1, pp 1–19.

Birkin F. 2000, 'The art of accounting for science: a prerequisite for sustainable development?', *Critical Perspectives on Accounting*, vol. 11, pp 289–309.

Black E. 2001, *IBM and the Holocaust: the strategic alliance between Nazi Germany and America's most powerful corporation*, Crown, New York.

Black J. 2003, *A dictionary of economics* (2nd edn), Oxford University Press, Oxford.

Bladen V.W. 1974, *From Adam Smith to Maynard Keynes: the heritage of political economy*, University of Toronto Press, Toronto.

Blake D.H., Frederick, W.C., and Myers M.S. 1976, *Social auditing: evaluating the impact of corporate programs*, Praeger, New York.

Blanchard K.H., O'Connor M.J., and Ballard J. 1997, *Managing by values*, Berrett-Koehler, San Francisco, CA.

Block W. and Barnett W. 2005, 'A positive programme for laissez-faire capitalism', *Journal of Corporate Citizenship*, no. 19, Autumn, pp 31–42.

Blok V. 2017. Bridging the gap between individual and corporate responsible behaviour: toward a performative concept of corporate codes. *Philosophy of Management*, vol. 16, no. 2, pp 117–136.

Bloom D.E. and Canning D. 2006, 'Booms, busts, and echoes', *Finance and Development*, vol. 43, no. 3, pp 8–15.

Blowfield M.E. 1991, *Does Bo know Nike?*, Asian American Free Labor Institute, Jakarta, Indonesia.

Blowfield M.E. 2000a, *A guide to developing agricultural markets and agro-enterprises; fundamentals of ethical trading/sourcing in poorer countries*, World Bank, Washington, DC.

Blowfield M.E. 2000b, 'Ethical sourcing: a contribution to sustainability or a diversion?', *Sustainable Development*, vol. 8, no. 4, pp 191–200.

Blowfield M.E. 2002, 'ETI—a multi-stakeholder approach', in Jenkins, R.O., Pearson, R., and Seyfang, G. (eds), *Corporate responsibility and ethical trade: codes of conduct in the global economy*, Earthscan, London, pp 184–195.

Blowfield M.E. 2003, 'Ethical trade: the negotiation of a global ethic', doctoral dissertation, University of Sussex, Falmer, East Sussex.

Blowfield M.E. 2004, 'Implementation deficits of ethical trade systems: lessons from the Indonesian cocoa and timber industries', *Journal of Corporate Citizenship*, no. 13, Spring, pp 77–90.

Blowfield M.E. 2005a, 'Corporate social responsibility—the failing discipline and why it matters for international relations', *International Relations*, vol. 19, no. 2, pp 173–191.

Blowfield M.E. 2005b, *Does society want business leadership? An overview of attitudes and thinking*, Center for Corporate Citizenship at Boston College, Chestnut Hill, MA.

Blowfield M.E. 2007, 'Reasons to be cheerful? What we know about CSR's impact', *Third World Quarterly*, vol. 28, no. 4, pp 683–695.

Blowfield M.E. 2010, 'Business and poverty reduction', in Utting P. and Marques J.C. (eds), *Corporate social responsibility and regulatory governance: towards inclusive development?*, Palgrave Macmillan, Basingstoke.

Blowfield M.E. 2012, *Business and sustainability*, Oxford University Press, Oxford.

Blowfield M.E. 2018, 'Climate change, business transformation' in Boeger N. and Villiers C. (eds), *Shaping the corporate landscape: towards corporate reform and enterprise diversity*, Bloomsbury Publishing.

Blowfield M.E. and Dolan C. 2008, 'Stewards of virtue: the ethical dilemma of CSR in Africa', *Development and Change*, vol. 39, no. 1, pp 1–23.

Blowfield M. and Dolan C. 2010, 'Outsourcing governance: fairtrade's message for C21 global governance', *Corporate Governance*, vol. 10, no. 4, pp 484–499.

Blowfield M. and Dolan C. 2014, 'Business as a development agent: evidence of possibility and improbability', *Third World Quarterly*, vol. 35, no. 1, pp 22–42.

Blowfield M.E. and Frynas J.G. 2005, 'Setting new agendas: critical perspectives on corporate social responsibility in the developing world', *International Affairs*, vol. 81, no. 3, pp 499–513.

Blowfield M.E. and Googins B. 2007, *Step up: a call for business leadership in society—CEOs examine role of business in the 21st century*, Center for Corporate Citizenship at Boston College, Chestnut Hill, MA.

Blowfield M.E. and Johnson L. 2013, *Turnaround challenge: business and the city of the future*, Oxford University Press, Oxford.

Blyth M. 2002, *Great transformations: economic ideas and institutional change in the twentieth century*, Cambridge University Press, New York.

Boeger N. and Villiers C. (eds) 2018, *Shaping the corporate landscape: towards corporate reform and enterprise diversity*, Hart Publishing, Oxford.

Bogle J.C. 2005, *The battle for the soul of capitalism*, Yale University Press, New Haven, CT.

Bogle J.C. 2009, *Enough: true measures of money, business, and life*, John Wiley, Hoboken, NJ.

Bond P. 2006, 'Global governance campaigning and MDGs: from top-down to bottom-up anti-poverty work', *Third World Quarterly*, vol. 27, no. 2, pp 339–354.

Bornstein D. 2007, *How to change the world* (updated edn), Oxford University Press, Oxford.

Børsting C. and Thomsen S. 2016, 'Foundation ownership and labour', *Oxford Review of Economic Policy*, vol. 33, no. 2, pp 317–338.

Bounds A. 2009, 'Ethiopian refugees discover benefits of coffee', *Financial Times*, 7 May. Available online at https://www.ft.com/content/f9b9f260-3a93-11de-8a2d-00144feabdc0, accessed 3 October 2018.

Boutilier R. 2009, *Stakeholder politics: social capital, sustainable development, and the corporation*, Stanford University Press, Stanford, CA.

Bowd R., Bowd L., and Harris P. 2006, 'Communicating corporate social responsibility: an exploratory case study of a major UK retail centre', *Journal of Public Affairs*, vol. 6, no. 2, pp 147–155.

Bowen A. and Hepburn C. 2014, 'Green growth: an assessment', *Oxford Review of Economic Policy*, vol. 30, no. 3, pp. 407-422.

Bowen H.R. 1953, *Social responsibilities of the businessman*, Harper, New York.

Bower T. 1988, *Maxwell: the outsider*, Aurum Press, London.

Bower T. 1996, *Maxwell: the final verdict*, HarperCollins, London.

Bowie N. 2018, *Business ethics in the 21st century (issues in business ethics)*, Springer, Dordrecht, The Netherlands.

Bowman E.H. 1973, 'Corporate social responsibility and the investor', *Journal of Contemporary Business*, Winter, pp 21–43.

Bowman E.H. and Haire M. 1976, 'Social impact disclosure and corporate annual reports', *Accounting, Organizations and Society*, vol. 1, no. 1, pp 11–21.

BP Sustainability Review, 2012, available online at https://www.bp.com/content/dam/bp/pdf/sustainability/group-reports/BP_Sustainability_Review_2012.pdf, accessed 6 December 2018.

Bracking S. 2009, *Hiding conflict over industry returns: a stakeholder analysis of the extractive industries transparency initiative*, Working Paper Series, Brooks World Poverty Institute, University of Manchester.

Brady K. 1984, *Ida Tarbell: portrait of a muckraker*, Seaview/Putnam, New York.

Brainard L. 2006, *Transforming the development landscape: the role of the private sector*, Brookings Institution Press, Washington, DC.

Braithwaite J. and Drahos P. 2000, *Global business regulation*, Cambridge University Press, Cambridge.

Brammer S., Jackson G., and Matten D. 2012, 'Corporate social responsibility and institutional theory: new perspectives on private governance', *Socio-Economic Review*, vol. 10, no. 1, pp 3–28.

Brand S. 1999, *The clock of the long now: time and responsibility*, Basic Books, New York.

Branson R. 2011, *Screw business as usual*, Virgin Books, London.

Bridge G., Bouzarovski S., Bradshaw M., and Eyre N. 2013, 'Geographies of energy transition: space, place and the low-carbon economy', *Energy Policy*, vol. 53, pp. 331-340.

Broad R. (ed.) 2002, *Global backlash: citizen initiatives for a just world economy*, Rowman and Littlefield, Lanham, MD.

Brooke H. 2010, *The silent state*, Heinemann, London.

Brooke P. A. and Penrice D. 2009, *A vision for venture capital: realizing the promise of global venture capital and private equity*, New Ventures Press/University Press of New England, Lebanon, NH.

Brower M., Leon W., and Union of Concerned Scientists 1999, *The consumer's guide to effective environmental choices: practical advice from the Union of Concerned Scientists*, Three Rivers Press, New York.

Brown C.C. 1979, *Beyond the bottom line*, Macmillan, New York.

Brown D.K. 2004, *Improving working conditions: what works and what doesn't—existing empirical evidence and historical experience*, presented at Globalization and Labor in Developing Countries Conference, Brown University, Providence, RI.

Brown T.J. and Dacin P.A. 1997, 'The company and the product: corporate associations and consumer product responses', *Journal of Marketing*, vol. 61, pp 68–84.

Brown W.S., McCabe D., and Primeaux P. 2003, 'Business ethics in transitional economies: introduction', *Journal of Business Ethics*, vol. 47, no. 4, pp 295–297.

Browne J. 2004, 'Beyond Kyoto', *Foreign Affairs*, vol. 83, no. 4, pp 20–32.

Browne M.N. and Haas P.F. 1974, 'Social responsibility: the uncertain hypothesis', *MSU Business Topics*, vol. 22, no. 3, pp 47–51.

Brugmann J. and Prahalad C.K. 2007, 'Cocreating business's new social compact', *Harvard Business Review*, February, pp 80–90.

BSR 2002, *Designing a CSR structure: a step-by-step guide including leadership examples and decision-making tools*, Business for Social Responsibility, San Francisco, CA.

BSR 2005, *Reporting on economic impacts*, Business for Social Responsibility, San Francisco, CA.

BT 2005, *BT social and environmental report*, BT Group, London.

Buchanan A.E. 1985, *Ethics, efficiency, and the market*, Rowman and Littlefield, Totowa, NJ.

Buchanan J.M. and Yoon Y.J. 2002, 'Globalization as framed by the two logics of trade', *Independent Review*, vol. 6, no. 3, pp 399–405.

Buchholz R.A., Marcus A.A., and Post J.E. 1992, *Managing environmental issues: a casebook*, Prentice Hall, Englewood Cliffs, NJ.

Bugg-Levine A. and Emerson J. 2011, 'Impact investing: transforming how we make money while making a difference', *Innovations*, vol. 6, no. 3, pp 9–18.

Bugg-Levine A., Kogut B., and Kulatilaka N. 2012, 'A new approach to funding social enterprises', *Harvard Business Review*, vol. 90, no. 1/2, pp 118–123.

Bulkeley, H. and Newell, P. 2015, *Governing climate change*, Routledge, Abingdon, Oxon.

Bulloch G. 2009, *Development collaboration: none of our business?*, Accenture, London.

Bunting M. 2005, 'Africa's flash moment', *Guardian*, London, 20 June. Available online at https://www.theguardian.com/society/2005/jun/20/internationalaidanddevelopment.live8, accessed 4 October 2018.

Burns P. 2001, *Entrepreneurship and small business*, Palgrave, London.

Burns, P. (2014) *New venture creation: a framework for entrepreneurial start-ups*, Palgrave Macmillan.

Burrough B. and Helyar J. 1999, *Barbarians at the gate*, Jonathan Cape, London.

Business for Social Responsibility various dates, *Sustainable business survey*, Business for Social Responsibility, San Francisco.

Business Week 2005, 'Social issues retailing: can Wal-Mart fit into a white hat?', *Business Week*, 2 October.

Butler E. 1985, *Hayek: his contribution to the political and economic thought of our time*, Universe Books, New York.

Byron N. and Arnold M. 1998, *What futures for the people of the tropical forests?* Centre for International Forestry Research, Bogor, Indonesia.

Cadbury S.A. 1992, *Report of the Committee on the Financial Aspects of Corporate Governance*, London, Gee.

CAFOD 2005, *'Clean up your computer' progress report*, CAFOD, London.

Cairncross F. 1995, *Green, Inc.: a guide to business and the environment*, Island Press, Washington, DC.

Cairns, G. and Sliwa, M. 2017, *A very short, fairly interesting and reasonably cheap book about international business*, SAGE Publications, London.

Calabrese A., Costa R., Menichini T., Rosati F., and Sanfelice G. 2013, 'Turning corporate social responsibility-driven opportunities in competitive advantages: a two-dimensional model', *Knowledge and Process Management*, vol. 20, no. 1, pp 50–58.

Callahan D. 2002, *Kindred spirits: Harvard Business School's extraordinary class of 1949 and how they transformed American business*, John Wiley, Hoboken, NJ.

Cannon T. 1994, *Corporate responsibility: a textbook on business ethics, governance, environment: roles and responsibilities*, Pitman, London.

Cantino V., and Cortese D. 2017, 'Integrated report system in Italian law', *Symphonya.Emerging Issues in Management*, , no. 1, pp. 83–94.

Caplan K. 2003, 'The purist's partnership: debunking the terminology of partnerships', *Partnership Matters*, vol. 1, pp 31–35.

Carnegie A. 1889, *The gospel of wealth*, F.C. Hagen, London.

Carney, M. 2016, *Resolving the climate paradox*, Bank of England, London.

Carney W.J. 1998, 'Limited liability', *Encyclopedia of law and economics*, Edward Elgar, Cheltenham, pp 659–691.

Carrington M., Zwick D., and Neville B. 2018, 'Activism and abdication on the inside: the effect of everyday practice on corporate responsibility', *Journal of Business Ethics*. DOI: 10.1007/s10551-018-3814-5.

Carroll A.B. 1977, *Managing corporate social responsibility*, Little, Brown, Boston, MA.

Carroll A.B. 1979, 'A three-dimensional conceptual model of corporate performance', *Academy of Management Review*, vol. 4, no. 4, pp 497–505.

Carroll A.B. 1999, 'Corporate social responsibility: evolution of a definitional construct', *Business & Society*, vol. 38, no. 3, pp 268–295.

Carroll A.B. 2000, 'A commentary and an overview of key questions on corporate social performance measurement', *Business & Society*, vol. 39, no. 4, pp 466–478.

Carroll A.B. and Buchholtz A.K. 2006, *Business and society: ethics and stakeholder management* (6th edn), Thomson/South-Western, Mason, OH.

Carroll A.B. and Shabana K.M. 2010, 'The business case for corporate social responsibility: a review of concepts, research and practice', *International Journal of Management Reviews*, vol. 12, no. 1, pp 85–105.

Carroll S.J. and Gannon M.J. 1997, *Ethical dimensions of international management*, SAGE Publications, Thousand Oaks, CA.

Carson R. 1962, *Silent spring*, Houghton Mifflin, Boston, MA.

Carswell J. 1960, *The South Sea Bubble*, Stanford University Press, Stanford, CA.

Carter D.A., Simkins B.J., and Simpson W.G. 2003, 'Corporate governance, board diversity, and firm value', *Financial Review*, vol. 38, no. 1, pp 33–53.

Casey T. 2018, 'When boycotts work: a guide to the Facebook/Cambridge Analytica scandal', 2 April. Available online at https://www.triplepundit.com/2018/04/boycotts-work-guide-facebook-cambridge-analytica-scandal, accessed 19 July 2018.

Castells M. 2017, *Another economy is possible: culture and economy in a time of crisis*, John Wiley and Sons.

Caufield C. 1996, *Masters of illusion: the World Bank and the poverty of nations*, Henry Holt, New York.

CCC 2005a, *Going global: how US-based multinationals are operationalizing corporate citizenship on a global platform*, Center for Corporate Citizenship, Boston College, Chestnut Hill, MA.

CCC 2005b, *Integration: critical link for corporate citizenship*, Center for Corporate Citizenship, Boston College, Chestnut Hill, MA.

CCC 2005c, *State of corporate citizenship in the US: business perspectives in 2005*, Center for Corporate Citizenship, Boston College, Chestnut Hill, MA.

CECP 2006, *Giving in numbers 2006*, Committee Encouraging Corporate Philanthropy, New York.

CEP 1997, *SA8000*, Council on Economic Priorities, New York.

CEPAA 1999, *Guidance document for Social Accountability 8000*, New York.

CERES undated, *CERES principles*, Coalition for Environmentally Responsible Economies, Boston, MA.

CFS/CIS 2005, *Sustainability report 2004*, Cooperative Financial Services, Manchester.

Chamberlain N.W. 1973, *The limits of corporate responsibility*, Basic Books, New York.

Chan A. and Siu K. 2007, 'Wal-Mart's CSR and labor standards in China', presented at International Network on Business, Development and Society Workshop, 12–14 September 2007.

Chan C.C.C. and Milne M.J. 1999, 'Investor reactions to corporate environmental saints and sinners: an experimental analysis', *Accounting and Business Research*, vol. 29, no. 4, pp 265–279.

Chan Kim W. and Mauborgne R. 2005, *Blue ocean strategy: how to create uncontested market space and make the competition irrelevant*, Harvard Business School, Boston, MA.

Chandler A.D. and Mazlish B. (eds) 2005, *Leviathans: multinational corporations and the new global history*, Cambridge University Press, Cambridge.

Chandler, D. 2016, *Strategic Corporate Social Responsibility: Sustainable Value Creation* (4th edn), Harvard University Press, Cambridge, MA.

Chang H. 2002, *Kicking away the ladder: development strategy in historical perspective*, Anthem, London.

Chang H. 2007, *Bad Samaritans: rich nations, poor policies, and the threat to the developing world*, Random House Business, London.

Chang H. 2010, *23 things they don't tell you about capitalism*, Allen Lane, London.

Charkham J. 2005, *Keeping better company*, Oxford, Oxford University Press.

Charkham J. 2008, *Keeping better company*, Oxford, Oxford University Press.

Chatterji A. and Levine D. 2006, 'Breaking down the wall of codes: evaluating non-financial performance measurement', *California Management Review*, vol. 48, no. 2, pp 29–51.

Chaudhury, V. 2017, *We're cheated, first in India, then in Qatar': how World Cup workers are deceived*, Guardian Books, London.

Chenall R.H. and Juchau R. 1977, 'Investor information needs: an Australian study', *Accounting and Business Research*, vol. 7, no. 26, pp 111–119.

Chenoweth J. and Bird J. 2005, *The business of water and sustainable development*, Greenleaf, Sheffield.

Cheung R. 2008, 'China', in Krosinsky C. and Robins N. (eds), *Sustainable investing: the art of long-term performance*, Earthscan, London, pp 149–164.

Christian Aid 1997, *Change at the check-out? Supermarkets and ethical business*, Christian Aid, London.

Christian Aid 2004, *Behind the mask: the real face of corporate social responsibility*, Christian Aid, London.

Christian Aid 2005, *The shirts off their backs: how tax policies fleece the poor*, Christian Aid, London.

Christian Aid, ASH, and Friends of the Earth 2005. *BAT in its own words*, Christian Aid, Action on Smoking and Health (ASH), and Friends of the Earth, London.

Chryssides G.D. and Kaler J.H. 1993, *An introduction to business ethics*, Chapman & Hall, London.

Chua W.F. 1986, 'Radical developments in accounting thought', *Accounting Review*, vol. 61, no. 4, pp 601–632.

CIE 2003, *The Global Alliance: benefit-cost framework and application*, Centre for International Economics, Canberra.

Clark J.M. 1939, *Social control of business* (2nd edn), McGraw-Hill, New York.

Clarke E. 2005, *Manufacturing the evidence*. Available online at http://www.supplymanagement.com, accessed 22 November 2018.

Clarke T. 1993, 'Case study. Robert Maxwell: master of corporate malfeasance', *Corporate Governance*, vol. 1, no, 3, pp 141–151.

Clarkson M.B. 1995, 'A stakeholder framework for analyzing and evaluating corporate social performance', *Academy of Management Review*, vol. 20, no. 1, pp 92–117.

Clay J. 2005, *Exploring the links between international business and poverty reduction: a case study of Unilever in Indonesia*, Oxfam, Oxford.

Coase R. 1937, 'The nature of the firm', *Economica*, vol. 4, no. 16, pp 386–405.

Cobb G., Collison D.J., Power D.M., and Stevenson L.A. 2005, *FTSE4Good: perceptions and performance*, Certified Accountants Educational Trust, London.

Coffee J.C. 2000, *The rise of dispersed ownership: the role of law in the separation of ownership and control*, Columbia Law and Economics Working Paper, Columbia University, New York.

Cogan D. 2004, *Corporate governance and climate change: making the connection*, CERES, Boston, MA.

Colchester M. 2014, *Lloyds settles rate-rig probe*, Wall Street Journal, New York.

Coleman J. 2002, 'Gender, power and post-structuralism in corporate citizenship', *Journal of Corporate Citizenship*, no. 5, Spring, pp 17–25.

Collinson C. 2001, *The business costs of ethical supply chain management: Kenya flower industry case study*, Natural Resources Institute, Chatham, Kent.

Collinson C. and Leon M. 2000, *Economic viability of ethical cocoa trading in Ecuador*, Natural Resources Institute, Chatham, Kent.

Collison D.J., Cobb G., Power D.M., and Stevenson L.A. 2008, 'The financial performance of the FTSE4Good indices', *Corporate Social Responsibility and Environmental Management*, vol. 15, no. 1, pp. 14–28.

Colwell D. 2002, 'Levis: made in China?' Available online at https://www.alternet.org/story/13095/levis%3A_made_in_china, accessed 3 October 2018.

Combined Code 1998, *The Combined Code, Principles of Corporate Governance*, Gee, London.

Combined Code 2003, *The Combined Code on Corporate Governance*, Financial Reporting Council, London.

Combined Code 2008, *The Combined Code on Corporate Governance*, Financial Reporting Council, London.

Cone M.H. 2003, 'Corporate citizenship: the role of commercial organisations in an Islamic society', *Journal of Corporate Citizenship*, no. 9, Spring, pp 49–66.

Cooper, S. 2004, *Corporate social performance: a stakeholder approach*, Routledge, Abingdon, Oxfordshire.

Corcoran T., 2006, 'Just say no to NGOs', *National Post*, 1 April.

Corkery J., Mikalsen M., and Allan K. 2017, *Corporate social responsibility: the good corporation*, Centre for Commercial Law, Bond University, Queensland, Australia.

Cornell B. and Shapiro A.C. 1987, 'Corporate stakeholders and corporate finance', *Financial Management*, vol. 16, no. 1, pp 5–14.

Cooperative Financial Services/CIS 2005, *Sustainability report 2004*, Cooperative Financial Services.

Courville S. 2000, *Promoting biological diversity through sustainable certification and fair trade*, Institute for Agriculture and Trade Policy, Minneapolis, MN.

Cowe R. 2002, *No scruples? Managing to be responsible in a turbulent world*, Spiro, London.

Cowen S.S., Ferreri L.B., and Parker L.D. 1987, 'The impact of corporate characteristics on social responsibility disclosure: a typology and frequency based analysis', *Accounting, Organizations and Society*, vol. 12, no. 2, pp 111–122.

Cragg W. and McKague K. 2003, *Compendium of ethics codes and instruments of corporate responsibility*, Schulich School of Business, York University.

Cramer J. 2006, *Corporate social responsibility and globalisation: an action plan for business*, Greenleaf, Sheffield.

Crane, A. and Matten, D. 2015, *Business ethics: managing corporate citizenship and sustainability in the age of globalization* (4th edn), Oxford University Press, Oxford.

Crane A., Matten D., and Moon J. 2008, *Corporations and citizenship*, Cambridge University Press, Cambridge.

Crane A., Matten D., and Spence L.J. 2013, 'Corporate social responsibility in a global context', in Crane A., Matten D., and Spence L.J. (eds), *Corporate social responsibility: readings and cases in a global context* (2nd edn), Routledge, Abingdon, Oxfordshire.

Crenson M.A. and Ginsberg B. 2002, *Downsizing democracy: how America sidelined its citizens and privatized its public*, Johns Hopkins University Press, Baltimore, MD.

Crowther D. and Caliyurt K.T. 2006, *Globalisation and social responsibility*, Cambridge Scholars Press, Newcastle upon Tyne.

Cummins A. 2004, 'The Marine Stewardship Council: a multi-stakeholder approach to sustainable fishing', *Corporate Social Responsibility and Environmental Management*, vol. 11, no. 2, pp 85–94.

Currans, E. 2017, *Marching dykes, liberated sluts, and concerned mothers: women transforming public space*, University of Illinois Press, Urbana-Champaign, IL.

Dallas G. (ed.) 2005, *Governance and risk: an analytical handbook for investors, managers, directors and stakeholders*, McGraw-Hill, New York.

Daly H.E. 1996, *Beyond growth: the economics of sustainable development*, Beacon Press, Boston, MA.

Damle, P., More, K., and Dereddy, S.R. 2017, 'Integrated reporting: comparative case study of 2016 annual reports of five companies', *International Journal of Engineering Technology Science and Research*, vol. 4, no. 9, pp 188-198.

Dando N. and Swift T. 2003, 'Transparency and assurance: minding the credibility gap', *Journal of Business Ethics*, vol. 44, no. 2/3, pp 195-200.

Danone undated, 'The 1972 speech: a milestone of Danone's history turns 40'. Available online at http://downtoearth.danone.com/2012/11/16/the-1972-speech-a-milestone-of-danones-history-turns-40, accessed 22 November 2018.

Darnton R. 2009, 'Google and the new digital future', *New York Review of Books*, vol. 56, no. 20.

Daum J.H. 2003, *Intangible assets and value creation*, John Wiley, Chichester.

Davies P.W.F. 1997, *Current issues in business ethics*, Routledge, London.

Davis K. 1960, 'Can business afford to ignore social responsibilities?', *California Management Review*, vol. 2, no. 3, pp 70-76.

Davis K. 1973, 'The case for and against business assumption of social responsibilities', *Academy of Management Review*, vol. 16, no. 2, pp 312-322.

Davis I. 2005, 'The biggest contract', *The Economist*, 26 May. Available online at http://piglossary.pbworks.com/f/Davis+-+the+Biggest+Comtract.pdf, accessed 6 December 2018.

Davis S.M., Lukomnik J., and Pitt-Watson D. 2006, *The new capitalists: how citizen investors are reshaping the corporate agenda*, Harvard Business School Press, Boston, MA.

Davy A. 2004a, 'Companies in conflict situations: a role for partnerships?' in Warner M. and Sullivan R. (eds), *Putting partnerships to work*, Greenleaf, Sheffield, pp 220-229.

Davy A. 2004b, 'Ownership and control of outcomes' in Warner M. and Sullivan R. (eds), Greenleaf, Sheffield, pp 210-219.

DCCA 2008, *Small suppliers in global supply chains: how multinationals can target small and medium-sized suppliers in their global supply chains*, Danish Commerce and Companies Agency/Hewlett Packard, Copenhagen.

de Oliveira J.A.P. 2006, 'Corporate citizenship in Latin America', *Journal of Corporate Citizenship*, no. 21, Spring, pp 17-20.

Deegan C. 2002, ' The legitimising effect of social and environmental disclosures—a theoretical foundation', *Accounting, Auditing and Accountability Journal*, vol. 15, no. 3, 282-311.

Dees J.G. 1998, *The meaning of 'social entrepreneurship'*, Social Entrepreneurship Funders Working Group. Available online at http://www.caseatduke.org/documents/dees_sedef.pdf, accessed 22 November 2018.

Dees J.G., Emerson J., and Economy P. 2002, *Strategic tools for social entrepreneurs: enhancing the performance of your enterprising nonprofit*, John Wiley, Chichester.

DeGhetto K., Sutton A., Holcomb T. and Holmes R. 2016, 'It's who you know and what you do: how SMEs from emerging economies capitalize on founder ties to create bargaining power with foreign multinational alliance partners', in Das, T.K. (ed.), *Strategic Alliances for SME Development*, Information Age Publishing, Charlotte, NC.

Della Croce R., Kaminker C., and Stewart F. 2011, *The role of pension funds in financing green growth initiatives*, OECD, Paris.

Demirag I. 2005, *Corporate social responsibility, accountability and governance*, Greenleaf, Sheffield.

Dempsey, A.L. 2017, *Evolutions in corporate governance: towards an ethical framework for business conduct*, Routledge, Abingdon, Oxfordshire.

Department of Trade and Industry 1971, *Report on the affairs of International Learning Systems Corporation Ltd, and Interim report on the affairs of Pergamon Press Ltd*, HMSO, London.

Department of Trade and Industry 2001, *Business and society: developing corporate social responsibility in the UK*, Department of Trade and Industry, London.

Deng X. and Xu Y., 2017. 'Consumers' responses to corporate social responsibility initiatives: The mediating role of consumer-company identification', *Journal of Business Ethics*, vol. 142, no. (3), pp 515-526.

Derber C. 1998, *Corporation nation: how corporations are taking over our lives and what we can do about it*, St Martin's Press, New York.

Devinney T.M., Auger P., Eckhardt G., and Birtchnell T. 2006, 'The other CSR', *Stanford Social Innovation Review*, vol. 4, no. 3, pp 30, 32-33, 35-37.

DFID 2002, *The challenges of assessing the poverty impact of ethical trading. What can be learnt from fair trade initiatives and the sustainable livelihoods approach*, Department for International Development, London.

Dicken P. 2003, *Global shift: reshaping the global economic map in the 21st century* (4th edn), SAGE Publications, London.

Diehl S., Karmasin M., Mueller B., Terlutter R., and Weder F. 2017, *Handbook of integrated CSR communication*, Springer, Basel, Switzerland.

Dillard J. and Murray A. 2012, 'Deciphering the domain of corporate social responsibility', in Haynes K., Murray A., and Dillard J. (eds), *Corporate social responsibility: a research handbook*, Routledge, Abingdon, Oxfordshire.

DiLorenzo T.J. 2004, *How capitalism saved America: the untold history of our country, from the Pilgrims to the present*, Crown Forum, New York.

Dion M. 2001, 'Corporate citizenship as an ethic of care, corporate values, codes of ethics and global governance', in Andriof J. and McIntosh M. (eds), *Perspectives on corporate citizenship*, Greenleaf, Sheffield, pp 118–138.

Doane D. 2005, 'The myth of CSR: the problem with assuming that companies can do well while also doing good is that markets don't really work that way', *Stanford Social Innovation Review*, Fall, pp 23–29.

Dobb M.H. 1973, *Theories of value and distribution since Adam Smith; ideology and economic theory*, Cambridge University Press, Cambridge.

Doherty B., Davies I.A., and Tranchell S. 2013, 'Where now for fair trade?', *Business History*, vol. 55, no. 2, pp 161–189.

Dolan C. and Humphrey J. 2004, 'Changing governance patterns in the trade in fresh vegetables between Africa and the United Kingdom', *Environment and Planning A*, vol. 36, no. 3, pp 491–509.

Dolan C.S. and Opondo M. 2005, 'Seeking common ground', *Journal of Corporate Citizenship*, no. 18, Summer, pp 87–98.

Donaldson T. 1989, *The ethics of international business*, Oxford University Press, New York.

Donaldson T. 2003, 'Ethics away from home', in Thomas D.C. (ed.), *Readings and cases in international management: a cross-cultural perspective*, SAGE Publications, Thousand Oaks, CA, pp 133–140.

Donaldson T. and Dunfee T.W. 1999, *Ties that bind: a social contracts approach to business ethics*, Harvard Business School Press, Boston, MA.

Donaldson T. and Gini A. 1996, *Case studies in business ethics* (4th edn), Prentice Hall, Upper Saddle River, NJ.

Donaldson T., Werhane P.H., and Cording M. 2002, *Ethical issues in business: a philosophical approach*, Prentice Hall, Upper Saddle River, NJ.

Donaldson T., Werhane P.H. and Van Zandt J. 2008, *Ethical issues in business: a philosophical approach* (8th edn), Pearson Prentice Hall, Upper Saddle River, NJ.

Donnan, S. 2018, 'Levi Strauss to replace workers with lasers', *Financial Times*, 27 February. Available online at https://www.ft.com/content/b95da4ec-1b75-11e8-aaca-4574d7dabfb6, accessed 28 November 2018.

Doppelt B. 2003, *Leading change towards sustainability: a change-management guide for business, government and civil society*, Greenleaf, Sheffield.

Drayton W. 2002, 'The citizen sector: becoming as entrepreneurial and competitive as business', *California Management Review*, vol. 44, no. 3, pp 120–132.

Drucker P.F. 1946, *Concept of the corporation*, John Day, New York.

DTI 2004, *DTI international CSR strategy consultation*, UK Department for Trade and Industry, London.

Du Cann R. 1993, *The art of the advocate* (revised edn), Penguin, Harmondsworth.

Dunn E. 2004, 'Standards and person-making in east central Europe', in Ong A. and Collier S.J. (eds), *Global assemblages*, Blackwell, New York.

Durkheim E. and Halls W.D. 1984, *The division of labor in society*, Free Press, New York.

Dyllick T. and Hockerts K. 2002, 'Beyond the business case for corporate sustainability', *Business Strategy and the Environment*, vol. 11, no. 2, pp 130–141.

Easterly W.R. 2006, *The white man's burden: why the West's efforts to aid the rest have done so much ill and so little good*, Oxford University Press, Oxford.

Eccles, R.G. and Krzus, M.P. 2014, *The Integrated Reporting Movement: Meaning, Momentum, Motives, and Materiality*, John Wiley and Sons.

Economist 1999, 'The key to industrial capitalism: limited liability', 23 December. Available online at http://www.economist.com/node/347323, accessed 3 October 2018.

Economist, 2004, 'Two-faced capitalism', 22 January. Available online at http://www.economist.com/node/2369912, accessed 3 October 2018.

Economist 2005a, 'The good company', 20 January. Available online at http://www.economist.com/node/3555212, accessed 3 October 2018.

Economist 2005b, 'The union of concerned executives', 20 January. Available online at http://www.economist.com/node/3555194, accessed 3 October 2018.

Economist 2005c, 'The world according to CSR', 20 January. Available online at http://www.economist.com/node/3555272, accessed 3 October 2018.

Economist 2005d, 'Profit and the public good', 20 January. Available online at http://www.economistcom/node/3555259, accessed 3 October 2018.

Economist 2005e, 'The ethics of business', *The Economist*, 20 January. Available online at http://www.economist.com/node/3555286, accessed 3 October 2018.

Economist 2006, 'Macro credit: Muhammad Yunus has won the Nobel peace prize for his role in promoting financial services for the poor', 19 October. Available online at http://www.economist.com/node/8049829, accessed 3 October 2018).

Economist 2007, 'Eco-warriors at the gate', 3 March. Available online at http://www.economist.com/node/8776388, accessed 3 October 2018.

Economist 2008, 'Just good business', 17 January. Available online at http://www.economist.com/node/10491077, accessed 3 October 2018.

Economist 2017, 'America's Department of Commerce imposes a tariff of 292% on Bombardier's C-Series jets', 20 December, Available online at https://www.economist.com/gulliver/2017/12/20/americas-department-of-commerce-imposes-a-tariff-of-292-on-bombardiers-c-series-jets, accessed 3 October 2018.

Economy E. 2004, *The river runs black: the environmental challenge to China's future*, Cornell University Press, Ithaca, NY.

Edwards M. 2010, *Small change: why business won't save the world*, Berrett-Koehler, San Francisco, CA.

Edwards M., Hulme D., and Save the Children Fund 1995, *Non-governmental organisations: performance and accountability: beyond the magic bullet*, Earthscan, London.

Efstathiou J. 2008, 'Carbon trading can raise billions of dollars to save forests', *Independent*, Dublin, 16 April. Available online at https://www.independent.ie/business/technology/carbon-trading-can-raise-billions-of-dollars-to-save-forests-26436189.html, accessed 3 October 2018.

Egbon O., Idemudia U., and Amaeshi K. 2018, 'Shell Nigeria's Global Memorandum of Understanding and corporate-community accountability relations: a critical appraisal', *Accounting, Auditing and Accountability Journal*, vol. 31, no. 1, pp. 51–74.

Ehrenreich B. 2001, *Nickel and dimed: on (not) getting by in America*, Metropolitan Books, New York.

Eisinger J. 2017, *The chickenshit club: why the Justice Department fails to prosecute executives*, Simon and Schuster, New York.

EITI 2005, *Extractive Industries Transparency Initiative source book*, Extractive Industries Transparency Initiative, London.

EIU 2010, *Global trends in sustainability performance management*, Economist Intelligence Unit, London.

Elfstrom G. 2000, 'The ethical responsibilities of multinational corporations: the case of the North American aluminum companies in Jamaica', in Vallis A. (ed.), *Ethics in international affairs*, Rowman and Littlefield, New York, pp 185–200.

Elkington J. 1998, *Cannibals with forks: the triple bottom line of 21st century business*, New Society, Gabriola Island, BC/Stony Creek, CT.

Elkington J. and Hartigan P. 2008, *The power of unreasonable people: how social entrepreneurs create markets that change the world*, Harvard Business School Press, Boston, MA.

Elkington J. and Lee M. 2006, 'It's the economics stupid. Has the corporate responsibility movement lost sight of the big picture?', *Grist Magazine*, 9 May. Available online at http://grist.org/article/lee, accessed 22 November 2018.

Elliott K.A. and Freeman R.B. 2003, *Can labor standards improve under globalization?* Institute for International Economics, Washington, DC.

Ellsworth R.R. 2002, *Leading with purpose: the new corporate realities*, Stanford Business Books, Stanford, CA.

Elson C.M. and Goossen N.J., 2017, 'E. Merrick Dodd and the rise and fall of corporate stakeholder theory'. Available online at https://www.researchgate.net/publication/322064935_E_Merrick_Dodd_and_the_rise_and_fall_of_corporate_stakeholder_theory, accessed 4 October 2018.

Elyachar J. 2012, 'Next practices: knowledge, infrastructure, and public goods at the bottom of the pyramid', *Public Culture*, vol. 24, no. 166, pp 109–129.

Emerson J. 2003, 'The blended value proposition: integrating social and financial returns', *California Management Review*, vol. 45, no. 4, pp 35–51.

Enderle G. 2004, 'Global competition and corporate responsibilities of small and medium-sized enterprises', *Business Ethics*, vol. 13, no. 1, pp 50–63.

Engfeldt L.-G. 2002, 'The road from Stockholm to Johannesburg', *UN Chronicle*, vol. 39, no. 3.

Englander E. and Kaufman A. 2004, 'The end of managerial ideology: from corporate social responsibility to corporate social indifference', *Enterprise and Society*, vol. 5, no. 3, pp 404–450.

Epstein M.J. 2018, *Making sustainability work: best practices in managing and measuring corporate social, environmental and economic impacts*, Routledge, London.

Epstein M.J. and Buhovac A.R., 2017. *Making sustainability work: best practices in managing and measuring corporate social, environmental and economic impacts*, routledge, Abingdon, Oxfordshire.

Epstein M.J. and Yuthas K., 2017. *Measuring and improving social impacts: a guide for nonprofits, companies and impact investors*, Routledge , Abingdon, Oxfordshire..

Ernst & Ernst 1976, *Social responsibility disclosure*, Ernst & Ernst, Cleveland, OH.

Ernst & Young, KPMG, PWC, and House of Mandrag Morgan 1999, *The Copenhagen charter: a management guide to stakeholder reporting*, House of Mandrag Morgan, Copenhagen.

ESRA 2004, *European Sustainability Reporting Awards 2004: report of the judges*, European Sustainability Reporting Association, Paris.

Estes J. 1976, *Social responsibility disclosure*, John Wiley, New York.

Estes R.W. 1975, 'A comprehensive social reporting model', in Seidler L.J. and Seidler L.L. (eds), *Social accounting: theory, issues and cases*, John Wiley, New York.

Estes R.W. 1976, *Corporate social accounting*, John Wiley, New York.

Estes R.W. 1996, *Tyranny of the bottom line: why corporations make good people do bad things*, Berrett-Koehler, San Francisco, CA.

Ethical Corporation 2005a, *The role of the big four in shaping corporate responsibility*, Ethical Corporation, London.

Ethical Corporation 2005b, *Why* The Economist *is wrong about CSR*, Ethical Corporation, London.

Ethical Corporation 2006, *Multi-fibre agreement forum in Bangladesh*, Ethical Corporation, London

Ethical Corporation and Nima Hunter Inc. 2003, *The business of business: managing corporate social responsibility. What business leaders are saying and doing 2002–2007*, Nima Hunter Inc., London.

Ethical Performance 2004, 'Angry critics run boycott over "slow" CSR progress', *Ethical Performance*, July 2004. Available online at http://www.ethicalperformance.com/news/article/2783, accessed 28 November 2018..

Ethical Performance 2005a, 'Firms put on notice as UN Compact gets teeth', *Ethical Performance*, October.

Ethical Performance 2005b, 'The United Nations deserves some credit', *Ethical Performance*, October.

Ethical Performance 2005c, 'Ruggie takes on delicate task of considering UN norms', *Ethical Performance*, October.

Ethical Performance 2006a, 'Caterpillar gets reprieve', *Ethical Performance*, April.

Ethical Performance 2006b, 'Criticisms augur end of "flawed" human rights norms', *Ethical Performance*, April.

Ethical Performance 2006c, 'EC white paper unveils European CSR alliance', *Ethical Performance*, April.

Ethical Performance 2006d, 'Sliding ingloriously down the pole of excellence', *Ethical Performance*, April.

Ethical Performance 2007, 'Facebook generation puts firms in the dock', *Ethical Performance*, November.

Ethical Performance 2008, 'Presenting case studies of corporate social responsibility', *Ethical Performance Best Practice*, Ethical Performance, London.

ETI 1998, *Purpose, principles, programme, membership information*, Ethical Trading Initiative, London.

ETI 1999, *Learning from doing review: a report on company progress in implementing ethical sourcing policies and practices*, Ethical Trading Initiative, London.

ETI 2001, *From good intentions to good practice: annual report 2003*, Ethical Trading Initiative, London.

ETI 2003, *Raising the stakes: annual report 2003*, Ethical Trading Initiative, London.

ETI 2004, *Putting ethics to work: annual report 2003/2004*, Ethical Trading Initiative, London.

ETI 2005a, *Addressing labour practices on Kenyan flower farms: report of ETI involvement 2002–2004*, Ethical Trading Initiative, London.

ETI 2005b, *ETI smallholder guidelines*, Ethical Trading Initiative, London.

ETI 2005c, *Driving change: annual report 2004–2005*, Ethical Trading Initiative, London.

ETI 2005d, *Managing compliance with labour codes at supplier level. A more sustainable way of improving working conditions?*, Ethical Trading Initiative, London.

ETI 2005e, *Moving production: stalling the race to the bottom*, Ethical Trading Initiative, London.

ETI 2006, *Ethical trade: a comprehensive guide for companies*, Ethical Trading Initiative, London.

ETI 2007, *Getting smarter at auditing: tackling the growing crisis in ethical trade auditing*, Ethical Trading Initiative, London.

ETI 2009a, *Marking our first decade: annual review 2007–2008*, Ethical Trading Initiative, London.

ETI 2009b, *ETI impact assessment*, Ethical Trading Initiative, 2009.

Etzion D. and Ferraro F. 2010, 'The role of analogy in the institutionalization of sustainability reporting', *Organization Science*, vol. 21, no. 5, pp 1092–1107.

European Commission 2002, 'Companies face their social responsibilities in Europe and abroad', *Social Agenda No. 3*, Directorate-General for Employment and Social Affairs, European Commission, Brussels.

European Social Investment Forum, 2006, *European SRI Study 2006*, Eurosif, Paris.

Evan W.M. and Freeman R.E. 1988, 'A stakeholder theory of the modern corporation: Kantian capitalism', in Beauchamp T. L. and Bowie N.E. (eds), *Ethical theory and business* (3rd edn), Prentice Hall, Upper Saddle River, NJ, pp 97–106.

Evans E.J. 1983, *The forging of the modern state: early industrial Britain 1783–1870*, Pearson Education, London.

Evers H. and Schrader H. 1994, *The moral economy of trade: ethnicity and developing markets*, Routledge, London.

FAO 2003, *Agriculture, food and water*, Food and Agriculture Organisation, Rome.

Farman J.C., Gardiner B.G. and Shanklin J.D. 1985, 'Large losses of total ozone in Antarctica reveal seasonal ClOx/NOx interaction', *Nature*, vol. 315, pp 207–210.

Farmer R.N. and Hogue W.D. 1985, *Corporate social responsibility*, Lexington Books, Lexington, MA.

Feldberg M. 1974, 'Defining social responsibility', *Long Range Planning*, vol. 7, pp 39–44.

Felix D. 1995, *Biography of an idea: John Maynard Keynes and the general theory of employment, interest and money*, Transaction, New Brunswick, NJ.

Ferguson C. 1998, *A review of UK company codes of conduct*, Department for International Development, London, August 1998.

Ferguson C. 1999, *Global social policy principles: human rights and social justice*. Available online at https://books.google.co.uk/books/about/Global_Social_Policy_Principles.html?id=6M7UNAAACAAJ&redir_esc=y, accessed 6 December 2018.

Ferguson I. 2003, *Corporate timelines*. Available online at http://www.openDemocracy.net, accessed 22 November 2018.

Ferguson J. 1990, *The anti-politics machine: 'development', depoliticization, and bureaucratic power in Lesotho*, Cambridge University Press, Cambridge.

Ferguson N. 2003, *Empire: how Britain made the modern world*, Allen Lane, London.

Fig D. 2005, 'Manufacturing amnesia: corporate social responsibility in South Africa', *International Affairs*, vol. 81, no. 3, pp 599–618.

Fig D. 2007, *Corporations and moral purpose: South Africa's Truth and Reconciliation Commission and business responsibility for apartheid*, BDS Working Paper 3, Copenhagen Business School, Copenhagen.

Fitzpatrick M. 2004, 'Business case for sustainability: finding a new state of equilibrium', Keynote address, Green Chemistry and Engineering Conference, Washington DC, 29 June 2004.

Fleming P. and Jones M.T. 2013, *The end of corporate social responsibility: crisis and critique*, SAGE Publications, London.

Foer F. 2004, *How soccer explains the world: an unlikely theory of globalization*, HarperCollins, New York.

Forum for the Future 2006, *Clean capital: financing clean technology firms in the UK*, Forum for the Future, London.

Foster R.N. and Kaplan S. 2001, *Creative destruction: why companies that are built to last underperform the market, and how to successfully transform them*, Currency/Doubleday, New York.

Fourie A. and Eloff T. 2005, 'The case for collective business action to achieve systems change: exploring the contributions made by the private sector to the social, economic and political transformation process in South Africa', *Journal of Corporate Citizenship*, no. 18, Summer, pp 39–48.

Fowler A. 2000, 'NGDOs as a moment in history: beyond aid to social entrepreneurship or civic innovation?', *Third World Quarterly*, vol. 21, no. 4, pp 637-654.

Fox Gorte J. 2008, 'Investors: a force for sustainability', in Krosinsky C. and Robins N. (eds), *Sustainable investing: the art of long-term performance*, Earthscan, London, pp 31–40.

Fox T. and Prescott D. 2004, 'Exploring the role of development cooperation agencies in corporate responsibility', presented at Conference on Development Cooperation and Corporate Social Responsibility, Stockholm, 22–23 March 2004.

Frangos, A. 2017, 'Airbus has trouble in the cockpit, *Wall Street Journal*, 15 December. Available online at https://www.wsj.com/articles/airbus-has-trouble-in-the-cockpit-1513345428, accessed 28 November 2018.

Frank A.G. 1979, *Dependent accumulation and underdevelopment*, Monthly Review Press, New York.

Frank, M., Roehrig P. and Pring B. 2017, *What to do when machines do everything: how to get ahead in a world of AI, algorithms, bots, and big data*, Wiley, Chichester.

Frankfurt School-UNEP Centre 2017, *Global trends in renewable energy investment 2017*, Frankfurt School-UNEP Centre, Frankfurt.

Fankhauser S., Bowen A., Calel R., Dechezleprêtre A., Grover D., Rydge J., and Sato M. 2013, 'Who will win the green race? In search of environmental competitiveness and innovation', *Global Environmental Change*, vol. 23, no. 5, pp. 902-913.

Fransen L. and Burgoon B. 2017, 'Introduction to the Special Issue: public and private labor standards policy in the global economy', *Global Policy*, vol. 8, pp 5–14.

Franks J.R. and Mayer C. 2017, 'Evolution of ownership and control around the world: the changing face of capitalism', Saïd Business School Research Papers. Available online at http://eureka.sbs.ox.ac.uk/6414/1/2017-08.pdf, accessed 4 October 2018.

FRC 2012, *The UK Corporate Governance Code*, Financial Reporting Council, London.

FRC 2016, *UK Corporate Governance Code*, Financial Reporting Council, London.

Frederick W.C. 1960, 'The growing concern over business responsibility', *California Management Review*, vol. 2, no. 4, pp 54–61.

Frederick W.C. 1995, *Values, nature, and culture in the American corporation*, Oxford University Press, New York.

Frederick W.C. 2006, *Corporation be good! The story of corporate social responsibility*, Dog Ear Publishing, Indianapolis, IN.

Freeman D. 2003, 'Homeworkers in global supply chains', *Greener Management International*, vol. 43, pp 107–118.

Freeman R.E. 1984, *Strategic management: a stakeholder approach*, Pitman, Boston, MA.

Freeman R.E. 2010, *Strategic management: a stakeholder approach*, Cambridge University Press, New York.

Freeman R.E. 2017, 'Five challenges to stakeholder theory: a report on research in progress', in Wasieleski D.M. and Weber J. (eds), *Stakeholder management*. Emerald Publishing, Bingley, West Yorkshire, pp 1–20.

Freeman R.E., Pierce J., and Dodd R. 2000, *Environmentalism and the new logic of business*, Oxford University Press, Oxford.

French P.A. 1984, *Collective and corporate responsibility*, Columbia University Press, New York.

Friede, G., Busch, T. and Bassen, A., 2015. 'ESG and financial performance: aggregated evidence from more than 2000 empirical studies', *Journal of Sustainable Finance and Investment*, vol. 5, no. 4, pp 210–233.

Friedman A.L. and Miles S. 2001, 'Socially responsible investment and corporate social and environmental reporting in the UK: an exploratory study', *British Accounting Review*, vol. 33, pp 523–548.

Friedman M. 1962, *Capitalism and freedom*, University of Chicago Press, Chicago, IL.

Friedman M. and Selden R.T. 1975, *Capitalism and freedom: problems and prospects*, University Press of Virginia, Charlottesville, VA.

Friedman T.L. 2000, *The lexus and the olive tree* (revised), Farrar, Straus & Giroux, New York.

Friedman T.L. 2005, *The world is flat: a brief history of the globalized world in the twenty-first century*, Allen Lane, London.

Friends of the Earth 2005, *Hidden voices: the CBI, corporate lobbying and sustainability*, Friends of the Earth, London.

Frynas J.G. 2005, 'False promises: evidence from multinational oil companies', *International Affairs*, vol. 81, no. 3, pp 581–598.

FT Reporters 2018, Escalating trade war shakes investors, *Financial Times*, 11 July. Available online at https://www.ft.com/content/799c584a-8528-11e8-a29d-73e3d454535d, accessed 22 November 2018.

FTSE4Good 2005, *Impact of new criteria and future direction: 2004–2005 report*, FTSE, London.

Fukuyama F. 1989, 'The end of history', *National History*, Summer, pp 1–18.

Fussler C., Cramer A., and van der Vegt S. (eds) 2004, *Raising the bar: creating value with the United Nations Global Compact*, Greenleaf, Sheffield.

Gabor A. 1999, *The capitalist philosophers: the geniuses of modern business—their lives, times, and ideas*, Times Business, New York.

Gabriel Y. and Lang T. 1995, *The unmanageable consumer: contemporary consumption and its fragmentation*, SAGE Publications, London.

Galbraith J.K. 1952, *American capitalism: the concept of countervailing power*, Houghton Mifflin, Boston, MA.

Galbraith J.K. 1967, *The new industrial state*, Houghton Mifflin, Boston, MA.

Galbraith J.K. 1972, 'The emerging public corporation', *Business and Society Review*, vol. 1, pp 54–56.

Galea C. 2004, *Teaching business sustainability*, Greenleaf, Sheffield.

Gao Y., Gao X., and Zhang X. 2017, 'The 2 °c global temperature target and the evolution of the long-term goal of addressing climate change—from the United Nations Framework Convention on Climate Change to the Paris Agreement', *Engineering*, vol. 3, no. 2 (April), pp 272–278.

Gaol F.L., Kadry S., Taylor M., and Li P.S. (eds), 'Recent trends in social and behaviour sciences: proceedings of the 2nd International Congress on Interdisciplinary Behavior and Social Sciences 2013', (ICIBSoS 2013), Jakarta, Indonesia, 4–5 November 2013.

Gangi F. and D'Angelo E., 2017. '"Make" or "buy" the choice of governance modes for corporate social responsibility projects from a stakeholder management perspective', *International Business Research*, vol. 10, no. 8, p 80.

Gardetti M.Á., and Torres A.L. (eds) 2014, *Sustainable luxury: managing social and environmental performance in iconic brands*, Greenleaf, Sheffield.

Gardner S. 2006, *Pushing business-driven corporate citizenship*. Ethical Corporation, London.

Gascoigne C. 2007, 'Good for the planet, good for profits', *Sunday Times*, London, 28 January. Available online at business.timesonline.co.uk

GE 2005, *Solving big needs: GE corporate citizenship report 2005*, General Electric, Fairfield, CT.

GE 2017, *5 ways companies can weave sustainability into their DNA*, GE online report. Available online at https://www.ge.com/reports/5-ways-companies-can-weave-sustainability-dna, accessed 22 November 2018).

GEE 2002, *Corporate social responsibility monitor*, GEE, London.

Geertz C. 1963, *Peddlers and princes; social change and economic modernization in two Indonesian towns*, University of Chicago Press, Chicago, IL.

Geisst C.R. 2004, *Wall Street: a history: from its beginnings to the fall of Enron* (revised edn), Oxford University Press, Oxford.

Gereffi G., Humphrey J., and Sturgeon T. 2005, 'The governance of global value chains', *Review of International Political Economy*, vol. 12, no. 1, pp 78–104.

Germain R.D. 2000, *Globalization and its critics: perspectives from political economy*, Palgrave Macmillan, Basingstoke.

Ghazali B.H. and Simula M. 1996, *Study on the development and formulation and implementation of certification schemes for all internationally traded timber and timber products*, International Timber Trade Organisation, Manila.

Ghemawat P. 2011, *World 3.0: Global prosperity and how to achieve it*, Harvard Business Review Press, Boston, MA.

Gibb F., and Webster P. 2008, 'High Court rules that the halt to BAE investigation was "unlawful, a threat to British justice"', *The Times*, 11 April. Available at https://www.thetimes.co.uk/article/high-court-rules-that-the-halt-to-bae-investigation-was-unlawful-a-threat-to-british-justice-tq9bxnzkcsw, accessed 4 October 2018.

Gibson K. 2000, 'The moral basis of stakeholder theory', *Journal of Business Ethics*, vol. 26, pp 245–257.

Giddens A. 1990, *The consequences of modernity*, Stanford University Press, Stanford, CA.

Giddens A. 1991, *Modernity and self-identity: self and society in the late modern age*, Stanford University Press, Stanford, CA.

Giddens A. 1994, *Beyond left and right: the future of radical politics*, Polity Press, Cambridge.

Giddens A. 2000, *The third way and its critics*, Polity Press, Cambridge.

Giddens A. and Hutton W. 2000, *On the edge: living with global capitalism*, Jonathan Cape, London.

GIIN 2017, *Evidence on the Financial Performance of Impact Investments*, Global Impact Investing Network.

Gillon R. and Lloyd A. 1994, *Principles of health care ethics*, John Wiley, Chichester.

Gilpin R. and Gilpin J.M. 1987, *The political economy of international relations*, Princeton University Press, Princeton, NJ.

Ginsberg T. 2005, 'Threats to critics of Vioxx alleged', *Philadelphia Inquirer*, 5 June, p A01.

Glasbeek H.J. 2002, *Wealth by stealth: corporate crime, corporate law, and the perversion of democracy*, Between the Lines, Toronto.

Gleick P.H. 1999, *The world's water 1998–1999: the biennial report on freshwater resources*, Island Press, Washington, DC.

Global Reporting Initiative, 2007, 'The G8 encourage GRI reporting to promote development and support investors'. Press release, 8 June, Amsterdam.

Glover D. 2007, 'Monsanto and smallholder farmers: a case study in CSR', *Third World Quarterly*, vol. 28, no. 4, pp 851–867.

Godfrey A., Huane K., Liying L., Witchalls B., and Yambayamba E. 2005, 'Findings from a learning partnership', *Partnership Matters*, vol. 3, pp 37–39.

Goffee R. and Scase R. 1995, *Corporate realities: the dynamics of large and small organisations*, Thomson Learning EMEA, London.

Goldacre B. 2012, *Bad pharma: how drug companies mislead doctors and harm patients*, Fourth Estate, London.

Goodijk R. 2000, 'Corporate governance and workers' participation', *Corporate Governance*, vol. 8, no. 8, pp 303–310.

Goodpaster K.E. 2002, 'Stakeholder thinking: beyond paradox to practicality', in Andriof J., Waddock S.A., Husted B., and Rahman S.S. (eds), *Unfolding stakeholder thinking: theory, responsibility and engagement*, Greenleaf, Sheffield, pp 43–64.

Gordon, R.J. 2016, *The rise and fall of American growth: The US standard of living since the civil war*, Princeton University Press, Princeton, NJ.

Gore A. 2006, *An inconvenient truth*, Bloomsbury, London.

Gore A. and Blood D. 2012, 'A manifesto for sustainable capitalism with commentary', *Sustainability*, vol. 5, no. 2, pp 66–69.

Goyal S., Sergi B.S. and Kapoor A., 2017. Emerging role of for-profit social enterprises at the base of the pyramid: the case of Selco. *Journal of Management Development*, vol. 36, no. 1, pp 97–108.

Graham D. and Woods N. 2006, 'Making corporate self-regulation effective in developing countries', *World Development*, vol. 34, no. 5, pp 868–883.

Grande C. 2007, 'Ethical consumption makes mark on branding', *Financial Times*, London, 20 February. Available online at http://www.ft.com, accessed 22 November 2018.

Grappi S., Romani S., and Bagozzi R.P. 2013, 'Consumer response to corporate irresponsible behavior: moral emotions and virtues', *Journal of Business Research*, vol. 66, no. 10, pp 1814–1821.

Gray R.H. 1996, *Accounting and accountability: changes and challenges in corporate social and environmental reporting*, Prentice Hall, London.

Gray R. 2001, *Accounting for the environment* (2nd edn), SAGE Publications, London.

Gray R. 2002a, 'The social accounting project and accounting organizations and society. Privileging engagement, imaginings, new accountings and pragmatism over critique?', *Accounting, Organizations and Society*, vol. 27, no. 7, pp 687–708.

Gray R. 2002b, 'Of messines, systems and sustainability: towards a more social and environmental finance and accounting', *British Accounting Review*, vol. 34, no. 4, pp 357–386.

Gray R.H. 2003, *Social and environmental accounting and reporting. From ridicule to revolution? From hope to hubris?*, Centre for Social and Environmental Accounting Research, University of St Andrews.

Gray R.H. 2006a, 'Does sustainability reporting improve corporate behaviour? Wrong question? Right time?', *Accounting and Business Research*, vol. 36, suppl. 1, pp 65–88.

Gray R.H. 2006b, 'Social, environmental and sustainability reporting and organisational value creation. Whose value? Whose creation?', *Accounting, Auditing and Accountability Journal*, vol. 19, no. 6, pp 793–819.

Gray R.H. and Bebbington K.J. 2000, 'Environmental accounting, managerialism and sustainability. Is the planet safe in the hands of business and accounting?', *Advances in Environmental Accounting and Management*, vol. 1, pp 1–44.

Gray R.H., Owen D., and Maunders K. 1987, *Corporate social reporting*, Prentice Hall, Upper Saddle River, NJ.

Gray R.H., Kouhy R., and Lavers S. 1995a, 'Constructing a research database of social and environmental reporting by UK companies: a methodological note', *Accounting, Auditing and Accountability Journal*, vol. 8, no. 2, pp 78–101.

Gray R.H., Kouhy R., and Lavers S. 1995b, 'Corporate social and environmental reporting: a review of the literature and a longitudinal study of UK disclosure', *Accounting, Auditing and Accountability Journal*, vol. 8, no. 2, pp 47–77.

Gray R.H., Kouhy R. and Lavers S. 1996a, 'Corporate social and environmental reporting: a review of the literature and a longitudinal study of UK disclosure', *Accounting Auditing and Accountability Journal*, vol. 8, no. 2, pp 47–77.

Gray R.H., Owen D., and Adams C. 1996b, *Accounting and accountability: changes and challenges in corporate social and environmental reporting*, Prentice Hall, London.

Gray R.H., Javad M., Power D.M., and Sinclair C.D. 2001, 'Social and environmental disclosure and corporate characteristics: a research note and extension', *Journal of Business Finance and Accounting*, vol. 28, no. 3–4, pp 327–356.

Gray R.H., Dillard J., and Spence C. 2009, 'Social accounting as if the world matters: towards absurdia and a new postalgia', *Public Management Review*, vol. 11, no. 5, pp 545–573.

Gray R.H., Owen D., and Adams C. 2010, 'Some theories for social accounting? A review essay and a tentative pedagogic categorization of theorizations around social accounting', in Freedman M. and Jaggi B. (eds), *Sustainability, environmental performance and disclosures*, Emerald Group, Bingley, West Yorkshire.

Grayson D. and Dodd T. 2007, *Small is sustainable (and beautiful!): encouraging European smaller enterprises to be sustainable*, Doughty Centre for Corporate Responsibility, Cranfield.

Grayson D. and Hodges A. 2004, *Corporate social opportunity: seven steps to make corporate social responsibility work for your business*, Greenleaf, Sheffield.

Grayson, D. and Hodges, A. (2017). *Corporate social opportunity!*, London: Routledge.

Grayson D. and Nelson J. 2013, *Corporate responsibility coalitions: the past, present, and future of alliances for sustainable capitalism*, Stanford University Press, Stanford, CA.

Grecco C, 2007, 'The Bovespa social stock exchange', in Koch-Weser M. and Jacobs W. (eds), *Financing the future: innovative funding mechanisms at work*, Terra Media Verlag, Berlin.

Green S. 2009, *Good value: reflections on money, morality and an uncertain world*, Allen Lane, London.

Greenbury S.R. 1995. *Directors' remuneration: report of a study group chaired by Sir Richard Greenbury*, Gee, London.

Greenfield K. 2006, *The failure of corporate law: fundamental flaws and progressive possibilities*, University of Chicago Press, Chicago, IL.

Greenfield K. 2008 'Reclaiming corporate law in a new gilded age', *Harvard Law and Policy Review*, vol. 2, pp 1–32.

Gregoriou, G.N., Micocci, M., and Masala, G.B., (eds) 2017, *Pension fund risk management: financial and actuarial modeling*, Chapman and Hall/CRC Finance Series.

Gregory A., Matatko J., and Luther R. 1997, 'Ethical unit trust financial performance: small company effects and fund size effects', *Journal of Business Finance and Accounting*, vol. 24, pp 705–725.

Gregory C.A. 1982, *Gifts and commodities*, Academic Press, New York.

Greider W. 1997, *One world, ready or not: the manic logic of global capitalism*, Simon and Schuster, New York.

Greider W. 2003, *The soul of capitalism: opening paths to a moral economy*, Simon and Schuster, New York.

Greider W., 2006, 'The future is now', *The Nation*, 26 June, pp 23–26.

GRI 2002, *Sustainability reporting guidelines*, Global Reporting Initiative, Boston, MA.

Gribben C. and Olsen L. 2004, *An anchor—not the answer: trends in social and sustainable development reporting*, Ashridge Centre for Business and Society, Berkhamsted, Hertfordshire.

Griesgraber J.M. and Gunter B.G. 1997, *World trade: toward a fair and free trade in the twenty-first century*, Pluto Press, London.

Griffin J.J. and Mahon J.F. 1997, 'The corporate social performance and corporate financial performance debate: twenty-five years of incomparable research', *Business and Society*, vol. 36, no. 1, pp 5–31.

Grinspun R. and Cameron M.A. 1993, *The political economy of North American free trade*, St Martin's Press, New York.

Gröschl S., Gabaldón P., and Hahn T. 2017, 'The co-evolution of leaders' cognitive complexity and corporate sustainability: the case of the CEO of Puma', *Journal of Business Ethics*, pp 1–22. DOI: 10.1007/s10551-017-3508-4.

Grosser K. and Moon J. 2005, 'Gender mainstreaming and corporate social responsibility: reporting workplace issues', *Journal of Business Ethics*, vol. 62, no. 4, pp 327–340.

Grubb M., Thompson K., and Sullivan F. 1993, *The Earth Summit agreements: a guide and assessment*, Earthscan, London.

Gunther M. 2008, 'Merrill Lynch's carbon bet. Why a Wall Street firm wants to save a forest in Sumatra', *Fortune*, 18 April. Available online at http://archive.fortune.com/2008/04/17/technology/carbon_farming.fortune/index.htm, accessed 6 December 2018.

Guo B. 2009, 'Social progress and challenges: building a comprehensive strategy for China's environmental clean-up', *China Currents*, vol. 8, no.2.

Guthrie J. and Parker L.D. 1989, 'Corporate social reporting: a rebuttal of legitimacy theory', *Accounting and Business Research*, vol. 19, pp 343–352.

Habisch A., Jonker J., Wegner M., and Schmidpeter R. (eds) 2005, *Corporate social responsibility across Europe*, Springer, New York.

Hale A. and Shaw L.M. 2001, 'Women workers and the promise of ethical trade in the globalised garment industry: a serious beginning?', *Antipode*, vol. 33, no. 3, pp 510–530.

Hale B. 2009, 'Oxfam is the new Tesco say angry independent bookshops being driven to the wall by charity shop's growth', *Daily Mail*, London, 4 August. Available online at http://www.dailymail.co.uk, accessed 22 November 2018.

Hale T. and Held D. (eds) 2018. *The handbook of transnational governance: institutions and innovations*, John Wiley & Sons, Chichester.

Hamann R. 2004, 'Kelian Equatorial Mining: mine closure', in Warner M. and Sullivan R. (eds), *Putting partnerships to work*, Greenleaf, Sheffield, pp 138–150.

Hamann R. and Boulogne F. 2008, 'Partnerships and cross-sector collaboration', in Hamann R. (ed.), *The business of sustainable development in Africa: human rights, partnerships, alternative business models*, Unisa Press, Pretoria, pp 54–82.

Hamann R., Agbazue T., Kapelus P., and Hein A. 2005, 'Universalizing corporate social responsibility? South African challenges to the international organization for standardization's new social responsibility standard', *Business and Society Review*, vol. 110, no. 1, pp 1–19.

Hamann R., Sinha P., Kapfudzaruwa F., and Schild C. 2009a, 'Business and human rights in South Africa: an analysis of antecedents of human rights due diligence', *Journal of Business Ethics*, vol. 87, no. 2, pp 453–473.

Hamann R., Woolman S., and Sprague C. 2009b, *The business of sustainable development in Africa: human rights, partnerships, alternative business models*, Unisa Press, Pretoria.

Hammond A.L., Kramer W.J., Katz R.S., Tran J.T., and Walker C. 2007, *The next four billion: market size and business strategy at the base of the pyramid*, International Finance Corporation/World Resources Institute, Washington, DC.

Hampden-Turner C. and Trompenaars A. 1993, *The seven cultures of capitalism: value systems for creating wealth in the United States, Japan, Germany, France, Britain, Sweden, and the Netherlands*, Currency/Doubleday, New York.

Hampel S. R. 1998, *Committee on Corporate Governance: final report*, Gee, London.

Handy C. 2002, 'What's a business for?', *Harvard Business Review*, December, pp 49–55.

Handy C.B. 1998, *The hungry spirit. Beyond capitalism: a quest for purpose in the modern world*, Broadway Books, New York.

Hannerz U. 1996, *Transnational connections: culture, people, places*, Routledge, London.

Hardt M. and Negri A. 2000, *Empire*, Harvard University Press, Cambridge, MA.

Harris D.L. and Twomey D.F. 2010, 'The enterprise perspective: a new mind-set for competitiveness and sustainability', *Competitiveness Review*, vol. 20, no. 3, pp 258–266.

Harrison A. and Scorse, J. 2004, *Moving up or moving out? Anti-sweatshop activists and labor market outcomes*. National Bureaus of Economic Research, Washington, DC.

Harrison R. 1964, *Animal machines*, Vincent Stuart, London.

Harrison R., Newholm T., and Shaw D. 2005, *The ethical consumer*, SAGE Publications, London.

Hart S.L. 2005, *Capitalism at the crossroads: the unlimited business opportunities in solving the world's most difficult problems*, Prentice Hall, Upper Saddle River, NJ.

Hart S.L. and Christensen C.M. 2002, 'The great leap: driving innovation from the base of the pyramid', *Sloan Management Review*, vol. 44, no. 1, pp 51–56.

Hartman L.P., Shaw B., and Stevenson R. 2003, 'Exploring the ethics and economics of global labor standards: a challenge to integrated social contract theory', *Business Ethics Quarterly*, vol. 13, no. 2, pp 193–220.

Harvey-Jones J. 1988, *Making it happen: reflections on leadership*, Collins, London.

Harwood I. and Humby S. 2008, 'Embedding corporate responsibility into supply: a snapshot of progress', *European Management Journal*, vol. 26, no. 3, pp 166–174.

Hasseldine J., Salama A.I., and Toms J.S. 2005, 'Quantity versus quality: the impact of environmental disclosures on the reputations of UK PLCs', *British Accounting Review*, vol. 37, no. 2, pp 231–248.

Haugh H. 2006, 'Social enterprise: beyond economic outcomes and individual returns', in Mair J., Robinson J., and Hockerts K. (eds), *Social entrepreneurship*, Palgrave Macmillan, Basingstoke, pp 180–206.

Hawken P. 1993, *The ecology of commerce: a declaration of sustainability*, HarperCollins, New York.

Hawken P. 2004, *Socially responsible investing. How the SRI industry has failed to respond to people who want to invest with conscience and what can be done to change it*, Natural Capital Institute, Sausalito, CA.

Hawken P., Lovins A.B., and Lovins L.H. 1999, *Natural capitalism: creating the next industrial revolution*, Little, Brown, Boston, MA.

Hawkins D. 2006, *Corporate social responsibility: balancing tomorrow's sustainability and today's profitability*, Palgrave Macmillan, Basingstoke.

Headd B. 2000, 'The characteristics of small-business employees', *Monthly Labor Review*, vol. 123, no. 4, pp 13–18.

Heal G.M. 2008, *When principles pay: corporate social responsibility and the bottom line*, Columbia Business School, New York.

Heald M. 1970, *The social responsibilities of business, company, and community, 1900–1960*, Case Western Reserve University Press, Cleveland, OH.

Hebrew Union College-Jewish Institute of Religion 1980, *Ethics and corporate responsibility*, Hebrew Union College-Jewish Institute of Religion, Cincinnati, OH.

Held D. and McGrew A.G. 2003, *The global transformations reader: an introduction to the globalization debate* (2nd edn), Polity Press, Cambridge.

Hemingway C.A. and MacLagan P.W. 2004, 'Managers' personal values as drivers of corporate social responsibility', *Journal of Business Ethics*, vol. 50, no. 1, pp 33–44.

Hemp P. and Stewart T. 2004, 'Leading change when business is good', *Harvard Business Review*, vol. 82, no. 12, pp 61–70.

Henderson D. 2001, *Misguided virtue: false notions of corporate social responsibility*, Institute of Economic Affairs, London.

Henderson D. 2004, *The role of business in the modern world*, Institute of Economic Affairs, London.

Hennigfeld J., Pohl M., and Tolhurst N. 2006, *The ICCA handbook on corporate social responsibility*, John Wiley, Chichester.

Henriques A. 2010, *Corporate impact: measuring and managing your social footprint*, Earthscan, London.

Henriques A. and Richardson J.A. 2004, *The triple bottom line, does it all add up? Assessing the sustainability of business and CSR*, Earthscan, London.

Hermes N. and Lensink R. 2011, 'Microfinance: its impact, outreach, and sustainability', *World Development*, vol. 39, no. 6, pp 875–881.

Herrera M.E. 2012, *Towards strategic CSR: aligning CSR with the business and embedding CSR into the organization (a manual for practitioners)*, Asian Institute of Management, Makati, Philippines.

Hertz N. 2001, *The silent takeover: global capitalism and the death of democracy*, Heinemann, London.

Hesse A. 2006, *Sustained added value*, Deloitte and German Federal Ministry of the Environment, Bonn.

Higgs D. 2003, *Review of the role and effectiveness of non-executive directors*, DTI, London.

Hill P. 1970, *Studies in rural capitalism in West Africa*, Cambridge University Press, Cambridge.

Hillary R. 2000a, *ISO 14001: case studies and practical experiences*, Greenleaf, Sheffield.

Hillary R. 2000b, *The risk society and beyond: critical issues for social theory*, SAGE Publications, London.

Hinrichsen D. 1987, *Our common future: a reader's guide*, Earthscan, London.

Hirst P.Q. and Thompson G. 1999, *Globalization in question: the international economy and the possibilities of governance*, Polity Press, Cambridge.

Hogner R.H. 1982, 'Corporate social reporting: eight decades of development at US Steel', *Research in Corporate Social Performance and Policy*, vol. 4, pp 243–250.

Holbeche, L. 2018, *The agile organization: how to build an innovative, sustainable and resilient business*, Kogan Page, London.

Hollender J. and Breen B. 2010, *The responsibility revolution: how the next generation of businesses will win*, Jossey-Bass, San Francisco, CA.

Holliday C.O., Schmidheiny S., Watts P., and World Business Council for Sustainable Development 2002, *Walking the talk: the business case for sustainable development*, Greenleaf, Sheffield.

Holliday I. 2005, 'Doing business with rights violating regimes: corporate social responsibility and Myanmar's military junta', *Journal of Business Ethics*, vol. 61, no. 4, pp 329–342.

Holpuch A. 2013, 'Google's Eric Schmidt says government spying is "the nature of our society" ', *Guardian*, London, 13 September. Available online at http://www.theguardian.com, accessed 22 November 2018.

Hoogvelt A.M.M. 2001, *Globalization and the postcolonial world: the new political economy of development*, Johns Hopkins University Press, Baltimore, MD.

Hopkins K. 2009, ' "Public must learn to tolerate the inequality of bonuses", says Goldman Sachs vice-chairman', *Guardian*, 21 October. Available online at https://www.theguardian.com/business/2009/oct/21/executive-pay-bonuses-goldmansachs, accessed 4 October 2018.

Hopkins M. 2003, *The planetary bargain: corporate social responsibility matters*, Earthscan, London.

House of Commons 1999, *House of Commons Select Committee on Trade and Industry. Sixth report: ethical trading*, House of Commons, London.

Howard, B. 2016, *Financial regulator FCA denies 'going soft' on banks*, BBC, London.

HSBC Global Research 2012, *Coal and carbon-stranded assets: assessing the risk*, HSBC, London.

Huang H.H., Sun L., and Tong R.Y. 2017, 'Are socially responsible firms less likely to expatriate? An examination of corporate inversions', *Journal of the American Taxation Association*, vol. 39, no. 2, Fall, pp 43–62.

Hudson W.H. 1996, *An introduction to the philosophy of Herbert Spencer*, Routledge/Thoemmes, London.

Hughes N. and Lonie S. 2007, 'M-Pesa: mobile money for the "unbanked"—turning cellphones into 24-hour tellers in Kenya', *Innovations*, vol. 2, no. 1-2, pp 63–81.

Hughes P. and Demetrious K. 2006, 'Engaging with stakeholders or constructing them?', *Journal of Corporate Citizenship*, no. 23, Autumn, pp 93–101.

Humphrey J. and Schmitz H. 2001, 'Governance in global value chains', *IDS Bulletin*, vol. 32, no. 3, pp 19–29.

Huntington S.P. 1996, *The clash of civilizations and the remaking of world order*, Simon and Schuster, New York.

Husain, S. and Lund-Thomsen, P. 2015, 'CSR and sexual and reproductive health: a case study among women workers in the football manufacturing industry of Sialkot, Pakistan', in Blowfield, M., Karam, C., and Jamali, D. (eds), *Development-oriented corporate social responsibility. volume 1, multinational corporations and the global context*, Greenleaf, Sheffield, pp. 189–202.

Husted B. 2011, *Corporate social strategy: stakeholder engagement and competitive advantage*, Cambridge University Press, Cambridge.

Hutton W. 1995. *The state we're in*, Jonathan Cape, London.

Hutton W. and Giddens A. 2000, *Global capitalism*, New Press, New York.

Ibrahim S., Jamali D., and Karatas-Ozkan M. 2012, 'Corporate social responsibility (CSR) in small and medium-sized enterprises: a developing country perspective', *Contemporary Issues in Entrepreneurship Research*, vol. 2, pp 167–192.

ICC 2000, *The business charter for sustainable development*, International Chamber of Commerce, Paris.

ICGN 2009, *ICGN Global Corporate Governance principles: revised (2009)*, International Corporate Governance Network, London.

IFAT 2006, *Fair trade in Europe 2005: facts and figures on Fair Trade in 25 European countries*, International Fair Trade Association.

Igalens J. and Gond J. 2005, 'Measuring corporate social performance in France: a critical and empirical analysis of ARESE data', *Journal of Business Ethics*, no. 56, pp 131–148.

IITA and ILO 2002, *Child labour in the cocoa sector of West Africa*, International Institute of Tropical Agriculture and International Labour Organisation, Ibadan.

ILO 1998, *Declaration on fundamental principles and rights at work and its follow-up*, International Labour Organisation, Geneva.

Impactt 2005, *Changing over time: tackling supply chain labour issues through business practice*, Impactt Ltd, London.

Inglis F. 2000, *Clifford Geertz: culture, custom, and ethics*, Polity Press, Cambridge.

Ingram R.W. 1978, 'The investigation of the information content of (certain) social responsibility disclosures', *Journal of Accounting Research*, vol. 16, no. 2, pp 270–285.

Innovest 2005, *Intangible value assessment: Swiss Reinsurance Company*, Innovest Strategic Value Advisors, London.

Innovest and Environment Agency 2004, *Corporate environmental governance: a study into the influence of environmental governance on financial performance*, Environment Agency, London.

INSEAD 2007, *RESPONSE: Understanding and responding to societal demands on corporate responsibility*, INSEAD, Brussels.

Institutional Shareholders' Committee 2005, *The responsibilities of institutional shareholders and agents—statement of principles*. Available online at http://www.ecgi.org/codes/documents/isc_statement_of_principles.pdf, accessed 4 October 2018.

Investopedia nd, 'Community investing'. Available online at https://www.investopedia.com/terms/c/community_investing.asp, accessed 3 October 2018.

International Association of Engineers 2013, *IAENG transactions on engineering sciences: special issue of the International MultiConference of Engineers and Computer Scientists 2013 and World Congress on Engineering 2013*, ed. S. Ao, A.H.S. Chan, H. Katagiri, L. Xu, International Association of Engineers, Taiwan.

IPCC 2007, *Fourth assessment report*. WMO/Intergovernmental Panel on Climate Change, Geneva.

IPCC 2013–2014. *Fifth assessment report*. WMO/Intergovenmental Panel on Climate Change, Geneva.

Ireland P. and Pillay R. 2009, 'Corporate social responsibility and the new constitutionalism', presented at the Business, Social Policy and Corporate Political Influence in Developing Countries UNRISD Conference, Geneva, 12-13 November 2007.

ISEA 1999, *Accountability 1000: overview of standard and its applications*, Institute of Social and Ethical Accountability, London.

Ite U.E. 2004, 'Multinationals and corporate social responsibility in developing countries: a case study of Nigeria', *Corporate Social Responsibility and Environmental Management*, vol. 11, no. 1, pp 1–11.

Jack, W. and Suri, T. 2011, *Mobile money: the economics of M-PESA*, NBER Working Paper No. 16721. Available online at http://www.nber.org/papers/w16721, accessed 4 October 2018.

Jacks D.S. 2013, *From boom to bust: a typology of real commodity prices in the long run*, Working Paper 18874, National Bureau of Economic Research, Cambridge, MA.

Jackson I.A. and Nelson J. 2004, *Profits with principles: seven strategies for delivering value with values*, Currency/Doubleday, New York.

Jackson, T. 2011, *Prosperity without growth: economics for a finite planet*, Routledge, London.

Jacoby N.H. 1973, *Corporate power and social responsibility; a blueprint for the future*, Macmillan, New York.

Jacoby S. 2007, 'Principles and agents: CalPERS and corporate governance in Japan', *Corporate Governance*, vol. 15, no. 1, pp 5–15.

Jahdi K.S. and Acikdilli G. 2009, 'Marketing communications and corporate social responsibility (CSR): marriage of convenience or shotgun wedding?', *Journal of Business Ethics*, vol. 88, no. 1, pp 103–113.

Jamali, D. and Carroll, A. 2017, 'Capturing advances in CSR: developed versus developing country perspectives', *Business Ethics*, vol. 26, pp 321–325.

Jamali D. and Mirshak R. 2007, 'Corporate social responsibility (CSR): theory and practice in a developing country context', *Journal of Business Ethics*, vol. 72, no. 3, pp 243–262.

Jamali D., Zanhour M., and Keshishian T. 2009, 'Peculiar strengths and relational attributes of SMEs in the context of CSR', *Journal of Business Ethics*, vol. 87, no. 3, pp 355–377.

Jamali D., Karam C., and Blowfield M. (eds) 2015, *Development-oriented corporate social responsibility. volume 1, multinational corporations and the global context*, Greenleaf, Sheffield.

Jamali, D., Lund-Thomsen, P., and Jeppesen, S. 2017, 'SMEs and CSR in developing countries', *Business and Society*, vol. 56, no. 1, pp. 11–22.

Jamison L. and Murdoch H. 2004, *Taking the temperature: ethical supply chain management*, Institute of Business Ethics, London.

Jenkins H. 2004, 'A critique of conventional CSR theory: an SME perspective', *Journal of General Management*, vol. 29, pp 37–57.

Jenkins H. 2006, 'Small business champions for corporate social responsibility', *Journal of Business Ethics*, vol. 67, no. 3, pp 241–256.

Jenkins H. 2009, 'A "business opportunity" model of corporate social responsibility for small- and medium-sized enterprises', *Business Ethics*, vol. 18, no. 1, pp 21–36.

Jenkins R.O. 1999, 'The changing relationship between emerging markets and multinational enterprises', in Buckley P.J. and Ghauri P.N. (eds), *Multinational enterprises and emerging markets: managing increasing interdependence*, Pergamon Press, Oxford.

Jenkins R.O. 2001, *Corporate codes of conduct: self-regulation in a global economy*, UNRISD, Geneva.

Jenkins R.O. 2002, 'The political economy of codes of conduct', in Jenkins R.O., Pearson R., and Seyfang G. (eds), *Corporate responsibility and labour rights: codes of conduct in the global economy*, Earthscan, London, pp 13–30.

Jenkins R.O. 2005, 'Globalization, corporate social responsibility and poverty', *International Affairs*, vol. 81, no. 3, pp 525-540.

Jenkins R.O., Pearson R., and Seyfang G. (eds) 2002, *Corporate responsibility and labour rights: codes of conduct in the global economy*, Earthscan, London.

Jensen M.C. 1986, 'Agency costs of free cash flow, corporate finance, and takeovers', *American Economic Review*, vol. 76, no. 2, pp 323–329.

Jensen M. C. 2000, *A theory of the firm: governance, residual claims, and organizational forms*, Harvard University Press, Cambridge, MA.

Jensen M. C. 2001. 'Value maximisation, stakeholder theory, and the corporate objective function', *European Financial Management*, vol. 7, no. 3, pp 297–317.

Jensen M.C. and Meckling W.H. 1976, 'Theory of the firm: managerial behavior, agency costs and ownership structure', *Journal of Financial Economics*, vol. 3, no. 4, pp 305–360.

Jeucken M. 2001, *Sustainable finance and banking: the financial sector and the future of the planet*, Earthscan, London.

Jewson Associates 2008. *The costs of ethical investing*, Jewson Associates, London.

John R. 2007, *Beyond the cheque: how venture philanthropists add value*, interim report for Finance for Change, Skoll World Forum, 29 March, Oxford.

Johnson J. 2004, 'Global trends in employment, productivity and poverty', presented at the Conference on Globalization and Labor in Developing Countries, Watson Institute for International Studies, Brown University, 10–11 December 2004.

Johnston D.C. 2003, *Perfectly legal: the covert campaign to rig our tax system to benefit the super rich—and cheat everybody else*, Portfolio, New York.

Jones K.A. 2004, *Who's afraid of the WTO?*, Oxford University Press, Oxford.

Jones L.B. 1995, *Jesus, CEO: using ancient wisdom for visionary leadership*, Hyperion, New York.

Jones O. and Tilley F. 2003, *Competitive advantage in SMEs: organising for innovation and change*, John Wiley, Chichester.

Jonkers J. 2005, 'CSR wonderland: navigating between movement, community and organisation', *Journal of Corporate Citizenship*, no. 20, Winter, pp 19–22.

Kabeer N. 2000, *The power to choose: Bangladeshi women and labour market decisions in London and Dhaka*, Verso, London.

Kadarusman, Y.B., and Herabadi, A.G. 2018, 'Improving sustainable development within Indonesian Palm Oil: the importance of the reward system', *Sustainable Development*, no. 6, pp 422-434.

Kakabadse A.P. 2006, 'Management thinking: making CSR work', *Ethical Corporation*, 20 June. Available online at http://www.ethicalcorp.com, accessed 22 November 2018.

Kamara J. 1986, *Socially responsible investment and economic development*, Division of Research, Michigan School of Business, University of Michigan, Ann Arbor, MI.

Kaminker C. and Stewart F. 2012, *The role of institutional investors in financing clean energy*, OECD, Paris.

Kaminsky J.S. 1995, *Corporate responsibility in the Hebrew Bible*, Sheffield Academic Press, Sheffield.

Kangogo J., Guyo W., Bowen M., and Ragui M. 2013, 'Supply chain disruption in the Kenya floriculture industry: a case study of Equator Flowers', *European Journal of Business and Management*, vol. 5, no. 7, pp 246–253.

Kanter R.M. 1999, 'From spare change to real change: the social sector as beta site for business innovation', *Harvard Business Review*, vol. 77, no. 3, pp 122–132, 210.

Kanter R.M. 2009, *Supercorp: how vanguard companies create innovation, profits, growth, and social good*, Crown Business, New York.

Kaplan R.E.B. and Berenbeim J.M. 2004, *Ethics programs: the role of the board—a global study*, Conference Board, New York.

Kapstein E.B. 2008, *Measuring Unilever's economic footprint: the case of South Africa*, Unilever, London.

Kaptein M. 2004, 'Business codes of multinational firms. What do they say?', *Journal of Business Ethics*, vol. 50, pp 13–31.

Karnani A. 2007, 'The mirage of marketing to the bottom of the pyramid', *California Management Review*, vol. 49, no. 4, pp 90.

Kauffman M. and Chedekel L. 2004, 'As colleges profit, sweatshops worsen', *Hartford Courant*, 12 December.

Kavlianz P. 2009, 'Mattel fined $2.3 million over lead in toys'. Available online at http://www.CNNMoney.com, accessed 4 October 2018.

Kay J. 2012, *The Kay review of UK equity markets and long-term decision making, final report (July)*, Department for Business, Innovation and Skills, London.

Kechiche A. and Soparnot R. 2012, 'CSR within SMEs: literature review', *International Business Research*, vol. 5, no. 7, pp 97–104.

Keefe J.F. 2007, 'From socially responsible investing to sustainable investing', *Green Money Journal*. Available online at https://greenmoneyjournal.com/.

Kell G. 2013, '12 years later: reflections on the growth of the UN Global Compact', *Business and Society*, vol. 52, no. 1, pp 31–52.

Kell G. and Levin D. 2003, 'The Global Compact network: an historic experiment in learning and action', *Business and Society Review*, vol. 108, no. 2, pp 151–181.

Kelly M. 2001, *The divine right of capital: dethroning the corporate aristocracy*, Berrett-Koehler, San Francisco, CA.

Kelly P.J. 1990, *Utilitarianism and distributive justice: Jeremy Bentham and the civil law*, Clarendon Press, Oxford.

Kennedy A. 2000, *The end of shareholder value*, Orion Business, London.

Kennedy P.M. 1987, *The rise and fall of the great powers: economic change and military conflict from 1500 to 2000*, Random House, New York.

Keyes, J. 2014, *BYOD for Healthcare*, CRC Press, Boca Raton, FL.

Khurana R. 2007, *From higher aims to hired hands: the social transformation of American business schools and the unfulfilled promise of management as a profession*, Princeton University Press, Princeton, NJ.

Kiernan M. 2005, 'Sustainable development', in Dallas G. (ed.), *Governance and risk*, McGraw-Hill, New York:

Kilic M. and Kuzey C. 2017, 'Factors influencing sustainability reporting: evidence from Turkey'. DOI: 10.2139/ssrn.3098812.

Killick N. 2004, 'BP and others, Azerbaijan: conflict prevention'; in Warner M. and Sullivan R. (eds), *Putting partnerships to work*, Greenleaf, Sheffield, pp 98–107.

King F., Marcus R., and Fabian T. 2000, *Big business, small hands: responsible approaches to child labour*, Save the Children, London.

Klein, A. 2017, 'Pioneering extractive sector transparency. A PWYP perspective on 15 years of EITI', *The Extractive Industries and Society*, vol. 4, no. 4, pp 771–774.

Klein G.D. 1978, 'Corporate social responsibility: an assessment of the enlightened self-interest model', *Academy of Management Review*, vol. 3, no. 1, pp 32–39.

Klein N. 1999, *No logo: taking aim at the brand bullies*, Picador, New York.

Klein, N. 2015, *This changes everything: Capitalism vs. the climate*. Simon and Schuster, New York.

Klein T.A. 1977, *Social costs and benefits of business*, Prentice-Hall, Englewood Cliffs, NJ.

Klimkiewicz, K. and Oltra, V. 2017, 'Does CSR enhance employer attractiveness? The role of millennial job seekers' attitudes', *Corporate Social Responsibility and Environmental Management*. DOI: 10.1002/csr.1419.

Knights D. and Tinker T. 1997, *Financial institutions and social transformations: international studies of a sector*, St Martin's Press, New York.

Koch C.G. 2015, *Good profit: how creating value for others built one of the world's most successful companies*, Piatkus, London.

Koch K. 1974, *War and peace in Jalémó: the management of conflict in highland New Guinea*, Harvard University Press, Cambridge, MA.

Kolb R.W. 2008, *Encyclopedia of business ethics and society*, SAGE Publications, Thousand Oaks, CA.

Koliba C. 2010, *Governance networks in public administration and public policy [electronic resource]*, CRC Press, Boca Raton, FL.

Kolk A. 2003, 'Trends in sustainability reporting by the Fortune Global 250', *Business Strategy and the Environment*, vol. 12, no. 5, pp 279–291.

Kolk A. 2004, 'A decade of sustainability reporting: developments and significance', *International Journal of Environment and Sustainable Development*, vol. 3, no. 1, pp 51–64.

Kolk A. and Pinkse J. 2010, *The climate change-development nexus and tripartite partnerships*, Working Paper 006, University of Amsterdam Business School.

Kolk A. and van Tulder R. 2002, 'Child labor and multinational conduct: a comparison of international business and stakeholder codes', *Journal of Business Ethics*, vol. 36, no. 3, pp 91–301.

Kolk A. and van Tulder R. 2006, 'Poverty alleviation as business strategy? Evaluating commitments of frontrunner multinational corporations', *World Development*, vol. 34, no. 5, pp 542.

Kolk A., van Tulder R., and Welters C. 1999, 'International codes of conduct and corporate social responsibility: can transnational corporations regulate themselves?', *Transnational Corporations*, vol. 8, no. 1, pp 143–180.

Korten D.C. 1995, *When corporations rule the world*, Kumarian Press, Bloomfield, CT/Berrett-Koehler, San Francisco, CA.

Korten D.C. 1999, *The post-corporate world: life after capitalism*, Berrett-Koehler, San Francisco, CA.

Kourula A. and Halme M. 2008, 'Types of corporate responsibility and engagement with NGOs: an exploration of business and societal outcomes', *Corporate Governance*, vol. 8, no. 4, pp 557–570.

KPMG 1993, *International survey of environmental reporting*, KPMG International, Amsterdam.

KPMG 1996, *International survey of environmental reporting*, KPMG International, Amsterdam.

KPMG 1999, *International survey of environmental reporting*, KPMG International, Amsterdam.

KPMG 2002, *International survey of corporate sustainability reporting 2002*, KPMG International, Amsterdam.

KPMG 2005, *International survey of corporate sustainability reporting 2005*, KPMG International, Amsterdam.

KPMG 2008, *International survey of corporate sustainability reporting 2008*, KPMG International, Amsterdam.

KPMG 2011, *International survey of corporate sustainability reporting 2011*, KPMG International, Amsterdam.

KPMG 2017, *The road ahead: the KPMG Survey of Corporate Responsibility Reporting 2017*, KPMG, London.

Kramer M. and Kania J. 2006, 'Changing the game: leading corporations switch from defense to offense in solving global problems', *Stanford Social Innovation Review*, Spring, pp 20–27.

Krawcheck, S., 2017, *Own it: the power of women at work*, Crown Business, New York.

Kreander N., Gray R., Power D., and Sinclair C. 2002, 'The financial performance of European ethical funds 1996–1998', *Journal of Accounting and Finance*, vol. 1, pp 3–22.

Kreander N., Gray R., Power D., and Sinclair C. 2005, 'Evaluating the performance of ethical and non-ethical funds: a matched pair analysis', *Journal of Business Finance and Accounting*, vol. 32, no. 7–8, pp 1465–1493.

Kreps T.J. and Murphy, K.R. 1940, *Measurement of the social performance of business*, U.S.Government Printing Office, Washington, DC.

Krosinsky C. 2008, 'Sustainable equity investing: the market-beating strategy', in Krosinsky C. and Robins N. (eds), *Sustainable investing: the art of long-term performance*, Earthscan, London, pp 19–30.

Krosinsky C. and Robins N. (eds) 2008, *Sustainable investing: the art of long-term performance*, Earthscan, London.

Krugman P. 1998a, *Why aren't we all Keynesians yet?* Available online at http://web.mit.edu/krugman/wwwkeynes.html, accessed 28 November 2018.

Krugman P. 1998b, *The accidental theorist: and other dispatches from the dismal science*, Norton, New York.

Krumbiegel, K., Maertens, M. and Wollni, M. 2018, 'The role of fairtrade certification for wages and job satisfaction of plantation workers', *World Development*, vol. 102, pp 195–212.

Krumsiek B. 2004, 'Voluntary codes of conduct for multinational corporations: promises and challenges', *Business and Society Review*, vol. 109, no. 4, pp 583–593.

Kuada J. and Hinson R.E. 2012, 'Corporate social responsibility (CSR) practices of foreign and local companies in Ghana', *Thunderbird International Business Review*, vol. 54, no. 4, pp 521–536.

Kukathas C. 1989, *Hayek and modern liberalism*, Clarendon Press, Oxford.

Kuriyan R., Nafus D., and Mainwaring S. 2012, 'Consumption, technology, and development: the "poor" as "consumer" ', *Information Technologies and International Development*, vol. 8, no. 1, pp 1–12.

Kurtenbach E. 2005, 'Chinese sofa factory workers go on strike'. Available online at http://www.globallabourrights.org, accessed 28 November 2018.

Kuzey, C. and Uyar, A. 2017, 'Determinants of sustainability reporting and its impact on firm value: Evidence from the emerging market of Turkey', *Journal of Cleaner Production*, vol. 143, pp 27–39.

Kwan A. and Frost S. 2002, 'Made in China: rules and regulations versus codes of conduct in the toy sector', in Jenkins R.O., Pearson R., and Seyfang G. (eds), *Corporate responsibility and ethical trade: codes of conduct in the global economy*, Earthscan, London, pp 124–134.

Ladbury S., Young G., and Gibbons S. 2000, *Mid-term review of the ETI: a review of the progress of the Ethical Trading Initiative*, Department for International Development, London.

Ladkin D. 2006, 'When deontology and utilitarianism aren't enough: how Heidegger's notion of "dwelling" might help organisational leaders resolve ethical issues', *Journal of Business Ethics*, vol. 65, no. 1, pp 87–98.

LaFeber W. 2002, *Michael Jordan and the new global capitalism* (new edn), W.W. Norton, New York.

Laffer A.B. and Miles M.A. 1982, *International economics in an integrated world*, Scott, Foresman, Glenview, IL.

Lakatos, Z. 2013, *Corporate social performance in emerging markets: sustainable leadership in an interdependent world*, Routledge, New York.

Lamberti L. and Noci G. 2012, 'The relationship between CSR and corporate strategy in medium-sized companies: evidence from Italy', *Business Ethics*, vol. 21, no. 4, pp 402–416.

Lash S. 2002, *Critique of information*, SAGE Publications, London.

Laszlo C. 2003, *The sustainable company: how to create lasting value through social and environmental performance*, Island Press, Washington, DC.

Laszlo E. 2006, *The chaos point: the world at the crossroads*, Hampton Roads Publishing, Charlottesville, VA.

Lawrence A.T., Weber J., and Post J.E. 2005, *Business and society: stakeholders, ethics, public policy* (11th edn), McGraw-Hill, New Yprk.

Leadbeater C. 1997, *The rise of the social entrepreneur*, Demos, London.

Leadbeater C. 2004, *Personalisation through participation: a new script for public services*, Demos, London.

Lee C.K., Kim J.S., and Kim J.S. 2018, 'Impact of a gaming company's CSR on residents' perceived benefits, quality of life, and support', *Tourism Management*, vol. 64, pp 281–290.

Legrand W., Sloan P., and Chen J.S. 2016, *Sustainability in the hospitality industry: principles of sustainable operations*, Routledge, Abingdon, Oxfordshire.

Lehman C. 1992, *Accounting's changing roles in social conflict*, London, Paul Chapman.

Leipziger D. 2001, *SA8000: the definitive guide to the new social standard*, Financial Times/Prentice Hall, Harlow.

Leipziger D. 2010, *The corporate responsibility code book* (2nd edn), Greenleaf, Sheffield.

Lenox M.J. and Nash J. 2003, 'Industry self-regulation and adverse selection: a comparison across four trade association programs', *Business Strategy and the Environment*, vol. 12, no. 6, pp 343–356.

Levy D.L. and Newell P. 2002, 'Business strategy and international environmental governance: toward a neo-Gramscian synthesis', *Global Environmental Politics*, vol. 2, no. 4, pp 84–101.

Levy D.L. and Newell P. 2005, *The business of global environmental governance*, MIT Press, Cambridge, MA.

Lewis M. 2011, *The big short: inside the Doomsday Machine*, Penguin, London.

Lewis N., Parker, L.D., and Sutcliffe, P. 1984, 'Financial reporting to employees: the pattern of development 1919–1979', *Accounting Organizations and Society*, vol. 9, no. 3–4, pp 275–289.

Light A. and Rolston H. 2003, *Environmental ethics: an anthology*, Blackwell, Malden, MA.

Light A. and Smith J.M. 1997, *Space, place, and environmental ethics*, Rowman and Littlefield, Lanham, MD.

Lim A. and Tsutsui K. 2012, 'Globalization and commitment in corporate social responsibility: cross-national analyses of institutional and political-economy effects', *American Sociological Review*, vol. 77, no. 1, pp 69–98.

Lindblom C.K. 1994, 'The implications of organizational legitimacy for corporate social performance and disclosure', paper presented at the Critical Perspectives on Accounting Conference, New York.

Lindberg, S. 2017, 'Encouragement for sustainable pension: A better understanding for sustainability in regards to pension savings', master's thesis, KTH Royal Institute of Technology, Stockholm. Available online at http://www.diva-portal.org/smash/get/diva2:1111203/FULLTEXT01.pdf, accessed 4 October 2018.

Lindgreen A., Kotler P., and Maon F. 2012, *A stakeholder approach to corporate social responsibility: pressures, conflicts, and reconciliation*, Gower, Farnham, Surrey.

Lindgreen, A., Maon, L., Vanhamme, J., Palacios Florencio, B., Strong, C., Vallaster, C., eds. 2018, *Engaging with stakeholders: a relational perspective on responsible business*, Routledge, London.

Lindsay J. 1975, *William Morris: his life and work*, Constable, London.

Lindsey B. 2002, *Against the dead hand: the uncertain struggle for global capitalism*, John Wiley, New York.

Lins K.V., Servaes H., and Tamayo A. 2017, 'Social capital, trust, and firm performance: the value of corporate social responsibility during the financial crisis', *The Journal of Finance*, vol. 72, no. 4, pp 1785–1824.

Little W.G. 2002, *The waste fix: seizures of the sacred from Upton Sinclair to The Sopranos*, Routledge, New York.

Litvin D.B. 2003, *Empires of profit: commerce, conquest and corporate responsibility*, Texere, New York.

Locke R., Fei Q., and Brause A. 2006, *Does monitoring improve labor standards? Lessons from Nike*, Working Paper 4612-06, MIT Sloan School of Management, Cambridge, MA.

Lodge G.C. 2006, *A corporate solution to global poverty: how multinationals can help the poor and invigorate their own legitimacy*, Princeton University Press, Princeton, NJ.

Loftus P. 2009, 'Merck sees $80 million Vioxx settlement', *Wall Street Journal*, New York, 3 August. Available online at http://online.wsj.com, accessed 22 November 2018.

Logan D. 1997, *The case for business action on family planning and AIDS prevention in Ghana*, Corporate Citizenship Company, London.

Logsdon J.M. 2004, 'Global business citizenship: applications to environmental issues', *Business and Society Review*, vol. 109, no. 1, p 67.

London T. and Hart S.L. 2010, *Next generation business strategies for the base of the pyramid: new approaches for building mutual value*, FT Press, Upper Saddle River, NJ.

Long J.C. 2008, 'From cocoa to CSR: finding sustainability in a cup of hot chocolate', *Thunderbird International Business Review*, vol. 50, no. 5, pp 315-320.

Lort-Phillips L, 2006, 'China: one country, two systems', *Corporate Citizenship Briefing*, December/January. Available online at http://www.ccbriefing.co.uk, accessed 22 November 2018.

Louche C. and Lydenberg S.D. 2011, *Dilemmas in responsible investment*, Greenleaf, Sheffield.

Lucas-Lecin V. and Nahal S. 2008, 'Sustainability analysis', in Krosinsky C. and Robins N. (eds), *Sustainable investing: the art of long-term performance*, Earthscan, London, pp 41-56.

Lukes S, 1974, *Power: a radical view*, London: Macmillan.

Lund-Thomsen P. 2005, 'Corporate accountability in South Africa: the role of community mobilizing in environmental governance', *International Affairs*, vol. 81, no. 3, pp 619-634.

Lund-Thomsen P., and Coe N.M. 2013, 'Corporate social responsibility and labour agency: the case of Nike in Pakistan', *Journal of Economic Geography*, vol. 15, no. 2, pp. 275-296.

Lund-Thomsen P. and Lindgreen A. 2013, 'Corporate social responsibility in global value chains: where are we now and where are we going?', *Journal of Business Ethics*, July, pp 1-12.

Lund-Thomsen P., and Lindgreen A. 2018, 'Is there a sweet spot in ethical trade? A critical appraisal of the potential for aligning buyer, supplier and worker interests in global production networks', *Geoforum*, vol. 90, pp. 84-90.

Lund-Thomsen P., Nadvi K., Chan A., Khara N., and Xue H. 2012, 'Labour in global value chains: work conditions in football manufacturing in China, India and Pakistan', *Development and Change*, vol. 43, no. 6, pp 1211-1237.

Lund-Thomsen, P., Lindgreen A., and Vanhamme J. 2016, 'Industrial clusters and corporate social responsibility in developing countries: what we know, what we do not know, and what we need to know', *Journal of Business Ethics*, vol. 133, no. 1, pp. 9-24.

Lussier R.N. and Hendon, J.R. 2012, *Human resource management: functions, applications, and skill development*. SAGE Publications, Thousand Oaks, CA.

Lydenberg S.D. 2005, *Corporations and the public interest: guiding the invisible hand*, Berrett-Koehler Publishers, San Francisco, CA.

Lyon F. 2003, 'Community groups and livelihoods in remote rural areas of Ghana: how small-scale farmers sustain collective action', *Community Development Journal*, vol. 38, no. 4, pp 323-331.

Lyon F. and Bertotti M. 2007, 'Measuring the contributions of small firms to reducing poverty and increasing social inclusion in the UK', in Stoner J.A. and Wankel C. (eds), *Innovative approaches to reducing global poverty*, Information Age Publishing, Charlotte, NC.

Lyon F. and Vickers I. 2009, 'Challenges of encouraging enterprise in deprived areas', in Southern A. (ed.), *Enterprise and deprivation: small business, social exclusion and sustainable communities*, John Wiley, Basingstoke.

Lyon S. and Moberg M. (eds) 2010, *Fair trade and social justice: global ethnographies*, NYU Press, New York.

McCarthy R.J. 2006, 'Venture capitalists flock to green stocks', *Inc.*, 28 March. Available online at http://www.inc.com, accessed 28 November 2018.

McCord N. 1970, *Free trade: theory and practice from Adam Smith to Keynes*, David and Charles, Newton Abbot.

McDonough W. and Braungart M. 2002, *Cradle to cradle: remaking the way we make things*, North Point Press, New York.

McEwan T. 2001, *Managing values and beliefs in organisations*, Financial Times/Prentice Hall, Harlow.

McGee R.W. 1994, *A trade policy for free societies: the case against protectionism*, Quorum Books, Westport, CT.

McGreal C. 2009, 'Revealed: millions spent by lobby firms fighting Obama health reforms', *Guardian*, 1 October. Available online at https://www.theguardian.com/world/2009/oct/01/lobbyists-millions-obama-healthcare-reform, accessed 4 October 2018.

McGregor R, 2007, 'China's good corporate citizens find their voice', *Financial Times*, 25 February. Available online at http://www.ft.com, accessed 28 November 2018.

McGuire J.W. 1963, *Business and society*, McGraw-Hill, New York.

McInnes W. 2012, *Culture shock: a handbook for 21st century business*, John Wiley, Hoboken, NJ.

McIntosh A. 2002, *Soil and soul: people versus corporate power*, Aurum, London.

McIntosh M. 2003a, *Living corporate citizenship: strategic routes to socially responsible business*, Financial Times/ Prentice Hall, Harlow.

McIntosh M. 2003b, *Raising a ladder to the moon: the complexities of corporate social and environmental responsibility*, Palgrave Macmillan, Basingstoke.

McIntosh M. and Thomas R. 2000, *Global companies in the twentieth century: selected archival histories*, Routledge, Abingdon, Oxfordshire.

McIntosh M., Leipziger D., Jones K., and Coleman G. 1998, *Corporate citizenship: successful strategies for responsible companies*, Financial Times/Prentice Hall, Harlow.

McIntosh M., Waddock S.A., and Kell G. (eds) 2004, *Learning to talk: corporate citizenship and the development of the UN Global Compact*, Greenleaf, Sheffield.

Maas K. and Grieco C. 2017, 'Distinguishing game changers from boastful charlatans: which social enterprises measure their impact?', *Journal of Social Entrepreneurship*, vol. 8, no. 1, pp 110–128.

Macdonald K. 2007, *Globalising justice within coffee supply chains? Fair Trade, Starbucks and the transformation of supply chain governance*, Third World Foundation for Social and Economic Studies, London.

Macdonald K. and Marshall S.E. 2010, *Fair trade, corporate accountability and beyond: experiments in globalizing justice*, Ashgate, Farnham, Surrey.

MacGillivray A. and Zadek, S. 1995, *Accounting for change: indicators for sustainable development*, New Economics Foundation, London.

Mackey, J. and Sisodia, R. 2013, *Conscious capitalism: liberating the heroic spirit of business*, Harvard Business Review Press, Boston, MA.

MacKenzie D.A. 2006, *An engine, not a camera: how financial models shape markets*, MIT Press, Cambridge, MA.

McLean B. and Elkind P. 2003, *The smartest guys in the room: the amazing rise and scandalous fall of Enron*, Portfolio, New York.

MacLean J. 1999, 'Towards a political economy of agency in contemporary international relations', in Shaw M. (ed.), *Politics and globalisation: knowledge, ethics and agency*, Routledge, London.

MacLean J. 2000, 'Philosophical roots of globalization and philosophical roots to globalization', in Germain R.D. (ed.), *Globalization and its critics: perspectives from political economy*, Macmillan, Basingstoke, pp 3–65.

McLellan D. 1972, *Marx's Grundrisse*, Harper and Row, New York.

McMichael P. 2004, *Development and social change: a global perspective* (3rd edn), Pine Forge Press, Thousand Oaks, CA.

McMichael P. 2009, *Contesting development: critical struggles for social change*, Routledge, Abingdon, Oxfordshire.

McMurtry J. 2002, *Value wars: the global market versus the life economy*, Pluto Press, London.

McPhail K. 2008, 'Contributing to sustainable development through multi-stakeholder processes: practical steps to avoid the "resource curse" ', *Corporate Governance*, vol. 8, no. 4, pp 471–481.

McQuaid K. 1977, 'Young, Swope and General Electric's new capitalism: a study in corporate liberalism 1920–33', *American Journal of Economics and Sociology*, vol. 36, no. 3, pp 323–334.

McWilliams A. and Siegel D. 2000, 'Corporate social responsibility and financial performance: correlation or misspecification?', *Strategic Management Journal*, vol. 21, no. 5, pp 603–609.

Mackey J. and Sisodia R. 2013, *Conscious capitalism: liberating the heroic spirit of business*, Harvard Business Review Press, Boston, MA.

Mahapatra S. 1984, 'Investor reaction to corporate social accounting', *Journal of Business Finance and Accounting*, vol. 11, no. 1, pp 29–40.

Mahon J. and Wartick S.L. 2012, 'Corporate social performance profiling: using multiple stakeholder perceptions to assess a corporate reputation', *Journal of Public Affairs*, vol. 12, no. 1, pp 12–28.

Mair J. and Noboa E. 2006, 'Social entrepreneurship: how intentions to create social venture are formed', in Mair J., Robinson J., and Hockerts K. (eds), *Social entrepreneurship*, Palgrave Macmillan, Basingstoke, pp 121–136.

Mair J., Robinson J., and Hockerts K.E. 2006, 'Introduction', in Mair J., Robinson J., and Hockerts K. (eds), *Social entrepreneurship*, Palgrave Macmillan, Basingstoke, pp 1–14.

Maitland A, 2005, 'Big business starts to scratch the surface', *Financial Times*, 14 September. Available online at http://www.ft.com, accessed 22 November 2018.

Maitland A, 2006, 'A responsible balancing act', *Financial Times*, 1 June. Available online at http://www.ft.com, accessed 22 November 2018.

Mallen C.A, 2012, *Corporate governance*, Oxford University Press, New York.

Maltzman, R. and Shirley, D. 2010, *Green project management*, CRC Press, Boca Raton, FL.

Mamic I. 2004, *Implementing codes of conduct: how businesses manage social performance in global supply chains*, Greenleaf, Sheffield, and ILO, Geneva.

Mander J. and Goldsmith E. 1996, *The case against the global economy: and for a turn toward the local*, Sierra Club Books, San Francisco, CA.

Manga J.E., Mirvis P., Rochlin S.A., and Zecchi K. 2005, *Integration: critical link for corporate citizenship. Strategies and stories from eight companies*, Center for Corporate Citizenship at Boston College, Chestnut Hill, MA.

Manheim J.B. 2000, *The death of a thousand cuts: corporate campaigns and the attack on the corporation*, Lawrence Erlbaum, Mahwah, NJ.

Manheim J.B. 2004, *Biz-war and the out-of-power elite: the progressive-left attack on the corporation*, Lawrence Erlbaum, Mahwah, NJ.

Manne H. and Wallich H.C. 1972, *The modern corporation and social responsibility*, American Enterprise Institute for Public Policy Research, Washington, DC.

Margolis J.D. and Walsh J.P. 2001, *People and profits? The search for a link between a company's social and financial performance*, Lawrence Erlbaum, Mahwah, NJ.

Margolis J.D. and Walsh J.P. 2003, 'Misery loves companies: rethinking social initiatives by business', *Administrative Science Quarterly*, vol. 48, no. 2, pp 268–305.

Margolis J.D., Elfenbein H.A., and James P.W. 2008, 'Do well by doing good? Don't count on it', *Harvard Business Review*, vol. 86, no. 1, pp 19.

Markopolos H. 2010, *No one would listen: a true financial thriller*, John Wiley, Hoboken, NJ.

Markopoulos M. 1998, *Impacts of certification on community forest enterprises: a case study of the Lomerio Community Forest Management Project, Bolivia*, Department for International Development, London.

Markopoulos M. 1999, *Community forest enterprise and certification in Mexico: a review of experience*, Oxford University Press, Oxford.

Marland G., Boden T.A., and Andres R.J. 2003, 'Global, regional, and national CO2 emissions,' in *Trends: A Compendium of Data on Global Change*, Carbon Dioxide Information Analysis Center, Oak Ridge National Laboratory, Oak Ridge, TN.

Marling W.H. 2006, *How 'American' is globalization?* Johns Hopkins University Press, Baltimore, MD.

Martin R.L. 2002, 'The virtue matrix: calculating the return on corporate responsibility', *Harvard Business Review*, vol. 80, no. 3, pp 68.

Marx, K. 1865, *Value, price, and profit: an introduction to the theory of capitalism*, abridged by P. Zarembka, 2000, JAI/Elsevier Science, Amsterdam, New York. Available online at https://www.marxists.org/archive/marx/works/download/pdf/value-price-profit.pdf, accessed 22 November 2018.

Marx K. 1973, *Grundrisse. Foundations of the critique of political economy*, Vintage Books, New York.

Marx K., Moore S., Aveling E.B., Engels F., and Besant A.W. 1887, *Capital: a critical analysis of capitalist production*, S. Sonnenschein Lowrey and Co., London.

Mason E.S. 1960, *The corporation in modern society*, Harvard University Press, Cambridge, MA.

Mason, P. 2015, *PostCapitalism: a guide to our future*, Allen Lane, London.

Mathews M.R., 1993, *Socially responsible accounting*, Chapman and Hall, London.

Mathews M.R. 1996, 'Twenty-five years of social and environmental accounting research. Is there a silver jubilee to celebrate?', *Accounting, Auditing and Accountability Journal*, vol. 10, no. 4, pp 481–531.

Mattar H. 2001, 'Ethical portals as inducers of corporate social responsibility', in Zadek S., Hojensgard N., and Raynard P. (eds), *Perspectives on the new economy of corporate citizenship*, Copenhagen Centre, Copenhagen, pp 113–121.

Matten D. and Crane A. 2005, 'Corporate citizenship: toward an extended theoretical conceptualization', *Academy of Management Review*, vol. 30, no. 1, pp 166–180.

Matten D. and Moon J. 2008, '"Implicit" and "explicit" CSR: a conceptual framework for a comparative understanding of corporate social responsibility', *Academy of Management Review*, vol. 33, no. 2, pp 404–424.

Matten, D., Crane, A., and Moon, J. 2017, 'Corporate power and responsibility: a citizenship perspective' in *Corporate citizenship, contractarianism and ethical theory*, Routledge, London, pp 19–38.

Mattingly J.E. and Berman S.L. 2006, 'Measurement of corporate social action: discovering taxonomy in the Kinder Lydenberg Domini ratings data', *Business and Society*, vol. 45, no. 1, pp 20–46.

Mawson A. 2008, *The social entrepreneur: making communities work*, Atlantic, London.

Maxwell S. 2005, *The Washington Consensus is dead! Long live the meta-narrative*, Working Paper 243, Overseas Development Institute, London.

May S., Cheney G., and Roper J. 2007, *The debate over corporate social responsibility*, Oxford University Press, New York.

Meadows D., Randers J., and Meadows D.L. 2004, *Limits to growth: the 30-year update*, Earthscan, London.

Meh A. 2004, 'Uneasy partnerships and contradictions: corporate social and environmental responsibility', presented at the 3rd Annual Global Studies Association Conference, Brandeis University.

Melcrum 2005, *How to structure the corporate responsibility function*, Melcrum, London.

Mervelskemper, L. and Streit, D. 2017, 'Enhancing market valuation of ESG performance: is integrated reporting keeping its promise?', *Business Strategy and the Environment*, vol. 26, no. 4, pp 536–549.

Mesure S. 2007, 'Tesco follows M&S with climate change move', *Independent*, London, 16 January. Available online at https://www.independent.co.uk/news/business/news/tesco-follows-mamps-with-climate-change-move-432341.html, accessed 4 October 2018.

Miles, S. 2017, 'Stakeholder theory classification: a theoretical and empirical evaluation of definitions', *Journal of Business Ethics*, vol. 142, no. 3, pp 437–459.

Mill J.S. 1987, *Utilitarianism*, Prometheus Books, Buffalo, NY.

Mill J.S. 2002, *The basic writings of John Stuart Mill*, Modern Library, New York.

Milligan, B. 2015, *PwC promoted tax avoidance 'on industrial scale', say MPs*, BBC, London.

Milne M.J. and Chan C.C.C. 1999, 'Narrative corporate social disclosures. How much of a difference do they make to investment decision-making?', *British Accounting Review*, vol. 31, no. 4, pp 439–457.

Milne, R. 2015, 'Volkswagen: system failure', *Financial Times*, 4 November. Available online at https://www.ft.com/content/47f233f0-816b-11e5-a01c-8650859a4767, accessed 3 October 2018.

Mirvis P. and Googins B.K. 2006, *Stages of corporate citizenship: a developmental framework*, Center for Corporate Citizenship at Boston College, Chestnut Hill, MA.

Mirvis P.H. 2000, 'Transformation at Shell: commerce and citizenship', *Business and Society Review*, vol. 105, no. 1, p 63.

Mitchell A. and Sikka P. 2004, 'Accountability of the accountancy bodies: the peculiarities of a British accountancy body', *British Accounting Review*, vol. 36, no. 4, pp 395–414.

Mitchell A., Sikka P., Puxty T., and Willmott H. 1991, *Accounting for change: proposals for reform of audit and accounting*, Discussion Paper No. 7, Fabian Society, London.

Mitchell A., Sikka P., Cooper C., Willmott H., and Arnold P. 2001, *The BCCI cover-up*, Association for Accountancy and Business Affairs, Basildon.

Mitchell J., Shankleman J., and Warner M. 2004, 'Measuring the added value of partnerships', in Warner M. and Sullivan R. (eds), *Putting partnerships to work*, Greenleaf, Sheffield, pp 191–200.

Mitchell L.E. 2001, *Corporate irresponsibility: America's newest export*, Yale University Press, New Haven, CT.

Mitchell L.E. 2005, 'Roles and incentives: the core problems of corporate social responsibility', *Ethical Corporation Magazine*, October, pp 46–50.

Mitnick B.M. 2000, 'Commitment, revelation, and the testaments of belief: the metrics of measurement of corporate social performance', *Business and Society*, vol. 39, no. 4, pp 419–465.

Mittelman J.H. 2000, *The globalization syndrome: transformation and resistance*, Princeton University Press, Princeton, NJ.

Monaghan, A. 2016, *No letup in executive pay rises, says thinktank, Guardian*, London, 13 April, p 18.

Monaghan, A. 2017, 'Rolls-Royce trio plead guilty to corruption charges in US', *Guardian*, 8 November. Available online at http://www.theguardian.com, accessed 22 November 2018.

Monbiot, G., 2005, 'Africa's new best friends', *Guardian*, 5 July. Available online at https://www.theguardian.com/politics/2005/jul/05/internationalaidanddevelopment.development, accessed 4 October 2018.

Monitor 2009, *Investing for social and environmental impact*, Monitor Group, Boston, MA.

Monks R.A.G. and Minow N. 1991, *Power and accountability*, HarperCollins, London.

Moody-Stuart S.M. 2004, 'The role of business in developing countries', *Business Ethics*, vol. 13, no. 1, pp 41–49.

Moon, J. 2014, *Corporate social responsibility: a very short introduction*, Oxford University Press, Oxford.

Moon J., Crane A., and Matten D. 2005, 'Can corporations be citizens? Corporate citizenship as a metaphor for business participation in society', *Business Ethics Quarterly*, vol. 15, no. 3, pp 427–451.

Mooney A. 2016, *Sharia-compliant fund sales plummet 75%*, Financial Times, London.

Moore B. 1966, *Social origins of dictatorship and democracy; lord and peasant in the making of the modern world*, Beacon Press, Boston, MA.

Moorhead J. 2007, 'Milking it', *Guardian*, London, 15 May. Available online at http://www.theguardian.com, accessed 22 November 2018.

Moratis, L. and Brandt, S. 2017, 'Corporate stakeholder responsiveness? Exploring the state and quality of GRI-based stakeholder engagement disclosures of European firms', *Corporate Social Responsibility and Environmental Management*, vol. 24, no. 4, pp 312–325.

Morgan, B. 2018, 'Telling stories beautifully: hybrid legal forms in the new economy', *Journal of Law and Society*, vol. 45, no. 1, pp 64–83.

Morris C.W. 1999, *The social contract theorists: critical essays on Hobbes, Locke, and Rousseau*, Rowman and Littlefield, Lanham, MD.

Morsing M. and Perrini F. 2009, 'CSR in SMEs: do SMEs matter for the CSR agenda?', *Business Ethics*, vol. 18, no. 1, pp 1-6.

Mosley L. 2011, *Labor rights and multinational production*, Cambridge University Press, New York.

Moss D.A. 2002, *When all else fails: government as the ultimate risk manager*, Harvard University Press, Cambridge, MA.

Mouan L.C. 2010, 'Exploring the potential benefits of Asian participation in the Extractive Industries Transparency Initiative: the case of China', *Business Strategy and the Environment*, vol. 19, no. 6, pp 367-376.

Muirhead S.A. 2006, *Philanthropy and business: the changing agenda*, Conference Board, New York.

Mullins J.W. 2006, *The new business road test: what entrepreneurs and executives should do before writing a business plan* (2nd edn), Financial Times/Prentice Hall, Harlow.

Mullins J.W. and Komisar R. 2009, *Getting to plan B: breaking through to a better business model*, Harvard Business School Press, Boston, MA.

Murillo D. and Lozano J.M. 2006, 'SMEs and CSR: an approach to CSR in their own words', *Journal of Business Ethics*, vol. 67, no. 3, pp 227-240.

Murphy D.Y. and Bendell J. 1999, *Partners in time? Business, NGOs and sustainable development*, UN Resarch Institute for Social Development, Geneva.

Murphy R. 2007, *Platinum performers must shine all the way through*, Ethical Performance, London.

Murray A., Sinclair D., Power D., and Gray, R. 2006, 'Do financial markets care about social and environmental disclosure? Further evidence and exploration from the UK', *Accounting, Auditing and Accountability Journal*, vol. 19, no. 2, pp 228-255.

Murray A.S. 2007, *Revolt in the boardroom: the new rules of power in corporate America*, Collins, New York.

Murray J. 2002, 'Labour rights/corporate responsibilities: the role of ILO labour standards', in Jenkins R.O., Pearson R., and Seyfang G. (eds), *Corporate responsibility and labour rights: codes of conduct in the global economy*, Earthscan, London, pp 31-42.

Muthuri J.N. 2013, 'Corporate social responsibility in Africa', in Lituchi T., Punnett B.J., and Puplampu B.B. (eds), *Management in Africa: macro and micro perspectives*, Routledge, Abingdon, Oxfordshire, pp 90-111.

Nader R. and Taylor W. 1986, *The big boys: power and position in American business*, Pantheon Books, New York.

Nair C. 2006, 'Eyes wide shut: corporate citizenship in Asia', *Ethical Corporation Magazine*, May, pp 46-47.

Narlikar A. 2005, *The World Trade Organization: a very short introduction*, Oxford University Press, Oxford.

Nash L.L. and Kantrow A.M. 1987, 'Multinational corporations and economic development', in Berger P.L. (ed.), *Capitalism and equality in the Third World*, Rowman and Littlefield, Lanham, MD.

Neergaard, P. and Pedersen, E.R. 2017, 'Between the rules of the game and the law of the jungle', in McIntosh, M. (ed.), *Business, capitalism and corporate citizenship: a collection of seminal essays*, Routledge, London.

Nelson J. 1996, *Business as partners in development: creating wealth for countries, companies and communities*, Prince of Wales Business Leaders' Forum, London.

Nelson J. 1998, *Building competitiveness and communities: how world class companies are creating shareholder value and societal value*, Prince of Wales Business Leaders' Forum, London.

Nelson J. 2007, *Building linkages for competitive and responsible entrepreneurship*, UNIDO, Vienna, and John F Kennedy School of Government, Harvard University, Cambridge, MA.

Nelson J. and Zadek S. 2000, *Partnership alchemy: new social partnerships in Europe*, The Copenhagen Centre, Copenhagen.

Nelson J., Gambhir, A., and Ekins-Daukes N. 2014, *Solar power for CO_2 mitigation*, Imperial College, Grantham Briefing Paper 11, London.

Nelson V. and Galvez M. 2000, *Social impact of ethical and conventional brazil nut trading on forest-dependent people in Peru*, Working Paper, Natural Resources Institute, University of Greenwich, Chatham.

Nelson V. and Pound B. 2009, *The last ten years: a comprehensive review of the literature on the impact of fairtrade*, Working Paper, Natural Resources Institute, University of Greenwich, Chatham.

Nelson V. and Tallontire A. 2002, 'Assessing the benefits of ethical trade schemes in cocoa (Ecuador) and Brazil nuts (Peru) for forest-dependent people and their livelihoods', *International Forestry Review*, vol. 4, no. 2, pp 99-109.

Nelson V., Martin A. and Ewert J. 2007, 'The impacts of codes of practice on worker livelihoods: empirical evidence from the South African wine and Kenyan cut flower industries', *Journal of Corporate Citizenship*, no. 28, Winter, pp 61-72.

Newark, D. 2018, 'Leadership and the logic of absurdity', *Academy of Management Review*, vol. 43, no. 2, pp 198-216.

Newell P. 2005, 'Citizenship, accountability and community: the limitations of the CSR agenda', *International Affairs*, vol. 81, no. 3, pp 541–558.

Newell P. and Frynas J.G. 2007, 'Beyond CSR? Business, poverty and social justice: an introduction', *Third World Quarterly*, vol. 28, no. 4, pp. 669–681.

Newell P. and Muro A. 2006, 'Corporate social and environmental responsibility in Argentina: the evolution of an agenda', *Journal of Corporate Citizenship*, no. 24, Winter, pp 49–68.

Newman P. and Hotchner A.E. 2003, *Shameless exploitation in pursuit of the common good*, Nan A. Talese, New York.

Newton A. 2005, 'Defining the art of conversation', *Ethical Corporation Magazine*, November, pp 46–47.

Nguyen, B., Melewar, T.C. and Schultz, D. 2016, *Asia branding: connecting brands, consumers and companies*, Macmillan, Basingstoke.

Nicholls A. 2008, *Social entrepreneurship: new models of sustainable social change* (2nd edn), Oxford University Press, Oxford.

Nicholls A. 2010, 'The institutionalization of social investment: the interplay of investment logics and investor rationalities', *Journal of Social Entrepreneurship*, vol. 1, no. 1, pp 70–100.

Nicholls A. and Opal C. 2005, *Fair trade: market-driven ethical consumption*, SAGE Publications, London.

Nicholls A. and Teasdale S. 2017, 'Neoliberalism by stealth? Exploring continuity and change within the UK social enterprise policy paradigm', *Policy and Politics*, vol. 45, no. 3, pp 323–341.

Nielsen A.E. and Thomsen C. 2012, 'Corporate social responsibility (CSR) management and marketing communication: research streams and themes', *Hermes–Journal of Language and Communication in Business*, vol. 49, pp 49–65.

Nielsen M.E. 2005, 'Child labour in the Bangladeshi garment industry', *International Affairs*, vol. 81, no. 3, pp 559–580.

Nieto M.L. 2014, *Human resource management [electronic resource]*, Palgrave Macmillan, Basingstoke.

Nikoloyuk J., Burns T.R., and de Man R. 2010, 'The promise and limitations of partnered governance: the case of sustainable palm oil', *Corporate Governance*, vol. 10, no. 1, pp 59–72.

Nocera J. 2006, 'The board wore chicken suits', *New York Times*, 27 May. Available online at https://www.nytimes.com/2006/05/27/business/27nocera.html, accessed 6 December 2018.

Novak M. 1982, *Spirit of democratic capitalism*, Simon and Schuster, New York.

Nozick R. 1974, *Anarchy, state, and utopia*, Basic Books, New York.

NRET 1999, 'Ethical trade and sustainable rural livelihoods', in Carney D. (ed.), *Sustainable rural livelihoods. What contribution can we make?*, Department for International Development, London, pp 107–129.

Nussbaum M.C. and Sen A.K. (eds) 1993, *The quality of life*, Clarendon Press, Oxford.

O'Connor, S. 2017, '"Gig economy" panel eyes boost for worker rights', *Financial Times*, 14 February, p. 3.

Odell A.M. 2007, 'Principles for responsible investment quadruples assets in first year', *Social Funds*, 1 June. Available online at http://www.socialfunds.com, accessed 28 November 2018.

O'Dwyer B. and Owen D.L. 2005, 'Assurance statement practice in environmental, social and sustainability reporting: a critical evaluation', *British Accounting Review*, 37, no. 2, pp 205–229.

OECD 1999, *Principles of corporate governance*, Organisation for Economic Co-operation and Development, Paris.

OECD/G20 2015, *G20/OECD Principles of corporate governance* , Organisation for Economic Co-operation and Development, Paris.

Okali C. 1983, *Cocoa and kinship in Ghana: the matrilineal Akan of Ghana*, Kegan Paul International, London.

Olsen L. 2004, *Making corporate responsibility work: lessons from real business*, Ashridge Centre for Business and Society/British Quality Forum, Berkhamsted, Hertfordshire.

Ong A. 1999, *Flexible citizenship: the cultural logics of transnationality*, Duke University Press, Durham, NC.

Onzivu W. 2013, '(Re)invigorating the health protection objective of the Basel Convention on Transboundary Movement of Hazardous Wastes and Their Disposal', *Legal Studies*, vol. 33, no. 4, pp 621–649.

Orange R., 20113, 'Swedish riots spark surprise and anger', *Guardian*, 25 May. Available online at https://www.theguardian.com/world/2013/may/25/sweden-europe-news?, accessed 3 October 2018.

O'Rourke D. 2003, 'Outsourcing regulation: non-governmental systems of labor standards and monitoring', *Policy Studies Journal*, vol. 31, no. 1, pp 1–29.

O'Rourke D. 2006, 'Multi-stakeholder regulation: privatizing or socializing global labor standards?', *World Development*, vol. 34, no. 5, pp 899–918.

O'Rourke K.H. 2005, *The international trading system, globalization, and history*, Edward Elgar, Cheltenham.

O'Rourke K.H. and Williamson J.G. 1999, *Globalization and history: the evolution of a nineteenth-century Atlantic economy*, MIT Press, Cambridge, MA.

Orr D. 2005, 'The triumph of neo-liberalism but will it really make poverty history?', *Independent*, London, 25 June. Available online at https://www.independent.co.uk/voices/commentators/deborah-orr/deborah-orr-the-triumph-of-neo-liberalism-but-will-it-really-make-poverty-history-294681.html, accessed 6 December 2018.

Oterberg R. 1993, *Corporate renaissance: business as an adventure in human development*, Paraview, New York.

Owen D. 2003. *Recent developments in European social and environmental reporting and auditing practice—a critical evaluation and tentative prognosis*, ICCSR Research Paper Series, University of Nottingham.

Owen D.L., Swift T.A., Humphrey C., and Bowerman M. 2000, 'The new social audits: accountability, managerial capture or the agenda of social champions?', *European Accounting Review*, vol. 9, no. 1, pp 81-98.

Paine L., Deshpande R., Margolis J.D., and Bettcher K.E. 2005, 'Up to code: does your company's conduct meet world-class standards?', *Harvard Business Review*, vol. 83, no. 12, pp 122-133, 154.

Palazzo G. and Richter U. 2005, 'CSR business as usual? The case of the tobacco industry', *Journal of Business Ethics*, vol. 61, pp 387-401.

Papista E. and Dimitriadis S. 2012, 'Exploring consumer-brand relationship quality and identification: qualitative evidence from cosmetics brands', *Qualitative Market Research*, vol. 15, no. 1, pp 33-56.

Parker J. 1998, *Citizenship, work, and welfare: searching for the good society*, Macmillan, Basingstoke.

Parket R. and Eilbirt H. 1975, 'The practice of social responsibility: the underlying factors', *Business Horizons*, 18, no. 4, pp 5-10.

Parmar B.L., Freeman R.E., Harrison J.S., Wicks A.C., Purnell L., and De Colle S. 2010, 'Stakeholder theory: the state of the art', *Academy of Management Annals*, vol. 4, no. 1, pp 403-445.

Patricof A. and Sunderland J. 2006, 'Venture capital for development', in Brainard L. (ed.), *Transforming the development landscape: the role of the private sector*, Brookings Institution Press, Washington, DC, pp 74-84.

Patrisia, D. 2016, 'The relationship between corporate diversification, corporate governance and corporate social performance in Indonesian companies', doctoral thesis, University of Huddersfield.

Paulden P. 2009, 'TXU LBO "disaster" punishes bondholders with offer'. Available online at http://www.bloomberg.com, accessed 22 November 2018.

Pava M.L. and Krausz J. 1995, *Corporate responsibility and financial performance: the paradox of social cost*, Quorum Books, Westport, CT.

Pearson R. 2007, 'Beyond women workers: gendering CSR', *Third World Quarterly*, vol. 28, no. 4, pp 731-749.

Pearson R. and Seyfang G. 2001, 'New hope or false dawn? Voluntary codes of conduct, labour regulation and social policy in a globalizing world', *Global Social Policy*, vol. 1, no. 1, pp 49-78.

Pedersen E.R. 2005, 'Guiding the invisible hand: the role of development agencies in driving corporate citizenship', *Journal of Corporate Citizenship*, no. 20, Winter, pp 77-91.

Pedersen E.R. 2006, 'Making corporate social responsibility (CSR) operable: how companies translate stakeholder dialogue into practice', *Business and Society Review*, vol. 111, no. 2, pp 137-163.

Pedersen E.R. 2009, 'The many and the few: rounding up the SMEs that manage CSR in the supply chain', *Supply Chain Management*, vol. 14, no. 2, pp 109-116.

Pedersen E.R. and Huniche M. (eds) 2006, *Corporate citizenship in developing countries: new partnership perspectives*, Copenhagen Business School Press, Copenhagen.

Peinado-Vara E. 2006, 'Corporate social responsibility in Latin America', *Journal of Corporate Citizenship*, no. 21, Spring, pp 61-69.

People & Profit 2007, *People and profit: a practical guide to corporate social responsibility*, Danish Commerce and Companies Agency, Copenhagen, Denmark. Available online at http://csrgov.dk/file/318759/people_profit_practical_guide_april_2008.pdf, accessed 4 October 2018.

Perez C. 2002, *Technological revolutions and financial capital: the dynamics of bubbles and golden ages*, Edward Elgar, Cheltenham.

Perkins R. 2004, 'Sweeter partnerships? An NGO's engagement with the sugar sector', *Partnership Matters*, vol. 2, pp 33-35.

Perrini F., Russo A., and Tencati A. 2007, 'CSR strategies of SMEs and large firms: evidence from Italy', *Journal of Business Ethics*, vol. 74, no. 3, pp 285-300.

Peters G. 1999, *Waltzing with the raptors: a practical roadmap to protecting your company's reputation*, John Wiley, New York.

Peters T.J. 1995, *In search of excellence: lessons from America's best-run companies*, HarperCollins, London.

Pettit, J. 2017, *The final frontier: E&P's low-cost operating model*, Wiley, Chichester.

Phillips K.P. 2002, *Wealth and democracy: a political history of the American rich*, Broadway Books, New York.

Phillips R. 2003, *Stakeholder theory and organizational ethics*, Berrett-Koehler, San Francisco, CA.

Phillips R. and Caldwell C.B. 2005, 'Value chain responsibility: a farewell to arm's length', *Business and Society Review*, vol. 110, no. 4, pp 345-370.

Phillips R., Freeman R.E., and Wicks A.C. 2003, 'What stakeholder theory is not', *Business Ethics Quarterly*, vol. 13, no. 4, pp 479–502.

Phylmar Group 2006, *Phylmar Enews*, February 2006.

Piketty, T. 2017, *Capital in the twenty-first century*, Harvard University Press, Cambridge, MA.

Pilger J. 2002, *The new rulers of the world*, Verso, London.

Pinchot G. 1985, *Intrapreneuring: why you don't have to leave the corporation to become an entrepreneur*, Harper and Row, New York.

Pinkse J. and Kolk A. 2009, *International business and global climate change*, Routledge, Abingdon, Oxfordshire.

Pio E. 2005, 'Eastern karma: perspectives on corporate citizenship', *Journal of Corporate Citizenship*, no. 19, Summer, pp 65–78.

Plender J. 1997, *A stake in the future: the stakeholding solution*, Nicholas Brealey, London.

Plender J. 2003, *Going off the rails: global capital and the crisis of legitimacy*, John Wiley, Chichester.

Polanyi K. 1944, *The great transformation*, Farrar and Rinehart, New York.

Pomeranz K. and Topik S. 2006, *The world that trade created: society, culture, and the world economy, 1400 to present*, M.E. Sharpe, Armonk, NY.

Ponte S., Gibbon P., and Vestergaard J. 2011, 'Governing through standards: an introduction', in Ponte S., Gibbon P., and Vestergaard J. (eds), *Governing through standards: origins, drivers and limitations*, Palgrave Macmillan, Basingstoke, pp 1–23.

Porritt J. 2005, *Capitalism: as if the world matters*, Earthscan, London.

Porter M.E. 1990, *The competitive advantage of nations*, Free Press, New York.

Porter M.E. and Kramer M.R. 2002, 'The competitive advantage of corporate philanthropy', *Harvard Business Review*, vol. 80, no. 12, pp 56–68.

Porter M.E. and Kramer M. 2006, 'Strategy and society: the link between competitive advantage and corporate social responsibility', *Harvard Business Review*, vol. 84, no. 12, pp 78–92.

Porter M.E. and Kramer M. 2011, 'The big idea: creating shared value', *Harvard Business Review*, vol. 89, no. 1–2, pp 62–77.

Porter M.E. and van der Linde C. 1995, 'Green and competitive: ending the stalemate', *Harvard Business Review*, vol. 73, no. 5, pp 120–134.

Posner R.A. 1981, *The economics of justice*, Harvard University Press, Cambridge, MA.

Post J.E. and Altman B.W. 1992, 'Models of corporate greening: how corporate social policy and organizational learning inform leading-edge environmental management', *Research in Corporate Social Performance and Policy*, vol. 13, pp 3–29.

Post J.E., Lawrence A.T., and Weber J. 1999, *Business and society: corporate strategy, public policy, ethics* (9th edn), Irwin/McGraw-Hill, Boston, MA.

Post J.E., Preston L.E., and Sauter-Sachs S. 2002, *Redefining the corporation: stakeholder management and organizational wealth*, Stanford Business Books, Stanford, CA.

Prahalad C.K. 2005, *The fortune at the bottom of the pyramid*, Prentice Hall, Upper Saddle River, NJ.

Prahalad C.K. and Hart S.L. 2002, 'The fortune at the bottom of the pyramid', *Strategy+Business*, no. 26, pp 2–14.

Prakash S. 2006, 'Conflicted safety panel let Vioxx study continue', 8 June, National Public Radio, Washington, DC. Available online at http://www.npr.org, accessed 22 November 2018.

Prentice R. and De Neve G. 2017, *Unmaking the global sweatshop: health and safety of the world's garment workers*, University of Pennsylvania Press, Philadelphia, PA.

Preston L.E. and O'Bannon D.P. 1997, 'The corporate social-financial performance relationship: a typology and analysis', *Business and Society*, vol. 36, no. 4, pp 419–428.

Preston L.E. and Post J.E. 1975, *Private management and public policy: the principle of public responsibility*, Prentice-Hall, Englewood Cliffs, NJ.

Preston L.E. and Sapienza H.J. 1990, 'Stakeholder management and corporate performance', *Journal of Behavioral Economics*, vol. 19, no. 4, pp 361–375.

PR News 2006, *Guide to best practices in corporate social responsibility*. Available online at http://www.prnewsonline.com, accessed 28 November 2018.

Putnam R.D. 2000, *Bowling alone: the collapse and revival of American community*, Simon and Schuster, New York.

PWBLF 1998, *Managing partnerships: tools for managing the public sector, business and civil society as partners in development*, Prince of Wales Business Leaders' Forum, London.

PWC 2006, *Corporate responsibility: strategy, management and value*, PricewaterhouseCoopers, London.

Quayle M. 2003, 'A study of supply chain management practice in UK industrial SMEs', *Supply Chain Management*, vol. 8, no. 1, pp 79–86.

Quinn J. 2009, 'Goldman chairman admits Wall St greed', *Daily Telegraph*, London, 7 April. Available online at http://www.telegraph.co.uk/finance, accessed 22 November 2018.

Quinn T.K. 1962, *Unconscious public enemies*, Citadel Press, New York.

Rachels J. 1999, *The elements of moral philosophy* (3rd edn), McGraw-Hill, New York.

Radin T.J. and Werhane P.H. 2003, 'Employment-at-will, employee rights, and future directions for employment', *Business Ethics Quarterly*, vol. 13, no. 2, pp 113–130.

Rai, N., Best, S. and Soanes, M. 2016, *Unlocking climate finance for decentralised energy access*, IIED, London.

Raimbaev A. 2009, 'Corporate social responsibility among SMEs in Uzbekistan', in Aras G. and Crowther D. (eds), *Global Perspectives on Corporate Governance and CSR*, Gower, Farnham, Surrey, pp 187–196.

Rajak D. 2006, 'The gift of CSR: power and the pursuit of responsibility in the mining industry', in Visser W., McIntosh M., and Middleton C. (eds), *Corporate citizenship in Africa: lessons from the past, paths to the future*, Greenleaf, Sheffield.

Rajak D. 2008, '"Uplift and empower": the market, the gift and corporate social responsibility on South Africa's platinum belt', *Research in Economic Anthropology*, vol. 28, pp 297–324.

Rajak D. 2011, *In good company: an anatomy of corporate social responsibility*, Stanford University Press, Stanford, CA.

Ram A. 2018, 'Cambridge Analytica ex-chief's answers fuel further questions', *Financial Times*, 10 June. Available online at https://www.ft.com/content/bc9ffd28-6b28-11e8-8cf3-0c230fa67aec, accessed 3 October 2018.

Ram A. and Thompson B. 2018, 'Facebook hit with first fine over Cambridge Analytica data scandal', *Financial Times*, 11 July. Available online at https://www.ft.com/content/b7c2e7ba-8460-11e8-96dd-fa565ec55929, accessed 3 October 2018.

Ramanathan K.V. 1976, 'Towards a theory of corporate social accounting', *Accounting Review*, vol. 52, no. 4, pp 516–528.

Rand A. 1966, *Capitalism, the unknown ideal*, New American Library, New York.

Rangan V.K., Quelch J.A., and Herrero G. (eds) 2007, *Business solutions for the social poor: creating social and economic value*, Jossey-Bass, San Francisco, CA.

Ranganathan J. 1998, *Sustainability rulers: measuring corporate, social, environmental and social performance*, World Resources Institute, Washington, DC.

Ranganathan J. 1999, 'Signs of sustainability: measuring corporate environmental and social performance', in Bennett M. and James P. (eds), *Sustainable measures: evaluation and reporting of environmental and social performance*, Greenleaf, Sheffield, pp 475–495.

Rao K. and Tilt C.A. 2013, 'Corporate governance and corporate social responsibility: a critical review', in Kokubu K., Sawabe N., and Sakaue M. (eds), Proceedings of the 7th Asia Pacific Interdisciplinary Research in Accounting Conference. Available online at http://www.apira2013.org/proceedings/pdfs/K167.pdf, accessed 28 November 2018.

Rapier, R. 2016, 'A record year for renewable energy', *Forbes.com*, no. 3 June, pp. 3. Available online at http://www.forbes.com/sites/rrapier/2016/06/03/a-record-year-for-renewable-energy/#4a11e6ff2066, accessed 22 November 2018.

Rasche A. 2010, 'The limits of corporate responsibility standards', *Business Ethics*, vol. 19, no. 3, pp 280–291.

Rasche A. and Esser D.E. 2006, 'From stakeholder management to stakeholder accountability: applying Habermasian discourse ethics to accountability research', *Journal of Business Ethics*, no. 65, pp 251–267.

Rasche A. and Kell G. 2010, *The United Nations Global Compact: achievements, trends and challenges*, Cambridge University Press, New York.

Rasche A., De Bakker F.G., and Moon J. 2013a, 'Complete and partial organizing for corporate social responsibility', *Journal of Business Ethics*, vol. 115, no. 4, pp 651–663.

Rasche A., Waddock, S., and McIntosh M. 2013b, 'The United Nations Global Compact: retrospect and prospect', *Business and Society*, vol. 52, no. 1, pp 6–30.

Rasche, A., Larsen, M.L., Gwozdz, W., and Moon, J. 2017, 'What firms leave multi-stakeholder initiatives?: an analysis of delistings from the UN Global Compact', *The 33rd EGOS Colloquium 2017*.

Ratcliffe, R. and Quinn, B. 2018, 'Oxfam: fresh claims that staff used prostitutes in Chad', *Guardian*, 11 February. Available online at https://www.theguardian.com/world/2018/feb/10/oxfam-faces-allegations-staff-paid-prostitutes-in-chad, accessed 3 October 2018.

Raufflet E. and Mills A.J. (eds) 2009, *The dark side: critical cases on the downside of business*, Greenleaf, Sheffield.

Rawls J. 1971, *A theory of justice*, Belknap Press, Cambridge, MA.

Rayman-Bacchus, L. 2017, *Perspectives on corporate social responsibility*, Routledge, New York.

Raynolds, L.T. 2017, 'Fairtrade labour certification: the contested incorporation of plantations and workers', *Third World Quarterly*, vol. 38, no. 7, pp 1–20.

Raynolds L.T., Murray D., and Taylor P.L. 2004, 'Fair trade coffee: building producer capacity via global networks', *Journal of International Development*, vol. 16, no. 8, pp 1109–1121.

Redclift M.R. 2000, *Sustainability: life chances and livelihoods*, Routledge, Abingdon, Oxfordshire.

Reddy D. 2008, 'India', in Krosinsky C. and Robins N. (eds), *Sustainable investing: the art of long-term performance*, Earthscan, London, pp 165–176.

Reddy P.L.S. 2002, 'Corporate governance—emerging trends', *Corporate Governance*, vol. 1, no. 1.

Reed M.M. and Neubert M.J. 2012, 'General Electric: ecomagination as a CSR initiative', *Journal of Business Ethics Education*, vol. 8, no. 1, pp 245–254.

Reich R.B. 2007, *Supercapitalism: the transformation of business, democracy, and everyday life*, Alfred A. Knopf, New York.

Rembert T.C. 2005, 'CSR in the crosshairs: a broad counter-attack against corporate reform is growing. (Could that be a sign of progress?)', *Business Ethics*, Spring, pp 30–35.

REN21 2016, *Renewable Global Status Report 2016*, REN21, Paris.

Rennison, J. 2016, 'Barclays and Credit Suisse to pay $154m over dark pools', *Financial Times*, 31 January. Available online at https://www.ft.com/content/d160fc2a-c84c-11e5-be0b-b7ece4e953a0, accessed 3 October 2018.

Revelli C. and Viviani J.L. 2015, 'Financial performance of socially responsible investing (SRI): what have we learned? A meta-analysis', *Business Ethics: A European Review*, vol. 24, no. 2, pp 158–185.

REWE 2012, *Ensure a successful 'energy transition' in Germany—provide predictability and fair allocation*, REWE, Cologne.

Rezaee Z. 2015, *Business sustainability: performance, compliance, accountability and integrated reporting*, Routledge, Abingdon, Oxfordshire.

Ricardo D. 1817, *On the principles of political economy, and taxation*, John Murray, London.

Richter, B. 2014, *Beyond smoke and mirrors: climate change and energy in the 21st century*, Cambridge University Press, Cambridge.

Ridley-Duff, R. 2015, *Understanding social enterprise: theory and practice* (2nd edn), SAGE Publications, London.

Ring P.S., Bigley G.A., D'Aunoo T., and Khanna T. 2005, 'Perspectives on how governments matter', *Academy of Management Review*, vol. 30, no. 2, pp 308–320.

Roberts R.W. 1992, 'Determinants of corporate social responsibility disclosure: An application of stakeholder theory', *Accounting, Organizations and Society*, vol. 17, no. 6, 595–612.

Robertson R. 1992, *Globalization: social theory and global culture*, SAGE Publications, London.

Robins N. 2007, 'The imperious company', *Journal of Corporate Citizenship*, no. 25, Spring, pp 31–42.

Robins N. 2008, 'The emergence of sustainable investing' in Krosinsky C. and Robins N. (eds), *Sustainable investing: the art of long-term performance*, Earthscan, London, pp 3–17.

Robins N. 2012, *The corporation that changed the world. How the East India Company shaped the modern multinational* (2nd edn), Pluto Press, London.

Roche C. 1999, *Impact assessment for development agencies: learning to value change*, Oxfam, Oxford.

Rockoff J. and Kendall B. 2009, 'Pfizer to plead guilty to improper marketing', *Wall Street Journal*, New York, 3 September. Available online at http://online.wsj.com/news, accessed 22 November 2018.

Roddick A. 2000, *Business as unusual*, Thorsons, London.

Rodrik D. 1997, *Has globalization gone too far?* Institute for International Economics, Washington, DC.

Rodrik, D. 2017, *Straight talk on trade: ideas for a sane world economy*, Princeton University Press, Princeton NJ.

Rogers, D. 2018, 'Analysis: Carillion by numbers', *Building*, 12 July.

Roodman, D.M. 2012, *Due diligence: an impertinent inquiry into microfinance*, Center for Global Development, Washington, D.C.

Ronchi L. 2002, *Impact of fair trade on producers and their organisations: a case study with Coocafe in Costa Rica*, Poverty Research Unit, University of Sussex, Falmer, East Sussex.

Rondinelli D.A. 2002, 'Transnational corporations: international citizens or new sovereigns?', *Business and Society Review*, vol. 107, no. 4, pp 391–413.

Rose C. 2007a, 'Does female board representation influence firm performance? The Danish evidence', *Corporate Governance*, vol. 15, pp 404–413.

Rose S. 2007b, 'Back in fashion: how we're reviving a British icon (Marks & Spencer)', *Harvard Business Review*, May, pp 51–57.

Rosenberg H. 1999, *A traitor to his class: Robert A.G. Monks and the battle to change corporate America*, John Wiley, New York.

Rosenberg J. 2000, *The follies of globalisation theory: polemical essays*, Verso, London.

Rowledge L.R. 1999, *Mapping the journey: case studies in strategy and action toward sustainable development*, Greenleaf, Sheffield.

Rowley T.J. and Moldoveanu M. 2003, 'When will stakeholder groups act? An interest- and identity-based model of stakeholder group mobilization', *Academy of Management Review*, vol. 28, no. 2, pp 204–219.

Ruggie J.G. 2003, 'Taking embedded liberalism global: the corporate connection', in Held D. and Koenig-Archibugi M. (eds), *Taming globalization: frontiers of governance*, Polity Press, Cambridge.

Ruggie, J.G. 2017, 'Corporate social responsibility and the global compact', in McIntosh, M. (ed.), *Business, capitalism and corporate citizenship: a collection of seminal essays*, Routledge, London.

Ruggie J.G., Wright M., and Lehr A. 2006, *Business recognition of human rights: global patterns, regional and sectoral variations*, UN Human Rights Commission, Geneva.

Rulli M.C., Saviori A., and d'Odorico P. 2013, 'Global land and water grabbing', *Proceedings of the National Academy of Sciences*, vol. 110, no. 3, pp 892–897.

Runciman D. 2003, 'Partnering the state', *Partnership Matters*, vol. 1, pp 12–15.

Runhaar H. and Lafferty H. 2009, 'Governing corporate social responsibility: an assessment of the contribution of the UN Global Compact to CSR strategies in the telecommunications industry', *Journal of Business Ethics*, vol. 84, no. 4, pp 479–495.

Runping Y. 2006, 'Business starts taking social responsibility seriously', *China View*, 17 May. Available online at http://news.xinhuanet.com, accessed 22 November 2018.

Rupley K.H., Brown D., and Marshall S. 2017, 'Evolution of corporate reporting: from stand-alone corporate social responsibility reporting to integrated reporting', *Research in Accounting Regulation*, vol. 29, no. 2, pp 172–176.

Rusbridger A. 2009, 'A chill on *The Guardian*', *New York Review of Books*, 15 January. Available online at http://www.nybooks.com, accessed 22 November 2018.

Russo A. and Perrini F. 2010, 'Investigating stakeholder theory and social capital: CSR in large firms and SMEs', *Journal of Business Ethics*, vol. 91, no. 2, pp 207–221.

Russo A. and Tencati A. 2009, 'Formal vs. informal CSR strategies: evidence from Italian micro, small, medium-sized, and large firms', *Journal of Business Ethics*, vol. 85, pp 339–353.

Rustad S.A., Le Billon P., and Lujala P. 2017, 'Has the Extractive Industries Transparency Initiative been a success? Identifying and evaluating EITI goals', *Resources Policy*, vol. 51, pp 151–162.

Sabapathy J., Swift T., Weiser J., and Polycarpe M. (2002), *Innovation through partnership*, Institute of Social and Ethical Accountability, London.

Sage, A. 2017, 'Airbus has trouble in the cockpit', *The Times*, 16 December.

Saha P. 2005, 'Shopping around: a leaked company document may dampen the Christmas spirit at Asda', *Ethical Corporation Magazine*, December. Available online at http://www.ethicalcorp.com, accessed 22 November 2018.

Saha P, 2006, 'Doing ethics the Tata way', *Ethical Corporation Magazine*, June, pp 26–28.

SAI 1999, *Guidance document for social accountability 8000*, Social Accountability International, New York.

Saith A. 2006, 'From universal values to millennium development goals: lost in translation', *Development and Change*, vol. 37, no. 6, pp 1167–1199.

Salamon L.M. 2003, *The resilient sector: the state of nonprofit America*, Brookings Institution Press, Washington, DC.

Salzmann O., Ionescu-Somers A., and Steger U. 2005, 'The business case for corporate sustainability: literature review and research options', *European Management Journal*, vol. 23, no. 1, pp 27–36.

Sampson G.P. 2001, *The role of the World Trade Organization in global governance*, United Nations University Press, Tokyo.

Sampson G.P. 2005, *The World Trade Organization and sustainable development*, United Nations University Press, Tokyo.

SAM-PWC 2008, *Sustainability year book 2008*, Sustainable Asset Management, Zurich and PricewaterhouseCoopers, London.

Sargeant, A. 2017, 'Centre voluntary sector management', in Sargeant, Adrian and Shang, J. (eds), *Fundraising Principles and Practice*, 2nd edn, Wiley, Chichester.

Satre L.J. 2005, *Chocolate on trial: slavery, politics, and the ethics of business*, Ohio University Press, Athens, OH.

Sauka A. and Chepurenko A. (eds) 2017, *Entrepreneurship in transition economies: diversity, trends, and perspectives*, Springer.

Scammell M. 2000, 'The internet and civic engagement: the age of the citizen-consumer', *Political Communication*, vol. 17, no. 4, pp 351–355.

Schafer H. 2005. 'International corporate social responsibility rating systems: conceptual outline and empirical results', *Journal of Corporate Citizenship*, no. 20, Winter, pp 107–120.

Schaltegger S., Burritt R., and Petersen, H. (eds) 2003, *An introduction to corporate environmental management: striving for sustainability*, Greenleaf, Sheffield.

Schaltegger S., Lüdeke-Freund F., and Hansen E.G. 2012, 'Business cases for sustainability: the role of business model innovation for corporate sustainability', *International Journal of Innovation and Sustainable Development*, vol. 6, no. 2, pp 95–119.

Scherer A.G. and Palazzo G. 2007, 'Toward a political conception of corporate responsibility: business and society seen from a Habermasian perspective', *Academy of Management Review*, vol. 32, pp 1096–1120.

Schiller B. 2006, 'Turkish progress: sampling the delights of corporate responsibility', *Ethical Corporation*

Magazine, June 2006. Available online at http://www.ethicalcorp.com, accessed 28 November 2018.

Schipper I. and de Haan E. 2005, *CSR issues in the ICT hardware manufacturing sector*, SOMO, Amsterdam.

Schirato T. and Webb J. 2003, *Understanding globalization*, SAGE Publications, London.

Schmidheiny S. 1992, *Changing course: a global business perspective on development and the environment*, MIT Press, Cambridge, MA.

Schmidheiny S. 2006, 'A view of corporate citizenship in Latin America', *Journal of Corporate Citizenship*, no. 21, Spring, pp 21–24.

Schmidheiny S. and WBCSD 1996, *Financing change: the financial community, eco-efficiency, and sustainable development*, MIT Press, Cambridge, MA.

Schmidheiny S. and Zorraquin F. 1996, *Financing change: the financial community, eco-efficiency, and sustainable development*, MIT Press, Cambridge, MA.

Scholte J.A. 2000, *Globalization: a critical introduction*, St Martin's Press, New York.

Schouten G. and Glasbergen P. 2011, 'Creating legitimacy in global private governance: rhe case of the roundtable on sustainable palm oil', *Ecological Economics*, vol. 70, no. 11, pp 1891–1899.

Schreck P. 2011, 'Reviewing the business case for corporate social responsibility: new evidence and analysis', *Journal of Business Ethics*, vol. 103, no. 2, pp 167–188.

Schröder M. 2005, *Is there a difference? The performance characteristics of SRI equity indexes*, Working Paper, Centre for European Economic Research (ZEW), Mannheim.

Schuler, D.A., and Cording, M. 2006, 'A corporate social performance-corporate financial performance behavioral model for consumers', *The Academy of Management Review*, vol. 31, no. 3, pp. 540–558.

Schwartz, M.S. 2017, *Corporate social responsibility*, Routledge, London.

Schwartz M.S. and Carroll A.B. 2003, 'Corporate social responsibility: a three domain approach', *Business Ethics Quarterly*, vol. 13, no. 4, pp 503–530.

Schwartz P. and Gibb B. 1999, *When good companies do bad things: responsibility and risk in an age of globalization*, John Wiley, New York.

Schwittay A. 2011, 'The marketization of poverty', *Current Anthropology*, vol. 52, no. S3, S71–S82.

Scott L. 2005, *Twenty first century leadership*. Available online at http://news.walmart.com, accessed 22 November 2018.

Scrase H., Wenban-Smith M., and Judd N. 1999, *Certification of forest products for small businesses: improving access—issues and options. Final report*, Department for International Development, London. Available online at https://www.gov.uk/dfid-research-outputs/certification-of-foreset-products-for-small-businesses-improving-access-issues-and-options-final-report, accessed 6 December 2018.

Searcy C. 2012, 'Corporate sustainability performance measurement systems: a review and research agenda', *Journal of Business Ethics*, vol. 107, no. 3, pp 239–253.

Seeger M.W. and Ulmer R.R. 2001, 'Virtuous responses to organizational crisis: Aaron Feuerstein and Milt Colt', *Journal of Business Ethics*, vol. 31, no. 4, pp 369–376.

Seidman G.W. 2003, 'Monitoring multinationals: lessons from the anti-apartheid era', *Politics and Society*, vol. 31, no. 3, pp 381–406.

Seidman G.W., 2004, 'Deflated citizenship: labor rights in a global era', in Brysk A. and Shafir G. (eds), *People out of place: globalization, human rights, and the citizenship gap*, Routledge, New York, pp 109–129.

Seitanidi M.M. 2010, *The politics of partnerships: a critical examination of nonprofit-business partnerships*, Springer, Dordrecht, The Netherlands.

Sen A.K. 2000, *Development as freedom*, Anchor Books, New York.

Senge P.M. 2008, *The necessary revolution: how individuals and organizations are working together to create a sustainable world*, Nicholas Brealey, London.

Sennett, R., 2007. *The culture of the new capitalism*. Yale University Press.

Servaes, H., and Tamayo, A. 2013, 'The impact of corporate social responsibility on firm value: the role of customer awareness', *Management Science*, vol. 59, no. 5, pp 1045–1061.

Sethi S.P. 1975, 'Dimensions of corporate social performance: an analytical framework', *California Management Review*, vol. 17, no. 3, pp 58–65.

Sethi S.P. 2003, *Setting global standards: guidelines for creating codes of conduct in multinational corporations*, John Wiley, Hoboken, NJ.

Sewing T, 2006, 'Mired in the regulation debate', *Ethical Corporation Magazine*, January, pp 13–14.

Shabib F. and Ganguli S. 2017, 'Impact of CSR on consumer behavior of Bahraini women in the cosmetics industry', *World Journal of Entrepreneurship, Management and Sustainable Development*, vol. 13, no. 3, pp 174–203.

Sharkey L., Barrett M., and Goldsmith, M. 2017, *The future-proof workplace: six strategies to accelerate talent development, reshape your culture, and succeed with purpose*, Wiley, Chichester.

Shaw M. 2000, *Theory of the global state: globality as unfinished revolution*, Cambridge University Press, Cambridge.

Shaw M. (ed.) 1999, *Politics and globalisation: knowledge, ethics and agency*, Routledge, London.

Shearman and Sterling LLP 2005, *Trends in the corporate governance practices of the 100 largest US public companies*. Available online at https://www.shearman.com/~/media/Files/NewsInsights/Publications/2006/01/Trends-in-the-Corporate-Governance-Practices-of-__/Files/View-2005-Corporate-Governance-Survey-of-the-100__/FileAttachment/2005-Corporate-Governance-Survey.pdf, accessed 4 October 2018.

Shell 2011, *Signals and signposts: Shell energy scenarios to 2050—an era of volatile transitions*, Shell International BV, Rotterdam.

Shell 2013, *New lens scenarios*, Shell International BV, Rotterdam.

Shleifer A. and Vishney R.W. 1997, 'A survey of corporate governance', *Journal of Finance*, vol. 52, no. 2, pp 737–783.

Sikka P. 2001, 'Regulation of accountancy and the power of capital: some observations', *Critical Perspectives on Accounting*, vol. 12, no. 2, pp 199–211.

Sikka, R. 2016, *What bank would flee this cushy paradise*, Guardian, London.

Sikka P. and Willmott H. 1995a, 'Illuminating the state-profession relationship: accountants acting as Department of Trade and Industry investigators', *Critical Perspectives on Accounting*, vol. 6, no. 4, pp 341–369.

Sikka P. and Willmott H. 1995b, 'The power of "independence": defending and extending the jurisdiction of accounting in the United Kingdom', *Accounting, Organizations and Society*, vol. 20, no. 6, pp 547–581.

Sikka P., Puxty A., Willmott H., and Cooper C. 1998, 'The impossibility of eliminating the expectations gap: Some theory and evidence', *Critical Perspectives on Accounting*, vol. 9, no. 3, pp 299–330.

Singer N. 2009, 'Judge orders former Bristol-Myers executive to write book', *New York Times*, 8 June. Available online at http://www.nytimes.com, accessed 28 November 2018.

Singer P. 1972, 'Famine, affluence, and morality', *Philosophy and Public Affairs*, vol. 1, no. 1, pp 229–243.

Skapkinker M. 2009, 'Consumers are savvy about organic food', *Financial Times*, London, 18 May. Available online at http://www.ft.com, accessed 22 November 2018.

Sklair L. 2002, *Globalization: capitalism and its alternatives*, Oxford University Press, Oxford.

Skocpol T. 2003, *Diminished democracy: from membership to management in American civic life*, University of Oklahoma Press, Norman, OK.

Smart J.J.C. and Williams B.A.O. 1973, *Utilitarianism; for and against*, Cambridge University Press, Cambridge.

Smith A. 1776, *An inquiry into the nature and causes of the wealth of nations*, Whitestone, Dublin.

Smith A. 1976, *The theory of moral sentiments*, Clarendon Press, Oxford (originally published by A. Millar, London, 1759).

Smith N.C. 2003, 'Corporate social responsibility: whether or how?', *California Management Review*, vol. 45, no. 14, pp 52–76.

Smith R. 2003, *Audit committees: combined code guidance*, Financial Reporting Council, London.

Smith R. and Carlton J. 2007, 'Environmentalist groups feud over terms of the TXU buyout', *Wall Street Journal*, New York, 3 March, A-1. Available online at http://online.wsj.com, accessed 22 November 2018.

Smith N.C. and Lenssen G. 2009, *Mainstreaming corporate responsibility*, John Wiley, Chichester.

Smith N.C. and McCormick E. 2019, 'Uber and the ethics of sharing: exploring the societal promises and responsibilities of the sharing economy', in Lenssen, G.G. and Smith, N.C (eds), *Managing Sustainable Business*, Springer, Dordrecht, The Netherlands, pp 579–611.

Smith N.C., Bhattacharya C.B., Vogel D., and Levine D.I. 2010, *Global challenges in responsible business*, Cambridge University Press, New York.

Smith N.V. 2016, 'Exploring regional-level impact of corruption and crime on multinational and domestic firms: the evidence from Russia', in Tüselmann H., Buzdugan S., Cao Q., Freund D., and Golesorkhi S. (eds), *Impact of international business*, The Academy of International Business. Palgrave Macmillan, London.

Social Investment Forum, 2006, *2005 Report on socially responsible investing trends in the United States*, Social Investment Forum, Washington, DC.

Solomon J. 2013, *Corporate governance and accountability* (4th edn), John Wiley, Chichester.

Sorell T. and Hendry J. 1994, *Business ethics*, Butterworth-Heinemann, Oxford.

Soros G. 2008, *The new paradigm for financial markets: the credit crisis of 2008 and what it means*, PublicAffairs, New York.

Soros G. 2009, 'Capitalism versus Open Society', *Financial Times*, 30 October. Available online at https://www.ft.com/content/d55926e8-bfea-11de-aed2-00144feab49a, accessed 30 October 2009.

Soundararajan V., Spence L.J. and Rees C. 2016, 'Small business and social irresponsibility in developing countries: Working conditions and "evasion" institutional work', *Business and Society*. DOI: 10.1177/0007650316644261.

Southern A. 2009, *Enterprise and deprivation: small business, social exclusion and sustainable communities*, Routledge, Abingdon, Oxfordshire.

Sparkes R. 2002, *Socially responsible investment: a global revolution*, John Wiley, New York.

Spence L.J. 2007, 'CSR and small business in a European policy context: the five C's of CSR and small business research agenda 2007', *Business and Society Review*, vol. 112, no. 4, pp 533–552.

Spence, L.J. 2016, 'Small business social responsibility: expanding core CSR theory', *Business and Society*, vol. 55, no. 1, pp 23–55.

Spence L.J. and Rutherfoord R. 2001, 'Social responsibility, profit maximisation and the small firm owner-manager', *Journal of Small Business and Enterprise Development*, vol. 8, no. 2, pp 126–139.

Spence L.J., Schmidpeter R., and Habisch A. 2003, 'Assessing social capital: small and medium sized enterprises in Germany and the UK', *Journal of Business Ethics*, vol. 47, no. 1, pp 17–29.

Stacey J. 2003, 'A global partnership with a mining multinational: exploring and realising the capacity for strategic biodiversity conservation', *Partnership Matters*, vol. 1, pp 25–29.

Stachowicz-Stanusch A. 2015, *Corporate social performance: paradoxes, pitfalls and pathways to the better world*, Information Age Publishing, Charlotte, NC.

Stachowicz-Stanusch A. (ed.) 2017a, *Corporate social performance: reflecting on the past and investing in the future*, Information Age Publishing, Charlotte NC.

Stachowicz-Stanusch A. (ed.) 2017b, *Organizational social irresponsibility: tools and theoretical insights*, Information Age Publishing, Charlotte, NC.

Stachowicz-Stanusch A., Amann W., and Mangia G. (eds) 2017, *Corporate social irresponsibility: individual behaviors and organizational practices*, Information Age Publishing Inc., Charlotte, NC.

Standing G. 2016, *The precariat: the new dangerous class*, Bloomsbury Publishing.

Starbuck W.H. 2005, 'Four great conflicts of the twenty-first century', in Cooper C.L. (ed.), *Leadership and management in the twenty-first century*, Oxford University Press, Oxford, pp 21–55.

Statman M. 2000. 'Socially reponsible mutual funds', *Financial Analysts Journal*, vol. 56, no. 3, pp 30–39.

Steger M.B. 2003, *Globalization: a very short introduction*, Oxford University Press, Oxford.

Steger U. 2004, *The business of sustainability: building industry cases for corporate sustainability*, Palgrave Macmillan, Basingstoke.

Steger U. 2009, *Sustainability partnerships: the manager's handbook*, Palgrave Macmillan, Basingstoke.

Stearns, P.N. 2016, *Globalization in world history*, Routledge.

Stern N. 2007, *Stern Review on the economics of climate change*, H.M. Treasury, London.

Stern N.H. 2009, *A blueprint for a safer planet: how to manage climate change and create a new era of progress and prosperity*, Bodley Head, London.

Stern S. 2006, 'Corporate responsibility and the curse of the three-letter acronym', *Financial Times*, 30 May. Available online at http://www.ft.com, accessed 22 November 2018.

Sternberg E. 1996, 'Stakeholder theory exposed', *Economic Affairs*, vol. 16, no. 3, pp 36–38.

Sterngold J, 1993, 'Japanese companies rebuff mighty US pension funds', *New York Times*, 30 June. Available online at http://www.nytimes.com, accessed 22 November 2018.

Stevens D., Kim A., Mukhamedova L., Mukimova M., and Wagner R. 2008, 'How far can CSR travel? Reflections on the applicability of the concept to SMEs in Uzbekistan', in Crowther D. and Capaldi N. (eds), *The Ashgate research companion to corporate social responsibility*, Ashgate, Aldershot, Hampshire, p 319.

Stewart J. and Konieczny K. 1996, 'The voluntary disclosure of environmental information—a comparison of investor and company perceptions', *Accounting Research Journal*, vol. 9, pp 29–39.

Stewart T.A. and Immelt J. 2006, 'Growth as a process', *Harvard Business Review*, June, pp 60–70.

Stiglitz J.E. 2002, *Globalization and its discontents*, W.W. Norton, New York.

Stiglitz J.E. 2005, *Fair trade for all: how trade can promote development*, Oxford University Press, Oxford.

Stopford J.M., Strange S., and Henley J.S. 1991, *Rival states, rival firms: competition for world market shares*, Cambridge University Press, Cambridge.

Stott P.A., Gillett N.P., Hegerl G.C., Karoly, D.J., Stone, D.A., et al. 2010, 'Detection and attribution of climate change: a regional perspective', *Wiley Interdisciplinary Reviews: Climate Change*, vol. 1, no. 2, pp 192–211.

Strand R. 2013, 'The chief officer of corporate social responsibility: a study of its presence in top management teams', *Journal of Business Ethics*, vol. 112, no. 4, pp 721–734.

Strange S. 1996, *The retreat of the state: the diffusion of power in the world economy*, Cambridge University Press, New York.

Sullivan R. 2003, *Business and human rights: dilemmas and solutions*, Greenleaf, Sheffield.

Sum N.L. 2009, 'Controlling the supply chain through CSR: Wal-Martization in China', in Utting P. and Marques J.C. (eds), *Corporate social responsibility and regulatory governance: towards inclusive development?*, Palgrave Macmillan, Basingstoke.

Suranyi M. 2000, *Blind to sustainability: stock markets and the environment*, Forum for the Future, London.

SustainAbility and UNEP 2001, *Buried treasure: uncovering the business case for corporate sustainability*, SustainAbility, London.

SustainAbility and UNEP 2002, *Trust us: the global reporters' 2002 survey of corporate sustainability reporting*, SustainAbility, London.

SustainAbility, IFC, and Ethos, 2002, *Developing value: the business case for sustainability in emerging markets*, SustainAbility, London.

Sutcliffe H. 2005, 'Finding the CR structure that fits your organization', in *How to structure the corporate responsibility function*, Melcrum, London, pp 6–10.

Svendsen A. and Laberge M. 2005, 'Convening stakeholder networks: a new way of thinking, being and engaging', *Journal of Corporate Citizenship*, no. 19, Autumn, pp 91–104.

Swenson P. 1989, *Fair shares: unions, pay, and politics in Sweden and West Germany*, Cornell University Press, Ithaca, NY.

Syed, J. and Kramar, R. 2017, *Human resource management: a global and critical perspective*, 2nd edn, Palgrave Macmillan.

Taibbi M. 2009, *Inside the great American bubble machine*, Rolling Stone, San Francisco, CA.

Tallontire A. and Blowfield M.E. 2000. 'Will the WTO prevent the growth of ethical trade: implications of the international policy environment for ethical trade schemes', *Journal of International Development*, vol. 12, no. 4, pp 571–584.

Taylor P.L. 2005, 'In the market but not of it: Fairtrade coffee and Forest Stewardship Council Certification as market-based social change', *World Development*, vol. 33, no. 1, pp 129–147.

Tencati A., Russo A., and Quaglia V. 2008, 'Unintended consequences of CSR: protectionism and collateral damage in global supply chains—the case of Vietnam', *Corporate Governance*, vol. 8, no. 4, pp 518–531.

Teoh S.H., Welch I., and Wazzah C.P., 1995, *The effect of socially activist investment policies on the financial markets: evidence from South African boycott*, Working paper 222, London Business School Institute of Finance and Accounting, London.

Testa, F., Gusmerottia, N.M., Corsini, F., Passetti, E., and Iraldo, F. 2016, 'Factors affecting environmental management by small and micro firms: the importance of entrepreneurs' attitudes and environmental investment', *Corporate Social Responsibility and Environmental Management*, vol. 23, no. 6, pp 373–385.

Thankappan S., Hitchens D., and Trainor M. 2004, *Dichotomy between attitudes and environmental performance: a case of European SMEs*, Centre for Business Relationships, Accountability, Sustainability and Society at Cardiff University, Cardiff.

Tharoor S. 2001, 'Are human rights universal?', *New Internationalist*, vol. 332, pp 34–35.

Thomas, D. 2017, 'Fiat accused over emissions software', BBC News, 13 January. Available online at https://www.bbc.co.uk/news/business-38600012, accessed 16 January 2017.

Thompson, E.P. 1963, *The making of the English working class*, Victor Gollancz, London.

Thornber K. 1999, *An overview of global trends in FSC certification*, International Institute for Environment and Development, London.

Thornber K. 2000, *Impacts of certification on forests, stakeholders and markets. Case study: Bainings ecoforestry project*, International Institute for Environment and Development, London.

Thurow L.C. 1996, *The future of capitalism: how today's economic forces shape tomorrow's world*, W. Morrow, New York.

Tilley F.J. 2000, 'Small firm environmental ethics: how deep do they go?', *Business Ethics*, vol. 9, pp 31–41.

Tinker A.M. and Lowe E.A. 1980, 'Rationale for corporate social reporting: theory, evidence from organizational research', *Journal of Business Finance and Accounting*, vol. 7, no. 1, pp 1–17.

Tinker T. 1985, *Paper prophets: a social critique of accounting*, Praeger, New York.

Tobin R. 1997, 'Encouraging signs. Is the corporate world developing a social vision?' *CHAC Review*, vol. 25, no. 1, pp 19–21.

Todd, M.K. 2012, *Physician integration and alignment: IPA, PHO, ACOs and beyond*, Taylor and Francis, Boca Raton, FL.

Toffler A. 1980, *The third wave*, W. Morrow, New York.

Tolba M. and El-Kholy A. 1992, *The world environment 1972–1992: two decades of challenge*, Chapman and Hall, London.

Toms J.S. 2002, 'Firm resources, quality signals and the determinants of corporate environmental reputation: some UK evidence', *British Accounting Review*, vol. 34, no. 3, pp 257–282.

Traidcraft 2005, *Traidcraft social accounts 2004–2005*, Traidcraft, Gateshead.

Treanor, J. 2017, 'World's biggest banks face £264bn bill for poor conduct', *Guardian*, 14 August. Available online at https://www.theguardian.com/business/2017/aug/14/worlds-biggest-banks-face-264bn-bill-for-poor-conduct, accessed 19 July 2018.

Tropenbos 1997, *Hierarchical framework for the formulation of sustainable forest management standards: principles, criteria and indicators*, Tropenbos Foundation, Leiden.

Trotman K.T. and Bradley G.W. 1981, 'Association between social responsibility disclosure and characteristics of companies', *Accounting, Organizations and Society*, vol. 6, no. 4, pp 355–362.

Tsalikis J. and Seaton B. 2008, 'Consumer perceptions of business ethical behavior in former Eastern Block countries', *Journal of Business Ethics*, vol. 82, no. 4, pp 919–928.

Tschopp D.J. 2005, 'Corporate social responsibility: a comparison between the United States and the European Union', *Corporate Social Responsibility and Environmental Management*, vol. 12, no. 1, pp 55–59.

Tsoukas H. and Knudsen C. 2003, *The Oxford handbook of organization theory*, Oxford University Press, Oxford.

Tucker R. 2006, 'The next level of corporate responsibility', *Women's Wear Daily*, 16 May. Available online at http://www.wwd.com, accessed 22 November 2018.

Turnbull N. 1999, *Internal control: guidance for directors on the Combined Code*, Institute of Chartered Accountants in England and Wales, London.

Turner R.K. 1994, *Environmental economics: an elementary introduction*, Pearson Education, London.

Tyson L. D'A. 2003, *The Tyson Report on the recruitment and development of non-executive directors*, London Business School, London.

UKSIF 2009, *Responsible business: sustainable investment*, UK Social Investment Forum, London.

Ullmann A. 1985, 'Data in search of a theory: a critical examination of the relationship among social performance, social disclosure, and economic performance', *Academy of Management Review*, vol. 10, no. 3, pp 540–557.

UN 2003, *Water for people, water for life: world water development report*, United Nations, New York.

UN 2005, *Business UNusual*, United Nations, New York.

UNDP 2009, *Global Compact—small and medium-sized enterprises on their way towards global responsibility*, UN Development Programme, New York.

UNEP 1987, *Environmental perspectives to the year 2000 and beyond*, UN Environment Programme, Nairobi, Kenya.

UNEP 2005, *Millennium ecosystem assessment—living beyond our means—statement from the Board*, United Nations Foundation, New York.

UNEP 2010, *Africa water atlas*, UN Environment Programme, Nairobi, Kenya.

UNEP 2012, GEO5 *Global environmental outlook: environment for the future we want*, UN Environment Programme, Nairobi, Kenya.

UNEP, Accountability, and Stakeholder Research Associates 2005, *Stakeholder engagement manual—from words to action*. vol. 1: *The guide to practioners' perspectives on stakeholder engagement*, UN Environmental Programme, Accountability, and Stakeholder Research Associates, New York.

UNEP, SustainAbility, and Standard & Poors 2006, *Tomorrow's value: the global reporters 2006 survey of corporate sustainability reporting*, SustainAbility, London.

UNEP FI and Mercer 2007, *Demystifying responsible investment performance: a review of key academic and broker research on ESG factors*, UNEP Finance Initiative, Geneva, and Mercer, New York.

UNGC 2013, *Global corporate sustainability report 2013*, United Nations Global Compact, New York.

UNGC, 2017, *United Nations Global Compact progress report: business solutions to sustainable development*, United Nations Global Compact, New York.

Unerman J. 2003, 'Enhancing organizational global hegemony with narrative accounting disclosures: an early example', *Accounting Forum*, vol. 27, pp 425–448.

UNIDO 2002, *Corporate social responsibility: implications for small and medium enterprises in developing countries*, UN Industrial Development Organization, Vienna.

Unilever 2005, *Environmental report 2004*, Unilever, London.

Uphoff N.T. 1996, *Learning from Gal Oya: possibilities for participatory development and post-Newtonian social science*, Intermediate Technology Publications, London.

Upton C. and Bass S. 1995, *The forest certification handbook*, Earthscan, London.

Uren S. 2007, 'Hall of shame: which companies are the worst polluters?', *Guardian*, London, 5 November Available online at http://www.theguardian.com, accessed 22 November 2018.

Utting P. 2005, *Rethinking business regulation: from self-regulation to social control*, UN Research Institute for Social Development, Geneva.

Utting P. 2007, *CSR and equality*, Third World Foundation for Social and Economic Studies, London.

Utting P. and Marques J.C. (eds) 2009, *Corporate social responsibility and regulatory governance: towards inclusive development?*, Palgrave Macmillan, Basingstoke.

Utting P. and Marques J.C. (eds) 2010, *Business, politics and public policy: implications for inclusive development*, Palgrave Macmillan, Basingstoke.

Utting P. and Zammit A. 2006, *Beyond pragmatism: appraising UN–business partnerships*, UN Research Institute for Social Development, Geneva.

van Dijk M.P. and Trienekens J.H. 2012, *Global value chains: linking local producers from developing countries to international markets*, Amsterdam University Press, Amsterdam.

van Gaal, M. 2014, 'Dutch bankers swear to God as trust in lenders slumps to record low', Bloomberg. Available online at https://www.bloomberg.com/news/articles/2014-02-05/dutch-bankers-swear-to-god-as-trust-in-lenders-slumps-to-record, accessed 4 October 2018.

van Tilburg, R., Francken, M., and da Rosa, A. 2013, *Managing the transition to a sustainable enterprise: lessons from frontrunner companies*, Routledge, Abingdon, Oxfordshire.

van Tulder R. 2006, *International business–society management: linking corporate responsibility and globalization*, Routledge, Abingdon, Oxfordshire.

van Tulder R., van Tilburg R., Francken M., and da Rosa A. 2013, *Managing the transition to a sustainable enterprise: lessons from frontrunner companies*, Routledge, Abingdon, Oxfordshire.

Varley P., Mathiasen C., and Voorhes M. 1998, *The sweatshop quandary: corporate responsibility on the global frontier*, Investor Responsibility Research Center, Washington, DC.

Vass, S. 2013. 'Scottish Coal liquidation leads to dispute over clean-ups', *The Herald*, 12 May. Available online at http://www.heraldscotland.com/business/company-news/scottish-coal-liquidation-leads-to-dispute-over-clean-ups.21050751, accessed 4 October 2018.

Veblen T.B. 1904, *The theory of business enterprise*, Charles Scribner's Sons, New York.

Verhoef P.C., Beckers S.F., and van Doorn J. 2013, 'Understand the perils of co-creation', *Harvard Business Review*, September. Available online at http://hbr.org/2013/09/understand-the-perils-of-co-creation/ar/1, accessed 22 November 2018.

Velasco G. 2005, 'Cross-sector partnership in action: a framework for knowledge management', *Partnership Matters*, vol. 3, pp 10–14.

Verité 2004, 'Excessive overtime in Chinese supplier factories: causes, impacts and recommendations for action', Research Paper, Verité, Amherst, MA.

Vernon P. 2007, 'Saint Stuart—the man who is turning M&S green', *Observer*, London, 14 April. Available online at http://www.theguardian.com, accessed 22 November 2018.

Vidal J. 1997, *McLibel: burger culture on trial*, New Press, New York.

Vigar D. 2006, *From challenge to opportunity: the role of business in tomorrow's society*, WBCSD, Geneva.

Virilio P. 2000, *The information bomb*, Verso, New York.

Visser W. 2006, 'Revisiting Carroll's pyramid: an African perspective', in Pedersen E.R. and Huniche M. (eds), *Corporate citizenship in developing countries*, Copenhagen Centre, Copenhagen.

Visser W. and Tolhurst N. (eds) 2010, *The world guide to CSR*, Greenleaf, Sheffield.

Visser W., McIntosh M., and Middleton C. (eds) 2006, *Corporate citizenship in Africa: lessons from the past; paths to the future*, Greenleaf, Sheffield.

Visser W., Matten D., Pohl M., and Tolhurst N. (eds) 2007, *The A to Z of corporate social responsibility: a complete reference guide to concepts, codes and organisations*, John Wiley, Chichester.

Vogel D. 2005, *The market for virtue: the potential and limits of corporate social responsibility*, Brookings Institution Press, Washington, DC.

Vogel D. 2008, 'CSR doesn't pay', *Forbes*, 16 October. Available online at https://www.forbes.com/2008/10/16/csr-doesnt-pay-lead-corprespons08-cx_dv_1016vogel.html#16f2cfe362a8, accessed 4 October 2018.

Vogel D. 2012, *The Politics of precaution: regulating health, safety, and environmental risks in Europe and the United States*, Princeton University Press, Princeton, NJ.

von Hayek F.A. 1944, *The road to serfdom*, Routledge, London.

von Hayek F.A. 1960, *The constitution of liberty*, University of Chicago Press, Chicago, IL.

Wackernagel M., Rees W.E., and Testemale P. 1996, *Our ecological footprint: reducing human impact on the Earth*, New Society, Gabriola Island, BC.

Waddell S. 2000, 'New institutions for the practice of corporate citizenship: historical, intersectoral, and developmental perspectives', *Business and Society Review*, vol. 105, no. 1, pp 107–126.

Waddock S. 2001, 'Integrity and mindfulness: foundations of corporate citizenship', *Journal of Corporate Citizenship*, no. 1, Spring, pp 25–37.

Waddock S. 2007, 'Corporate citizenship: the dark-side paradoxes of success', in May S.K., Cheney G., and Roper J. (eds), *The debate over corporate responsibility*, Oxford University Press, New York.

Waddock S. and Bodwell C. 2002, 'From TQM to TRM: total responsibility management approaches', *Journal of Corporate Citizenship*, no. 7, Autumn, p 113.

Waddock S.A. 2006, *Leading corporate citizens: vision, values, value-added* (2nd edn), McGraw-Hill, Boston, MA.

Waddock S.A. and Graves S.B. 1997, 'The corporate social performance–financial performance link',

Strategic Management Journal, vol. 18, no. 4, pp 303–319.

Walker R.B.J. 1994, 'Social movements/world politics', *Millennium: Journal of International Studies*, vol. 23, no. 3, pp 669–700.

Wall C. 2007, 'Kazakh public policy and corporate social responsibility: an analysis of health care provision in an era of CSR and Kazakh nationalism', presented at the Conference on Business, Social Policy and Corporate Political Influence in Developing Countries, 12–13 November, 2007, Geneva, Switzerland.

Wallerstein I.M. 1974, *The modern world-system*, Academic Press, New York.

Wallerstein I.M. 1978, *The capitalist world-economy*, Cambridge University Press, Cambridge.

Wall Street Journal 2005, 'Corporate social concerns: are they good citizenship or a rip-off for investors?', *Wall Street Journal*, New York, 6 December. Available online at https://www.wsj.com/articles/SB113355105439712626, accessed 4 October 2018.

Walsh J.P. 2005, 'Book review essay: Taking stock of stakeholder management', *Academy of Management Review*, vol. 30, no. 2, pp 426–452.

War on Want 2005, *Caterpillar: the alternative report*, War on Want, London.

War on Want and GMB 2005, *Asda Wal-Mart: the alternative report*, War on Want, London.

Ward H. 2003, *Legal issues in corporate citizenship*, International Institute for Environment and Development, London.

Warhurst, A. (ed.) 1998, *Mining and the environment: case studies from the Americas*, International Development Research Centre, Ottawa.

Warhurst A. and Noronha L. 2000, *Environmental policy in mining: corporate strategy and planning for closure*, Lewis, Boca Raton, FL.

Warner M. 2004, 'Getting started', in Warner M. and Sullivan R. (eds), *Putting partnerships to work*, Greenleaf, Sheffield, pp 166–181.

Warner M. and Sullivan R. (eds) 2004, *Putting partnerships to work*, Greenleaf, Sheffield.

Wartick S.L. and Cochran P.L., 1985, 'The evolution of the corporate social performance model', *Academy of Management Review*, vol. 10, no. 4, pp 758–769.

Waters M. 2001, *Globalization* (2nd edn), Routledge, Abingdon, Oxfordshire.

Waters R. 2010, 'Google in fresh retreat on Buzz', *Financial Times*, London, 15 February. Available online at http://www.ft.com, accessed 22 November 2018.

Watkins K. 1997, *Globalization and liberalization: implications for poverty, distribution and inequality*, UN Development Programme, New York.

Watkins K. and Fowler P. 2005, *Rigged rules and double standards: trade, globalisation and poverty*, Oxfam, Oxford.

Watson, B. 2015, 'Do boycotts really work?' *Guardian*, 6 January. Available online at https://www.theguardian.com/vital-signs/2015/jan/06/boycotts-shopping-protests-activists-consumers, accessed 19 July 2018.

Watts R. 2009, 'Google avoids £100m UK tax', *Sunday Times*, London, 19 April. Available online at http://www.thesundaytimes.co.uk, accessed 22 November 2018.

WBCSD 2005, *Business for development: business solutions in support of the Millennium Development Goals*, World Business Council for Sustainable Development, Geneva.

WBCSD 2006, *Doing business with the world: the new role of corporate leadership in global development*, World Business Council for Sustainable Development, Geneva.

WBCSD 2007, *Doing business with the world: the new role of corporate leadership in global development*, World Business Council for Sustainable Development, Geneva.

WCED, 1987, *Our common future*, World Commission on Environment and Development. Oxford University Press, Oxford.

WDM, War on Want, NUS, and Friends of the Earth 2005, *2005 and sustainable development*, World Development Movement/War on Want/National Union of Students/Friends of the Earth, London.

Weber M., Parsons T., and Giddens A. 1992, *The Protestant ethic and the spirit of capitalism*, Routledge, London.

WEF and Accenture 2012, *More with less: scaling sustainable consumption and efficiency*, World Economic Forum, Geneva.

WEF and Deloitte 2011, *Consumption dilemma: leverage ponts for accelerating sustainable growth*, World Economic Forum, Geneva.

Weinberg A. and Weinberg L.S. 1961, *The muckrakers. The era in journalism that moved America to reform—the most significant magazine articles of 1902–1912*, Simon and Schuster, New York.

Weinstein J.R. 2001, *On Adam Smith*, Thomson Learning, Stamford, CT.

Weiser J. and Rochlin S. 2004, 'Walking in order to run: practical challenges in measuring community and economic development', *AccountAbility Forum*, vol. 1, no. 1, pp 26–32.

Weiser J. and Zadek S. 2000, *Conversations with disbelievers: persuading companies to address social challenges*, BrodyWeiser, New York.

Weiser J., Kahane M., Rochlin S., and Landis J. 2006, *Untapped assets: creating value in underserved markets*, Berrett-Koehler, San Francisco, CA.

Wei-Skillern J. 2004, 'The evolution of Shell's stakeholder approach: a case study', *Business Ethics Quarterly*, vol. 14, no. 4, pp 713–728.

Weiss L. 1998, *The myth of the powerless state*, Cornell University Press, Ithaca, NY.

Welford R. 1995, *Environmental strategy and sustainable development: the corporate challenge for the 21st century*, Routledge, London.

Welford R. 2005, 'Corporate social responsibility in Europe, North America and Asia: 2004 survey results', *Journal of Corporate Citizenship*, no. 17, Spring, pp 33–52.

Weng X. and Buckley L. 2016, 'Chinese Businesses in Africa. Perspectives on corporate social responsibility and the role of Chinese government policies', IIED Discussion Paper, IIED, London.

Wenner G., Bram J.T., Marino M., Obeysekare E., and Mehta K. 2017, 'Organizational models of mobile payment systems in low-resource environments', *Information Technology for Development*, pp 1–25. DOI: 10.1080/02681102.2017.1311830.

Werhane P.H. and Freeman R.E. 1997, *The Blackwell encyclopedic dictionary of business ethics*, Blackwell, Oxford.

Werther, W.B., 2016, *Strategic corporate social responsibility: sustainable value creation*, SAGE Publications, Thousand Oaks, CA.

Werther W.B. and Chandler D. 2011, *Strategic corporate social responsibility: stakeholders in a global environment* (2nd edn), SAGE Publications, Thousand Oaks, CA.

Wettstein F. 2005, 'For causality to capability: toward a new understanding of the multinational corporation's enlarged social responsibilities', *Journal of Corporate Citizenship*, no. 19, Autumn, pp 105–117.

Weybrecht G. 2009, *The sustainable MBA: the manager's guide to green business*, John Wiley, Hoboken, NJ.

Whalley J. 2001, 'World Trade Organization', in Smelser N.J. and Baltes P.B. (eds), *International encyclopedia of the social and behavioral sciences*, Elsevier Science, Oxford, pp 16,613–16,616.

White A. 2005, 'Fade, integrate or transform? The future of CSR', *BSR Newsletter*, August 2005. Available online at http://www.jussemper.org/Newsletters/Resources/BSR_Allen-White.pdf, accessed 28 November 2018..

White C. 2006, 'The spirit of disobedience', *Harpers*, April 2006, pp 31–40.

WHO Tobacco Free Initiative 2008, *Evolution of the tobacco industry positions on addiction to nicotine*, World Health Organization, Geneva.

Wick A. 2001, *Workers' tool or PR ploy? A guide to codes of international labour practice*, Friedrich-Ebert-Stiftung/SÜDWIND Institut für Öknomie und Ökumene, Bonn.

Wiesmann G. and Simensen I. 2007, 'German blue chips ponder switch to SE format', *Financial Times*, London, 12 April.

Wijnberg N. 2000, 'Normative stakeholder theory and Aristotle: the link between ethics and politics', *Journal of Business Ethics*, vol. 25, no. 4, pp 329–342.

Willard B. 2002, *The sustainability advantage: seven business case benefits of a triple bottom line*, New Society, Gabriola Island, BC.

Williams O.F. 2004, 'The UN Global Compact: the challenge and the promise', *Business Ethics Quarterly*, vol. 14, no. 4, pp 755–774.

Williams R. and Elliott L. 2010, *Crisis and recovery: ethics, economics and justice*, Palgrave Macmillan, Basingstoke.

Willums J. 1998, *The sustainable business challenge: a briefing for tomorrow's business leaders*, with World Business Council for Sustainable Development, UN Environment Programme, Bellagio Forum for Sustainable Development, and Foundation for Business and Sustainable Development, Greenleaf, Sheffield.

Wilkinson A., Redman T., and Dundon T. 2016, *Contemporary human resource management: text and cases*, 5th edn, Pearson.

Wilson C. 2006, *Make poverty business: increase profits and reduce risks by engaging with the poor*, Greenleaf, Sheffield.

Windsor D. 2001, 'Corporate citizenship: evolution and interpretation', in Andriof J. and McIntosh M. (eds), *Perspectives on corporate citizenship*, Greenleaf, Sheffield, pp 39–52.

Windsor, D. 2017, 'A corporate social responsibility calculus: global dialogue and local discourses', in Blowfield M., Karam C., and Jamali D. (eds), *Development-Oriented Corporate Social Responsibility*, vol. 1, Routledge, Abingdon, Oxfordshire, pp 27-42.

Wines M. 2010, 'Is Google case a rights bellwether?', *International Herald Tribune*, Paris.

Wohlmeyer H. and Quendler, T. (eds) 2001, *The WTO, agriculture and sustainable development*, Greenleaf, Sheffield.

Woidtke T., Bierman L., and Tuggle C. 2003, 'Reining in activist funds', *Harvard Business Review*, March.

Wolf M. 2004, *Why globalization works*, Yale University Press, New Haven, CT.

Wolff J. 1991, *Robert Nozick: property, justice, and the minimal state*, Stanford University Press, Stanford, CA.

Wood D. 2000, 'Theory and integrity in business and society', *Business and Society*, vol. 39, no. 4, pp 359–378.

Wood D.J. and Logsdon J.M. 2001, 'Theorising business citizenship', in Andriof J. and McIntosh M. (eds), *Perspectives on corporate citizenship*, Greenleaf, Sheffield, pp 83–103.

Wood D.J. and Logsdon J.M. 2002, 'Business citizenship: from individuals to organizations', *Ethics and Entrepreneurship*, vol. 3, pp 59–94.

Wood D.J., Logsdon J.M., Lewellyn P.G., and Davenport P.G. 2006, *Global business citizenship: a transformative framework for ethics and sustainable capitalism*, M.E. Sharpe, Armonk, NY.

Wood E.M. 1995, *Democracy against capitalism: renewing historical materialism*, Cambridge University Press, Cambridge.

World Bank 2003, *Strengthening the implementation of corporate social responsibility in global supply chains*, World Bank, Washington, DC.

World Bank 2005, *World development report 2005. Better investment climate for everyone*, World Bank, Washington, DC.

World Bank 2006, *World development report 2006. Equity and development*, World Bank, Washington, DC.

World Bank Group 2003, *Company codes of conduct and international standards: an analytical comparison*, vol. 1, World Bank Group, Washington, DC.

World Commission on Environment and Development and Brundtland, G.H. 1987, *Our common future*, Oxford University Press, Oxford.

World Economic Forum 2006, *Harnessing private sector capabilities to meet public needs: the potential of partnerships to advance progress on hunger, malaria and basic education*, World Economic Forum, Geneva.

WRI 2002, *Tomorrow's markets: global trends and their implications for business*, World Business Council for Sustainable Development, Washington, DC.

WRI and WBCSD 2004, *The greenhouse gas protocol: a corporate accounting and reporting standard*, World Resources Institute/World Business Council for Sustainable Development, Washington, DC.

Wright C. and Rwabizambuga A. 2006, 'Institutional pressures, corporate reputation, and voluntary codes of conduct: an examination of the Equator Principles', *Business and Society Review*, vol. 111, no. 1, pp 89–117.

Wright S. and Rees S. (eds) 2000, *Human rights, corporate responsibility*, Pluto Press, London.

Wright T. 2007, 'Indonesian proposal: pay us not to chop down our trees', *Wall Street Journal*, New York, 10 August. Available online at https://www.wsj.com/articles/SB118668871988593367, accessed 4 October 2018.

Wu G.C. 2017, 'Effects of socially responsible supplier development and sustainability-oriented innovation on sustainable development: empirical evidence from SMEs', *Corporate Social Responsibility and Environmental Management*, vol. 24, no. 6, pp 661–675.

WWF 2010, *WWF–Living Planet Report*, World Wide Fund For Nature. Available online http://wwf.panda.org/knowledge_hub/all_publications/living_planet_report_timeline/lpr_2010/, accessed 5 June 2016.

WWF 2012, *Living planet report: biodiversity, biocapacity and better choices*, WWF International, Gland, Switzerland.

WWF and SustainAbility 2005, *Influencing power: reviewing the conduct and content of corporate lobbying*, WWF, Gland, Switzerland, and Sustainability, London.

Xenikou, A. and Furnham, A. 2012, *Group dynamics and organizational culture: effective work groups and organizations*, Palgrave Macmillan, Basingstoke.

Yunus M. 1998, *Banker to the poor: the autobiography of Muhammad Yunus, founder of the Grameen Bank*, Aurum, London.

Zadek S. 2000, *Doing good and doing well: making the business case for corporate citizenship*, Conference Board, New York.

Zadek S. 2001a, *The civil corporation: the new economy of corporate citizenship*, Earthscan, London.

Zadek S. 2001b, *Third generation corporate citizenship: public policy and business in society*, Foreign Policy Centre/AccountAbility, London.

Zadek S. 2002, *Third generation corporate citizenship*, Foreign Policy Centre/AccountAbility, London.

Zadek S. 2004, 'The path to corporate responsibility', *Harvard Business Review*, vol. 82, no. 12, pp 125–133.

Zadek S., Pruzan P.M., and Evans R. 1997, *Building corporate accountability: emerging practices in social and ethical accounting, auditing and reporting*, Earthscan, London.

Zadek S., Sabapathy J., Dossing H., and Swift T. 2003, *Responsible competitiveness: corporate responsibility clusters in action*, AccountAbility, London.

Zadek S., Raynard P., and Oliveira C. 2005, *Responsible competitiveness: reshaping global markets through responsible business practices*, AccountAbility, London.

Zakhem A.J., Palmer D.E., and Stoll M.L. 2007, *Stakeholder theory: essential readings in ethical leadership and management*, Prometheus Books, Amherst, NY.

Zeitz J. and Grün A. 2013, *The manager and the monk: a discourse on prayer, profit, and principles*, Jossey-Bass, San Francisco, CA.

Zenisek T.J. 1979, 'Corporate social responsibility: a conceptualization based on organizational literature', *Academy of Management Review*, vol. 4, no. 3, pp 359–369.

Zheng, D. (ed.) 2014, *Education Management and Management Science: Proceedings of the International Conference on Education Management and Management Science (ICEMMS 2014), August 7–8, 2014*, Tianjin, China.

Zimmerman A., Matthews, R.G., and Hudson, C. 2005, 'Can employers alter hiring policies to cut health costs?', *Wall Street Journal*, New York, 27 October. Available online at https://www.wsj.com/articles/SB113036976015880610, accessed 4 October 2018.

Index